P9-AOT-578

The Politics
of American
Economic
Policy Making

The Politics
of American
Economic
Policy Making

Edited by

Paul Peretz

M. E. Sharpe, Inc.
ARMONK, NEW YORK
LONDON, ENGLAND

To my mother and father

Library of Congress Cataloging in Publication Data

The Politics of American economic policy making.

    Bibliography: p.
    1. Finance, Public—United States. 2. Industry and state—United
States. 3. Fiscal policy—United States. 4. United States—Economic
policy. 5. United States—Politics and government. I. Peretz, Paul.
HJ257.P59   1987   338.973   87-12827
ISBN 0-87332-406-4
ISBN 0-87332-407-2 (pbk.)

Printed in the United States of America

Contents

The Politics
of American
Economic
Policy Making

Introduction

The importance of economic policy

Anyone who has turned on the evening news cannot help but be struck by the degree to which foreign affairs and foreign policy, economic conditions and economic policy, dominate national reporting. In a way, it is easy to understand why foreign affairs should receive such extensive coverage. Whether we go to war or not is obviously a matter of concern to every citizen, and the possibility of nuclear war means that what happens in such remote flashpoints as Lebanon, Afghanistan, and Central America may affect all of us.

By contrast, what is reported about our own economy—about indexes and indicators, rising rates, falling rates, and seasonal fluctuations, the size of the money supply and the value of the dollar—is often obscure, even for reasonably well-informed viewers. Yet, economic policy has unmistakable direct and indirect impacts on our daily lives. The single most important effect is on employment. Psychologists say that becoming unemployed is one of life's major traumas, on a par with divorce or severe illness. In good times, when unemployment is low, around four million people are unemployed in the United States. In bad times, such as 1982, the number rises; in that year there were nearly eleven million unemployed.

National economic policy plays a critical role in determining the levels of employment and unemployment. It also helps determine food and clothing prices, salaries and wages, mortgage and tax rates; it affects the safety of the goods we buy and the cost of a hospital stay. In the long run it determines the prosperity of the United States in comparison to other countries, and the standard of living of the average citizen.

Economic policy has myriad indirect effects as well. It helps determine the amounts available to be spent (if we so decide) on public goods. It is the arena in which we decide what resources to allocate to national defense, medical research, crime control, pensions for the elderly, and the clean-up of toxic waste dumps. Regulation of the economy helps determine all sorts of things, from whether we have local train service and pollution-free air and water, to whether minorities are hired in the construction industry.

During the 1980s the United States has seen a burst of economic policy activism on the part of the federal government, sparked by low growth, high unemployment, lagging productivity, and a president who was committed to making changes in economic policy. There has been extensive deregulation in some industries, accompanied by increasing regulation in others. There have been three major tax bills—one lowering business and individual income taxes, one increasing them both, and one simplifying the income tax and shifting some of the burden from consumer to business taxes. There have been two major revisions of Social Security financing, together with several minor ones. There has been a large increase in the defense budget and large cuts in the funding of domestic programs. There was an abrupt shift to a tight monetary policy in 1979 and a slow retreat in 1985 and 1986. These policies have brought reduced inflation, increased unemployment, slightly below-average growth, a huge trade deficit, and the largest peacetime federal deficit in our history.

The purpose of this book

The recent intensity of economic policy activity, together with the somewhat lackluster economic performance that has accompanied it, has greatly increased interest among economists and political scientists in the relationship between government and the economy. The essays collected in this volume are some of the best efforts to explore this question. In making the selections my intention was to cover most of the central areas of concern and to maintain a balance between older, classic pieces and newer articles that represent the latest research in each area. What I would like to do here is to survey the field and show how the essays that follow complement each other and where they fit in the context of broader political-economic research.

The first section of the book presents some *broad theories* about the relationship between government and the economy. We start by looking at the standard view of that relationship held by most American economists, which is that government has an important role to play in the economy. In this view it is the responsibility of government not only to provide public goods such as defense, but also to stabilize the economy and redistribute resources as needed to aid those requiring special assistance. We then look at a conservative challenge to this view which holds that government should play a minimal role in economic affairs. Next we look at a neo-Marxist view, which holds that government has no choice but to play an active role in the economy, to preserve the capitalist system. Finally, we examine a supply-side view, which argues that the capitalist economy is best served by keeping the government's role minimal and taxes low in order to preserve incentives for private initiative.

The second section of the book looks at the relationship of government to private business. It has two parts. In part A we look at *government regulation of business*. We first consider the view that regulation is the result of periodic attempts by consumers to curb the excesses of business. We then examine the argument, made by many in the field, that regulated businesses use the power of government to gain advantages against consumers and other businesses. Finally, we look at the possibility that regulatory agencies have power that is independent both of voters and of big business.

In part B of this section we review the debate over *government planning* or *"industrial policy,"* which has reemerged in recent years in the face of Japan's spectacular successes in manufacturing. We look at the argument that U.S. attempts to imitate Japanese planning are inappropriate and that we should maintain an unplanned economy. We consider the argument that the United States in effect already has an industrial policy and can only benefit by pursuing it in a more conscious, systematic manner. We close this section with an appraisal of the current state of the debate.

In the third section of the book we look at policies that determine the overall state of the economy. These are generally referred to as macroeconomic policies—as distinguished from microeconomic policies, which seek to influence individual business decisions. The three chief instruments that can be used to affect the overall health of the economy are changes in government spending, changes in taxes, and changes in the quantity of money created.

In part A of this section we investigate factors influencing *government expenditures* in the short term—that is, the federal budget. We focus on the generally accepted view that changes in government expenditures tend to be incremental, or primarily determined by reference to expenditure levels in previous years, and secondarily determined by changes in the administration in power. We present strong arguments in support of this view and equally strong arguments against it.

In part B we look at some causes of changes in *taxes*. We begin by asking what determines the structure of the tax system in the long term. We look at an argument that major changes in taxation occur only rarely, when cataclysmic events (for example the Civil War or the Great Depression) lead to a major shift in political power. We also look at an alternative view, that changes in the tax system take place only if they are in the interest of the most powerful elements in society. We then examine recent, Reagan-era tax changes and assess the evidence that they have resulted in extensive redistribution in favor of the wealthy.

Taken together, changes in expenditures and taxes, or fiscal policy, constitute one of the major means of affecting the health of the economy. The other major economic tool is monetary policy. Changing the amount of money that is created has the effect of raising or lowering interest rates. This in turn leads to expansion or contraction in areas of the economy that are dependent on interest rates, such as housing, and to increases or reductions in the amount of business investment. These eventually affect the entire economy, including the rates of unemployment, inflation, and growth.

In part C of the third section we look at the question of control of *monetary policy*. We first examine the argument that monetary policy, because it is made by the Federal Reserve Board, an appointed body of banking experts with no formal accountability to the people, is not subject to democratic control. We then look at the argument that the President is largely in control of the Federal Reserve Board and hence of monetary policy. We finally consider the argument that the Board, although it appears to control monetary policy, is really the scapegoat for unpopular contractionary policies that actually are decided by the President and Congress.

The fourth section of the book looks at the impact of politics on some important economic outcomes. Part A investigates the short-term effects of elections on the health of the economy. The primary focus is on a theory claiming that governments, in an effort to get reelected, spark temporary booms in periods just preceding elections, which are paid for with postelection recessions. This theory of *"political business cycles"* is of central importance if correct, for it means that the health of our economy is dependent not on prudent economic management but on political party competition. We will examine arguments both for and against the existence of political business cycles.

In part B we move from the short-term effects of politics on the economy to the long-term trend of *growth of government*, something that has immense significance in the daily lives of all Americans. The most vexing question about the growth of government is . . . what causes it? We look briefly at a number of the more important theories that have been advanced to explain this phenomenon and then focus on two that are particularly interesting. One argues that government growth tends to occur during and after wars and other major crises that can be dealt with only by governments. The other argues that the openness of the economy to trade and the ideology of the government in power are central determinants of government size.

Finally, in section 5 we look at *economic policy making in the 1980s*, in the light of the perspectives developed in preceding sections of the book. We look at the policies that were adopted, and examine their effects on the economic welfare of citizens. And, of course, we will ask whether the events of the 1980s confirm or disconfirm our central theories.

I would like to note that, while I made a conscious effort to avoid selecting especially difficult pieces for inclusion in this collection, this is a highly technical literature and it is inevitable that some readers will have difficulty with some of the articles. For this reason I have provided headnotes, to help readers new to the terrain to proceed through the articles with more confidence. I need hardly add (which of course is why I am adding it) that these summaries are, at best, aids to understanding and *not* substitutes for the material in the articles.

*   *   *

No book is complete without thanks to those who helped make it possible. My primary thanks must go to Patricia Kolb, my editor at M. E. Sharpe, Inc. It was she who first suggested that I put together a book of this type. It was she who guided me through the perilous paths of seeking permissions from publishers. It was she who bullied me into abandoning my normally obscure writing style for the somewhat more comprehensible one in this book. In short, she has been a veritable paragon among editors.

I would also like to thank my wife, Jean Schroedel, who read the drafts of my essays in this volume and made valuable suggestions. I thank Don McCrone, Dennis Quinn, Neil Berch, and Chris Heaphy for a number of helpful conversations on various of the topics in this book. Steven Rose and Alexander Hicks gave me some useful reading suggestions. A course I taught jointly with Tom Anton first got me to look seriously at economic policy in the 1980s.

Lastly I would like to thank my students, both at Brown University and at the University of Washington, for pre-testing much of the material in this book and—most important—turning thumbs down on some of the material not in this book.

1. Broad Theories

Those who analyze the relation between government and the economic system are guided in their analyses by broad theories about the way that government actions affect the economy. In this section we look at four such theories.

In economics this area of inquiry is called *public finance*. Public finance economists see government as having a number of goals and an array of economic tools that can be used to achieve those goals. Government is charged with pursuing its goals in the most efficient manner and managing programs that yield more benefits than costs. But this is no simple task. The policy tools that government possesses are often inexact. Moreover, government goals can, and often do, conflict with one another. And there is no insurance that government will always pursue goals and policies that are in the best interest of the governed.

The authors of the four readings in this section differ in their views of the goals that government should pursue and the means that should be used to reach those goals. They also disagree on such matters as the functioning of the economic system and the relationship between government and the private economy—what it is and what it should be.

The reading by Richard Musgrave and Peggy Musgrave is representative of mainline thinking in the field of public finance, which holds that government has an important part to play in the guidance of the economy. This active role is forced on it by the fact that, in the absence of substantial government intervention, imperfections in the free-market system will lead to inequities, economic recessions, and a lack of public goods. Nonetheless, most advocates of this view think that, in most cases, the private economy produces most goods more efficiently than government and should be left to do so.

Milton Friedman's essay is representative of a more conservative view, which sees the proper role of government as considerably more limited. Those in this camp find few if any imperfections in the free-market system, and they are concerned that conventional wisdom underestimates the inefficiency of government efforts to produce goods or manage the economy. They believe that the proper role of government is to provide conditions ensuring that free markets can operate and to leave as much as possible to that market.

The selection from James O'Connor is representative of neo-Marxist analysis, which sees government in a capitalist society as operating primarily to assist those who control economic resources. Accordingly, O'Connor and others do not see the economy as neatly divided into public and private sectors, and they argue that most government actions—including those that appear to be in aid of the average citizen or even the disadvantaged—can be shown to have the underlying purpose of maintaining the status quo—that is, inequality.

Finally, the reading by Jude Wanniski is representative of the supply-side thinking that has so heavily influenced the Reagan Administration. Although the supply-siders resemble conservatives in many ways, they place more emphasis on policies that encourage investment and they put greater faith in the positive effect of tax cuts.

For further reading

Virtually any introductory economics textbook devotes at least some attention to economic philosophies. Three personal favorites are Paul Samuelson's *Economics* and, for a higher-level approach, Edmund Phelp's *Political Economy* and Robert Gordon's *Macroeconomics*. A good source for the development of economic theory over the last two hundred years is Mark Blaug's *Economic Theory in Retrospect*. E.K. Hunt and Howard Sherman's *Economics: An Introduction to Traditional and Radical Views* gives a good introduction to leftist economic theory. Lester Thurow's *Dangerous Currents: The State of Economics* has good sections on supply-side and expectations theory. Two accessible journals that frequently feature articles in this area are *Challenge: The Magazine of Economic Affairs* and *The Journal of Economic Literature*.

Bibliography

Blaug, Mark, *Economic Theory in Retrospect*, 4th ed. (New York: Cambridge University Press, 1985).
Gordon, Robert J., *Macroeconomics*, 3rd ed. (Boston: Little Brown, 1984).
Hunt, E.K. and Howard J. Sherman, *Economics: An Introduction to Traditional and Radical Views*, 5th ed. (New York: Harper and Row, 1985).
Phelps, Edmund S., *Political Economy: An Introductory Text* (New York: W.W. Norton, 1985).
Samuelson, Paul and William Nordhaus, *Economics*, 12th ed. (New York: McGraw Hill, 1985).
Thurow, Lester, *Dangerous Currents: The State of Economics* (New York: Random House, 1983).

1.1. Fiscal Functions
An Overview

RICHARD A. MUSGRAVE and PEGGY MUSGRAVE

The branch of economics that deals with the relation between government and the economy is called public finance. *This essay by Peggy Musgrave and Richard A. Musgrave, one of the fathers of the field, outlines what most regard as the central theoretical framework in public finance.*

The authors argue that the most useful way of looking at the role of government is to see it as having three primary tasks—distribution, stabilization, and allocation. A government performs its distributive *function when it alters the income shares that result from the operation of free-market forces, in order better to approximate society's judgment as to what is fair. For example, society may tax an employed executive and then provide support payments to an elderly blind person. Stabilization is the task of maintaining a reasonable growth rate and keeping unemployment as low as possible, without setting off inflation or incurring large debts to other countries. Allocation* is decision-making on how much society should spend on "public goods" *such as defense and sewage treatment, which are more efficiently provided by government, as opposed to private goods such as food and clothing, which are most efficiently provided by the free market.*

The reader should keep in mind that while almost all economists agree that most governments perform these three functions in some measure, they tend to disagree over the proper scope of the government role in each area. Disagreement is especially strong over the extent to which government should redistribute income.

A. Introduction

Need for public sector

. . . From the normative view, why is it that a public sector is required? If one starts with the premises, generally accepted in our society, that (1) the composi-

Reprinted with permission from *Public Finance in Theory and Practice*, 3rd ed., by Richard A. Musgrave and Peggy Musgrave (New York: McGraw-Hill, 1980), pp. 5–23. Copyright 1980 by McGraw-Hill Book Company.

tion of output should be in line with the preferences of individual consumers and that (2) there is a preference for decentralized decision making, why may not the entire economy be left to the private sector? Or, putting it differently, why is it that in a supposedly private enterprise economy, a substantial part of the economy is subject to some form of government direction, rather than left to the "invisible hand" of market forces?

In part, the prevalence of government may reflect the presence of political and social ideologies which depart from the premises of consumer choice and decentralized decision making. But this is only a minor part of the story. More important, there is the fact that the market mechanism alone cannot perform all economic functions. Public policy is needed to guide, correct, and supplement it in certain respects. It is important to realize this fact since it implies that the proper size of the public sector is, to a significant degree, a technical rather than an ideological issue. A variety of reasons explain why this is the case, including the following:

1. The claim that the market mechanism leads to efficient resource use (i.e., produces what consumers want most and does so in the cheapest way) is based on the condition of competitive factor and product markets. This means that there must be no obstacles to free entry and that consumers and producers must have full market knowledge. Government regulation or other measures are needed to secure these conditions.

2. They are needed also where, due to decreasing cost, competition is inefficient.

3. More generally, the contractual arrangements and exchanges needed for market operation cannot exist without the protection and enforcement of a governmentally provided legal structure.

4. Even if the legal structure were provided, and all barriers to competition were removed, the production or consumption characteristics of certain goods are such that these goods cannot be provided for through the market. Problems of "externalities" arise which lead to "market failure" and require solution through the public sector.

5. Social values may require adjustments in the distribution of income and wealth which results from the market system and from the transmission of property rights through inheritance.

6. The market system, especially in a highly developed financial economy, does not necessarily bring high employment, price level stability, and the socially desired rate of economic growth. Public policy is needed to secure these objectives.

7. The rate of discount used in the valuing of future (relative to present) consumption may differ as seen from a public and a private point of view.

As we shall see later on, items 3 through 7 are of particular importance from the viewpoint of budget policy.

To argue that these limitations of the market mechanism call for corrective or compensating measures of public policy does not prove, of course, that any policy measure which is undertaken will in fact improve the performance of the economic system. Public policy, no less than private policy, can err and be inefficient; and the basic purpose of our study of public finance is precisely that of exploring how the effectiveness of policy formulation and application can be improved.

Major functions

Although particular tax or expenditure measures affect the economy in many ways and may be designed to serve a variety of purposes, several more or less distinct policy objectives may be set forth. They include:

1. The provision for social goods, or the process by which total resource use is divided between private and social goods and by which the mix of social goods is chosen. This provision may be termed the *allocation function* of budget policy. Regulatory policies, which may also be considered a part of the allocation function, are not included here because they are not primarily a problem of budget policy.

2. Adjustment of the distribution of income and wealth to assure conformance with what society considers a "fair" or "just" state of distribution, here referred to as the *distribution function*.

3. The use of budget policy as a means of maintaining high employment, a reasonable degree of price level stability, and an appropriate rate of economic growth, with allowance for effects on trade and on the balance of payments. We refer to all these objectives as the *stabilization function*.

B. The allocation function

We begin with the allocation function and the proposition that certain goods— referred to here as *social* as distinct from *private* goods—cannot be provided for through the market system, i.e., by transactions between individual consumers and producers. In some cases the market fails entirely, while in others it can function only in an inefficient way. Why is this the case?

Social goods and market failure

The basic reason for market failure in the provision of social goods is not that the need for such goods is "felt" collectively, whereas that for private goods is felt individually. While people's preferences are influenced by their social environment, in the last resort wants and preferences are experienced by individuals and not by society as a whole. Moreover, both social and private goods are included in their preference maps. Just as I can rank my preferences among housing and backyard facilities, so I may also rank my preferences among my private yard and my use of public parks. Rather, the difference arises because the benefits to which social goods give rise are not limited to one particular consumer who purchases the good, as is the case for private goods, but become available to others as well.

If I consume a hamburger or wear a pair of shoes, these particular products will not be available to other individuals. My and their consumption stand in a rival relationship. This is the situation with private goods. But now consider measures to reduce air pollution. If a given air quality improvement is obtained, the resulting gain will be available to all who breathe. In other words, consumption of such products by various individuals is "nonrival," in the sense that one person's partaking of benefits does not reduce the benefits available to others. To put it differently, the benefits derived by anyone's consuming a social good are "externalized" in that they become available to all others. This is the situation with social goods. In the case of private goods, the benefits of consumption are "internalized" with a particular consumer, whose consumption excludes consumption by others.

The market mechanism is well suited for the provision of private goods. It is based on exchange, and exchange can occur only where there is an exclusive title to the property which is to be exchanged. In fact, the market system may be viewed as a giant auction where consumers bid for products and producers sell to the highest bidders. Thus the market furnishes a signaling system whereby producers are guided by consumer demands. For goods such as hamburgers or pairs of shoes this is an efficient mechanism. Nothing is lost and much is gained when consumers are excluded unless they pay. Application of the exclusion principle tends to be an efficient solution.

But not so in the case of social goods. For one thing, it would be inefficient to exclude any one consumer from partaking in the benefits, when such participation would not reduce consumption by anyone else. The application of exclusion would thus be undesirable, even if it were readily feasible. Furthermore, the application of exclusion is frequently impossible or prohibitively expensive. Gains from air-cleaning measures cannot readily be withheld from particular consumers, streetlights shine upon all who pass by, and so forth. Given these conditions, the benefits from social goods are not vested in the property rights of certain individuals, and the market cannot function. In other instances, such as provision of sewer lines, fees can be charged and the government can function on a market basis.

But where the benefits are available to all, consumers will not voluntarily offer payments to the suppliers of social goods. I will benefit as much from the consumption of others as from my own, and with thousands or millions of other consumers present, my payment is only an insignificant part of the total. Hence, no voluntary payment is made, especially where many consumers are involved. The linkage between producer and consumer is broken and the government must step in to provide for such goods.

Public provision for social goods

The problem, then, is how the government should determine how much of such goods is to be provided. Refusal of voluntary payment is not the basic difficulty. The problem could be solved readily, at least from the theoretical point of view, if the task were merely one of sending the tax collector to those consumers to whom the benefits of social goods accrue. But matters are not this simple. The difficulty lies in deciding the type and quality of a social good that should be supplied to begin with and how much a particular consumer should be asked to pay. It may be reasonable to rule that the individual should pay for the benefits received, as in the case of private goods, but this does not solve the problem; the fundamental difficulty lies in how these benefits are valued by the recipient.

Just as individual consumers have no reason to offer voluntary payments to the private producer, so they have no reason to reveal to the government how highly they value the public service. If I am only one member in a large group of consumers, the total supply available to me is not affected significantly by my own contribution. Consumers have no reason to step forward and declare what the service is truly worth to them individually unless they are assured that others will do the same. Placing tax contributions on a voluntary basis would, therefore, be to no avail. People will prefer to enjoy as "free riders" what is provided by others. A different technique is needed by which the supply of social goods and the cost allocation thereof can be determined.

This is where the political process enters the picture as a substitute for the market mechanism. Voting by ballot must be resorted to in place of dollar voting. Since voters know that they will be subject to the voting decision (be it simple majority or some other voting rule), they will find it in their interest to vote so as to let the outcome fall closer to their own preferences. Thus decision making by voting becomes a substitute for preference revelation through the market. The results will not please everyone, but they will approximate an efficient solution. They will do so more or less perfectly, depending on the efficiency of the voting process and the homogeneity of the community's preferences in the matter.[1]

National and local social goods

Although social goods are available equally to those concerned, their benefits may be spatially limited. Thus, the benefits from national defense accrue nation-wide while those from streetlights are of concern only to local residents. This suggests that the nature of social goods has some interesting bearing on the issue of fiscal centralization. A good case can be made for letting national public services be provided by national government and local public services by local government.

Public provision versus public production

Before considering how such public provision is to be arranged, a clear distinction must be drawn between public *provision* for social goods, as the term is used here, and public *production*. These are two distinct and indeed unrelated concepts which should not be confused with each other.

Private goods may be produced and sold to private buyers either by private firms, as is normally done, or by public enterprises, such as public power and

Table 1

Forms of Production and Types of Goods
(United States data for 1977)

	Privately purchased goods (private goods) (I)	Goods provided through budgets (social goods) (II)	Total (III)
1. Public production, billions of dollars	25[a]	208[b]	233
2. Private production, billions of dollars	1,468	186	1,654
3. Total, billions of dollars	1,493	394[c]	1,887[d]
4. Percentage publicly produced	1.7	52.8	12.4
5. Percentage privately produced	98.3	47.2	87.6
6. Percentage, both forms	100.0	100.0	100.0
7. Percentage of public production	10.7	89.3	100.0
8. Percentage of private production	88.8	11.2	100.0
9. Percentage of total production	79.5	20.5	100.0

Notes: a. Equals income originating in public enterprise. (*Survey*, table 1-14.)
   b. Equals income originating in government. (*Survey*, table 1-14.)
   c. Equals government purchases. (*Survey*, table 1-1.)
   d. Equals GNP. (*Survey*, table 1-1.) Other items are residuals.
Source: U.S. Department of Commerce, *Survey of Current Business*, July 1978.

transportation authorities or the nationalized British coal industry. Social goods, such as spaceships or military hardware, similarly may be produced by private firms and sold to government; or they may be produced directly under public management, as are services rendered by civil servants or municipal enterprises. If we say that social goods are provided publicly, we mean that they are financed through the budget and made available free of direct charge. How they are produced does not matter.

This distinction is brought out in the estimates of Table 1, where the total product of the United States economy is broken down according to (1) whether the goods and services are purchased privately or provided through the budget (corresponding roughly to our distinction between private and social goods), and (2) whether they have been produced publicly or by private firms. We find that only 12.4 percent of total production is in the public sector (line 4, column III), while 20.5 percent of output is provided through the budget (line 9, column II). We also note that 52.8 percent of the social goods provided through the budget involves public production (line 4, column II), while this ratio is only 1.7 percent for private goods (line 4, column I). Finally, 89.3 percent of public production consists of social goods (line 7, column II) as against 11.2 percent of private production (line 8, column II). In short, production in the United States is undertaken almost entirely in the private sector, although social goods constitute a substantial part of total output; and such public production as exists is very largely for the provision of social goods. Public production for sale (public enterprise) plays only a very minor role.

A similar analysis for other countries[2] shows that the United States ranks low in the public production share, as does Canada. The share rises as we move to the United Kingdom and Sweden, where public enterprise is more important. It becomes much larger for the case of socialist economies such as the USSR, where the bulk of production is by public enterprise. But one also finds that the share of total output going into social goods differs much less. This is true even with regard to the USSR, provided that investment in public enterprise is excluded and that the comparison is limited to final goods. It is thus evident that the decision whether to allocate resources to social goods or to private goods is quite different from that whether to produce any good (private or social) in a public or a private enterprise. A socialist economy, in which most production is public, may produce largely private goods, while a capitalist economy, where all production is private, may produce a larger share of social goods. In fact, provision for social goods poses much the same problem in the capitalist (private firm) as in the socialist (public enterprise) setting. In both cases, it is difficult to determine how such goods are valued by consumers. At the same time, provision for social goods requires taxation, which may interfere with incentives. As explained later, this may be more damaging in the capitalist than in the socialist setting.[3]

C. The distribution function

The allocation function of securing an efficient provision of social goods poses the type of problem with which economic analysis has traditionally been concerned, but the problem of distribution is more difficult to handle. Yet, distribution issues are a major (frequently the major) point of controversy in the determination of public policy. In particular, they play a key role in determining tax and transfer policies.

Determinants of distribution

In the absence of policy measures to adjust the prevailing state of distribution, the distribution of income and wealth depends first of all on the distribution of factor endowments. Earnings abilities differ, as does the ownership of inherited wealth. The distribution of income, based on this distribution of factor endowments, is then determined by the process of factor pricing, which, in a competitive market, sets factor returns equal to the value of the marginal product. The distribution of income among individuals thus depends on their factor supplies and the prices which they fetch in the market.

This distribution of income may or may not be in line with what society considers fair or just. A distinction must be drawn between (1) the principle that efficient factor use requires factor inputs to be valued in line with competitive factor pricing, and (2) the proposition that the distribution of income among families should be fixed by the market process. Principle 1 is an economic rule that must be observed if there is to be efficient use of resources. But, proposition 2 is a different matter. For one thing, factor prices as determined in the market may not correspond with the competitive norm. But even if all factor prices, including wages and other returns to personal services, were determined competitively, the resulting pattern of distribution might not be acceptable. It involves a substantial degree of inequality, especially in the distribution of capital income; and though views on distributive justice differ, most would agree that some adjustments are required.

Optimal distribution

This being the case, one must consider what constitutes a fair or just state of distribution. Modern economic analysis has steered shy of this problem. The essence of modern welfare economics has been to define economic efficiency in terms which exclude distributional considerations. A change in economic conditions is said to be efficient (i.e., to improve welfare) if, and only if, the position of some person, say A, is improved without that of anyone else, including B and C, being worsened. This criterion, which may be qualified and amended in various ways, cannot be applied to a redistributional measure which by definition improves A's position at the expense of B's and C's. While the "someone gains, no one loses" rule has served well in assessing the efficiency of markets and of certain aspects of public policy, it contributes little to solving the basic social issues of distribution and redistribution.

The answer to the question of fair distribution involves considerations of social philosophy and value judgment. Philosophers have come up with a variety of answers, including the view that persons have the right to the fruits derived from their particular endowments, that distribution should be arranged so as to maximize total happiness or satisfaction, and that distribution should meet certain standards of equity, which, in a limiting case, may be egalitarian. The choice among these criteria is not simple, nor is it easy to translate any one criterion into the corresponding "correct" pattern of distribution. We shall encounter these difficulties when dealing with redistribution policy and again in interpreting the widely accepted proposition that people should be taxed in line with their "ability to pay."

There are two major problems involved in the translation of a justice rule into an actual state of income distribution. First, it is difficult or impossible to compare the levels of utility which various individuals derive from their income. There is no simple way of adding up utilities, so that criteria based on such comparisons are not operational. This limitation has led people to think in terms of social evaluation rather than subjective utility measurement. The other difficulty arises from the fact that the size of the pie which is available for distribution is not unrelated to how it is to be distributed. We shall find that redistribution policies may involve an efficiency cost which must be taken into account when one is deciding on the extent to which equity objectives should be pursued.

Notwithstanding these difficulties, however, distributional considerations have remained an important issue of public policy. Attention appears to be shifting from the traditional concern with relative income positions, with the overall state of equality, and with excessive income at the top of the scale, to adequacy of income at the lower end. Thus the current discussion emphasizes prevention of poverty, setting what is considered a tolerable cutoff line or floor at the lower end rather than putting a ceiling at the top, as was once the popular view.

Fiscal instruments of distribution policy

Among various fiscal devices, redistribution is implemented most directly by (1) a tax-transfer scheme, combining progressive income taxation of high-income households with a subsidy to low-income households.[4] Alternatively, redistribution may be implemented by (2) progressive income taxes used to finance public services, especially those such as public housing, which particularly benefit low-income households. Finally, redistribution may be achieved by (3) a combination of taxes on goods purchased largely by high-income consumers with subsidies to other goods which are used chiefly by low-income consumers.[5]

In choosing among alternative policy instruments, allowance must be made for resulting "deadweight losses" or efficiency costs, i.e., costs which arise as consumer or producer choices are interfered with. Redistribution via an income tax–transfer mechanism has the advantage that it does not interfere with particular consumption or production choices. However, even this mechanism is not without its "efficiency cost," since the choice between income and leisure remains affected. But chances are that the distortion will be less than with more selective measures, so that we shall think of the function of the distribution branch as being discharged by a set of direct income taxes and transfers, a process to be examined later under the heading of "Negative Income Tax."

Where redistribution involves an efficiency cost, this consequence by itself establishes no conclusive case against such policies. It merely tells us that (1) any given distributional change should be accomplished at least efficiency cost, and that (2) a need exists for balancing conflicting policy objectives. Efficiency in the broad sense, i.e., an optimally conducted policy, must allow for both concerns.

D. The stabilization function

Having dealt with the bearing of budget policy on matters of allocation and distribution, we must now examine its role as an instrument of macroeconomic policy. Fiscal policy must be designed to maintain or achieve the goals of high employment, a reasonable degree of price level stability, soundness of foreign accounts, and an acceptable rate of economic growth.

Need for stabilization

Fiscal policy is needed for stabilization, since full employment and price stability do not come about automatically in a market economy but require public policy guidance. Without it, the economy tends to be subject to substantial fluctuations, and it may suffer from sustained periods of unemployment or inflation. To make matters worse, unemployment and inflation may exist at the same time. To hold that public policy is needed to deal with these contingencies does not preclude the possibility that public policy, if poorly conducted, may itself be a destabilizer. The purpose of our study, as noted before, is to see how policy can be shaped more effectively.

The overall level of employment and prices in the economy depends upon the level of aggregate demand, relative to potential or capacity output valued at prevailing prices. The level of demand is a function of the spending decisions of millions of consumers, corporate managers, financial investors, and unincorporated operators. These decisions in turn depend upon many factors, such as past and present income, wealth position, credit availability, and expectations. In any one period, the level of expenditures may be insufficient to secure full employment of labor and other resources. Because wages and prices are downward rigid and for other reasons, there is no ready mechanism by which such employment will restore itself automatically. Expansionary measures to raise aggregate demand are needed. At other times, expenditures may exceed the available output under conditions of high employment and thus may cause inflation. In such situations, restrictive conditions are needed to reduce demand. Furthermore, just as deficient demand may generate further deficiency, so may an increase in prices generate further expectations of price rise, leading to renewed inflation. In neither case is there an adjustment process by which the economy is automatically returned to high employment and stability.

A wide range of models may be constructed on the drawing boards of economic theory, some of which are explosively unstable, while others are characterized by dampened oscillations or continuous, limited fluctuations. As we know from the world around us, the actual behavior of the economy is fortunately not explosive. Built-in stabilizers exist which limit fluctuations. There remains, however, a band of instability which is sufficiently serious to require stabilizing action.

This task is complicated by the fact that economies do not operate in isolation but are linked to one another by trade and capital flows. Policies which affect the level of domestic income and prices also affect a country's exports, imports, and balance of payments. This in turn affects the economic position of other countries. Stabilization policy thus must be conducted in a way which involves the complex problems of international policy coordination.

Whereas, in the thirties and forties, the problem of stabilization was mainly seen as one of reaching full employment within a given level of potential output, developments since the fifties have shifted attention to the rate of growth of potential output and inflation. Given the rate of increase in population and/or productivity, the level of aggregate expenditures must be adjusted to rise accordingly, so as to permit demand to expand in line with potential output. This objective will require periodic adjustments in fiscal policy. Furthermore, public policy may not accept the rate of growth of potential output as determined by market forces, but may wish to influence this rate. Since growth depends, among other things, upon the rate of capital formation, the rate of saving and investment incentives become of strategic importance.[6]

Most recently, primary focus has been on inflation. After a high level of employment was reached in the mid-sixties, the problem became one of restraining inflation without losing the full-employment objective. As the experience of the seventies has shown, policy may have to fight inflation and unemployment at the same time. As we shall see, the appearance of "stagflation" has raised doubts regarding the effectiveness of traditional fiscal measures and has called for new approaches.

Fiscal instruments of stabilization policy

The very existence of the fiscal system has an immediate and inevitable influence on the level and structure of demand. Even if fiscal policy was intended to be "neutral," it would be necessary to consider effects on aggregate demand to secure such neutrality. Moreover, changes in budget policy may be used as a positive means of obtaining or offsetting changes in demand.

Leverage effects of a given budget. Government expenditures add to total (private plus public) demand, while taxes reduce it. This suggests that budgetary effects on demand will be the larger the higher is the level of expenditures and the lower that of tax revenue. Deficits are expansionary and surpluses are restrictive, but even a balanced budget has an expansionary effect.

Changes in budget policy. Discretionary policy measures may thus be taken to affect the level of aggregate demand. The government may raise its expenditures or reduce tax rates if demand is to be expanded and vice versa if it is to be contracted. Depending on the type of expenditure or tax adjustments made, consumption or investment in the private sector may be affected, and the promptness of the expenditure response may differ. The policy problem, therefore, is not only one of direction of change but also of selecting the proper type and magnitude of change.

Built-in responses. Not only may changes in the level of public expenditures or tax rates be used to affect the overall level of demand, but changes in the level of economic activity will also affect public expenditures and tax revenue. Thus, the level of expenditure under any given program may vary with economic activity, most obviously so in the case of unemployment benefits and welfare. More important, the revenue obtained from given tax rates will rise or fall with changes in the level of income or sales subject to tax. Thus, the fiscal system possesses a "built-in flexibility" which responds to changes in the economic scene, even though no changes in policy (changes in tax rates or expenditure legislation) are made. As we shall see later, these built-in responses are helpful under some, and harmful under other, circumstances.

Monetary instruments

While the market mechanism, if it functions well, may be relied upon to determine the allocation of resources among private goods, economists agree that it cannot by itself regulate the proper money supply. As Walter Bagehot pointed out a century ago, "Money does not control itself." The banking system if left to its own devices will not generate just that money supply which is compatible with economic stability, but will—in response to the credit demands of the market—accentuate prevailing tendencies to fluctuation. Therefore, the money supply must be controlled by the central banking system and be adjusted to the needs of the economy in terms of both short-run stability and longer-run growth. Monetary policy—including the devices of reserve requirements, discount rates, open market policy, and selective credit controls—is thus an indispensable component of stabilization policy.

Policy mix

Although monetary and fiscal measures supplement each other, they differ in their impact. By using them in proper combination, it is possible to achieve more objectives than would be possible with the use of one policy instrument alone. Thus, a mix of easy money (permitting high expenditures, particularly investment) and a tight budget (reducing the level of aggregate expenditures, particularly consumption) is favorable to economic growth. Given fixed exchange rates, we shall note that monetary policy has a special advantage (due to its effects on international capital movements) in securing balance-of-payments adjustments, while fiscal policy is more effective in dealing with domestic needs. Monetary and fiscal policies, therefore, are linked by the need for obtaining a policy mix which will permit the pursuit of multiple policy objectives.

Moreover, there is a mechanical link between fiscal and monetary measures. While budgetary imbalance (surplus or deficit, depending on the needs of the situation) is an important tool of fiscal policy, this means that the structure of claims, including money and public debt, is changed in the process. These "claim effects" are an inevitable by-product of budgetary imbalance, providing an important link between fiscal and monetary policy.

Fiscal and monetary policies thus interact and complement each other in important ways. But they also suffer from the same weakness. So long as the problems of unemployment and inflation are merely due to a deficiency or excess of aggregate demand, measures aimed at controlling aggregate demand are likely to be effective, but they become less so in dealing with stagflation, where structural maladjustments in various markets are at the root of the problem. As noted before, new uses of the old tools or indeed new tools may be needed to deal with these problems.

E. Coordination or conflict of functions

It remains to consider how the three basic functions of fiscal policy—allocation, distribution, and stabilization—can be coordinated into an overall pattern of budget policy. Here in particular, our earlier distinction between a normative and a descriptive (or predictive) view of the fiscal process must be kept in mind. Although fully coordinated policy determination permits simultaneous achievement of the various objectives, actual practice gives rise to multiple conflicts.

Coordination

Consider first the coordinated approach as it would proceed under a normative or optimally conducted fiscal process. In dealing with the analysis of public policy, economists have shown that the number of available policy tools must match the number of policy targets. If the tools are insufficient, a conflict among targets must be accepted. Given our three targets—(1) provision for social goods, (2) adjustments in distribution, (3) stabilization—three policy instruments are needed to meet them. Let us think of them as three separate subbudgets or fiscal branches, each designed for the implementation of its particular objective.

The manager of the distribution-branch budget will design a tax-transfer plan to secure the desired adjustment in distribution. For this purpose a full-employment level of income will be assumed. The manager also assumes that the allocation branch provides for public services financed by taxes imposed in line with consumer evaluation thereof. The subbudget of the distribution branch, by its very nature, will be balanced. The manager of the allocation branch in turn will provide for social goods and finance them by taxes imposed in line with consumer evaluation thereof. In so doing, this manager will assume that the distribution branch has secured the "proper" state of income distribution and that the stabilization branch has secured full employment. Again, this will involve a balanced budget.[7] The manager of the stabilization branch, finally, will provide for the necessary adjustment in aggregate demand, again proceeding on the assumption that the other two branches have met their tasks. By its nature this final budget will consist of either taxes or transfers and thus usually be in imbalance. Taxes and transfers used to accomplish the stabilization task may be designed so as not to interfere with the "proper" distribution as provided by the distribution branch, i.e., they will be proportional to the "proper" pattern of income distribution.

The reader may wonder how this can be done, since the respective plans of the three branches are closely interdependent. The answer is that the system may be solved by simultaneous determination.[8] When the three budgets have been determined in this fashion, it would then be cumbersome for administrative purposes to carry out each budget separately. Rather it will be convenient to clear the taxes imposed by the allocation branch, the taxes and transfers of the distribution branch, and the taxes and transfers of the stabilization branch against each other and to implement only the resulting net transfers and taxes with regard to each consumer. In addition to these net taxes and transfers, government must undertake the purchases of products or resources needed to provide for the services of the allocation branch.

The combined or net budget may thus be viewed as a composite of the three subbudgets. It will have a deficit or surplus, depending on the position of the stabilization branch. Whether the net payment system will be progressive, proportional, or regressive is not obvious. The distribution branch component would tend to make it progressive, but it remains to be seen how the allocation component will look.[9]

This system has been spelled out not as a description of the actual budget process, but to show how the various objectives could be coordinated and pursued without interference with one another. We now turn to the real world of fiscal politics, where the situation is quite different.

Conflict

The distinction among the allocation, distribution, and stabilization aspects of fiscal policy is helpful not only in separating more or less distinct policy objectives but also as a guide to fiscal politics. In the real world setting, budget planning frequently does not permit evaluation of the various policy objectives on their own merits. Individual and group interests clash in their implementation so that achievement of one objective is frequently accomplished at the cost of another. The history of fiscal politics abounds with illustrations of this sort.

Allocation and distribution. Consider first the relationship between allocation and redistribution measures. Although redistribution is accomplished most directly through tax-transfer schemes, it is achieved also by progressive tax finance of the provision for social goods. This is based on an "ability-to-pay approach," by which the distribution of the tax burden is determined by the ability of a taxpayer to sustain the sacrifice of income reduction, independent of the mix of social goods which is supplied and the benefits derived therefrom. Because of this, the degree of redistribution tends to depend on the levels of programs which are to be financed, thus associating extensive provision for social goods with extensive redistribution.

This approach furthered the cause of redistribution when budgets were small and the additional burden could be imposed on high-income recipients. But over time as budgets have increased relative to national income, additional finance had to be drawn more largely from the middle- and low-income groups, thus reversing this effect. In either case, the linkage between expenditure levels and redistribution does not make for efficiency from a normative point of view. People's attitudes toward redistribution need not coincide with their preferences for social goods. A person who wants public services should not have to oppose them because he or she dislikes redistribution, or vice versa. A better policy choice will be made, therefore, if each issue is taken up on its merits.

Allocation and stabilization. Now take the relationship between considerations of allocation and stabilization. In times of unemployment, when an expansion of aggregate demand is needed, an increase in government expenditures is often proposed as a remedy. Similarly, at times of inflation, when demand is to be restricted, a case is made for a reduction in such expenditure.

While it is proper for social goods to share in a general expansion or restriction of expenditures, there is no reason why they should account for the entire or major part of the change. As we have seen, the stabilizing adjustment can also be made through increase or reduction in taxes, or reduction or increase in transfers, while leaving the provision for social goods (appropriate at full-employment income levels) unaffected.

Mixing the issues leads to an oversupply of social goods or to wasteful public expenditures when expansion is needed; and to a no less wasteful undersupply when restriction is called for. Moreover, mixing the issues leads to opposition to expansionary fiscal measures by those who oppose high provision for such goods and to opposition to restrictive measures by those who favor high provision of social goods. If the issues are separated, reasonable people may agree on the need for stabilizing action while differing, in line with their preferences, on the appropriate scale at which social goods are to be provided.

Distribution and stabilization. Finally, consider the relationship between distribution and stabilization objectives. In the past it has been argued during periods of severe unemployment that lower-income groups should be given greater tax relief, since they are likely to spend more of their tax savings than higher-income recipients. The opposite case has been made in times of inflation, namely that taxes on low-income groups should be raised, since they are more potent in reducing demand than taxes on the higher incomes.

Again, proper stabilization action may be interfered with, or redistributional action may be biased, because the two objectives are linked. This is unnecessary since the stabilization adjustment can be made with distributionally neutral taxes—or, for that matter, any pattern of tax distribution—provided only that the overall level of taxation is raised or reduced by a sufficient amount.

Distribution and growth. Similar problems arise if the growth objective is introduced. A higher rate of growth may call for a higher rate of capital formation, which calls for increased saving and investment. Since the marginal propensity to save is higher among high-income recipients than among low-income groups, and since high-income taxpayers undertake most investment, it would seem that the tax structure should be such as to concentrate on lower incomes. Again the conclusion need not follow if we permit the possibility of public saving which, for any given tax-burden distribution, may be achieved through higher tax rates. But, as we shall see, the conflict may not be resolved as easily if effects of taxation on investment incentives are considered. Unless larger reliance on public investment is introduced, a higher rate of growth may be in conflict with redistribution objectives.

As we view these potential conflicts, it becomes evident that the normative view of neatly attuned subbudgets is not a realistic description of the fiscal process. Rather, it must be understood as a standard against which actual performance may be measured and the quality of existing fiscal institutions may be assessed.

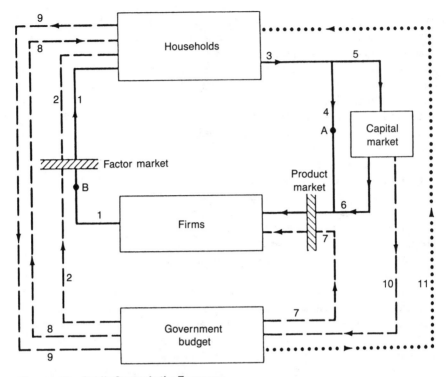

Figure 1 **The Public Sector in the Economy**

F. Interaction of private and public sectors

It will be evident from the preceding review that the functions of the public sector differ sharply from those pursued by private households or firms. At the same time, both sectors interact and are linked in the overall economic process. This interdependence is illustrated in Figure 1, which presents a highly simplified picture of the circular flow of income and expenditure in the economy. We disregard business saving and the foreign sector and assume that all tax revenue derives from the income tax.

Income and expenditure flows. The solid lines of Figure 1 show income and expenditure flows in the private sector; the broken lines show public sector flows. Suppose first that there is no public sector. Moving clockwise along the solid lines, we note how households obtain income through the sale of factors in the factor market (line 1), income which is then spent (line 4) or saved (line 5). Saving in turn finances investment expenditure (line 6).[10] Lines 4 and 6, combining in the purchase of products in the product market, give rise to the receipts of firms, which in turn are used for the purchase of factor services.

When the government is introduced, we note that factors are bought by the public sector (line 2) as well as by the private sector, and that output of private firms is purchased by government (line 7) as well as by private buyers. In addition to factor and product purchases, the government also makes transfer payments (line 8). Government revenue in turn is derived from taxes (line 9) and from borrowing (line 10).

As this diagram shows, the private and public sector flows are closely inter-twined. Note especially that the public sector participates as a buyer in both the factor and the product markets. Its operations are thus an integral part of the pricing system. This is why it is necessary, in designing fiscal policies, to allow for how the private sector will respond. Imposition of a tax at one point in the system—for instance, at point A or point B—may lead to responses which will shift the burden to a quite different point. Moreover, the government not only diverts private income to public use, but through factor and product purchases also contributes to the income flow to households. It is thus misleading to think of the public sector as being ''superimposed'' on the private sector. Rather, they are both integral and interacting parts of what in fact is a mixed economic system.

Factor and product flows. Instead of viewing Figure 1 in terms of income and expenditure flows, it may also be interpreted as showing the real flows of factor inputs and product outputs. Reversing the arrows and moving now in a counter-clockwise direction, lines 1 and 2 show the flow of factor inputs into the private and public sectors, respectively, while lines 4, 6, and 7 show the flow of firm outputs to private and government buyers, respectively.[11] We must now add dotted line 11 to show the flow of public goods and services which are provided free of direct charge to the consumer. This flow, which bypasses the product market, is financed not through sales proceeds but through taxation or through borrowing. Note also that the goods and services which government thus pro-vides (line 11) are only in part produced by government (based on the factor inputs of line 2); the remainder is privately produced (and sold to government as shown in line 7).

G. Summary

This chapter, being itself in the form of a summary, can hardly be summarized further. However, the main ideas presented are these:

1. Modern so-called capitalist economies are in fact ''mixed'' economies, with one-third or more of economic activity occurring in the public sector.

2. . . . The term ''public sector'' is used to refer to those parts of govern-mental economic policy which find their expression in budgetary (expenditure and revenue) measures.

3. Three major types of budgetary activity are distinguished, namely, (1) the public provision of certain goods and services, referred to as ''social goods''; (2) adjustments in the state of distribution of income and wealth; and (3) mea-sures to stabilize the level of economic activity in the economy at large.

4. In discussing the provision of social goods (the allocation function), reference is made to payment for certain goods and services through budgetary finance. Whether the production of these goods is under public management, or whether the goods and services are purchased from private firms, is a different matter.

5. Provision for so-called social goods poses problems which differ from those that arise in connection with private goods. The main point of difference is that social goods tend to be nonrival in consumption and that consumer preferences with regard to such goods are not revealed by consumer bidding in the market. Therefore a political process is required.

6. The pattern of distribution that results from the existing pattern of factor endowments and from the sale of factor services in the market is not necessarily one that society considers as fair. Distributional adjustments may be called for, and tax and transfer policies offer an effective means of implementing them, thus calling for a distribution function in budget policy.

7. Tax and expenditure policies affect aggregate demand and the level of economic activity. They are also an important instrument in maintaining economic stability, including high employment and control of inflation. Hence, the stabilization function enters as the third budgetary function.

8. Fiscal policies may be conducted in centralized or decentralized fashion, with different budgetary functions being more or less appropriate at various levels of governmental activity.

9. Theoretically, budget policies can be designed so that allocation, distribution, and stabilization objectives are accomplished without conflict. But in practice, conflicts are frequent and distortions arise.

10. Although the functions of the public and private sectors differ in important respects, the operations of both interact in the product and factor markets as well as in the income and expenditure flows of the economy.

Notes

1. This summary of the allocation function oversimplifies matters in various respects. Two major qualifications . . . are:
(a) It is unrealistic to think of all goods as being divided into those which are private and those which are social. The existence of externalities and the social-goods problems to which they give rise are a matter of degree, and many goods carry both characteristics. Your education, for instance, will benefit not only you (we hope) but also others.
(b) In some instances, government decides to interfere with consumer preferences. Certain goods may be considered meritorious (milk), whereas others are considered harmful (liquor), so that one is subsidized while the other is taxed. This practice does not fit into the above framework and requires further explanation. See p. 84 [of *Public Finance in Theory and Practice*].
2. See Richard A. Musgrave, *Fiscal Systems*, New Haven, Conn.: Yale, 1969, chap. 2.
3. See p. 100 [of *Public Finance in Theory and Practice*].
4. A *progressive tax* is defined as one in which the ratio of tax to income rises with income.
5. We disregard here other and nonfiscal approaches to distribution policy, such as manpower and education policies or policies designed to counteract discrimination. These measures, of course, also have an important part to play.
6. Since the choice of a desirable rate of growth is essentially a question of present versus future consumption, it may be argued that this is a problem of resource allocation rather than of stabilization, and that policy decisions to affect the rate of growth are in fact

allocation decisions. There is much to be said for this point of view, but the close link to other aspects of stabilization policy renders it convenient to treat growth in this macropolicy context.

7. Subject, however, to the qualification given in connection with considerations of intergeneration equity. See p. 706 [of *Public Finance in Theory and Practice*.]

8. For further discussion, see Richard A. Musgrave, *The Theory of Public Finance*, New York: McGraw-Hill, 1959, chap. 2.

9. See p. 239 [of *Public Finance in Theory and Practice*].

10. For a discussion of what happens if people wish to invest more or less than others intend to save, see p. 593 [of *Public Finance in Theory and Practice*].

11. Since public sector sales (the role of public enterprise) are quite small in the United States economy, this item has been omitted in Figure 1. We may think of government enterprises as included under private firms.

Further readings

Buchanan, J.: "Social Choice, Democracy and Free Markets," *Journal of Political Economy*, December 1954.

Colm, G.: *Essays in Public Finance and Fiscal Policy*, New York: Oxford University Press, 1955, chap. 1.

Houghton, R. W. (ed.): *Public Finance*, Baltimore: Penguin, 1970.

Musgrave, R. A.: *The Theory of Public Finance*, New York: McGraw-Hill, 1959, chaps. 1, 2.

Pigou, A. C.: *A Study in Public Finance*, London: Macmillan, 1928, part I.

Stigler, George F.: *The Citizen and the State*, Chicago: University of Chicago Press, 1975, chaps. 1, 2, 5.

1.2. The Role of Government in a Free Society

MILTON FRIEDMAN

In this reading, Nobel Prize winner Milton Friedman presents a somewhat more restrictive view of the proper role of government than that offered by Musgrave and Musgrave. Arguing that it is imperative to maintain the maximum freedom for individuals, he maintains that the government's role should be limited primarily to three tasks: establishing the conditions for the functioning of free markets, providing law and order, and dealing with what Friedman terms "neighborhood effects." All of these are forms of what are called "public goods" (the Musgraves refer to them as "social goods"). Friedman also argues that many of the services currently performed by government could be better provided by the private market.

Many of the policy changes introduced by the Reagan Administration can be considered applications of Friedman's views. The reader should note that Friedman places less stress than do the Musgraves on redistribution, that he thinks fewer things can properly be called public goods, and that he thinks stabilization is best assured if government sets unchanging policy goals rather than trying to fine-tune the economy.

The reader should also note that the author tends to see freedom as freedom from state interference rather than as freedom from coercion by powerful private actors such as large businesses. In the nineteenth century this view was referred to as liberalism, and so Friedman refers to himself as a liberal, although he is generally characterized as a conservative.

A common objection to totalitarian societies is that they regard the end as justifying the means. Taken literally, this objection is clearly illogical. If the end does not justify the means, what does? But this easy answer does not dispose of the objection; it simply shows that the objection is not well put. To deny that the end justifies the means is indirectly to assert that the end in question is not the ultimate end, that the ultimate end is itself the use of the proper means. Desirable or not, any end that can be attained only by the use of bad means must give way to the more basic end of the use of acceptable means.

To the liberal, the appropriate means are free discussion and voluntary co-operation, which implies that any form of coercion is inappropriate. The ideal is unanimity among responsible individuals achieved on the basis of free and full discussion. This is another way of expressing the goal of freedom. . . .

From this standpoint, the role of the market, as already noted, is that it permits unanimity without conformity; that it is a system of effectively proportional representation. On the other hand, the characteristic feature of action through explicitly political channels is that it tends to require or to enforce substantial conformity. The typical issue must be decided "yes" or "no"; at most, provision can be made for a fairly limited number of alternatives. Even the use of proportional representation in its explicitly political form does not alter this conclusion. The number of separate groups that can in fact be represented is narrowly limited, enormously so by comparison with the proportional representation of the market. More important, the fact that the final outcome generally must be a law applicable to all groups, rather than separate legislative enactments for each "party" represented, means that proportional representation in its political version, far from permitting unanimity without conformity, tends toward ineffectiveness and fragmentation. It thereby operates to destroy any consensus on which unanimity with conformity can rest.

There are clearly some matters with respect to which effective proportional representation is impossible. I cannot get the amount of national defense I want and you, a different amount. With respect to such indivisible matters we can discuss, and argue, and vote. But having decided, we must conform. It is precisely the existence of such indivisible matters—protection of the individual and the nation from coercion are clearly the most basic—that prevents exclusive reliance on individual action through the market. If we are to use some of our resources for such indivisible items, we must employ political channels to reconcile differences.

The use of political channels, while inevitable, tends to strain the social cohesion essential for a stable society. The strain is least if agreement for joint action need be reached only on a limited range of issues on which people in any event have common views. Every extension of the range of issues for which explicit agreement is sought strains further the delicate threads that hold society together. If it goes so far as to touch an issue on which men feel deeply yet differently, it may well disrupt the society. Fundamental differences in basic values can seldom if ever be resolved at the ballot box; ultimately they can only be decided, though not resolved, by conflict. The religious and civil wars of history are a bloody testament to this judgment.

The widespread use of the market reduces the strain on the social fabric by rendering conformity unnecessary with respect to any activities it encompasses. The wider the range of activities covered by the market, the fewer are the issues on which explicitly political decisions are required and hence on which it is necessary to achieve agreement. In turn, the fewer the issues on which agreement is necessary, the greater is the likelihood of getting agreement while maintaining a free society.

Unanimity is, of course, an ideal. In practice, we can afford neither the time nor the effort that would be required to achieve complete unanimity on every issue. We must perforce accept something less. We are thus led to accept majority rule in one form or another as an expedient. That majority rule is an expedient rather than itself a basic principle is clearly shown by the fact that our willingness to resort to majority rule, and the size of the majority we require, themselves depend on the seriousness of the issue involved. If the matter is of little moment and the minority has no strong feelings about being overruled, a bare plurality will suffice. On the other hand, if the minority feels strongly about the issue involved, even a bare majority will not do. Few of us would be willing to have issues of free speech, for example, decided by a bare majority. Our legal structure is full of such distinctions among kinds of issues that require different kinds of majorities. At the extreme are those issues embodied in the Constitution. These are the principles that are so important that we are willing to make minimal concessions to expediency. Something like essential consensus was achieved initially in accepting them, and we require something like essential consensus for a change in them.

The self-denying ordinance to refrain from majority rule on certain kinds of issues that is embodied in our Constitution and in similar written or unwritten constitutions elsewhere, and the specific provisions in these constitutions or their equivalents prohibiting coercion of individuals, are themselves to be regarded as reached by free discussion and as reflecting essential unanimity about means.

I turn now to consider more specifically, though still in very broad terms, what the areas are that cannot be handled through the market at all, or can be handled only at so great a cost that the use of political channels may be preferable.

Government as rule-maker and umpire

It is important to distinguish the day-to-day activities of people from the general customary and legal framework within which these take place. The day-to-day activities are like the actions of the participants in a game when they are playing it; the framework, like the rules of the game they play. And just as a good game requires acceptance by the players both of the rules and of the umpire to interpret and enforce them, so a good society requires that its members agree on the general conditions that will govern relations among them, on some means of arbitrating different interpretations of these conditions, and on some device for enforcing compliance with the generally accepted rules. As in games, so also in society, most of the general conditions are the unintended outcome of custom, accepted unthinkingly. At most, we consider explicitly only minor modifications in them, though the cumulative effect of a series of minor modifications may be a drastic alteration in the character of the game or of the society. In both games and society also, no set of rules can prevail unless most participants most of the time conform to them without external sanctions; unless that is, there is a broad underlying social consensus. But we cannot rely on custom or on this consensus alone to interpret and to enforce the rules; we need an umpire. These then are the basic roles of government in a free society: to provide a means whereby we can modify the rules, to mediate differences among us on the meaning of the rules, and to enforce compliance with the rules on the part of those few who would otherwise not play the game.

The need for government in these respects arises because absolute freedom is impossible. However attractive anarchy may be as a philosophy, it is not feasible in a world of imperfect men. Men's freedoms can conflict, and when they do, one man's freedom must be limited to preserve another's—as a Supreme Court Justice once put it, "My freedom to move my fist must be limited by the proximity of your chin."

The major problem in deciding the appropriate activities of government is how to resolve such conflicts among the freedoms of different individuals. In some cases, the answer is easy. There is little difficulty in attaining near unanimity to the proposition that one man's freedom to murder his neighbor must be sacrificed to preserve the freedom of the other man to live. In other cases, the answer is difficult. In the economic area, a major problem arises in respect of the conflict between freedom to combine and freedom to compete. What meaning is to be attributed to "free" as modifying "enterprise"? In the United States, "free" has been understood to mean that anyone is free to set up an enterprise, which means that existing enterprises are not free to keep out competitors except by selling a better product at the same price or the same product at a lower price. In the continental tradition, on the other hand, the meaning has generally been that enterprises are free to do what they want, including the fixing of prices, division of markets, and the adoption of other techniques to keep out potential competitors. Perhaps the most difficult specific problem in this area arises with respect to combinations among laborers, where the problem of freedom to combine and freedom to compete is particularly acute.

A still more basic economic area in which the answer is both difficult and important is the definition of property rights. The notion of property, as it has developed over centuries and as it is embodied in our legal codes, has become so much a part of us that we tend to take it for granted, and fail to recognize the extent to which just what constitutes property and what rights the ownership of property confers are complex social creations rather than self-evident propositions. Does my having title to land, for example, and my freedom to use my property as I wish, permit me to deny to someone else the right to fly over my land in his airplane? Or does his right to use his airplane take precedence? Or does this depend on how high he flies? Or how much noise he makes? Does voluntary exchange require that he pay me for the privilege of flying over my land? Or that I must pay him to refrain from flying over it? The mere mention of royalties, copyrights, patents; shares of stock in corporations; riparian rights, and the like, may perhaps emphasize the role of generally accepted social rules in the very definition of property. It may suggest also that, in many cases, the existence of a well specified and generally accepted definition of property is far more important than just what the definition is.

Another economic area that raises particularly difficult problems is the monetary system. Government responsibility for the monetary system has long been recognized. It is explicitly provided for in the constitutional provision which gives Congress the power "to coin money, regulate the value thereof, and of foreign coin." There is probably no other area of economic activity with respect to which government action has been so uniformly accepted. This habitual and by now almost unthinking acceptance of governmental repsonsibility makes thorough understanding of the grounds for such responsibility all the more necessary, since it enhances the danger that the scope of government will spread from activities that are, to those that are not, appropriate in a free society, from providing a monetary framework to determining the allocation of resources among individuals. . . .

In summary, the organization of economic activity through voluntary exchange presumes that we have provided, through government, for the maintenance of law and order to prevent coercion of one individual by another, the enforcement of contracts voluntarily entered into, the definition of the meaning of property rights, the interpretation and enforcement of such rights, and the provision of a monetary framework.

Action through government on grounds of technical monopoly and neighborhood effects

The role of government just considered is to do something that the market cannot do for itself, namely, to determine, arbitrate, and enforce the rules of the game. We may also want to do through government some things that might conceivably be done through the market but that technical or similar conditions render it difficult to do in that way. These all reduce to cases in which strictly voluntary exchange is either exceedingly costly or practically impossible. There are two general classes of such cases: monopoly and similar market imperfections, and neighborhood effects.

Exchange is truly voluntary only when nearly equivalent alternatives exist. Monopoly implies the absence of alternatives and thereby inhibits effective freedom of exchange. In practice, monopoly frequently, if not generally, arises from government support or from collusive agreements among individuals. With respect to these, the problem is either to avoid governmental fostering of monopoly or to stimulate the effective enforcement of rules such as those embodied in our anti-trust laws. However, monopoly may also arise because it is technically efficient to have a single producer or enterprise. I venture to suggest that such cases are more limited than is supposed but they unquestionably do arise. A

simple example is perhaps the provision of telephone services within a community. I shall refer to such cases as "technical" monopoly.

When technical conditions make a monopoly the natural outcome of competitive market forces, there are only three alternatives that seem available: private
monopoly, public monopoly, or public regulation. All three are bad so we must
choose among evils. Henry Simons, observing public regulation of monopoly in
the United States, found the results so distasteful that he concluded public monopoly would be a lesser evil. Walter Eucken, a noted German liberal, observing
public monopoly in German railroads, found the results so distasteful that he
concluded public regulation would be a lesser evil. Having learned from both, I
reluctantly conclude that, if tolerable, private monopoly may be the least of the
evils.

If society were static so that the conditions which give rise to a technical
monopoly were sure to remain, I would have little confidence in this solution. In a
rapidly changing society, however, the conditions making for technical monopoly
frequently change and I suspect that both public regulation and public monopoly
are likely to be less responsive to such changes in conditions, to be less readily
capable of elimination, than private monopoly.

Railroads in the United States are an excellent example. A large degree of
monopoly in railroads was perhaps inevitable on technical grounds in the nineteenth century. This was the justification for the Interstate Commerce Commission. But conditions have changed. The emergence of road and air transport has
reduced the monopoly element in railroads to negligible proportions. Yet we have
not eliminated the ICC. On the contrary, the ICC, which started out as an agency
to protect the public from exploitation by the railroads, has become an agency to
protect railroads from competition by trucks and other means of transport, and
more recently even to protect existing truck companies from competition by new
entrants. Similarly, in England, when the railroads were nationalized, trucking
was at first brought into the state monopoly. If railroads had never been subjected
to regulation in the United States, it is nearly certain that by now transportation,
including railroads, would be a highly competitive industry with little or no
remaining monopoly elements.

The choice between the evils of private monopoly, public monopoly, and public
regulation cannot, however, be made once and for all, independently of the factual
circumstances. If the technical monopoly is of a service or commodity that is
regarded as essential and if its monopoly power is sizable, even the short-run
effects of private unregulated monopoly may not be tolerable, and either public
regulation or ownership may be a lesser evil.

Technical monopoly may on occasion justify a *de facto* public monopoly. It
cannot by itself justify a public monopoly achieved by making it illegal for anyone
else to compete. For example, there is no way to justify our present public
monopoly of the post office. It may be argued that the carrying of mail is a
technical monopoly and that a government monopoly is the least of evils. Along
these lines, one could perhaps justify a government post office but not the present

law, which makes it illegal for anybody else to carry mail. If the delivery of mail is a technical monopoly, no one will be able to succeed in competition with the government. If it is not, there is no reason why the government should be engaged in it. The only way to find out is to leave other people free to enter.

The historical reason why we have a post office monopoly is because the Pony Express did such a good job of carrying the mail across the continent that, when the government introduced transcontinental service, it couldn't compete effectively and lost money. The result was a law making it illegal for anybody else to carry the mail. That is why the Adams Express Company is an investment trust today instead of an operating company. I conjecture that if entry into the mail-carrying business were open to all, there would be a large number of firms entering it and this archaic industry would become revolutionized in short order.

A second general class of cases in which strictly voluntary exchange is impossible arises when actions of individuals have effects on other individuals for which it is not feasible to charge or recompense them. This is the problem of "neighborhood effects." An obvious example is the pollution of a stream. The man who pollutes a stream is in effect forcing others to exchange good water for bad. These others might be willing to make the exchange at a price. But it is not feasible for them, acting individually, to avoid the exchange or to enforce appropriate compensation.

A less obvious example is the provision of highways. In this case, it is technically possible to identify and hence charge individuals for their use of the roads and so to have private operation. However, for general access roads, involving many points of entry and exit, the costs of collection would be extremely high if a charge were to be made for the specific services received by each individual, because of the necessity of establishing toll booths or the equivalent at all entrances. The gasoline tax is a much cheaper method of charging individuals roughly in proportion to their use of the roads. This method, however, is one in which the particular payment cannot be identified closely with the particular use. Hence, it is hardly feasible to have private enterprise provide the service and collect the charge without establishing extensive private monopoly.

These considerations do not apply to long-distance turnpikes with high density of traffic and limited access. For these, the costs of collection are small and in many cases are now being paid, and there are often numerous alternatives, so that there is no serious monopoly problem. Hence, there is every reason why these should be privately owned and operated. If so owned and operated, the enterprise running the highway should receive the gasoline taxes paid on account of travel on it.

Parks are an interesting example because they illustrate the difference between cases that can and cases that cannot be justified by neighborhood effects, and because almost everyone at first sight regards the conduct of National Parks as obviously a valid function of government. In fact, however, neighborhood effects may justify a city park; they do not justify a national park, like Yellowstone

National Park or the Grand Canyon. What is the fundamental difference between the two? For the city park, it is extremely difficult to identify the people who benefit from it and to charge them for the benefits which they receive. If there is a park in the middle of the city, the houses on all sides get the benefit of the open space, and people who walk through it or by it also benefit. To maintain toll collectors at the gates or to impose annual charges per window overlooking the park would be very expensive and difficult. The entrances to a national park like Yellowstone, on the other hand, are few; most of the people who come stay for a considerable period of time and it is perfectly feasible to set up toll gates and collect admission charges. This is indeed now done, though the charges do not cover the whole costs. If the public wants this kind of an activity enough to pay for it, private enterprises will have every incentive to provide such parks. And, of course, there are many private enterprises of this nature now in existence. I cannot myself conjure up any neighborhood effects or important monopoly effects that would justify governmental activity in this area.

Considerations like those I have treated under the heading of neighborhood effects have been used to rationalize almost every conceivable intervention. In many instances, however, this rationalization is special pleading rather than a legitimate application of the concept of neighborhood effects. Neighborhood effects cut both ways. They can be a reason for limiting the activities of government as well as for expanding them. Neighborhood effects impede voluntary exchange because it is difficult to identify the effects on third parties and to measure their magnitude; but this difficulty is present in governmental activity as well. It is hard to know when neighborhood effects are sufficiently large to justify particular costs in overcoming them and even harder to distribute the costs in an appropriate fashion. Consequently, when government engages in activities to overcome neighborhood effects, it will in part introduce an additional set of neighborhood effects by failing to charge or to compensate individuals properly. Whether the original or the new neighborhood effects are the more serious can only be judged by the facts of the individual case, and even then, only very approximately. Furthermore, the use of government to overcome neighborhood effects itself has an extremely important neighborhood effect which is unrelated to the particular occasion for government action. Every act of government intervention limits the area of individual freedom directly and threatens the preservation of freedom indirectly. . . .

Our principles offer no hard and fast line how far it is appropriate to use government to accomplish jointly what it is difficult or impossible for us to accomplish separately through strictly voluntary exchange. In any particular case of proposed intervention, we must make up a balance sheet, listing separately the advantages and disadvantages. Our principles tell us what items to put on the one side and what items on the other and they give us some basis for attaching importance to the different items. In particular, we shall always want to enter on the liability side of any proposed government intervention, its neighborhood effect in threatening freedom, and give this effect considerable weight. Just how much weight to give to it, as to other items, depends upon the circumstances. If, for example, existing government intervention is minor, we shall attach a smaller weight to the negative effects of additional government intervention. This is an important reason why many earlier liberals, like Henry Simons, writing at a time when government was small by today's standards, were willing to have government undertake activities that today's liberals would not accept now that government has become so overgrown.

Action through government on paternalistic grounds

Freedom is a tenable objective only for responsible individuals. We do not believe in freedom for madmen or children. The necessity of drawing a line between responsible individuals and others is inescapable, yet it means that there is an essential ambiguity in our ultimate objective of freedom. Paternalism is inescapable for those whom we designate as not responsible.

The clearest case, perhaps, is that of madmen. We are willing neither to permit them freedom nor to shoot them. It would be nice if we could rely on voluntary activities of individuals to house and care for the madmen. But I think we cannot rule out the possibility that such charitable activities will be inadequate, if only because of the neighborhood effect involved in the fact that I benefit if another man contributes to the care of the insane. For this reason, we may be willing to arrange for their care through government.

Children offer a more difficult case. The ultimate operative unit in our society is the family, not the individual. Yet the acceptance of the family as the unit rests in considerable part on expediency rather than principle. We believe that parents are generally best able to protect their children and to provide for their development into responsible individuals for whom freedom is appropriate. But we do not believe in the freedom of parents to do what they will with other people. The children are responsible individuals in embryo, and a believer in freedom believes in protecting their ultimate rights.

To put this in a different and what may seem a more callous way, children are at one and the same time consumer goods and potentially responsible members of society. The freedom of individuals to use their economic resources as they want includes the freedom to use them to have children—to buy, as it were, the services of children as a particular form of consumption. But once this choice is exercised, the children have a value in and of themselves and have a freedom of their own that is not simply an extension of the freedom of the parents.

The paternalistic ground for governmental activity is in many ways the most troublesome to a liberal; for it involves the acceptance of a principle—that some shall decide for others—which he finds objectionable in most applications and which he rightly regards as a hallmark of his chief intellectual opponents, the proponents of collectivism in one or another of its guises, whether it be communism, socialism, or a welfare state. Yet there is no use pretending that problems are simpler than in fact they are. There is no avoiding the need for some measure of paternalism. As Dicey wrote in 1914 about an act for the protection of mental defectives, "The Mental Deficiency Act is the first step along a path on which no sane man can decline to enter, but which, if too far pursued, will bring statesmen across difficulties hard to meet without considerable interference with individual liberty."[1] There is no formula that can tell us where to stop. We must rely on our fallible judgment and having reached a judgment, on our ability to persuade our fellow men that it is a correct judgment, or their ability to persuade us to modify our views. We must put our faith, here as elsewhere, in a consensus reached by imperfect and biased men through free discussion and trial and error.

Conclusion

A government which maintained law and order, defined property rights, served as a means whereby we could modify property rights and other rules of the economic game, adjudicated disputes about the interpretation of the rules, enforced contracts, promoted competition, provided a monetary framework, engaged in activities to counter technical monopolies and to overcome neighborhood effects widely regarded as sufficiently important to justify government intervention, and which supplemented private charity and the private family in protecting the irresponsible, whether madman or child—such a government would clearly have important functions to perform. The consistent liberal is not an anarchist.

Yet it is also true that such a government would have clearly limited functions and would refrain from a host of activities that are now undertaken by federal and state governments in the United States, and their counterparts in other Western countries. . . . [I]t may help to give a sense of proportion about the role that a liberal would assign government simply to list, in closing this chapter, some activities currently undertaken by government in the U.S., that cannot, so far as I can see, validly be justified in terms of the principles outlined above:

1. Parity price support programs for agriculture.
2. Tariffs on imports or restrictions on exports, such as current oil import quotas, sugar quotas, etc.
3. Governmental control of output, such as through the farm program, or through prorationing of oil as is done by the Texas Railroad Commission.
4. Rent control, such as is still practiced in New York, or more general price and wage controls such as were imposed during and just after World War II.
5. Legal minimum wage rates, or legal maximum prices, such as the legal maximum of zero on the rate of interest that can be paid on demand deposits by commercial banks, or the legally fixed maximum rates that can be paid on savings and time deposits.
6. Detailed regulation of industries, such as the regulation of transportation by the Interstate Commerce Commission. This had some justification on technical monopoly grounds when initially introduced for railroads; it has none now for

any means of transport. Another example is detailed regulation of banking.

7. A similar example, but one which deserves special mention because of its implicit censorship and violation of free speech, is the control of radio and television by the Federal Communications Commission.

8. Present social security programs, especially the old-age and retirement programs compelling people in effect (*a*) to spend a specified fraction of their income on the purchase of retirement annuity, (*b*) to buy the annuity from a publicly operated enterprise.

9. Licensure provisions in various cities and states which restrict particular enterprises or occupations or professions to people who have a license, where the license is more than a receipt for a tax which anyone who wishes to enter the activity may pay.

10. So-called "public-housing" and the host of other subsidy programs directed at fostering residential construction such as F.H.A. and V.A. guarantee of mortgage, and the like.

11. Conscription to man the military services in peacetime. The appropriate free market arrangement is volunteer military forces; which is to say, hiring men to serve. There is no justification for not paying whatever price is necessary to attract the required number of men. Present arrangements are inequitable and arbitrary, seriously interfere with the freedom of young men to shape their lives, and probably are even more costly than the market alternative. (Universal military training to provide a reserve for war time is a different problem and may be justified on liberal grounds.)

12. National parks, as noted above.

13. The legal prohibition on the carrying of mail for profit.

14. Publicly owned and operated toll roads, as noted above.

This list is far from comprehensive.

Note

1. A. V. Dicey, *Lectures on the Relation between Law and Public Opinion in England during the Nineteenth Century* (2d. ed.; London: Macmillan & Co., 1914), p. li.

1.3. The Fiscal Crisis of the State

JAMES O'CONNOR

In this introduction to his fascinating but controversial book, The Fiscal Crisis of the State, *James O'Connor outlines a very different model for looking at the role of government in the economy. He starts by claiming that governments have two basic functions. One is to maintain the process of investment, which keeps the capitalist system running. O'Connor calls this the* capital accumulation *function. The second is to maintain the support of the people for the current unequal distribution of economic, social, and political power. He calls this the* legitimacy *function.*

O'Connor's central argument is that these two functions necessarily conflict. The state is subject to pressure simultaneously from large firms, which want the government to cover an ever-increasing share of their real costs, and from taxpayers, who resent having to pay higher and higher taxes to support these subsidies. Governments attempt makeshift solutions, but these rapidly degenerate, giving rise to new crises. It will be interesting for the reader to ask how well this reading from 1973 predicts the large federal deficits and other economic problems of the 1980s.

"Lockheed Gets Loan Guarantees," "President Says, 'No Vietnam Dividend,'" "New $50 Million BART Issue," "Medicare Spending Up 20%," "30% City Budget Increase," "Teachers' Strike Begins Third Week," "Violence Mars Welfare Rights Demonstration"—these were some of the typical headlines of the 1960s and early 1970s. Each is a variation on the same theme: Corporations want government to build more freeways; bankers and investors want government to underwrite more loans and investments; small businessmen and farmers want more subsidies; organized labor wants more social insurance; welfare rights groups want higher income allowances, more housing, and better public health services; government employees want higher wages and salaries; and government agencies want more appropriations.

Other familiar headlines—"School Bond Issue Voted Down," "Gallup Poll: Tax Relief Top Worry," "Unified School District Referendum Defeated," "Commuter Tax Declared Unconstitutional," "Homeowners Vote to Shift Tax to Downtown Business," "Reagan Supports State Withholding Tax"—tell a similar story. Large corporations and wealthy investors want working people and small businessmen to foot the bill for airport modernization, freeway expansion, rapid transit, water investment projects, and pollution control. Small business-men and homeowners want property tax relief. Middle-income wage and salary earners want income tax relief. Poor people want tax relief, period. Suburbanites don't want to pay taxes in the central city where they work, and they don't want central-city residents to get any of the taxes that they pay in the suburbs.

Every economic and social class and group wants government to spend more and more money on more and more things. But no one wants to pay new taxes or higher rates on old taxes. Indeed, nearly everyone wants lower taxes, and many groups have agitated successfully for tax relief. Society's demands on local and state budgets seemingly are unlimited, but people's willingness and capacity to pay for these demands appear to be narrowly limited. And at the federal level expenditures have increased significantly faster than the growth of total produc-tion. In the words of the head of the Federal Reserve System,

> We stand at a crossroads in our fiscal arrangements. Many of our citizens are alarmed by the increasing share of their incomes that is taken away by Federal, State, and local taxes. . . . The propensity to spend more than we are prepared to finance through taxes is becoming deep-seated and ominous. An early end to Federal deficits is not now in sight. Numerous Federal programs have a huge growth of expenditures built into them, and there are proposals presently before the Congress that would raise expenditures by vast amounts in coming years.[1]

We have termed this tendency for government expenditures to outrace rev-enues the "fiscal crisis of the state." There is no iron law that expenditures must always rise more rapidly than revenues, but it is a fact that growing needs which only the state can meet create ever greater claims on the state budget. Several factors, singly or in combination, may offset the crisis. People who need govern-ment-provided services may be ignored and their need neglected, as happened in New York's welfare cutback during the 1970–1971 recession. Corporations that want loans and subsidies from the government may not get them, as happened in the Congressional defeat of proposed subsidies for the development of the SST. Government-employee income may fall behind private sector income or below the cost of living, but this does not mean that these workers get automatic pay increases. In fact, the government may even freeze wages and salaries in an attempt to ameliorate the fiscal crisis. Furthermore, people can be forced to pay higher taxes. Should they be unwilling to pay taxes directly because large num-bers oppose particular spending programs, the government can force them to pay taxes indirectly by financing increased expenditures via inflation or credit expan-sion—as the Johnson Administration did during the peak years of American aggression in Southeast Asia.

A combination of some of these countertendencies resulted in budgetary surpluses in many state and local governments in 1972. According to one "optimistic" estimate, state and local governments will be able to meet their normal needs through 1975 by increasing tax rates by not more than 5 percent.[2]

The volume and composition of government expenditures and the distribution of the tax burden are not determined by the laws of the market but rather reflect and are structurally determined by social and economic conflicts between classes and groups. The English Prime Minister Gladstone once said that "budgets are not merely matters of arithmetic, but in a thousand ways go to the root of prosperity of individuals, and relations of classes, and the strength of Kingdoms." The "relations of classes" were then expressed in many ways that today are of only historical interest. In modern America individual well-being, class relationships, and national wealth and power are bound up in the agony of the cities, poverty and racism, profits of big and small business, inflation, unemployment, the balance-of-payments problem, imperialism and war, and other crises that seem a permanent part of daily life. No one is exempt from the fiscal crisis and the underlying social crisis which it aggravates. We need a way to think about and ultimately act on this fiscal crisis that clarifies the contradictory processes which find both their reflection and cause in the government budget. We need a theory of government budget and a method for discovering the meaning for the political economy and society as a whole.

Perhaps then we will be able to answer such questions as: Who will pay for rising government expenditures? Will some kinds of spending rise while others are cut back? Can the government deliver more services for less taxes? Why don't Americans want to pay for services that presumably benefit the "people"? Can the fiscal system survive in its present form? Political-economic analysis is needed to answer these and dozens of other equally important related questions.

The theoretical bankruptcy of traditional economics

The theory of government budget put forth in this work is based on the study of fiscal politics, an investigation of the sociological foundations of government or state finances.[3] The main concerns of fiscal politics are to discover the principles governing the volume and allocation of state finances and expenditures and the distribution of the tax burden among various economic classes. The major work of the German Marxist Rudolph Goldscheid, founder of the contemporary science of fiscal politics, appeared in the second decade of this century.[4] A few years thereafter Joseph Schumpeter wrote glowingly of the promise of fiscal politics:

> The public finances are one of the best starting points for an investigation of society, especially though not exclusively of its political life. The full fruitfulness of this approach is seen particularly at those turning points, or better epochs, during which existing forms begin to die off and to change into something new.

> This is true both of the causal significance of fiscal policy (insofar as fiscal events are an important element in the causation of all change) and of the symptomatic significance (insofar as everything that happens has its fiscal reflection). Notwithstanding all the qualifications which always have to be made . . . we may surely speak of . . . a special field: fiscal sociology, of which much may be expected.[5]

Schumpeter's optimism proved to be premature. The budget remains, in his words, a "collection of hard, naked facts" not yet "drawn into the realm of sociology." "Unfortunately," one scholar confesses, "there exists no integrated theory of the economics and politics of public finance which would serve as a framework for analyzing [state] finance."[6] No blunter admission of theoretical bankruptcy can be found than the declaration that within the mainstream of Western economic thought,

> public finance, traditionally, has neither contained a theory of demand nor one of supply. . . . The scholar from outer space, coming to earth in the post-Marshallian era, might have concluded on perusing the English-language literature that governments exist wholly apart from their citizens, that these units impose taxes on individuals and firms primarily to nourish the state; and he might have thought that positive public finance consists in predicting the effects of these taxes.[7]

The "scholar from outer space" would have been only partly right. Orthodox public finance theorists are concerned not only with the economic effects of taxation (and expenditures), but also with the problem of what the government should take away in taxes (and provide in expenditures). For example, in his study of state enterprise Ralph Turvey writes that "because it is public, what interests us about public enterprise is how it ought to behave. . . . [W]e are not so much concerned with understanding its behavior and making predictions as with criticizing and making recommendations."[8] Turvey's interest lies in how the behavior of state enterprise can be made to conform to a preconceived notion of economic optimum. This is the focus of the best known treatise on public finance, Richard Musgrave's *The Theory of Public Finance*. Musgrave tries to synthesize the entire modern literature on government finance and, in particular, "to state the rules and principles that make for an efficient conduct of the public economy." Musgrave devises an "optimal budget plan on the basis of initially defined conditions" and then tries to "see how it can be achieved." He calls it "a normative or optimal theory of the public household."[9]

The effect of this emphasis on normative theory has been to ignore the application of the theory of economic growth. The absence of an "integrated theory of the economics and politics of public finance" (or "a theory of demand and supply of public goods and services") has compelled economists to adopt an almost metaphysical attitude toward government spending. For example, the Keynesian Evsey Domar theorized that government expenditures can be dealt with (1) by assuming that they are exogenous, or determined by forces outside the economic system; (2) by merging them with consumption expenditures; or (3) by assuming them away altogether. The last alternative is obviously completely unsatisfactory, and to assume that government spending is determined by undefinable outside forces is to beg the question. And merging all government spending with private consumption is merely a convenient fiction. Methods of analysis such as this have led two public finance specialists to write that "growth models in their present form cannot be treated as anything more than exercises in a technique of arrangement."[10]

As government expenditures come to constitute a larger and larger share of total spending in advanced capitalist countries, economic theorists who ignore the impact of the state budget do so at their own (and capitalism's) peril. Currently, economists do not consider actual determinants in their theoretical models but rather restrict themselves to estimates of the volume of state spending necessary to effect desired changes such as high employment or more rapid accumulation and growth. Their premise is that the government budget should and can be increased or lowered to compensate for reduced or increased private spending. Many orthodox economists believe that the volume of federal spending (if not its composition) is determined by and inversely related to the volume of private spending.

As will be seen in the course of this study, the orthodox approach is at best simplistic. Although changes in tax rates and tax structure have been increasingly used to regulate private economic activity, the growth of federal spending over the past two or three decades has not resulted from the government's adopting compensatory fiscal policies, "except perhaps to a very limited degree."[11] Particular expenditures and programs and the budget as a whole are explicable only in terms of power relationships within the private economy.

Summation of the theory of the fiscal crisis

To avoid "exercises in a technique of arrangement," we have attempted to develop a theory of economic growth that is rooted in the basic economic and political facts of late capitalist society. We hope to elucidate the relationship between the private and state sectors and between private and state spending. Although we believe that many of the ideas presented can be adapted to the experience of other advanced capitalist countries, the focus is on the post–World War II United States. Basically an interpretation of the period's economic development and crisis tendencies, this study does not offer a comprehensive analysis of state budgetary planning and policy or a comprehensive guide to state finance. Many of the data presented have been chosen more to illustrate a line of theoretical argument than to verify a set of hypotheses.

The categories that make up this theoretical framework are drawn from Marxist economics and adapted to the problem of budgetary analysis. Our first premise is that the capitalistic state must try to fulfill two basic and often mutually contradictory functions—*accumulation* and *legitimization*. This means that the state must try to maintain or create the conditions in which profitable capital accumulation is possible. However, the state also must try to maintain or create the conditions for social harmony. A capitalist state that openly uses its coercive forces to help one class accumulate capital at the expense of other classes loses its legitimacy and hence undermines the basis of its loyalty and support. But a state that ignores the necessity of assisting the process of capital accumulation risks drying up the source of its own power, the economy's surplus production capacity and the taxes drawn from this surplus (and other forms of capital). This contradiction explains why President Nixon calls a legislated increase in profit rates a "job development credit," why the government announces that new fiscal policies are aimed at "stability and growth" when in fact their purpose is to keep profits high and growing, why the tax system is nominally progressive and theoretically based on "ability to pay" when in fact the system is regressive. The state must involve itself in the accumulation process, but it must either mystify its policies by calling them something that they are not, or it must try to conceal them (e.g., by making them into administrative, not political, issues).

Our second premise is that the fiscal crisis can be understood only in terms of the basic Marxist economic categories (adapted to the problems taken up here). State expenditures have a twofold character corresponding to the capitalist state's two basic functions: social capital and social expenses. *Social capital* is expenditures required for profitable private accumulation; it is indirectly productive (in Marxist terms, social capital indirectly expands surplus value). There are two kinds of social capital: social investment and social consumption (in Marxist terms, social constant capital and social variable capital). *Social investment* consists of projects and services that increase the productivity of a given amount of laborpower and, other factors being equal, increase the rate of profit. A good example is state-financed industrial-development parks. *Social consumption* consists of projects and services that lower the reproduction costs of labor and, other factors being equal, increase the rate of profit. An example of this is social insurance, which expands the reproductive powers of the work force while simultaneously lowering labor costs. The second category, *social expenses*, consists of projects and services which are required to maintain social harmony—to fulfill the state's "legitimization" function. They are not even indirectly productive. The best example is the welfare system, which is designed chiefly to keep social peace among unemployed workers. (The costs of politically repressed populations in revolt would also constitute a part of social expenses.)

Because of the dual and contradictory character of the capitalist state, nearly every state agency is involved in the accumulation and legitimization functions, and nearly every state expenditure has this twofold character. For example, some education spending constitutes social capital (e.g., teachers and equipment needed to reproduce and expand work-force technical and skill levels), whereas other outlays constitute social expenses (e.g., salaries of campus policemen). To take another example, the main purpose of some transfer payments (e.g., social insurance) is to reproduce the work force, whereas the purpose of others (e.g., income subsidies to the poor) is to pacify and control the surplus population. The national income accounts lump the various categories of state spending together. (The state does not analyze its budget in class terms.) Clearly, the different categories cannot be separated if each budget item is not examined.

Furthermore, precisely because of the social character of social capital and social expenses, nearly every state expenditure serves these two (or more) purposes simultaneously, so that few state outlays can be classified unambiguously. For example, freeways move workers to and from work and are therefore items of social consumption, but they also transport commercial freight and are therefore a form of social investment. And, when used for either purpose, they may be considered forms of social capital. However, the Pentagon also needs freeways; therefore they in part constitute social expenses. Despite this complex social character of state outlays we can determine the political-economic forces served by any budgetary decision, and thus the main purpose (or purposes) of each budgetary item.

The first basic thesis presented here is that the growth of the state sector and state spending is functioning increasingly as the basis for the growth of the monopoly sector and total production. Conversely, it is argued that the growth of state spending and state programs is the result of the growth of the monopoly industries. In other words, the growth of the state is both a cause and effect of the expansion of monopoly capital.

More specifically, the socialization of the cost of social investment and social consumption capital increases over time and increasingly is needed for profitable accumulation by monopoly capital. The general reason is that the increase in the social character of production (specialization, division of labor, interdependency, the growth of new social forms of capital such as education, etc.) either prohibits or renders unprofitable the private accumulation of constant and variable capital. The growth of the monopoly sector is irrational in the sense that it is accompanied by unemployment, poverty, economic stagnation, and so on. To insure mass loyalty and maintain its legitimacy, the state must meet various demands of those who suffer the "costs" of economic growth.

It might help to compare our approach with traditional economic theory. Bourgeois economists have shown that increases in private consumption beget increases in private investment via the accelerator effect. In turn, increases in private investment beget increases in private consumption via the multiplier effect. Similarly, we argue that greater social investment and social consumption spending generate greater private investment and private consumption spending, which in turn generate surplus capital (surplus productive capacity and a surplus population) and a larger volume of social expenses. Briefly, the supply of social capital creates the demand for social expenses. In effect, we work with a model of expanded reproduction (or a model of the economy as a whole) which is generalized to take into account the socialization of constant and variable capital costs and the costs of social expenses.[12] The impact of the budget depends on the volume and indirect productivity of social capital and the volume of social expenses. On the one hand, social capital outlays indirectly increase productive capacity and simultaneously increase aggregate demand. On the other hand, social expense outlays do not increase productive capacity, although they do expand aggregate demand. Whether the growth of productive capacity runs ahead or behind the growth of demand thus depends on the composition of the state budget. In this way, we can see that the theory of economic growth depends on class and political analyses of the determinants of the budget.

This view contrasts sharply with modern conservative thought, which asserts that the state sector grows at the expense of private industry. We argue that the growth of the state sector is indispensable to the expansion of private industry, particularly monopoly industries. Our thesis also contrasts sharply with a basic tenet of modern liberal thought—that the expansion of monopoly industries inhibits the growth of the state sector.[13] The fact of the matter is that the growth of monopoly capital generates increased expansion of social expenses. In sum, the greater the growth of social capital, the greater the growth of the monopoly sector. And the greater the growth of the monopoly sector, the greater the state's expenditures on social expenses of production.

The second basic thesis in this study is that the accumulation of social capital and social expenses is a contradictory process which creates tendencies toward economic, social, and political crises. Two separate but related lines of analysis are explored.

First, we argue that although the state has socialized more and more capital costs, the social surplus (including profits) continues to be appropriated privately. The socialization of costs and the private appropriation of profits creates a fiscal crisis, or "structural gap," between state expenditures and state revenues. The result is a tendency for state expenditures to increase more rapidly than the means of financing them.[14] While the accumulation of social capital indirectly increases total production and society's surplus and thus in principle appears to underwrite the expansion of social expenses, large monopoly-sector corporations and unions strongly resist the appropriation of this surplus for new social capital or social expense outlays.

Second, we argue that the fiscal crisis is exacerbated by the private appropriation of state power for particularistic ends. A host of "special interests"—corporations, industries, regional and other business interests—make claims on the budget for various kinds of social investment. (These claims are politically processed in ways that must either be legitimated or obscured from public view.) Organized labor and workers generally make various claims for different kinds of social consumption, and the unemployed and poor (together with businessmen in financial trouble) stake their claims for expanded social expenses. Few if any claims are coordinated by the market. Most are processed by the political system and are won or lost as a result of political struggle. Precisely because the accumulation of social capital and social expenses occurs within a political framework, there is a great deal of waste, duplication, and overlapping of state projects and services. Some claims conflict and cancel one another out. Others are mutually contradictory in a variety of ways. The accumulation of social capital and social expenses is a highly irrational process from the standpoint of administrative coherence, fiscal stability, and potentially profitable private capital accumulation. We discuss the ways in which struggles around the control of the budget have developed in recent years and the ways in which these struggles impair the fiscal capacity of the system and potentially threaten the capacity of the system to produce surplus.

Notes and references

1. Arthur F. Burns, statement to the Joint Economic Committee, July 26, 1972, *Federal Reserve Bulletin*, August 1972, p. 699. Burns concludes that "the fundamental problem . . . is how to regain control over Federal expenditures." As this study will attempt to show, the lack of control of federal expenditures is merely a symptom of a much more deep-rooted problem.

2. Richard Musgrave and A. Mitchell Polinsky: cited by Edward C. Banfield, "Revenue Sharing in Theory and Practice," *The Public Interest*, 33 (Spring 1971), 35.

3. The conventional phrase "public finance" reveals the ideological content of orthodox economic thought by prejudging the question of the real purposes of the budget. The phrase "state finance" is preferable to "public finance" (and "state sector" to "public sector," etc.) precisely because it remains to be investigated how "public" are the real and financial transactions that take place in the state sector. For example, many so-called public investments are merely special forms of private investments.

4. Rudolf Goldscheid, "A Sociological Approach to the Problem of Public Finance," reprinted in translation in Richard Musgrave and Alan T. Peacock, eds., *Classics in the Theory of Public Finance* (New York: 1958); *Staatssozialismus oder Staatskapitalismus* (Wien-Leipzig, 1917); *Sozialisierung der Wirtschaft oder Staatsbankerott* (Leipzig-Wien, 1919).

5. Joseph Schumpeter, "The Crisis of the Tax State," reprinted in *International Economic Papers*, No. 4 (1954), p. 7. Schumpeter was expecting much of the mainstream of economic thought (the orthodox or bourgeois economists). Fiscal sociology has always been central to the Marxist tradition. Marx himself wrote extensively on the subject. For example, compare Marx's conclusion that "tax struggle is the oldest form of class struggle" with the contemporary English Marxist John Eaton's statement that "state expenditure is . . . unceasingly the battleground of class interests."

6. Glenn W. Fisher, *Taxes and Politics, A Study of Illinois Public Finance* (Urbana, Ill.: 1969), p. 3.

7. James M. Buchanan, *The Demand and Supply of Public Goods* (Chicago: 1968), p. v. Political scientists also have tended to take the state and political order for granted in their analyses of politics and administration as natural phenomena. See Theodore Lowi, "Decision Making vs. Policy Making: Toward an Antidote for Technocracy," *Public Administration Review*, 30:3 (May/June 1970).

8. Ralph Turvey, *Public Enterprise* (Baltimore: 1968).

9. Richard A. Musgrave, *The Theory of Public Finance* (New York: 1959), p. 4. Musgrave's treatise is a perfect example of what Paul Baran was talking about years ago when he wrote that "in our time . . . faith in the manipulative omnipotence of the State has all but displaced analysis of its social structure and understanding of its political and economic functions." Paul A. Baran, *The Longer View* (New York: 1969), p. 262.

10. Evsey Domar, *Essays in the Theory of Economic Growth* (New York: 1957), p. 6; Alan T. Peacock and Jack Wiseman, *The Growth of Public Expenditures in the United Kingdom* (Princeton, N.J.: 1961), p. 10.

11. Herbert Stein, *The Fiscal Revolution in America* (Chicago: 1969), p. 69. Stein is an establishment economist who participated in many crucial corporate and government decisions in the 1950s and 1960s. He was associated for a long time with the corporate-dominated Committee for Economic Development and was chief economic advisor to

President Nixon in 1971–1972. "[A] very limited degree" means that Congress is more receptive to new spending bills during periods of recession. Three other exceptions to the general rule should be noted: (1) In 1958, the federal government began extending unemployment insurance programs to give workers additional purchasing power and thus offset expected declines in private spending (the policy has been applied fitfully since 1958). (2) Federal highway expenditures have been adjusted to smooth out fluctuations in the economy. However, fiscal policy probably has affected the timing of government outlays much more than the total volume of highway spending. (3) The President has tried to regulate spending by impounding funds (impounded funds rose from about 3.5 percent of total appropriations in 1964 to roughly 5.5 percent in 1971).

12. We have not presented a theory of the relationship between private investment and private consumption in either the short run or long run. Nor have we worked out in detail the dialectical movements between the different kinds of state expenditures. Consider, briefly, education expenditures. Education spending does double-duty as both constant and variable capital. The education system also temporarily takes surplus population off the labor market. In other words, the growth of education simultaneously absorbs surplus labor and expands productivity (and thus creates more surplus labor). In short, education spending creates and eliminates surplus capital simultaneously. Any detailed study of the education system would have to take this basic contradiction into account. A further complication arises to the degree that the growth of the education establishment and the growth of militarism are inseparable processes (as they seem to have been in the United States). It is probably true that one of the reasons that state-financed higher education in Europe is relatively undeveloped is that military and related spending is comparatively small.

Finally, it might be added that both Marx's notion of realization crises and Keynesian notions of crises of effective demand require emendation. The reason is that "supply creates its own demand" in ways that neoclassical economics never dreamed of.

13. The standard conservative work is Milton Friedman's *Capitalism and Freedom* (Chicago: 1962). The standard liberal work is John Kenneth Galbraith's *The Affluent Society* (Boston: 1958).

14. The socialization of profits consists of the redistribution of productive wealth from capital to labor, or the confiscation of the owning classes by the working class. Although wealth and profits as a whole have not been socialized, a portion of surplus value is appropriated by the state and used to finance expanded social capital and social expense outlays. Instead of private capital "plowing back" a portion of surplus value into expanded reproduction (net capital formation) in a particular corporation or industry, the state "plows back" that part of the pool of surplus value that it appropriated into expanded social reproduction (new social capital formation) in industry as a whole. However, the state also appropriates part of constant and variable capital. Because capital's and labor's claims on budgetary resources are processed by the political mechanism, there is rarely a one-to-one correspondence between sources of financing and the uses of tax monies. On the one hand, taxes must appear to conform to bourgeois democratic norms of "equity" and "ability to pay." On the other hand, the mixed character of social capital and social expense outlays makes it difficult to develop clearly defined criteria for identifying state expenditures empirically. Perhaps the closest correspondence between private and social forms of capital is the tax on payrolls (levied on private variable capital or wages) which is used to finance social insurance (a form of social variable capital).

1.4. Taxes, Revenues, and the "Laffer Curve"

JUDE WANNISKI

In the last decade, supply-side economics, which was once regarded as a foolish notion espoused only by radical right-wingers, has exerted considerable influence on government policy making. Much of the attractiveness of this theory comes from its promise that it is possible to stimulate the economy and raise total revenues by cutting taxes. This is a proposition with obvious attractions for politicians, who are normally under pressure from voters to increase expenditures while at the same time reducing taxes. This reading by Jude Wanniski explains why supply-siders think this feat is possible.

The central argument is that progressive taxes, which take an increasing percentage of one's income as that income rises, act to discourage people from working and saving. This is because people think they will keep less of what they earn if they work harder or more efficiently, as government takes a larger and larger bite of each increment of extra income. If this is true, it follows that lowering tax rates would encourage people to work harder and longer and to save more. This would lead to increases in employment and the amount of goods produced, which in turn would increase the revenue government gets through taxes on employment and sales of products.

The reader should note that most economists, while conceding that this effect is real, believe that it is often offset by what they term the "income effect." This holds that if individuals require a certain amount of income to meet their needs, their response to higher taxes may be to work more, not less, in order to meet their income target. In the following essay, Jude Wanniski, seeking to deal with this objection, expounds a more sophisticated version of supply-side theory. He claims that even if increasing taxes has the effect of increasing work effort, higher taxes may drive people into the untaxed underground economy, with the result that revenues are reduced.

Reprinted with permission of the author from *The Public Interest*, No. 50 (Winter 1978), pp. 3–16. © 1978 by National Affairs, Inc.

As Arthur Laffer has noted, "there are always two tax rates that yield the same revenues." When an aide to President Gerald Ford asked him once to elaborate, Laffer (who is Professor of Business Economics at the University of Southern California) drew a simple curve, shown on the next page, to illustrate his point. The point, too, is simple enough—though, like so many simple points, it is also powerful in its implications.

When the tax rate is 100 percent, all production ceases in the money economy (as distinct from the barter economy, which exists largely to escape taxation). People will not work in the money economy if all the fruits of their labors are confiscated by the government. And because production ceases, there is nothing for the 100-percent rate to confiscate, so government revenues are zero.

On the other hand, if the tax rate is zero, people can keep 100 percent of what they produce in the money economy. There is no governmental "wedge" between earnings and after-tax income, and thus no governmental barrier to production. Production is therefore maximized, and the output of the money economy is limited only by the desire of workers for leisure. But because the tax rate is zero, government revenues are again zero, and there can be no government. So at a 0-percent tax rate the economy is in a state of anarchy, and at a 100-percent tax rate the economy is functioning entirely through barter.

In between lies the curve. If the government reduces its rate to something less than 100 percent, say to point A, some segment of the barter economy will be able to gain so many efficiencies by being in the money economy that, even with near-confiscatory tax rates, after-tax production would still exceed that of the barter economy. Production will start up, and revenues will flow into the government treasury. By lowering the tax rate, we find an increase in revenues.

On the bottom end of the curve, the same thing is happening. If people feel that they need a minimal government and thus institute a low tax rate, some segment of the economy, finding that the marginal loss of income exceeds the efficiencies gained in the money economy, is shifted into either barter or leisure. But with that tax rate, revenues do flow into the government treasury. This is the situation at point B. Point A represents a very high tax rate and very low production. Point B represents a very low tax rate and very high production. Yet they both yield the same revenue to the government.

The same is true of points C and D. The government finds that by a further lowering of the tax rate, say from point A to point C, revenues increase with the further expansion of output. And by raising the tax rate, say from point B to point D, revenues also increase, by the same amount.

Revenues and production are maximized at point E. If, at point E, the government lowers the tax rate again, output will increase, but revenues will fall. And if, at point E, the tax rate is raised, both output and revenue will decline. The shaded area is *the prohibitive range for government*, where rates are unnecessarily high and can be reduced with gains in *both* output and revenue.

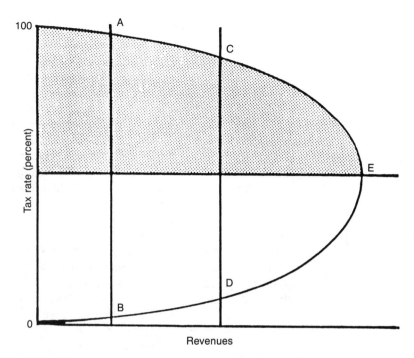

The Laffer Curve

Tax rates and tax revenues

The next important thing to observe is that, except for the 0-percent and 100-percent rates, there are no numbers along the "Laffer curve." Point E is not 50 percent, although it may be, but rather a variable number: *It is the point at which the electorate desires to be taxed.* At points B and D, the electorate desires more government goods and services and is willing—without reducing its productivity—to pay the higher rates consistent with the revenues at point E. And at points A and C, the electorate desires more private goods and services in the money economy, and wishes to pay the lower rates consistent with the revenues at point E. It is the task of the statesman to determine the location of point E, and follow its variations as closely as possible.

This is true whether the political leader heads a nation or a family. The father who disciplines his son at point A, imposing harsh penalties for violating both major and minor rules, only invites sullen rebellion, stealth, and lying (tax evasion, on the national level). The permissive father who disciplines casually at point B invites open, reckless rebellion: His son's independence and relatively unfettered growth comes at the expense of the rest of the family. The wise parent seeks point E, which will probably vary from one child to another, from son to daughter.

For the political leader on the national level, point E can represent a very low or a very high number. When the nation is at war, point E can approach 100 percent. At the siege of Leningrad in World War II, for example, the people of the city produced for 900 days at tax rates approaching 100 percent. Russian soldiers and civilians worked to their physical limits, receiving as "pay" only the barest of rations. Had the citizens of Leningrad not wished to be taxed at that high rate, which was required to hold off the Nazi army, the city would have fallen.

The number represented by point E will change abruptly if the nation is at war one day and at peace the next. The electorate's demand for military goods and services from the government will fall sharply; the electorate will therefore desire to be taxed at a lower rate. If rates are not lowered consistent with this new lower level of demand, output will fall to some level consistent with a point along the prohibitive side of the "Laffer curve." Following World War I, for example, the wartime tax rates were left in place and greatly contributed to the recession of 1919–20. Warren G. Harding ran for President in 1920 on a slogan promising a "return to normalcy" regarding tax rates; he was elected in a landslide. The subsequent rolling back of the rates ushered in the economic expansion of the "Roaring Twenties." After World War II, wartime tax rates were quickly reduced, and the American economy enjoyed a smooth transition to peacetime. In Japan and West Germany, however, there was no adjustment of the rates; as a result, postwar economic recovery was delayed. Germany's recovery began in 1948, when personal income-tax rates were reduced under Finance Minister Ludwig Erhard, and much of the government regulation of commerce came to an end. Japan's recovery did not begin until 1950, when wartime tax rates were finally rolled back. In each case, reduced *rates* produced increased *revenues* for the government. The political leader must fully appreciate the distinction between tax rates and tax revenues to discern the desires of the electorate.

The easiest way for a political leader to determine whether an increase in rates will produce more rather than less revenues is to put the proposition to the electorate. It is not enough for the politician to propose an increase from, say, point B to point D on the curve. He must also specify how the anticipated revenues will be spent. When voters approve a bond issue for schools, highways, or bridges, they are explicitly telling the politician that they are willing to pay the high tax rates required to finance the bonds. In rejecting a bond issue, however, the electorate is not necessarily telling the politician that taxes are already high enough, or that point E (or beyond) has been reached. The only message is that the proposed tax rates are too high a price to pay for the specific goods and services offered by the government.

Only a tiny fraction of all government expenditures are determined in this fashion, to be sure. Most judgments regarding tax rates and expenditures are made by individual politicians. Andrew Mellon became a national hero for engineering the rate reductions of the 1920's and was called "the greatest Treasury Secretary since Alexander Hamilton." The financial policies of Ludwig Erhard were responsible for what was hailed as "an economic miracle"—the postwar recovery of Germany. Throughout history, however, it has been the exception rather than the rule that politicians, by accident or design, have sought to increase revenues by lowering rates.

Work vs. productivity

The idea behind the "Laffer curve" is no doubt as old as civilization, but unfortunately politicians have always had trouble grasping it. In his essay, *Of Taxes*, written in 1756, David Hume pondered the problem:

> Exorbitant taxes, like extreme necessity, destroy industry by producing despair; and even before they reach this pitch, they raise the wages of the labourer and manufacturer, and heighten the price of all commodities. An attentive disinterested legislature will observe the point when the emolument ceases, and the prejudice begins. But as the contrary character is much more common, 'tis to be feared that taxes all over Europe are multiplying to such a degree as will entirely crush all art and industry; tho' perhaps, their first increase, together with other circumstances, might have contributed to the growth of these advantages.

The chief reason politicians and economists throughout history have failed to grasp the idea behind the "Laffer curve" is their confusion of work and productivity. Through both introspection and observation, the politician understands that when tax rates are raised, there is a tendency to work harder and longer to maintain after-tax income. What is not so apparent, because it requires analysis *at the margin*, is this: As taxes are raised, individuals in the system may indeed work harder, but their productivity declines. Hume himself had some trouble with this point:

> There is a prevailing maxim, among some reasoners, that every new tax creates a new ability in the subject to bear it, and that each increase of public burdens increases proportionably the industry of the people. This maxim is of such a nature as is most likely to be abused; and is so much the more dangerous as its truth cannot be altogether denied: But it must be owned, when kept within certain bounds, to have some foundation in reason and experience.

Twenty years later, in *The Wealth of Nations*, Adam Smith had no such problem: In his hypothetical pin factory, what is important to a nation is not the effort of individuals but the productivity of *individuals working together*. When the tax rates are raised, the workers themselves may work harder in an effort to maintain their income level. But if the pin-making entrepreneur is a marginal manufacturer, the increased tax rate will cause him to shift into the leisure sphere or into a lower level of economic activity, and the *system* will lose *all* the production of the pin factory. The politician who stands in the midst of this situation may correctly conclude that the increase in tax rates causes people to work harder. But it is not so easy for him to realize that they are now less efficient in their work and are producing less.

To see this in another way, imagine that there are three men who are skilled at building houses. If they work together, one works on the foundation, one on the frame, and the third on the roof. Together they can build three houses in three months. If they work separately, each building his own home, they need six months to build the three houses. If the tax rate on homebuilding is 49 percent, they will work together, since the government leaves them a small gain from their division of labor. But if the tax rate goes to 51 percent, they suffer a net loss because of their teamwork, and so they will work separately. When they were pooling their efforts, since they could produce six houses in the same time it would take them to build three houses working alone, the government was collecting revenues almost equivalent to the value of three completed homes. At the 51-percent tax rate, however, the government loses all the revenue, and the economy loses the production of the three extra homes that could have been built by their joint effort.

The worst mistakes in history are made by political leaders who, instead of realizing that revenues could be gained by lowering tax rates, become alarmed at the fall in revenues that results when citizens seek to escape high tax rates through barter and do-it-yourself labor. Their impulse is to impose taxes that cannot be escaped, the most onerous of which is a poll tax or head tax, which must be paid annually for the mere privilege of living. Hume had no difficulty in pointing out the fallacy of that line of thinking:

> Historians inform us that one of the chief causes of the destruction of the Roman state was the alteration which Constantine introduced into the finances, by substituting a universal poll tax in lieu of almost all the tithes, customs, and excises which formerly composed the revenue of the empire. The people, in all the provinces, were so grinded and oppressed by the publicans [tax collectors] that they were glad to take refuge under the conquering arms of the barbarians, whose dominion, as they had fewer necessities and less art, was found preferable to the refined tyranny of the Romans.

The trouble with a poll tax, as Hume noted, is that it *can* be escaped—one method being not to defend your country against an aggressor who promises to remove the tax as soon as he has gained power. Montesquieu made a similar observation in Book XIII of *The Spirit of the Laws:*

> Because a moderate government has been productive of admirable effects, this moderation has been laid aside; because great taxes have been raised, they wanted to carry them to excess; and ungrateful to the hand of liberty, of whom they received this present, they addressed themselves to slavery, who never grants the least favor.
>
> Liberty produces excessive taxes; the effect of excessive taxes is slavery; and slavery produces diminution of tribute. . . .

It was this excess of taxes that occasioned the prodigious facility with which the Mahommedans carried on their conquests. Instead of a continual series of extortions devised by the subtle avarices of the Greek emperors, the people were subjected to a simple tribute which was paid and collected with ease. Thus they were far happier in obeying a barbarous nation than a corrupt government, in which they suffered every inconvenience of lost liberty, with all the horror of present slavery.

Modern governments have at least abandoned the notion of using a poll tax to generate revenues. Instead, they often go directly to the barter economy in search of revenues. Activities previously not admitted to the money economy and public marketplace because of public disapproval—e.g., gambling and pornography— are welcomed because of the promise of revenues. But this process tends to lower the quality of the marketplace itself, hastening the exodus or discouraging the entry of enterprises that have earned public approbation.

"Cracking down"

Another timeless remedy of governments that find revenues falling on the face of rising tax rates is to increase the numbers and power of the tax collectors. Invariably, this method further reduces the flow of revenues to the treasury. Yet even with a thousand-year history of failure, the policy of "cracking down" on tax evasion remains a favorite of modern governments. Here is Adam Smith, in *The Wealth of Nations*, on why such policies are doomed from the start:

Every tax ought to be so contrived as both to take out and to keep out of the pockets of the people as little as possible, over and above what it brings into the public treasury of the state. A tax may either take out or keep out of the pockets of the people a great deal more than it brings into the public treasury in the four following ways.

First, the levying of it may require a great number of officers, whose salaries may eat up the greater part of the produce of the tax, and whose perquisites may impose another additional tax upon the people.

Secondly, it may obstruct the industry of the people, and discourage them from applying to certain branches of business which might give maintenance and employment to great multitudes. While it obliges the people to pay, it may thus diminish, or perhaps destroy, some of the funds which might enable them to do so.

Thirdly, by the forfeitures and other penalties which these unfortunate individuals incur who attempt unsuccessfully to evade the tax, it may frequently ruin them, and thereby put an end to the benefit which the community might have received from the employment of their capitals. An injudicious tax offers a great temptation to smuggling. But the penalties of smuggling must rise in proportion to the temptation. The law, contrary to all the ordinary principles of justice, first creates the temptation, and then punishes those who yield to it; and it commonly enhances the punishment too in proportion to the very circumstances which ought certainly to alleviate it, the temptation to commit the crime.

Fourthly, by subjecting the people to the frequent visits and odious examination of the tax-gatherers, it may expose them to much unnecessary trouble, vexation, and oppression; and though vexation is not, strictly speaking, expense, it is certainly equivalent to the expense at which every man would be willing to redeem himself from it.

Adam Smith's point about smuggling may now seem obscure. After all, smuggling was something that went on in the 18th century, wasn't it? Consider the following excerpts from a recent editorial in *The Wall Street Journal*, which urged New York State and New York City to reduce their combined cigarette tax from 26ᶜ to 10ᶜ a pack:

Through our browsings in the *United States Tobacco Journal* we have learned of estimates that half the cigarettes smoked in New York City are smuggled in from North Carolina, where the tax is 2ᶜ a pack. State Senator Roy M. Goodman, a Manhattan Republican, says the state and city are losing $93 million a year in this fashion. The smugglers load 40-foot trailers with 60,000 cartons purchased legally at $2.40 each and peddle them in the city via the organized crime network for $3.75, which is $1.25 or more below legitimate retail.

Mr. Goodman recommends a one-year suspension of the city's 8ᶜ-a-pack tax in order to break up the smuggling, plus an increase in the state enforcement field staff to 250 from the current 50, plus five years in jail for anyone caught smuggling 20,000 cartons or more. Last year only nine smugglers were jailed, each for a few months, with the common penalty $10 or $15.

If Mr. Goodman's solution were adopted, at the end of the year the smugglers would be back, and the state would have a bigger bureaucracy. More smugglers would be caught, more judges and bailiffs and clerks would have to be hired, more jails would have to be built and more jailers hired. The wives and children of the jailed smugglers would go on welfare.

Cutting the tax to 10ᶜ avoids all that. It immediately becomes uneconomic to smuggle. The enforcement staff of 50 can be assigned to more useful work, the state saving $1 million on that count alone. The courts would be less clogged with agents and smugglers, and the taxpayers would save court costs, as well as the costs of confining convicted smugglers and caring for their families.

The state and city would *appear* to face a loss of $50 million or $60 million in revenues, but of course smokers would now buy their cigarettes through legitimate channels and the 10ᶜ a pack would yield about as much in revenues as 26ᶜ a pack yields now. But that's not all. Legitimate dealers would double their cigarette sales, earning higher business profits and personal income that the city and state then taxes.

And don't forget the impact on the millions of cigarette smokers who would save 16ᶜ a pack. At a pack a day, that's $58.40 per year. At average marginal tax rates, a smoker has to earn more than $80 before Federal, state, and city taxes are deducted to get that amount. He can thus maintain his or her standard of living on $80 less in gross wage demands per year, which means it becomes economic for the marginal employer to do business in New York, increasing the number of jobs of all varieties and reducing cost and tax pressure on social services.

Among other benefits, the industrious smugglers would have to find legitimate employment. It might be argued that they would be thrown on the welfare rolls. But if we know New York City, they are already on the welfare rolls, and would be forced to get off once they have visible jobs.

The Finance Office of New York City, unwilling to take the advice of either Adam Smith or *The Wall Street Journal*, simply rejected the idea that lowering rates would produce expanded revenues. But Adam Smith's advice was not even taken in England at the time he tendered it. The theory was not tested until 1827, and then only by accident, by an Act of Parliament. Oddly enough, the incident in question involved tobacco smuggling. Stephen Dowell gives the following account in *A History of Taxation and Taxes in England*:

> The consumption of tobacco had failed to increase in proportion to the increase in the population. A curious circumstance had happened as regards the duty on tobacco. In effecting the statutory rearrangement of the duties in the previous year, the draughtsman of the Bill, in error, allowed one fourth of the duty to lapse in July. Unconsciously he had accomplished a master stroke, for his reduction in the duty was followed by a decrease in smuggling so considerable as to induce [Chancellor of the Exchequer] Robinson to allow his [budget] surplus, estimated at about £700,000, to go to continue the reduction thus unconsciously effected.

The Politburo of the Soviet Union has the same problem as the Finance Office of New York City: It also rejects the idea behind the "Laffer curve." The greatest burden to Soviet economic development is Soviet agriculture. Roughly 34.3 million Soviet citizens, out of a total population of 250 million, are engaged in producing food for the nation—and there is never enough. The United States, by contrast, employs only 4.3 million workers in food production, out of a total population of 200 million, generating an annual surplus for export equivalent to one-fourth the entire Soviet output. The drain on the Soviet economy is not only the low productivity of the farm sector. Because there are always shortages, and the state puts farm goods on the market at regulated prices rather than using the market system to allocate what is available, Soviet citizens spend billions of hours annually waiting on lines. If food were produced in plentiful quantities, it could still be allocated through regulated prices in conformance with Soviet ideology, but most of the lines would disappear, and the talents and energies of the urban work force would not be wasted in long lines.

The real source of this problem is the high marginal tax rates exacted on the state's collective farms. The state provides land, capital, housing, and other necessities on its collectives. It also permits the workers to keep 10 percent of the value of their production. The marginal tax rate is thus 90 percent. In agriculture, a small expenditure of effort might yield, say, 100 units of production; but twice the effort might be required for 150 units, and four times the effort for 200 units. The worker on the collective thus faces a progressive tax schedule so withering that any incentive to expend anything beyond a minimal effort is lost. With minimum work, he gets land, capital, housing, and other necessities, as well as 10 units of output. By quadrupling his effort (not necessarily physical effort, but perhaps increased attentiveness to details), he gets the same services and only 10 more units of output.

Meanwhile, however, the peasants on the collective farms are also permitted to tend private plots, the entire output of which is theirs to keep. The tax rate on these private plots is zero. Here is the result, as detailed by Hedrick Smith in *The Russians*:

> Twenty-seven percent of the total value of Soviet farm output—about $32.5 billion worth a year—comes from private plots that occupy less than 1 percent of the nation's agricultural lands (about 26 million acres). At that rate, private plots are roughly 40 times as efficient as the land worked collectively. . . . Peasants farm their own plots much more intensively than they do collective land.
>
> Ultimately, the Communist ideal is to have this last embarrassing but necessary vestige of private enterprise wither away as industrialized state farming grows in scale and output. Nikita Khrushchev, in spite of rural roots, pursued that end vigorously and earned the enmity of the peasantry. He cut the size of private plots to a maximum of half an acre and made life difficult for the farm market trade. I was told by Russian friends that Ukrainian peasants became so irate that they stopped selling eggs as food and made paint out of them.
>
> Under Brezhnev things have improved. The maximum plot went back up to an acre and measures were taken to improve farm market operations. Soviet figures show the private farm output grew nearly 15 percent from 1966 to 1973.

In terms of the "Laffer curve," what Khrushchev did by reducing the size of the private plots from one acre to one-half acre was to increase the marginal tax rate of the *system* from point C to point A. This was undoubtedly a major cause of his political downfall. On the other hand, Brezhnev moved the marginal tax rate of the system back to point C, increasing output and revenues to the previous levels. This was an "economic miracle" of minor dimensions, but it has undoubtedly contributed heavily to Brezhnev's durability as a political leader.

The politics of the "Laffer curve"

The "Laffer curve" is a simple but exceedingly powerful analytical tool. In one way or another, all transactions, even the simplest, take place along it. The homely adage, "You can catch more flies with molasses than with vinegar," expresses the essence of the curve. But empires are built on the bottom of this simple curve and crushed against the top of it. The Caesars understood this, and so did Napoleon (up to a point) and the greatest of the Chinese emperors. The Founding Fathers of the United States knew it well; the arguments for union (in *The Federalist Papers*) made by Hamilton, Madison, and Jay reveal an understanding of the notion. Until World War I—when progressive taxation was sharply increased to help finance it—the United States successfully remained out of the "prohibitive range."

In the 20th century, especially since World War I, there has been a constant struggle by all the nations of the world to get down the curve. The United States managed to do so in the 1920's, because Andrew Mellon understood the lessons of the "Laffer curve" for the domestic economy. Mellon argued that there are always two prices in the private market that will produce the same revenues. Henry Ford, for example, could get the same revenue by selling a few cars for $100,000 each, or a great number for $1,000 each. (Of course, Ford was forced by the threat of competition to sell at the low price.) The tax rate, said Mellon, is the "price of government." But the nature of government is monopolistic; government itself must find the lowest rate that yields the desired revenue.

Because Mellon was successful in persuading Republican Presidents—first Warren G. Harding and then Calvin Coolidge—of the truth of his ideas the high wartime tax rates were steadily cut back. The excess-profits tax on industry was repealed, and the 77-percent rate on the highest bracket of personal income was rolled back in stages, so that by 1925 it stood at 25 percent. As a result, the period 1921–29 was one of phenomenal economic expansion: G.N.P. grew from $69.6 billion to $103.1 billion. And because prices fell during this period, G.N.P. grew even faster in real terms, by 54 percent. At the lower rates, revenues grew sufficiently to enable Mellon to reduce the national debt from $24.3 billion to $16.9 billion.

The stock market crash of 1929 and the subsequent global depression occurred because Herbert Hoover unwittingly contracted the world economy with his high-tariff policies, which pushed the West, as an economic unit, up the "Laffer curve." Hoover compounded the problem in 1932 by raising personal tax rates almost up to the levels of 1920.

The most important economic event following World War II was also the work of a finance minister who implicitly understood the importance of the "Laffer curve." Germany had been pinned to the uppermost ranges of the curve since World War I. It took a financial panic in the spring of 1948 to shake Germany loose. At that point, German citizens were still paying a 50-percent marginal tax rate on incomes of $600 and a 95-percent rate on incomes above $15,000. On

June 22, 1948, Finance Minister Ludwig Erhard announced cuts that raised the 50-percent bracket to $2,200 and the 95-percent bracket to $63,000. The financial panic ended, and economic expansion began. It was Erhard, not the Marshall Plan, who saved Europe from Communist encroachment. In the decade that followed, Erhard again and again slashed the tax rates, bringing the German economy farther down the curve and into a higher level of prosperity. In 1951 the 50-percent bracket was pushed up to $5,000 and in 1953 to $9,000, while at the same time the rate for the top bracket was reduced to 82 percent. In 1954, the rate for the top bracket was reduced again, to 80 percent, and in 1955 it was pulled down sharply, to 63 percent on incomes above $250,000; the 50-percent bracket was pushed up to $42,000. Yet another tax reform took place in 1958: The government exempted the first $400 of income and brought the rate for the top bracket down to 53 percent. It was this systematic lowering of unnecessarily high tax rates that produced the German "economic miracle." As national income rose in Germany throughout the 1950's, so did revenues, enabling the government to construct its "welfare state" as well as its powerful national defense system.

The British empire was built on the lower end of the "Laffer curve" and dismantled on the upper end. The high wartime rates imposed to finance the Napoleonic wars were cut back sharply in 1816, despite warnings from "fiscal experts" that the high rates were needed to reduce the enormous public debt of £900 million. For the following 60 years, the British economy grew at an unprecedented pace, as a series of finance ministers used ever-expanding revenues to lower steadily the tax rates and tariffs.

In Britain, though, unlike the United States, there was no Mellon to risk lowering the extremely high tax rates imposed to finance World War I. As a result, the British economy struggled through the 1920's and 1930's. After World War II, the British government again made the mistake of not sufficiently lowering tax rates to spur individual initiative. Instead, the postwar Labour government concentrated on using tax policy for Keynesian objectives—i.e., increasing consumer demand to expand output. On October 23, 1945, tax rates were cut on lower-income brackets and surtaxes were added to the already high rates on the upper-income brackets. Taxes on higher incomes were increased, according to Chancellor of the Exchequer Hugh Dalton, in order to "continue that steady advance toward economic and social equality which we have made during the war and which the Government firmly intends to continue in peace."

From that day in 1945, there has been no concerted political voice in Britain arguing for a reduction of the high tax rates. Conservatives have supported and won tax reductions for business, especially investment-tax income credits. But while arguing for a reduction of the 83-percent rate on incomes above £20,000 (roughly $35,000 at current exchange rates) of earned income and the 98-percent rate on "unearned income" from investments, they have insisted that government *first* lower its spending, in order to permit the rate reductions. Somehow, the spending levels never can be cut. Only in the last several months of 1977 has

Margaret Thatcher, the leader of the opposition Conservative Party, spoken of reducing the high tax rates as a way of expanding revenues.

In the United States, in September 1977, the Republican National Committee unanimously endorsed the plan of Representative Jack Kemp of New York for cutting tax rates as a way of expanding revenues through increased business activity. This was the first time since 1953 that the GOP had embraced the concept of tax cuts! In contrast, the Democrats under President Kennedy sharply cut tax rates in 1962–64 (though making their case in Keynesian terms). The reductions successfully moved the United States economy down the "Laffer curve," expanding the economy and revenues.

It is crucial to Western economic expansion, peace, and prosperity that "conservative" parties move in this direction. They are, after all, traditionally in favor of income growth, with "liberals" providing the necessary political push for income redistribution. A welfare state is perfectly consistent with the "Laffer curve," and can function successfully along its lower range. But there must be income before there can be income redistribution. Most of the economic failures of the century can rightly be charged to the failure of conservatives to press for tax rates along the lower range of the "Laffer curve." Presidents Eisenhower, Nixon, and Ford were timid in this crucial area of public policy. The Goldwater Republicans of 1963–64, in fact, emphatically opposed the Kennedy tax-rate cuts!

If, during the remainder of this decade, the United States and Great Britain demonstrate the power of the "Laffer curve" as an analytical tool, its use will spread, in the developing countries as well as the developed world. Politicians who understand the curve will find that they can defeat politicians who do not, other things being equal. Electorates all over the world always know when they are unnecessarily perched along the upper edge of the "Laffer curve," and will support political leaders who can bring them back down.

2. Public Regulation of the Private Economy

2A. Business Regulation

Government can affect economic outcomes by influencing the total demand for goods, by choosing to produce certain goods itself, or by enacting rules that prescribe how private industry can operate. The most common way in which government sets rules for private industry is through the regulation of business activity.

Business regulation may be enacted for a number of reasons. Generally the stated aim is to benefit the consumer by preventing business from doing things that are considered harmful to people's interests.

One type of harm can occur when we have what is called a natural monopoly situation. For example, in industries such as gas, electrical power, and communications it is most efficient for one firm to supply the whole market. In such cases the industry can name its price for a product, and the consumer has no option but to pay or do without. This gives the industry an incentive to supply minimum service at the maximum price. Regulation is required to keep the quantity up and the price down.

Another type of harm can occur when firms, attempting to cut costs in order to gain a competitive advantage against other firms, use production methods that inflict harm on the general public. Air pollution is an example of this process of "rational exploitation." Here regulation is needed in order to force firms to produce in a way that, even if it is more costly, is less harmful to the general public.

In the case of health and safety regulation, it is more efficient for the government to set standards and to test drugs and other products for safety than for each consumer to attempt to make these determinations.

The use of public property by private interests is also regulated, for example the use of the public airwaves by television and radio stations, or the logging of national forests by private companies.

All these are examples of business activity being regulated in the interest of the public. But regulation can also occur for less noble motives. The most common is what I term "producer regulation," referring to cases where industries seek government intervention in order to reduce the rigors of market competition. Through government regulation, for example, prices can be set at higher levels than would occur under free competition, and licensing rules can be used to prevent new firms from entering the market. This happens at the expense of consumers, who have to pay more for the good or service. In the opinion of some authors, a great deal of regulation is instituted for this reason. And some think that a number of regulatory agencies initially set up to help the consumer have since been "captured" by the industries they regulate.

Another, more ambiguous reason for regulation might be termed cross-subsidization. In this case, regulators raise the price of a good for one group of consumers in order to lower the price for another group. Examples are special, lower utility rates for the aged, or the requirement that railroads provide service on certain uneconomic routes.

There is considerable disagreement within the literature over which of these many motives is behind most government regulation of business, or whether a mixture of motives is typical (Gilligan et al. 1987). This argument is important in the context of the debate over whether we need more or less regulation and whether we ought to deregulate certain industries. We will survey the argument over regulation in this section of the book.

The first article in this section, by Anthony Downs, is representative of the literature that sees regulation as primarily a response to public outcry over abuses by industry. Downs argues that, although it may be intense at first, regulation will decline in severity over time, as public attention to an issue recedes. In Samuel Huntington's view, the public's short attention span means that regulatory agencies quickly become vulnerable to "capture" by the industries they regulate. Huntington's essay is a classic statement of the argument that much regulation is "producer regulation," which in the end harms the consumer. The third essay, by Kenneth Meier, looks at regulatory agencies themselves to see what political resources they have that might enable them to avoid capture and under what circumstances they are most vulnerable to capture.

For further reading

Two good general introductions to the politics of regulation are Kenneth Meier's *Regulation: Politics, Bureaucracy and Economics* and Alan Stone's *Regulation and its Alternatives*. A sound, recent introduction to the economic considerations involved in regulation is Douglas Needham's *The Economics and Politics of Regulation: A Behavioral Approach*. James Q. Wilson's *The Politics of Regulation* contains a number of interesting case studies of different regulatory agencies. George Stigler's article "The Theory of Economic Regulation" is a classic statement of the case for producer regulation. Richard Posner's "Taxation by Regulation" expounds the notion that taxation is a motive for regulation. Barry

Mitnick's *The Political Economy of Regulation* and Paul Quirk's *Industry Influence in Regulatory Agencies* outline and analyze most of the major political theories about regulation. *The Federal Regulatory Directory*, published by *The Congressional Quarterly*, gives up-to-date facts about regulatory agencies. Murray Weidenbaum's *The Future of Business Regulation: Private Action and Public Demand* outlines a regulatory reform program which served as a guide for the Reagan Administration's efforts at deregulation. Leonard Weiss and Michael Klass's *Regulatory Reform: What Actually Happened* examines the effects of deregulation under the Carter and Reagan Administrations.

Bibliography

Congressional Quarterly Press, *Federal Regulatory Directory*, 5th ed. (Washington D.C.: Congressional Quarterly Press, 1986).

Gilligan, Thomas W., William J. Marsall, and Barry R. Weingast, "Regulation and the Theory of Legislative Choice: The Interstate Commerce Act of 1887," California Institute of Technology Social Science Working Paper, January 1987.

Meier, Kenneth J., *Regulation: Politics, Bureaucracy and Economics* (New York: St. Martin's Press, 1985).

Mitnick, Barry, *The Political Economy of Regulation* (New York: Columbia University Press, 1980).

Needham, Douglas, *The Economics and Politics of Regulation: A Behavioral Approach* (Boston: Little Brown, 1983).

Posner, Richard A., "Taxation by Regulation," *Bell Journal of Economics and Management Science* (Spring 1971).

Quirk, Paul J., *Industry Influence in Regulatory Agencies* (Princeton, N.J.: Princeton University Press, 1981).

Stigler, George, "The Theory of Economic Regulation," *Bell Journal of Economics and Management Science* (Spring 1971).

Stone, Alan, *Regulation and Its Alternatives* (Washington D.C.: Congressional Quarterly Press, 1982).

Weidenbaum, Murray, *The Future of Business Regulation: Private Action and Public Demand* (New York: AMACOM, 1979).

Weiss, Leonard W. and Michael W. Klass, eds. *Regulatory Reform: What Actually Happened* (Boston: Little Brown, 1986).

Wilson, James Q., ed. *The Politics of Regulation* (New York: Basic Books, 1980).

2A.1. Up and Down with Ecology
The "Issue-Attention Cycle"

ANTHONY DOWNS

We typically think of business regulation as an attempt by the public, or consumers, to curb the excesses of private business. Such regulation becomes necessary when businesses, in their effort to reduce costs and increase profits in the face of competition, undertake practices that could harm their customers or the surrounding community. In this essay Anthony Downs tries to show the circumstances under which such excesses will be curbed in a democracy.

Downs outlines a five-part "issue-attention cycle," which he then applies to the great wave of environmental regulation that took place in the 1960s and early 1970s. In the first stage, a problem exists but the general public is not aware of it. In the second stage, the public discovers the problem and there is public outrage, followed by demands for regulation. In the third stage, attempts to solve the problem make the public aware of the (generally high) costs of solving the problem. In the fourth stage, the issue becomes less popular and is replaced in the public consciousness by new problems whose solution costs are not yet publicly perceived. In the fifth and final stage, the original issue sinks into the background at a higher level of public consciousness than before the issue was raised, but at a far lower level than was true before the costs of solving the problem became apparent.

It is important to note that Downs here views regulation as taking place for the benefit of the general public. He also sees the degree of public support as the crucial variable both in establishing and in maintaining regulation. Thus Downs implicitly assumes that regulatory policy is produced through an open democratic process aimed at satisfying the needs of the average consumer.

American public attention rarely remains sharply focused upon any one domestic issue for very long—even if it involves a continuing problem of crucial importance to society. Instead, a systematic "issue-attention cycle" seems

Reprinted with permission of the author from *The Public Interest*, No. 28 (Summer 1972): 38–50. © 1972 by National Affairs, Inc.

strongly to influence public attitudes and behavior concerning most key domestic problems. Each of these problems suddenly leaps into prominence, remains there for a short time, and then—though still largely unresolved—gradually fades from the center of public attention. A study of the way this cycle operates provides insights into how long public attention is likely to remain sufficiently focused upon any given issue to generate enough political pressure to cause effective change.

The shaping of American attitudes toward improving the quality of our environment provides both an example and a potential test of this "issue-attention cycle." In the past few years, there has been a remarkably widespread upsurge of interest in the quality of our environment. This change in public attitudes has been much faster than any changes in the environment itself. What has caused this shift in public attention? Why did this issue suddenly assume so high a priority among our domestic concerns? And how long will the American public sustain high-intensity interest in ecological matters? I believe that answers to these questions can be derived from analyzing the "issue-attention cycle."

The dynamics of the "issue-attention cycle"

Public perception of most "crises" in American domestic life does not reflect changes in real conditions as much as it reflects the operation of a systematic cycle of heightening public interest and then increasing boredom with major issues. This "issue-attention cycle" is rooted both in the nature of certain domestic problems and in the way major communications media interact with the public. The cycle itself has five stages, which may vary in duration depending upon the particular issue involved, but which almost always occur in the following sequence:

1. The pre-problem stage

This prevails when some highly undesirable social condition exists but has not yet captured much public attention, even though some experts or interest groups may already be alarmed by it. *Usually, objective conditions regarding the problem are far worse during the pre-problem stage than they are by the time the public becomes interested in it.* For example, this was true of racism, poverty, and malnutrition in the United States.

2. Alarmed discovery and euphoric enthusiasm

As a result of some dramatic series of events (like the ghetto riots in 1965 to 1967), or for other reasons, the public suddenly becomes both aware of and alarmed about the evils of a particular problem. This alarmed discovery is invariably accompanied by euphoric enthusiasm about society's ability to "solve this problem" or "do something effective" within a relatively short time. The combination of alarm and confidence results in part from the strong public pressure in America for political leaders to claim that every problem can be "solved." This outlook is rooted in the great American tradition of optimistically viewing most obstacles to social progress as *external* to the structure of society itself. The implication is that every obstacle can be eliminated and every problem solved *without any fundamental reordering of society itself*, if only we devote sufficient effort to it. In older and perhaps wiser cultures, there is an underlying sense of irony or even pessimism which springs from a widespread and often confirmed belief that many problems cannot be "solved" *at all* in any complete sense. Only recently has this more pessimistic view begun to develop in our culture.

3. *Realizing the cost of significant progress*

The third stage consists of a gradually spreading realization that the cost of "solving" the problem is very high indeed. Really doing so would not only take a great deal of money but would also require major sacrifices by large groups in the population. The public thus begins to realize that part of the problem results from arrangements that are providing significant benefits to someone—often to millions. For example, traffic congestion and a great deal of smog are caused by increasing automobile usage. Yet this also enhances the mobility of millions of Americans who continue to purchase more vehicles to obtain these advantages.

In certain cases, technological progress can eliminate some of the undesirable results of a problem without causing any major restructuring of society or any loss of present benefits by others (except for higher money costs). In the optimistic American tradition, such a technological solution is initially assumed to be possible in the case of nearly every problem. Our most pressing social problems, however, usually involve either deliberate or unconscious exploitation of one group in society by another, or the prevention of one group from enjoying something that others want to keep for themselves. For example, most upper-middle-class whites value geographic separation from poor people and blacks. Hence any equality of access to the advantages of suburban living for the poor and for blacks cannot be achieved without some sacrifice by middle-class whites of the "benefits" of separation. The increasing recognition that there is this type of relationship between the problem and its "solution" constitutes a key part of the third stage.

4. *Gradual decline of intense public interest*

The previous stage becomes almost imperceptibly transformed into the fourth stage: a gradual decline in the intensity of public interest in the problem. As more and more people realize how difficult, and how costly to themselves, a solution to the problem would be, three reactions set in. Some people just get discouraged. Others feel positively threatened by thinking about the problem; so they suppress such thoughts. Still others become bored by the issue. Most people experience some combination of these feelings. Consequently, public desire to keep attention focused on the issue wanes. And by this time, some other issue is usually entering Stage Two; so it exerts a more novel and thus more powerful claim upon public attention.

5. The post-problem stage

In the final stage, an issue that has been replaced at the center of public concern moves into a prolonged limbo—a twilight realm of lesser attention or spasmodic recurrences of interest. However, the issue now has a different relation to public attention than that which prevailed in the "pre-problem" stage. For one thing, during the time that interest was sharply focused on this problem, new institutions, programs, and policies may have been created to help solve it. These entities almost always persist and often have some impact even after public attention has shifted elsewhere. For example, during the early stages of the "War on Poverty," the Office of Economic Opportunity (OEO) was established, and it initiated many new programs. Although poverty has now faded as a central public issue, OEO still exists. Moreover, many of its programs have experienced significant success, even though funded at a far lower level than would be necessary to reduce poverty decisively.

Any major problem that once was elevated to national prominence may sporadically recapture public interest; or important aspects of it may become attached to some other problem that subsequently dominates center stage. Therefore, problems that have gone through the cycle almost always receive a higher average level of attention, public effort, and general concern than those still in the pre-discovery stage.

Which problems are likely to go through the cycle?

Not all major social problems go through this "issue-attention cycle." Those that do generally possess to some degree three specific characteristics. First, the majority of persons in society are not suffering from the problem nearly as much as some minority (a *numerical* minority, not necessarily an *ethnic* one). This is true of many pressing social problems in America today—poverty, racism, poor public transportation, low-quality education, crime, drug addiction, and unemployment, among others. The number of persons suffering from each of these ills is very large *absolutely*—in the millions. But the numbers are small *relatively*—usually less than 15 percent of the entire population. Therefore, most people do not suffer directly enough from such problems to keep their attention riveted on them.

Second, the sufferings caused by the problem are generated by social arrangements that provide significant benefits to a majority or a powerful minority of the population. For example, Americans who own cars—plus the powerful automobile and highway lobbies—receive short-run benefits from the prohibition of using motor-fuel tax revenues for financing public transportation systems, even though such systems are desperately needed by the urban poor.

Third, the problem has no intrinsically exciting qualities—or no longer has them. When big-city racial riots were being shown nightly on the nation's television screens, public attention naturally focused upon their causes and consequences. but when they ceased (or at least the media stopped reporting them so intensively), public interest in the problems related to them declined sharply. Similarly, as long as the National Aeronautics and Space Administration (NASA) was able to stage a series of ever more thrilling space shots, culminating in the worldwide television spectacular of Americans walking on the moon, it generated sufficient public support to sustain high-level Congressional appropriations. But NASA had nothing half so dramatic for an encore, and repetition of the same feat proved less and less exciting (though a near disaster on the third try did revive audience interest). So NASA's Congressional appropriations plummeted.

A problem must be dramatic and exciting to maintain public interest because news is "consumed" by much of the American public (and by publics everywhere) largely as a form of entertainment. As such, it competes with other types of entertainment for a share of each person's time. Every day, there is a fierce struggle for space in the highly limited universe of newsprint and television viewing time. Each issue vies not only with all other social problems and public events, but also with a multitude of "non-news" items that are often far more pleasant to contemplate. These include sporting news, weather reports, crossword puzzles, fashion accounts, comics, and daily horoscopes. In fact, the amount of television time and newspaper space devoted to sports coverage, as compared to international events, is a striking commentary on the relative value that the public places on knowing about these two subjects.

When all three of the above conditions exist concerning a given problem that has somehow captured public attention, the odds are great that it will soon move through the entire "issue-attention cycle"—and therefore will gradually fade from the center of the stage. The first condition means that most people will not be continually reminded of the problem by their own suffering from it. The second condition means that solving the problem requires sustained attention and effort, plus fundamental changes in social institutions or behavior. This in turn means that significant attempts to solve it are threatening to important groups in society. The third condition means that the media's sustained focus on this problem soon bores a majority of the public. As soon as the media realize that their emphasis on this problem is threatening many people and boring even more, they will shift their focus to some "new" problem. This is particularly likely in America because nearly all the media are run for profit, and they make the most money by appealing to the largest possible audiences. Thus, as Marshall McLuhan has pointed out, it is largely the audience itself—the American public—that "manages the news" by maintaining or losing interest in a given subject. As long as this pattern persists, we will continue to be confronted by a stream of "crises" involving particular social problems. Each will rise into public view, capture center stage for a while, and then gradually fade away as it is replaced by more fashionable issues moving into their "crisis" phases.

The rise of environmental concern

Public interest in the quality of the environment now appears to be about midway through the "issue-attention cycle." Gradually, more and more people are beginning to realize the immensity of the social and financial costs of cleaning up our air and water and of preserving and restoring open spaces. Hence much of the enthusiasm about prompt, dramatic improvement in the environment is fading. There is still a great deal of public interest, however, so it cannot be said that the "post-problem stage" has been reached. In fact, as will be discussed later, the environmental issue may well retain more attention than social problems that affect smaller proportions of the population. Before evaluating the prospects of long-term interest in the environment, though, it is helpful to analyze how environmental concern passed through the earlier stages in the "issue-attention cycle."

The most obvious reason for the initial rise in concern about the environment is the recent deterioration of certain easily perceived environmental conditions. A whole catalogue of symptoms can be arrayed, including ubiquitous urban smog, greater proliferation of solid waste, oceanic oil spills, greater pollution of water supplies by DDT and other poisons, the threatened disappearance of many wildlife species, and the overcrowding of a variety of facilities from commuter expressways to National Parks. Millions of citizens observing these worsening conditions became convinced that *someone* ought to "do something" about them. But "doing something" to reduce environmental deterioration is not easy. For many of our environmental problems have been caused by developments that are highly valued by most Americans.

The very abundance of our production and consumption of material goods is responsible for an immense amount of environmental pollution. For example, electric power generation, if based on fossil fuels, creates smoke and air pollution or, if based on nuclear fuels, causes rising water temperatures. Yet a key foundation for rising living standards in the United States during this century has been the doubling of electric power consumption every 10 years. So more pollution is the price we have paid for the tremendous advantages of being able to use more and more electricity. Similarly, much of the litter blighting even our remotest landscapes stems from the convenience of using "throwaway packages." Thus, to regard environmental pollution as a purely external negative factor would be to ignore its direct linkage with material advantages most citizens enjoy.

Another otherwise favorable development that has led to rising environmental pollution is what I would call the democratization of privilege. Many more Americans are now able to participate in certain activities that were formerly available only to a small, wealthy minority. Some members of that minority are incensed by the consequences of having their formerly esoteric advantages spread to "the common man." The most frequent irritant caused by the democratization of privilege is congestion. Rising highway congestion, for example, is denounced almost everywhere. Yet its main cause is the rapid spread of automobile owner-ship and usage. In 1950, about 59 percent of all families had at least one auto-mobile, and seven percent owned two or more. By 1968, the proportion of families owning at least one automobile had climbed to 79 percent, and 26 percent had two or more cars. In the 10 years from 1960 to 1970, the total number of registered automotive vehicles rose by 35 million (or 47 percent), as compared to a rise in human population of 23 million (or only 13 percent). Moreover, it has been estimated that motor vehicles cause approximately 60 percent of all air pollution. So the tremendous increase in smog does not result primarily from larger population, but rather from the democratization of automobile ownership.

The democratization of privilege also causes crowding in National Parks, rising suburban housing density, the expansion of new subdivisions into formerly picturesque farms and orchards, and the transformation of once tranquil resort areas like Waikiki Beach into forests of high-rise buildings. It is now difficult for the wealthy to flee from busy urban areas to places of quiet seclusion, because so many more people can afford to go with them. *The elite's environmental deterio-ration is often the common man's improved standard of living.*

Our soaring aspirations

A somewhat different factor which has contributed to greater concern with environmental quality is a marked increase in our aspirations and standards concerning what our environment ought to be like. In my opinion, rising dissatis-faction with the "system" in the United States does not result primarily from poorer performance by that system. Rather, it stems mainly from a rapid escala-tion of our aspirations as to what the system's performance ought to be. Nowhere is this phenomenon more striking than in regard to the quality of the environment. One hundred years ago, white Americans were eliminating whole Indian tribes without a qualm. Today, many serious-minded citizens seek to make important issues out of the potential disappearance of the whooping crane, the timber wolf, and other exotic creatures. Meanwhile, thousands of Indians in Brazil are still being murdered each year—but American conservationists are not focusing on that human massacre. Similarly, some aesthetes decry "galloping sprawl" in metropolitan fringe areas, while they ignore acres of rat-infested housing a few miles away. Hence, the escalation of our environmental aspirations is more selective than might at first appear.

Yet regarding many forms of pollution, we are now rightly upset over practices and conditions that have largely been ignored for decades. An example is our alarm about the dumping of industrial wastes and sewage into rivers and lakes. This increase in our environmental aspirations is part of a general cultural phenomenon stimulated both by our success in raising living standards and by the recent emphases of the communications media. Another cause of the rapid rise in interest in environmental pollution is the "explosion" of alarmist rhetoric on this subject. According to some well-publicized experts, all life on earth is threatened by an "environmental crisis." Some claim human life will end within three decades or less if we do not do something drastic about current behavior patterns.

Are things really that bad? Frankly, I am not enough of an ecological expert to know. But I am skeptical concerning all highly alarmist views because so many previous prophets of doom and disaster have been so wrong concerning many other so-called "crises" in our society.

There are two reasonable definitions of "crisis." One kind of crisis consists of a rapidly deteriorating situation moving towards a single disastrous event at some future moment. The second kind consists of a more gradually deteriorating situation that will eventually pass some subtle "point of no return." At present, I do not believe either of these definitions applies to most American domestic problems. Although many social critics hate to admit it, the American "system" actually serves the majority of citizens rather well in terms of most indicators of well-being. Concerning such things as real income, personal mobility, variety and choice of consumption patterns, longevity, health, leisure time, and quality of housing, most Americans are better off today than they have ever been and extraordinarily better off than most of mankind. What is *not* improving is the gap between society's performance and what most people—or at least highly vocal minorities—believe society *ought* to be doing to solve these problems. Our aspirations and standards have risen far faster than the beneficial outputs of our social system. Therefore, although most Americans, including most of the poor, are receiving more now, they are enjoying it less.

This conclusion should not be confused with the complacency of some super-patriots. It would be unrealistic to deny certain important negative trends in American life. Some conditions are indeed getting worse for nearly everyone. Examples are air quality and freedom from thievery. Moreover, congestion and environmental deterioration might forever destroy certain valuable national amenities if they are not checked. Finally, there has probably been a general rise in personal and social anxiety in recent years. I believe this is due to increased tensions caused by our rapid rate of technical and social change, plus the increase in worldwide communication through the media. These developments rightly cause serious and genuine concern among millions of Americans.

The future of the environmental issue

Concern about the environment has passed through the first two stages of the "issue-attention cycle" and is by now well into the third. In fact, we have already begun to move toward the fourth stage, in which the intensity of public interest in environmental improvement must inexorably decline. And this raises an interesting question: Will the issue of environmental quality then move on into the "post-problem" stage of the cycle?

My answer to this question is: Yes, but not soon, because certain characteristics of this issue will protect it from the rapid decline in public interest typical of many other recent issues. First of all, many kinds of environmental pollution are much more visible and more clearly threatening than most other social problems. This is particularly true of air pollution. The greater the apparent threat from visible forms of pollution and the more vividly this can be dramatized, the more public support environmental improvement will receive and the longer it will sustain public interest. Ironically, the cause of ecologists would therefore benefit from an environmental disaster like a "killer smog" that would choke thousands to death in a few days. Actually, this is nothing new; every cause from early Christianity to the Black Panthers has benefited from martyrs. Yet even the most powerful symbols lose their impact if they are constantly repeated. The piteous sight of an oil-soaked seagull or a dead soldier pales after it has been viewed even a dozen times. Moreover, some of the worst environmental threats come from forms of pollution that are invisible. Thus, our propensity to focus attention on what is most visible may cause us to clean up the pollution we can easily perceive while ignoring even more dangerous but hidden threats.

Pollution is also likely to be kept in the public eye because it is an issue that threatens almost everyone, not just a small percentage of the population. Since it is not politically divisive, politicians can safely pursue it without fearing adverse repercussions. Attacking environmental pollution is therefore much safer than attacking racism or poverty. For an attack upon the latter antagonizes important blocs of voters who benefit from the sufferings of others or at least are not threatened enough by such suffering to favor spending substantial amounts of their money to reduce it.

A third strength of the environmental issue is that much of the "blame" for pollution can be attributed to a small group of "villains" whose wealth and power make them excellent scapegoats. Environmental defenders can therefore "courageously" attack these scapegoats without antagonizing most citizens. Moreover, at least in regard to air pollution, that small group actually has enough power greatly to reduce pollution if it really tries. If leaders of the nation's top auto-producing, power-generating, and fuel-supplying firms would change their behavior significantly, a drastic decline in air pollution could be achieved very quickly. This has been demonstrated at many locations already.

Gathering support for attacking any problem is always easier if its ills can be blamed on a small number of "public enemies"—as is shown by the success of Ralph Nader. This tactic is especially effective if the "enemies" exhibit extreme wealth and power, eccentric dress and manners, obscene language, or some other uncommon traits. Then society can aim its outrage at a small, alien group without having to face up to the need to alter its own behavior. It is easier to find such scapegoats for almost all forms of pollution than for other major problems like poverty, poor housing, or racism. Solutions to those problems would require millions of Americans to change their own behavior patterns, to accept higher taxes, or both.

The possibility that technological solutions can be devised for most pollution problems may also lengthen the public prominence of this issue. To the extent that pollution can be reduced through technological change, most people's basic attitudes, expectations, and behavior patterns will not have to be altered. The traumatic difficulties of achieving major institutional change could thus be escaped through the "magic" of purely technical improvements in automobile engines, water purification devices, fuel composition, and sewage treatment facilities.

Financing the fight against pollution

Another aspect of anti-pollution efforts that will strengthen their political support is that most of the costs can be passed on to the public through higher product prices rather than higher taxes. Therefore, politicians can demand enforcement of costly environmental quality standards without paying the high political price of raising the required funds through taxes. True, water pollution is caused mainly by the actions of public bodies, especially municipal sewer systems, and effective remedies for this form of pollution require higher taxes or at least higher prices for public services. But the major costs of reducing most kinds of pollution can be added to product prices and thereby quietly shifted to the ultimate consumers of the outputs concerned. This is a politically painless way to pay for attacking a major social problem. In contrast, effectively combatting most social problems requires large-scale income redistribution attainable only through both higher taxes and higher transfer payments or subsidies. Examples of such politically costly problems are poverty, slum housing, low-quality health care for the poor, and inadequate public transportation.

Many ecologists oppose paying for a cleaner environment through higher product prices. They would rather force the polluting firms to bear the required costs through lower profits. In a few oligopolistic industries, like petroleum and automobile production, this might work. But in the long run, not much of the total cost could be paid this way without driving capital out of the industries concerned and thereby eventually forcing product prices upwards. Furthermore, it is just that those who use any given product should pay the full cost of making it—including the cost of avoiding excessive pollution in its production. Such payment is best made through higher product prices. In my opinion, it would be unwise in most cases to try to pay these costs by means of government subsidies in order to avoid shifting the load onto consumers. We need to conserve our politically limited taxing capabilities to attack those problems that cannot be dealt with in any other way.

Still another reason why the cleaner-environment issue may last a long time is that it could generate a large private industry with strong vested interests in continued spending against pollution. Already dozens of firms with "eco-" or "environ-" in their names have sprung up to exploit supposedly burgeoning anti-pollution markets. In time, we might even generate an "environmental-industrial complex" about which some future President could vainly warn us in his retirement speech! Any issue gains longevity if its sources of political support and the programs related to it can be institutionalized in large bureaucracies. Such organizations have a powerful desire to keep public attention focused on the problems that support them. However, it is doubtful that the anti-pollution industry will ever come close to the defense industry in size and power. Effective anti-pollution activities cannot be carried out separately from society as a whole because they require changes in behavior by millions of people. In contrast, weapons are produced by an industry that imposes no behavioral changes (other than higher taxes) on the average citizen.

Finally, environmental issues may remain at center stage longer than most domestic issues because of their very ambiguity. "Improving the environment" is a tremendously broad and all-encompassing objective. Almost everyone can plausibly claim that his or her particular cause is another way to upgrade the quality of our life. This ambiguity will make it easier to form a majority-sized coalition favoring a variety of social changes associated with improving the environment. The inability to form such a coalition regarding problems that adversely affect only minority-sized groups usually hastens the exit of such problems from the center of public attention.

All the factors set forth above indicate that circumstances are unusually favorable for launching and sustaining major efforts to improve the quality of our environment. Yet we should not underestimate the American public's capacity to become bored—especially with something that does not immediately threaten them, or promise huge benefits for a majority, or strongly appeal to their sense of injustice. In the present mood of the nation, I believe most citizens do not want to confront the need for major social changes on any issues except those that seem directly to threaten them—such as crime and other urban violence. And even in regard to crime, the public does not yet wish to support really effective changes in our basic system of justice. The present Administration has apparently concluded that a relatively "low-profile" government—one that does not try to lead the public into accepting truly significant institutional changes—will most please the majority of Americans at this point. Regardless of the accuracy of this view, if it remains dominant within the federal government, then no major environmental programs are likely to receive long-sustained public attention or support.

Some proponents of improving the environment are relying on the support of students and other young people to keep this issue at the center of public attention. Such support, however, is not adequate as a long-term foundation. Young people form a highly unstable base for the support of any policy because they have such short-lived "staying power." For one thing, they do not long enjoy the large amount of free time they possess while in college. Also, as new individuals enter the category of "young people" and older ones leave it, different issues are stressed and accumulated skills in marshaling opinion are dissipated. Moreover, the radicalism of the young has been immensely exaggerated by the media's tendency to focus attention upon those with extremist views. In their attitudes toward political issues, most young people are not very different from their parents.

There is good reason, then, to believe that the bundle of issues called "improving the environment" will also suffer the gradual loss of public attention characteristic of the later stages of the "issue-attention cycle." However, it will be eclipsed at a much slower rate than other recent domestic issues. So it may be possible to accomplish some significant improvements in environmental quality—if those seeking them work fast.

2A.2. The Marasmus of the ICC
The Commission, the Railroads, and the Public Interest

SAMUEL P. HUNTINGTON

As we have seen, many think that much business regulation originates as a govern-ment response to an aroused citizenry. There is, however, a quite different view of the reason for government regulation of business. George Stigler (1971) points out that business can gain from regulation, if that regulation is undertaken in its interest. This is because government is able to, for example, put barriers in the way of new firms and set prices at higher than free-market levels. The taxicab industry, the undertaking industry, and the marine industry are often cited as instances.

In this reading Samuel Huntington puts forward a somewhat more sophisticated version of this view. He argues that, even when regulation is originally undertaken to benefit the general public, over time it may instead come to benefit the industry being regulated. This happens, he argues, because over time, the success of the regulatory agency in correcting the original abuses makes the issue less *central to the general public but* more *central to the industry being regulated. Because the agency needs outside political support if it is to continue to secure adequate funding, it is forced to shift its base from the general public to the industry. But this political support comes at a price. Bit by bit, the agency begins to slant its decisions in such a way as to favor the industry being regulated and even to protect it from new competition.*

The reader should note that it is quite possible that some regulation may be undertaken to benefit the general public and some to benefit the industry being regulated. It is also possible that the process Huntington outlines may happen in some cases but not others.

. . . **Successful adaptation to changing environmental circumstances** is the secret of health and longevity for administrative as well as biological organisms. Every government agency must reflect to some degree the "felt needs" of its

Reprinted by permission of The Yale Law Journal Company and Fred B. Rothman & Company from *The Yale Law Journal*, Vol. 61, No. 4 (April 1952), pp. 467–509 (with deletions).

time. In the realm of government, felt needs are expressed through political demands and political pressures. These demands and pressures may come from the president, other administrative agencies and officials, congressmen, political interest groups, and the general public. If any agency is to be viable it must adapt itself to the pressures from these sources so as to maintain a net preponderance of political support over political opposition.[1] It must have sufficient support to maintain and, if necessary, expand its statutory authority, to protect it against attempts to abolish it or subordinate it to other agencies, and to secure for it necessary appropriations. Consequently, to remain viable over a period of time, an agency must adjust its sources of support so as to corrrespond with changes in the strength of their political pressures. If the agency fails to make this adjustment, its political support decreases relative to its political opposition, and it may be said to suffer from administrative marasmus.[2] The decline of the ICC may be attributed to its susceptibility to this malady.

I. Historical background

The history of the ICC in terms of its political support divides naturally into two fairly distinct periods. The Commission was created in 1887 after the Supreme Court invalidated state attempts to regulate the railroads' abuse of their monopoly power.[3] The driving force behind these early state regulatory laws and commissions were the farmers, who had suffered severely from exorbitant rates and discriminatory practices. This group plus equally dissatisfied commercial shippers were the political force responsible for the Act to Regulate Commerce.[4] In addition, general public indignation and disgust at railroad financial and business practices provided a favorable climate of opinion for the creation of the Commission. President Cleveland endorsed the legislation and enhanced the Commission's reputation by appointing Judge Cooley and other prominent figures as its first members.[5]

From 1887 down to the First World War the support of the Commission came primarily from the groups responsible for its creation. Opposition came principally from the railroads and the courts. In its first two decades the Commission was severely hampered by the combined action of these two groups.[6] Subsequently farmer and shipper interests with the vigorous support of President Roosevelt secured the passage of the Hepburn Act of 1906. This enlarged the Commission, extended its jurisdiction, gave it the power to prescribe future maximum rates, and prohibited railroads from owning the products they transported. The decade which followed the passage of this Act was the peak of the Commission's power and prestige while still dependent upon consumer, public and presidential support.[7]

The end of the First World War marked a definite change in the nature of the transportation problem and in the attitudes of the various interests towards railroad regulation. The vigorous actions of the ICC in the period immediately prior to the war had eliminated the worst discriminatory practices and had convinced the railroads that the path of wisdom was to accept regulation and to learn to live with the Commission. This domestication of the carriers consequently reduced the interest and political activity of shipper groups. And increased urbanization reduced the power of farm groups which had been such a significant source of support to the Commission. Finally, "normalcy" had supplanted progressivism and Harding and Coolidge were significantly different from T. Roosevelt and Wilson. Consequently there was little likelihood that restrictive regulation would find much support from either the public or the White House.

All these factors dictated not only the shift in public policy which was made in the Transportation Act of 1920 but also a shift by the Commission in the sources to which it looked for support.[8] Continued reliance upon the old sources of support would have resulted in decreasing viability. Therefore the Commission turned more and more to the railroad industry itself, particularly the railroad management group. This development was aided by the expansion of the Commission's activities and the resulting increased dependence of the Commission upon the cooperation of regulated groups for the successful administration of its program.[9] The support which the Commission received from the railroads sustained it down to World War II and enabled it both to expand its authority over other carrier groups and to defend itself against attempts to subject it to executive control.

The present marasmus of the ICC is due to continued dependence upon railroad support. The transportation industry is not only large, it is also dynamic. Technological changes and economic development are basically altering the nation's transportation pattern. The tremendous expansion of air and motor transport, the resulting increase in competition, the economic development of the South and West, the rise of private carriage, and the increased significance of defense considerations all make today's transportation system fundamentally different from that of twenty-five years ago. These technological and economic developments have given rise to new political demands and pressures, and have drastically altered the old balance of political forces in the tranportation arena. A quarter of a century ago commercial transportation was railroad transportation. Today, railroads are a declining, although still major, segment of the transportation industry. Their economic decline has been matched by a decrease in political influence. The ICC, however, remains primarily a "railroad" agency. It has not responded to the demands of the new forces in transportation. It has not duplicated the successful adjustment of its source of political support that it carried out after World War I. Consequently, it is losing its leadership to those agenies which are more responsive to the needs and demands of the times.

II. Railroad support of the ICC

Railroad praise of the ICC

The attitude of the railroads towards the Commission since 1935 can only be described as one of satisfaction, approbation, and confidence. At times the railroads have been almost effusive in their praise of the Commission. The ICC, one sub-committee of the Association of American Railroads has declared, "is eminently qualified by nearly sixty years of experience to handle transportation matters with a maximum of satisfaction to management, labor and the public."[10] Another representative of the same association has similarly stated that "[w]hat is needed for the solution of the tremendously important problems of transport regulation is the impartiality, deliberation, expertness, and continuity of policy that have marked the history of the Interstate Commerce Commission."[11] Railroad officials and lawyers have commended the Commission as a "conspicuous success," a "contructive force," and as a "veteran and generally respected tribunal."[12] The American Short Line Railroad Association has commented upon the "fair, intelligent treatment" its members have been accorded by the Commission, and the Pennsylvania Railroad has been lavish in its praise of the latter's policies.[13] The ICC is probably the only regulatory body in the federal government which can boast that a book has been written about it by counsel for a regulated interest in order to demonstrate "how well" the Commission has "performed its duty."[14]

The railroads and the Commission have both praised their harmonious relations. "The railroad industry," it has been said, "in wide contrast to other industry, has learned to live under government regulation."[15] The editors of *Railway Age* have similarly spoken highly of the "collaboration" which exists between the Commission and its regulated enterprises and have remarked that this "stands out in strong contrast to the animosity and distrust which now separates many regulatory bodies from the areas of industry which they supervise."[16] The Commission itself has noted with pride the lack of criticism which its administration of the Interstate Commerce Act has received from the carriers and has pointed out that while some interests have urged the abandonment of regulation the "railroads have never joined in that suggestion."[17]

Railroad defense of Commission independence

The railroads have vigorously defended the independence of the ICC from control by other governmental units and have opposed all attempts to subordinate it to other agencies or to transfer from the Commission any of its functions. This support for the Commission has taken three principal forms.

Opposition to ICC reorganization. The railroads have successfully opposed all reorganization proposals to subordinate the ICC or transfer any of its functions to the executive branch. . . .

Opposition to the creation of new agencies which might rival the ICC. Within the last decade the railroads have generally opposed the establishment of new agencies which might in any way infringe upon or limit the powers of the ICC. . . .

Expansion of ICC regulatory authority over unregulated railroad-competitive groups. During the 1930's the railroads consistently urged the extension of ICC authority over unregulated carriers, particularly motor and inland water carriers. Their efforts in regard to the former achieved success in the Motor Carrier Act of 1935, which was the culmination of a determined legislative push by the railroads and the ICC. . . .

Railroad support in all its forms has been the basis of the Interstate Commerce Commission's viability. Other interests have at times supported individual actions of the Commission or defended the Commission against specific attempts to curb its authority. But such action on the part of these interests has always been sporadic and balanced by severe criticism of the Commission and opposition to it in other lines of policy. The railroads are alone among the interests surrounding the Commission in their constant and comprehensive support of that body. By their continuous praise of the Commission, by their defense of its independence and by their efforts to protect and to extend its authority the railroads have made the Commission the beneficiary of what has been their not inconsiderable political power. But in the rough world of competitive politics nothing comes for free. Political support must be purchased, and the price which the ICC has paid for its railroad support may be traced through almost all important phases of its policy and behavior.

III. ICC aid to the railroads

An exhaustive analysis of the ramifications of the ICC-railroad affiliation throughout Commission policy is obviously beyond the scope of this article. Instead it is here proposed to indicate briefly the consequences of this affiliation in four major areas of Commission activity: (1) the level of rates and fares; (2) monopoly and antitrust; (3) rail-motor competition; (4) rail-water competition.

The level of rates and fares

The ease with which the railroads in recent years have obtained advances in rates and fares from the ICC has been the subject of considerable unfavorable comment.[18] The significance of this Commission acquiescence to railroad demands can only be appreciated by a comparison of ICC policy in this field before and after it became dependent upon railroad support. The Commission received the power to prescribe future maximum rates in the Hepburn Act of 1906. The first general request for rate advances came from the carriers in 1911 after the Mann-Elkins Act had broadened the Commission's powers in this area. These requests were denied, with the Commission laying down rigorous criteria for the justification of rate advances.[19] During the next few years, in a series of general rate cases, the Commission either denied the railroad requests for increases or granted only a minor fraction of their demands.[20] As a consequence of this policy, freight rates remained stable and in general harmony with wholesale prices from 1908 through 1915.[21] In 1916, however, wholesale prices started to skyrocket, and the railroads renewed their demands for rate advances. But the ICC remained adamant throughout 1917, and it was not until March 1918 that the railroads were able to secure any substantial relief.[22] ICC policy during this period directly reflects its shipper and farmer sources of political support.

In 1920, as its support from non-railroad sources was beginning to weaken, the Commission approved a major increase in railroad rates.[23] After prices plummeted in 1921, freight rates were considerably out of line, and the Commission in 1922 ordered a ten per cent decrease.[24] Despite the pressure of agricultural interests, however, the Commission did not restore the prewar relationship between prices and rates. Instead, the Commission from 1924 through 1929 stabilized freight rates at about 165% of the 1913 level, whereas prices had fallen back to about 140% of that level. It was during this period that the Commission lost its farmer and shipper support and developed close railroad affiliations. The changing attitudes of the former toward the Commission are reflected in the Hoch-Smith resolution of 1925, and the year 1926 marks the last time that the Commission denied in toto a railroad request for a general rate advance.[25]

By the advent of the thirties the ICC was exercising a benevolent paternalism in regard to the rate level. Whereas in 1932 the wholesale price index had fallen off over 30% from its 1929 level, the Commission by granting "emergency" increases had actually slightly increased the level of freight rates. Throughout the depression the Commission maintained the rate level by approval of additional "emergency" increases and surcharges, by the rejection in 1933 of a shipper petition for rate reduction, and by the approval in 1938 of a general ten per cent rise. The result was that freight rates never dropped more than eleven per cent from their 1929 level. When wholesale prices increased in the early forties, freight rates went up also: the price index for 1945 was 151.6 and the freight rate index 173.8. Thus from 1924 through 1945 the Commission was able to maintain the rate level well above the price level. The significant gap between wholesale prices and freight rates during this period is graphic measure of the price of railroad support. (See graph.)

The removal of price controls in 1946 sent wholesale prices shooting upward. In three years the wholesale index had risen to 236.4. The ICC made valiant efforts to keep up with these skyrocketing prices. In June 1946 the Commission approved the first of a series of ten general rate increases embodied in four major proceedings.[26] By September 1951 the cumulative percentage increases granted by the Commission amounted to an increase of 67.6% in basic freight rates over the June 1946 level. The actual increase in the rate level from 1946 to 1950 was 35.6%. The drastic rise in wholesale prices has made it impossible for the Commission to maintain the 1945 cushion between prices and rates. The Commission has, however, been successful in preserving the 1913 relationship: in 1949 the rate index was 231.2, the price index 222.1; in 1950 the rate index was 229.5 and the price index 231.4. Considering the normal tendency of regulated and administered prices to lag far behind violent fluctuations in the general price level, the action of the Commission in moving rates up along with prices is

Railroad Freight Rates and Wholesale Prices
1913 = 100

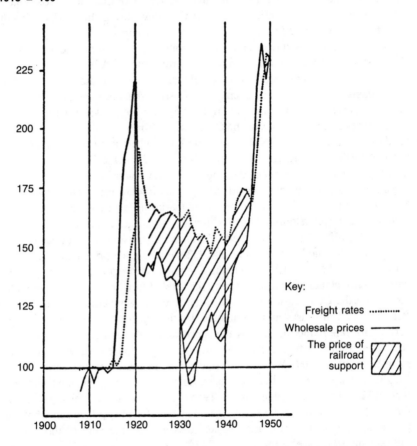

Source: For indexes from 1908 through 1947 the source is Transcript of Record, p. 3, Exhibit No. 54, testimony of C. E. Childe, *Ex Parte* No. 168, Increased Freight Rates, 1948, 272 I.C.C. 695 (1948), 276 I.C.C. 9 (1949). For indexes from 1948 through 1950 the source is letter of C. E. Childe to the author, Jan. 23, 1952. Mr. Childe compiled the freight rate level index from data in the annual issues of ICC, *Statistics of Railways in the United States*. The figures for the years from 1908 through 1949 are all steam railways. The figures for 1950 are based upon data for Class I steam railways only. The wholesale price index is calculated from the index published by the Bureau of Labor Statistics.

eloquent testimony to its sensitivity to railroad interests. The speed of the ICC in increasing freight rates during this period contrasts with its tardiness during the World War I inflation and has evoked praise from the railroads and envy from other carrier groups regulated by less considerate commissions.[27] . . .

Monopoly and antitrust

The Commission received its principal powers with respect to combinations and competition in the Transportation Act of 1920.[28] Consequently it was only rarely that it acted in this area while dependent upon shipper and public support. In the few instances in which it did consider problems of monopoly prior to 1920 it was vigorously critical of the railroads.[29] Its interpretations of the Transportation Act of 1920, on the other hand, have always been colored by its dependence upon railroad support. The Commission has advanced the individual and collective interests of the railroads by facilitating the reduction of competition among them and by aiding their development of cooperative devices designed to increase group solidarity.

In carrying out this necessary consequence of its railroad affiliation, the Commission has repeatedly come into conflict with the Antitrust Division and other groups interested in the maintenance of competition. The Commission early adopted the views of the railroads that collective price-fixing through rate bureaus and conferences was not only necessary and legal but also highly desirable.[30] This position conflicts with judicial interpretations of the Sherman Act holding (1) that the act is applicable to carriers regulated by the Commission, and (2) that cooperative price-fixing by competing companies is per se a violation of the antitrust laws.[31] It is, hence, significant that of eleven major antitrust proceedings instituted between 1935 and 1948 by the Department of Justice against carriers subject to ICC regulation, only one, which was against a motor carrier rate bureau, was based upon information referred to the Department by the ICC.[32] In another suit, also against a motor carrier, there was "close cooperation" between the Division and the Commission in the investigation preceding the indictment.[33] In regard to the railroads, however, the Commission has not turned over to the Department evidence of antitrust violations uncovered in the performance of its duties. . . .

Going beyond non-cooperation, the Commission has in some instances positively affected the conclusion of antitrust suits by the Government. Since it began to become dependent upon railroad support the Commission has in effect reversed successful antitrust suits by approving under Section 5 of the Interstate Commerce Act, and thereby exempting from the antitrust laws, practices which had previously been found to be in violation of those laws.[34] Similarly, in the recent *Pullman* case the Commission approved the sale of the Pullman operating company to the railroads over the objections of the Antitrust Division.[35] Also, the approval by the Commission of the Western Traffic Association Agreement after the passage of the Reed-Bulwinkle Bill has obstructed the Justice Department's suit against the western railroads.[36] . . .

Rail-motor competition

The affiliation of the ICC with the railroads has resulted in an ambiguous relationship between the Commission and the principal railroad-competitive group, the motor carriers. On the one hand, there is a close affiliation between the motor carrier industry and the ICC's Bureau of Motor Carriers, with the two cooperating in the enforcement of the Motor Carrier Act of 1935. The Bureau has consequently been praised by the motor carriers and criticized by the railroads.[37] On the other hand, the relationship between the motor carrier industry and the Commission apart from the BMC has been cool and frequently antagonistic. The reason for this is Commission partiality towards the railroads in conflicts of interest between the two carrier groups. The price of railroad affiliation has been motor carrier alienation.

Because a large portion of railroad traffic is non-competitive and must move by rail, the Commission has been able to aid the railroads by permitting selective rate-cutting during periods of intense rail-motor competition such as that from 1935 through 1941. For three years from 1937 to 1940 the Commission required motor carriers to bear the burden of proof in making competitive rate cuts while at the same time not requiring the railroads to do so. This policy was continued after Congress in 1938 amended the Motor Carrier Act to make its provisions concerning burden of proof identical with those applicable to the railroads.[38] During this same period the Commission put further barriers in the way of motor carrier competition by prescribing comprehensive minimum rate levels for motor carriers in the northeast and middle west.[39] Although initially requested by the motor carriers, the subsequent effect of these orders was, as Commissioner Eastman pionted out in one dissent, to substitute a much more difficult procedure for motor carriers wishing to lower rates than for railroads.[40] The Commission rejected, however, motor carrier petitions to remedy the situation.[41] Throughout this period the Commission in a number of cases encouraged the railroads to exercise their managerial discretion by meeting motor carrier competition through various devices.[42] . . . On the other hand, attempts by the motor carriers to meet railroad competition or to undercut railroads were usually disapproved by the Commission.[43] . . .

While competitive rate-making has been the single most important field of Commission behavior favoring railroads in their struggle with the motor carriers, other actions and policies of the Commission also deserve mention. In the discussion prior to the passage of the Motor Carrier Act the industry only consented to regulation by the "railroad-minded" ICC on the condition that a separate motor carrier bureau and division be established.[44] These two bodies became the representatives of the industry within the Commission and as such anathemas to the railroads, who consistently urged the Commission to organize itself on a "functional" rather than an "industry" basis.[45] In line with these desires the Commission has gradually emasculated the motor carrier units. The division has been stripped of its repsonsibilities in regard to rates, securities, consolidations, mergers, purchases, accounts, and penalties; the bureau has lost its Section of Traffic, its Section of Accounts, and its functions in connection with motor carrier securities.[46] In other fields of activity, the Commission has narrowly interpreted the "grandfather clause" (statutory authorization of operating rights to carriers for bona fide operations on a given date) so as to deny certificates and permits to many operating truck lines.[47] When it has approved such rights it has frequently severely restricted them as to the territory or classes of shippers which might be served or the commodities which might be transported.[48] For almost a decade the Commission interpreted the acquisition, certificate, and affiliation clauses of the Interstate Commerce Act in such a manner as to facilitate railroad penetration into the motor carrier industry and to raise genuine fears in the motor carriers as to the extent to which the Commission really wished to preserve the independent trucker.[49] Only recently the Commission announced a policy which would seem to indicate that motor carriers are to be barred from operating upon a transcontinental scale.[50]

The cumulative result of these ICC policies has been the alienation of the motor carriers from the Commission. Motor carrier criticism of the ICC has been consistent and vigorous.[51] At the end of the war, the truckers seriously considered initiating a drive to free themselves from ICC control.[52] After much discussion and the consideration of alternative plans, the industry now supports the break-up of the ICC into separate regulatory commissions for each type of transportation with an appellate commission to have jurisdiction over controversies involving two or more classes of carriers, the transfer of the executive functions of the ICC to an executive agency, and the further development of a general control over transportation by the Undersecretary of Commerce.[53]

Rail-water competition

Its affiliation with the railroads has dominated Commission action concerning water carriers and rail-water competition since the middle twenties when the Commission became dependent upon railroad support. Previous to this time the Commission had, with the exception of its administration of the Panama Canal Act, adequately balanced the interests of the two types of carriers.[54] Beginning in this period, however, the railroads instituted a concerted competitive drive against the water carriers. In this they had the virtually complete cooperation of the ICC. The twenty per cent differential which had been established by the Director General of the railroads during World War I for water rail-competitive rates was reduced to ten or fifteen per cent in a number of cases.[55] The persistent refusal of the railroads to enter into joint rates and through routes with the water carriers was acquiesced in by the Commission despite congressional pressure to the contrary.[56] Where joint rates were established, the participating water carrier was made to bear the full burden of the differential, and the Commission on occasion even permitted the railroad division of the joint rate to be considerably higher than the local rate to the point of interchange, thus virtually penalizing the water carrier for entering into such a relationship.[57] Reversing a previous policy adopted when it was dependent upon farmer and shipper support, the Commission began to permit railroads to charge discriminatory rates on traffic which had a prior or subsequent haul by water.[58] Liberal use was made of the provisions of the Fourth Section of the Interstate Commerce Act allowing the ICC to permit railroads to charge a higher rate for a shorter haul than for a longer one, and the

Commission frequently granted "flexible" relief permitting the railroads to meet automatically any competitive reductions by the water carriers.[59] In many cases, the Commission cooperated with the railroads to evade the statutory requirement that railroads not be allowed to raise depressed rates solely because of the elimination of water competition.[60] In approving general rate increases during this period the Commission frequently acquiesced to railroad requests for the exemption from such increases of heavily water-competitive traffic.[61] The Commission also showed a marked tendency to permit the railroads to lower rates on highly competitive items, at times such reductions going below the fully compensatory level.[62] . . .

As a result of these policies the water carriers, during the thirties, struggled against the extension over them of the power of the "railroad-minded" ICC. Unlike the motor carriers, they never acquiesced to Commission regulation.[63] In 1940, however, the railroads and the Commission triumphed and the water carrier industry was brought under a comprehensive system of control.[64] This did not ameliorate the antagonism between the water carriers and the Commission, and, again unlike the motor carriers, the water carrier industry never developed affiliations with any significant segment of the ICC. The Commission does not have a separate water carrier division, and, whereas the Bureau of Motor Carriers is the Commission's largest bureau, the Bureau of Water Carriers and Freight Forwarders is one of its smallest. In 1950 this bureau had only twenty-one employees,[65] and in addition to its water carrier duties it also supervised the regulation of freight forwarders and rate bureaus. The water carriers have consequently frequently complained that their interests are neglected, but these complaints have not produced any remedies.[66] The Commission has remained closely affiliated with the railroads. . . .

While the barge lines have suffered from the Commission's railroad partiality, they have at least been able to stay in business. Such has not been the case with the coastwise and intercoastal carriers. The combination of the war, railroad competition, and the unsympathetic attitude of the ICC has drastically weakened the domestic ocean shipping industry.[67] Service was suspended during the war, the traffic went to the rails, and with ICC concurrence it has stayed there. For a year and a half, from the end of the war until July 1947, the War Shipping Administration and the Maritime Commission operated a common and contract carrier service in the intercoastal and coastwise trades.[68] The difficulties encountered in this operation made it clear that the resumption of private service would be dependent upon a readjustment of railroad water-competitive rates. Consequently in March 1946 the two maritime agencies asked the Commission to initiate an investigation of these rates. Nine months later the ICC began to comply wih this request and instituted the first of five major investigations into water-rail competitive rates.[69] The net result of these investigations has been virtually inconsequential. The water carriers have repeatedly been denied substantial relief which would permit them to resume operations on anything remotely resembling their prewar scale. Practically the only rate increases which have been ordered have been minor ones readily acquiesced to by the railroads.[70] At the same time the Commission allowed the railroads to introduce lower increases on water-competitive traffic in their general rate advance cases, and also to put into effect in the last few years new lower rates on highly competitive individual items.[71] The result of these policies has been vigorous criticism of the Commission by the alienated water carriers, and various suggestions from them for the reorganization of water carrier regulation.[72]

IV. Railroad affiliation and Commission viability

The pattern of affiliation of the Commission with the railroads described in the preceding pages is the basic reason for the decreasing viability of the Commission. This decline has four significant aspects:

(1) The alienation of non-railroad interest groups. This process has been described in regard to the water carriers and motor carriers. The fourth major type of transportation, the air carriers, also recognize the Commission's railroad affiliations and have blocked the extension of Commission power into their field.[73] Among shippers the Commission can only command qualified support from the large industrial shippers of the National Industrial Traffic League, which has always been closely associated with the railroads. Other shippers, and agricultural groups in particular, are generally hostile towards the Commission.[74]

(2) The alienation of other government agencies. With some agencies, such as the Department of Agriculture and the Maritime Commission, estrangement has developed because these bodies are closely affiliated with interest groups alienated from the Commission. In a larger number of instances, however, it has been because the Commission's espousal of the relatively narrow interests of the railroads has conflicted with the responsibility felt by these other agencies to some broader interest and their dependence upon some broader basis of political support. This is particularly true of such agencies as the Departments of Commerce, Interior, and Defense, the Antitrust Division, and the price stabilization agencies.[75]

(3) Subversion of congressional intent. In interpreting the Interstate Commerce Act in the interests of the railroads it is quite obvious that the Commission is applying the law in a manner not intended by the Congress. In 1940 Congress declared the national transportation policy to include ''fair and impartial regulation of all modes of transportation.'' Congress also wrote into the acts of 1935 and 1940 various provisions designed to insure that this policy would be carried out. The failure of the Commission to do this has resulted in increased criticism of the Commission in Congress.[76]

(4) Passivity and loss of leadership. The general purpose of the railroads during the past quarter century has been first the preservation, and then subsequently, after it had been lost, the restoration of their transportation monopoly. Because of its affiliation with the railroads the Commission has, like them, become a defender of the status quo. To this end it has maintained an outdated,

formalistic type of procedure.[77] It has been slow to introduce the most simple and accepted new techniques of modern management.[78] It has failed to develop effective devices for representing the public interest.[79] It has neglected administrative planning, and has failed to develop a coherent transportation policy aside from that of giving the railroads what they want.[80] As a result, it has been slow to recognize and deal with obvious evils, such as the freight classification problem or the question of state limitations on truck sizes and weights. It has also been unable to adjust its thinking and actions to the new demands of an era in which defense considerations are paramount. These failures of the Commission have inevitably led to the formation within the executive branch of a responsible office which can take the lead in national transportation policy and planning.

Given this situation in regard to the ICC, what, then, is desirable public policy? The independence of a regulatory commission is based upon the premise that this independence will aid it in being objective and impartial. When such a commission loses its objectivity and impartiality by becoming dependent upon the support of a single narrow interest group, obviously the rationale for maintaining its independence has ceased to exist, and it becomes necessary to subordinate this agency to some other agency possessing a broader outlook and a broader basis of political support. It is undoubtedly desirable to have an agency within the federal government affiliated with the railroads and able to represent their interests. It is undoubtedly undesirable to have such an agency independent of all administrative supervision, masquerading as an impartial tribunal, and controlling competing carrier groups. Fortunately the recent reorganization of the Maritime Commission suggests a pattern for application to the ICC.

The Interstate Commerce Commission should be abolished as an independent agency. Its executive functions should be transferred, as the Hoover Commission recommended, to the Secretary of Commerce. The motor and water carriers should be emancipated by dividing the regulatory functions of the ICC among three separate commissions dealing respectively with rail, water, and highway transportation. These three commissions should all be placed within the Department of Commerce in a position similar to that of the Maritime Board and subject to the same general policy guidance of the Secretary.[81]

The Supreme Court of the United States once remarked that:

> "The outlook of the Commission and its powers must be greater than the interest of the railroads or of that which may affect those interests. It must be as comprehensive as the interest of the whole country."[82]

This is not only a norm of public policy; it is also a requisite for administrative viability. The railroads may still, at least in the immediate future, furnish the Commission with powerful political support. But the prolonged failure of the Commission to adhere to the Court's standard must eventually make the Commission unviable and lead to its replacement by other instrumentalities better able to act in the public interest.

Notes

1. For thorough discussion of agency support theory, see Simon, Smithburg, & Thompson, *Public Administration* cc. 18, 19 (1950); Long, Power and Administration, 9 *Pub. Admin. Rev.* 257-64 (1949); Truman, *The Governmental Process* 395-478 (1951).

2. "ma-ras'-mus . . . n. Pathol. A gradual and continuous wasting away of the bulk of the body from some morbid cause. [Gr. *marasmos, maraino*, waste]." Funk & Wagnalls, *New Standard Dictionary of the English Language* (1935).

3. Wabash, St. L. & P.R. *v.* Illinois, 118 U.S. 577 (1886).

4. Fainsod & Gordon, *Government and the American Economy* 245 (1941).

5. See Middleton, *Railways and Public Opinion: Eleven Decades* 75-91 (1941).

6. Counselman *v.* Hitchcock, 142 U.S. 547 (1892); C., N.O. and Texas-Pacific Ry. *v.* ICC, 162 U.S. 184 (1896).

7. See *e.g.*, Miller, *The Interstate Commerce Commission—Past and Present* 800 (1946); Sen. Rep. No. 597, 63rd Cong., 2d Sess. 6, 10 (1914); H.R. Rep. No. 553, 63d Cong., 2d Sess. 8 (1914). According to Mansfield, *The Lake Cargo Coal Rate Controversy* 141 (1932), the ICC had by this time "gained a place near the Supreme Court in public estimation. . . ." The increase in the Commission's viability was marked by a steady stream of legislation increasing its powers, Hepburn Act, 34 Stat. 584 (1906), Mann-Elkins Act, 36 Stat. 539 (1910), Locomotive Boiler Inspection Act, 36 Stat. 913 (1911), Panama Canal Act, 37 Stat. 560 (1912), Valuation Act, 37 Stat. 701 (1913), Clayton Antitrust Act, 38 Stat. 730 (1914), and by a more respectful attitude from the Courts.

8. The Transportation Act of 1920 required the Commission to fix rates so that the railroad industry as a whole would earn a "fair return upon the aggregate value" of its invested capital.

9. See Herring, *Public Administration and the Public Interest* 183-93 (1936).

10. Ass'n of American Railroads, Railroad Committee for the Study of Transportation, *Report on Coordination* 26.

11. *Hearings before Senate Committee on Interstate and Foreign Commerce on Domestic Land and Water Transportation*, 81st Cong., 2d Sess. 495 (1950).

12. Wham, Railroads and The National Transportation Policy, 7 *John Marshall L. Q.* 168-9 (1941); Drayton, *Transportation Under Two Masters* 3 (1946).

13. House Committee on Interstate and Foreign Commerce, Special Subcommittee on Transportation, *National Transportation Inquiry* 17, 266 (1946).

14. Walter, Introduction to Drayton, *Transportation Under Two Masters*, xii (1946).

15. Ass'n of American Railroads, *op. cit. supra* note 10, at 26.

16. 112 *Railway Age* 324 (Feb. 7, 1942).

17. 52 ICC *Ann. Rep.* 8 (1938).

18. *Hearings before the Senate Committee on Interstate and Foreign Commerce on the Reappointment of J. Monroe Johnson to be a Member of the Interstate Commerce Commission*, 81st Cong. 1st Sess. 10 (1949) 10-11; *N.Y. Times*, April 15, 1950, p. 21, col. 5; Askwith, *Our Pampered Railroads*, 168; *Nation* 556-7 (1949).

19. 36 Stat. 539 (1910); Advances in Rates, Eastern Case, 20 I.C.C. 243 (1911); Advances in Rates, Western Case, 20 I.C.C. 307 (1911).

20. The Five Per Cent Case, 31 I.C.C. 351 (1914), 32 I.C.C. 325 (1914); 1915 Western Rate Advance Case, 35 I.C.C. 497 (1915), 37 I.C.C. 114 (1915); Western Trunk Line Rate Increases, 43 I.C.C. 481 (1917); The Fifteen Per Cent Case, 45 I.C.C. 303 (1917); Proposed Increases in New England, 49 I.C.C. 421 (1918).

21. The source for this and subsequent figures on the level of freight rates and wholesale prices is Exhibit 54, p. 3, Testimony of C. E. Childe, *Ex Parte* No. 168, Increased Freight Rates 1948, 276 I.C.C. 9 (1949). For both the rate and price indexes 1913 equals 100. Mr. Childe compiled these indexes from data furnished by the Commission and the Bureau of Labor Statistics. Index figures for 1948 through 1950 have been supplied directly to the author by Mr. Childe.

22. 3B Sharfman, *Interstate Commerce Commission* 83–98 (1936); General Order No. 28, United States Railroad Administration, dated May 25, 1918, amended June 12, 1918, effective June 25, 1918.

23. Increased Rates, 1920, 58 I.C.C. 220 (1920); Authority to Increase Rates, 58 I.C.C. 302 (1920).

24. Reduced Rates, 1922, 68 I.C.C. 676 (1922).

25. 43 Stat. 801 (1925); Revenues in Western District, 113 I.C.C. 3 (1926). In following the mandate of the resolution the Commission in one case, Calif. Growers' and Shippers' Protective League *v.* So. Pac. Co., 129 I.C.C. 25 (1927), 132 I.C.C. 582 (1927), ordered a reduction in rates, but this was reversed by the Supreme Court on the grounds that the resolution was a mere expression of Congressional opinion and did not change the existing law. Ann Arbor Railroad *v.* United States, 281 U.S. 658 (1930). For a description of the alienation of the shipper and farmer groups from the Commission, see Fainsod & Gordon, *Government and the American Economy* 269 (1941).

26. Increased Railway Rates, Fares, and Charges, 1942, 248 I.C.C. 545 (1942) authorized a six per cent increase, which was suspended, 255 I.C.C. 357 (1943), and restored, 264 I.C.C. 695 (1946). . . . The ICC has not been unaware of the harmful effects of its policy: "One consequence of the cumulative rate increases of the past 3 years undoubtedly has been a disturbance of many processes of production and distribution with permanent changes in the economic map of the country, although other factors have also contributed to the same result." 63 ICC *Ann. Rep.* 2–3 (1949).

27. *Hearings before the House Committee on Interstate and Foreign Commerce on National Transportation Policy*, 80th Cong., 2d Sess. (1948), at 82–3, 440–1; *Hearings on Domestic Land and Water Transportation*, *supra* note 11, at 209, 257–9. For the dissident voice of Robert R. Young, see *Hearings on National Transportation Policy*, *supra* at 320, and 12 *Law & Contemp. Prob.* 627–9; for the envious voice of W. A. Patterson, president of United Air Lines, see 49 *Aviation Week* 43 (Nov. 8, 1948); *Stewardship of the Airlines by the CAB*, 15 J. of *Air L. & Commerce* 391–2 (1948).

28. Section 407, Transportation Act of 1920, 41 Stat. 480–2 (1920).

29. See, *e.g.*, *In re* Financial Investigation of the N.Y., N.H. & Hartford R. R. Co., 31 I.C.C. 32 (1914), especially at pp. 65–70 for a hard-hitting and incisive attack on the New Haven's "policy of transportation monopoly."

30. *In re* Transcontinental Freight Bureau, 77 I.C.C. 252 (1923); Rates between Ariz., Calif., N. M., and Texas, 3 M.C.C. 505 (1937).

31. United States *v.* Trans-Missouri Freight Ass'n, 166 U.S. 290 (1897); United States *v.* Joint Traffic Ass'n; 171 U.S. 505 (1898); United States *v.* Trenton Potteries Co., 273 U.S. 392 (1927); United States *v.* Socony-Vacuum Oil Co., 310 U.S. 150 (1940).

32. United States *v.* Middlewest M. Frt. Bur., Crim No. 9905 (D. Colo. 1944); *Hearings on S. 942, supra* note 21, at 267–9; 58 ICC Ann. Rep. 30 (1944).

33. United States *v.* Freightways, Civil No. 22075-R (N.D. Calif. 1944); *Transport Topics*, Feb. 9, 1942; 112 *Railway Age* 353 (Feb. 7, 1942).

34. United States *v.* Southern Pacific Co., 259 U.S. 214 (1922), 290 Fed. 443 (D. Utah 1923), Control of Central Pacific by Southern Pacific, 76 I.C.C. 508 (1923).

35. United States *v.* Pullman Co., 50 F. Supp. 123 (E.D. Pa. 1943), 53 F. Supp. 908 (E.D. Pa. 1944), 55 F. Supp. 985 (E.D. Pa. 1944), 64 F. Supp. 108 (E.D. Pa. 1945), 330 U.S. 806 (1947), *rehearing denied*, 331 U.S. 865 (1947); Proposed Pooling of Railroad

Earnings and Service Involved in the Operation of the Pullman Co. under Railroad Ownership, 268 I.C.C. 473 (1947).

36. *Transport Topics*, Nov. 29, 1948; CCH Trade Reg. Rep. ¶¶ 61, 168.

37. *Transport Topics*, Oct. 11, 25, 1937, Jan. 31, Oct 17, 1938, Feb. 20, July 3, 1939, March 19, 1945, Feb. 4, 1946, Jan. 17, 24, Aug. 29, 1949; 104 *Railway Age* 19 (March 12, 1938); 106 *id*. at 21 (Feb. 11, 1939), 550 (April 1, 1939); 108 *id*. at 9 (Jan. 13, 1940), 43 (Feb. 24, 1940), 395 (March 2, 1940); 109 *id*. at 389 (Sept. 21, 1940); 110 *id*. at 240 (Feb. 1, 1941); 111 *id*. at 940 (Dec. 6, 1941).

38. See Northcutt Minimum Charges, Ariz. and Calif.—N.M., 14 M.C.C. 611 (1939); Split Deliveries in Chicago Union Stockyards, 14 M.C.C. 743 (1939); Packing House Products—Portland, Ore.—Wash., 17 M.C.C. 255 (1939).

39. Rates over Freight Forwarders, Inc., 4 M.C.C. 68 (1937); Central Territory M.C. Rates, 8 M.C.C. 233 (1938); N. Eng. Terr. M.C. Rates, 8 M.C.C. 287 (1938); Trunk Line Terr. M.C. Rates, 24 M.C.C. 501 (1940); 57 I.C.C. Ann. Rep. 97-8 (1943).

40. Trunk Line Terr. M.C. Rates, 24 M.C.C. 501, 625 (1940).

41. *Transport Topics*, Feb. 10, 1941.

42. Western Trunk Line Class Rates, 210 I.C.C. 312 (1935); Emergency Freight Charges, 1935, 215 I.C.C. 439 (1936); Fuel & Gas Oil to Memphis, Tenn., 218 I.C.C. 106 (1936); All Freight from Chicago & St. Louis to Birmingham, 226 I.C.C. 455 (1938); Sand, Gravel & Stone to Champaign & Urbana, 237 I.C.C. 773 (1940); Bags & Bagging from Portland & Seattle, 238 I.C.C. 717 (1940).

43. 124 Cotton Fabrics & Cotton Piece Goods, 10 M.C.C. 275 (1938); Mine Cars & Machinery between Denver & El Paso, 22 M.C.C. 317 (1940); Trunk Line Terr. M.C. Rates, 24 M.C.C. 501 (1940); Fruit from New York to Philadelphia, 24 M.C.C. 760 (1940). Many of these cases involved competition between motor carriers as well as between motor carriers and railroads.

44. See *Hearings before the House Committee on Interstate and Foreign Commerce on H.R.6836*, 73rd Con., 2d. Sess. 14 *et seq*. (1934); *Hearings before the Senate Committee on Interstate and Foreign Commerce on S.1629, S.1632, S.1635*, 74th Cong., 1st Sess., 116 *et seq*. (1935).

45. *Recommendations upon the General Transportation Situation* 14 (1938); 109 *Railway Age* 503 (Oct. 12, 1940); *Transport Topics*, Feb. 20, March 6, 1939, Feb. 6, 1946.

46. 53 ICC *Ann. Rep*. 1-5 (1939); *Transport Topics*, Dec. 25, 1944, March 11, Apr. 1, 1946, March 8, 15, 1948.

47. Vedder Oil Contract Car. App., 1 M.C.C. 758 (1936); McDonald v. Thompson, 305 U.S. 263 (1938); Gregg Cartage & Storage Co. v. United States 316 U.S. 74 (1942).

48. See, generally, Board of Investigation and Research, Federal Regulatory Restrictions upon Motor and Water Carriers, Sen. Doc. No. 78, 79th Cong., 1st Sess. (1945).

49. Pennsylvania Truck Lines—Control—Barker, 1 M.C.C. 101 (1936), 5 M.C.C. 9 (1937); Pacific Motor Trucking Co.—Control—Pacific, 35 M.C.C. 353 (1940); Rock Island M. Transit Co.—Purchase—White Line, 40 M.C.C. 457 (1946), 55 M.C.C. 567 (1949).

50. Pacific Intermountain Express Co.—Control and Purchase—Keeshin Freight Lines, 57 M.C.C. 341, 379 (1950): "In the administration of the national transportation policy the inherent advantages of rail transportation on volume movements of transcontinental traffic are to be preserved."

51. *Transport Topics*, Dec. 26, 1938, April 17, Oct. 9, 1939, Feb. 24, May 26, 1941, Oct. 22, 1945, March 29, 1948; 86 *Traffic World* 73 (Feb. 2, 1951); 1 *National Transportation Inquiry* 11, 37-8.

52. *Transport Topics*, Jan. 31, 1946.

53. *Hearings on Domestic Land and Water Transportation* 862-7.

54. See *e.g., Hearings on S.1629, S.1632, S.1635.*

55. Through Routes and Joint Rates, Inland Waterways Corp., 153 I.C.C. 129 (1929): Application of Mississippi Valley Barge Line Co., 167 I.C.C. 41 (1930).

56. Dep't War v. Abilene & S. Ry. Co., 77 I.C.C. 317 (1923), 92 I.C.C. 528 (1924); Through Routes & Joint Rates, Inland Waterways Corp., 167 I.C.C. 385 (1930), 192 I.C.C. 173 (1933); *Hearings on S.1629, S.1632, S.1635, supra* note 44, at 858-9.

57. See. *e.g.,* Inland Waterways Corp. v. Ala. G.S.R. Co., 151 I.C.C. 126 (1929); *Hearings on S.1629, S.1632, S.1635, supra* note 44, 786-7.

58. Ex-River Grain from St. Louis to the South, 203 I.C.C. 385 (1934); Raw Sugar, New Orleans to Grammercy and Reserve, La., 206 I.C.C. 231 (1935).

59. Pacific Coast Fourth Section Applications, 129 I.C.C. 3 (1927), 165 I.C.C. 373 (1930), 173 I.C.C. 577 (1931), 190 I.C.C. 273 (1932), 196 I.C.C. 296 (1933), 200 I.C.C. 259 (1934), Citrus Fruit from Fla. to North Atlantic Ports, 211 I.C.C. 535 (1935).

60. Interstate Commerce Act §4(2). This was done by granting only temporary relief from the requirements of the Fourth Section. Consequently when the temporary order expired the previous rates could be automatically reinstated if the water competition has been eliminated, or if it has not been eliminated, the relief could be extended. Temporary relief was granted in 35 of the 88 cases mentioned in note 59 *supra* where Fourth Section applications were approved. See *Hearings on S.1629, S.1632, S.1635,* 857, 866-7.

61. Emergency Freight Charges, 1935, 208 I.C.C. 4 (1935); General Commodity Rate Increases, 1937, 223 I.C.C. 657 (1937); Fifteen Per Cent Case, 1937-1938, 226 I.C.C. 41 (1938).

62. Petroleum from New Orleans, 194 I.C.C. 31 (1933); Malt Liquors from River Crossings to Fla., 227 I.C.C. 285 (1938); Lumber from N.C. to N.Y., 245 I.C.C. 231 (1941).

63. See *Hearings on S.1629, S.1632, S.1635, supra* note 44.

64. 54 Stat. 929 (1940). This became Part III of the Interstate Commerce Act.

65. *Hearings on Independent Offices Appropriation Bill for 1951* 788-9. This was just one per cent of the Commission's staff.

66. *Hearings before Senate Committee on Interstate and Foreign Commerce on the Merchant Marine Study and Investigation,* 81st Cong., 2d Sess. 1158-60, 1201 (1950); *Commission on Organization* III-34, III-38.

67. On June 30, 1939 there were 235 vessels of 1,187,000 deadweight tonnage in the coastwise trades and 143 vessels (1,377,000 deadweight tons) in intercoastal service. On Dec. 31, 1949 there were 78 vessels (including 6 government ships operating under charter) with a tonnage of 552,000 deadweight tons in the coastwise trade and 58 vessels (including 32 government ships under charter) of 651,000 deadweight tons in the inter- coastal trade. *Hearings on Merchant Marine Study and Investigation, supra* note 66, 1186.

68. War Shipping Administration Temporary Authority Application (Coastwise and Intercoastal), 260 I.C.C. 589 (1945); 60 ICC Ann. Rep. 34-5 (1946).

69. 60 ICC *Ann. Rep.* 32-4 (1946); Trancontinental Rail Rates, 268 I.C.C. 567, 569- 70 (1947); 1 *National Transportation Inquiry* 232-4.

70. 61 ICC *Ann. Rep.* 47-9 (1947); 62 *id* at 6, 49-52 (1948); 64 *id.* at 51 (1950).

71. Increased Railway Rates, Fares, and Charges, 1946, 266 I.C.C. 537 (1946); Increased Freight Rates, 1947, 270 I.C.C. 403 (1948); 1 *National Transportation Inquiry* 231; ICC Problems in the Regulation of Domestic Transportation by Water 343; 62 ICC *Ann. Rep.* 48 (1948); *Hearings on Merchant Marine Study and Investigation, supra* note 66, 1236-7.

72. *Hearings on Domestic Land and Water Transportation* 1251, 1371 *et. seq.; Hearings on National Transportation Policy* 170, 176-7; *Hearings on Merchant Marine Study and Investigation, supra* note 66, 1157-67, 1265-6, 1270-1, 1276-7,1274-5; Commis- sion on Organization, *Staff Report of the Interstate Commerce Commission,* III-10-11,

III–34, III–38.

73. 1 *National Transportation Inquiry* 25–30; *Hearings on National Transportation Policy* 4–8, 22–4; Barker, *State of the Industry*, 5 *Air Transport* 3 (Oct. 1947).

74. See 21 *Nation's Agriculture* 18 (Jan. 1946), 23 *id.* at 16 (Feb. 1948); Amer. Farm Bureau Federation, 25 *Official News Letters* 5 (Dec. 25, 1946), 1, 4 (May 1, 1946); 27 *id.* 5–6 (Dec. 22, 1948); 25 *National Union Farmer* 1–2 (April 15, 1946), 5 (May 1, 1946); 27 *id.* at 7 (Oct. 1949); 95 *Cong. Rec.* A–2002–05 (1949).

There have been frequent conflicts between the Commission and various government agencies in the latters' capacities as shippers. See Commission on Organization, *op. cit. supra* note 72, at III–20–21. The most notable instance of this nature has been the attempt by the Department of Justice to secure refunds of several hundred million dollars in overcharges paid by the government to the railroads during the war. The ICC has resolutely sided with the carriers in this conflict and the government has been unsuccessful in getting its money back.

75. See, in general, Commission on Organization, *op. cit. supra* note 72, at III–14, III–19, III–22–23, IV–7; Stern, "Inconsistency" in Government Litigation, 65 *Harv. L. Rev.* 762–3 (1951).

76. Two examples of the results of Congress' fear that the ICC was "railroad-minded" are found in the Transportation Act of 1940: the Whittington Amendment providing that all the provisions of the Interstate Commerce Act shall be administered and enforced with a view to carrying out the National Transportation Policy and the revision of the rule of ratemaking to protect motor and water carriers against "umbrella" ratemaking on behalf of the railroads. 54 *Stat.* 899, 912, 924, 938 (1940).

77. Attorney General's Committee on Administrative Procedure, *op. cit. supra* note 65, *passim*; Commission on Organization, *op. cit. supra* note 72, at I–52—59, II–19, IV–32; 61 ICC Ann. Rep. 14–19 (1947). The Hoover Commission staff report stated (p. II–24): "To a remarkable extent the Commission has operated by judicial processes, although allowing somewhat more flexibility than is the practice of the courts. Its procedures appear to have become more and more formalized as the volume of its work has increased, its bar has become organized, and its tradition has grown."

78. Commission on Organization, *op. cit. supra* note 72, at I–23–24: "The Commission completely lacks any provision of organization and management personnel in its administrative set-up. As a result such changes in organization as occur come about in somewhat haphazard way, largely as changes in personnel or other matters of expediency require or suggest."

79. This deficiency and the manner in which it benefits the railroads is discussed at length in Davis, *Official Notice*, 62 *Harv. L. Rev.* 542–5 (1949) and Williams, *supra* note 76, at 1364–6.

80. The failure of the ICC in this area is best indicated by the recurring creation of temporary transportation planning agencies, *e.g.* National Transportation Committee, 1933, Federal Coordinator of Transportation, 1933–36, the Committee of Three, 1938, the Committee of Six, 1938, the Board of Investigation and Research, 1940–44.

81. See Commission on Organization, The Independent Regulatory Commission 12 (1949) for the recommendation of the transfer of the executive functions of the carriers who have also gone on record in favor of separate industry commissions with an appellate commission to resolve conflicting decisions. *Hearings on S. Res. 253, 254, 255, 256, supra* note 35, at 162–3; *Hearings on Domestic Land and Water Transportation* 862–7; *Transport Topics*, Feb. 5, 1951.

82. ICC *v.* Chicago, R.I. & Pac. Ry. Co., 218 U.S. 88, 103 (1910).

2A.3. Regulatory Agencies
Inside the Black Box

KENNETH J. MEIER

Many observers of regulatory politics hold that once a regulatory agency becomes established it exerts an independent influence on what regulation is undertaken in its area. In this excerpt from his book Regulation, *Kenneth J. Meier develops the view that agencies can to some degree insulate themselves from immediate political pressures such as those Huntington discusses. The primary reason they are able to do so is that they possess more expertise than others. However, agencies are not all equally insulated. The degree of freedom from outside political pressure depends on such factors as the complexity of the area being regulated, the degree of cohesion and leadership in the agency, and the independent authority granted to the agency when it was established.*

The reader should note that agency independence (to the degree that it exists) can be a two-edged sword. That is, although it may enable the agency to fend off attempts by special interests to control it, by the same token, such independence may make it possible for the agency to act in ways contrary to public preferences. However, many experts believe that regulatory agencies develop a sense of mission which motivates them to strive to accomplish the job they were set up to do. If this is true, then the sort of diminution of public issue activism over time that is discussed by Downs and Huntington need not translate into a diminution of regulatory activity.

Government agencies are not passive actors pushed along at the whim of other subsystem members. They shape as well as respond to pressures from the subsystem (Rourke, 1984). The U.S. Department of Agriculture (USDA), for example, played a role in creating and developing the American Farm Bureau; Farm Bureau members, in turn, assisted the USDA in crop regulation. The Environmental Protection Agency funds academic research on pollution; such research is then used in debates over environmental protection. In a sense, both agencies helped create a portion of the subsystem. If bureaus can take an active role in structuring their environments, they need not passively respond to subsystem pressures. They can actively seek to influence the forces impinging on regulatory policy. To understand the policy actions of regulatory agencies, two variables—goals and resources—must be discussed.

Agency goals

Every regulatory agency has goals including policy goals that agency employees wish to attain. Environmental Protection Agency employees seek cleaner air and water; FDA personnel pursue safe and effective drugs. Although this contention may seem trivial, many treatments of bureaucracy either assume an organization's sole goal is to survive or that the bureaucrats' goal is to maximize their income (e.g., see Niskanen, 1971). Both approaches provide a misleading view of regulatory agencies.

This distinction merits some discussion. If we assume, as Niskanen does, that bureaucrats are rational utility maximizers, regulators clearly seek goals other than income maximization. Because incomes are higher in the regulated industry, an income maximizer would choose to work for the regulated industry rather than the regulatory agency.[1] The choice to enter the public sector is not dictated by inferior skills because studies show that public sector employees in jobs similar to private sector ones have greater skills and better training (Guyot, 1979). A public sector bureaucrat, therefore, must be maximizing something other than income; the most logical thing to maximize is policy goals.

Ascribing regulatory policy goals to bureaucrats is consistent with motivation theory (e.g., Maslow, 1970) and empirical evidence. Employees work for the Office of Civil Rights because they believe in racial equality (Romzek and Hendricks, 1982). Individuals work for OSHA because they desire to improve workplace safety (Kelman, 1980). In the long run, most agency employees become advocates of the agency and its goals (Downs, 1967). Those interested in higher incomes or in the goals of the regulated industry will probably leave the agency.

Having policy goals does not mean that bureaucrats would not like to see their organization survive, all things being equal. Survival, after all, is necessary to obtain most policy goals. In some cases, the present Civil Aeronautics Board bureaucrats, for example, are content to accomplish policy objectives that will eventually eliminate the agency. In sum then, regulators regulate because they wish to attain policy goals; without understanding that regulators are goal-seeking and without determining what those goals are, regulatory behavior will appear random to the outside observer.

Also important in terms of regulatory goals is the potential for goal conflict within an agency. Such lack of consensus might result from several different conflicts within the organization: central staff versus field personnel, professionals versus administrators, one profession versus another profession, career staff versus political appointees. The last source of conflict is especially important. Career staff are more likely to identify with the agency and be strongly committed to its programs (Heclo, 1977). Political appointees are more likely to see themselves as the president's representative (Welborn, 1977) and therefore, hold different views.

Resources

In pursuit of policy goals, regulatory agencies have access to five resources—expertise, cohesion, legislative authority, policy salience, and leadership.[2] Access to such resources determines the value of the agency's participation to other subsystem members. The greater a regulatory agency's resources, the more likely the agency will be able to resist industry pressures for regulation solely in the interests of the industry.

Expertise

Bureaucratic organizations are designed to develop and store knowledge. To a degree greater than legislatures or courts, bureaucracies can divide tasks and gain knowledge via specialization (Rourke, 1984: 16). An EPA employee, for example, could spend an entire career dealing with the intricacies of regulating the pesticide mirex. As part of specialization, American government bureaucracies recruit skilled technocrats as employees, and the agencies become professionalized. A professionalized agency often adopts the values of the predominant profession; the values of safety and health professionals in the Occupational Safety and Health Administration, for example, are the reason why OSHA relies on engineering standards (Kelman, 1980).

Professionalization and specialization permit an agency to develop independent sources of knowledge so that the agency need not rely on the industry (or others) for its information. Although the levels of professionalism and specialization in regulatory agencies cannot rival those of such agencies as the National Institutes of Health, they are a factor. The Nobel laureate Glenn Seaborg's appointment to head the Atomic Energy Commission (AEC; now the Nuclear Regulatory Commission) increased the AEC's reputation for expertise. Similarly, the creation of a separate research arm for the Environmental Protection Agency provided the EPA with expertise it could use in its political battles (Davies and Davies, 1975).

Professionalism does not mean that an agency is dominated by a single profession. At times one or more professions may be struggling for control of the agency. In the Federal Trade Commission (FTC), for example, economists and lawyers have long fought over control of the FTC's antitrust functions. The professional conflict, in fact, has major policy implications. Lawyers prefer

cases that can be quickly brought to trial like Robinson-Patman cases. Economists favor either major structural monopoly cases that will significantly increase
competition or cases against collusion.

Cohesion

A second resource permitting the agency to affect public policy is the cohesive-
ness of the bureau's personnel. If agency personnel are united in pursuit of their
goals, coalitions opposed to agency actions will need to develop their own
sources of information to challenge agency decisions. A cohesive agency is far
more difficult to resist than an agency that engages in public disputes over policy
direction. Cohesion, in turn, is a function of an agency's goals and its ability to
socialize members to accept these goals. Some public agencies such as the Marine
Corps or the Forest Service even go so far as to create an organizational ideology
for their members. Although no regulatory agency engages in the same degree of
socialization that the Marine Corps does, they do seek consciously or unconsciously to influence the values of employees. Bureaucrats in the Environmental
Protection Agency, for example, show much greater concern for environmental
protection than for compliance costs. The Office of Education in the 1960s was a
zealous advocate of school desegregation.

Legislative authority

All regulatory agencies must have legislative authority to operate, but all grants
of legislative authority are not equal (see Sabatier, 1977: 424–431).[3] Five important differences in legislative authority exist and contribute to agency resources.
First, policy goals as expressed in legislation can be specific or vague. Before
1973, Congress specified agricultural price support levels exactly, leaving little
discretion for Agriculture Department regulators. In contrast, the Interstate
Commerce Commission regulates interstate commerce with the general goal that
regulation should be in the public interest. The more vague the legislative expression of goals, the greater the agency's ability to set regulatory policy. Specific
policy goals should be correlated with regulation in the interests of whichever
group has the best access to Congress. Consequently, specific goals are associated
both with the regulation in the interests of the regulated (e.g., agriculture) and
with regulation for the benefit of the nonregulated (e.g., environmental protection; see Marcus, 1980).
    Second, legislative delegations vary in the scope of authority they grant. Some
agencies have jurisdiction over every firm in the industry (e.g., EPA). Other
agencies might be denied jurisdiction over portions of their industry; OSHA's
law, for example, exempts small farms. An agency with limited authority cannot
affect the behavior of those outside its jurisdiction. The greater the limitations
and restrictions on a regulatory agency, the more likely such an agency will

regulate in the interest of the regulated industry.

Third, legislative delegations vary in the sanctions permitted to an agency. Bank regulators possess a wide variety of sanctions that can greatly influence the profits and viability of financial institutions. In contrast, the Equal Employment Opportunity Commission (EEOC) has no sanctions and must rely on court action to extract compliance. The greater the range of sanctions available to a regulatory agency, the more likely the agency will regulate in the interests of the nonregulated.

Fourth, regulatory agencies differ in their organizational structure. The two most common structural forms are the department regulatory agency (an agency headed by one person within a larger executive department) and the independent regulatory commission (a multimember board that reports directly to the legislature). Although the different structures do not appear related to performance (see Meier, 1980; Welborn, 1977), often independent regulatory commissions are subjected to other restraints. At the state level, regulatory commissions are often by law composed of members of the regulated industry. When selection restrictions such as this occur, regulation in the interests of the regulated is a given.

Fifth, legislative grants of authority often specify agency procedures. The FTC must follow the lengthy *formal* rule-making process to issue rules, and the Consumer Product Safety Commission was handicapped until recently with a cumbersome "offeror" procedure. Other agencies such as the EEOC and the antitrust regulators are limited further because they must use the courts to set policy and resolve disputes. The more restrictive an agency's procedures are, the less likely the agency will be able to regulate the industry closely.

Political salience

The salience of a regulatory issue (i.e., its perceived importance by the public) can be used as a resource in the agency's regulatory battles. Regulatory issues vary greatly in salience. Nuclear plant regulation after the Three Mile Island accident was a highly salient issue to political elites and the general public. State regulation of barbers, on the other hand, is rarely salient. Not only does salience vary across issue areas, it also varies across time within an issue area. Banking regulation was highly salient in 1933 but not so in 1973.

According to William Gormley (1983), salience determines the willingness of political elites to intervene in the regulatory process. When issues become salient, the rewards for successful intervention are greater for elected officials. In salient issue areas, therefore, regulators will find their actions closely watched by political elites whereas in nonsalient areas regulatory discretion is likely to go unchecked. A lack of salience should be to the advantage of the regulated industry because it will have little opposition to its demands.

Leadership

The final regulatory resource is the agency's leadership. Unlike the career bureaucracy, which is fairly stable, leadership positions turn over frequently. Two elements of leadership are important—quality and the leader's goals. Quality of leadership is a nebulous resource that, though difficult to define, is clearly a factor. The leadership abilities of Alfred Kahn as Civil Aeronautics Board chairperson were instrumental in deregulating airlines; the absence of strong leadership in Federal Trade Commission chairman Paul Rand Dixon was often cited as a reason for poor performance by the pre-1969 FTC.

Essential to understanding the impact of leadership are the policy goals of regulatory agency heads. Through the leadership of Caspar Weinberger, Miles Kirkpatrick, and Michael Pertschuk, the Federal Trade Commission became less tied to the interests of the regulated industry and more interested in consumer issues. The appointment of Reese Taylor to head the Interstate Commerce Commission in 1981 signaled an end to the rapid movement toward deregulation of the trucking industry.

Leadership is especially important because the agency head is the focal point for interaction with the subsystem. In such interactions, the agency head is constrained by the expertise, cohesion, legislative authority, issue salience, and policy goals of the agency. An agency head who acts in opposition to the values and normal policy activities of the career staff risks political opposition from within the agency. Anne Burford's effort to alter environmental policy in the 1980s and the response of the EPA career staff is a classic example of this.

Agency discretion: a recapitulation

Regulatory agencies, therefore, exercise some discretion in regulatory policy. This discretion is not limitless, however. The amount of discretion accorded an agency is a function of its resources (expertise, cohesion, legislative authority, policy salience, and leadership) and the tolerances of other actors in the political system. Each actor has a zone of acceptance (see Simon, 1957); and if agency decisions fall within that zone, no action will be taken. Because regulatory policy is more important to subsystem actors, the zone of acceptance for subsystem actors is probably narrower than that for macropolitical system actors (e.g., the president). Consequently, subsystem actors will be more active.

As long as the regulatory subsystem produces policies within the zone of acceptance of Congress, the president, and the courts, then these actors will permit the subsystem some autonomy. Actions outside the zone of acceptance will bring attempts to intervene. The size of the zones of acceptance should vary with both salience and complexity (see Gormley, 1983). Salience increases the benefits of successful intervention to a political actor, and complexity increases the costs of intervention. All things being equal, therefore, political actors will be more likely to intervene in policies that are salient but not complex (Gormley, 1983).

Notes

1. One might argue that working for a regulatory agency increases one's value to industry in the future. Such a calculation ignores both the careerist orientation of the regulatory agency's career staff (see McGregor, 1974) and the fact that regulators such as Joan Claybrook are unlikely to accept industry employment.

2. The section on bureaucratic variables relies heavily on Rourke (1984) and Sabatier (1977). The most applicable parts of the writings of each are used. In some cases, the impact of the variables reflects my interpretation of their work rather than their interpretation.

3. The analysis of legislative authority follows that of Sabatier (1977). I have added the category of procedure and shortened his discussion of structure.

References

Davies, J. Clarence, and Barbara S. Davies. 1975. *The Politics of Pollution*, 2d ed. Indianapolis: Pegasus.

Downs, Anthony. 1967. *Inside Bureaucracy*. Boston: Little, Brown.

Gormley, William T. 1983. "Regulatory Issue Networks in a Federal System." Paper presented at the annual meeting of the American Political Science Association, Chicago.

Guyot, James F. 1979. "The Convergence of Public and Private Sector Bureaucracies." Paper presented at the annual meeting of the American Political Science Association, Washington, D.C.

Heclo, Hugh. 1977. *Government of Strangers*. Washington, D.C.: Brookings.

Kelman, Steven. 1980. "Occupational Safety and Health Administration." In James Q. Wilson, ed., *The Politics of Regulation*. New York: Basic Books, pp. 236–266.

Marcus, Alfred. 1980. "Environmental Protection Agency." In James Q. Wilson, ed., *The Politics of Regulation*. New York: Basic Books, pp. 267–303.

Maslow, Abraham H. 1970. *Motivation and Personality*. 2d ed. New York: Harper & Row.

McGregor, Eugene B., 1974. "Politics and Career Mobility of Civil Servants." *American Political Science Review* 68 (March), 18–26.

Meier, Kenneth J. 1980. "The Impact of Regulatory Agency Structure: IRCs or DRAs." *Southern Review of Public Administration* 3 (March), 427–443.

Niskanen, William. 1971. *Bureaucracy and Representative Government*. Chicago: Aldine.

Romzek, Barbara S., and J. Stephen Hendricks. 1982. "Organizational Involvement and Representative Bureaucracy." *American Political Science Review* 76 (March), 75–82.

Rourke, Francis E. 1984. *Bureaucracy, Politics, and Public Policy.* Boston: Little, Brown.

Sabatier, Paul A. 1977. "Regulatory Policy Making: Toward a Framework of Analysis." *National Resources Journal* 17 (July), 415–460.

Simon, Herbert A. 1957. *Administrative Behavior*. New York: Free Press.

Welborn, David M. 1977. *The Governance of Federal Regulatory Agencies*. Knoxville: University of Tennessee Press.

2B. Industrial Policy

In many industrial countries government not only regulates industry but takes an active part in planning industrial change. This practice is obviously most prevalent in the communist countries, where almost all industries are owned by the state, their development guided by five-year plans. However, there is a milder form of planning, nowadays often referred to as industrial policy, in which governments formulate development plans in consultation with industry and provide incentives for their implementation. This system is found in many Western European countries and in Japan (Shonfield 1969; Johnson 1982).

Thoughout the 1970s and 1980s the United States has experienced weak economic growth and slow productivity increases. A number of experts have proposed that what America needs to do is imitate its more successful rivals and implement some form of industrial policy (Vogel 1979). They argue that the incentive structure facing managers in our free-market system encourages them to emphasize short-term gains at the expense of long-term growth. They point out that other countries, having systematically investigated and successfully anticipated future trends, have been able to build industries that have a head start on our own. Robert Reich is one expert who sees the United States as ripe for industrial policy. In Reich's view, since economic policies already have a significant effect on corporate planning, what is really needed is for government to take a longer view, and manage economic policy in a more conscious and coordinated manner. This way of thinking about industrial policy has had a great deal of appeal for some liberal Democrats.

As one might expect, industrial policy has its detractors as well as its proponents. The issue is especially heated inasmuch as industrial policy, as a form of economic planning, could increase government power at the expense of private firms. Most who oppose it argue that in general, the managers of firms will do better than government planners in evaluating future trends (Schultze 1983). Further, they argue that while a case can be made for government planning in theory, in practice governments have shown themselves most responsive to appeals to preserve the *status quo* by giving assistance and subsidies to declining industries and inefficient firms (Olson 1982).

Would an American industrial policy be a good thing? Before we can formulate an answer to this question, we need to resolve a number of not very simple prior questions. Is it in fact true that American industry is becoming less competitive over time (Lawrence 1984)? If it is true, can we be sure that the decline is a result of lack of planning, or might it be due to such things as low tariffs, shifts in the value of the dollar, higher labor costs, or poor management practices? This in turn raises the question of whether the success of countries such as Korea and Japan is in fact a result of government planning (Abramovitz 1979; Roy 1982). Finally, even among those who favor industrial policy, there is disagreement over how comprehensive it should be.

The reading in this section by Amitai Etzioni is an argument *for* a limited industrial policy, confined largely to research, and *against* a more active industrial policy. The general notion that Japanese success is due to the intervention of MITI, the Japanese Ministry of International Trade and Industry, is, in Etzioni's view, largely mistaken. And in any case, many Japanese techniques simply are not transferable to the United States.

The article by Robert Reich argues for an active, wide-ranging industrial policy. In Reich's view, we already have a *de facto* industrial policy, and the real choice is whether it is to be effective or ineffective. Finally, Patrick Norton surveys the development of the debate on industrial policy and looks at some of the most important arguments for and against it.

For further reading

An early book advocating indicative planning was Andrew Shonfield's *Modern Capitalism*; a more recent one is Ezra Vogel's *Japan as Number 1*. A good history of attempts to institute planning in this country is Otis Graham's *Toward a Planned Society: From Roosevelt to Nixon*. Ira Magaziner and Robert Reich's *Minding America's Business: The Decline and Rise of the American Economy* is a recent work that was largely responsible for reviving the debate over American industrial policy. Patrick Norton's article "Industrial Policy and American Renewal," from which our third reading is drawn, is the most comprehensive analysis of recent developments in the debate.

Bibliography

Abramovitz, Moses, "Rapid Growth Potential and its Realization: The Experience of Capitalist Economies in the Postwar Period," in Edmond Malinvaud, ed., *Economic Growth and Resources*. Vol. 1, *The Major Issues* (New York: The Macmillan Press, 1979) pp. 1–51.

Graham, Otis L. Jr., *Toward a Planned Society: From Roosevelt to Nixon* (New York: Oxford University Press, 1976).

Johnson, Chalmers, *MITI and the Japanese Miracle: The Growth of Industrial Policy*

1925-1975 (Stanford: Stanford University Press, 1982).

Lawrence, Robert Z., *Can America Compete?* (Washington D.C.: The Brookings Institution, 1984).

Magaziner, Ira C. and Robert B. Reich, *Minding America's Business: The Decline and Rise of the American Economy* (New York: Harcourt Brace Jovanovich, 1982).

Norton, Patrick, "Industrial Policy and American Renewal," *Journal of Economic Literature* 24 (March 1986):33–40.

Olson, Mancur, *The Rise and Decline of Nations: Economic Growth, Stagflation and Social Rigidities* (New Haven: Yale University Press, 1982).

Roy, A.D., "Labor Productivity in 1980: An International Comparison," *National Institute Economic Review* 101 (August 1982):26–37.

Shonfield, Andrew, *Modern Capitalism: The Changing Balance of Public and Private Power* (London: Oxford University Press, 1969).

Schultze, Charles L., "Industrial Policy: A Dissent," *Brookings Review* 2(1) (Fall 1983):3–12.

Vogel, Ezra F., *Japan as Number 1: Lessons for America* (New York: Harper, 1979).

2B.1. The MITIzation of America?

AMITAI ETZIONI

In this essay Amitai Etzioni argues against some proposals for a Japanese-style industrial policy that were advanced by Ira Magaziner and Robert Reich in a book called Minding America's Business. *Etzioni argues that industrial policy has been less successful in Japan than many of its American proponents contend. He also underscores the fact that the United States is not Japan, and that many of the conditions that made industrial policy workable in Japan do not hold here. However, Etzioni does think that some government action to create economic incentives and set national priorities is appropriate, especially in the area of research and development.*

From half a dozen Democratic study groups, caucuses, a think tank, and—more indirectly—from statements by several Democratic presidential hopefuls, a new theme is rising: industrial policy. It calls for the next Democratic administration, in consultation with business and labor, to formulate a set of industrial priorities. Chosen industries (high tech, especially computers, usually lead the list) are to be showered with public funds and benefits. Losing industries (autos and steel, for example) are to be "sunset" and their workers moved to other industries after "retraining." (Some suggest reconstructing the losing industries—with public funds and guidance—to become winners.) In these ways the government is to help American business adapt more rapidly to the changing technological environment and to the competitive world overseas. An often repeated line is, "We did Japan and Germany a favor by bombing out their steel mills; now we must take out our own obsolescent ones."

The model that several proponents of industrial policy seek to emulate is Japan. The Ministry of International Trade and Industry (MITI) of Japan is credited with successfully managing Japan's economy as if it were one corporation. Hence references to "Japan, Inc.," and a standard question from the left: "If corporations have a planning committee, what's wrong with having one for

Reprinted with permission of the author from *The Public Interest*, No. 73 (Summer 1983), pp. 44–51. © 1983 by National Affairs, Inc.

the U.S.?'' Indeed, the MITIzation of America is openly advocated.

One American version of MITI calls for the Department of Commerce to be transformed into a Department of Trade and Development, with a desk and a trilateral committee (made up of government, business, and labor) for each industry, from ball bearings to shoes. Each desk would analyze its industry and determine whether it had a promising future in terms of productivity, export potential, technological innovation, labor intensiveness, ''added-value,'' and other such criteria. The industries ranked at the top would be granted whatever they need to thrive, based on trilateral consultations. (''Consensus'' is another Japanese characteristic the new industrial world is to emulate.)

The people who most explicitly call for an industrial policy based on identification of winners and losers are the left-liberal Gar Alperowitz, co-director of the Center for Economic Alternatives, and Arny Packer, an Assistant Secretary of Labor in the Carter administration. Robert Reich, a former planning director of the Federal Trade Commission and currently a professor at Harvard's Kennedy School of Government, is widely considered the spokesman for Democratic industrial policy. A book he co-authored with Ira C. Magaziner, *Minding America's Business*, is often cited in discussions of industrial policy. Reich does not use the terms ''winners'' and ''losers'' and objects to being identified with the Alperowitz-Packer position. Nevertheless, he does call for identifying and assisting those industries with a ''high added-value.''

Reich never clearly defines what ''high added-value'' is. The problems in predicting which industries will have a high added-value in the future are similar, if not identical, to those of picking winners and losers. Indeed, in their book, Magaziner and Reich talk about ''declining'' and ''growing'' businesses as if there were labels pinned to their smokestacks or written on their laboratory flat-roofs. While it might be relatively easy to tell who is currently on the decline, this is by no means an easy business to predict. Losers turn into winners in a few short years, and vice versa, a catch Reich and others ignore.

As I see it, America cannot be MITI-ized, nor should it be. Before indicating why, I ought to make it clear that the Democratic Party has not adopted the idea as part of its platform or official policy, both because Democrats are still actively debating the idea and because the 1984 elections still seem far away. Now, before a commitment has been made, is the best time to raise questions about industrial policy. (Republican readers may feel that they could not care less—or would even find it welcome—if the Democrats lock into a wrong-headed strategy. But there is always a certain statistical probability that the Democrats will win, and the last thing the country needs is another round of experimentation with faulty economic theory.)

The cultural gap

Before evaluating what MITI has to offer America, we ought to ask how well it has done for Japan. In the mood of self-flagellation which prevailed on these shores in the late 1970s, Japan was credited with almost unbelievable prowess.

For instance, Harvard sociologist Ezra Vogel found Japan first not only in economic achievement, but also in education, crime control, equality of income distribution, environmental protection, and health. The guiding spirit in this account—the consensus-builder, the administrator-coordinator, the promoter of productivity, export, research and development (R&D), good labor relations and wise investment decisions—is, you guessed it, MITI.

Others disagree. They point to MITI failures. For example, in 1955 MITI wanted Japanese auto makers to concentrate on a single car model, the "People's Car," and it took lobbying in the Japanese parliament to allow the auto makers to keep a more varied line, which has been part of their marketing success. Not long before, MITI officials had told Japanese auto makers not to waste resources trying to export—on the assumption that they could never penetrate foreign markets! In the 1960s, Honda and Mitsubishi succeeded by staying out of MITI-guided cartels and going it alone. More recently, Japan's MITI-ized steel mills have been operating for years at 70 percent of capacity.

But more to the point, whatever MITI does or does not do for Japan, it cannot be Xeroxed and shipped to the U.S. Major institutions do not travel well across international boundaries. It suffices to remember that our Constitution has been copied by some of the republics of Latin America, which have frequently used it to impose the rule of generals, not to sustain democracy. Japan is a far more homogeneous society than the U.S., and its people have a strongly shared national mentality, fostered by a sense of vulnerability due to their isolation and the absence of most natural resources. They pull together much more readily than do the people of continent-sized, pluralistic America. Executives in Japan often have secure, lifelong employment commitments. Many employees live on corporate campuses and many labor unions are, in effect, company-controlled. To put it succinctly, there probably is not a major industrial country from which the U.S. can copy *less* than from Japan.

The essential feature of MITIzation is that it presupposes an intensive and extensive role for government in planning and managing the economy. Nothing could be further from the political philosophy to which most Americans subscribe. The American antipathy for government, and the corresponding belief in individualism, competition, and the marketplace, go back to the days of the founding. In recent years, in a reaction to the liberal decades of the New Frontier and the Great Society, these beliefs have been strongly reaffirmed. After all, not just Reagan but Carter, too, rode on an anti-big-government wave. If Reaganomics fails, some backlash may develop, which could carry us either to *greater* opposition to government, or to some new willingness to draw on it for economic revitalization. But I cannot imagine that by 1984 or 1988 the public will embrace a MITI-ized economy. To advocate it is, at least politically, a losing proposition.

The political gap

Nor is a MITI compatible with the way America is governed. In Congress we find a strong expression of local interests and, increasingly, of other special interests. We may leave to another occasion the question whether this makes for a wholesome, pluralistic, representative system or for a semi-corrupt PACed Congress. The fact is that a national economic plan cannot be formed and implemented under our political institutions, if it can be done at all. When our social engineers wanted to test the Model Cities plan in six sites during the 1960s, members of Congress, long before the data were in, demanded the program for "their" cities, extending it to 75, soon 150, cities. The Economic Development Administration was to allot funds for selected economically depressed counties; soon, under Congressional pressure, 84.5 percent of *all* U.S. counties qualified, turning the program into an open pork barrel and completely defeating its purpose. Essentially the same thing happened to Trade Adjustment Assistance and to the tax code, the latter becoming so riddled with special favors that some have proposed turning to a flat rate tax.

Moreover, the "losing" industries are usually the oldest and best-established ones, and therefore have the most political influence, while newer, more innovative industries often have relatively little. Bio-engineering is lost among the farm, bank, labor, real estate, steel, and auto lobbies. Thus the American political process tends to channel resources to obsolescent industries, to the relative neglect of the new, with-it ones. President Carter's short-lived 1980 economic revitalization drive started with the auto and steel industries—both obsolescent and in need of being scaled back—not because his staff believed they were the engines of America's future, but because their labor unions were flirting with the idea of endorsing Senator Kennedy.

It has been suggested that the American MITI, like the Federal Reserve, would be an independent authority, insulated from Congress. But would Congress agree to keep its hands off a comprehensive national planning and management agency? And could the economy run if we had *two* economic policy-making institutions independent from one another—and from general national policy making? (Some feel one is too many.) Sometimes the bark of the proponents of industrial policy is worse than their bite. Reich calls for "government management" of capital markets, which is enough to drive most American businessmen, investors, and voters up the wall (and over it, to relocate overseas). Actually, he does not quite mean a government-run investment decision-making apparatus for the American economy, only introduction of "public investment criteria" into allocations of loan guarantees, insurance subsidies, and tax and credit subsidies.

The knowledge gap

Other advocates of industrial policy, such as Lester Thurow and Felix Rohatyn, are much more moderate. They favor directing *some* capital to where it is needed—perhaps through a Reconstruction Finance Corporation (RFC) on the order of $50 billion a year—which is a long way from "managing the American capital market." Indeed, the size of the intervention is as important as its tightness of grip. A small RFC might be wasteful, a nuisance, a symbol of relying on government rather than the market; a major one would constitute an attempt to plan the economy through a central financial authority. Gar Alperowitz, for instance, recently called for "coordinated overall planning." Recognizing that this notion is not very popular, he has returned to an old-left chestnut, expecting the forthcoming crisis to raise people's "consciousness." He writes, "Probably the new approach will have to linger on the sidelines . . . until the economic disarray explodes into crisis and the people demand that something be done."

Last but not least, the identification of "winners" and "losers," the cornerstone of industrial policy, is a near-impossible task. To identify a winning industry requires predicting the future, determining what product line will succeed, taking into account future technological developments, changes in the general level of economic activity, actions by our competitors, and so on. The fact is that American industries that in the past were considered sure losers—textiles, shoes—have become winners, *without* industrial policy, and an industry that until recently seemed an American winner—airplane manufacturing—may turn sour (and then again may not). It is hard to foretell. I find it very revealing when people who put their faith in forecasting do not engage in studies of the validity of past forecasts. (Do not trust a broker who will not provide—or keep—a performance record.)

At one point Magaziner and Reich announce that "the governments must be capable of distinguishing between major structural declines and temporary problems that can be overcome with adequate funding." Maybe they must, maybe they do not—but *can* they? So far as one can tell from historical and anecdotal information, and as the preceding examples illustrate, successful long-run identification of winners or losers is beyond our current intellectual and technical capacity.

Learning from the American experience

All this does not mean that the only alternative is to sit back and await the results of the vicissitudes of the marketplace. As long as there is a government (even for defense only) there will be a tax system and public policy decisions as to how to distribute its burdens, not only among various social groups, but between consumption and investment and production. (For instance, shall there be a tax on corporations or only on individuals? On capital gains or only on earned income?) Similarly, monetary policy and the level of government activities, especially deficits, affect the availability of credit to the private sector. In effect, both the tax and the credit systems are used daily by the government—including the Reagan administration—to transmit national priorities to the economy.

These sorts of signals differ from those sent by MITI in that they are economic incentives, not administrative decrees, regulations, or public financing. Moreover, these incentives are focused on wide sectors of the economy, not specific industries. For example, to favor investment in capital goods over collectibles and residential real estate (as most items of the 1981 Economic Recovery Act do) is not to favor tin over silver, or slurry pipelines over railroads. Because they are broad, these incentives are much less subject to political pork-barreling; most political corruption enters when economic incentives are tied to a narrow, specific constituency. In addition, they can work well even if we cannot forecast precisely. To favor R&D in general, for instance, does not require forecasting *which* specific R&D projects, or even which line of investigation, will "win," or which new technology will pay off.

A major study of "industrial innovation policy" published in *Science* illustrates the point.[1] The authors identified three ways the U.S. government historically has supported R&D. Before one rushes to condemn all government support for R&D it should be noted that a good part of this support is directly related to U.S. national security. And all but the most extreme free market purists recognize the need for the government to support some shared goods which have no profit potential, among which basic scientific research ranks second only to defense. Support, of course, does not mean government administration, production, or control. Support of R&D currently takes the form of appropriation of needed funds. The question under study is what kind of government guidance—if any—should be built into the ways the funds are allotted.

The study found two ways that worked well and one that clearly does not. Support for items in which the government has a "strong and direct procurement interest" (e.g., missiles) works well, as does support for "generic" research *between* basic and applied (e.g., accelerating the transition of basic work in chemistry and biology to applied R&D carried out by the private sector). What "unequivocally" did *not* work, say the researchers, is the government's trying to "pick winners." In the SST project and Operation Breakthrough (a HUD housing development), the government "did not attempt to create a framework in which scientific and user interests could guide allocation; rather than federal agencies attempting to insert themselves directly into the business of developing particular technologies for a commercial market in which they had little or no procurement interest." This "targeted" form of support for R&D failed, while the indirect—or *semi*-targeted—approach worked quite effectively.

All specific economic decisions can be left to the private marketplace within a framework that encourages what I have called reindustrialization—that is, shoring up the infrastructure and capital goods sectors, the sectors favored by the first industrialization of America. Others may call such an approach "industrial policy II" or "MITI-minus." By whatever name, such an economic policy may foster American economic reconstruction, as long as it does not look like or attempt to work like MITI in Japan. Incentives and broad-gauged signaling of priorities might help; national planning and managing the economy will not.

Note

1. Richard R. Nelson and Richard N. Langlois, "Industrial Innovation Policy: Lessons from American History," *Science* (February 18, 1983): 814–818.

2B.2. An Industrial Policy of the Right

ROBERT B. REICH

Amitai Etzioni is not alone in his belief that a full-scale industrial policy would be unsuitable for American conditions, but there are some who think that an industrial policy is exactly what is needed to revive American productivity. Robert Reich is one of the foremost proponents of the view that, because of imperfections in the free market, it is essential that government play a part both in research and development and in the planning of the nation's industrial development. In this essay Reich argues that it is impossible for the United States to avoid having an industrial policy, and that the real question is whether it will be an implicit industrial policy, with large but unplanned effects, or a more coordinated policy with planned effects.

Industrial policy has become something of a political Rorschach test. The term somehow summons each person's fondest hopes or direst fears. Direct evidence of this phenomenon is to be found in the last issue of *The Public Interest*, in which Professor Amitai Etzioni [in ''The MITIzation of America?''] casts a caricature of Japan's ''MITI'' and then proceeds to show why such a straw man could not (and should not) survive in the United States; and George Gilder claims that industrial policy is at best no more than supply-side economics in rather perverse disguise.[1] Lost in this ideological shuffle are the facts about what America's *actual* industrial policy is coming to look like, and an explanation of the central questions it raises for our republic.

A nation's industrial policy is the sum of its microeconomic policies—like tax rules, research and development grants, credit subsidies, and import restrictions—as they affect the pace and direction of industrial change. Every advanced nation has an industrial policy, just as it has fiscal and monetary policies. And just as fiscal and monetary policies may be deemed ''good'' or ''bad''—depending on how one values and ranks the ultimate goals to be achieved, and on empirical

Reprinted with permission of the author from *The Public Interest* No. 73 (Fall 1983), pp. 3–17. © 1983 by National Affairs, Inc.

assumptions about how the economy responds to various policy choices along the way—so too can a nation's industrial policy be judged by the values it serves and the economic logic on which it depends.

U.S. industrial policy today

What is the industrial policy of the United States? One clue can be found in Table 1, which reveals sharp disparities in the effective rate of corporate income tax paid by various industries in 1981. The industries with the lowest effective tax rate, interestingly, are either service industries largely sheltered from international competition (retailing, finance, airlines, utilities, commercial banks, railroads), or natural-resource industries (oil and oil refining, petrochemicals, crude oil, and paper and wood products). Aerospace and metal-manufacturing also fare relatively well. Manufacturers of automobiles, trucks, pharmaceuticals, appliances and electronics, on the other hand, bear a relatively high effective tax.

We get a somewhat different picture if we look at another set of disparities— the percentage of industrial research and development funded by the federal government (Table 2). The federal government supports roughly half of all research and development undertaken in the United States, and upwards of 75 percent of basic research. (This sample is from 1977, the most recent year for which such data are available.)

Here aerospace again is among the winners, and automobiles and pharmaceuticals among the losers. But the petrochemical industry now becomes something of a loser, while electrical equipment moves into the winner's camp. Nor does this allocation of research and development subsidies reveal the same bias against internationally-traded manufacturing industries as does the effective tax rate.

This inventory could go on. In the cases of federally-subsidized loans (amounting to some $56 billion in new loans to specific industries in 1982) and loan guarantees ($36 billion), the biggest winners by far are housing construction and agriculture, with aerospace and aircraft equipment coming in a distant third.[2] On the other hand, the major industrial beneficiaries of import restrictions are steel, textiles, apparel, and automobiles (together comprising approximately one-fourth of all U.S. merchandise imports). And the federal government obligingly purchases most of the output of the firms that produce aircraft, communications equipment, super computers, and lasers.

What is the net result of all this? We cannot really know without charting the interdependencies among our industries, and measuring how disparities in government treatment alter their profitability—how, for example, differences in effective tax rates or research and development grants affect cost structures, ease of entry or exit, and the speed with which new market opportunities can be exploited.

What we do know, however, is that the current patchwork of policies yields some odd results. For example, the United States automobile industry (on which one out of every six American workers directly or indirectly depended for a

Table 1

Effective Rate of Corporate Income Tax, by Industry

Automobiles	48%	Airlines	16%
Trucking	46%	Metal manufacturing	10%
Pharmaceuticals	36%	Utilities	9%
Electronics, appliances	29%	Aerospace	7%
Food processing	27%	Petrochemicals	5%
Industrial and farm equipment	24%	Crude oil	3%
Retailing	23%	Commercial banks	2%
Oil and refining	19%	Railroads	− 8%
Diversified financial	17%	Paper and wood	−14%

Source: Joint Committee on Taxation, *Taxation of Banks and Thrift Institutions* (March 9, 1983): Table 2. (There are a number of ways to compute effective tax rates, and some computations generate results slightly different from these; but regardless of methodology, great disparities exist.)

Table 2

Percentage of Research and Development Funded by the Federal Government, by Industry

Aircraft and parts	70%	Motor vehicles	8%
Transportation equipment (excludes autos)	55%	Non-electric machinery	7%
Fabricated metals	53%	Petrochemicals	2%
Communications equipment, electronic components	49%	Primary metals	2%
Electrical equipment (excludes communications)	26%	Drugs and medicines	<1%
Scientific instruments	22%	Textiles and apparel	<1%

Source: National Science Board, *Science Indicators*, 1978 (Washington, D.C.: 1979).

livelihood in 1980) owes its present condition, at least in part, to a mixture of generous import restrictions and loan guarantees, onerous environmental regulations, relatively high effective tax rates, and little or no government-supported research. On the other hand, the housing-construction industry has been the indirect beneficiary of large credit and tax subsidies to American homeowners, the cumulative effect of which has been to help channel approximately one-third of U.S. gross domestic fixed investment over the last dozen years into housing and to transform our housing stock into a form of savings for countless middle-class families. The federal government spends five times more on research and development for commercial fisheries than it does for steel. As of 1980, the government was providing $455 million annually in tax breaks for timber and none for semiconductors. And the fact that substantial benefits go to industries sheltered from international competition notwithstanding, some of the chief recipients of government largesse—like aircraft, communications equipment, electronic components, wheat, and soybeans—are among our most successful exporters.

Clearly, government strongly affects the pattern of industrial development in the United States. But does this amount to an industrial "policy"? The term suggests some intention, purpose, plan. Yet these patterns appear to be nothing but the fallout from separate government programs designed to achieve all manner of things—ensure national security, provide Americans with decent housing, protect domestic energy supplies, and so on. The programs are not intended to advance (or retard) the development of specific industries. No one picks the winner and losers; they are anointed inadvertently.

Tell that to the National Association of Home Builders, the lobbyists for General Motors or Boeing, lawyers representing the nation's largest banks before the Internal Revenue Service, the government relations staffs at General Dynamics and TRW, and members of the House Ways and Means Committee. They will be amused. True, the official language appearing in the *Congressional Record* and in administrative rulings—justifying this or that tax credit, loan guarantee, or research subsidy—typically makes at least vague reference to the public interest. It would be unseemly not to. And all but the most confirmed cynics would concede that many of these programs do benefit broad segments of the public. After all, we do want an effective national defense and affordable housing. But the fact is that these public benefits are often incidental to the choice of what industry (or what segment of what industry) actually comes out the winner.[3] Those who promote and shape public policy in America usually know fairly well how a given policy will affect the development of a specific industry. Indeed, such a purpose often lies at the very heart of the initiative, encased within layers of public justifications bearing no direct relation to it. And more often than not, the most heated legislative and administrative battles concern not the wisdom of the policy itself but the underlying heart of the matter—which industry will win and which will lose by it. Winners and losers are picked all the time; the picking is the stuff of politics.

Nor is it possible *not* to have an industrial policy. Laws and agency rulings need not specifically target winners and losers in order for their effects to be highly discriminatory. Because each industry (or industrial segment) has a distinct competitive position relative to all others—based upon the costs it bears and markets it serves—any seemingly even-handed program is likely to affect it differently from others. Even something so apparently neutral as a tax credit for new capital investment favors industries whose competitive success hinges on continually updating plant and equipment, relative to industries that depend on the careful hiring and training of personnel or on the use of sophisticated marketing techniques. (Thus, the disparities noted above in effective rates of corporate income tax are due not so much to tax breaks targeted to particular industries as to differences in the ability of industries to take advantage of superficially neutral deductions and credits.) Most industry lobbyists—and not a few legislators and government officials—well understand that no tax, credit, or subsidy program, however neutral in appearance, is neutral in competitive effect.[4]

Disparities like these are inevitable so long as government has any role to play in the economy, even the minimal roles of setting the rules of the game (should copyright protection be extended to cover the circuitry etched on computer chips? should coal slurry pipelines have "eminent domain" authority to run beneath railroad lines?), and purchasing "public goods" (national defense alone will continue to consume 5 to 10 percent of our gross national product, largely in the form of procurement contracts and subsidies conferred discriminately on the private sector). Beyond these basic functions, other aspects of government involvement are appropriate to an advanced industrial nation. For example, in many industries the social return to investment in new products and processes is substantially higher than the private return to individual investors, because new knowledge "leaks" out into the market. Thus individual investors left to their own devices will systematically underinvest in our industrial future. For this reason, all governments busily support commercial research and development; ours is no exception. And finally, at the other end of the industrial spectrum, there is the political certainty that industries seriously threatened by imports will demand and often obtain protection, unless or until their capital and labor can easily shift to new undertakings.

In short, the United States has an industrial policy. It always has and always will. But our present industrial policy is of the "do-it-yourself" variety—spearheaded by our most politically active and sophisticated industries and firms. Industrial development is the goal, but not the nation's overall industrial development. There are winners and losers, but they bear no particular relation to those industries or segments that could be expected either to advance or decline as the national economy moved rapidly to a more productive and internationally competitive industrial base. Our industrial policy lies buried, and the choices it embodies are never clearly posed: Should we be channeling so much of our nation's capital into home construction, and so little into, say, machine tools? Could we achieve national defense objectives equally well by nurturing technologies with more direct commercial applications? Should we help our steel and automobile industries reduce and consolidate their operations—granting them relief from antitrust laws and subsidizing employee retraining—instead of merely continuing to protect these industries from international competition? We do not know the answers to questions like these, in large part because we lack any institutional mechanism for asking them.

The limits of macroeconomics

We could continue to ignore our industrial policy if fiscal and monetary policies were up to the task of supporting the economy on their own. But fiscal and monetary policies have revealed troublesome shortcomings of late. For example, no one any longer knows how to control the money supply because no one any longer knows what money is. With the recent explosion of financial services, money held in cash or checking accounts quickly transmogrifies into all manner of things, and then back again. What is more, financial capital now sloshes across national borders with scant respect for macroeconomic managers. As France has painfully discovered, any attempt to expand a single economy if others are not following suit causes imports to rise, the domestic currency to depreciate, and import prices thereby to increase, with inflationary consequences. On the other hand, our current experience confirms that high real interest rates at home attract foreign savings, raise the value of the domestic currency in international exchange, and thus cripple exports. None of this is meant to suggest that macroeconomic management is a futile exercise, only that it is becoming ever more constrained.

Even more telling is the dismal performance of the American economy over the last dozen years. As I write this the nation appears to be recovering from one of the worst recessions in the postwar era. Let us hope that as you read this the recovery is still progressing. But the longer-term trends are less encouraging. More than ten million Americans are jobless, with millions more either too discouraged to look for work or working at part-time jobs when they want full-time. Each downturn in the business cycle has been progressively worse in this regard: Two recessions before this one (1970 and 1975) claimed, respectively, 6 percent and 8.2 percent of the workforce; down to 5.8 percent and 7.7 percent, respectively, in the first year of recovery. Our Council of Economic Advisors now speaks of a new "natural" rate of unemployment in the neighborhood of 6 or 7 percent; a dozen years ago it was 3.5 percent. Each upturn in the business cycle, meanwhile, has brought worse bouts of inflation. At the same time productivity improvements have steadily declined, from a yearly average of 3.2 percent between 1948 and 1965 to 2.4 percent between 1965 and 1973, to 1.8 percent between 1973 and 1978, with an actual decline in productivity since then. And, largely in consequence, increases in real after-tax pay of production workers in America (a group comprising over 80 percent of the workforce, which is almost entirely dependent on wage and salary income) began slowing between 1966 and 1975, reached a standstill around 1978, and have declined since then; by 1981, real pay levels were at their lowest since 1961.[5]

Viewed in this long-term perspective, several other industrial nations have fared better than the United States, particularly in maintaining productivity growth, keeping a lid on unemployment, and enhancing their citizens' real incomes. In the recession just ended, the United States suffered more severe plunges in productivity and output (in 1982, −1 percent and −8.8 percent, respectively) than Japan (1 percent and .3 percent), West Germany (1.7 percent and −2.7 percent), France (6.9 percent, −.1 percent), Italy (1.3 percent, −1.8 percent), and even Great Britain (3.4 percent, −.8 percent). I have treated longer-term comparisons at length elsewhere.[6] To be sure, the United States did create some 22 million new jobs during the 1970s, while several Western European nations did just the opposite—ridding themselves of "guest" workers. But the vast majority of the jobs created in America were very low paying, in service sectors of the economy sheltered from international trade; and the "guest" workers of our trading partners comprised a very small percentage of the work forces from which they were disinvited.

Some view all of the recent United States economic history as a kind of "molting" of the industrial base, as it moves out of heavy industries and into high technologies and services. They ignore several facts. First, high technology, standing alone, promises to generate relatively few new jobs, and many of those that it does create are rapidly shifting to nations with far lower wage rates (witness Atari's recent farewell to America). Only as high technologies are embedded within the products and processes of our older industries—thereby rendering them more competitive internationally—can we expect to generate more jobs with higher real incomes. And for some industries this needed restructuring is likely to be so costly, over so many years, that neither private lenders nor private investors can be expected to foot the bill entirely on their own.

They also ignore the telling fact that we are losing the international "race" in many key technologies. While exports of our ten most research-intensive product groups grew from 29 percent of total U.S. exports in 1974 to 32 percent in 1981, imports of these same products grew more precipitously, from 13 percent to 19 percent of total imports over the same interval.[7] Even before the dollar became overvalued, the United States already was losing world market share in a broad array of high technologies: in computers and office machines, from 38.4 percent in 1970 to 28.4 percent in 1980; semiconductors, 39.5 percent to 22.7 percent; aircraft, 67.3 percent to 53 percent; scientific, medical, and controlling equipment, 32 percent to 29 percent; and so on.[8] We have lost ground most dramatically in the sophisticated, highest value-added segments of these industries, particularly in industrial technologies on which our future manufacturing base is likely to be dependent. And again, the start of this decline predated the current overvalued dollar: In semiconductor memory chips, the Japanese by 1979 had gained a major share of the market for 16K RAMs; they subsequently claimed most of the market for 64K RAMs, and appear to have taken the lead in the next generation, 256K RAMs. A similar story can be told about numerically-controlled machine tools (with both the West Germans and the Japanese dominating the United States and world markets), robots, industrial sensors, advanced fiber-optics, and composite new materials like fine ceramics and high-strength plastics.

The problem is not a failure of American inventiveness; we continue to innovate like mad. The problem is that we have failed fully to use our human and capital resources to transform these innovations into competitive commercial products. Commercialization of new invention requires a steady supply of "patient" capital and skilled workers. But our mounting unemployment, falling productivity, and underutilized industrial capacity have constrained the growth of both these resources.

Fiscal and monetary policies have not been the cause of our problems; they simply have not been capable of setting things right during these last dozen years of economic turbulence. Every other industrial nation also has endured contractions in recent years under the combined weight of oil shocks, the emergence of highly competitive, newly industrialized countries, and domestic regulatory and welfare burdens. That several of these nations have managed to ride out the storm more successfully than we have is attributable, at least in part, to their willingness to use all three legs of the stool—fiscal, monetary, *and* industrial policies. They have understood the value, during this period of global change, of an explicitly *strategic* industrial policy—one in which the inevitable choices embedded in tax, research and development, credit, trade, government procurement, and antitrust rules are made with reference to the increasing productivity and competitiveness of their national economies, and the fuller utilization of their capital and labor during the transition. They have viewed industrial policy not as a substitute for sound fiscal and monetary policies, or for good management at the level of the individual firm, but as a necessary complement. Yes, they have made mistakes in their industrial policies, just as they (and we) have made mistakes in fashioning fiscal and monetary policies. But they have at least tried, as we have not, to bring industrial policies into line with national goals. That they have succeeded at all suggests that we should try as well.

The defense connection

At its base, industrial policy raises questions more political than economic. The fear is often expressed that any effort to render more coherent our industrial policy is doomed by the same special interests that have fashioned it in the first place. Indeed, it is feared that any more explicit recognition of U.S. industrial policy and centralization of its administration merely would encourage more special pleadings and politicize the economy to an even greater degree. A counter-hypothesis holds just the opposite: that the *only* way to transform our present industrial policy from a "do-it-yourself" hodgepodge—heavily weighted toward subsidizing service industries sheltered from international trade and maintaining aging segments of our older industries—into a form for positive economic change is by centralizing its administration and enhancing its visibility. Choices still would have to be made, of course, but at least they could then be informed by public debate and the participation of other industries, unions, and industry analysts. The experiences of other democratic industrial nations, and our own history, provide some evidence for both points of view, although I believe somewhat more evidence for the latter.

But it is imperative that we engage these political issues head on, rather than continue to bury them under ideological platitudes about the relative merits of "markets" or "planning." The United States already is moving at a rapid clip toward the institutionalization of a more centralized and strategic industrial policy, but is doing so with almost no public understanding of its main features or debate over its merits. The shift comes as an inevitable response to the long-term decline in American competitiveness in world markets, now growing more serious as the globalization of markets proceeds apace. Of course, the present Republican administration, committed as it is to the "magic of the marketplace," does not refer to this shift as "an industrial policy." The term sounds too much like planning. But all the elements are coming to be there: enhanced government support for high technology, active government involvement in restructuring older industries, and a vast consolidation of government authority over both of these ends of the industrial spectrum.

United States industrial policy for high technologies increasingly is being planned and executed by the Pentagon. This is partly due to the current defense build-up. The Congressional Budget Office estimates that by 1984 federal research and development spending will have increased 13 percent in real terms over 1980 levels. Approximately 70 percent of this increase—amounting to some $32 billion—will be related to defense. Federal spending for basic research alone will rise to an expected $6.62 billion in current dollars; again, the bulk will be defense-related. In addition to these sums, some $88 billion will be spent in 1984 on procuring new weapons, many of which will incorporate the most sophisticated technologies.[9] At the same time, and largely because of this infusion of federal funds, several of the government's other industrial programs have been brought within the Pentagon's orbit. Management of the Space Shuttle, for example, is shifting from NASA to the Department of Defense.

The development of many advanced products and processes will be spurred by this infusion of federal defense dollars. Between 1982 and 1987, for example, defense spending for semiconductors is expected to increase by 18.3 percent, while commercial semiconductor purchases will increase by only 11.8 percent. A similarly divergent growth pattern is expected for computer sales (16.4 percent for defense, 11.8 percent for commercial purposes), engineering and scientific equipment sales (9 percent for defense, 5.6 percent for commercial purposes), and sales of communications technologies (11.6 percent for defense, 5.3 percent for commercial purposes).[10]

But the Pentagon's high-tech industrial policy is also being driven by a fear even more palpable than the Soviet threat. It is the fear that other nations, particularly the Japanese, are gaining a lead in new "strategic" technologies—incorporating innovations that will be critical to America's capacity to wage war in an era of advanced electronics. Lest this nation become dependent on another's high-tech mastery, therefore, the Department of Defense has launched an all-out effort to maintain leadership in these areas.

Under the Defense Advanced Research Projects Agency, several specific programs are now underway: a $500 million effort to accelerate the development of very-large-scale integrated circuits (the next generations of logic and memory chips), a $250 million per year research and development drive in advanced lasers, $40 million per year in fiber optics, and research programs in an array of related technologies, such as computer software and composite materials. In addition, the Reagan administration has announced with unusual fanfare the start of a five-year, $1 billion program designed to maintain America's lead in "super-computers"—capable of significantly faster computations than today's most advanced computers. On each of these projects groups of U.S. companies are working in tandem with several universities and government laboratories. At the same time the Central Intelligence Agency is undertaking major studies of the industrial policies of other nations, presumably in order to gain further insight into how and where "strategic" technologies are being targeted.

These "strategic" technologies are likely to be important to America's economic development if only because Japan has deemed them critical to its continued commercial success in the years ahead. All have been anointed "industries of the future" by Japan's notorious Ministry of International Trade and Industry (MITI), which is precisely why the Pentagon is concerned enough to want to speed their development here. Thus it is not without some irony that Japan's choices of high-tech "winners" are becoming our own, albeit through the back door of national security.

But if this emerging institutionalization of U.S. high-tech industrial policy resembles your vision of the role of MITI, you are mistaken. MITI does not intervene as directly in the Japanese economy as does the Department of Defense in the U.S., nor does the Japanese government directly finance nearly so great a percentage of industrial research and development. The Japanese do target certain emerging technologies, to be sure, but decisions about which ones deserve certain tax and credit treatment are arrived at consensually, through ongoing conversations among trading companies, industry groups, and government analysts. The Pentagon and CIA are not known to be models of decision-making by consensus. Most importantly, and most obviously, MITI is concerned about commercial competitiveness; the Pentagon seeks industrial competitiveness only to the extent that it undergirds the nation's defense capabilities.

A new (Republican) coherence?

At the other end of America's industrial spectrum, meanwhile, there is a similar trend. Industrial policy for declining industries increasingly is falling under the twin domains of the Office of the U.S. Special Trade Representative and the Commerce Department. If the Reagan Administration has its way, both will be consolidated into a new cabinet-level Department of International Trade and Industry (DITI). It is difficult to know precisely how DITI will function, but already there are indications of a new industrial policy for declining industries, one that most likely will come to pass even if DITI does not.

To understand this policy, one must first note the potent protectionist forces that have been brought to bear on our political process as America's heavy industries have lost ground to international competition. The Reagan Administration, its free-market rhetoric notwithstanding, has been no less susceptible to these pressures than its predecessors. If anything, the pressures have increased, and the current administration's record is in fact more protectionist than the last: We now have bilaterally-negotiated quotas against the importation of basic steel from Western Europe and automobiles from Japan, quotas on textile and apparel imports from Southeast Asia more stringent than at any time in recent history, and a ten-fold increase in tariffs on motorcycles from Japan. Even in the wake of the Williamsburg summit's call for a reduction in worldwide import barriers, the Reagan administration decided to increase tariffs and impose quotas on stainless steel imports.

The Reagan administration, anxious to develop politically acceptable alternatives to blunt protectionism, increasingly is negotiating with distressed industries. The "voluntary" quota against European steel was the product of such a negotiation with U.S. steel producers, who in return agreed to forgo more onerous countervailing duties and penalties. As another example, the Harley Davidson Company (the single U.S.-owned manufacturer of motorcycles) agreed to a plan for upgrading its facilities in return for the administration's willingness to increase tariffs on imported motorcycles for a limited period of time. In one pending case the administration is considering channeling tariff proceeds to the protected industry on condition that the industry use the proceeds to retool its aging plant and equipment and retrain its workers for higher value-added production. Another industry in distress has been promised export assistance and stepped-up government procurement for its willingness to forgo anti-dumping levies and countervailing duties on foreign imports.

The trend is clear. Protection will be granted only on condition that the industry seeking it devise a "workable plan" for restructuring itself in a more competitive mold. The terms of such plans will be negotiated between the industry or firm and government officials. And the administration will seek to buy off the petitioning industry with assistance other than outright protection—subsidized loans, research grants, tax breaks, export financing. A new DITI, combining all major international trade programs under one roof, will make it administratively easier to negotiate such restructuring plans and to deliver such packages of assistance in return. Industry specialists from what formerly had been the Commerce Department's Bureau of Industry Analysis can review the feasibility of restructuring plans and monitor their execution; assistance programs from anywhere within the newly-consolidated Department, and even some without, can be targeted (perish the word) to the industries in need.

The drift toward a more coherent industrial policy for both high technologies and declining industries is not the result of any grand plan on the part of the Reagan administration. (Indeed, members of the administration may be aghast to see in these pages the pattern that is emerging.) Rather, the gradual institutionalization and management of industrial policy is the consequence of increasingly intense international competition, as mediated through our domestic politics. Another administration, less avowedly wedded to free market principles, would find itself drifting precisely in the same direction. Instead of the Pentagon and DITI as the institutional centers of its industrial policy, the Democratic alternative might feature a hierarchy of "tripartite" boards comprised of the elites of organized labor, big business, and finance. But in all likelihood the boards would find themselves following Japan's lead in selecting high technologies for special treatment, and simultaneously would be negotiating with distressed industries about the means necessary to restructure them toward more competitive production. If the current administration is drifting toward a strategic industrial policy more speedily than a Democratic administration might be expected to move, that probably is because this administration has less ideological terrain to its right with which to contend. A coherent industrial policy may be politically easier for Republicans than for Democrats to attain, just as was President Nixon's historic overture to Peking.

All of this suggests that the central question with which we must deal, and deal soon, concerns not the economic wisdom of industrial policy but its political form. The mounting pressures of international competition inevitably are reshaping our governing institutions—consolidating authority over the economy, and forcing a closer strategic link between business and government. This reshaping transcends ideological and political lines. At the same time, as America's industrial base dramatically transforms itself with government's help, the stakes for both winners and losers will grow significantly larger. Thus the process by which industrial policy is formulated raises anew one of the most perplexing issues of political legitimacy. How can we insulate it from the predations of narrow interest groups and the vagaries of partisan politics while ensuring that it is democratically accountable? Republican or Democrat, liberal or conservative, that question will continue to be with us.

Notes

1. George Gilder, "A Supply-Side Economics of the Left," and Amitai Etzioni, "The MITIzation of America?" *The Public Interest* 72 (Summer 1983).

2. This tally of subsidized loans and loan guarantees does not include such welfare and relief programs as housing for the elderly and handicapped, low-rent public housing, SBA disaster loans, and veterans' programs.

3. "Industries" are of course convenient constructs, referring to clusters of firms sharing similar situations of supply and demand. Much of the stuff of politics occurs *within* industries, between smaller clusters (or "segments") of firms serving different groups of customers within the same market, and facing different cost structures.

4. This political and economic reality apparently has been lost on several otherwise thoughtful commentators. For example, Professor Amitai Etzioni in these pages argued against a targeted industrial policy in favor of a system of government "incentives . . . focused on wide sectors of the eocnomy, not specific industries . . . [which] are much less subject to political pork-barreling. . . ."

5. S. Bowles, D. Gordon, T. Weisskopf, "A Continuous Series on Real Spendable Hourly Earnings," Technical Note, Economics Institute of the Center for Democratic Alternatives (1982).

6. See Robert B. Reich, *The Next American Frontier* (New York: Times Books, 1983), chapter 1; and Ira C. Magaziner and Robert B. Reich, *Minding America's Business* (New York: Harcourt Brace Jovanovich, 1982), chapters 1–4.

7. United States Department of Commerce, *Business America* (October 18, 1982).

8. United States Department of Labor, *Trends in Technology Intensive Trade* (Washington, D.C.: 1980); Office of Economic Cooperation and Development, *Foreign Trade Series C* (Paris: 1981).

9. Congressional Budget Office, internal memorandum (May 11, 1983).

10. See George F. Brown, Jr., *Defense and the American Economy: An Analysis of the Reagan Administration's Programs* (Lexington, MA: Data Resources, April 1982).

2B.3. A Reader's Guide to Industrial Policy

PATRICK NORTON

How is one to decide whether having an industrial policy is a good or a bad idea? The argument turns on two questions. The first is whether a free-market economy can produce more efficiently in the long term than an economy with mixed public and private planning. The second is whether the United States actually has a free, competitive market economy, as the defenders of a laissez-faire approach contend. Those who favor industrial policy raise such issues as the desirability of protecting fledgling industries, the distorting effects of our foreign competitors' government-subsidized production, the short-term orientation of American business and its neglect of long-term growth issues, and firms' lack of incentives to invest in research whose benefits quickly become available to the competition.

In this reading, taken from a longer article on industrial policy, Patrick Norton reviews the current state of the debate. He first outlines the views of the proponents, including both "soft" proponents such as Etzioni and "hard" proponents such as Reich. He then deals with the objections raised against industrial policy by many free-market economists and identifies some specific situations where the best case can be made for such a policy.

The summer of 1980 saw various manifestos urging America's "reindustrialization." Such proposals preceded the idea of a targeted industrial policy for the U.S. They centered on more general tax and regulatory reforms to restore the nation's competitive vigor and rebuild its decaying infrastructure (and, in some versions, to mend its decadent values). Among the most influential advocates were Lester Thurow, *Business Week* magazine, and Amitai Etzioni.

Thurow's *The Zero-Sum Society* introduced a neo-liberal theme of what might be termed *productive justice*. Central to his call for a freeze on consumption levels so as to boost investment and productivity growth was an emphasis on

Reprinted with permission of the author from *Journal of Economic Literature*, Vol. XXIV (March 1986), pp. 33–40. Copyright 1986 by the American Economics Association.

equal sacrifice, or shared austerity. The zero-sum reference was to the nation's apparent political impasse. Because of declining productivity growth, the de facto U.S. approach to inequality (rising standards of living, but with constant shares of the income pie) had broken down. In turn, the deadlock over shares barred any major new political initiatives that might help break the society out of its underinvestment mode (Thurow 1980).

The solution? Abolish the corporation income tax (i.e., integrate it with the personal income tax), thus boosting after-tax rates of return and stimulating investment. In a variant, Thurow would later propose a consumption tax as an alternative to the administration's individual income-tax cuts; the latter, he said, would favor consumption at the expense of investment. A value-added tax of 10 percent, he contended, could replace the corporation income and social security taxes, and spur incentives to work and to save (Thurow 1981; Barry Bosworth 1983).

All this sparked an enthusiastic review in *Business Week*, which soon devoted a full issue to "The Reindustrialization of America" (1980). The message reinforced Thurow's, while lending it the mantle of centrist corporate respectability. Management, labor, government, and affluence—all were to blame for American economic decline. Accordingly, what was needed was a new "social contract," which in the book version (1982) was replaced by the phrase "new social consensus." The goals: to allocate sacrifice fairly as steps were taken to (1) raise investment's GNP share; (2) stimulate work, saving, innovation, and export performance; and (3) rebuild the social infrastructure.

Meantime, Amitai Etzioni (a sociologist and policy planner in the Carter Administration) had written a series of articles that would eventually be published as *An Immodest Agenda: Rebuilding America Before the Twenty-first Century* (1983). Etzioni likened the U.S. to a "mature and aging" community in need of an infusion of capital for new infrastructure. His thesis was that over the period 1950–1980, "overconsumption—public and private—and underinvestment have created a maintenance gap, and an adaptation lag, due to insufficiently innovative response to changes in the outside world" (p. 191).

Etzioni saw three distinct policy strategies as possible:

1. On the right, supply-side economics was insufficiently targeted, and would spur consumption, not investment.

2. On the left was a targeted industrial policy, which to Etzioni connoted unwanted bureaucracy.

3. The third option was "semitargeted" reindustrialization.

In the last, preferred option, the idea was to "release resources to the private sector, but channel them to the infrastructure and capital goods sectors, away from public and private consumption" (p. 315).

What actually happened, of course, was option 1, the Reagan tax program. In turn, passage of the Reagan program in mid-1981 was greeted with numerous counterproposals for option 2, a targeted industrial policy, typically along the lines suggested by Japan's Ministry of International Trade and Investment (MITI).

The preservationists versus the modernizers

Thurow had not used the term *industrial policy*. But in that direction, and as a means of raising productivity growth, he did call for an updated version of the Reconstruction Finance Corporation. Contending that "disinvestment is what our economy does worst" (p. 77), he saw a role for "the national equivalent of a corporate investment committee to redirect investment flows from our 'sunset' industries to our 'sunrise' industries" (p. 95). In this view, the problem was that market forces failed to shift capital to growing industries fast enough.

In contrast, *Business Week* would soon call for targeted sectoral policies to counter—not to accelerate—market forces. In another special issue on America's restructured economy (*Business Week* 1981), the case was made that the U.S. economy had "evolved into five separate economies [old-line and high-tech manufacturing, energy, agriculture, and services] that no longer act as one" (p. 56). This approach to the economy's evolving structure seemed mystifying, at least until the policy punchline.

The policy problem, in this view, was that without targeted sectoral policies, "the market will continue to steer all funds" to the energy and high-tech sectors of the South and West, thus further weakening the old-line manufacturing sector and the North. Therefore "government policies will have to be carefully targeted to meet special needs. . . . The government needs a new set of fiscal policies aimed at bringing out capital and channeling it in the right directions" (p. 100). So market forces work to hurt the basic industries of the North—and should be countered.

This dichotomy would prove characteristic of proposals for targeted industrial policies. On the one hand, the modernizers like Thurow (and Reich and Frank Weil) argued that without an industrial policy, the American economy would suffer a further relative decline within the world economy. Meantime, others argued for the restoration or at least support of declining industries and places—a preservationist strategy.

The distinction between modernizers and preservationists is highlighted by General Electric's marketing maxim, "Automate, emigrate, or evaporate." It arises also when an OECD report refers to "the two strategies of the mature industrial countries," that is, switching to automated methods or abandoning basic industries to LDCs (OECD 1980, p. 83). Productivity growth via robotic processes and other labor-saving innovations (or by abandoning older industries) may be lauded by modernizers, but not by job-oriented preservationists. The latter are more likely to be troubled by the specter of "jobless growth" (Colin Norman 1980, p. 35) and to turn to a third strategy, protectionism, to maintain jobs.

A key preservationist is Felix Rohatyn, the investment banker who presided over the Municipal Assistance Corporation which arranged New York's fiscal reorganization. His premise is that "market forces are destroying our basic industries, possibly permanently, but these market forces are by no means free" (Rohatyn 1983, p. 14). Hence they should be resisted.

Arguing for a "continuing institutionalized response" to the policies of other governments, Rohatyn advocates the kind of mandated cooperation among labor, business, and government that proved workable in New York. To this end, a new Reconstruction Finance Corporation "would be able to provide (or withhold) capital in exchange for concessions (from management, labor, banks, suppliers, local governments)" (p. 15). In sum, intervention is required to counter the tactics of other governments.

Perhaps the most fully developed rationale for an industrial policy comes from Reich—in the main, a modernizer. Having set forth a well-documented indictment of American management with Ira Magaziner in a 1982 book, Reich went on to write *The Next American Frontier*, renowned in part for its appeal to Walter Mondale as a blueprint for the Democratic party electoral campaign (Reich 1983).

Reich posits a divergence between two distinct cultures in the U.S.: the managerial (in which efficiency is the dominant value) and the civic (which values community and harmony). In nations forced to rebuild after World War II, economic natinalism reconciled these two strands. "These societies almost naturally connect economic development with social change" (p. 16). As a result, he contends, "since 1970 many of these other nations have been more successful . . . in adjusting to the new realities of international competition" (p. 17). Hence the book's title. "Adaptation is America's challenge. It is America's next frontier" (p. 21).

In Reich's view, "American producers have not fared well in [the] new contest" for world markets since roughly 1965 (p. 121). Japan, France, and Germany, he contends, have recognized that their comparative advantage in the new world economy lies in activities requiring skilled labor, such as precision, custom, and technology-intensive products. Such commodities "are relatively secure against low-wage competition because they depend on high-level skills" (p. 128). In contrast, American management, labor, and government have clung to arrangements left over from a bygone era of mass production.

The reasons he advances for failure to adjust lie in what he sees as the extreme hierarchy or separation of managers from workers in Britain and the U.S. In particular, "the radical distinction heretofore drawn between those who plan work and those who execute it is inappropriate to flexible-system production," the system required in the new international competition (p. 135). Instead of adjusting, the U.S. suffers from maladies that Reich terms (1) paper entrepreneurialism, (2) historic preservation (protection), and (3) a dead end for many American workers.

What is needed, as spelled out earlier in a 1982 article, "Industrial Policy: Ten

Concrete Practical Steps . . . ,'' are policies to speed the shift of capital and labor into high value-added activities. (In this respect, Reich's program harmonizes with Thurow's sunset-sunrise investment policy.) Examples of such policy innovations are employment vouchers, a human-capital tax credit, regional development banks, and, to monitor government influences on capital allocation, a national industrial board.

Reich's larger—and more persuasive—message is that an industrial policy already exists in piecemeal form, through tax, regulatory, and protectionist policies. Accordingly, he contends that the relevant question is not whether to have an industrial policy. Instead, it is whether to monitor, coordinate, and improve upon the de facto industrial policy the U.S. already has.

The rebuttal

Economists have replied to proposals for industrial policy with telling criticisms on three divergent counts. (1) As a matter of *theory*, the critics question the assumption of market failure implicit in calls for government intervention. (2) As a matter of *practice*, they argue that an undesirable bureaucratic layer would be required to administer a targeted program—and that such a program would inevitably revert to protectionism (or, in a radical variant, that it would become a captive of big business). (3) As a matter of *evidence*, some economists reject the notion of a fundamental decline in U.S. trade competitiveness.

1. The problem in theory (Branson and Krugman)

National security is sometimes invoked (especially by preservationists) as a reason to sustain industries like steel through some form of industrial policy. Branson assays this proposition in terms of two separate tests:

> First, supply interruption must be plausible. It is not enough to note that effective defense requires chromium, or basic steel, or automotive products. It should also be plausible that the United States could be cut off from supply, implying that there are few enough sellers, concentrated in a hostile or potentially inaccessible area. Second, if the supply cut-off test is passed, the question remains whether to protect the domestic industry or to stockpile. (1981, p. 397)

While stockpiling may make sense for some raw materials (platinum, chromium, and manganese), the manufacturing industries sometimes cited as candidates for protection (autos and steel) do not pass the first test. The reason is the extreme improbability of an effective supply cut-off in either industry, given the present dispersion of worldwide capacity.

A separate issue arises in Marina Whitman's case for temporary protection of Detroit. In our terms, Whitman offers a modernizer's rationale for the preservationist position. By the same token, Branson questions whether "assembled autos are high on the list of skill and technology-intensive components of industry that are the future growth sector in the United States'' (Branson 1981, pp. 400–401; Whitman 1981). In his view, then, neither defense nor growth potential provides a persuasive rationale for the quotas the U.S. would impose on Japan.

In "Targeted Industrial Policies: Theory and Evidence" (1983), Paul Krugman also criticizes the concept and feasibility of targeting industries for government support. The key tactical question is which industries to support; that is, what criteria should be used to select them? The paper lists popular and more technical criteria for picking industries to target. Krugman rejects the first set of guidelines but is ambivalent about the second. His reasoning is worth recounting.

Among the popular criteria for targeting, various writers have suggested the following types of industries for support:

(A) High value-added per worker. Magaziner and Reich (1982) propose accelerating the shift of labor and capital to high-value-added industries. The result, they believe, would be to raise productivity and incomes.

Krugman counters this proposal by pointing out that what makes some jobs high in value-added is a combination of acquired skills and large capital backups. Shifting capital to such sectors (i.e., with high capital-output and capital-labor ratios) when market signals do not warrant it would actually reduce output and especially job growth.

(B) Linkage industries. Other writers urge support for such basic industries as steel because steel is an input for many other industries (Elinor Hadley 1983). Krugman replies that only if there is market failure would there be a case for promoting home production of a widely used intermediate good. Otherwise the inputs should be purchased at home or abroad, whichever offers the lower price, as usual.

(C) Future competitiveness. A number of writers have made the infant-industry case that the capacity to earn future export earnings is a good test of whether an industry merits current support (John Diebold 1980; F. Gerard Adams 1983). One criticism here is that with sufficient help, some industries may indeed succeed in world markets—but still fail a cost-benefit test for the assistance. If so, "eventual competitiveness is not a useful guide to selecting targets" (Krugman, p. 132). The standard caveats for aiding infant industries might also be mentioned: the problem of picking the right industry, and that of turning off the aid once the industry is on its feet.

(D) Fighting fire with fire. Rohatyn and others say the U.S. must target industry assistance to counter foreign subsidies. In practice, and as the examples of wheat and steel illustrate, this is likely to lead to subsidies for industries that already suffer from excess capacity worldwide, not a promising approach.

On the other hand, Krugman adds, *some types of deviation from the competitive model may make targeting defensible,* though here the problem is one of adequate information for policy makers.

(E) Duopoly with steep experience curves. In the presence of learning by doing, and with only two serious competitors, say one American and one Japa-

nese, the firm that can demonstrate its willingness to incur current losses to gain market share and move down its experience curve may be able to drive the other firm out of the world industry. A temporary government subsidy may then help the U.S. firm move down the curve, winning the market. The assumption here is that government would be more willing to underwrite temporary losses than the market would be.

(F) External economies and R&D appropriability. Where the full benefits of R&D are spread beyond the firm paying for the research, there is a textbook justification for government support of industrial research. But Krugman questions whether government could act competently and also whether firms do indeed underinvest in R&D (cf. Thurow 1980, pp. 94–95; Richard Nelson 1982; Bosworth 1983; Edwin Mansfield 1983).

(G) Offsetting other government policies. In general, where specific government policies have created inappropriate incentives, the corrective should be general, not industry specific. If, as seems likely, tax provisions combined with inflation to favor housing investment over plant and equipment during the 1970s, then the response should be tax reform, not industrial targeting.

In sum, "If we must have a targeted industrial policy, it would probably be best to target the high technology industries, which have both important dynamic scale economies [i.e., steep experience curves] and important externalities. But we have no assurance that this is actually the right policy" (p. 138).

2. The problem in practice: more planning, more politics

In an attack on the whole idea of industrial policy as a new task for government, Charles Schultze (chairman of the CEA in the Carter Administration) charges that such proposals would needlessly add a new layer of bureaucracy to the federal government (Schultze 1983). From a different perspective, Samuel Bowles, David M. Gordon, and Thomas E. Weisskopf share Schultze's unease as regards industrial policy in practice. They charge that Rohatyn's plan amounts to a kind of "corporatism" that would elevate the interests of business over those of consumers, labor, and others (Bowles et al. 1983, ch. 9).

Reich summarizes such misgivings in his comments on Rhode Island's defeated bond issue (1984, p. 32):

> Americans don't like central planning, they don't like complicated plans, and they especially don't trust business-government-and-labor elites to do the planning. These biases are as populist as apple pie, running clear across the political spectrum and rooted deep in our political history.

The political lesson: A U.S. adjustment plan should be fashioned within the existing institutional framework, free from the kind of tripartite administrative apparatus used in Japan and Europe.

3. Evidence: what decline?

Schultze's wide-ranging attack contends that industrial policy proposals rest on four premises:

- that the U.S. economy was deindustrialized in the 1970s,
- that MITI enabled Japan to avoid a similar fate,
- that government here is capable of picking winners, and
- that it could then politically impose its choices.

Schultze rejects all four premises as invalid. His reasoning on the latter two points parallels that of Krugman, while reflecting the administrative experience he had as head of the CEA. As for MITI, Schultze contends that it is as much a symptom as a cause of Japan's cultural capacity for pursuing a catch-up strategy. Finally, his rejection of deindustrialization reflects the arguments outlined in the body of this paper.

This review brings us into the mid-1980s, when the debate shifts toward the dollar's role—and to the question of whether a currency's depreciation is too great a price to pay for restored competitiveness (Thurow 1984).

References

Adams, F. Gerard. "Criteria for U.S. Industrial Policy Strategies," in F. Gerard Adams and Lawrence R. Klein, *Industrial Policies for Growth and Competitiveness*. Lexington, Ma: Lexington Books, 1983, pp. 393–420.

Bluestone, Barry and Harrison, Bennett. *The Deindustrialization of America*. NY: Basic Books, 1982.

Bosworth, Barry. "Capital Formation, Technology, and Economic Policy," in Federal Reserve Bank of Kansas City, *Industrial Change and Public Policy*. Kansas City, 1983, pp. 231–59.

Bowles, Samuel; Gordon, David M. and Weisskopf, Thomas E. *Beyond the Waste Land: A Democratic Alternative to Economic Decline*. Garden City, NY: Anchor Press/Doubleday, 1983.

Branson, William H. "Industrial Policy and U.S. International Trade," in Michael L. Wachter and Susan M. Wachter, *Toward a New U.S. Industrial Policy?* Philadelphia: University of Pennsylvania Press, 1981, pp. 378–408.

Business Week. America's Restructured Economy. Special issue. 1 June 1981, pp. 55–100.

Business Week. The Reindustrialization of America. NY: McGraw-Hill, 1982 (Based on a special issue of *Business Week*, 30 June 1980, pp. 55–146).

Diebold, John. *Industrial Policy as an International Issue*. NY: McGraw-Hill, 1980.

Etzioni, Amitai. *An Immodest Agenda: Rebuilding America before the Twenty-first Century*. NY: New Press, 1983.

Hadley, Elinor M. "The Secret of Japan's Success," *Challenge* May/June 1983 26(2), pp. 4–10.

Krugman, Paul, R. "Targeted Industrial Policies: Theory and Evidence," in Federal Reserve Bank of Kansas City, 1983, pp. 123–55.

Lawrence, Robert Z. "Is Trade Deindustrializing America? A Medium Term Perspective," *Brookings Pap. Econ. Act.*, 1983:1, pp. 129–71.

————. *Can America Compete?* Washington, DC: Brookings Institution, 1984.

Magaziner, Ira C. and Reich, Robert B. *Minding America's Business: The Decline and Rise of the American Economy.* NY: Harcourt Brace Jovanovich, 1982.

Mansfield, Edwin. "Commentary," in Federal Reserve Bank of Kansas City, 1983, pp. 261–65.

Nelson, Richard R., ed. *Government and Technical Progress: A Cross-Industry Analysis.* NY: Pergamon Press, 1982.

Norman, Colin. *Microelectronics at Work: Productivity and Jobs in the World Economy.* Washington, DC: Worldwatch Institute, 1980.

Organization for Economic Cooperation and Development (OECD). *Technical Change and Economic Policy: Science and Technology in the New Economic and Social Context.* Paris: OECD, 1980.

Reich, Robert B. "Industrial Policy: Ten Concrete, Practical Steps to Building a Dynamic, Growing and Fair American Economy," *The New Republic*, March 31, 1982, *186*, pp. 28–31.

————. *The Next American Frontier.* NY: Penguin Books, 1983.

————. "Small State, Big Lesson," *The Boston Observer*, July 1984, *3*(7), p. 32.

Rohatyn, Felix. *The Twenty-Year Century: Essays on Economics and Public Finance.* NY: Random House, 1983.

Schultze, Charles L. "Industrial Policy: A Dissent," *Brookings Review*, Fall 1983, *2*(1), pp. 3–12.

Thurow, Lester, *The Zero-Sum Society.* NY: Basic Books, 1980.

————. "Getting Serious About Tax Reform," *The Atlantic*, March 1981, *247*, pp. 68–72.

————. "Losing the Economic Race," *New York Review of Books*, September 27, 1984, pp. 29–31.

Whitman, Marina v. N. "International Trade and Investment: Two Perspectives." Graham Memorial Lecture, Princeton U., Princeton, NJ, March 1981.

3. Fiscal and Monetary Policy

There are many policy tools that can be used to change economic behavior. Trade policies and exchange rate policies can be used to change the balance between imports and exports. Labor market policies can be used to influence underlying unemployment. Immigration policies can affect the supply of labor. Research and development spending can affect productivity. Wage-price policies can affect short-run inflation.

But of all the policy tools available to government, the most powerful by far are fiscal and monetary policies. Traditionally these are studied together, as the policies pursued in one area act to constrain what is possible or desirable in the other. The standard macroeconomics course is largely an examination of how these policies interact and how they affect the economy.

However, when we examine the politics of economic policymaking, it is advisable to look at monetary policy, tax policy, and expenditure policy separately. In part this is because there are few if any overarching theories in political science to explain interaction among the different policies, and in part it is because the political systems surrounding the three areas are much more distinctly separate than the economic systems.

There are exceptions to this generalization. Both Bach (1971) and Pierce (1971) have written books that make some attempt at integration. Much of the writing about applied policy looks at how outcomes in one area constrain the others. Some analysts have tried to apply incrementalist theory to the three types of policy (Wildavsky 1964, Sharkansky 1969, Knott 1983). The political business cycle theory has been tested against both monetary and fiscal policy outcomes. (Tufte 1978, Beck 1987). But, on the whole, the literature tends to concentrate on one area at a time.

The plan of this book generally follows this tendency, and looks at the three policies separately. However, I thought it would be useful to begin part three with an essay that talked about the three types of policy and their relation to one another. Therefore I include a brief piece that introduces readers to the different policy areas and points out the similarities and differences between them.

For further reading

See the comments in this section in parts 3A, 3B, and 3C.

Bibliography

Bach, George L., *Making Monetary and Fiscal Policy* (Washington D.C.: The Brookings Institution, 1971).

Beck, Nathaniel, "Elections and the Fed: Is There a Political Monetary Cycle?" *American Journal of Political Science*, 3:1 (February 1987): 194–216.

Knott, Jack, "Uncertainty and Federal Reserve Decision Making," Paper presented at the annual meeting of the American Political Science Association, Chicago, Ill., September 1–4, 1983.

Pierce, Lawrence C., *The Politics of Fiscal Policy Formation* (Pacific Palisades, Ca.: Goodyear, 1971).

Sharkansky, Ira, *The Politics of Taxing and Spending* (Indianopolis, Ind.: University of Indiana, 1969).

Tufte, Edward, *Political Control of the Economy* (Princeton, N.J.: Princeton University Press, 1978).

Wildavsky, Aaron, *The Politics of the Budgetary Process*, 1st ed. (Boston: Little Brown, 1964).

3.1. The Politics of Fiscal and Monetary Policy

PAUL PERETZ

This essay is intended as a brief introduction to macroeconomic policymaking in the United States. It attempts to identify the most important actors in the determination of policy outcomes and the degree to which the different kinds of macroeconomic policy are coordinated. Two general points are developed. The first is that the three major types of economic policy—that is, expenditure policy, tax policy, and monetary policy—are less coordinated than most economists would recommend, because different "subgovernments" with different policy processes control these policy areas. The second is that each type of policy tends to specialize in different economic tasks, with monetary policy concentrating on stabilizing the economy, tax policy concentrating on determining the allocation between public and private goods, and expenditure policy concentrating on redistribution and allocating between different public goods. While there are important exceptions to both of these statements, the existence of the tendencies does to some degree explain economic outcomes.

The economic policy process

There are three primary methods for affecting the overall shape of the economy: changing the supply of money, changing the level of taxation, and changing the level of government spending. When we alter the amount of money in circulation with the aim of raising or lowering interest rates, we call this *monetary policy*; tax and expenditure policies together are called *fiscal policy.*

All three means can be used to expand the economy. Raising government expenditures creates work in the government sector or gives money to those who receive government payments, such as the aged. In turn, the newly hired workers or recipients of transfer payments spend much of their money in the private sector. This raises the demand for goods such as clothing and automobiles, which means that new workers will be hired in these industries and business will have good reason to invest in new plants and machinery.

We can achieve much the same effect by lowering taxes. This leaves more money in people's pockets, money they can then spend on consumer goods. This again causes more people to be employed in consumer industries and gives business a reason to invest in new capital.

Finally, monetary policy achieves similar results through somewhat different means. When the government increases the supply of money, those who need to borrow money find it easier to obtain and hence can borrow at lower interest rates. When interest rates go down, consumers borrow more money to buy goods such as automobiles and houses. This increases employment in those sectors. At the same time businesses are more likely to invest, because the cost of the money they borrow to finance their investments has gone down. This leads to new hiring in the investment sector of the economy.

As we have seen, changes in both monetary and fiscal policy can be used to expand or contract the economy. Some administrations place more weight on one type of policy than another. Typically, Republican administrations place more weight on monetary policy, Democratic administrations on fiscal policy (Peretz 1983). Which policy should be relied on to carry most of the burden is a function of the administration's other aims, the length of time it takes for the policies to affect the economy, and the economic beliefs of the political actors.

The point about the other aims is fairly straightforward. If, for example, one wishes to stimulate the economy while aiding the poor at the same time, one might, like President Johnson, increase transfer payments to the elderly and those on welfare. If, on the other hand, one wished to help the well-off, one might, like President Reagan, cut the taxes of those with the highest rates.

The point about the length of time it takes for a policy to have impact is somewhat more complex. In general, one would like one's policy to affect the economy in the shortest possible time. This is because it is difficult to forecast very far in advance where the economy is going; hence, the longer the lag time, the more likely it is that the stimulus will be too late. Much depends, of course, on the time it takes for the policy to work its way through the political process (the inside lag); then comes the time it takes to affect the economy once it goes into operation (the outside lag) (Pierce 1971). In general monetary policy has the shortest inside lag but the longest outside lag. Expenditure changes have the longest inside lag but the shortest outside lag. Tax policy is intermediate for both types of lag.

The point about the beliefs of actors should be fairly clear. Economists do not all agree on the relative usefulness of the different policy tools. Monetarists, for example, tend to believe that the quantity of money is the most important tool, especially for controlling inflation. Keynesians place more weight on the independent effect of fiscal policy. Expectations theorists believe that economic policy has less effect than we suppose, because the market successfully anticipates what will be done. Over the last thirty years different administrations have been dominated by those with one or another set of beliefs. In general, monetarists have been more influential during Republican administrations and Keynesians during Democratic ones.

The interdependence of monetary and fiscal policy

It is generally agreed by economists that it is best to coordinate tax and expenditure policies, to move the economy in one and the same direction. It is also generally agreed that the economy performs better when monetary policy is coordinated with both types of fiscal policy.

When policy makers fail to coordinate the three policy tools, two negative effects occur. One is that the policies tend to cancel one another out, failing to produce the intended effects. The other is that when different policy tools pull in different directions, distortions are introduced which serve to make the economy less efficient or to produce new problems for the future. For example, it was the combination of a stimulative fiscal policy and a restrictive monetary policy that placed disproportionate burdens on the housing and automotive industries in the early part of the Reagan Administration.

The political separation of monetary, tax, and expenditure policy

We have seen that there are good reasons to coordinate the two kinds of fiscal policy as well as fiscal and monetary policy. What is most notable about the way that these policies are made in the United States, however, is the degree to which different players and different institutions have political control over the different policy tools. While there are some actors who have influence in all three areas, and while there are some similarities in the ways the policies are made, what is most notable is that the policies are made separately and that the mechanisms set up to coordinate the three policies are weak.

The greatest coordination occurs between the two types of fiscal policy; the least between monetary policy and fiscal policy. But the overall separation is sufficiently great to make it productive to look at expenditure, tax, and monetary policy making in terms of little subgovernments arrayed around each policy area.

Expenditure policy

The process

Government expenditures are determined in a long and complex budgetary process that stretches over two and a half years. In March to June of the first year, agencies review current operations and receive estimates from their subunits. Around June, the Office of Management and Budget (OMB), working with the President and his economic advisers, produces rough guidelines for agency spending totals and gives them to the agencies. Over the succeeding summer, the agencies decide on their spending priorities in consultation with those in the OMB who have responsibility for their programs. This generally results in cuts in the amounts that their subunits had requested.

Around October, the agencies submit their budgets to the OMB. In the period between October and January, the OMB, the Treasury, and the Council of Economic Advisers prepare economic forecasts as well as forecasts of revenues for the financial year beginning in October of the second year. Generally these revenue forecasts are lower than the amount requested by the agencies, and, as a consequence, the budgets requested by most of them are cut. However, some favored programs that are high on the President's agenda are cut only minimally or may even be enhanced.

In January of the second year, the OMB submits a budget to Congress, while the Council of Economic Advisers submits a report outlining the economic assumptions behind the budget. The budget is then referred to the budget committees in the House of Representatives and the Senate. Their responsibility is to look at the broad revenue and expenditure totals proposed and then to decide whether the totals are reasonable and how the money will be divided between the major categories of spending. At the same time, the appropriations committees in the House and the Senate examines the details of the proposed expenditures. If tax changes are proposed, these are studied by the Ways and Means committee in the House and the Finance Committee in the Senate.

The Congressional budget process from this point on is currently in flux. Until 1985 the budget committees established sets of provisional targets for spending and taxes, to be passed by the House and Senate by April 15. The spending bills were then examined by the appropriations committees and their dozen or so subcommittees. By September the appropriations committees were supposed to pass the bills and send them back to the budget committees. A binding budget resolution was to be passed by September 15, in time for the beginning of the fiscal year—October 1.

This process was altered by the Gramm-Rudman-Hollings bill of 1985. This legislation set steadily declining yearly targets for the federal deficit. Both the budget submitted by the President and the April 15 resolution were supposed to be below these totals. Action on spending by the appropriations and budget committees was to be completed by June 30. The period July to September was to be spent determining whether the budget met the deficit targets. If the budget total was too high, across-the-board cuts were to be made by the President. Congress could react to the cuts in September by reordering priorities within the new total (LeLoup 1986).

However, a Supreme Court decision in 1986 declared the mechanism for automatic cuts unconstitutional, taking the teeth from the Act. While the provisions were roughly adhered to in 1986, by 1987 both the President and Congress were extending the timetables and cheating on the requirement that their budgets fall below the target level.

Under both mechanisms, the budget and the individual spending bills in each area are supposed to be passed before the fiscal year begins on October 1. In recent years, however, it has been unusual for all the bills to be passed in time (Senate Budget Committee 1985, p. 11). To finance the government in the interim period, Congress passes bills that continue spending at around the level of the previous year, until the new bills are completed. Generally, presidents sign these automatically, as failure to do so will mean that people do not get paid. But in recent years President Reagan has several times refused to sign these bills, on the grounds that Congress should fund the agencies at a somewhat lower level.

During the fiscal year, supplemental spending bills are sometimes passed in order to deal with unanticipated spending needs. At the end of the fiscal year (that is, in October of the third year), there is an audit of expenditures by the General Accounting Office, to ensure that appropriated funds were spent as intended and not misappropriated or spent on other programs.

As even the highly simplified account above indicates, this is a long and involved process in which many players participate. In general, the process is one in which initially high expenditure requests get continually reduced, first by the agency, next by the Office of Management and Budget, and then by Congress. In recent years, however, this pattern has changed a little. It has been usual for the Reagan Administration to ask for very large cuts in domestic programs and large increases in military spending. The Congress has continued to cut the military spending requests but has often restored domestic spending that, in its view, was reduced too far by the Office of Management and Budget.

The major players

The expenditure process involves a large number of actors and engenders considerable political conflict. As a process, it is almost a model for what political scientists call *pluralism*, with large numbers of players joining together in groups and coalitions in order to realize their political ends.

We saw above that many different groups in both the executive branch and the legislative branch have an influence on the budget. To these must be added the vast number of interest groups representing those who are the beneficiaries of government spending or who will pay the bill. These interest groups lobby at all stages of the budgetary process. They pressure the White House to give priority to their concerns, they urge the agencies to request more money to benefit their constituents, and they pressure congressional committees to authorize the spending.

Interest groups are most likely to apply political pressure when benefits that they previously received are threatened; for example, when cuts in Social Security or Medicare are proposed, organizations representing the elderly mobilize an opposition. Thousands of groups have permanent offices in Washington, so that their representatives can participate on a more routine basis, often in alliance with bureaucrats in the spending agencies. In most cases the groups concentrate on the particular category of spending of most concern to their constituents. But some of the larger "peak" organizations representing broader groups, such as labor and business, also attempt to influence the total amount to be spent on defense and domestic programs.

Despite the multitude of participants in the process, one should not infer that all actors are of equal importance. Within the executive branch the White House and the Office of Management and Budget are the central actors—increasingly so in recent years (Heclo 1984; Greider 1985). The White House is important in setting the general priorities within which the executive branch operates. President Reagan, for example, has been quite successful in shifting spending from domestic programs to defense. The OMB is extremely important in deciding which agencies and programs are to receive more funding and which will receive less. Traditionally, the OMB has tried to apply professional criteria while working within the President's priorities. But, although this is still largely true, there has been some politicization of the agency, especially during the Reagan Administration.

Within Congress, the two budget committees, the two appropriation committees, and the House and Senate leadership are most important. The budget committees, first established in 1974, are primarily important in setting total spending levels. Their record in terms of ability to make their divisions of those totals stick is somewhat mixed. The budget committees are important—but less powerful than their central role in the process makes them appear to be. "Both committees," it has been observed, "are in truth adding machine committees that take the demands of spending committees and impose as much constraint on them as the current Congressional mood allows" (Ippolito 1981, p. 104). The appropriations committees are still the most important center of power over expenditures in the legislative branch. That power, however, lies not in the full committees, but in their subcommittees. It is here that the budget proposed by the executive is closely scrutinized and detailed allocations are made. As many observers have noted, this results in considerable fragmentation and makes detailed trade-offs between different areas virtually impossible (Shepsle and Weingast 1984). Finally, the House and Senate leaderships are important primarily in managing the budget, making sure that deadlines are met, and resolving impasses over such things as the deficit.

Why so many players?

Despite recent attempts to centralize it, decision making on expenditure policy remains quite fragmented. Indeed, much of the conflict in our political system revolves around the making of the budget, with vast numbers of groups both inside and outside the government struggling to influence the result. As we shall see, this is is much less true of tax and monetary policy making.

Why does expenditure policy involve so many players and so much effort? The primary reason is that expenditure policy is far more than simply a means of controlling the economy. Large numbers of people, ranging from defense contractors to residents of nursing homes, are directly or indirectly dependent on government payments and have good reason to favor expansion of "their" programs. But, since all spending programs compete for a limited total of funds, the beneficiaries of a program often have to battle other, similarly motivated people. Moreover, much of the battle over redistribution (from the rich to the poor, or vice versa) occurs over budget expenditures. Because spending programs are biased toward those who are less well off, there are continual attempts by those representing the better off to cut expenditures, and by those representing the less well off to maintain or increase them.

For both these reasons, the struggle over the budget is one of the central struggles in our society.

Tax policy

Tax policy would seem logically to connect with expenditure policy as part of the budgetary process described above. But, despite recent reforms aimed at integrating tax and expenditure policy, the two processes remain separate for all but the most routine tax decisions. The tendency in the budgetary process is to treat current tax laws as fixed and simply project the amount of revenue that current taxes will generate. Sometimes, when the deficit appears frighteningly large, Congress will legislate small tax increases or user fees as part of the budgetary process. But in general, tax changes, though sometimes sparked by projected revenue shortfalls, take place through a rather different process.

In the executive branch, the primary responsibility for tax policy lies with the Treasury. Within the Treasury, the Internal Revenue Service is responsible for tax collection and produces rules applying the general laws passed by Congress to particular cases. But the primary responsibility for tax changes lies with the economists in the Office of Tax Analysis and the lawyers on the Tax Legislative Council (Reese 1979). The Treasury, and especially the Office of Tax Analysis, tends to have what might be termed a conservative, pro-revenue orientation. While often loath to embark on major changes in taxes, the Treasury continually seeks to close the loopholes in existing tax laws.

Under most presidents the Treasury shares the responsibility for major tax changes with the Office of Management and Budget and the Council of Economic Advisers. The latter has in the past been important in recommending major tax increases or decreases, with the Kennedy tax cut of 1964 being especially notable.

Presidents and their major policy advisers also have some tax ideas of their own. Generally these are distributional in character, as in the case of President Carter's efforts to make the Social Security tax more progressive. The pattern has been that Democrats seek to redistribute resources to the working class, and Republicans to the upper middle class and the wealthy, but this is not invariably true. In the last thirty years only two presidents, Kennedy and Reagan, have taken a major interest in taxes. Both pushed successfully for major cuts in the income tax, although Kennedy's cuts were both smaller and more successful than Reagan's.

In Congress, the major responsibility for taxes lies with the Ways and Means Committee in the House and the Finance Committee in the Senate, with the former being generally regarded as slightly more important. Tax changes that are proposed in the budget are referred to these committees after little or no "preprocessing" in the budget committees. Many major tax change proposals bypass the budgetary route altogether and are referred directly to the committees. Although the loss of the legendary Ways and Means Chairman Wilbur Mills and Finance Committee Chairman Russell Long weakened both bodies, they still are the crucial gatekeepers for any tax change, as the conflict over the 1986 income and corporate tax reform shows (Congressional Quarterly 1985, 1986).

Interest-group participation in tax policy, while considerable, is far less than it is in expenditure policy. This is for two primary reasons. One is the sheer complexity of tax policy. It takes a considerable investment in learning to be able to participate in any but the most peripheral way, and many people who might participate simply do not understand the effects of current or proposed taxes on them. The other is the "free rider" phenomenon. People may be completely dependent on government spending, but taxes represent only a portion of their income. Given the high costs of participation, and the low likelihood that it will pay off, most people leave it to others to participate.

The result is that interest group participation in tax policy making has a distinctly upper-income bias. Because they earn a lot, and because the income tax is progressive, corporations and wealthy individuals consider it worth their while to pay the high costs of participation. Few other groups do, except for academics, some public-interest tax groups of both the left and the right, and the major "peak" organizations. Consequently, most of the interest group participation in tax policy making at the federal level centers around an endless search for tax breaks and exemptions of certain kinds of income (Reese 1979).

Outcomes

The differences between the tax and expenditure policy processes lead to some important differences in the outcomes of the two policies. The most marked is the effect of the two types of policy on the distribution of income. In terms of pure economics, there is no reason why redistribution cannot be accomplished equally well through expenditures or taxes. However, in the United States, as in most other developed nations, most redistribution from the better off to the less well off is achieved through government expenditures (Musgrave and Musgrave 1980).

People often assume that taxes redistribute from the rich to the poor. However, if one takes into consideration the combined effect of federal, state, and local taxes in the United States, taxes have little net impact on the distribution of income, as regressive Social Security and sales taxes offset the mildly progressive federal income tax. There is reason to think that the recent changes in the federal income tax code, by increasing the taxation of wage and salary income, have shifted more of the tax burden to the middle classes.

Expenditures, on the other hand, are strongly progressive. This is for two reasons, one obvious and one not so obvious. The obvious one is that over a third of the federal budget and a significant part of every state budget is spent on transfer payments—such as Social Security, Medicaid, and food stamps—which are biased toward those with low incomes. The less obvious reason is that the benefits of federal expenditures constitute a relatively larger percent of the income of the poor. For example, if a person who earns $10,000 a year and has one car, and another person who earns $100,000 a year and has one car, each pay 10 percent of their income to fund the building of a road, the rich person will pay ten times as much but will get roughly the same benefit.

While the reasons for expenditures being so much more progressive than taxes are open to conjecture, the observer cannot help but be struck by the fact that expenditure policy, with a relatively wide base of political participation, redistributes to the less well off, while tax policy, dominated by more affluent participants, redistributes far less. An implication of this is that the well-off have an incentive to reduce government spending. However, because they are more powerful in the tax area, and because taxes are always unpopular, it is easier for these groups to seek to lower taxes, in an effort to constrain the growth in government revenue. If taxes are reduced, but spending continues to increase, the result is likely to be a growing federal deficit. This may help explain why deficits in the last forty years have been generally higher under Republican than under Democratic presidents.

Monetary policy

The formal process

Monetary policy is even more insulated from democratic participation than is tax policy. Formally, the process through which monetary policy is determined is far removed from the hurly-burly of the political arena. The Federal Reserve system, a complex web of bodies with appointed members, has major responsibility for determining policy. The web consists of twelve regional banks, the Open Market Committee, and the Federal Reserve Board, together with a number of advisory bodies. The key players in this web are the Chairman and six additional Governors of the Federal Reserve Board. They are responsible for determining the money supply, thus influencing interest rates and, through these, the operation of the economy (Bach 1971).

Members of the Board are appointed by the President for fourteen-year terms. Federal Reserve Board chairmen are appointed to four-year terms, but two and a half years after the presidential election. This means that the members of the Board, more than any other economic agency, are independent of the President and Congress. Formally, the only real limit on what the Board does is the possibility that Congress could restrict its powers, but this is not likely to happen (Weintraub 1978).

The Governors of the Federal Reserve conduct a process of economic forecasting and targeting, having in mind a number of important goals. These are the achievement of a reasonably low rate of unemployment, moderate and steady growth, low inflation, and an even balance of payments. The goal of low inflation is usually given priority. If their forecasts indicate that the economy is moving in an undesired direction, the Governors take corrective action—usually by buying or selling government bonds. This has the effect of increasing or decreasing the amount of money, and hence expanding or contracting the economy.

About once a year the Governors announce economic targets based on their forecasts, giving private actors some indication of the sorts of decisions the Board is likely to be making. Usually these targets are bands within which the Board intends monetary growth to occur. They might, for example, announce that M1 (money, narrowly defined) will grow between 6 and 9 percent in the coming year. They then try to stay within that band, making adjustments on the basis of their forecasts. But it is not unusual for monetary growth to exceed the board's self-imposed targets.

The Federal Reserve Board's power to influence the economy is differently valued by different observers. On the good side, it has been argued that the Governors are experts; that they are freer of political pressures than the President and Congress; that they are needed to keep inflation from getting out of hand; and that they can act more expeditiously than the President and Congress.

On the bad side, it has been argued that economic policy in a democracy should be decided by elected officials; that the Governors represent a very narrow range of interests, preeminently in banking; that the conservative bent of the Governors inclines them to tolerate and even cause unacceptably—and unnecessarily—high unemployment rates; and finally, that the Board's policies often are very often wrong and ill-timed (Reagan 1961).

The informal process

Thus far, our discussion has assumed that the Federal Reserve system does in fact control monetary policy. Yet, most observers agree that the President, despite his limited formal power in this area, has influence over the Fed, whether or not he can limit its independence (Woolley 1984). Some argue that Congress, too, has more power than one would initially expect, but others maintain that Congress is essentially powerless to alter Federal Reserve policy.

The claim of presidential influence over the Fed is usually based on the memoirs of Federal Reserve Governors or other evidence that on some occasions monetary policy changed in accord with a President's priorities, with the reasons for this usually being left obscure. What is perhaps the most plausible explanation of congruence between Federal Reserve policy and a President's policies is the

Board's recognition of a practical need to coordinate its policies with the fiscal policies pursued by the President and Congress. It is also possible that the Board, conscious that it lacks legitimating electoral support, is reluctant to oppose the will of elected officials too strongly.

To the degree that Congress has power to influence economic policy, it generally acts to promote economic expansion. During recessions Congress attempts to influence the Fed to refloat the economy. Presidents also tend to favor expansion. Even conservative presidents like Reagan and Nixon have pushed for looser monetary policies, especially during periods of economic downturn. And it is not unknown for presidents to try to generate economic expansion near election time (Rose 1974).

There is no substantial interest group pressure on monetary policy, unlike spending and tax policy. But bankers, monetarist economists, and the conglomerate of financial interests usually described as "Wall Street" have privileged access to the Federal Reserve system and do exert influence on it.

The obscurity of monetary policy and its consequences

Monetary policy is much more insulated from the political process than is fiscal policy, even if not as insulated as a formal account of the policy process would lead one to expect. This independence springs from three sources. One is the sheer difficulty of understanding monetary policy. Its effects are only dimly understood by the general public, few of whom are able to connect changes in monetary policy with their own lives. The second is that monetary policy has less immediate effects on the distribution of income and the allocation of public and private goods than tax and expenditure policy. Because taxing and spending have clear immediate effects and are conflictual issues for most political players, they feel impelled to participate in fiscal policy making. Finally, the structure of governance in monetary policy is designed to restrict participation, and those who attempt it open themselves to the charge that they are interfering in matters where they have no place.

This insulation has two major effects. One is that it is easier to use the monetary policy tool. The time between deciding on a policy and implementing it can be as little as a day, versus the months or years it can take to change expenditure and tax policy. An ironic result of this is that presidents often rely on monetary policy for short-term manipulation of the economy, and that it is their own relative lack of control over the policy that enables them to do so.

The other major effect is that monetary policy is generally more deflationary than fiscal policy. Many think that this is because Federal Reserve Governors—unlike presidents and members of Congress, who need to win elections—have little incentive to expand the economy. Reinforcing factors here may be the predominantly conservative, upper-income background of the members of the board and the influence of bankers on their decisions.

Conclusions

Despite surface similarities, the three major economic policy tools involve political processes that differ in important respects. While each policy area has participation from the executive branch, the legislative branch, and interest groups, different groups within those broad categories are important for each type of policy. The political processes are sufficiently dissimilar that outcomes in the three areas diverge substantially, making policy coordination all the more difficult.

These differences are not accidental. They stem from three basic factors. One is the degree to which the ends sought in each policy area involve conflict. The health of the economy is a non–zero-sum game, in which all players can win, even if some may win more than others. Issues of distribution and allocation are more zero-sum in character. Wins for one side tend to spell losses for the other side, and this draws many highly motivated participants into the fray.

The second factor is the effect of policy changes on individuals. While expenditure policy involves decisions that can determine someone's livelihood, the effects of tax and monetary policy on individual well-being are usually more indirect and partial.

The third factor is the complexity of the issues. Issues of spending are easy to grasp and their implications are relatively straightforward. Tax issues are more complex and their consequences are less obvious. Monetary policy is opaque to the average citizen and the impact of changes in monetary policy on an individual's welfare are usually a mystery.

These three factors all work in the same direction. Each tends to increase participation in expenditure policy, reduce participation in monetary policy, and produce intermediate participation in tax policy.

I would argue that these differences have implications for democracy in the United States. While economic policies are usually the most significant of all public policies for the welfare of individuals, participation in economic policy making is on balance not very extensive. While this may make it easier to reach policy decisions, it should be seen as problematic by those who believe that the American people should control the policies that most affect their lives.

Bibliography

Bach, George L., *Making Monetary and Fiscal Policy* (Washington D.C.: The Brookings Institution, 1971)

Congressional Quarterly Weekly Report, July 6, 1985, pp. 1315–22; June 14, 1986, pp. 1377–79; June 14 1986, pp. 1311–13.

Greider, William, *The Education of David Stockman and Other Americans* (New York: E.P. Dutton, 1985).

Heclo, Hugh, "Executive Budget Making," in Gregory B. Mills and John L. Palmer, *Federal Budget Policy in the 1980s* (Washington D.C.: The Urban Institute Press, 1984).

Ippolito, Dennis S., *Congressional Spending* (Ithaca, N.Y.: Cornell University Press, 1981).

LeLoup, Lance T., *Budgetary Politics*, 3rd ed. (Brunswick, Ohio: Kings Court, 1986).

Musgrave, Richard A., and Peggy Musgrave, *Public Finance in Theory and Practice*, 3rd ed. (New York, McGraw Hill, 1980).

Peretz, Paul, *The Political Economy of Inflation in the United States* (Chicago: University of Chicago Press, 1983).

Pierce, Lawrence C. *The Politics of Fiscal Policy Formation* (Pacific Palisades, Ca.: Goodyear, 1971).

Reagan, Michael D., "The Political Structure of the Federal Reserve System," *American Political Science Review* 55 (March 1961).

Reese, T.J., *The Politics of Taxation* (Westport, Conn., Quorum, 1979).

Rose, Sanford, "The Agony of the Federal Reserve," *Fortune* (January 1974).

Senate Budget Committee, *The Congressional Budget Process: How it Works* (Washington D.C.: U.S. Government Printing Office, 1985).

Shepsle, Kenneth A. and Barry R. Weingast, "Legislative Politics and Budget Outcomes," in Gregory B. Mills and John L. Palmer, *Federal Budget Policy in the 1980s* (Washington D.C.: The Urban Institute Press, 1984).

Weintraub, Robert, "Congressional Supervision of Monetary Policy," *Journal of Monetary Economics* 4 (April 1978).

Woolley, John T., *Monetary Politics* (New York: Cambridge University Press, 1984).

3A. Budgetary Policy

Most studies of the budget are concerned with the political processes through which government expenditures are determined, and the reasons why governments spend more on some things than on others. In the United States the three major types of expenditure are *defense* expenditures, the provision of *services* such as education and police which cannot efficiently be provided by the free market, and *transfer payments* such as Social Security, which take money from one group of people and give it to a different group. In terms of the categories developed in the article by Musgrave in part 1, most of the expenditures on defense and services are on public goods, while most transfers are intended to redistribute to those perceived to be particularly deserving of public aid.

Until the late 1950s political scientists viewed the budgetary process as a complex struggle between actors in the legislative and executive branches—with considerable prompting from interest groups (see Smithies 1955 or Burkhead 1956 for a review of the early literature). Economists, on the other hand, tended to believe that public expenditures were a rough-and-ready approximation to the desires of the public, and that their job was to show how one could change expenditures to increase the benefits to the public and reduce the costs. In the late 1950s a new model, initially expounded by Wildavsky and Lindblom and elaborated by people such as Barber (1966) and Sharkansky (1969), challenged the conventional wisdom, and in a few years became the conventional wisdom itself.

This model, termed *incrementalism*, held that because of the immense complexity of the budgetary process, it was necessary for legislators to adopt simple rules to allow speedy decisions while minimizing political conflict. They did this, it was argued, by accepting the expenditures made in the preceding period (the base) without reexamining them closely and by concentrating their attention on the generally small increases (the increment) proposed by the departments responsible for the policies. This, it was argued, led to a slow but steady increase in government expenditures. The theory was backed up with evidence showing that government expenditures for each department did in fact increase at a slow but steady rate.

In the 1970s this model ran into two major types of objection. One group held that while incrementalists were correct in thinking that expenditures in each policy area increased slowly but steadily, they were wrong about the reason for this. These increases, they pointed out, could be the result of slow changes in need, locked-in spending on interest, multi-year contracts and entitlement programs, overall limits on what was available to be spent, a stable balance of power between contending forces, or the tendency of programs to build their own constituencies (Crecine 1969; Wanat 1978; Le Loup 1978). The other group held that the incrementalists were wrong in asserting that expenditures in each category all grew slowly, and argued that if one looked at more detailed policies, examined changes made within the executive branch, included defense agencies, or looked at agency budgets over longer periods, rather than year-to-year changes, one would find much more variability in the budgets than incrementalists allowed for (Bailey and O'Connor 1975; Gist 1976; Le Loup 1978; Wanat 1978).

While much of the more recent quantitative work in this field has continued to accept the idea of incrementalism, there has been a tendency to break up expenditures into different types and argue that some of the variability in growth can be explained by other factors (Fischer and Kamlet 1984). In the nonquantitative work there has been a renewed interest in the institutional structure within which budgets are made in Congress, and in the role of party ideology in determining budget outcomes. Some hold that these are important in explaining some of the distinctly nonincremental character of expenditure change under the Reagan administration (Penner 1979; Wander et al. 1984).

The readings in this section examine the arguments for and against incrementalism. Charles Lindblom's essay argues that, although incrementalist decision-making processes may seem at first glance to be less rational than the kind of cost-benefit analyses normally advocated by economists, closer examination reveals a hidden logic to incrementalist decision making. The article by Davis, Dempster, and Wildavsky seeks to show that the United States budget is in fact made using incrementalist methods. The essay by Natchez and Bupp is representative of the challenge to incrementalism by those who believe that slow, steady increase is not characteristic of all budget decisions.

For further reading

Good introductions to American budgeting at the federal level are Lance Le-Loup's *Budgetary Politics* and Aaron Wildavsky's *The Politics of the Budgetary Process*. The latter book also gives a detailed exposition of the incrementalist view of budgeting. The classic books on state and local budgeting are Ira Sharkansky's *The Politics of Taxing and Spending* and Thomas Anton's *The Politics of State Expenditure in Illinois*, though both are now a little out of date. Most public finance books contain chapters on budgeting. Thomas Lynch's *Public Budgeting in America* is a good general book on how to construct a public budget. Haveman and Margolis's *Public Expenditure and Policy Analysis* contains useful articles on cost-benefit analysis. Ott and Ott's *Federal Budget Policy* gives the economist's perspective. John Wanat's *Introduction to Budgeting* contains a useful summary of the incrementalist/anti-incrementalist debate.

Bibliography

Anton, Thomas, *The Politics of State Expenditures in Illinois* (Urbana, Ill.: University of Illinois Press, 1966).

Barber, James D., *Power in Committees: An Experiment in Governmental Process* (Chicago: Rand McNally, 1966).

Bailey, John J. and Robert J. O'Connor, "Operationalizing Incrementalism: Measuring the Muddles," *Public Administration Review* (January/February 1975).

Burkhead, Jesse, *Governmental Budgeting* (New York: John Wiley, 1956).

Crecine, John P., *Defense Budgeting: Constraints and Organizational Adaptation*. Discussion Paper No. 6, University of Michigan, Institute of Public Policy Studies (1969).

Fischer, Gregory W. and Mark S. Kamlet, "Explaining Presidential Priorities: The Competing Aspiration Levels Model of Macrobudgetary Decision Making," *American Political Science Review* 78 (June 1984).

Gist, John R. "'Increment' and 'Base' in the Congressional Appropriations Process." Paper presented at the Midwest Political Science Association Meetings, Chicago, Ill., May 1, 1976.

Haveman, Robert H. and Julius Margolis, *Public Expenditure and Policy Analysis*, 3rd ed. (Boston: Houghton Mifflin, 1983).

Le Loup, Lance, "The Myth of Incrementalism: Analytical Choices in Budgetary Theory," *Polity* 10(4) (Summer 1978).

Le Loup, Lance, *Budgetary Politics*, 3rd ed. (Brunswick, Ohio: Kings Court Press, 1986).

Lynch, Thomas D., *Public Budgeting in America* (Englewood Cliffs, N.J.: Prentice Hall, 1979).

Ott, David J. and Attiat F. Ott, *Federal Budget Policy*, rev. ed. (Washington D.C. The Brookings Institution, 1969).

Penner, Rudolph G., ed. *The Congressional Budget Process after Five Years* (Washington D.C.: American Enterprise Institute, 1979).

Sharkansky, Ira, *The Politics of Taxing and Spending* (Indianopolis, Ind.: University of Indiana, 1969).

Smithies, Arthur, *The Budgeting Process in the United States* (New York: McGraw Hill, 1955).

Wanat, John, *Introduction to Budgeting* (North Scituate, Mass.: Duxbury Press, 1978).

Wander, W. Thomas, F. Ted Herbert and Gary W. Copeland, *Congressional Budgeting: Politics, Process and Power* (Baltimore: The Johns Hopkins University Press, 1984).

Wildavsky, Aaron, *The Politics of the Budgetary Process*, 4th ed. (Boston: Little Brown, 1984).

3A.1. The Science of "Muddling Through"

CHARLES E. LINDBLOM

Public-finance economists have long held that the best method for deciding which projects the government should undertake and how much it should spend on each is one in which the costs and benefits *of a program are weighed against alternative uses of the same funds. The aim is to ensure that only the most beneficial programs will be implemented. In this essay Charles Lindblom argues that this seemingly simple method is beset with hidden pitfalls, and he presents a defense of* incremental *policy making. With an incremental approach, existing programs are generally continued and attention is focused primarily on new proposals. Lindblom favors incremental methods both in light of the technical difficulty of doing cost-benefit analysis and because he considers incrementalism better suited to the American political system. Lindblom points out that cost-benefit analysis requires clear, unambiguous, agreed-upon goals against which a project can be evaluated; moreover, it assumes that one can readily evaluate a myriad of different approaches to each goal. In reality, however, it is difficult to obtain agreement on goals and difficult to find measures that would permit ready comparison of alternative means of reaching a given goal.*

On the political side, Lindblom notes that the U.S. budget, which encompasses thousands of complex programs, has to be approved by small and overburdened groups of decision makers. Ways must be found to reduce the information needs of decision makers. Placing primary reliance on past decisions, and examining only proposed changes, meets this need. Additionally, he argues that comparing actual changes against one another, rather than starting by deciding goals first, may facilitate decision making. It allows people with differing goals to form coalitions behind particular programs and thus reduces political conflict.

Suppose an administrator is given responsibility for formulating policy with respect to inflation. He might start by trying to list all related values in order of

Reprinted with permission of the author from *Public Administration Review* 60 (Spring 1959), pp. 77–88 (with deletions). Copyright 1959 by the American Society for Public Administration.

importance, e.g., full employment, reasonable business profit, protection of small savings, prevention of a stock market crash. Then all possible policy outcomes could be rated as more or less efficient in attaining a maximum of these values. This would of course require a prodigious inquiry into values held by members of society and an equally prodigious set of calculations on how much of each value is equal to how much of each other value. He could then proceed to outline all possible policy alternatives. In a third step, he would undertake systematic comparison of his multitude of alternatives to determine which attains the greatest amount of values.

In comparing policies, he would take advantage of any theory available that generalized about classes of policies. In considering inflation, for example, he would compare all policies in the light of the theory of prices. Since no alternatives are beyond his investigation, he would consider strict central control and the abolition of all prices and markets on the one hand and elimination of all public controls with reliance completely on the free market on the other, both in the light of whatever theoretical generalizations he could find on such hypothetical economies.

Finally, he would try to make the choice that would in fact maximize his values.

An alternative line of attack would be to set as his principal objective, either explicitly or without conscious thought, the relatively simple goal of keeping prices level. This objective might be compromised or complicated by only a few other goals, such as full employment. He would in fact disregard most other social values as beyond his present interest, and he would for the moment not even attempt to rank the few values that he regarded as immediately relevant. Were he pressed, he would quickly admit that he was ignoring many related values and many possible important consequences of his policies.

As a second step, he would outline those relatively few policy alternatives that occurred to him. He would then compare them. In comparing his limited number of alternatives, most of them familiar from past controversies, he would not ordinarily find a body of theory precise enough to carry him through a comparison of their respective consequences. Instead he would rely heavily on the record of past experience with small policy steps to predict the consequences of similar steps extended into the future.

Moreover, he would find that the policy alternatives combined objectives or values in different ways. For example, one policy might offer price level stability at the cost of some risk of unemployment; another might offer less price stability but also less risk of unemployment. Hence, the next step in his approach—the final selection—would combine into one the choice among values and the choice among instruments for reaching values. It would not, as in the first method of policymaking, approximate a more mechanical process of choosing the means that best satisfied goals that were previously clarified and ranked. Because practitioners of the second approach expect to achieve their goals only partially, they would expect to repeat endlessly the sequence just described, as conditions and aspirations changed and as accuracy of prediction improved.

By root or by branch

For complex problems, the first of these two approaches is of course impossible. Although such an approach can be described, it cannot be practiced except for relatively simple problems and even then only in a somewhat modified form. It assumes intellectual capacities and sources of information that men simply do not possess, and it is even more absurd as an approach to policy when the time and money that can be allocated to a policy problem is limited, as is always the case. Of particular importance to public administrators is the fact that public agencies are in effect usually instructed not to practice the first method. That is to say, their prescribed functions and constraints—the politically or legally possible—restrict their attention to relatively few values and relative few alternative policies among the countless alternatives that might be imagined. It is the second method that is practiced.

Curiously, however, the literatures of decision-making, policy formulation, planning, and public administration formalize the first approach rather than the second, leaving public administrators who handle complex decisions in the position of practicing what few preach. For emphasis I run some risk of overstatement. True enough, the literature is well aware of limits on man's capacities and of the inevitability that policies will be approached in some such style as the second. But attempts to formalize rational policy formulation—to lay out explicitly the necessary steps in the process—usually describe the first appoach and not the second.[1] . . .

Accordingly, I propose in this paper to clarify and formalize the second method, much neglected in the literature. This might be described as the method of *successive limited comparisons*. I will contrast it with the first approach, which might be called the rational-comprehensive method.[2] More impressionistically and briefly—and therefore generally used in this article—they could be characterized as the branch method and root method, the former continually building out from the current situation, step-by-step and by small degrees; the latter starting from fundamentals anew each time, building on the past only as experience is embodied in a theory, and always prepared to start completely from the ground up.

Let us put the characteristics of the two methods side by side in simplest terms (see opposite).

Assuming that the root method is familiar and understandable, we proceed directly to clarification of its alternative by contrast. In explaining the second, we shall be describing how most administrators do in fact approach complex questions, for the root method, the "best" way as a blueprint or model, is in fact not workable for complex policy questions, and administrators are forced to use the method of successive limited comparisons.

Rational comprehensive (Root)	Successive limited comparisons (Branch)
1a. Clarification of values or objectives distinct from and usually prerequisite to empirical analysis of alternative policies.	1b. Selection of value goals and empirical analysis of the needed action are not distinct from one another but are closely intertwined.
2a. Policy-formulation is therefore approached through means-end analysis: First the ends are isolated, then the means to achieve them are sought.	2b. Since means and ends are not distinct, means-end analysis is often inappropriate or limited.
3a. The test of a "good" policy is that it can be shown to be the most appropriate means to desired ends.	3b. The test of a "good" policy is typically that various analysts find themselves directly agreeing on a policy (without their agreeing that it is the most appropriate means to an agreed objective).
4a. Analysis is comprehensive; every important relevant factor is taken into account.	4b. Analysis is drastically limited: i. Important possible outcomes are neglected. ii. Important alternative potential policies are neglected. iii. Important affected values are neglected.
5a. Theory is often heavily relied upon.	5b. A succession of comparisons greatly reduces or eliminates reliance on theory

Intertwining evaluation and empirical analysis (1b)

The quickest way to understand how values are handled in the method of successive limited comparisons is to see how the root method often breaks down in *its* handling of values or objectives. The idea that values should be clarified, and in advance of the examination of alternative policies, is appealing. But what happens when we attempt it for complex social problems? The first difficulty is that on many critical values or objectives, citizens disagree, congressmen disagree, and public administrators disagree. Even where a fairly specific objective is prescribed for the administrator, there remains considerable room for disagreement on sub-objectives. Consider, for example, the conflict with respect to locating public housing, described in Meyerson and Banfield's study of the Chicago Housing Authority[3]—disagreement which occurred despite the clear objective of providing a certain number of public housing units in the city. Similarly conflicting are objectives in highway location, traffic control, minimum wage administration, development of tourist facilities in national parks, or insect control.

Administrators cannot escape these conflicts by ascertaining the majority's preference, for preferences have not been registered on most issues; indeed, there often *are* no preferences in the absence of public discussion sufficient to bring an issue to the attention of the electorate. Furthermore, there is a question of whether intensity of feeling should be considered as well as the number of persons preferring each alternative. By the impossibility of doing otherwise, administrators often are reduced to deciding policy without clarifying objectives first.

Even when an administrator resolves to follow his own values as a criterion for decisions, he often will not know how to rank them when they conflict with one another, as they usually do. Suppose, for example, that an administrator must relocate tenants living in tenements scheduled for destruction. One objective is to empty the buildings fairly promptly, another is to find suitable accommodation for persons displaced, another is to avoid friction with residents in other areas in which a large influx would be unwelcome, another is to deal with all concerned through persuasion if possible, and so on.

How does one state even to himself the relative importance of these partially conflicting values? A simple ranking of them is not enough; one needs ideally to know how much of one value is worth sacrificing for some of another value. The answer is that typically the administrator chooses—and must choose—directly among policies in which these values are combined in different ways. He cannot first clarify his values and then choose among policies.

A more subtle third point underlies both the first two. Social objectives do not always have the same relative values. One objective may be highly prized in one circumstance, another in another circumstance. If, for example, an administrator values highly both the dispatch with which his agency can carry through its projects *and* good public relations, it matters little which of the two possibly conflicting values he favors in some abstract or general sense. . . .

The value problem is, as the example shows, always a problem of adjustments at a margin. But there is no practicable way to state marginal objectives or values except in terms of particular policies. That one value is preferred to another in one decision situation does not mean that it will be preferred in another decision situation in which it can be had only at great sacrifice of another value. Attempts to rank or order values in general and abstract terms so that they do not shift from decision to decision end up by ignoring the relevant marginal preferences. The significance of this third point thus goes very far. Even if all administrators had at hand an agreed set of values, objectives, and constraints, and an agreed ranking of these values, objectives, and constraints, their marginal values in actual choice situations would be impossible to formulate.

Unable consequently to formulate the relevant values first and then choose among policies to achieve them, administrators must choose directly among alternative policies that offer different marginal combinations of values. Somewhat paradoxically, the only practicable way to disclose one's relevant marginal values even to oneself is to describe the policy one chooses to achieve them. Except roughly and vaguely, I know of no way to describe—or even to understand—what my relative evaluations are for, say, freedom and security, speed and accuracy in governmental decisions, or low taxes and better schools than to describe my preferences among specific policy choices that might be made between the alternatives in each of the pairs.

In summary, two aspects of the process by which values are actually handled can be distinguished. The first is clear: evaluation and empirical analysis are intertwined; that is, one chooses among values and among policies at one and the same time. Put a little more elaborately, one simultaneously chooses a policy to attain certain objectives and chooses the objectives themselves. The second aspect is related but distinct: the administrator focuses his attention on marginal or incremental values. Whether he is aware of it or not, he does not find general formulations of objectives very helpful and in fact makes specific marginal or incremental comparisons. . . . The only values that are relevant to his choice are these increments by which the two policies differ; and, when he finally chooses between the two marginal values, he does so by making a choice between policies.[4]

As to whether the attempt to clarify objectives in advance of policy selection is more or less rational than the close intertwining of marginal evaluation and empirical analysis, the principal difference established is that for complex problems the first is impossible and irrelevant, and the second is both possible and relevant. The second is possible because the administrator need not try to analyze any values except the values by which alternative policies differ and need not be concerned with them except as they differ marginally. His need for information on values or objectives is drastically reduced as compared with the root method; and his capacity for grasping, comprehending, and relating values to one another is not strained beyond the breaking point.

Relations between means and ends (2b)

Decision-making is ordinarily formalized as a means-ends relationship: means are conceived to be evaluated and chosen in the light of ends finally selected independently of and prior to the choice of means. This is the means-ends relationship of the root method. But it follows from all that has just been said that such a means-ends relationship is possible only to the extent that values are agreed upon, are reconcilable, and are stable at the margin. Typically, therefore, such a means-ends relationship is absent from the branch method, where means and ends are simultaneously chosen.

Yet any departure from the means-ends relationship of the root method will strike some readers as inconceivable. For it will appear to them that only in such a relationship is it possible to determine whether one policy choice is better or worse than another. How can an administrator know whether he has made a wise or foolish decision if he is without prior values or objectives by which to judge his decisions? The answer to this question calls up the third distinctive difference between root and branch methods: how to decide the best policy.

The test of "good" policy (3b)

In the root method, a decision is "correct," "good," or "rational" if it can be shown to attain some specified objective, where the objective can be specified without simply describing the decision itself. Where objectives are defined only through the marginal or incremental approach to values described above, it is still sometimes possible to test whether a policy does in fact attain the desired objectives; but a precise statement of the objectives takes the form of a description of the policy chosen or some alternative to it. To show that a policy is mistaken one cannot offer an abstract argument that important objectives are not achieved; one must instead argue that another policy is more to be preferred.

So far, the departure from customary ways of looking at problem-solving is not troublesome, for many administrators will be quick to agree that the most effective discussion of the correctness of policy does take the form of comparison with other policies that might have been chosen. But what of the situation in which administrators cannot agree on values or objectives, either abstractly or in marginal terms? What then is the test of "good" policy? For the root method, there is no test. Agreement on objectives failing, there is no standard of "correctness." For the method of successive limited comparisons, the test is agreement on policy itself, which remains possible even when agreement on values is not.

It has been suggested that continuing agreement in Congress on the desirability of extending old age insurance stems from liberal desires to strengthen the welfare programs of the federal government and from conservative desires to reduce union demands for private pension plans. If so, this is an excellent demonstration of the ease with which individuals of different ideologies often can agree on concrete policy. Labor mediators report a similar phenomenon: the contestants cannot agree on criteria for settling their disputes but can agree on specific proposals. Similarly, when one administrator's objective turns out to be another's means, they often can agree on policy.

Agreement on policy thus becomes the only practicable test of the policy's correctness. And for one administrator to seek to win the other over to agreement on ends as well would accomplish nothing and create quite unnecessary controversy.

If agreement directly on policy as a test for "best" policy seems a poor substitute for testing the policy against its objectives, it ought to be remembered that objectives themselves have no ultimate validity other than they are agreed upon. Hence agreement is the test of "best" policy in both methods. But where the root method requires agreement on what elements in the decision constitute objectives and on which of these objectives should be sought, the branch method falls back on agreement wherever it can be found.

In an important sense, therefore, it is not irrational for an administrator to defend a policy as good without being able to specify what it is good for.

Non-comprehensive analysis (4b)

Ideally, rational-comprehensive analysis leaves out nothing important. But it is impossible to take everything important into consideration unless "important" is so narrowly defined that analysis is in fact quite limited. Limits on human intellectual capacities and on available information set definite limits to man's capacity to be comprehensive. In actual fact, therefore, no one can practice the rational-comprehensive method for really complex problems, and every administrator faced with a sufficiently complex problem must find ways drastically to simplify.

An administrator assisting in the formulation of agricultural economic policy cannot in the first place be competent on all possible policies. He cannot even comprehend one policy entirely. In planning a soil bank program, he cannot successfully anticipate the impact of higher or lower farm income on, say, urbanization—the possible consequent loosening of family ties, possible consequent eventual need for revisions in social security and further implications for tax problems arising out of new federal responsibilities for social security and municipal responsibilities for urban services. Nor, to follow another line of repercussions, can he work through the soil bank program's effects on prices for agricultural products in foreign markets and consequent implications for foreign relations, including those arising out of economic rivalry between the United States and the USSR.

In the method of successive limited comparisons, simplification is systematically achieved in two principal ways. First, it is achieved through limitation of policy comparisons to those policies that differ in relatively small degree from policies presently in effect. Such a limitation immediately reduces the number of alternatives to be investigated and also drastically simplifies the character of the investigation of each. For it is not necessary to undertake fundamental inquiry into an alternative and its consequences; it is necessary only to study those respects in which the proposed alternative and its consequences differ from the status quo. The empirical comparison of marginal differences among alternative policies that differ only marginally is, of course, a counterpart to the incremental or marginal comparison of values discussed above.[5]

Relevance as well as realism

It is a matter of common observation that in Western democracies public administrators and policy analysts in general do largely limit their analyses to incremental or marginal differences in policies that are chosen to differ only incrementally. They do not do so, however, solely because they desperately need some way to simplify their problems; they also do so in order to be relevant. Democracies change their policies almost entirely through incremental adjustments. Policy does not move in leaps and bounds.

The incremental character of political change in the United States has often been remarked. The two major political parties agree on fundamentals; they offer alternative policies to the voters only on relatively small points of difference. Both parties favor full employment, but they define it somewhat differently; both favor the development of water power resources, but in slightly different ways; and both favor unemployment compensation, but not the same level of benefits. Similarly, shifts of policy within a party take place largely through a series of relatively small changes, as can be seen in their only gradual acceptance of the idea of governmental responsibility for support of the unemployed, a change in party positions beginning in the early 30's and culminating in a sense in the Employment Act of 1946.

Party behavior is in turn rooted in public attitudes, and political theorists cannot conceive of democracy's surviving in the United States in the absence of fundamental agreement on potentially disruptive issues, with consequent limitation of policy debates to relatively small differences in policy.

Since the policies ignored by the administrator are politically impossible and so irrelevant, the simplification of analysis achieved by concentrating on policies that differ only incrementally is not a capricious kind of simplification. In addition, it can be argued that, given the limits on knowledge within which policymakers are confined, simplifying by limiting the focus to small variations from present policy makes the most of available knowledge. Because policies being considered are like present and past policies, the administrator can obtain information and claim some insight. Non-incremental policy proposals are therefore typically not only politically irrelevant but also unpredictable in their consequences.

The second method of simplification of analysis is the practice of ignoring important possible consequences of possible policies, as well as the values attached to the neglected consequences. If this appears to disclose a shocking shortcoming of successive limited comparisons, it can be replied that, even if the exclusions are random, policies may nevertheless be more intelligently formulated than through futile attempts to achieve a comprehensiveness beyond human capacity. Actually, however, the exclusions, seeming arbitrary or random from one point of view, need be neither.

Achieving a degree of comprehensiveness

Suppose that each value neglected by one policy-making agency were a major concern of at least one other agency. In that case, a helpful division of labor would be achieved, and no agency need find its task beyond its capacities. The shortcomings of such a system would be that one agency might destroy a value either before another agency could be activated to safeguard it or in spite of another agency's efforts. But the possibility that important values may be lost is present in any form of organization, even where agencies attempt to comprehend in planning more than is humanly possible.

The virtue of such a hypothetical division of labor is that every important interest or value has its watchdog. And these watchdogs can protect the interests in their jurisdiction in two quite different ways: first, by redressing damages done by other agencies; and, second, by anticipating and heading off injury before it occurs.

In a society like that of the United States in which individuals are free to combine to pursue almost any possible common interest they might have and in which government agencies are sensitive to the pressures of these groups, the system described is approximated. Almost every interest has its watchdog. Without claiming that every interest has a sufficiently powerful watchdog, it can be argued that our system often can assure a more comprehensive regard for the values of the whole society than any attempt at intellectual comprehensiveness. . . .

Even partisanship and narrowness, to use pejorative terms, will sometimes be assets to rational decision-making, for they can doubly insure that what one agency neglects, another will not; they specialize personnel to distinct points of view. The claim is valid that effective rational coordination of the federal administration, if possible to achieve at all, would require an agreed set of values[6]—if "rational" is defined as the practice of the root method of decision-making. But a high degree of administrative coordination occurs as each agency adjusts its policies to the concerns of the other agencies in the process of fragmented decision-making I have just described.

For all the apparent shortcomings of the incremental approach to policy alternatives with its arbitrary exclusion coupled with fragmentation, when compared to the root method, the branch method often looks far superior. In the root method, the inevitable exclusion of factors is accidental, unsystematic, and not defensible by any argument so far developed, while in the branch method the exclusions are deliberate, systematic, and defensible. Ideally, of course, the root method does not exclude; in practice it must.

Nor does the branch method necessarily neglect long-run considerations and objectives. It is clear that important values must be omitted in considering policy, and sometimes the only way long-run objectives can be given adequate attention is through the neglect of short-run considerations. But the values omitted can be either long-run or short-run.

Succession of comparisons (5b)

The final distinctive element in the branch method is that the comparisons, together with the policy choice, proceed in a chronological series. Policy is not made once and for all; it is made and re-made endlessly. Policy-making is a process of successive approximation to some desired objectives in which what is desired itself continues to change under reconsideration.

Making policy is at best a very rough process. Neither social scientists, nor politicians, nor public administrators yet know enough about the social world to avoid repeated error in predicting the consequences of policy moves. A wise policy-maker consequently expects that his policies will achieve only part of what he hopes and at the same time will produce unanticipated consequences he would have preferred to avoid. If he proceeds through a *succession* of incremental changes, he avoids serious lasting mistakes in several ways.

In the first place, past sequences of policy steps have given him knowledge about the probable consequences of further similar steps. Second, he need not attempt big jumps toward his goals that would require predictions beyond his or anyone else's knowledge, because he never expects his policy to be a final resolution of a problem. His decision is only one step, one that if successful can quickly be followed by another. Third, he is in effect able to test his previous predictions as he moves on to each further step. Lastly, he often can remedy a past error fairly quickly—more quickly than if policy proceeded through more distinct steps widely spaced in time. . . .

The assumption of root analysts is that theory is the most systematic and economical way to bring relevant knowledge to bear on a specific problem. Granting the assumption, an unhappy fact is that we do not have adequate theory to apply to problems in any policy area, although theory is more adequate in some areas—monetary policy, for example—than in others. Comparative analysis, as in the branch method, is sometimes a systematic alternative to theory.

Suppose an administrator must choose among a small group of policies that differ only incrementally from each other and from present policy. He might aspire to "understand" each of the alternatives—for example, to know all the consequences of each aspect of each policy. If so, he would indeed require theory. In fact, however, he would usually decide that, *for policy-making purposes*, he need know, as explained above, only the consequences of each of those aspects of the policies in which they differed from one another. For this much more modest aspiration, he requires no theory (although it might be helpful, if available), for he can proceed to isolate probable differences by examining the differences in consequences associated with past differences in policies, a feasible program because he can take his observations from a long sequence of incremental changes. . . .

Theorists often ask the administrator to go the long way round to the solution of his problems, in effect ask him to follow the best canons of the scientific method, when the administrator knows that the best available theory will work less well than more modest incremental comparisons. Theorists do not realize that the administrator is often in fact practicing a systematic method. . . .

Successive comparison as a system

Successive limited comparison is, then, indeed a method or system; it is not a failure of method for which administrators ought to apologize. Nonetheless, its imperfections, which have not been explored in this paper, are many. For example, the method is without a built-in safeguard for all relevant values, and it also may lead the decision-maker to overlook excellent policies for no other reason than that they are not suggested by the chain of successive policy steps leading up to the present. Hence, it ought to be said that under this method, as well as under some of the most sophisticated variants of the root method—operations research, for example—policies will continue to be as foolish as they are wise.

Why then bother to describe the method in all the above detail? Because it is in fact a common method of policy formulation, and is, for complex problems, the principal reliance of administrators as well as of other policy analysts.[7] And because it will be superior to any other decision-making method available for complex problems in many circumstances, certainly superior to a futile attempt at superhuman comprehensiveness. The reaction of the public administrator to the exposition of method doubtless will be less a discovery of a new method than a better acquaintance with an old. But by becoming more conscious of their practice of this method, administrators might practice it with more skill and know when to extend or constrict its use. . . .

Notes

1. James G. March and Herbert A. Simon similarly characterize the literature. They also take some important steps, as have Simon's recent articles, to describe a less heroic model of policy-making. See *Organizations* (John Wiley and Sons, 1958). p. 137.

2. I am assuming that administrators often make policy and advise in the making of policy and am treating decision-making and policy-making as synonymous for purposes of this paper.

3. Martin Meyerson and Edward C. Banfield, *Politics, Planning and the Public Interest* (The Free Press, 1955).

4. The line of argument is, of course, an extension of the theory of market choice, especially the theory of consumer choice, to public policy choices.

5. A more precise definition of incremental policies and a discussion of whether a change that appears "small" to one observer might be seen differently by another is to be found in my "Policy Analysis," 48 *American Economic Review* 298 (June, 1958).

6. Herbert Simon, Donald W. Smithburg, and Victor A. Thompson, *Public Administration* (Alfred A. Knopf, 1950), p. 434.

7. Elsewhere I have explored this same method of policy formulation as practiced by academic analysts of policy ("Policy Analysis," 48 *American Economic Review* 298 [June, 1958]). Although it has been here presented as a method for public administrators, it

is no less necessary to analysts more removed from immediate policy questions, despite their tendencies to describe their own analytical efforts as though they were the rational-comprehensive method with an especially heavy use of theory. Similarly, this same method is inevitably resorted to in personal problem-solving, where means and ends are sometimes impossible to separate, where aspirations or objectives undergo constant development, and where drastic simplification of the complexity of the real world is urgent if problems are to be solved in the time that can be given to them. To an economist accustomed to dealing with the marginal or incremental concept in market processes, the central idea in the method is that both evaluation and empirical analysis are incremental. Accordingly I have referred to the method elsewhere as "the incremental method."

3A.2. A Theory of the Budgetary Process

OTTO A. DAVIS, M.A.H. DEMPSTER, and AARON WILDAVSKY

The preceding essay raised the important question of which budgeting method is best. In the pathbreaking article below, Davis, Dempster, and Wildavsky examine the way budgets are actually made in the United States. The authors provide evidence that what they term the incrementalist *method best describes the budgetary process. They reach this conclusion in four steps.*

In the first section Wildavsky makes a qualitative argument that incrementalism makes considerable sense in the American political system, and that the incremental pattern of slow change over time fits what we know about how the system works.

The authors then argue that if their theory is correct there should be small, slow increases over time in the funding each agency receives. They test this in two ways. First, they look to see how the amounts requested by the Bureau of the Budget on behalf of each agency vary from the amounts each agency was given by Congress the previous year (equation 1). Second, they determine how much Congress changes these requests (equation 2).

In their results, shown in Table 1, they find that Congress makes little change in most of the agency budgets submitted by the Bureau of the Budget, and that most of the budgets submitted by the Bureau on behalf of each agency are similar in size to the those approved by Congress in the previous year. However, the latter result is less strong than the former (in general, receiving a correlation coefficient greater than .90 is taken as strong evidence that the factors the researcher thinks might be important are in fact important). Because the correlations for each agency generally exceed this figure, the results have been seen as strong evidence of an incremental process.

Finally, in a third step the authors look at the cases where their theory does not appear to hold well and show that most of them are associated with something they expected to have an independent effect—a new President taking office.

The material in this essay, especially in parts II–IV, is technically quite difficult,

Reprinted with permission from *The American Political Science Review* 60, *3* (September 1966), pp. 529–47. Copyright 1966 by the American Political Science Association.

but it has been included here because it is the seminal article on incrementalism, and to permit comparison with the next essay (by Natchez and Bupp). The reader should note that this essay includes an appendix which explains some of the terminology.

There are striking regularities in the budgetary process. The evidence from over half of the non-defense agencies indicates that the behavior of the budgetary process of the United States government results in aggregate decisions similar to those produced by a set of simple decision rules that are linear and temporally stable. For the agencies considered, certain equations are specified and compared with data composed of agency requests (through the Bureau of the Budget) and Congressional appropriations from 1947 through 1963. The comparison indicates that these equations summarize accurately aggregate outcomes of the budgetary process for each agency.

In the first section of the paper we present an analytic summary of the federal budgetary process, and we explain why basic features of the process lead us to believe that it can be represented by simple models which are stable over periods of time, linear, and stochastic.[1] In the second section we propose and discuss the alternative specifications for the agency–Budget Bureau and Congressional decision equations. The empirical results are presented in section three. In section four we provide evidence on deviant cases, discuss predictions, and future work to explore some of the problems indicated by this kind of analysis. An appendix contains informal definitions and a discussion of the statistical terminology used in the paper.

I. The budgetary process

Decisions depend upon calculation of which alternatives to consider and to choose.[2] A major clue toward understanding budgeting is the extraordinary complexity of the calculations involved. There are a huge number of items to be considered, many of which are of considerable technical difficulty. There is, however, little or no theory in most areas of policy which would enable practitioners to predict the consequences of alternative moves and the probability of their occurring. Nor has anyone solved the imposing problem of the inter-personal comparison of utilities. Outside of the political process, there is no agreed upon way of comparing and evaluating the merits of different programs for different people whose preferences vary in kind and in intensity.

Participants in budgeting deal with their overwhelming burdens by adopting aids to calculation. By far the most important aid to calculation is the incremental method. Budgets are almost never actively reviewed as a whole in the sense of considering at once the value of all existing programs as compared to all possible alternatives. Instead, this year's budget is based on last year's budget, with special attention given to a narrow range of increases or decreases.

Incremental calculations proceed from an existing base. (By "base" we refer to commonly held expectations among participants in budgeting that programs will be carried out at close to the going level of expenditures.) The widespread sharing of deeply held expectations concerning the organization's base provides a powerful (although informal) means of securing stability.

The most effective coordinating mechanisms in budgeting undoubtedly stem from the roles adopted by the major participants. Roles (the expectations of behavior attached to institutional positions) are parts of the division of labor. They are calculating mechanisms. In American national government, the administrative agencies act as advocates of increased expenditure, the Bureau of the Budget acts as Presidential servant with a cutting bias, the House Appropriations Committee functions as a guardian of the Treasury, and the Senate Appropriations Committee as an appeals court to which agencies carry their disagreements with House action. The roles fit in with one another and set up patterns of mutual expectations which markedly reduce the burden of calculation for the participants. Since the agencies can be depended upon to advance all the programs for which there is prospect of support, the Budget Bureau and the Appropriations Committees respectively can concentrate on fitting them into the President's program or paring them down.

Possessing the greatest expertise and the largest numbers, working in the closest proximity to their policy problems and clientele groups, and desiring to expand their horizons, administrative agencies generate action through advocacy. But if they ask for amounts much larger than the appropriating bodies believe reasonable, the agencies' credibility will suffer a drastic decline. In such circumstances, the reviewing organs are likely to cut deeply, with the result that the agency gets much less than it might have with a more moderate request. So the first guide for decision is: do not come in *too* high. Yet the agencies must also not come in too low, for the reviewing bodies assume that if agency advocates do not ask for funds they do not need them. Thus, the agency decision rule might read: come in a little too high (padding), but not too high (loss of confidence).

Agencies engage in strategic planning to secure these budgetary goals. Strategies are the links between the goals of the agencies and their perceptions of the kinds of actions which will be effective in their political environment. Budget officers in American national government uniformly believe that being a good politician—cultivation of an active clientele, development of confidence by other officials (particularly the appropriations subcommittees), and skill in following strategies which exploit opportunities—is more important in obtaining funds than demonstration of agency efficiency.

In deciding how much money to recommend for specific purposes, the House Appropriations Committee breaks down into largely autonomous subcommittees in which the norm of reciprocity is carefully followed. Specialization is carried further as subcommittee members develop limited areas of competence and jurisdiction. Budgeting is both incremental and fragmented as the subcommittees deal with adjustments to the historical base of each agency. Fragmentation and specialization are increased through the appeals functions of the Senate Appropriations Committee, which deals with what has become (through House action) a fragment of a fragment. With so many participants continually engaged in taking others into account, a great many adjustments are made in the light of what others are likely to do.

This qualitative account of the budgetary process contains clear indications of the kind of quantitative models we wish to develop. It is evident, for example, that decision-makers in the budgetary process think in terms of percentages. Agencies talk of expanding their base by a certain percentage. The Bureau of the Budget is concerned about the growth rates for certain agencies and programs. The House Appropriations Committee deals with percentage cuts, and the Senate Appropriations Committee with the question of whether or not to restore percentage cuts. These considerations suggest that the quantitative relationships among the decisions of the participants in the budget process are linear in form.

The attitudes and calculations of participants in budgeting seem stable over time. The prominence of the agency's "base" is a sign of stability. The roles of the major participants are powerful, persistent, and strongly grounded in the expectations of others as well as in the internal requirements of the positions. Stability is also suggested by the specialization that occurs among the participants, the long service of committee members, the adoption of incremental practices such as comparisons with the previous year, the fragmentation of appropriations by program and item, the treatments of appropriations as continuously variable sums of money rather than as perpetual reconsiderations of the worth of programs, and the practice of allowing past decisions to stand while coordinating decision-making only if difficulties arise. Since the budgetary process appears to be stable over periods of time, it is reasonable to estimate the relationships in budgeting on the basis of time series data.

Special events that upset the apparent stability of the budgetary process can and do occur. Occasionally, world events take an unexpected turn, a new President occupies the White House, some agencies act with exceptional zeal, others suffer drastic losses of confidence on the part of the appropriations subcommittees, and so on. It seems plausible to represent such transient events as random shocks to an otherwise deterministic system. Therefore, our model is stochastic rather than deterministic.

The Politics of the Budgetary Process contains a description of strategies which various participants in budgeting use to further their aims. Some of these strategies are quite complicated. However, a large part of the process can be explained by some of the simpler strategies which are based on the relationship between agency requests for funds (through the Budget Bureau) and Congressional appropriations. Because these figures are made public and are known to all participants, because they are directly perceived and communicated without fear of information loss or bias, and because the participants react to these figures, they are ideal for feedback purposes. It is true that there are other indicators—special events, crises, technological developments, actions of clientele groups—which are attended to by participants in the budgetary process. But if these indicators have impact, they must quickly be reflected in the formal feedback mechanisms—the actions of departments, the Bureau of the Budget, and Congress—to which they are directed. Some of these indicators (see section IV) are represented by the stochastic disturbances. Furthermore, the formal indicators are more precise, more simple, more available, more easily interpreted than the others. They are, therefore, likely to be used by participants in the budgetary process year in and year out. Present decisions are based largely on past experience, and this lore is encapsulated in the amounts which the agencies receive as they go through the steps in the budgetary cycle.

For all the reasons discussed in this section, our models of the budgetary process are linear, stable over periods of time, stochastic, and strategic in character. They are "as if" models: an excellent fit for a given model means only that the actual behavior of the participants has an effect equivalent to the equations of the model. The models, taken as a whole, represent a set of decision rules for Congress and the agencies.

II. The models

In our models we aggregate elements of the decision-making structure. The Budget Bureau submissions for the agency are used instead of separate figures for the two kinds of organizations. Similarly, at this stage in our analysis, we use final Congressional appropriations instead of separating out committee action, floor action, conference committee recommendations, and so on. We wish to emphasize that although there may be some aggregation bias in the estimation of the postulated structure of decision, this does not affect the linearity of the aggregate relationships. If the decisions of an agency and the Bureau of the Budget with regard to that agency depend linearly upon the same variable (as we hypothesize), then the aggregate decision rule of the two, treated as a single entity, will depend linearly upon that variable. By a similar argument, the various Congressional participants can be grouped together so that Congress can be regarded as a single decision-making entity. While the aggregating procedure may result in grouping positive and negative influences together, this manifestly does not affect the legitimacy of the procedure; linearity is maintained.[3]

Our models concern only the requests presented in the President's budget for an individual agency and the behavior of Congress as a whole with regard to the agency's appropriation. The models do not attempt to estimate the complete decision-making structure for each agency from bureau requests to departments to submission through the Budget Bureau to possible final action in the Senate and House. There are several reasons for remaining content with the aggregated figures we use. First, the number of possible decision rules which must be considered grows rapidly as each new participant is added. We would soon be overwhelmed by the sheer number of rules invoked. Second, there are genuine restrictions placed on the number of structural parameters we can estimate because (a) some data, such as bureau requests to departments, are unavailable, and (b) only short time series are meaningful for most agencies. It would make no sense, for example, to go back in time beyond the end of World War II when most domestic activity was disrupted.[4]

Since the agencies use various strategies and Congress may respond to them in various ways, we propose several alternative systems of equations. These equations represent alternative decision rules which may be followed by Congressional and agency–Budget Bureau participants in the budgetary process. One important piece of data for agency–Budget Bureau personnel who are formulating appropriations requests is the most recent Congressional appropriation. Thus, we make considerable use of the concept "base," operationally defined as the previous Congressional appropriation for an agency, in formulating our decision rules. Since the immediate past exercises such a heavy influence on budgetary outcomes, Markov (simultaneous, difference) equations are particularly useful. In these Markov processes, the value of certain variables at one point in time is dependent on their value at one or more immediately previous periods as well as on the particular circumstances of the time.

We postulate several decision rules for both the agency–Budget Bureau requests and for Congressional action on these requests. For each series of requests or appropriations, we select from the postulated decision rules that rule which most closely represents the behavior of the aggregated entities. We use the variables

y_t the appropriation passed by Congress for any given agency in the year t. Supplemental appropriations are not included in the y_t.

x_t the appropriation requested by the Bureau of the Budget for any given agency for the year t. The x_t constitutes the President's budget request for an agency.

We will also introduce certain symbols representing random disturbances of each of the postulated relationships. These symbols are explained as they are introduced.

A. Equations for agency–Budget Bureau decision rules. The possibility that different agencies use different strategies makes it necessary to construct alternative equations representing these various strategies. Then, for each agency in our sample, we use time series data to select that equation which seems to describe best the budgetary decisions of that agency. In this section we present three simple models of agency requests. The first states agency requests as a function of the previous year's appropriation. The second states requests as a function of the previous appropriation as well as a function of the differences between the agency request and appropriation in the previous year. The third states requests as a function of the previous year's request. In all three linear models provision is made for a random variable to take into account the special circumstances of the time.

An agency, while convinced of the worth of its programs, tends to be aware that extraordinarily large or small requests are likely to be viewed with suspicion by Congress; an agency does not consider it desirable to make extraordinary

requests, which might precipitate unfavorable Congressional reaction. Therefore, the agency usually requests a percentage (generally greater than one hundred percent) of its previous year's appropriation. This percentage is not fixed; in
the event of favorable circumstances, the request is a larger percentage of the
previous year's appropriation than would otherwise be the case; similarly, the
percentage might be reduced in the event of unfavorable circumstances.

Decisions made in the manner described above may be represented by a simple
equation. If we take the average of the percentages that are implicitly or explicitly
used by budget officers, then any request can be represented by the sum of this
average percentage of the previous year's appropriation plus the increment or
decrement due to the favorable or unfavorable circumstances. Thus

(1) $$x_t = \beta_0 y_{t-1} + \epsilon_t$$

> The agency request (through the Budget Bureau) for a certain year is a fixed
> mean percentage of the Congressional appropriation for that agency in the pre-
> vious year plus a random variable (normally distributed with mean zero and
> unknown but finite variance) for that year.

is an equation representing this type of behavior. The average or mean percentage
is represented by β_0. The increment or decrement due to circumstances is represented by ϵ_t, a variable which requires some special explanation. It is difficult to
predict what circumstances will occur at what time to put an agency in a favorable
or unfavorable position. Numerous events could influence Congress's (and the
public's) perception of an agency and its programs—the occurrence of a destructive hurricane in the case of the Weather Bureau, the death by cancer of a friend of
an influential congressman, in the case of the National Institutes of Health, the
hiring (or losing) of an especially effective lobbyist by some interest group, the
President's becoming especially interested in a program of some agency as
Kennedy was in mental health, and so on. (Of course, some of them may be more
or less "predictable" at certain times to an experienced observer, but this fact
causes no difficulty here.) Following common statistical practice we may represent the sum of the effects of all such events by a random variable that is an
increment or decrement to the usual percentage of the previous year's appropriation. In equation (1), then, ϵ_t represents the value which this random variable
assumes in year t.

We have chosen to view the special events of each year for each agency as
random phenomena that are capable of being described by a probability density or
distribution. We assume here that the random variable is normally distributed
with mean zero and an unknown but finite variance. Given this specification of the
random variable, the agency makes its budgeting decisions as if it were operating
by the postulated decision rule given by equation (1).

An agency, although operating somewhat like the organizations described by
equation (1), may wish to take into account an additional strategic consideration:

while this agency makes a request which is roughly a fixed percentage of the previous year's appropriation, it also desires to smooth out its stream of appropriations by taking into account the difference between its request and appropriation for the previous year. If there were an unusually large cut in the previous year's request, the agency submits a "padded" estimate to make up for the loss in expected funds; an unusual increase is followed by a reduced estimate to avoid unspent appropriations. This behavior may be represented by equation or decision rule where

(2) $$x_t = \beta_1 y_{t-1} + \beta_2 (y_{t-1} - x_{t-1}) + \chi_t$$

> The agency request (through the Budget Bureau) for a certain year is a fixed mean percentage of the Congressional appropriation for that agency in the previous year plus a fixed mean percentage of the difference between the Congressional appropriation and the agency request for the previous year plus a stochastic disturbance.

χ_t is a stochastic disturbance, which plays the role described for the random variable in equation (1), the β's are variables reflecting the aspects of the previous year's request and appropriation that an agency takes into account: β_1 represents the mean percentage of the previous year's request which is taken into account, and β_2 represents the mean percentage of the difference between the previous year's appropriation and request $(y_{t-1} - x_{t-1})$ which is taken into account. Note that $\beta_2 < 0$ is anticipated so that a large cut will (in the absence of the events represented by the stochastic disturbance) be followed by a padded estimate and vice-versa.[5]

Finally, an agency (or the President through the Bureau of the Budget), convinced of the worth of its programs, may decide to make requests without regard to previous Congressional action. This strategy appeals especially when Congress has so much confidence in the agency that it tends to give an appropriation which is almost identical to the request. Aside from special circumstances represented by stochastic disturbances, the agency's request in any given year tends to be approximately a fixed percentage of its request for the previous year. This behavior may be represented by

(3) $$x_t = \beta_3 x_{t-1} + \rho_t$$

> The agency request (through the Budget Bureau) for a certain year is a fixed mean percentage of the agency's request for the previous year plus a random variable (stochastic disturbance).

where ρ_t is a stochastic disturbance and β_3 is the average percentage. Note that if the agency believes its programs to be worthy, $\beta_3 > 1$ is expected.[6]

These three equations are not the only ones which may be capable of representing the actual behavior of the combined budgeting decisions of the agencies and the Bureau of the Budget. However, they represent the agency–Budget Bureau budgeting behavior better than all other decision rules we tried.[7]

B. *Equations for Congressional decision rules.* In considering Congressional behavior, we again postulate three decision equations from which a selection must be made that best represents the behavior of Congress in regard to an agency's appropriations. Since Congress may use various strategies in determining appropriations for different agencies, different Congressional decision equations may be selected as best representing Congressional appropriations for each agency in our sample. Our first model states Congressional appropriations as a function of the agency's request (through the Budget Bureau) to Congress. The second states appropriations as a function of the agency's request as well as a function of the deviation from the usual relationship between Congress and the agency in the previous year. The third model states appropriations as a function of that segment of the agency's request that is not part of its appropriation or request for the previous year. Random variables are included to take account of special circumstances.

If Congress believes that an agency's request, after passing through the hands of the Budget Bureau, is a relatively stable index of the funds needed by the agency to carry out its programs, Congress responds by appropriating a relatively fixed percentage of the agency's request. The term "relatively fixed" is used because Congress is likely to alter this percentage somewhat from year to year because of special events and circumstances relevant to particular years. As in the case of agency requests, these special circumstances may be viewed as random phenomena. One can view this behavior as if it were the result of Cognress' appropriating a fixed mean percentage of the agency requests; adding to the amount so derived a sum represented by a random variable. One may represent this behavior as if Congress were following the decision rule

(4) $$y_t = a_0 x_t + \eta_t$$

The Congressional appropriation for an agency in a certain year is a fixed mean percentage of the agency's request in that year plus a stochastic disturbance.

where a_0 represents the fixed average percentage and η_t represents the stochastic disturbance.

Although Congress usually grants an agency a fixed percentage of its request, this request sometimes represents an extension of the agency's programs above (or below) the size desired by Congress. This can occur when the agency and the Bureau of the Budget follow Presidential aims differing from those of Congress, or when Congress suspects that the agency is padding the current year's request. In such a situation Congress usually appropriates a sum different from the usual percentage. If a_1 represents the mean of the usual percentages, this behavior can be represented by equation or decision rule

(5) $y_t = a_1 x_t + v_t$

where v_t is a stochastic disturbance representing that part of the appropriations attributable to the special circumstances that cause Congress to deviate from a relatively fixed percentage. Therefore, when agency aims and Congressional desires markedly differ from usual (so that Congress may be said to depart from its usual rule) the stochastic disturbance takes on an unusually large positive or negative value. In order to distinguish this case from the previous one, more must be specified about the stochastic disturbance v_t. In a year following one in which agency aims and Congressional desires markedly differed, the agency makes a request closer to Congressional desires, and/or Congress shifts its desires closer to those of the agency (or the President). In the year after a deviation, then, assume that Congress will tend to make allowances to normalize the situation. Such behavior can be represented by having the stochastic disturbance v_t generated in accordance with a first order Markov scheme. The stochastic component in v_t is itself determined by a relation

(6) $v_t = a_2 v_{t-1} + \epsilon_t$

where ϵ_t is a random variable. The symbol v_t therefore stands for the stochastic disturbance in the previous year (v_{t-1}) as well as the new stochastic disturbance for the year involved (ϵ_t). Substituting (6) into (5) gives

(7) $y_t = a_1 x_t + a_2 v_{t-1} + \epsilon_t$

> The Congressional appropriation for an agency is a fixed mean percentage of the agency's request for that year plus a stochastic disturbance representing a deviation from the usual relationship between Congress and the agency in the previous year plus a random variable for the current year.

as a complete description of a second Congressional decision rule. If Congress never makes complete allowance for an initial "deviation," then $-1 < a_2 < 1$ is to be expected.

To complete the description of this second Congressional decision rule, we will suppose $0 < a_2 < 1$. Then, granted a deviation from its usual percentage, Congress tends to decrease subsequent deviations by moving steadily back toward its usual percentage (except for the unforeseeable events or special circumstances whose effects are represented by the random variable ϵ_t). For example, if in a particular year $v_{t-1} > 0$, and if in the following year there are no special circumstances so that $\xi_t = 0$, then $v_t = a_2 v_{t-1} < v_{t-1}$. The deviation in year t is smaller than the deviation in year $t - 1$. However, if $-1 < a_2 < 0$ after an initial deviation, Congress tends to move back to its usual rule (apart from the disturbances represented by the random variable ϵ_t) by making successively smaller deviations which differ in sign. For example, if $v_{t-1}>0$, then apart from the disturbance ϵ_t it is clear that $v_t = a_2 v_{t-1} < 0$, since $a_2 < 0$. Finally, if $a_2 = 0$, decision rule (7) is the same as the previous rule (4).

The specialization inherent in the appropriation process allows some members of Congress to have an intimate knowledge of the budgetary processes of the agencies and the Budget Bureau. Thus, Congress might consider that part of the agency's request (x_t) which is not based on the previous year's appropriation or request. This occurs when Congress believes that this positive or negative remainder represents padding or when it desires to smooth out the agency's rate of growth. If Congress knows the decision rule that an agency uses to formulate its budgetary request, we can let λ_t represent a dummy variable defined as $\lambda_t = \xi_t$ if the agency uses decision rule (1); $\lambda_t = \beta_2(y_{t-1} - x_{t-1}) + \chi_t$ if the agency uses decision rule (2); and, $\lambda_t = \rho_t$ if the agency uses decision rule (3). Suppose that Congress appropriates, on the average, an amount which is a relatively fixed percentage of the agency's request plus a percentage of this (positive or negative) remainder λ_t. This behavior can be represented by the "as if" decision rule

(8)
$$y_t = a_3 x_t + a_4 \lambda_t + v_t$$

The Congressional appropriation for an agency is a fixed mean percentage of the agency's request for a certain year plus a fixed mean percentage of a dummy variable which represents that part of the agency's request for the year at issue which is not part of the appropriation or request of the previous year plus a random variable representing the part of the appropriation attributable to the special circumstances of the year.

where v_t is a stochastic disturbrance whose value in any particular year represents the part of the appropriation attributable to the agency's special circumstances of the year. One might expect that Congress takes only "partial" account of the remainder represented by λ_t, so $0 < a_4 < 1$.

III. Empirical results

Times series data for the period 1947–1963 were studied for fifty-six non-defense agencies of the United States Government. The requests (x_t) of these agencies were taken to be the amounts presented to Congress in the President's budget. For eight sub-agencies from the National Institutes of Health, data for a shorter period of time were considered, and the requests (x_t) of these eight sub-agencies were taken to be their proposals to the Bureau of the Budget.[8] In all instances the Congressional decision variable (y_t) was taken to be the final appropriation before any supplemental additions. The total appropriations (without supplements) of the agencies studied amounted to aproximately twenty-seven percent of the non-defense budget in 1963. Over one-half of all non-defense agencies were investigated; the major omissions being the Post Office and many independent agencies.

A minimum of three agencies was examined from each of the Treasury, Justice, Interior, Agriculture, Commerce, Labor, and Health, Education and Welfare Departments.[9]

If the agency–Budget Bureau disturbance is independent of Congressional disturbance,[10] the use of ordinary least squares (OLS) to estimate most of the possible combinations of the proposed decision equations is justified. OLS is identical to the simultaneous full information maximum likelihood (FIML) technique for most of the present systems. This is not so, however, for some systems of equations because of the presence of an auto-correlated disturbance in one equation of the two and the consequent non-linearity of the estimating equations. In equation (6) the stochastic disturbance for year t is a function of the value of the disturbance in the previous year. In a system of equations in which auto-correlation occurs in the first equation, an appropriate procedure is to use OLS to estimate the alternative proposals for the other equation, decide by the selection criteria which best specifies the data, use the knowledge of this structure to estimate the first equation, and then decide, through use of appropriate criteria, which version of the first equation best specifies the data.

The principal selection criterion we used is that of maximum (adjusted) correlation coefficient (R). For a given dependent variable this criterion leads one to select from alternative specifications of the explanatory variables, that specification which leads to the highest sample correlation coefficient. The estimations of the alternative specifications must, of course, be made from the same data.[11] The second criterion involves the use of the d-statistic test for serial correlation of the estimated residuals of a single equation.[12] This statistic tests the null hypothesis of residual independence against the alternative of serial correlation. We used the significance points for the d-statistic of Theil and Nagar.[13] When the d-statistic was found to be significant in fitting the Congressional decision equation (4) to an agency's data, it was always found that equation (7) best specified Congressional behavior with respect to the appropriations of that agency in the sense of yielding the maximum correlation coefficient. A third criterion is based on a test of the significance of the sample correlation between the residuals of (4) and the estimated λ_t of the equation selected previously for a given agency. David's significance points for this statistic were used to make a two-tailed test at the five percent level of the null hypothesis that the residuals are uncorrelated.[14] When significant correlation occurred, it was always found that Congressional decision equation (8), in which a function of the deviation from the usual relationship between request and the previous year's appropriation enters explicitly, best specified appropriation behavior with respect to the agency in question.

The statistical procedures were programmed for the Carnegie Institute of Technology's Control Data G-21 electronic computer in the 20-Gate algebraic compiling language. The selection among alternate specifications according to the criteria established was not done automatically; otherwise all computations were performed by machine. Since the results for each agency are described in detail elsewhere,[15] and a full rendition would double the length of the paper, we

Table 1

Best Specifications for Each Agency Are High

Frequencies of correlation coefficients

	1 – .995	– .99	– .98	– .97	– .96	– .95	– .94	– .93	– .90	– .85	– 0
Congressional	21	8	15	4	5	2	2	1	5	2	2
Agency-Bureau	9	2	2	8	5	2	4	3	5	11	10

must restrict ourselves to summary statements.

The empirical results support the hypothesis that, up to a random error of reasonable magnitude, the budgetary process of the United States government is equivalent to a set of temporally stable linear decision rules. Estimated correlation coefficients for the best specification of each agency are generally high. Although the calculated values of the multiple correlation coefficients (R's) tend to run higher in time series than in cross-sectional analysis, the results are good. We leave little of the variance statistically unexplained. Moreover the estimated standard deviations of the coefficients are usually much smaller than one-half of the size of the estimated coefficients, a related indication of good results. Table 1 presents the frequencies of the correlation coefficients.

The fits between the decision rules and the time series data for the Congressional decision equations are, in general, better than those for the agency–Bureau of the Budget equations. Of the 64 agencies and sub-agencies studied, there are only 14 instances in which the correlation coefficient for the agency (or sub-agency) equation was higher than the one for the corresponding Congressional equation. We speculate that the estimated variances of the disturbances of the agency–Budget Bureau decision rules are usually larger because the agencies are closer than Congress to the actual sources that seek to add new programs or expand old ones.

Table 2 presents a summary of the combinations of the Agency–Bureau of the Budget and Congressional decision equations. For those agencies studied, the most popular combinations of behavior are the simple ones represented by equations (4) and (1) respectively. When Congress uses a sophisticated "gaming" strategy such as (7) or (8), the corresponding agency–Bureau of the Budget decision equation is the relatively simple (1). And, when Congress grants exactly or almost exactly the amount requested by an agency, the agency tends to use decision equation (3).

Our discussion thus far has assumed fixed values for the coefficients (parameters) of the equations we are using to explain the behavior underlying the budgetary process. In the light of many important events occurring in the period

Table 2

Budgetary Behavior Is Simple

Summary of decision equations

Agency-Budget Bureau		1	2	3
	4	44*	1	8
Congress	7	1	0	0
	8	12	0	0

*Including eight sub-agencies from the National Institutes of Health.

from 1946 to 1963, however, it seems reasonable to suppose that the appropriations structure of many government agencies was altered. If this is correct, the coefficients of the equations—literally, in this context, the values represented by the on-the-average percentages requested by the agencies and granted by Congress—should change from one period of time to the next. The equations would then be temporally stable for a period, but not forever. The year when the coefficient of an equation changes from one value to another is termed the "shift point." The time series we are using are so short that it is possible to find only one meaningful shift point in each of the two equations that describe the budget request and appropriation best fitting an agency. We, therefore, broke each time series into two parts and used Chow's F-statistic[16] to determine temporal stability by testing the null hypothesis that the underlying coefficients did not shift (against all alternatives) for the individual equations. We used four categories for the coefficients of a decision equation defined as follows:

> *Temporally very stable:* The F-statistic is small and the coefficients estimated from the first and last part of the series are virtually the same.
> *Temporally stable:* The F-statistic is small, but the coefficients estimated from the first and last parts of the series appear to be different.
> *Not temporally stable:* The F-statistic is large but not significant at the ten percent level and the coefficients estimated from the first and last parts of series appear to be different.
> *Temporally unstable:* The F-statistic is significant at the ten percent level.

Of the Congressional decision equations, six were temporally very stable, 12 were temporally stable, 12 were not temporally stable, and 28 were temporally unstable. Of the agency–Bureau of the Budget decision equations, four were temporally very stable, 18 were temporally stable, 18 were not temporally stable, and 18 were temporally unstable.[17] Since a substantial majority of cases fall into

Table 3

Congressional Behavior Tends to Become More Sophisticated

First period decision equations

	1	2	3
4	45	0	10
7	1	0	0
8	2	0	0

Second period decision equations

	1	2	3
4	35	1	9
7	1	0	0
8	12	0	0

the not temporally stable and temporally unstable categories, it is evident that while the process is temporally stable for short periods, it may not be stable for the whole period.

Table 3 presents a summary of the combinations of the agency–Bureau of the Budget and Congressional decision equations when each series is broken into two parts. These specifications are referred to as "first period" and "second period" for all agencies even though the years at which the time series were broken vary. While the most frequent combinations of behavior are the simple ones represented by equations (4) and (1) respectively, there is a marked tendency for Congressional behavior to become more sophisticated: the incidence of the gaming behavior represented by equation (8) increases over time.[18]

The budgetary process seems to become more linear over time in the sense that the importance of the "special circumstances" appears to diminish. Table 4 presents frequencies of the correlation coefficients for the first and second periods. Although there is a different number of correlation coefficients in each period (111 in the first period and 114 in the second)[19] Table 4 shows clearly that fits are better for the second period, which is sufficient evidence of increasing linear tendencies. To us it seems reasonable to expect an increasing use of simplifying rules of thumb as the budget grows in size and the pressure of time on key decision makers increases. Yet this is only one of a number of possible explanations. For example, the data are not deflated for changes in the price level during the early years. Since there were larger increases in the price level during

Table 4

The Budgetary Process Is Becoming More Linear

Frequencies of correlation coefficients

	1 – .995	– .99	– .98	– .97	– .96	– .94	– .92	– .90	– .80	– .60	– .0
First period	9	5	8	5	3	6	8	4	18	24	21
Second period	27	5	13	8	8	15	7	5	12	8	6

the early years, this might help explain why the fits are better during the second period.

When only one shift point is presumed, most shifts are discovered during the first two budgets of the Eisenhower Administration (1954–1955). Table 5 presents, for both Congressional and agency–Budget Bureau decision equations, frequencies of the shift points for (a) those equations whose coefficients are in the not temporally stable or temporally unstable categories and (b) those agencies for which the decision rules of the participants appeared to change. While it is certainly possible that shift points do not occur as dramatically and as sharply as shown here, and that it may take several years for actual behavior to change noticeably, Table 5 nevertheless makes it clear that likely shifts are concentrated in the first period of the Eisenhower administration.

We said, in Section II, that we expected $\beta_0, \beta_1, \beta_3$, to be greater than one, and β_2 to be negative. In 56 instances this expectation is satisfied, but eight exceptions were noted. In the two cases where the estimated $\beta_3 < 1$, explanations are immediately available. First, the fit for the Bureau of Employment Security is not good. Second, the Office of Territories evidences most un-Parkinsonian behavior: its activities decline with a decrease in the number of territories. In the six other exceptions, the estimated coefficient is $\beta_0 < 1$. For three of these, Congress tends to appropriate an amount greater than the request, and two of the three represent an interesting phenomenon. When those parts of requests and appropriations directly related to loans are omitted from the data for both the Rural Electrification Administration and the Federal Housing Administration, the estimated coefficients are of the magnitudes expected with $\beta_0 > 1$ and $a_0 < 1$. However, when the data relating to loans are included, then $\beta_0 < 1$ and $a_0 > 1$. Apparently, Congress favors the loan programs more than do the agencies or the Budget Bureau.

As a rule, the d-statistics resulting from fitting the best specifications were not significant. It would thus appear that all major underlying trended variables (with the possible exception of variables with the same trend) have been accounted for by these specifications. When an exception to this rule did exist, the authors made a careful examination of the residuals in an effort to determine the reason for such

Table 5

Likely Shift Points Are Concentrated in the First Years of the Eisenhower Administration

| | Frequencies of shift points | | | | | | | | | | | | | | | | |
Year	48	49	50	51	52	53	54	55	56	57	58	59	60	61	62	T	
Congressional	0	2	3	1	0	1	17	16	1	1	3	0	0	1	0	46	(40)
Agency-Bureau	0	2	4	0	2	3	15	13	3	0	2	1	0	2	1	37	(36)

a situation. It appeared that in most of these instances the cause was either (a) that the coefficients shifted slowly over several years and not abruptly at one point in time, or (b) that restricting the search to only one shift point left undetected an additional shift either very early or very late in the series.

In an attempt to unmask the trended variable most likely (in our opinion) to have been ignored, and to cast some light upon the notion of "fair share," final appropriations y_t for each agency were regressed on total non-defense appropriations z_t. This time series was taken from the *Statistical Abstract of the United States*. The results were poor. Indeed, the sample correlations between y_t and z_t are usually worse than those between y_t and x_t. Moreover, the d-statistics are usually highly significant and the residual patterns for the regression show the agency's proportion of the non-defense budget to be either increasing or decreasing over time. However, it should be noted that even those exceptional cases where the agency trend is close to that of the total non-defense appropriation do not invalidate the explicit decision structure fitted here. A similar study, with similar results, was conducted at the departmental level by regressing y_t for the eight National Institutes of Health on y_t for the Public Health Service, the agency of which they are a part. Finally, the y_t for selected pairs of agencies with "similar" interests were regressed on each other with uniformly poor results.

Although empirical evidence indicates that our models describe the budgetary process of the United States government, we are well aware of certain deficiencies in our work. One deficiency, omission of certain agencies from the study, is not serious because over one-half of all non-defense agencies were investigated. Nevertheless, the omission of certain agencies may have left undiscovered examples of additional decision rules. We will shortly study all agencies whose organizational structure can be traced. We will also include supplemental appropriations.

A more serious deficiency may lie in the fact that the sample sizes, of necessity, are small. The selection criterion of maximum sample correlation, therefore, lacks proper justification, and is only acceptable because of the lack of a better criterion. Further, full-information maximum likelihood estimators, and especially biased ones, even when they are known to be consistent, are not fully satisfactory in such a situation, although they may be the best available. However, the remedy for these deficiencies must await the results of future theoretical research on explosive or evolutionary processes.

IV. The deviant cases and prediction: Interpretation of the stochastic disturbances

The intent of this section is to clarify further the interpretation of the stochastic disturbances as special or unusual circumstances represented by random variables. While those influences present at a constant level during the period serve only to affect the magnitude of the coefficients, the special circumstances have an important, if subsidiary, place in these models. We have indicated that although outside observers can view the effects of special circumstances as a random variable, anyone familiar with all the facts available to the decision-makers at the time would be able to explain the special circumstances. It seems reasonable therefore to examine instances where, in estimating the coefficients, we find that the estimated values of the stochastic disturbances assume a large positive or negative value. Such instances appear as deviant cases in the sense that Congress or the agency–Budget Bureau actors affected by special circumstances (large positive or negative values of the random variable) do not appear to be closely following their usual decision rule at that time but base their decisions mostly on these circumstances. The use of case studies for the analyses of deviant phenomena, of course, presupposes our ability to explain most budgeting decisions by our original formulations. Deviant cases, then, are those instances in which particular decisions do not follow our equations. It is possible to determine these deviant instances simply by examining the residuals of the fitted equations: one observes a plot of the residuals, selects those which appear as extreme positive or negative values, determines the year to which these extreme residuals refer, and then examines evidence in the form of testimony at the Appropriations Committees, newspaper accounts and other sources. In this way it is possible to determine at least some of the circumstances of a budgetary decision and to investigate whether or not the use of the random variables is appropriate.[20]

Finally, it should be pointed out that in our model the occurrence of extreme disturbances represents deviant cases, or the temporary setting aside of their usual decision rules by the decision-makers in the process, while coefficient shifts represent a change (not necessarily in form) of these rules.

From the residuals of one-half of the estimated Congressional decision equations, a selection of 55 instances (approximately 14 percent of the 395 Congressional decisions under consideration) were identified as deviant.[21] Table 6 shows the yearly frequency of the occurrence of deviant cases. It is apparent that deviancy grows in years of political change; in 1948 the Republican 80th Congress made a determined effort to reduce appropriations submitted by the Democratic President; the years 1953 through 1955 mark the beginning of

Table 6

Deviant Cases Cluster in Years of Political Change

Year	'48	'49	'50	'51	'52	'53	'54	'55	'56	'57	'58	'59	'60	'61	'62	'63
Number of cases	8	2	1	1	1	4	6	4	1	1	2	3	4	2	8	7

Eisenhower's Presidency; the large number of deviant cases in 1962 and 1963 are related to the accession to office of Kennedy and Johnson. The latter category of deviant cases, we will explain later, may be mis-classifications in the sense that the passage of time and the corresponding accumulation of additional evidence may reveal shift points, i.e., changes in the "average percentages" of the decision porcesses, rather than "exceptional circumstances." Nevertheless, this fact causes no particular problem in light of our purposes here, and the cases may be viewed as if they are appropriately classified.

Table 7 categorizes the cases according to estimates of why deviance occurred. It should be noted that the largest category, significant policy change, involves the lack of a budgetary base for the agency in question. In order to highlight the meaning we give to random phenomena, an illustration of each category follows. This analysis explains why, although the deviant cases are understandable to an experienced observer or participant, an outsider would have to regard them as essentially random disturbances to an otherwise deterministic system. Indeed, no two events in the categories of Table 7 are likely, *a priori*, either to be the same or to occur in any particular year.

Significant policy change
The Southwestern Power Administration is typical of agencies whose appropriations fluctuate unduly because basic policy is being negotiated. Deviance was evident in 1948, 1949, 1954, and 1955. The SPA continually requested funds for the building of transmission lines, and Congress repeatedly eliminated the request from their appropriations, insisting that private enterprise would supply the necessary facilities. In 1948 the Bureau of the Budget recommended $7,600,000 of which only $125,000 was appropriated, with stringent and explicit instructions that printing and mailing of materials calculated to increase clientele among rural and municipal electrical cooperatives cease.

The Korean War increased demands for electric power. Deviance occurred in 1955 not because of appropriations cuts but because of House floor amendments and Senate Appropriations Committee increases. Public policy then became stabilized as Congress established a budgetary base. The following years fit our equations.

Table 7

Deviant Cases May Be Viewed As Random Events

Categories of deviance	Number of cases
Significant policy change	20
Fiscal policy change	8
Felt need of Congressional supervision	6
Amended estimate due to a time factor	6
Single event	5
Large new legislative program	4
Reorganization of agency	1
Non-identifiable	5
Total N =	55

Fiscal policy changes
The Foreign Agricultural Service's 1963 appropriation is deviant in appropriation figures, but, because $3,117,000 was provided by transferring funds from Sec. 32, the total budget for FAS is close to the Budget Bureau's initial request.

Felt need of Congressional supervision
The House Committee reports on Office of Territories for 1953 show a lack of confidence in the agency. The tenor can be judged by House Report 1622: ''The Department was advised last year that the Committee did not intend to provide appropriations for an endless chain of capital investment in the Alaska Railroads. Army testimony was conflicting as to the need for a road and railways. There is need for a coordinated plan before the Committee can act intelligently with regard to the railroad.''

Amended estimate due to time factor
Typical of this type of deviance is the Commodity Stabilization Service's appropriation for 1958. On the basis of figures from County Agricultural Agents, Secretary Ezra Taft Benson scaled down his request from $465 million to $298 million. A more accurate estimate was made possible because of added time.

Large new legislative program
This is especially apt to affect an agency if it is required to implement several new programs simultaneously. The Commissioner of Education said in reference to the student loan program, ''We have no way of knowing because we never had such a program, and many of the institutions never had them.'' The NDEA Act alone had ten new entitlements.

Reorganization of an agency
The only example is the Agricultural Marketing Service's appropriation for 1962. Funds were reduced because of a consolidation of diverse activities by the Secretary of Agriculture and not through reorganization as a result of Congressional demands.

Non-identifiable
This applies, for example, to the Public Health Service where a combination of lesser factors converge to make the agency extremely deviant for 1959, 1960, 1961, and 1962. Among the apparent causes of deviance are publicity factors, the roles of committee chairmen in both House and Senate, a high percentage of professionals in the agency, and the excellent press coverage of health research programs. No one factor appears primarily responsible for the deviance.

Our models are not predictive but explanatory. The alternate decision equations can be tried and the most appropriate one used when data on requests and appropriations are available. The appropriate equation explains the data in that, given a good fit, the process behaves "as if" the data were generated according to the equation. Thus, our explanatory models are backward looking; given a history of requests and appropriations, the data appear as if they were produced by the proposed and appropriately selected scheme.

The models are not predictive because the process is only temporally stable for short periods. We have found cases in which the coefficients of the equations change, i.e., cases in which there are alterations in the realized behavior of the processes. We have no *a priori* theory to predict the occurrence of these changes, but merely our *ad hoc* observation that most occurred during Eisenhower's first term. Predictions are necessarily based upon the estimated values of the coefficients and on the statistical properties of the stochastic disturbance (sometimes called the error term). Without a scientific method of predicting the shift points in our model, we cannot scientifically say that a request or an appropriation for some future year will fall within a prescribed range with a given level of confidence. We can predict only when the process remains stable in time. If the decision rules of the participants have changed, our predictions may be worthless: in our models, either the coefficients have shifted or, more seriously, the scheme has changed. Moreover, it is extremely difficult to determine whether or not the observation latest in time represents a shift point. A sudden change may be the result either of a change in the underlying process or a temporary setting aside of the usual decision rules in light of special circumstances. The data for several subsequent years are necessary to determine with any accuracy whether a change in decision rules indeed occurred.

It is possible, of course, to make conditional predictions by taking the estimated coefficients from the last shift point and assuming that no shift will occur. Limited predictions as to the next year's requests and appropriations could be made and might turn out to be reasonably accurate. However, scholarly efforts would be better directed toward knowledge of why, where and when changes in the process occur so that accurate predictions might be made.

The usual interpretation of stochastic (in lieu of deterministic) models may, of course, be made for the models of this paper, i.e., not all factors influencing the budgetary process have been included in the equations. Indeed, many factors often deemed most important, such as pressure from interest groups, are ignored. Part of the reason for this lies in the nature of the models: they describe the decision process in skeleton form. Further, since the estimations are made, of necessity, on the basis of time series data, it is apparent that any influences that were present at a constant level during the period are not susceptible to discovery by these methods. However, these influences do affect the budgetary process by determining the size of the estimated coefficients. Thus, this paper, in making a comparative study of the estimated coefficients for the various agencies, suggests a new way of approaching constant influences.

No theory can take every possible unexpected circumstance into account, but our theory can be enlarged to include several classes of events. The concentration of shift points in the first years of the Eisenhower administration implies that an empirical theory should take account of changes in the political party controlling the White House and Congress.

We also intend to determine indices of clientele and confidence so that their effects, when stable over time, can be gauged.[22] Presidents sometimes attempt to gear their budgetary requests to fit their desired notion of the rate of expenditures appropriate for the economic level they wish the country to achieve. By checking the Budget Message, contemporary accounts, and memoirs, we hope to include a term (as a dummy variable) which would enable us to predict high and low appropriations rates depending on the President's intentions.

V. Significance of the findings

We wish to consider the significance of (a) the fact that it is possible to find equations which explain major facets of the federal budgetary process and (b) the particular equations fitted to the time series. We will take up each point in order.

A. It is possible to find equations for the budgetary process. There has been controversy for some time over whether it is possible to find laws, even of a probabilistic character, which explain important aspects of the political process. The greatest skepticism is reserved for laws which would explain how policy is made or account for the outcomes of the political process. Without engaging in further abstract speculation, it is apparent that the best kind of proof would be a demonstration of the existence of some such laws. This, we believe, we have done.

Everyone agrees that the federal budget is terribly complex. Yet, as we have shown, the budgetary process can be described by very simple decision rules.

Work done by Simon, Newell, Reitman, Clarkson, Cyert and March, and others on simulating the solution of complex problems, has demonstrated that in complicated situations human beings are likely to use heuristic rules or rules of thumb to enable them to find satisfactory solutions.[23] Braybrooke and Lindblom have provided convincing arguments on this score for the political process.[24] Wildavsky's interviews with budget officers indicate that they, too, rely extensively on aids to calculation.[25] It is not surprising, therefore, as our work clearly shows, that a set of simple decision rules can explain or represent the behavior of participants in the federal budgetary process in their efforts to reach decisions in complex situations.

The most striking fact about the equations is their simplicity. This is perhaps partly because of the possibility that more complicated decision procedures are reserved for special circumstances represented by extreme values of the random variable. However, the fact that the decision rules generally fit the data very well is an indication that these simple equations have considerable explanatory power. Little of the variance is left unexplained.

What is the significance of the fact that the budgetary process follows rather simple laws for the general study of public policy? Perhaps the significance is limited; perhaps other policy processes are far more complex and cannot be reduced to simple laws. However, there is no reason to believe that this is the case. On the contrary, when one considers the central importance of budgeting the political process—few activities can be carried on without funds—and the extraordinary problems of calculation which budgeting presents, a case might better be made for its comparative complexity than for its simplicity. At present it is undoubtedly easier to demonstrate that laws, whether simple or complex, do underlie the budgetary process than to account for other classes of policy outcomes, because budgeting provides units of analysis (appropriations requests and grants) that are readily amenable to formulating and testing propositions statistically. The dollar figures are uniform, precise, numerous, comparable with others, and, most important, represent an important class of policy outcomes. Outside of matters involving voting or attitudes, however, it is difficult to think of general statements about public policy that can be said to have been verified. The problem is not that political science lacks propositions which might be tested. Works of genuine distinction like Herring's *The Politics of Democracy*, Truman's *The Governmental Process*, Hyneman's *Bureaucracy in a Democracy*, Neustadt's *Presidential Power*, Buchanan and Tullock's *The Calculus of Consent*, contain implicit or explicit propositions which appear to be at least as interesting as (and potentially more interesting than) the ones tested in this paper. The real difficulty is that political scientists have been unable to develop a unit of analysis (there is little agreement on what constitutes a decision) that would permit them to test the many propositions they have at their command. By taking one step toward demonstrating what can be done when a useful unit of analysis has been developed, we hope to highlight the tremendous importance that the development of units of analysis would have for the study of public policy.

B. The significance of the particular equations. Let us examine the concepts that have been built into the particular equations. First, the importance of the previous year's appropriation is an indication that the notion of the base is a very significant explanatory concept for the behavior of the agencies and the Budget Bureau. Similarly, the agency–Budget Bureau requests are important variables in the decisions of Congress. Second, some of the equations, notably (7) and (8) for Congress, and (2) for the agency–Budget Bureau, incorporate strategic concepts. On some occasions, then, budgeting on the federal level does involve an element of gaming. Neither the Congress nor the agencies can be depended upon to "take it lying down." Both attempt to achieve their own aims and goals. Finally, the budgetary process is only temporally stable. The occurrence of most changes of decision rules at a change in administration indicates that alterations in political party and personnel occupying high offices can exert some (but not total) influence upon the budgetary process.

Our decision rules may serve to cast some light on the problem of "power" in political analysis. The political scientist's dilemma is that it is hardly possible to think about politics without some concept of power, but that it is extremely difficult to create and then to use an operational definition in empirical work. Hence, James March makes the pessimistic conclusion that "The Power of Power" as a political variable may be rather low.[26] The problem is particularly acute when dealing with processes in which there is a high degree of mutual dependence among the participants. In budgeting, for example, the agency–Budget Bureau and Congressional relationships hardly permit a strict differentiation of the relative influence of the participants. Indeed, our equations are built on the observation of mutual dependence; and the empirical results show that how the agency–Budget Bureau participants behave depends on what Congress does (or has done) and that how Congress behaves depends on what the agency–Budget Bureau side is doing (or has done). Yet the concept of power does enter the analysis in calculations of the importance that each participant has for the other; it appears in the relative magnitude of the estimated coefficients. "Power" is saved because it is not required to carry too great a burden. It may be that theories which take power into account as part of the participants' calculations will prove of more use to social science research than attempts to measure the direct exercise of influence. At least we can say that theories of calculation, which animate the analysis of *The Politics of the Budgetary Process* and of this paper, do permit us to state and test propositions about the outcomes of a political process. Theories of power do not yet appear to have gone this far.

In the field of economics, work has long been done on organizational units called industrial firms. In political science, however, despite the flurry of excitement over organization theory, there has been no empirical demonstration of the value of dealing with various public organizations as comparable entities. By viewing governmental bodies not as distinctly different agencies but as having certain common properties (here, in budgetary calculations and strategies), we hope to have shown the utility to empirical theory of treating organizations *qua* organizations. Despite the differences among the organizations studied—some follow different decision rules and are affected by different random disturbances—it is analytically significant to explain their behavior by virtue of features they share as organizations.

It should be clear that we are dealing with general models of organizations and not with individual policies. One cannot say anything directly about water, land, health, or other transportation policies, from inspection of our models of a given agency. But this limit is not inherent in our approach. It is possible, for example, to calculate from our data present and future estimated rates of growth for virtually all domestic agencies since World War II. Agencies with similar growth rates may be segregated and examined for common features. The growth rates of agencies in similar areas of policy, such as public health and natural resources, may be compared, and the fortunes of policies in those areas deduced. Individual agencies may be broken down into sub-units or the courses of certain policy programs charted to explain the differential treatment they receive. While pursuing this type of analysis, we hope to have one advantage. We shall be working from a general model of the budgetary process. It will, therefore, be possible for us to locate our efforts within this larger scheme. To know whether one is dealing with a normal or deviant case, to know one's position in this larger universe, is to be able to give more general meaning to the individual and particular circumstances with which one must be involved in handling small parts of the total process.

The general mode of analysis we have developed here may be pursued in many different contexts. Similar studies could be undertaken in state and local governments as well as foreign countries.[27] Private firms and public agencies may be conceptualized in parallel terms through their budgetary mechanisms.[28] By comparing the processes underlying budgeting in a variety of political and economic systems, it may be possible to state more elegantly and precisely the conditions under which different forms of behavior would prevail.

Appendix

On the definition of terms

Certain of the technical terms required in the paper are here given informal definitions.

Coefficient: A coefficient of an equation is a parameter or number that is said to have some given but usually unknown value. The α's and β's used in the models are the coefficients of the equations in which they appear. Since the values of the coefficients are usually unknown, they must be estimated statistically from available data. In this paper, the coefficients (α's and β's) are average representations of the real percentages of requests made by agencies and appropriations granted by Congress.

Linear: An equation is linear if it has no square or higher order terms. Thus $y = \alpha x$ is linear whereas $y = \alpha x^2$ is not linear. (Remember that for two variables linear means "in a straight line.")

Stochastic: A variable is stochastic, a term meaning random, if the particular value that it assumes is a matter of chance and the set of values that it can assume is capable of being described by a probability distribution or density. The distribution gives the probability of the random variable assuming the various allowable values.

Variance: The variance is defined as $E(x - \mu)^2$ where x is a random variable, μ is its mean, and E stands for "the expected value of." One can think of variance as a measure of the dispersion or spread of the probability distribution governing the random variable.

Linear Regression Equation: A linear regression equation is a particular model of the relationship between two or more variables. The model has the form

$$y_i = \beta_0 + \beta_1 x_{1i} + \beta_2 x_{2i} + \cdots + \beta_k x_{ki} + \epsilon_i$$

where β_0 is the unknown constant term, the other β's are unknown coefficients, and ϵ_i is a random variable. In this notation, y_i represents the value of the dependent variable on the ith observation and $x_{1i} x_{2i}, \cdots, x_{ki}$ represents in a similar manner the values of the independent variables for the same observation. From a set of n observations, each of which consists of particular values for the dependent and independent variables, the regression operation estimates values for the unknown coefficients and the constant term; the regression operation also estimates n values of the random variable, which are called residuals. When the sets of observations on the dependent and independent variables refer to successive periods, the observations are called time series and we say that the values of y_i are generated by a stochastic process.

Stochastic Disturbance: This is a name for the random variable in a regession equation. It is also called the error term. Thus, in the equation $y_t = \alpha x_t + \epsilon_t$, the term ϵ_t represents a stochastic disturbance (or random variable), which is usually assumed to be normally distributed with mean zero and finite but unknown variance.

Difference Equation: An equation which describes the value of a variable in one period in terms of the value of either that variable or another variable in some previous period is a difference equation. For example, $x_t = \beta y_{t-1}$ is a difference equation. If a random variable is present, the equation is called a stochastic difference equation. Thus, if ϵ is a random variable, $x_t = \beta y_{t-1} + \epsilon_t$ is a stochastic difference equation and the successive values of x may be thought of as a stochastic process.

Unstable, Evolutionary or Explosive Process: A process is said to be unstable, evolutionary or explosive if the expected values of the successive values taken by the process are increasing. For example, the stochastic difference equation $y_t = \gamma y_{t-1} + \epsilon$, where $\chi > 1$, generates an evolutionary process.

Serially Independent: If successive realizations of a random variable are serially independent, the value it assumes in one period is independent of the value it assumed in a previous period. This can be described mathematically as $E(x_t | x_{t-})_1 = E(x_t)$, meaning that the expected value of random variable x at period t does not depend upon the value that the random variable x assumed at period $t-1$. It follows that the expected simple correlation between x_t and x_{t-1} will be zero, if the random variable x

is serially independent. For example, in our models, the assumption of serial independence of the disturbances reflects the belief that special circumstances in one year either do not affect special circumstances in succeeding years or that their influence enters explicitly into our model (as in equation (8) and the equations of footnote 4).

The meaning of a Markov process

For our purposes, a Markov process generating some random variable x, is a process for which the value of x at time t depends upon the values assumed by that random variable at one or more earlier periods plus the value assumed by some stochastic disturbance at time t. A Markov process is "first order" if the variable x_t takes on a value that depends only upon the value of the variable x_{t-1} in the previous period plus the value of a stochastic disturbance at time t. Thus

$$x_t = \alpha_{t-1} + \epsilon_t$$

is a first order Markov process where ϵ_t is a random variable with a given distribution and α is a non-zero constant. A second order Markov process can be described by

$$x_t = \alpha_1 x_{t-1} + \alpha_2 x_{t-2} + \epsilon_t$$

where both α_1 and α_2 are non-zero constants. The value of the variable x_t now depends upon its values in two previous periods.

On the meaning of goodness of fit

An intuitive notion of good fit for a linear regression equation is that in a scatter diagram the observations should cluster about the fitted line. Probably the most popular measure of good fit is the square of the multiple correlation coefficient (R^2), which may often be interpreted as the percentage of the variance of the dependent variable that is explained by the postulated linear relationship (regression). For our models however, this interpretation is not valid, although the adjusted R gives a rough measure of the goodness of fit. The closer to 1 that the adjusted R is, the better the fit.

On standard deviations of coefficient estimates

Speaking roughly, these standard deviations measure the reliability of the estimates of the coefficients. The smaller the estimated standard deviation, the more accurate the estimated coefficient is likely to be. If we had another series of data generated from the same process, the smaller the standard deviation of the coefficient (estimated from the first data) in relation to the size of this coefficient, the more likely it is that a new estimate made on the basis of the hypothetical new series of data would be close to the estimate made from the original data. Generally, one hopes the estimated standard deviation of the coefficient is at least as small as one-half the size of the estimated coefficient.

On biased and unbiased estimators

Think of the problem of trying to determine the average IQ of students at a large university. Suppose the administration would not allow access to records and one did not wish to give IQ tests to all students. One might select a certain number of students at random (a sample) and give them the tests. The test scores of these students are sample observations. One might compute the average of these test scores and claim that he has an estimate of the mean IQ of all students at the University. The estimator is the formula for the average of the sample observations. If he repeated the process, taking a new sample, it is possible that the estimator would produce a slightly different estimate of the mean. However, the estimator would still have a certain expected value. If the expected value of the estimator can be proven to equal the population parameter (the mean IQ of all the students for example) then the estimator is said to be unbiased. Otherwise, it is said to be biased.

On consistent estimators

An estimator is consistent if it approaches nearer and nearer to the true value of a parameter (in our case, a coefficient) as the size of the sample is increased. A consistent estimator may be biased (it may approach closer to but never actually equal the parameter), but if the sample from which it is estimated is large enough this bias will be small.

On least-squares estimators and the meaning of temporally stable processes

This discussion specifically refers to process (4) although it is equally applicable to all processes. Consider

$$y_t = \alpha_0 x_t + \eta_t$$

where α represents the coefficient of the equation or the "on the average" percentage of the request that is granted by Congress and η_t is a stochastic disturbance (random variable) that represents the variation in the request over time that may be assigned to special circumstances. We assume that η_t is normally distributed with mean zero and finite but unknown variance. The coefficient is unknown and must be estimated on the basis of available data. The data are the requests x_t and the corresponding appropriations y_t. We do not know the values assumed by the stochastic disturbance. Our estimates of the values assumed by the stochastic disturbance are the residuals of the fitted regression equation. If, for a given agency, we observe the requests and appropriations over a specified period of time, we could plot the data in a scatter

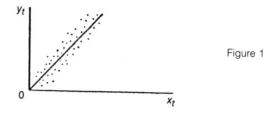

Figure 1

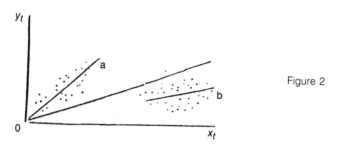

Figure 2

diagram (Figure 1). The line drawn in Figure 1 would be our estimated line (the line resulting from our estimate of α).

The vertical positive and negative distances of the points from the fitted line are the values of the residuals, our estimates of the values assumed by the stochastic disturbance. The least-squares estimates of the coefficients are those values of the coefficients which make the sum of the squares of these distances a minimum. In Figure 1, there is no discernible pattern of departure of the points from the line.

Thus, we can say that the process is temporally stable (i.e., fixed over time) and presume that the true value of the coefficient (we know only its estimated value) remained constant during the period under consideration. A temporally stable process is one in which the value of the true coefficient does not change during the period under consideration. This should not be confused with a stable or non-evolutionary process, i.e., one whose values do not tend to grow, but fluctuate about some level.

If we again plotted the requests and appropriations data for an agency and found the results to be as in Figure 2, the longest line would represent our first fitted equation (or the equation resulting from our first estimate of the value of the coefficient). The points (alternately the residuals) form a pattern of departure from the fitted line. In the early years (a) they fall mostly above the line and in the later years (b) they fall mostly below the line. The process must have been temporally unstable for the period as a whole, i.e., the coefficient had one true value during the first years of the period and a different true value during the last years.

A temporally unstable process is one in which the true coefficient assumes two or more values during the period under consideration. Since we only know the estimated coefficient, we must examine the residuals to determine whether such a pattern is present. Then, we select what appears to be the probable year of change, and fit two lines such as those drawn in above. We then compute the F Statistic to make our statistical test to determine, at a given level of significance, whether or not the true value of the coefficient shifted. If it was found to shift, the process was temporally stable for some period of time but not necessarily for the entire series of time periods examined.

The meaning of a shift point and a break point

The two second lines fitted to Figure 2 represent the true process. The year during which the coefficient changes (the year when the pattern shifts from clustering about line (a) to clustering about line (b) is referred to as a shift point. If what appears at first to be a shift in the true value of the coefficient is actually an alteration in behavior so that one equation fits the first sub-period, we still refer to the year of the change in realized behavior a shift point. Break point is the term used to describe a suspected shift point but for which the F-test indicates that the true coefficient value did not shift.

Notes

1. See the Appendix for explanations of terms and concepts.
2. The description which follows is taken from Aaron Wildavsky, *The Politics of the Budgetary Process* (Boston, 1964). Portions of the comments on the House Appropriations Committee are from Richard Fenno, "The House Appropriations Committee as a Political System: The Problem of Integration," this *Review*, 56 (1962), 310–324.
3. See H. Thiel, *Linear Aggregation of Economic Relations* (Amsterdam, 1954).
4. Our subsequent discussion of "shift" or "break" points should also make clear that it is not realistic to expect meaningful time series of great length to be accumulated for most agencies in the United States government.
5. Since some readers may not be familiar with the notation we are using, a brief explanation may be in order. As a coefficient of the equation, β_2 is an unknown number that must be estimated from the data, and this coefficient multiplies another number $(y_{t-1} - x_{t-1})$ that may be computed by subtracting last year's request from last year's appropriation. We want the equation to say that the agency will try to counteract large changes in their appropriations by changing their normal requests in the next year. If the agency asks for much more than it thinks it will get and its request is cut, for example, the expression $(y_{t-1} - x_{t-1})$ will be a negative number written in symbolic form as $(y_{t-1} - x_{t-1}) < 0$. A rule of multiplication says that a negative number multiplied by another negative number gives a positive number. If an agency pads its requests, however, it presumably follows a cut with a new request which incorporates an additional amount to make allowance for future cuts. In order to represent this behavior, that is to come out with a positive result incorporating the concept of padding, the unknown coefficient β_2 must be negative $(\beta_2 < 0)$.
6. The agency that favors its own programs should increase its requests over time. In the absence of the stochastic disturbance (when the random variable is 0), the request in a given year should be larger than the request in the previous year so that $x_t > {t-1}$. Therefore, the unknown coefficient β_2 must be larger than one $(\beta_3 > 1)$ since it multiplies last year's request.
7. Other gaming strategies are easily proposed. Suppose, for example, that a given

agency believes that it knows the decision rule that Congress uses in dealing with it, and that this decision rule can be represented by one of (4), (7), or (8), above. Presume, for reasons analogous to those outlined for (8), that this agency desires to take into account that positive or negative portion of the previous year's appropriation y_{t-1} that was not based on the previous year's request x_{t-1}. This consideration suggests

$$x_t = \beta_4 y_{t-1} + \beta_5 \Delta_{t-1} + \delta_t$$

as an agency decision rule where Δ_{t-1} is a dummy variable representing in year $t - 1$ the term not involving x_{t-1} in one of (4), (7) or (8) above. If one believes that agency and Bureau of the Budget personnel are sufficiently well acquainted with the senators and congressmen to be able to predict the value of the current stochastic disturbance, then it becomes reasonable to examine a decision rule of the form

$$x_t = \beta_6 y_{t-1} + \beta_7 \Delta_t + \sigma_t$$

where σ_t is defined as above. No evidence of either form of behavior was found, however, among the agencies that were investigated. We also estimated the parameters of the third order auto-regressive scheme for the requests of an individual agency

$$x_t + \beta_8 x_{t-1} + \beta_9 t_{-2} + \beta_{10} t_{-3} + \gamma_t$$

in an attempt to discover if naive models would fit as well as those above. In no case did this occur and generally the fits for this model were very poor. A similar scheme was estimated for the appropriations y_t of an individual agency with similar results with respect to equations (4), (7) and (8) above. Since the "d" statistic suggests that no higher order Markov process would be successful, no other rules for agency behavior were tried.

8. Agency proposals to the Bureau of the Budget are not reported to the public and could be obtained only for these eight sub-agencies.

9. Three interrelated difficulties arise in the analysis of the time series data x_t, y_t for an agency. The first problem is the choice of a technique for estimating the parameters of the alternative schemes in some optimal fashion. Given these estimates and their associated statistics, the second problem is the choice of criteria for selecting the model best specifying the system underlying the data. Finally, one is faced with the problem of examining the variability of the underlying parameters of the best specification. We believe that our solution to these problems, while far from optimal, is satisfactory given the present state of econometric knowledge. See our presentation in "On the Process of Budgeting: An Empirical Study of Congressional Appropriations," by Otto Davis, M. A. H. Dempster, and Aaron Wildavsky, to appear in Gordon Tullock (ed.), *Papers on Non-Market Decision Making*, Thomas Jefferson Center, University of Virginia. See especially section 4 and the appendix by Dempster, which contains discussions and derivations of estimation procedures, selection criteria and test statistics for the processes in Section II of this paper.

10. We make the assumption that these two disturbances are independent throughout the paper. Notice, however, that dependence between the disturbances explicitly enters decision equation (8) of section II and those of footnote 7. For these equations, the assumption refers to the disturbance of the current year. That is, we allow the possibility that special circumstances may affect a single participant (Bureau of the Budget or Congress) as well as both. When the latter case occurred, our selection criteria resulted in the choice of equation (8) as best specifying Congressional behavior.

11. We are estimating the unknown values of the coefficients (or parameters) of regression equations for each agency. All of our estimators are biased. We use biased

estimators for the simple reason that no unbiased estimators are known. The property of consistency is at least a small comfort. All of our estimators are consistent. It might be noted that all unbiased estimators are consistent, but not all consistent estimators are unbiased.

12. This statistic is known as the Durbin-Watson ratio. A description of the test may be found in J. Johnston, *Econometric Methods* (New York, 1963), p. 92.

13. H. Theil and A. L. Nagar, "Testing the Independence of Regressional Disturbances," *Journal of the American Statistical Association*, 56 (1961), 793–806. These significance points were used to construct further significance points when necessary. See Davis, Dempster, and Wildavsky, *op. cit.*

14. The test is described in T. W. Anderson, *An Introduction to Multivariate Analysis* (New York, 1958) pp. 69–71. See Dempster's appendix to Davis, Dempster, and Wildavsky, *op. cit.*, for some justification of the use of the test.

15. See Davis, Dempster, and Wildavsky, *op. cit.*

16. G. C. Chow, "Tests of Equality between Sets of Coefficients in Two Linear Regressions," *Econometrica*, 28 (1960), 591–605, and the appendix to Davis, Dempster, and Wildavsky, *op. cit.*

17. In a few instances an inspection of the residuals indicated that a shift point occurred so early or so late in the series that it was not possible to compute a meaningful stationarity F-Statistic. In these few cases the deviant observations were dropped and the usual analysis performed on the shortened time series. Thus we "forced" a break in every case in order to perform subsequent operations.

18. The apparent discrepancy between the latter part of Table 3 and Table 1 is caused by the fact that for two agencies, the Bureau of the Census and the Office of Education, although the Agency–Bureau of the Budget decision equations are temporally stable and best specified as (1), when a shift point is forced, the criteria indicate (3) for the latter period.

19. Some of the shift points appeared to occur so early in the series that it was not possible to calculate a correlation coefficient.

20. The importance of analyzing deviant cases is suggested in: Milton M. Gordon, "Sociological Law and the Deviant Case," *Sociometry*, 10 (1947); Patricia Kendall and Katharine Wolf, "The Two Purposes of Deviant Case Analysis," in Paul F. Lazarsfeld and Morris Rosenberg (eds.), *The Language of Social Research*, (Glencoe, 1962), pp. 103–137; Paul Horst, *The Prediction of Personal Adjustment: A Survey of the Logical Problems and Research Techniques* (New York, 1941); and Seymour Lipset, Martin Trow, and James Coleman, *Union Democracy* (New York, 1960).

21. We are indebted to Rose M. Kelly, a graduate student in the Department of Political Science, University of California, Berkeley, who did the research on the deviant cases and provided the data for Tables 6 and 7.

22. See Wildavsky, *op. cit.*, pp. 64–68, for a discussion of clientele and confidence. In his forthcoming book, *The Power of the Purse* (Boston, 1966), Richard Fenno provides further evidence of the usefulness of these categories.

23. Geoffrey P. E. Clarkson, *Portfolio Selection: A Simulation of Trust Investment* (Englewood Cliffs, N. J., 1962); G. P. E. Clarkson and H. A. Simon, "Simulation of Indiviudal and Group Behavior," *American Economic Review*, 50 (1960), 920–932; Richard Cyert and James March (eds.). *A Behavioral Theory of the Firm* (Englewood Cliffs, N. J., 1963); Allen Newell, "The Chess Machine: An Example of Dealing with a Complex Task by Adaptation," *Proceedings of the Western Joint Computer Conference* (1955), pp. 101–108; Allen Newell, J. C. Shaw, and H. A. Simon, "Elements of a Theory of Human Problem Solving," *Psychological Review*, 65 (1958), 151–166; Allen Newell and H. A. Simon, "The Logic Theory Machine: A Complex Information Processing System,"

Transactions on Information Theory (1956), 61–79; W. R. Reitman, "Programming Intelligent problem Solvers," *Transactions on Human Factors in Electronics*, HFE-2 (1961), pp. 26–33; H. A. Simon, "A Behavioral Model of Rational Choice," *Quarterly Journal of Economics*, 60 (1955), 99–118; and H. A. Simon, "Theories of Decision Making in Economics and Behavioral Science," *American Economic Review*, 49 (1959), 253–283.

24. David Braybrooke and Charles Lindblom, *A Strategy of Decision* (New York, 1964).

25. Wildavsky, *op. cit.*, pp. 8–63.

26. James March, "The Power of Power," in David Easton, editor, *Varieties of Political Theory* (Englewood Cliffs, N. J., 1966), pp. 39–70.

27. See the forthcoming studies by John P. Crecine on budgeting in Pittsburgh, Detroit and Cleveland, and by Donald Gerwin on the Pittsburgh School District. Aaron Wildavsky will attempt to apply variations of the models in this paper to Oakland, California.

28. Aaron Wildavsky, "Private Markets and Public Arenas," *The American Behavioral Scientist*, vol. 9 no. 7. (Sept. 1965), pp. 33–39.

3A.3. Policy and Priority in the Budgetary Process

PETER B. NATCHEZ and IRVIN C. BUPP

The incrementalist thesis challenged an extensive literature in political science ac-
cording to which budgets were formed through considerable political conflict, and so
would change with shifts in the power and influence of competing groups. In this
reading, Natchez and Bupp argue that the incrementalist thesis is overstated and that
the strong results achieved by Dempster, Davis, and Wildavsky are due to the particu-
lar data and methods they used.

While not denying that there is some truth to the concept of incrementalism, the
authors attempt to show that budgets are also determined by the sort of political
struggles that political scientists have always thought important. They argue that
incrementalists miss this struggle because of the type of evidence they use and the way
they analyze it. Especially important is the fact that incrementalists focus on agencies
rather than on programs. They thus miss the fact that programs within an agency may
have very different fates, even when the amount received by the agency as a whole
varies little over time. They also show that the fate of a program is affected by the
direction of even small changes—upward or downward—and whether growth is
steady or intermittent. They also demonstrate that rather small year-to-year changes
can amount to very large changes over time.

The authors seek to prove their point by examining programs within the Atomic
Energy Commission. They first demonstrate that the change in the Commission's
budget over time fits the pattern identified by Davis, Dempster, and Wildavsky. Then
they devise prosperity scores to measure the relative success of different programs
within the agency and show that in the 1958-1972 period the different programs had
markedly different budget histories. They attribute this to the importance of entrepre-
neurial political activity by both agency leaders and outside political actors.

Reprinted with permission of the author from *The American Political Science Review* 67, 3
(September 1973), pp. 951–63. Copyright 1973 by the American Political Science Association.

Politics and the budgetary process

By an impressive margin the federal government spends more money, does more things, and affects more people than it did twenty-five, or even ten, years ago. But the record of innovation and expansion has not been uniform; rather the prosperity of individual programs has varied widely during this period. Some programs have continuously prospered, grown, and evidently become permanent fixtures in the governmental system: farm commodity supports, highway construction, Social Security, and, most recently, health care. Others seem to have thrived only temporarily: aircraft nuclear propulsion, manned space flight, and the "Green Berets"; while still others have an uneven history of success and failure and are constantly involved in political turmoil: AID, Model Cities, and the Atomic Energy Commission's "Plowshare" program.

What is responsible for the success or failure of governmental programs? Who (or what) determines our national priorities? Political scientists have long regarded the budgetary process as the richest source of evidence on these matters. The assumption has been that the budgetary process, the most important "action forcing" mechanism in government, reflects the aspirations and controversies which cause some programs to be favored over others. Within the budgetary process clashes of interest and priority should be expressed in real dollar terms. Evidence concerning the goals of program directors and clients, the support of agency heads, the surveillance of the Office of Management and Budget (formerly the Bureau of the Budget), the strategic choices of the president, and the influence of Congress should all be contained in the data generated annually by the federal budget cycle.[1]

More recent quantitative analyses of the federal budgetary process do not, however, support these assumptions. Instead, a younger generation of political scientists has discovered "striking regularities" indicating that what happens in any given year closely resembles what had happened in the previous year.[2] Implicit in this approach is the view that the strategic and tactical choices, the interagency disputes and alliances, the battles with the Office of Management and Budget (OMB), and the appeals for presidential support, all make very little difference. In the end what happens during any given period pretty much determines what will happen in subsequent periods.

There is, of course, an important element of truth in these findings. Administrative budgets are not rewritten from scratch every year; and it is a little silly to judge the consequences of policy innovations as if they were. Further, it is undoubtedly true that political historians (and public administrators) often exaggerate the importance of particular policies, choices, and competing personalities. After all, they find the business of public administration interesting precisely because it embodies great controversies between powerful forces—conflicts which seem both to be inherent in and to shed light upon the process of popular government.

Still, the gap between traditional and quantitative approaches to the budget remains. It is not enough to dismiss the conclusions of the older school out of hand, as the product of too much enthusiasm for public administration and the inevitable result of unsystematic research. Much of the traditional literature comes from men who in fact have served in government—participant observers, if you will—and their description of the central role of the budgetary process as a policy vehicle is important if only because that is what they saw happening. The challenge of the quantitative budget studies is precisely over the question of how much public policy is embedded in the budgetary process. Their argument is that administrators rarely depart significantly from what they are already doing. They "muddle through" as best they can, making only marginal changes in the established operations of government. Consequently, agency budgets are massively stable from one year to the next.[3] Bureaucratic behavior and the budgets that result from it seem to reduce to a simple set of operating principles that, at the same time, leave no room for other explanations.

> The most striking fact about the equations [which describe the budgetary process] is their simplicity. This is perhaps partly because of the possibility that more complicated decision procedures are reserved for special circumstances represented by extreme values of the random variable. However, the fact that the decision rules generally fit the data very well is an indication that these simple questions have considerable explanatory power. Little of the variance is left unexplained.[4]

In the end, this line of reasoning may yet provide a new and strong foundation for the study of public administration. However, it may be also that the relationship between public policy and the budgetary process has been obscured by the way the problem has been quantified.

The theme of this essay is that the political choices and conflicts inherent in the administration of government have been unnecessary casualties of the quantitative revolution. The problem is essentially one of theory. After reviewing the theoretical underpinnings of the quantitative budget studies we will suggest an alternative approach to the manipulation of budgetary data, developing along the way a methodology that will uncover controversies over policy and priorities.

The incremental model of budgeting

The budgets of federal agencies are developed over a period which begins as much as eighteen months before appropriations requests are acted upon by the Congress. During this period agency budgets are typically formulated to meet the guidelines establishd by the OMB speaking for the president and his administration. The initial budgets normally undergo a sequence of successive reductions and appeals often culminating in a presidential review.

The budgetary process itself is composed of six stages, though the precise pattern that is followed may vary slightly by agency and department, particularly in the final stages of appeal and presidential review. The process begins with the budget guidelines that are sent down by the OMB. These are deliberately varied from year to year so as to communicate to the bureaucracy a sense of limited resources and to direct attention to items that happen to be of particular concern to the administration. Usually agencies will respond to the OMB by preparing "flash estimates" or "preview budgets." These budgets serve to begin the process of negotiation, and, in the weeks that follow, a series of informal estimates are established indicating how much expansion is likely to be considered reasonable in light of the administration's priorities.

On the basis of this information, the agency's comptroller begins to aggregate budget requests from the operating divisions within the department or agency. Of course, division requests regularly exceed the amount of money that, according to the OMB, will be available. Hence these estimates are worked over by the comptroller with an eye towards bringing them in line with administration expectations.

The comptroller's recommendations along with each division's request constitute the material from which an agency budget is produced. It is during this part of the process that competition *within* the agency (or department) reaches its greatest intensity. Each division struggles for funds against the budgetary interest of the other operating divisions, each trying to avoid the heavy hand of the comptroller by shifting the burden of budgetary cuts to some other division's programs.

The easiest way for a division to protect itself is, of course, to gain the support of the department secretary or agency chairman. But the competition for funds often extends beyond the administrative framework in which the operating divisions are located. Thus, it is not unusual to find program directors drawing in other elements of government—congressmen, other bureaus and departments, consultants, lobbyists, etc.—in order to gain some vital budgetary advantage. (Admiral Rickover, for one, was so skilled at managing his congressional support that he operated virtually outside the normal review procedures of the AEC.) The department or agency must now produce a series of budgetary settlements that compromise the demands of its working parts along with the push and pull of external political forces while, of course, trying to hold to OMB guidelines.

The budgetary outcomes at this stage of the process become formal requests to the president for funding and are sent to the OMB for review. Acting "in accordance with the President's program,"[5] the OMB "marks up" each budget, item by item, program by program—cutting away wherever it can, accepting other requests as submitted, and occasionally, adding money to some project that the administration looks upon with special favor. For the managers of the federal bureaucracy, this is the most difficult part of the process, because it threatens to unbalance the blend of policies and priorities that has been arranged among a department's working parts. Yet the entire thrust of the OMB at this point is to attack budget requests that have produced unnecessary and expensive settlements. Budgets then are normally marked up with a heavy hand and returned to those who wrote them for reconsideration.

Here the agency or department has a choice: it can accept the OMB's actions as they stand or it can appeal to the OMB for some measure of restoration. It is important to note here that any further budgetary action by either the president or the OMB occurs only over contested items in the budget. Those items not disputed by the OMB or subsequently returned to the OMB by appeal are regarded as a settled part of the administration's budget. Thus, the budget is now agreed upon for the most part with only a small number of controversies remaining.

The OMB reconsiders those matters that are still disputed and again leaves the agency or department with a choice. Again the decision of the OMB can be accepted, thus settling the matter. There is, however, also the alternative of appealing the OMB's final action directly to the president. It is understood that each agency chairman or department secretary can argue for restorations directly before the president, much like a knight pleading before his king for special favor. The president's decision, of course, ends the process and the results are printed up and sent along to Congress (where specific issues can be reopened). Several things ought to be noted about the presidential budgetary reviews. The first is that this stage is centered on specific budgetary items and does not usually include a general review of the agency's or department's budget. Second, it is in these last stages of appeals that the budgetary process varies most widely. These variations usually reflect the relative stature of particular branches of government. (Thus military budgets, for example, have a preferred status in the appeal process.) Also, it is at this point that the standing of the department's chief administrator is determined. It is he who must go before the president and argue for funds that are presumably vital to his department's functions. Consequently, the degree of success that he has with the president is widely regarded as an evaluation of his administrative worth and, at the same time, a measure of the importance that agency or department has in the administration.

By design, then, the budgetary process produces a climate of scarcity in which the success of those who participate is measured by the number of dollars they are able to win. Indeed, the entire process of formulating budgets within agencies plays upon the institutional interests of bureaucrats so as to produce the explicit competition between alternative "policies."[6]

This competition among alternative programs seems to have been all but lost in the work of Davis, Dempster, and Wildavsky. These scholars have argued that budgets are produced by relatively straightforward incremental strategies and hence are not often an especially interesting source of conflict, not to mention change and innovation.[7] Specifically, they have examined the variations in fifty-six nondefense federal agencies from 1947 to 1963 and discovered that they can be explained very simply by a "set of simple decision rules that are linear and temporally stable."[8] In their most sophisticated equation (decision rule), Davis, Dempster, and Wildavsky argue that the congressional appropriation of any agency is

. . . a fixed mean percentage of the agency's request for a certain year plus a fixed mean percentage of a dummy variable which represents that part of the agency's request for the year at issue which is not part of the appropriation or request of the previous year plus a random variable representing the part of the appropriation or request of the previous year plus a random variable representing the part of the appropriation attributable to the special circumstances of the year.[9]

This is to say that appropriations subcommittees normally give an agency some proportion of what it asked for, adjusted by things in dispute and special considerations peculiar to a particular year.

The point that Davis, Dempster, and Wildavsky most emphasize is that their decision rules fit the data: ". . . the results are very good. We leave very little of the variance statistically unexplained."[10] In fact, for the majority of congressional decisions (appropriations) their equations yield R^2s exceeding 99 per cent, and for all but two show R^2s above 90 per cent. Further, these decision rules seem to square neatly with other research which suggests that the budgetary process in appropriations subcommittees has become an institutionalized series of actions sanctioned by an elaborate set of norms and behaviors.[11]

The creative insights upon which Wildavsky and others have built are contained in the writings of Herbert Simon and his colleagues.[12] The theme of this work is that people are quite limited in their ability to process new information, generate alternatives, anticipate consequences, and weigh values. The Simon-Lindblom administrator faces a highly complicated world, a world of multiple values and goals related to each other in unknown ways. He has no very reliable way of predicting the consequences of alternative courses of action and little information pertinent to assessing these consequences even if he had an acceptable theory. As Crecine has put it,

> [He] is a man with limited knowledge, limited information, and limited cognitive ability, making a policy choice in an uncertain world by "drastically" simplifying the problem and making marginal adjustments in past "successful" policies to formulate current policies.[13]

The phrase that captures the essence of the administrative situation is "organized complexity."[14] And nowhere are its consequences more apparent than in the making of budgets. The budgetary process is, after all, a complicated procedure in which officials are usually under the intense pressure of time and circumstance. One expects that whatever decision rules have worked in the past will be used again in the solving of current disputes. Indeed, one does not expect the level of disagreement to be very high, because individual administrators can be expected to request funds for what they are already doing, give or take a little bit.

These observations are all quite true as far as they go. Across aggregations of decision-making units (federal agencies, municipal administrations or individual budget-makers), behavior at time "T" can be shown to be a robust function of comparable behavior at "T − 1." What is striking is that administrative behavior is so very similar in all sorts of diverse organizations. State governments, business organizations, labor unions, organizations of every sort seem to promote the same sort of responses from those who administer them, responses that are rationalized in budgetary processes that do not seem to vary widely in effect from organization to organization.[15]

The trouble is that in politics the budgetary process, while certainly responding to the requirements of administrative life, is also a battlefield for conflicting priorities and alternative policies. The categories of analysis established by Wildavsky, Crecine, and others help us to understand the behavior of the pertinent decision maker as he attempts to resolve the problems that he faces. But this line of reasoning does not shed much light upon the sort of things which over time cause some activities to become the continuing policies of government while others fade and are discarded. It is this variation in the *competitive* success of alternative *programs*, rather than the cognitive processes of decision makers, which is central to the politics of public administration. It is this aspect of government that the "problem solving" perspective is inherently unable to explain.

Let us stress again that we are not quarreling with descriptions of administrative behavior. Quite to the contrary, our argument is premised on the findings of Simon, Lindblom, Cyert and March, and Wildavsky. Administrators in complex organizations *behave similarly*. However, accounting for these patterns of administrative behavior—itself vital to the science of public administration—is not the focus of our problem. We want to explain why some programs are repeatedly funded while others are considerably less successful, *given* that the behavior of their administrators is likely to be quite similar. This is to say that we are looking at a diffferent level of public administration. Our focus is not on the behavior of administrators, *per se*, but on administrators as they are organized in terms of policy output, programs as they compete for dollars.

In a sense budget data present us with a measurement problem: *How are yearly government budgetary figures reordered so that they indicate policy choices and public priorities?* This is by no means an easy question to answer. For the budget reflects simultaneously a yearly *process of administration* and decisions among *alternative political priorities*. That is, budgets are at once measures of the way government is organized and of the policy decisions that the organization implements. Obviously, these are not the same things although they are nested within the very same data.

The fact that political choices and the budgetary process are so completely intertwined accounts for much of the confusion among approaches to public administration. What has happened is that the traditional scholars have spoken of public administration without placing it within the context of an annual, stable budgetary process. Thus, they have tended to write about policy as if that were the only thing that government was producing. In discovering that there is, in fact, a budgetary process in administration, younger and more quantitatively trained researchers assumed that the process of government, in addition to producing budgets, produced settlements on questions of public policy. Here the quantitative approach was a victim of its own theoretical and statistical precision. The budgetary process models worked so well that there simply did not seem to be anything left to explain.

The reason for the great statistical success of the quantitative budget studies lies in the fact that *agencies* were taken as the unit of analysis, yearly budget cycles being nothing more than replications of the same event over time. These data yielded to Wildavsky and his associates a simple set of equations (decision rules) that, by and large, seemed to describe how public policy is formulated while reserving more complex and sophisticated political strategies for a small number of "deviant cases." What has been captured—quite accurately—by this formulation is the great stability of the administrative structure of government. But because administrative categories have formed the basis of budgetary analysis, the entire process in which public policy is produced has been obscured.[16]

The first step, then, in untangling information on policy choices from data on the administration of government is to shift the level of analysis for agencies and departments to programs. This is to say that in the context of the budgetary process, programs are the operating units of public policy, that they provide "categories that are closer to being true outputs [of government] than the older categories."[17]

It should be noted, however, that it is difficult to make explicit comparisons *between* program budgets (although even with the data in this form a great deal can be done).[18] Programs vary widely in their scope, size, and content, and these differences are unfortunately reflected in their budgets. The amount of money necessary to fund a strong cancer research program differs substantially from the funding necessary to lift the incomes of the elderly above the "poverty line." Similarly, reducing the army's manpower budget by 100 million dollars has a markedly different effect from taking the same number of dollars away from OEO. In a fundamental way, then, all budgetary dollars are not equal; and while all policy outcomes are expressed in terms of dollars, some care must be taken to make this information commensurate across programs. This is to argue that merely shifting to programs as the basis of policy analysis is not in itself sufficient, that budgetary data organized by programs must themselves be transformed so that the relative prosperity of programs in the policy process can be measured and compared.

It should be added, finally, that programs have histories of support and opposition, and focusing explicitly on them returns this dimension to budgetary analyses. Agencies (or departments) usually do not have such histories associated with them (except in their first years of operation). They are normally accepted as part of the fixed institutional landscape, terrain that seems to change dramatically only during periods of great crisis and political turmoil. An important lesson of the Eisenhower and Nixon Administrations is that changing the party in power does not open up already establishd agencies to direct attack. However, the relative priorities for programs within an agency (and even the relative standing of the agency as a whole) do vary quite widely from administration to administration, even though the agency continues as an established part of government.

Thus, the salient characteristic of established agencies and departments is their stability—both organizational and budgetary. And again, it is this aspect of government that Wildavsky and others have captured so well. Yet within departmental and agency boundaries (and occasionally between them, e.g., the case of OEO) there is a constant struggle by program directors, lobbyists, congressmen, state and local politicians, and White House personnel to fund new ideas and to continue the funding of old ones. It is a competition that draws to it people and institutions with radically different ideas and purposes, and that decides, in the end, what public policies we are to have.

From this perspective the struggle to establish new public policies looks very much like the competitive ideal in nineteenth century capitalism. Entrepreneurs—"policy entrepreneurs," if you will—seek scarce resources for their programs. In their quest for funding and political authority, they use every available weapon: pressure from various constituencies and groups, aggressive selling inside government, attracting congressmen as innovators or as protectors (congressmen who in turn often lobby other congressmen), pressuring the White House as well as receiving pressure from the White House, and so on through a diverse range of opportunities and strategies. The fact that political strategies vary widely as a result of the peculiar combination of resources that happens to be available probably explains why "the case study method" of public administration was never able to produce a cogent set of generalizations. But this should not be taken as evidence that there is no struggle, that the process is one of slow, incremental change. Rather it suggests that the policy process in the United States is an open one where all sorts of influences are at play, and where—because the process is a long and complex one (six stages plus congressional action over more than eighteen months)—the competition between policies is reinforced and accentuated.

The case of the AEC

To make these thoughts more concrete, let us turn to the activities of a particular federal agency: the Atomic Energy Commission. Though now a mature agency with established purposes and programs, the AEC was created and in many ways has continued to exist in an atmosphere of uncertainty and conflict about the appropriate applications of a new and poorly understood technology.[19] Was nuclear technology to be applied exclusively to the development of weapons? Or were its applications ultimately to be essentially civilian and peaceful? Could peaceful applications be carried out with economy and safety? By whom, and under whose supervision? These and other questions have defined areas of sharp conflict among philosophies of government and among programs and personalities. The early history of these disputes has been compiled and is presently being published as a multivolume study of the Atomic Energy Commission.[20] A definitive account of the programs and controversies that developed over the years within the AEC, this material provides a rich historical context against which we can examine the AEC's activities as they are reflected in the agency's budgetary records. Perhaps more important, however, are the specific characteristics of the actual budgetary records upon which we have been able to draw. First, we have been able to identify and trace the histories in whole or in part of twenty-three distinct AEC programs during the period of 1958–1972. While these programs do not represent an exhaustive categorization of all AEC activities, they are all "real" programs as distinct from mere projects on the one hand or "accounting categories" on the other. The twenty-three identified programs are mutually exclusive but are not exhaustive of all Commission activities, comprising on the average about 90 per cent of any given year's total AEC operating budget.[21]

Second, within each of the fifteen "budget cycles," FY 1958–FY 1972, we have isolated six discrete stages beginning with the program divisions' requests to the Commission's general manager and ending with the official presidential budget for a given year. The intermediate stages represent the general manager's recommendation to the Commission; the Commission's "September" submission to the Administration; the OMB's "mark-up" of the submission, and the "appeal" of the "mark-up," either to the Office of Management and Budget or the president.[22] Consider now the data reflected in Table 1.

In Table 1 we have ignored the programmatic breakdown of the fifteen AEC budgets and have simply correlated the requests for allocations for each stage across the fiscal cycles for which we have data. For these fifteen observations, the funds requested at a given stage correlate almost perfectly with that requested at a previous stage and that granted at a subsequent stage. The perfection of these correlations is powerful support for Wildavsky's basic argument about the regularities of the budgetary process, but it suggests very little about the political conflicts which we *know* were taking place during the period spanned by this data. For, within this apparently stable framework, five substantial AEC programs were cancelled altogether, two major activities experienced a sharp monotonic decline in their fortunes, three grew impressively, and most others fluctuated widely. Moreover, the picture is not very much different at the program than at the agency level.

When requests and allocations are correlated at the program level there is on the whole less close association across stages but the average magnitude of the correlation coefficients is still quite high. Most are in the .80–.90 range, and out of twenty-three programs only four show associations of less than .70 between pairs of stages. So, even at places where conflict is *known* to have occurred, the budgetary process perspective merely uncovers "striking regularities." Simply changing the units of analysis, that is to say, does not uncover the underlying political competition that structures the process of policy formulation; a more profound change is required.

It is at this point that we come to manipulating budgetary data themselves, to transforming dollars so that they will better reflect the competitive struggle for growth, for continued (or renewed) prosperity. The elements that we have to work

Table 1

Correlations Between Budgetary Stages for 23 AEC Programs Pooled Across FY 1958–FY 1962

	Division	General manager	AEC	OMB	Appeal	Presidential
Division	1.000					
General manager	.996	1.000				
AEC	.997	.999	1.000			
OMB	.995	.998	.997	1.000		
Appeal	.996	.997	.997	.998	1.000	
Final	.995	.996	.997	.998	.999	1.000

with are: the agency in which programs operate (i.e., the administrative context), the past success or failure of a program in obtaining funds, and the action that is taken on program requests as they pass through the budgetary cycle (i.e., a program budget from initial request to final presidential decision).[23] The raw data, of course, come in the form of absolute dollar levels of programs from year to year. And it is by transforming and recombining these data that we hope to create an "index of prosperity" which will reflect the relative political success or failure of programs as they compete for scarce resources. Such an index has to meet two different problems of comparability.[24]

The first has to do with the variation in the total AEC operating budget between FY 1958 and FY 1972, which was, of course, by no means constant over that period. In Table 2 below, we have computed the sum at each stage of the twenty-three programs on which we have calculated data. It varies from year to year, ranging from a low of $2006.3 million in FY 1967 to a high of $2568.5 million in FY 1963.[25]

It seems reasonable to argue that programs are equally prosperous only if each preserves its proportion of the total even as the total changes *both* from year to year *and* across the stages of budgetary process. A first step, then, toward operationalizing the notion of "prosperity" is to divide all program allocations at all stages by the total for that stage. This procedure, however, leads to a second problem of comparability.

There is great variation in the absolute magnitude of program budgets. Among the twenty-three AEC programs for which we have data, several have budgets in the $5–10 million range, and a few have budgets that were greater than $400 million. The obvious consequence is that each of the smaller programs is a tiny proportion of the total agency budget and is thus "lost" for analytical purposes. For example, one of the most politically controversial AEC programs is "Plowshare," a project to develop nonweapons applications for nuclear explosives. This program has never commanded more than one per cent of the total Commission budget.

Table 2

Total at Each Budget Stage for 23 AEC Programs (in $ millions)

Fiscal year	Division request	General manager	Commission	OMB	Appeal	Final
1958	2170.9	2059.1	2199.1	2081.2	2083.2	2076.6
1959	2414.9	2235.4	2267.9	2253.9	2253.9	2252.3
1960	2575.7	2501.7	2510.9	2447.5	2472.7	2451.0
1961	2494.3	2409.6	2368.8	2206.6	2310.3	2296.4
1962	2538.7	2499.2	2491.1	2285.3	2306.5	2343.0
1963	2586.2	2428.7	2447.5	2389.8	2592.3	2568.5
1964	2781.2	2468.5	2586.6	2366.7	2548.3	2381.4
1965	2505.1	2428.1	2447.0	2294.5	2283.1	2239.6
1966	2323.8	2251.4	2257.4	2104.0	2195.3	2129.1
1967	2213.6	2098.1	2118.2	1986.0	2034.4	2006.3
1968	2399.9	1999.1	2110.1	2005.8	2053.6	2026.4
1969	2438.2	2272.8	2269.8	2151.7	2225.3	2180.5
1970	2376.0	2238.9	2274.4	2104.8	2169.9	2037.4
1971	2469.4	2285.1	2303.9	2024.4	2121.0	2013.7
1972	2420.7	2179.5	2150.7	1962.6	1990.2	1980.5

We need to normalize the percentages obtained by dividing each program budget by the appropriate total so that these small programs are not made to seem insignificant out of sheer tininess. To adjust for this problem we have first calculated for each budget stage a program's *mean* proportion of the total for that stage across either (a) all the years spanned by our data, or (b) when a program began or was cancelled within that period, the years during which the program existed. We have then divided a program proportion of the total for each stage/ year by this mean and multiplied the quotient by 100, converting to a percentage. The effect is to normalize these percentages so that they average 100 for the period FY 1958–FY 1972, or, when appropriate, for the years a program existed. We believe that the characteristics of this index and its behavior over time are highly suggestive of the process of competitive growth, i.e., "prosperity" in which we are interested. Eventually we shall want to use "prosperity change scores." This is the numerical difference of the prosperity scores across years for a given stage and will be zero when a program's proportion of the stage total does not change over the years.

At this point, it is useful to state these arguments more formally. For a full array of budget observations for programs over a number of years across each budget stage, $D_{(i,j,k)}$, where

i = programs (1–23 in the case of the AEC),
j = a specified budget stage (1–6),

k = years,

T = Total agency budget for the sum of all programs

the corresponding array of prosperity scores, $P_{(i,j,k)}$ is defined as:

$$P_{(i,j,k)} = (Pr_{(i,j,k)}/\text{mean } p_{(i,j)})*100$$

where

$$\text{(a) } Pr_{(i,j,k)} = D_{(i,j,k)}/T_{(j,k)}$$

for

$$T_{(j,k)} = \sum_{i-1}^{23} D_{(i,j,k)}',$$

and where

$$\text{(b) mean } p_{(i,k)} = Tp_{(i,j)}/Ic_{(i,j)}'$$

for

$$Tp_{(i,j)} = \sum_{k-1}^{15} Pr_{(i,j,k)}',$$

and

$Ic_{(i,j)}$ = the number of years for which the ith program in the jth stage >0.

In Table 3 we present the scores for four programs within the AEC, all of which show striking variance in prosperity. In fact, all twenty-three programs exhibited a lively and theoretically interesting variance, but limitations of space preclude discussing them all.[26]

We see quite vividly the growth, decay, and fluctuation of which we have spoken—all within the context of a roughly constant total budget. These variations were caused by political events, not the operation of a budgetary process. The sudden reversals in the fortunes of "Rover" were caused by various officials of three administrations having attached sharply different priorities to the undertaking. The competitive success of high energy physics resulted in part from the constant attention of the Atomic Energy Commission Chairman with a strong interest in pure research. High energy physics did not grow "accidentally" or "naturally"—indeed none of these curves represents any sort of "natural process." On the contrary, each is the record of a sequence of priority settings made within a political system. Programs do not naturally grow, decline, or remain

Table 3

Four AEC Program Histories Expressed as "Prosperity Scores"

Fiscal Year	Rover (Nuclear Space Rocket)	High Energy Physics	Sherwood (Controlled Thermonuclear Research)	Nuclear Weapons (Research, Development and Production)
1958	25	20	87	69
1959	19	25	95	75
1960	28	34	130	67
1961	34	36	95	68
1962	56	51	88	80
1963	128	82	86	94
1964	187	118	83	92
1965	165	107	80	109
1966	174	122	92	105
1967	173	144	103	104
1968	131	149	108	110
1969	145	147	109	122
1970	103	156	114	129
1971	94	154	123	133
1972	33	150	97	136

constant, or anything else. They are caused to do all of these by politicians and administrators making often difficult choices among competing claims upon scarce resources.

This "authoritative allocation of values" is the essence of the political process, that is vividly portrayed in these prosperity scores. The relative stability of "Sherwood" (controlled thermonuclear research) is not an illustration of organizational process in Lindblom's terms.[27] Sherwood has remained constant, has *resisted* competing claims upon its share of the Commission budget, only because it has been supported by the Commission, the Office of Management and Budget, and the president. Its constant level of prosperity is an indicator of stable political support, not of the operation of some "budgetary constant." Its support could have evaporated completely much like the nuclear rocket program's (Rover)—a program which received high priority in the early years of the Kennedy administration only to be completely abandoned.

Alternatively, consider the history of weapons. This has been a truly prosperous enterprise and one with an especially suggestive administrative history. The circumstances surrounding the 1950 presidential decision to build thermonuclear bombs left the Atomic Energy Commission with little influence over the future of this program.[28] The function of the Commission came to be one of merely fulfilling requirements for nuclear explosives in the establishment of which it played no role. The AEC, that is, played no role in setting the priority of weapons

Table 4

Arithmetic Mean of Prosperity Change Scores, FY 1958–FY 1972, 23 AEC Programs (Presidential Budget)

Rank	Program	Mean	Rank	Program	Mean
1	High Energy Physics	9.0	13	Sherwood	0.57
2	Nuclear Safety	8.1	14	Rover	.43
3	Program Direction and Administration	7.1	15	Euratom	.08
4	General Reactor Technology	6.1	16	Training, Education and Information	−2.2
5	Biology and Medicine	5.4	17	Advanced Systems	−2.8
6	Cooperative Power	5.1	18	Special Nuclear Materials	−3.5
7	Weapons	4.5	19	Pluto	−4.0
8	Naval Reactors	4.5	20	Army Reactors	−7.0
9	Civilian Power	4.3	21	Merchant Ship	−7.7
10	SNAP	4.1	22	Raw Materials	−13.6
11	Plowshare	3.5	23	Aircraft Nuclear Propulsion	−25.6
12	Isotopes	3.3			

relative to other nuclear activities or among types of weapons. The competition for resources among the latter took place with the relative priority of weapons already set by forces external to the Commission. The weapons program record of continuous prosperity is largely the story of the consequences of the actions taken in 1950. The program emerged from the "great thermonuclear debate" with a very real competitive advantage over other AEC programs. Weapons was a "stronger" program."[29]

These measures of prosperity permit us to summarize AEC program activities since 1956. We could, of course, just subtract a given program's prosperity in FY 1958 from its score in the FY 1972 and rank the program according to the numerical value of the result. The "net prosperity change" is not, however, an especially helpful number. Now, we can recover exactly the same rank ordering by working instead with "prosperity change scores." For any program, the mean of the distribution of these change scores across all fifteen yearly intervals is also an indicator of how that program has prospered during the period for which we have data. The numerical value of these indicators, moreover, has an instantly appealing interpretation. A glance at Table 4 shows that since FY 1958 fifteen programs have prospered and eight have not.

What does all this have to tell us about how priorities are established within government? There is growing interest in examining federal budgets to determine how the nation is allocating its resources and exercising its spending priorities. The authors of one of the best and most recent of such studies correctly point out that in order to understand what the federal budget for any one year says about the national priorities, one must pay attention to past trends.

> In determining priorities and formulating the federal budget, the President and his advisors do not start with a clean slate, deciding *de novo* how . . . the expenditures for fiscal 1972 should be allocated in meeting national goals. Recent history, prior commitments, current political realities, relations with Congress, economic and social events beyond the control of budget makers—all play a major role in limiting their ability to change radically the current shape of the budget. What they consider desirable must be tempered by what they consider feasible. . . . The margin of truly free choice is surprisingly small.[30]

Still, patterns of obligation and expenditure do change even at the aggregated federal level. Schultze and his colleagues, too, have found impressive variation in the objects of government expenditures over time. They proceed to infer changing priorities from changing absolute outlays.[31] But we also know that programs are in explicit competition with each other as they move jointly through the budget formulation process. A measure of relative priority levels must take account of this competition.

The prosperity index developed in the preceding pages does so; it extracts from each individual budgetary observation *a meaning determined by its context*. The essential idea here is that the individual budgetary figures must be seen as the product of two quite different processes. One is the *budgetary process*, the public accounting that organizations give for the dollars that they receive. The stress here is on organization, the continuing complex hierarchy of government— bureaus, divisions, agencies, and departments. And the key to understanding administrative behavior in these terms is in the incremental nature of the process. The other is the *policy process*. Here emphasis is on the competition among programs for scarce resources which are needed to expand, or to continue, or even to begin. The central problem in analyzing political competition between programs is to make the information about each comparable. Dollars are the operational unit of administration. Political competition is something else again. The great difficulty in untangling these two aspects of the budgetary process is that they occur simultaneously.

The methodological problem this poses can be handled by a series of transformations which in general affect different observations in different numerical ways but whose result is a set of numbers which now may be compared freely among themselves. Inspection of these numbers confirms the fundamental proposition of this preliminary analysis: in the context of the "massively stable" processes cited by other scholars, there is considerable variation in the fortunes of federal activities *at the program level*. We believe that the explanation of this variance constitutes the real challenge for further empirical analysis of budgetary data.

Table 5

Product-Moment Correlations Prosperity Change Scores, Presidential Budgets FY 1958–FY 1972 with Weapons Program

Raw Materials	−0.47	SNAP	−0.26
Special Nuclear Materials	−.25	General Reactor Technology	−.44
Civilian Power Reactors	−.13	Advanced Systems	−.10
Cooperative Power Reactors	−.32	High Energy Physics	−.29
		Sherwood	−.37
Euratom	−.19	Biology and Medicine	−.24
Merchant Ship Reactors	−.28	Training, Education, and Information	ns
Army Reactors	ns*		
Naval Reactors	ns	Isotopes	−.17
Aircraft Nuclear Propulsion	ns	Plowshare	−.25
Pluto	ns	Program Direction	−.23
Rover	ns		

*ns = not significant

Analyzing federal budgets

What has been the nature of the competition among programs? Has it been a "war of all against all" or are certain activities capable of causing other less strong programs to "pay" for their prosperity either by exercising first claim upon newly available resources or by actually growing at the expense of lower priority activities?

Professor Russett has suggested that we may be able to recover some evidence about the extent of such "benefits" or "payments" by examining the patterns of covariation among yearly changes in program levels.[32] Since we now have strong *a priori* reason to believe the Atomic Energy Commission's weapons program to have been independent of other Commission activities for the past twenty years, the intercorrelation of changes in weapons prosperity with those in the other twenty-two programs seems especially pertinent. They are reported in Table 5.

It is clear that everyone pays for defense. With the exception of the Commission's various military reactor enterprises (the largest group among those with insignificant correlations) all AEC programs change scores are negatively associated with changes in the weapons program. As anticipated, the relationship between prosperity changes in raw materials and weapons is high and negative. Decay in the prosperity of the former has been strongly associated with the growth of weapons. But the latter has evidently not only benefited from the decline of this program, it has also in Russett's sense been able to make other programs, notably general reactor technology and controlled thermonuclear research, "pay" for its prosperity.

The difficulty with such patterns of covariation is that, though fascinating, they may also be *wholly spurious*. Certainly they do not in themselves illuminate the real causal processes which produce variation in the prosperity of programs. At most, the *sign* of the associational measure, particularly when it is negative, may provide some clue about the right questions to be asked. Thus in the case of the AEC weapons program one could plausibly accept the overall pattern of inverse association as empirical confirmation of what we suspect on independent grounds. But positive correlations among prosperity change scores have no obvious causal interpretation and the meaning of differences in magnitude between any pair of negative coefficients is totally obscure. More important, the covariation patterns cannot tell us why some programs are stronger than others. Assuming the competitive struggle for limited funds is not exactly a war of all against all, what is it that makes some more equal than others? Is it strong directors who make for strong programs by "running a tight ship" and by "effectively generating support at the agency and congressional levels?"[33] Directors generating such support are able to neutralize opposition by the most potent natural enemy, the Office of Management and Budget. Programs which are supported at the Commission, the Office of Management and Budget, presidential and congressional levels are prosperous; programs which are not supported soon fall victim to the exigencies of the budgetary process.[34]

This widely accepted professional wisdom, then, contains a clear theory of the governmental process. National priorities are not set by administrators with national constituencies; they are set at the operating levels of federal bureaus—by program directors sensitive to their own clienteles. National priorities are established by bureaucratic entrepreneurship in a process which settles priorities without anyone being aware of them. In this regard, Davis, Dempster, and Wildavsky's stochastic models perpetuate a fundamental error about the way government operates. The whole metaphor of an inert bureaucratic machine doing the same thing this year that it did last year misses the basic point. Priority setting in the federal bureaucracy resembles nineteenth century capitalism: Priorities are established by aggressive entrepreneurs at the operating levels of government. Programs prosper because energetic division directors successfully build political support to withstand continuous attacks upon a program's resource base by competing claims. As a consequence, the only matters which reach the president are those already in dispute. At the presidential level the administrative process is less one of "policy-making"than "dispute-settling." It is at this level that things are accepted simply because they have been accepted, that the desirable has to be adjusted to the feasible. On the whole, the differences which count, the actions which produce the patterns of relative prosperity and strength we have discussed occur at lower levels of the administrative process.

All of this is missed by taking the Wildavsky and Lindblom perspective. By concentrating on the underlying regularities of the administrative process, these scholars are obliged to argue (in effect) that except for learning adjustments, no changes of any significance occur. We have seen that real change does occur within this "massive stability," reflecting real conflicts over purpose and priority. The more telling point about the process is that the program director, the operating-level bureaucrat, is a central figure in the determination of public policy. The history of the Atomic Energy Commission's weapons program is far more typical of the way public values are allocated than is the dramatic termination of the aircraft nuclear propulsion program.[35]

This is a strong theory, and we must be careful to stress that our discussion is limited to the single agency on which we have data. But if this fact makes us somewhat cautious, we also feel that the concepts we have specified and the theory which underlies them are probably more—not less—applicable to other areas of government. The Atomic Energy Commission has been a fairly stable agency both in administrative organization and actual spending levels for the last ten years. That we find such great variation in the relative prosperity of programs here seems to suggest that we can expect greater fluctuations elsewhere, particularly in the controversial areas of social policy.[36] Do program directors occupy the same crucial position throughout the government? Is there more or less presidential leadership in other policy areas? For what programs is congressional intervention truly a significant factor?

These are the type of questions that need to be asked. By translating budgetary data into actual operating units of government programs, students of public administration should be able to provide more than speculative answers. Prosperity scores are themselves an important step in this direction, for they establish a measure of program prosperity and decay.

Notes

1. The "traditional"literature on the budgetary process is immense. The text and references in either Arthur Smithies, *The Budgetary Process in the United States* (New York: McGraw-Hill Book Company, 1955), or Jesse Burkhead, *Governmental Budgeting* (New York: John Wiley and Sons, 1956), provide convenient guides. Of particular interest are: Richard E. Neustadt, "The Presidency and Legislation: The Growth of Central Clearance," *American Political Science Review*, 48 (September, 1954), 641–671; Arthur Maass, "In Accord with the President's Program," in C. J. Friedrich and K. Galbraith, eds., *Public Policy*, 4 (Harvard University Press, Cambridge, Mass., 1954), 77–93; Fritz Morstein Marx, "The Bureau of the Budget: Its Evolution and Present Role," I and II, *American Political Science Review*, 39 (August and October, 1945), 653–684 and 869–898; and Lucius Wilmerding, Jr., *The Spending Power* (New Haven: Yale University Press, 1943). The notion of an "action forcing" mechanism is, of course, Richard E. Neustadt's.

2. Aaron Wildavsky's highly influential *The Politics of the Budgetary Process* (Boston: Little, Brown and Co., 1964) is the watershed. The ideas embodied in this analysis were more precisely formulated in Otto A. Davis, M. A. H. Dempster and Aaron Wildavsky, "A Theory of the Budgetary Process," *American Political Science Review*, 60 (September 1966), 529–547. See also, by the same authors, "On the Process of Budgeting: An Empirical Study of Congressional Appropriations," in *Papers on Non-Market Decision Making*, ed. Gordon Tullock (Charlottesville: Thomas Jefferson Center for Political Economy, 1966), pp. 63–133. This general analytic approach has been importantly extended by John P. Crecine. See his "A Computer Simulation Model of Municipal Resource Allocation" (paper delivered at the Midwest Conference of Political Science,

April, 1966), as well as *Governmental Problem Solving* (Chicago, Ill.: Markham Pub. Co., 1969). See also Ira Sharkansky, *The Routines of Politics* (New York: Van Nostrand, 1969).

3. See in this regard Charles Lindblom, "The Science of 'Muddling Through,' " *Public Administration Review*, 29 (Spring, 1959), 79–88; and Charles Lindblom, *The Intelligence of Democracy: Decision Making Through Mutual Adjustment* (New York: The Free Press, 1965).

4. Davis, Dempster, and Wildavsky, p. 543.

5. See Arthur Maass, "In Accord with the President's Program," for an excellent discussion of the great subtlety and variation with which this phrase is used.

6. For a thorough review of one such cycle, see Irvin C. Bupp, "Priorities in Nuclear Technology: Program Prosperity and Decay in the USAEC, 1956–1971" (Ph.D. dissertation, Harvard University, 1971), chap. 1.

7. Davis, Dempster, and Wildavsky, pp. 540—543, do make explicit provision for deviant cases in their analysis. These are cases that lie beyond the normal rules of budgeting that they describe; they are also cases that presumably involve controversy, change and innovation in the budgetary process. This line of thought is further developed in their subsequent article: "On the Process of Budgeting II: an Empirical Study of Congressional Appropriations," *Studies in Budgeting*, eds. R. F. Byrne, A. Charnes, W. W. Cooper, and D. Gilfords (North Holland, Amsterdam, 1971), pp. 292–375.

8. Davis, Dempster, and Wildavsky, p. 529.

9. Davis, Dempster, and Wildavsky, p. 534.

10. Davis, Dempster, and Wildavsky, p. 537.

11. Richard Fenno, "The House Appropriations Committee as a Political System: The Problem of Integration," *American Political Science Review*, 56 (1962), 310–324. See also Richard Fenno, *The Power of the Purse: Appropriations Politics in Congress* (Boston: Little, Brown and Co., 1966).

12. Herbert A. Simon, *Administrative Behavior*, 2nd ed. (New York: Macmillan, 1957); Herbert A. Simon, *Models of Man* (New York: Wiley, 1957); Herbert A. Simon, Donald Smithburg, and Victor Thompson, *Public Administration* (New York: Knopf, 1950); David Braybrooke and Charles Lindblom, *A Strategy of Decision* (New York: The Free Press of Glencoe, 1963); Richard Cyert and James March, eds., *A Behavioral Theory of the Firm* (Englewood Cliffs: Prentice-Hall, 1963); H. A. Simon, "Theories of Decision Making in Economics and Behavioral Science," *American Economic Review*, 59 (June, 1959), 253–283; G. P. E. Clarkson and H. A. Simon, "Simulation of Individual Group Behavior," *American Economic Review*, 60 (Dec., 1960), 920–932.

13. Crecine, *Governmental Problem Solving*, p. 11.

14. Herbert Simon, "The Architecture of Complexity," Reprint No. 113 of the Graduate School of Industrial Administration, Carnegie Institute of Technology.

15. Compare: Thomas Dye, *Politics, Economics, and the Public: Policy Outcomes in the American States* (Chicago: Rand McNally and Co., 1966) with Cyert and March, and William Leiserson, *American Trade Union Democracy* (New York: Columbia University Press, 1959) with Crecine.

16. In policy terms the entire metaphor of normal and deviant cases is vastly misleading. With it, Davis, Dempster, and Wildavsky promote the idea that bureaucracy is largely inert, proceeding to do today essentially what it did yesterday, all without competition and controversy. The exceptions, by this logic, are reserved for a small number of deviant cases which involve "more complicated decision procedures."

The entire thrust of our argument is that the logic of the budgetary process involves public policies in a continuous struggle for scarce resources; that, if there is any "normal state of affairs" in the policy process, it is one of intense competition between programs for public funds. Further, this logic holds equally for policies that desire nothing more than to continue to do what they were doing last year. There is nothing simple or automatic about continuing. Again we must stress that we are speaking of policies and programs here, not the administrative framework in which they are managed. Thus when Davis, Dempster, and Wildavsky (pp. 544–545) suggest that the analysis of individual programs follow from the broad outlines established in their own work, we must respond that their emphasis on normal and deviant cases has started such research off in the wrong direction.

17. Roland N. McKean and Melvin Awshen, "Limitations, Risks and Problems," in *Program Budgeting: Program Analysis and the Federal Budget*, ed. David Novick (Cambridge, Mass.: Harvard University Press, 1965) p. 286.

18. For a thoughtful discussion which complements many of these points, see Charles L. Schultze, *The Politics and Economics of Public Spending* (Washington, D.C.: The Brookings Institution, 1968). Indirect, but vivid, support for many of the same arguments can be found in Charles L. Schultze, Edward R. Fried, Alice M. Rivlin, and Nancy H. Teeters, *Setting National Priorities: The 1972 Budget* (Washington, D.C.: The Brookings Institution, 1971). And at the municipal level see John E. Jackson's perceptive essay, "Politics and the Budgetary Process," *Social Science Research*, 1 (April, 1972) 35–60.

19. James R. Newman and Byron S. Miller, *The Control of Atomic Energy* (New York: McGraw-Hill Book Co., 1948). See also David E. Lilienthal, *The Atomic Energy Years, 1945–1950* (New York: Harper and Row, 1964).

20. Richard G. Hewlett and Oscar E. Anderson, Jr., *The New World, 1939–1946, A History of the USAEC*, Vol. 1 (University Park, Pennsylvania; Pennsylvania State University Press, 1962); Richard G. Hewlett and Francis Duncan, *Atomic Shield, 1947–1953, A History of the USAEC*, Vol. 2 (University Park, Pennsylvania: Pennsylvania State University Press, 1969). A separate study of the Naval Nuclear Propulsion Program has also been prepared by Richard Hewlett and Francis Duncan and is scheduled for publication in the Fall of 1973.

21. One of the authors (Irvin Bupp), was for several years on the staff of the secretariat of the AEC and hence had access to the agency's internal financial records. This association led to AEC support under the auspices of the Office of the Historian for the research reported here.

It is perhaps also worth noting that the AEC is one of the very few executive agencies to have followed a generally consistent "output" format in its budgetary practices since its creation. This fortunate circumstance considerably simplified the problem of isolating and tracing distinct programs.

22. This fifth "appeal" stage is the only one not strictly comparable across all fifteen years. Records of this process were often difficult to locate, and for FY 1959 and FY 1960 there is no evidence that an "appeal" as such was allowed at all.

23. Congressional action is not included in our calculations, although a good case could be made for doing so. Congress is, after all, quite active in the budgetary process through its committee and subcommittee system; see Fenno, *Power of the Purse*. We are concerned, however, with the formulation of program budgets, not with their review. Congressional review of the budget really moves on to a different level of analysis. Of course, much of congressional influence is informal. As such, it should be entered into any explanation of why some programs prosper and others fail. This is again a different analytical problem from developing an index of program prosperity—the results of which can then be searched for appropriate causes.

24. For a somewhat different, but also highly imaginative, approach to this problem, see John Jackson, "Politics and the Budgetary Process."

25. For any given year or stage, the totals reflected in Table 2 are equal to about 90 per cent of the comparable total operating budget, the remaining 10 per cent being that portion of the AEC budget which we were unable to allocate to meaningful output categories. Since we are explicitly interested in competition among programs, the aggregated totals shown have been used as the basis for the transformation described in the text.

26. For a full discussion of all twenty-three programs, see Bupp, chapters 1–3.

27. Cf. Lindblom, "The Science of 'Muddling Through.' "

28. Hewlett and Duncan, 362–409.

29. For a more careful definition of "program strength," see Bupp, chapter 2.

30. Schultze et al. (1971), *Setting National Priorities*.

31. Schultze et al., *Setting National Priorities*, 19–21.

32. Bruce Russett, "Who Pays for Defense?" *American Political Science Review*, 63 (June, 1969), 412–426. See also, Bruce Russett, *What Price Vigilance: The Burdens of National Defense* (New Haven: Yale University Press, 1970), especially chapters 5 and 6.

33. These observations are based on a series of interviews with officials in AEC and the Office of Management and Budget.

34. Russett's substantive conclusions have recently been challenged. See Jerry Hollenhorst and Gary Ault, "An Alternative Answer to: Who Pays for Defense," *American Political Science Review*, 65 (Sept., 1971), 760–764.

By respecifying Russett's regression model to include several dummy variables, Hollenhorst and Ault claim to detect important "sub-period effects." This more methodologically sophisticated approach, however, seems to us merely to compound the original theoretical error. The posited relationshps are spurious.

35. See, W. Henry Lambright, "Shooting Down the Nuclear Plane," Inter-University Case Program, ICP Case Series No. 104 (Indianapolis: Bobbs-Merrill, 1967).

36. Congress appears to be much more active in the area of social policy. An excellent account of administrative policy in this area refers again and again to congressional intervention in specific programs. See Gilbert Y. Steiner, *The State of Welfare* (Washington, D.C.: The Brookings Institution, 1971). Or in a different area, Arthur Maass, *Muddy Waters: The Army Engineers and the Nation's Rivers* (Cambridge, Mass.: Harvard University Press, 1951).

3B. Tax Policy

Tax policy is just as important as expenditure policy and some think that it can be explained in much the same way. Thus economists conduct cost-benefit studies of different taxes and some political scientists think that tax policy is incremental. There are, however, important differences between the two areas, and many think that these differences affect the process through which policy is made and the outcomes of that policy.

One important difference lies in the way that taxes and expenditures affect the general public. Expenditures confer large benefits on groups of individuals, which gives them a strong incentive to press for the establishment and maintenance of such benefits. Taxes impose smaller but discernible costs on the general public taken as a whole, giving almost everyone a reason to oppose new taxes and press for the reduction of existing ones (Buchanan 1967; Buchanan and Wagner 1977).

The other major difference arises from the complexity of taxes. Whereas everyone can understand that spending more on education benefits those with children more than those without, many fail to understand that taxes on business are largely paid for by consumers and that property taxes fall on renters as well as those who own houses. This complexity makes it more likely that people will support a tax structure that hurts them (Peretz 1983). It also means that many citizens lack the knowledge to get involved effectively in the political process.

Taken together these differences lead to a tax policy process in which smaller and more knowledgeable interests have more power than they do over expenditure policy, and where the continual question is, how can taxes be raised without provoking outrage from the general public? They also lead to the often observed fact that government expenditures are on balance beneficial to the less well off, while the tax structure is much less so.

Many see these characteristics of the tax process as dividing tax politics into three distinct types. One, which one might term *incidence politics*, occurs when small, organized, and knowledgeable groups, usually representing the well-off, seek special tax provisions that benefit themselves. The second, *extraction politics*, occurs when those in office are forced to seek new taxes to pay for rising government expenditures. The last, which we will call *populist politics*, occurs when the tax system departs sufficiently far from the wishes of the public that it takes a more active part in tax politics. Most students of tax politics consider what we are calling "incidence" and "extraction" politics to represent the normal situation. These lead to small, steady changes in the tax system. However, periodically the public takes a more active part and this sometimes leads to sharper and more important tax changes.

The readings in this section are primarily concerned with the underlying rationale of our tax system, the reasons why major shifts in taxes occur, and whether the recent tax changes under Ronald Reagan add up to a major shift in our tax system. James M. Buchanan is primarily interested in why taxes are less redistributive than we might expect. In an argument reminiscent of Rawls's (1971) "veil of ignorance," he suggests that this happens because people are uncertain whether they might in the future be in the position of having to pay the unfair taxes from which they currently benefit. Susan Hansen argues that major tax changes come about during periods of political realignment, when major social and economic changes lead to replacement of one political party by the other as the in-power majority party. In Ronald King's view, major tax changes occur both as the result of popular agitation and as the result of attempts by the elite to control and co-opt popular feeling. The final reading, by Joseph Pechman, represents an attempt to measure the effect of the large number of tax changes that have taken place in the wake of the California tax revolt and the election of Ronald Reagan. It shows that while there has been little overall change in the size of the tax burden or in the mix of taxes, there do appear to have been significant shifts in the tax burden of particular groups.

For further reading

A good introduction to the economic principles underlying taxation is Richard and Peggy Musgrave's *Public Finance in Theory and Practice*. A more conservative view is Edgar and Jacqueline Browning's *Public Finance and the Price System*. A good general book on tax politics in America is Susan Hansen's *The Politics of Taxation: Revenue Without Representation*. Two good books on how tax policy has been made in the last two decades are Lawrence Pierce's *The Politics of Fiscal Policy Formation* and Thomas Reese's *The Politics of Taxation*. Hulten and O'Neill's article "Tax Policy" gives an account of changes during the early Reagan Administration. Guy Peters's article "Determinants of Tax Policy," and James Alt's article "The Evolution of Tax Structures," outline some of the political theories in the area. Hibbs and Masden's article "Public Reaction to the Growth of Taxation and Government Expenditure" looks at public opinion on taxes. David Sears and Jack Citrin's book *Tax Revolt: Something for Nothing in*

California is a careful case study of the interaction between public opinion and tax reduction.

Bibliography

Alt, James, "The Evolution of Tax Structures," *Public Choice* 41:1 (1983): 181–222.

Browning, Edgar K. and Jacqueline M. Browning, *Public Finance and the Price System* (New York: Macmillan, 1979).

Buchanan, J.M., *Public Finance in Democratic Process: Fiscal Institutions and Democratic Choice* (Chapel Hill: University of North Carolina Press, 1967).

Buchanan, J.M. and R. Wagner, *Democracy in Deficit* (New York: Academic Press, 1977).

Hansen, Susan, *The Politics of Taxation: Revenue Without Representation* (New York: Praeger, 1983).

Hibbs, Douglas and H. Masden, "Public Reaction to the Growth of Taxation and Government Expenditure," *World Politics* 33 (April 1981):413–35.

Hulten, Charles R. and June O'Neill, "Tax Policy," in John L. Palmer and Isabel V. Sawhill, *The Reagan Experiment* (Washington D.C.: The Urban Institute Press, 1982).

Musgrave, Richard and Peggy Musgrave, *Public Finance in Theory and Practice* 3rd ed. (New York: McGraw Hill, 1980).

Pierce, Lawrence, *The Politics of Fiscal Policy Formation* (Pacific Palisades, Ca.: Goodyear, 1971).

Peretz, Paul, *The Political Economy of Inflation* (Chicago: University of Chicago Press, 1983).

Peters, B. Guy, "Determinants of Tax Policy," *Policy Studies Journal* 7 (Summer 1979): 787–93.

Rawls, J.A., *A Theory of Justice* (Cambridge, Mass.: Harvard University Press, 1971).

Reese, T.J., *The Politics of Taxation* (Westport, Conn.: Quorum Books, 1979).

Sears, David O. and Jack Citrin, *Tax Revolt: Something for Nothing in California*, enlarged ed. (Cambridge, Mass.: Harvard University Press, 1985).

3B.1. The Fiscal "Constitution"

JAMES M. BUCHANAN

Nobel Prize winner James Buchanan is regarded as a pioneer in the study of the relation between the tax structure and the individual incentives facing political actors. Two of Buchanan's contributions are particularly notable. One follows from his observation that obtaining revenues is a central problem of all governments. Given that taxes are much less popular than the expenditures they finance, governments have an incentive to give high visibility to expenditures and low visibility to the tax structure. Likewise, governments have an incentive to spend more than they tax. In light of this, Buchanan thinks there is good reason for a balanced-budget amendment to the Constitution. Buchanan's other major contribution is the notion that levying taxes can and should be considered a constitutional decision, rather than a short-term political one.

In this essay, Buchanan asks why taxes are not more unfair than they are. If taxes were decided in the short term, he argues, one would expect the politically powerful to place heavy taxes on others, to pay for expenditures that benefit them. Yet this is not what happens. According to Buchanan, we can explain the even distribution of tax burdens if we assume that forming the tax structure is analogous to making a constitution. Because we do not know how we, or our children, will fare in the future, we make tax decisions on the assumption that we might fall into the class of people bearing the tax burden. By spreading the load evenly, we reduce the risk of later having to bear a disproportionately heavy burden. Likewise, he argues, there is an incentive to make taxes mildly progressive, since if we turn out to be poor our load will be lighter, and if we turn out to be rich we will be better able to bear a heavier load.

In assessing Buchanan's argument the reader should ask whether the tax structure stays the same for long periods, whether people think in the way Buchanan expects when making tax policy, and whether our current tax structure is best explained by his logic.

Tax shares, divisibility, and zero-sum games

The reason why the tax question has been relatively neglected is that it is characteristically different from questions concerning budgetary size and allocation. The nature of taxation itself ensures this. Given any specified tax structure, one which relates tax obligations to an economic base or one that assigns tax shares among different persons and groups, we can analyze the fiscal decision process in terms of areas of agreement on the part of all persons or on the part of persons in a dominant majority coalition, agreement concerning the budgetary variables. Agreement here consists in the settlement on values for variables which all persons must commonly share. The final values chosen for budgetary size and composition must be available equally to all members of the community; these are indivisible in this sense.

We cannot, however, proceed in reverse order. We cannot, that is to say, assume that these budgetary variables, both as to size and composition, are fixed in advance and then proceed to analyze the process of group agreement on the allocation of tax shares among individuals and groups. The reason is that tax shares are measured in monetary units that are fully divisible as among separate persons. There is no area of agreement on such sharing, at least in simplified models where persons are assumed to be motivated primarily by their own economic well-being.[1] Taxation takes on all of the aspects of a zero-sum game. If one person succeeds in reducing his tax liability by a dollar, some other person or persons finds his or their liability increased by $1. Taxation takes on properties of either/or; either one man pays or the other.

When this very simple fact is recognized, the difficulties of securing any agreement at all on the allocation of tax shares becomes apparent. Collective decisions on tax systems and changes in these systems become extremely costly, and we may wonder that existing systems are ever changed once established. At a naïve level, any chosen allocation of tax shares would seem to represent the exploitation of the politically weak by the politically strong. In such a simplistic game theory model of taxation, we should expect that members of the dominant political coalition would pay little or no taxes while imposing heavy burdens on members of the powerless minority.

How can general taxes be explained?

Observations of fiscal structures falsify the predictions which the simple game theory model makes. Taxes are observed which are *general* in their imposition. All persons and groups, or substantially all, pay taxes, and individual shares seem to depend upon reasonably explicit criteria of economic status such as incomes, property holdings, consumption spending on all or on particular products and services. Can we possibly explain the generality of taxation by resort to simple and abstract models of democratic decision process?

Reconciliation is achieved when we recognize that collective decisions on taxing institutions are temporally different from those involving budgetary size and composition. Budgets are made within the restrictions of existing tax institutions. This is descriptively true, and the simple majority voting models yield fruitful insights. But tax share decisions are not made with the restrictions of existing budgets. Tax share choices are made independently, and they are made to be applicable over a much longer period of time than budgetary choices. The tax share choices are essentially *constitutional* in the descriptive meaning of this term. That is to say, tax institutions, which embody specific tax share allocations as among separate persons and groups, are collectively chosen as quasi-permanent fiscal devices, designed to yield revenues over a long sequence of budgetary periods and over many possible budgetary compositions. For this reason, it is appropriate that tax structures be conceived as inherent parts of a "fiscal constitution" that is changed only occasionally and then not in direct response to short-run modifications in the budgetary variables.

Consider the idealized selection of tax-sharing arrangements under this constitutional approach. Individuals are asked to select, to "vote for," tax-sharing alternatives on the assumption that the structure finally chosen will be used to finance budgets at all possible levels and of all possible combinations of spending items. If individuals are uncertain as to their own specific private economic status during future periods of time and also uncertain as to their own desires for specific public spending programs, they may think in terms of *general* taxing schemes, those that might be broadly acceptable over wide ranges of individual positions. In this choice setting, the conception of "fair" or "equitable" taxation takes on a meaning that is relevant for individual participation in such collective choice processes.

Even at this constitutional level of decision individuals will, of course, have differing notions as to preferred tax-sharing schemes. But a range of agreement does seem possible in this setting, and the zero-sum aspects of taxation in the single-period fixed budget setting largely disappear. The selection of a set of tax institutions here becomes analogous to the selection of rules for a game, by participants who do not fully know what their own positions will be in subsequent rounds of actual play. Each person will, in his own interest, be led to select a set of rules that he considers broadly "fair," so as to prevent undue penalization for those who may be, unpredictably, in unfavorable positions.

Why must all persons pay taxes in the same way?

The central question of this chapter is: How are taxes to be paid? As we have noted, tax payments made by an individual are measured in money, generalized purchasing power, and this is fully divisible as among persons. How is the question as to how taxes are to be paid any different from the question as to how prices are to be paid in the private economy? The essential difference here is that tax arrangements which are applicable to one person must be applicable to all persons in the community. Individuals cannot individually choose how they are to meet their obligations to the government. Ideally, this might seem to be an optimal arrangement. Suppose that each person owes a share in government financing amounting to $1,000. Why could we not allow each person to pay this sum in any way that he chooses? This procedure could, in fact, be followed if the size of the financial obligation should be fully independent of the means of payment. However, if we want to adopt tax-sharing institutions that are not directly related to budgetary size and composition, the means of payment become, in turn, a means for determining relative shares.

Progressive taxation and democratic consensus

We observe that progressive income taxation is an important revenue producer in the United States. Is it possible to explain the origins of this important tax institution in terms of the approach that is examined in this chapter? Opponents of progressive income taxation often denounce this institution as demonstrable exploitation of the rich by the poor who make up the dominant political majority. Proponents often defend the institution on purely ethical grounds without reference to any economic origins.

It seems probable that at least some support for progression, as a sharing scheme, does lie in the type of calculus suggested here. If an individual is faced with the choice among several taxing institutions, in the knowledge that the alternative selected will remain in effect over a long period of time, and if he is himself uncertain as to his own economic status over this period of time, he may well "vote for" progressive taxes on income. Under this institution, he knows that he will be subjected to heavy taxes only if he is fortunate enough to receive large incomes; if he is unlucky in the economic game and secures only small incomes, he is assured that his taxes will be more than proportionately reduced. On the basis of this sort of calculus, and quite apart from any feelings for his fellow man, feelings which can be partially translated into demands for explicit redistribution as a "public good," a certain logic of progressive taxation can be developed. Individuals may agree, within certain broad limits, on progressive income taxation as a part of their fiscal constitution. Progressive income taxation will be further analyzed for its economic effects and for its actual institutional form in the United States, but it is useful that its place in a democratic social process be recognized. To the extent that progressive rate structures are viewed by high-income earners and low-income earners alike as means through which the former are exploited by the latter through the fiscal process, democratic consensus has broken down.

Direct versus indirect taxation

The constitutional approach to the choice among tax institutions offers interesting insights into the age-old question concerning the desirability of direct versus indirect taxation. Direct taxation is defined as taxation imposed upon the person who is intended to be the final bearer of the burden of payment. Indirect taxation is defined as taxation imposed upon others than the person who is intended to bear the final burden. When participating in a choice among fiscal instruments, in the knowledge that the instrument selected is to remain in force over a whole sequence of budgetary periods, why should an individual prefer to pay a tax indirectly? Such a tax, which would normally be imposed on the purchase of a particular product or products, clearly distorts the individual budgetary allocation in the private market. Why should the individual choose this tax if he recognizes the presence of this predictable distortion?

A person may, quite rationally, select a tax which imposes such a distortion for the very reason of such distortion. This is the very essence of what is often called *sumptuary taxation*, defined as taxation that is designed to discourage the consumption of certain products and services. There are two separate elements involved in such taxation. By "voting for" a tax on a particular product, an individual may be indicating his preference for a scheme that discourages *others* from consuming products which he thinks they should not consume. This is the traditional interpretation that has been placed on the support for sumptuary taxation. However, the individual may select the indirect tax here because he wants to discourage his own consumption of the product in future periods. The constitutional approach allows us to isolate this second explanatory feature which the more traditional approach tended to ignore.

A second reason why the rational person may deliberately choose the taxation of specific consumption items is equivalent to the explanation of the support of progressive taxation outlined above. Certain consumption items may be quite closely correlated in usage with high-income levels; in addition, these items may be known to be displacable in time. The individual who is uncertain as to his income earning prospects may not be at all averse to placing a heavy burden of taxation on the consumption of items that he expects to demand only during periods of relative affluence.

Conclusion and summary

We have done little more than sketch out a beginning of a constitutional approach to the selection of tax-sharing institutions in this chapter. The summary treatment covers material that has been developed in more detail in other works. There remain many aspects of the "fiscal constitution" that have not been analyzed satisfactorily.

Note

1. Modifications on these simplified models will allow for some agreement on taxing schemes even for purely redistributive purposes, but these complications are ignored in this chapter.

3B.2. Partisan Realignment and Tax Policy 1789-1976

SUSAN B. HANSEN

Susan Hansen, like James Buchanan, sees the process by which tax policy is made as basically democratic in nature. Following Downs (1960), she argues that the combination of the unpopularity of taxes and the fact that control of government is often divided between the two major parties ensures that in normal times there will be only slow and cautious change in the tax structure.

However, Hansen points out that while this slow pattern of change seems to fit tax changes in the last twenty or thirty years, over the longer term there have been quite massive changes in the level of taxes, the type of tax relied on most heavily, and the degree to which taxes redistribute from the rich to the poor. She argues that these larger changes usually come about in the relatively brief periods when one party controls both the Presidency and Congress. Further, she claims that such changes are particularly likely when there has just been a partisan realignment—a massive shift of power away from one party and to the other. This is because the major changes in society that brought about the realignment are likely to call for tax changes, and at the same time the victorious party is likely to have an extraordinarily large majority and to be unusually unified, and so capable of making significant policy changes.

The reader should note that for Hansen's argument to be correct it is not necessary that all major tax changes take place during realignments, but only that there is greater tax change in realignment than in non-realignment periods.

. . . **Economic historians have suggested** three factors to account for historical changes in tax systems: economic development, war, and demand for new services. Thus, Musgrave (1969) argues that economic structure determines the sources and amount of revenue which can be raised. Simple taxes on land, mines, or agriculture may be imposed in underdeveloped extractive economies. Trading

Reprinted, in edited version, from *Realignment in American Policy: Towards a Theory*, edited by Bruce A. Campbell and Richard J. Trilling. Copyright © 1980. By permission of the author and the University of Texas Press.

nations can raise revenue from tariffs. But more sophisticated taxes (payroll, income, sales) require a money economy, an industrialized population, and a complex administrative system and thus appear at later stages of economic development. Further, tax revenues in nations among the American states tend to increase with urbanization and industrialization (Dye 1966: chap. 7).

Peacock and Wiseman (1961) stress the importance of wars in tax development. Extraordinary demands are imposed on a political system, so that new sources of revenue must be considered. Inflation or borrowing may of course be used instead of taxes, but Peacock and Wiseman argue that new taxes are likely to be imposed in wartime because citizen opposition to them may be diminished by patriotism. Their United Kingdom data suggest that those new taxes persist long after peace has returned—that both taxing and spending are displaced to new and higher plateaus by wars.

A third theory of tax development stresses demand for new services. Thus, Britain's adoption of an income tax was linked to the introduction of social security in 1906; gasoline taxes in the U.S. came into use to meet demands for roads for the new automobiles.

At a broad comparative level, these patterns describe changes in revenue patterns quite well. But they do not take into account the political factors which determine how a policy responds to the economic choices posed by war, economic development, or the need for new services. . . .

Taxes distribute the burden of government across different social or economic groups and as such represent the outcome of complex political bargaining. Further, tax policy decisions must be made by political actors operating under legal and electoral constraints. Aggregate measures of political variables can be added to the usual economic explanations, but feeding random political variables into a correlation matrix will not suffice.[1] A more general theory concerning the politics of tax outcomes is needed. The literature on realignment and the writings of the economist Anthony Downs suggest such a theory.

Realignment and tax policy: theory

Periodically in American history, critical elections have ushered in realignments in parties and voting patterns and have changed the political agenda. For two reasons, realigning elections should alter the relationship between elections and tax policy. First, the social or economic crisis which precipitates realignment may change perceptions of revenue needs: "politics as usual" could not deal with war (1860), with depression (1893, 1932), or with the tariff problems and governmental surpluses of the 1830s. Second, realigning elections have changed the nature of political opposition and support and thus could affect politicians' calculus of social forces favoring or opposing changes in the financing of government.

Most empirical analyses of political realignment have focused on the behavior of the American electorate. The central finding is that realignment is a response to a major social or economic crisis, when the electorate undergoes a large-scale transformation in its durable political attachments. In realigning elections, the coalitional base of the party system shifts (in Sundquist's terms) to a new axis. Burnham and others have documented these shifts with aggregate data on voter turnout, registration, and voting behavior (Burnham 1970; Sundquist 1973), and Seligman and King (1980) note major shifts in elite recruitment patterns.

But—then what? Are changes in the electorate and in government personnel followed by changes in the political agenda and in policy outputs and outcomes? Based on the small amount of research that has been done on these aspects of realignment, the answer must be "not necessarily." As Campbell and Trilling (1980, p. 10) note:

> The process may be aborted anywhere along the way—because the severity of the crisis ebbs by itself, or because party leaders waffle on the critical issues long enough to deny meaningful choice to voters, or because electoral change lacks the clarity and magnitude to transform the party system, or because institutional factors cause personnel turnover or policy change to lag substantially behind social and economic and electoral change, or because entrenched officials effectively engage in obstructionism, or because subsequent social and electoral conditions offset or reverse the realignment.

Sundquist's various scenarios for party realignment also suggest a multiplicity of possible outcomes. In several cases, the results may well be stalemated under our system of divided government and fragmented parties. Third parties could win a substantial proportion of votes or seats, the major parties could shift but divide the control of offices, or different parties might control different states or regions within our federal system. There is no a priori theory to suggest that major shifts in federal or state policy will follow a realigning election or a realigning era, even if the political agenda and the political decision makers change. And, if changes do occur, the analyst must ascertain whether electoral change was the proximate cause, because factors in the domestic or international environment (such as war or economic development) may produce policy changes which have little to do with the politics of realignment.

Even though the diffuse "theory" of realignment is of little help in predicting policy outcomes, there is empirical reason to believe that realigning elections will have more impact on public policy than "normal" elections. First, party polarization around some issue (old or new) has occurred during realigning elections, as suggested by Ginsberg's analysis (1976) of changes in the salience and direction of party stands on seven major issues from 1840 to 1968. Downs' spatial model (1957) would predict party convergence on issues in attempts to build majority support, but for several reasons this has not occurred during critical elections: the electorate may be changing, new elites may take over a party and impose a new agenda, the country may be undergoing a social or economic crisis. All these factors make strategic calculation of party stands difficult, especially in the days before mass survey techniques enabled politicians to calculate modal preferences with any accuracy.

Second, realigning elections have produced large and one-sided shifts in the control of government. The years following 1800, 1828, 1860, 1896, and 1932 (as well as the exceptional period following the nonrealigning election of 1920) are characterized (as Table 1 demonstrates) by a phenomenon otherwise rare in American political history: control of the House, the Senate, and the presidency for extended periods by members of the same political party.[2] In these high-stimulus elections, a switch of party alignments has been accompanied by a one-sided surge in support for one particular party. This of course does not guarantee unified control of government; the Supreme Court, the bueaucracy, and state governments may remain out of phase for years thereafter, and factional divisions may persist within the Congress (e.g., the southern Democrats who opposed Roosevelt and the New Deal).[3] Nevertheless, formal political control of the decision-making machinery of the federal government has been firmly in the hands of one political party by larger majorities and for longer periods of time after realignment than during the periods between critical elections.

This striking fact suggests that realignments may indeed affect policy outputs and outcomes because the machinery to do so is in the hands of one party. Advocates of responsible parties (such as Schattschneider 1942) have long argued for a system of party government which would facilitate public policy making. If their prognosis is correct, unified control of governments should produce changes in public policy. But divided control of government is even less likely to be associated with major policy changes, because of the greater need for compromise to insure that neither party gets the credit for policy leadership. If one can rely on Ginsberg's elaborate coding of federal statutes and his multiplicative measures (criticized by Neuman and Hicks 1977), it appears that new legislation has occurred corresponding to those elections usually defined as realigning (although the passage of laws does not mean that changes in policy outputs will occur). Brady (1980) shows *why* critical elections are associated with policy changes by analysis of the internal structuring of the House. Perhaps the unified control of government may offer a further explanation.[4]

If political realignment suggests major changes in taxes, the work of Downs (1960), based on "normal" politics, suggests why marginal and incremental changes more typically characterize tax policy. Downs' analysis rests on two key assumptions. The first is obvious: tax burdens are unpopular. The second is certainly plausible: tax burdens are more salient to citizens than are the benefits each person is supposed to receive from collective goods. He then argues that rational politicians will be reluctant to raise taxes (or impose new ones) because their perceived costs will outweigh any benefits that might be provided by these taxes. Further, in an earlier work (1957), Downs argued that parties tend to converge on highly salient issues (such as tax policy) or to avoid the issue altogether. Thus, the amount of collective goods provided in democracies is less than optimal; politicians fear electoral retribution for tax increases and are

Table 1

Periods of Unified Political Control of Presidency and Congress, 1791–1981

Date	Party	Years
1791–1793	Federalist	2
1795–1801	Federalist	6
1801–1825	Democrat-Republican	24
1829–1841	Democrat	12
1841–1843	Whig	2
1845–1847	Democrat	2
1853–1855	Democrat	2
1857–1859	Democrat	2
1861–1869	Republican/Unionist	8
1873–1875	Republican	2
1881–1883	Republican	2
1889–1891	Republican	2
1893–1895	Democrat	2
1897–1911	Republican	14
1913–1919	Democrat	6
1921–1931	Republican	10
1933–1947	Democrat	14
1949–1953	Democrat	4
1953–1955	Republican	2
1961–1969	Democrat	8
1977–1981	Democrat	4

constrained to avoid or hide them. Politicians of both parties have incentives to avoid making taxation an election issue and to keep budgets low.[5]

These theoretical considerations are generally supported by empirical analyses of state and local tax policy making. Taxes are raised (if at all) incrementally, indirectly, even deviously in order to minimize political fallout (Meltsner 1971; Fisher 1969). Sharkansky notes little difference in parties' positions on tax issues and suggests that economic or administrative criteria are paramount (1969: 19). Winters' (1976) longitudinal analysis of redistribution considered spending as well as taxation, but he found that political variables such as party competition, Democratic control, or the powers of the governor had little impact on redistribution ratios of tax burdens to benefits in the American states. Economic and demographic factors have generally proved to be better predictors of state tax policies than political variables.

The existing state and local studies have focused on a short time span and on incremental changes. If one looks at revenue patterns over all of U.S. history, however, a very different pattern emerges. First, taxes have increased from less than 1 percent of the GNP in 1789 to over 30 percent today, and dramatic increases are apparent even if one uses constant dollars or revenue per capita. Second, tax sources have shifted not once but several times from the tariff, to excise taxes, to the income tax, to increased reliance on payroll taxes.

Third, state tax patterns have also changed. State and local tax rates have increased faster than federal taxes, although they have remained fairly stable as a percentage of the GNP (Mosher and Poland 1964: 61–72). And, since 1900, almost all states have come to rely on income, sales, and excise taxes rather than property taxes for their revenues, considerable financial innovations which Walker's 1969 study did not consider. What extraordinary circumstances could explain these dramatic and nonincremental changes in tax policy? What factors have led politicians to implement policies fraught with such apparent political peril? Analyses such as Winters' or Sharkansky's, based only on recent and limited time periods, cannot help us to answer these questions. . . .

Realignment and tax policy: evidence

As figures 1 to 3 suggest, several changes in revenue, sources, and amounts have corresponded to periods of realignment. Thus, excise taxes vanished when the Jeffersonian Democrats took over from the Federalists. Land sales and tariff revenues soared under the Jacksonians. Income taxes were adopted in 1860 and 1892, also critical realignment periods, and the payroll tax appeared during the New Deal. Each of these new taxes shifted the costs of government to different groups in society. I will now examine more closely some reasons why critical elections (as opposed to the "normal" operations of parties and elections) have affected tax policy.

This account will focus on four variables: the salience of tax issues, party polarization over revenue, the actions taken by the newly dominant majority coalition, and the policy impact of those actions. I will compare the politics of realignment with tax politics during the periods between critical elections and also with other factors affecting tax policies: wars, economic growth, and revenue needs.

Tax policy after the first realignment

Tax questions figured prominently in national politics from the beginning. The first bill introduced into the House of Representatives was a revenue bill, and the first party system in the United States was based partly on profound conflicts over the appropriate financial program for the new nation. Hamilton and the Federalists proposed sound financial measures on the Continental model to pay off the war debt and establish the credit of the U.S.: national assumption of all debts, establishment of the first Bank of the United States, and excise taxes to finance the new government. The Jeffersonians felt that excise taxes, payable in coin or currency, were inappropriate for a barter economy, and they were convinced that

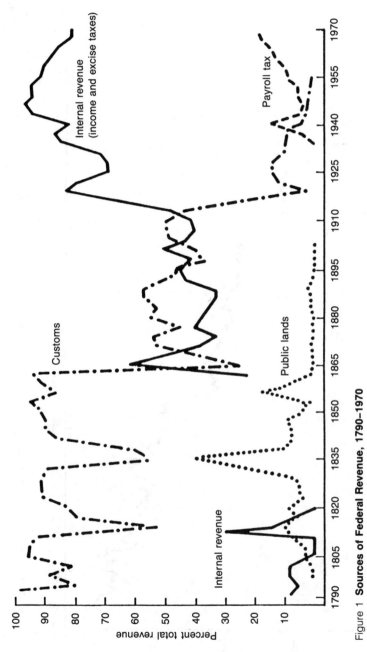

Figure 1 **Sources of Federal Revenue, 1790–1970**

Source: Historical Statistics of the United States 1975: tables Y567–Y568.

240

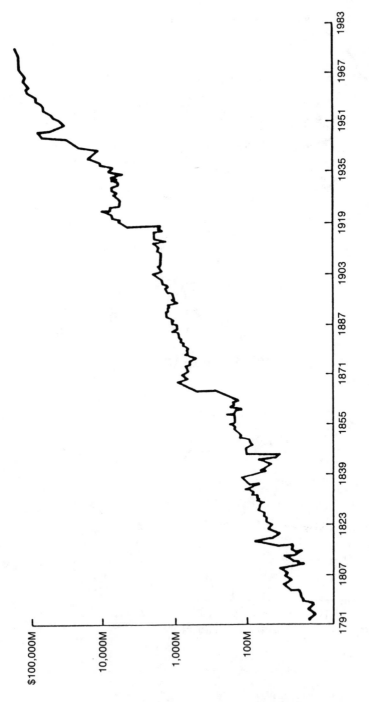

Figure 2 **Total Federal Revenue, 1791–1970 (Log$_n$), in constant dollars.**

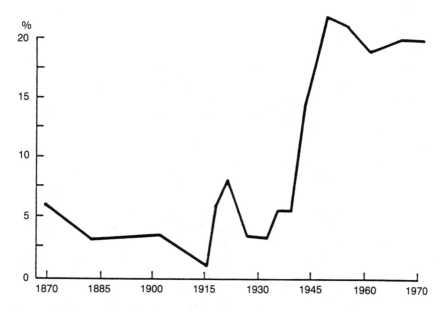

Figure 3 **Federal Revenue As a Percentage of the GNP, 1869–1970.**

the moneyed classes would benefit from Federalist banking and revenue measures. Excise taxes were thoroughly unpopular among people who had just rid themselves of British taxes, and the Jeffersonians were able to turn this discontent (evidenced by the Whisky Rebellion) to their own political advantage (Ratner 1942: 27).

When the Federalists lost Congress as well as the presidency in 1800, the result was predictable: "complete abolition of all of the taxes so laboriously established by Hamilton and his successors" (Howe 1896: 34) until the War of 1812 necessitated the imposition of taxes on consumer goods to provide revenue lost as the war cut income from the tariff. Although revenue from this was reduced by war and the Embargo Acts, Jefferson and his successors clearly differed from the Federalists regarding tax policy, and after 1800 they were able to abolish excise taxes, use land sales to help settlers, and keep the tariff lower (as desired by southern planters and western farmers) than Hamilton and the eastern industrialists might have desired (Paul 1954: 7). It seems clear, therefore, that the realigning election of 1800 produced changes in federal tax policy which accorded with the philosophy of the victors. The War of 1812, however, necessitated a temporary departure from that philosophy.

Jacksonian Democracy and tax policy

Changes in both revenue and expenditures occurred during the Jackson and Van Buren administrations. Revenue from the tariff and from sales of land increased sharply. The federal debt was retired completely in 1835, and in fact the treasury reported large surpluses from 1834 on.

But realignment did little to produce these changes. Although the Jacksonian Democrats tried to change the level and distribution of the federal tax burden, they lacked the fiscal and administrative means to do so. The dilemma was noted by Schlesinger (1946): the Jeffersonian philosophy of support for the interests of the common people (modified by the Jacksonians to include urban laborers as well as yeoman farmers) required Hamiltonian means to achieve its ends. But Jackson was limited by his strict constructionist philosophy of limited federal intervention in the economy, banking, and social investment.

How did this anomaly come about? Two conditions that I have established for the policy impact of elections were met. First, Jackson (and Van Buren after him) scored impressive victories, and the Democrats controlled both houses of Congress from 1829 until 1841. Further, the Jacksonian Democrats' ideas on taxation differed markedly from those of the opposition (which included National Republicans, Anti-Masonites, and Whigs). They opposed taxation for internal improvements and the infamous 1828 "Black Tariff," because high tariffs (the principal source of revenue) would have reduced the money capital of farmers. Jackson also favored reducing land prices and held that the public lands should not be made a source of revenue but should be sold at nominal cost to settlers (Dewey 1934: 218). Finally, Jackson and Van Buren were "hard money" advocates, compared to the Whigs, who favored easy money and the generous use of bank credit for financing of such internal improvements as roads and canals. The Jacksonians opposed the Second Bank of the United States and issued the Specie Circular of 1835 to 1837, because they assumed (mistakenly) that soft money benefited speculators and the rich at the expense of farmers and workers.

Despite their apparent political advantages, the Jacksonians had either no effect on revenues or precisely the opposite effect from that intended. The major reason for this was a lack of understanding of fiscal and monetary policy. Although Jackson possessed the formal political power to change the laws regarding federal revenue, his unstable political coalition of southern planters and New England industrialists probably would not have held together to support such changes.[6] Southerners and Westerners were strongly opposed to protectionism, but many compromises had to be engineered to gain sufficient support from other regions to pass the measure, and its major tariff reductions were scheduled far into the future.

Neither Jackson nor the Southerners were willing to reopen debate on the issue for fear of even higher tariffs. Thus, throughout Jackson's administration, revenue from the tariff remained embarrassingly high, because revenue derived from the tariff depended far more on business conditions than on the reductions in duties imposed on imports of 1830, 1832, and 1833. The same was true of land sales, which soared due to easy credit, population growth, and increased value and accessibility of western lands.

Although the overflowing treasury was not due to Jackson's policy choices, he took steps to decrease revenues: requiring land payments in specie, recalling federal bank loans so as to distribute federal funds among state "pet" banks, and distributing the treasury surplus to the states. But the consequences were disastrous, and the resulting severe economic depression fell most heavily on the small farmers and urban workers who had supported Jackson. Bank failures in Europe and crop failures in the U.S. aggravated the dismal situation, and economic problems helped defeat the Jacksonians in 1840.

The Jacksonians lacked economic knowledge of the causes of business-cycle fluctuations and of the government's responsibility for them. But, even if their economic theory had been more advanced, one must doubt whether they would have been willing to expand the powers of the federal government into regulation of the economy, or if they could have rallied the necessary political support from their southern populist-strict constructionist coalition.[7] Many elections would take place before persons opposed to the dominance of business interest would again attempt to shift the tax burden from consumers to producers.

Tax policy in the Civil War period

Major changes in government revenue occurred during and after the Civil War. Some of these (wartime income and excise taxes) were clearly due to the compelling need for revenue during the war, when sea blockades hindered trade and cut tariff revenue. These measures were repealed soon after the war, however. But the political history of wartime increases in tariff rates and their longevity after Appomattox suggest that a major switch back to a protective tariff occurred. This was the result not of the war but of Republican hegemony in Washington from 1860 until 1878, the outcome of the realigning elections of 1854 to 1860.

The Republican-sponsored changes began in 1858, when the Republicans gained control of the House of Representatives. The highly protectionist Morrill Tariff passed the House during the 1859 to 1860 session. This was not war legislation but an effort to attract Republican presidential votes in the upcoming presidential election in such protectionist states as Pennsylvania (Taussig 1966: 158) and to supplement revenue lost in the business panic of 1857.

After the Republicans gained control of the Senate in 1860, the bill passed that chamber before a single shot was fired in the South. The author of the act, Morrill, became chairman of the House Ways and Means Committee, and practically every month of the ensuing war saw tariff increases. Most of these high tariff duties remained in effect until 1892, when the Democrats finally regained control of the national government.

Two major changes in revenue were introduced during the Civil War: a progressive income tax and an inheritance tax. These, however, did not result from the 1860 election; neither party proposed them until the precarious state of Union finances made new sources of revenue mandatory, and both received support from Republicans as well as Union Democrats. It appears that the rich and the Republican party accepted a progressive tax on incomes as the lesser of two evils.

The financial condition of the north was so unstable, due to war losses, inflation, and the suspension of specie payments, that those in business realized that their investments would be better protected if taxes were raised.

As soon as the financial emergency of the war abated, however, the true colors of the Republican majority and the wealthy emerged. Income from stocks, bonds, and land sales was eliminated from the income tax (a forerunner of modern "capital gains" exclusions). The progressive rate structure was abandoned in 1867, and the income tax was repealed altogether in 1872. According to Ratner, President Grant's opposition to the income tax was "explained by his wish to strengthen his hold on the support of the great moneyed interests in the Presidential election of 1872" (1942: 96).

Three of my conditions for the policy impact of elections on revenue were therefore met after 1860: the parties differed (the Republicans had a strong protectionist plank in their 1860 platform), the Republicans controlled the government, and legislative changes were made. The impact of the high tariffs on total revenue was not immediately noticeable for two reasons. First, the war cut into tariff revenue. Second, tariffs as a proportion of total government revenue actually declined, since many new (and usually regressive) excise taxes were introduced. But the industries which supported the tariff certainly benefited from it: revenue from the tariff increased from 1866 on. This did *not* happen, as Taussig posits, because "all feeling of opposition to high import duties almost entirely disappeared" (1966: 166). Rather, it was the Democrats opposed to the tariff who all but vanished from the national government. The new Republican majority favored generous pensions for war veterans (who were, of course, mostly Republicans: Sanders 1976) and spending on internal improvements, especially railroads. Increased revenues from the new taxes underwrote those policies. These revenues were so large relative to the demand for their use that even the Republicans considered reforming or reducing tariff rates in the 1870s, but of course tariffs were more likely to be cut on items for which there was no domestic producers' lobby (Taussig 1966: 178–180).

Post-Civil War taxes clearly suited the needs of the growing industrial elite. Revenues declined as a percentage of the GNP: business profits could thus be directed toward investment or consumption, not toward the public sector or higher wages. Taxes fell much more heavily on consumption than on production, and excise taxes on liquor and tobacco, adopted for moral as well as revenue purposes, were in fact highly regressive (Trescott 1957: 66). Individual and corporate income and profits were not taxed, and high investment rates no doubt contributed to economic development. But farmers and urban workers had to pay the social and economic cost. Growing protest against high tariffs, hard money, and lack of credit laid the basis for the next period of realignment.

The 1894 income tax: aborted realignment

Support for an income tax continued after the 1861 tax was repealed. Revenue needs were *not* a major factor (Paul 1954: 27). Its advocates saw an income tax not only as an alternative to high tariff rates but as a means to redistribute income and to stop the piling up of pensions. The agrarian protest parties had long argued that government power should be used to control the economic monopoly on behalf of the public. The populists had included an income tax plank in their national platforms, stressing its value as a means of redistributing wealth, and, beginning about 1890, substantial numbers of people within the Democratic party (including Bryan) agreed with this view. Republicans strongly disagreed, and the vote on the bill was highly partisan. But the bill (part of the Wilson-Gorman bill to reduce tariffs) passed largely because in 1894 Democrats controlled the presidency and both houses of Congress for the first time since the Civil War.

Was this a result of realignment? Certainly some of Burnham's state data suggest that major changes in state voting patterns, as indicated by t-tests or his "discontinuity variable," began in 1892 or 1894, not 1896 (Burnham 1970: 22–23, table 2.4) and populists and other agrarian reformers carried many central and western states in the "prairie fire" of 1890. Sundquist, however, argues that 1892 was a deviating, not a realigning, election and did not produce fundamental shifts in party loyalty (1973: 145). But he also suggests that the severe depression of 1893, when a Democratic administration was in power, seriously hindered the efforts of the Populists and reform Democrats to consolidate their new majority. Also, the Supreme Court, dominated by Republicans, reversed a century of precedents to rule that a tax on incomes was a direct tax and therefore unconstitutional.[8] And the tax may have contributed to the Republican victory in 1896. Fearful of its reappearance, the Republicans outspent Bryan by at least $3.5 million to $650,000. Employers, the media, and the clergy were enlisted in the fight against the threat of social revolution posed by the income tax and by Bryan (Ratner 1942: 217ff.).

The 1894 income tax may be viewed as a consequence of two of my preconditions for policy consequences of elections: differing party stands on the issue and a shift to unified control of the government by one party (the Democrats). But the Democrats held control for only two years and did not control what proved to be a crucial branch of government. The 1896 realignment is the only one in American history *not* accompanied by a shift in control of government. The basis of Republican votes was certainly somewhat different after 1896 than before, but they remained the majority party. A consequence of the realignment of 1896 was not only a delay in consideration of the income tax in any form but also a return to high tariffs (the McKinley Tariff of 1898) as a means of financing the federal government.

Taxation in the New Deal: inverted realignment

Political realignment contributed substantially to the major changes in taxes which occurred during the New Deal. Federal revenue increased sharply over 1920 levels, in constant dollars, per capita, and as a percentage of the GNP.

Individual and corporate income tax rates were increased. After 1934, the tariff became an instrument of foreign policy, largely controlled by the president, instead of a domestic policy debated in Congress, and a payroll tax on employers and employees was introduced to finance the new social security system.

These tax changes, like the New Deal policies of deficit spending and government intervention in the economy, were clearly the responsibility of the overwhelming Democratic control of the national government. But New Deal policy was never presented to the electorate as the basis of choice in the 1932 election: as already mentioned, the party platforms differed little. The major revenue changes were largely initiated by the Roosevelt administration and underwent substantial changes in the nominally Democratic Congress. Further, although these policies were intended to aid the economic recovery and to shift the burden of government from the poor and middle classes to the rich, many of them had precisely the opposite effect. The evidence in fact suggests that New Deal policies prolonged the recession and made the tax burden more regressive.

The history of the New Deal revenue policy suggests a delicate political balancing act. The administration had liberal and labor support, but Roosevelt moved cautiously in many areas so as not to frighten off business investment.[9] In Congress, some Democrats supported the demands for redistribution voiced by Huey Long and the Townsendites. But in 1933 other House Democrats proposed what even Republicans called a "soak the poor" plan to increase taxes on small salary and wage earners, and in 1936 Southerners opposed many aspects of social security. Very few conservative Democrats suffered defeat in the 1932 and 1936 Democratic landslides. Their presence in Congress guaranteed trouble for Democrats who favored lower and less regressive taxes, since many of them gained leadership position because of increasing reliance on seniority (Brady 1973).

Even if these complex political considerations had not been present, economic confusion in this pre-Keynesian era produced policies whose impact differed greatly from their stated purpose. The Revenue Act of 1935, for example, increased taxes on the rich and on corporations. Liberals who urged even higher rates failed to realize that a considerable portion of corporate taxes are shifted to consumers. Taxes were *increased* every year from 1933 through 1938 to finance growing federal expenditures, but the economic impact of such increases was to decrease disposable income, remove money from the economy, and thus slow recovery (Trescott 1957; Brown 1956). The impact on redistribution was minimal (Lambert 1970). Also, several New Deal taxes were in fact regressive. The agricultural adjustment program was based on a "wickedly regressive processing tax" (Trescott 1957); the social security tax was levied only on the first $3,000 of income and was coupled with a deflationary reserve program. Congress also amended the Social Security Act to insure that the unemployment program would be administered at the state level, and the states varied widely in their distribution of unemployment benefits, with the poor states predictably providing the least assistance. Finally, many states, strapped for revenue, imposed new and regressive sales taxes which "diminished purchasing power more seriously than the

Federal income tax'' (Paul 1954: 245).

Unlike Jackson, Roosevelt was willing to use federal resources to counter the effects of business cycles. But, as with Jackson, he lacked both the political power and the economic theory to enable him to realize his policy goals. The realignment of 1928 to 1932 gave the New Dealers the power to make many changes in federal tax policy, but they did not fully control Congress, the Supreme Court, or state governments. It is therefore not surprising that the impact of the New Deal was not as great as its supporters had hoped or as its conservative opponents had feared.

Tax policy changes between realignments

Some changes in tax sources and amounts have occurred between realignments. These are attributable either to wars or to unified control of the national government by one political party. One of the ironies of American history is that one party has controlled the federal government during our major wars (1812, Civil War, both world wars, Korea, Vietnam), so that it is difficult to determine the independent effect of party control and war demands on tax policy.

Revenues have been increased (through deficit spending or the imposition of new taxes) during every war in which the U.S. has engaged since 1789. Revenue and expenditure levels have moved to new plateaus after wars. But considerable portions of the war-based taxes have been repealed or greatly reduced as soon as the wars ended, except for the high tariff following the Civil War, which (as described above) was not due to the war itself. Wars have not produced lasting changes in *sources* of revenues, but they provide the simplest explanation of changes in *amounts* of revenues. New sources of taxes and changes in tax incidence, however, are better explained by political factors. A partial exception may be the introduction of withholding in 1943, which resulted in a dramatic increase in the proportion of Americans filing federal tax returns[10] and gave the national government automatic access to wages and wage increases (Hughes 1977: 207). This also occurred under a unified government but under wartime conditions and with considerable Republican support. Administrative, political, and financial conditions were all involved.

Unified control of the national government has consistently been associated with tax policy changes. The Democrats were able to make some reductions in the tariff whenever they gained control of the national government during the nineteenth century (bills of 1846, 1857, and 1886 especially). Nevertheless, the tariff remained the major source of federal revenue throughout this period, except when the Civil War interrupted trade. Since Democrats also controlled Congress and the presidency in 1913, the first tax bill passed under the Seventeenth Amendment had progressive rates rather than the flat rates the Republicans preferred. When the Republicans regained control in the 1920s, Harding, Coolidge, and Treasury Secretary Mellon reversed this pattern: they eliminated the wartime ''excess profits'' tax, devised such new loopholes as the oil depletion allowance, and raised tariff rates, all over the protests of the Progressives and Democrats in Congress (Paul 1954: 128–132). They also delayed implementation of social security (Waltman 1976).

A major tax change which did *not* coincide with realignment of the major parties was the passage of a federal income tax amendment (as a provision of the Payne-Aldrich Tariff) in 1909. Republicans controlled both Congress and the presidency, but the major factor here was the strength of the Progressives in *both* parties and in the White House. If one accepts Sundquist's view, this was a realignment in the composition of both parties which was nevertheless contained within the framework of the existing party system (1973: 158–162). The process began with Theodore Roosevelt, who shocked his party in 1906 by advocating "the adoption of some such scheme as that of the progressive income tax on all fortunes" (Ratner 1942: 260) and gained fame as a trustbuster. Democratic Progressives gained seats in the previously Republican East, Republican Progressives in the West and Midwest. Many conservative Republicans also came to support an income tax, rather than continuation of high tariff rates, because during the 1890s the U.S. shifted from being a debtor to a creditor nation (Bauer et al. 1963: 18).[11] A country which was now a net exporter of manufactured goods quickly found the protective tariff a hindrance to trade. And, beginning in 1901, reciprocal provisions for bilateral trade agreements with such countries as France and Great Britain began to appear in tariff legislation. In short, a protective tariff was no longer economically necessary nor politically desirable. Another source of revenue had to be found, and the income tax was the most obvious alternative.

In the final House vote on the income tax amendment, fifty-five insurgent Republicans abstained because they saw the amendment as a strategy to defeat the income tax through a long ratification process in state legislatures and preferred a direct act of Congress (Ratner 1942: 301ff.). But a vote against the measure would have guaranteed defeat of the tax. Progressive Republicans and Democrats held the balance of power in Congress and thus assured a significant change in the source of federal revenue, although changes in the popular basis of party support and in the economy contributed to this far-reaching innovation.

Recent trends in the politics of taxation

This analysis has suggested that parties and elections have significantly shaped the development of U.S. tax policy, apparently contradicting recent empirical studies as well as Downs' theories concerning taxes and electoral strategy. Two recent trends in American history may account for this anomaly, however: the decline of political parties and the progressive depoliticization of tax policy making. Political parties have long served as a means, however minimal, of producing cooperation in policy making across different levels and units of government. But party strength has varied considerably throughout American history, reaching its peak during the 1890s. A major legacy of the Progressive Era was a general weakening of the party system, at least partially attributable to the "reforms" they introduced (nonpartisan election, direct primaries, voter registration requirements). As a result, the realignment of 1932 was far more diffuse than its predecessor (Burnham 1970: 91–110), and Burnham suggests that the "onward march of party decomposition" has made future realignments less likely. Unified party control of government today is likely to be far removed in practice from the "responsible party" model.

These developments have affected tax policy making as well. Opposition to tax changes should be less effective if it is diffuse rather than structured, whether in the electoral arena or in legislatures.[12] At the same time, advocates of tax policy innovation may be stymied by lack of organizational ability to initiate effective changes in the size, source, or distribution of the tax burden.

Party voting patterns on major revenue bills have varied considerably from the Jacksonian era to the present. As Table 2 shows, party cohesion on tax issues (as measured by Rice's index) was substantially higher in the nineteenth century, especially in the House of Representatives. It peaked in the 1890s with the vote on the 1894 income tax, declined somewhat with Republican insurgency in the Progressive Era (vote on the income tax amendment), increased slightly during the New Deal, but has declined steadily since. Some recent tax bills have been almost unanimously bipartisan (the Investment Tax Credit of 1967, for example, passed 386 to 2), while others were conflictual within rather than between parties (Vietnam surcharge, 1975 tax cut).

Factors other than party have become more important in tax policy formulation, so that even unified party control of the federal government is unlikely to produce major or predictable changes in federal revenue patterns. Perhaps not coincidentally, this pattern began to develop very shortly after the Seventeenth Amendment imposed direct federal income taxes on the American public. As taxes became more salient to citizens, individual politicians were motivated to find ways to insure that tax increases would not be linked to their political careers or positions on federal issues. O'Connor (1973: 67–73) further suggests that business and conservative forces represented in the Republican party were alarmed by the prospect of a dominant populist or liberally oriented party and took steps (creation of the Bureau of the Budget, city-manager government, Internal Revenue Service) to minimize the impact that any party could have on taxes on wealth or corporate profits.

An early step in this process was the fiscal dividend derived from progressive income tax rates: the government could reap an ever growing share of revenue from inflation and economic growth without changing tax rates. A second step was the creation of the Bureau of the Budget in 1921, when accountants and statisticians in the Budget Office in the executive branch began to take responsibility for coordinating taxing and spending decisions away from Congress. Since the 1920s, the Internal Revenue Service has been granted considerable authority to prescribe tax rules and regulations.

This trend continued in the 1930s. Congress delegated a major element of

Table 2

Party Votes on Tax Bills, House of Representatives, 1833–1975

	Rice Index of Party Cohesion	
Tax Bill	Republicans	Democrats
Compromise tariff of 1833	.49[a]	.51
1861 income tax	.52[b]	.58
1894 income tax	1.00	.84
1909 income tax	.73	.85
1936 social security	.54	.91
1969 Vietnam surcharge	.22	.33
1972 to index social security[c]	.25	.02
1975 tax cut	.14	.64

a. Includes Whigs and Anti-Masons.
b. Includes Whigs and Unionists.
c. Amendment to bill raising federal debt ceiling.

distributive policy (the tariff) to the executive but gained respite from the intense conflict generated over tariff rates. The Social Security Administration set up an independent trust fund operating at least in part on actuarial principles. Attempts to fund the reserves through general revenues have been stoutly resisted, from Conservative Coalition members in the 1930s down to Representative Al Ullman today. Benefits are now indexed to the cost of living and are due to legal entitlements, not legislative discretion. Such a system entails so little political risk that it is no wonder that increases in social security taxes as well as benefits are generally by nonpartisan votes. The House Ways and Means Committee still has a role to play in making tax policy, but there nonpartisanship is the norm, and most members are insulated from electoral control by seniority, incumbency, and the resulting large margins of victory in their districts (Manley 1970).

These national trends are reflected at state and local levels. City-manager governments, relying on uniform sales taxes and "businesslike" assessment procedures, have made local taxing less responsive to political demands and social needs (Lineberry and Fowler 1967). Many states have also adopted progressive income taxes and budget bureaus. Federal programs such as revenue sharing have also limited the impact that state parties or elections can have on either revenue or expenditures (Winters 1976).

Since the Keynesian revolution, tax policy has become an instrument of economic stabilization, left to the experts in the Treasury Department and the Council of Economic Advisers. Tax decisions are made far more on the basis of inflation and unemployment rates (determined by complex statistical procedures insulated from the political process: de Neufville 1975; Pierce 1971) than by demands for expenditures or for redistribution. Congress (over Nixon's objections) passed the Economic Stabilization Act of 1970, giving the president unprecedented authority over taxation and economic policy. This action made political sense, removing Congress even further from political fallout over taxes. The experts may be unable to use fiscal policy effectively to regulate the economy (Schultz and Dam 1977), but they have become increasingly less vulnerable to political control.

Conclusion

This analysis has shown that party control of government has been an important explanation for changes in federal tax policy. In American history, unified party control of the legislature and executive has shown a strong pattern of association with critical elections defined in terms of electoral shifts, and the economic crises so often associated with periods of realignment also contribute to demands for changes in the size and source of tax burdens. Tax changes between realignments have also coincided with unified control of the presidency and Congress. But realigning periods have been associated with larger tax changes than have interim years, perhaps because other political or economic considerations reduced the relative salience of tax questions.

These results are further strengthened by a study of tax innovations at the state level (Hansen 1978). State adoptions of sales and income taxes were more likely when the governor and legislature were controlled by the same party, and one-party states initiated these innovations many years earlier than more competitive states.

Two important caveats must be stressed, however, because party dominance is a necessary but hardly sufficient criterion for tax policy making. First, a party may be nominally in control but divided internally in many respects. On a highly disaggregated, distributive issue such as the tariff, or revisions in the Internal Revenue Code, party unity is not likely. Thus, even when Democrats controlled Congress before and after the Civil War, they were unable to make large downward revisions in tariff rates. Tariff reduction was a collective good with little political support: it was far easier politically to extend protection than to reduce rates (Bauer et al. 1963: 15–17). But efforts to impose entirely new sources of revenue cannot be so easily compromised within parties. Higher party unity should therefore prevail when new sources of revenue are being considered than when older ones are being adjusted.

Second, Downs' theory of budget making in democracies stressed that popular opposition to taxes would give parties little incentive to advocate tax changes or increases and that rational political actors would tend to avoid the issue altogether. But the salience of tax questions has varied throughout American history. Federal taxes have become more salient to the electorate since greatly increased tax rates and near universal withholding were instituted during World War II. Thus, recent platforms of both parties rituallly call for lower taxes. In earlier years, parties differed as to the sources and amounts of federal taxes, and parties in Congress were more highly polarized on revenue issues than is now the case. Under those conditions, unified control of the national government produced changes in tax policy. But this is less likely today, as parties have weakened and the tax process has become more insulated from political control. Downs' tax policy model based on political opposition must be expanded to allow for historical variation in its key parameters. . . .

Notes

1. See Tarschys (1975) for discussion of financial and tax-related perspectives on Wagner's Law and the growth of public expenditures. Pryor (1968) attempts a quantitative cross-cultural analysis. But the political variables for which he was able to find comparable data (such as party competition and voter turnout) had no theoretical linkage to government taxing or spending and, not surprisingly, accounted for little of the variance in either.

2. Campbell's "surge and decline" theory of electoral change (1966), based largely on survey data from the recent past, also appears to fit aggregate electoral data from earlier periods.

3. Brady (1973) has contrasted the strong leadership and party unity that prevailed after 1896 with the dispersion of power characteristic of the period since the New Deal and the rise of the Conservative Coalition.

4. Riker's (1962) theory of political coalitions suggests that a large majority for one legislative party may result in low cohesion and policy making characterized by stalemate and compromise. But this theory does not appear to fit congressional behavior after periods of realignment: very high party-unity scores prevailed after 1896 and from 1933 through 1936. See also the discussion and references in Hardin (1976).

5. Niskanen (1971) and Buchanan and Tullock (1962) describe processes internal to bureaucracies which may result in larger-than-optimal budgets. But larger budgets may *not* require tax increases, especially when a nation has a progressive income tax, a flexible debt ceiling, and the ability to print money (Hughes 1977: 224). The issue here is the amount of taxes, not budgets.

6. The nascent political parties of this period were divided regionally and ideologically: the Rice Index of Cohesion on the 1833 tariff was only .51 for the Jacksonian Democrats.

7. Trescott (1957) notes that such deficit spending may have eased the impact of the Depression, but such a "Keynesian" policy was hardly intentional: it simply resulted from a lag between federal revenues and expenditures. Nor did it absolve the Jacksonians from the responsibility of creating the Depression in the first place.

8. See Ratner (1942: 193ff.) for a detailed discussion of the political and legal ramifications of the Supreme Court's ruling on the 1894 income tax.

9. See Lambert (1970) for an analysis of Roosevelt's strategy in revenue matters during the New Deal.

10. The number of returns filed rose from seven million in 1939 to forty-four million in 1943, imposing direct federal taxes on a majority of Americans for the first time in U.S. history (*Historical Statistics of the United States* 1975: 1110).

11. The change in the balance of trade was noted in the 1900 Republican party platform, but its economic and political significance did not affect party policy for several years. See Stewart (1976) for an analysis of other reasons for changes in Republicans' attitudes toward the tariff and income tax.

12. As Buchanan noted, "the institutions through which costs and benefits are presented to the private citizen may affect his choices" (1967: 5). Market choice (correspondence between private costs and benefits) does not apply to collective, political choice processes. Individuals thus reduce information costs by choosing among parties, candidates, or other fiscal choice-making institutions.

Bibliography

Bauer, R. A., I. de S. Pool, and L. A. Dexter. 1963. *American Business and Public Policy*. New York: Atherton Press.

Brady, D. W. 1973. *Congressional Voting in a Partisan Era: A Comparison of the McKinley Houses to the Modern House*. Lawrence: University of Kansas Press.

——————. 1980. "Elections, Congress and Public Policy Changes: 1886–1960," in Bruce A. Campbell and Richard J. Trilling, *Realignment in American Politics: Toward a Theory*. Austin: University of Texas Press.

Brown, E. C. 1956. "Fiscal Policy in the Thirties: A Reappraisal." *American Economic Review* 46: 857–879.

Buchanan, J. M. 1967. *Public Finance in Democratic Process: Fiscal Institutions and the Individual Choice*. Chapel Hill: University of North Carolina Press.

Buchanan, J. M., and G. Tullock. 1962. *The Calculus of Consent*. Ann Arbor: University of Michigan Press.

Burnham, W. D. 1970. *Critical Elections and the Mainsprings of American Politics*. New York: W. W. Norton.

Campbell, A. 1966. "Surge and Decline: A Study of Electoral Change." In A. Campbell, P. E. Converse, W. E. Miller, and D. E. Stokes, *Elections and the Political Order*, pp. 40–62. New York: John Wiley & Sons.

Campbell, B. and R. J. Trilling. 1980. *Realignment in American Politics: Toward a Theory*. Austin: University of Texas Press.

De Neufville, J. I. 1975. *Social Indicators and Public Policy*. New York: Elsevier.

Dewey, D. R. 1934. *Financial History of the United States*. New York: Longmans, Green.

Downs. A. 1957. *An Economic Theory of Democracy*. New York: Harper & Row.

——————. 1960. "Why the Government Budget Is Too Small in a Democracy." *World Politics* 12: 541–563.

Dye, T. 1966. *Politics, Economics and the Public*. Chicago: Rand McNally.

Fisher, G. 1969. *Taxes and Politics: A Study of Illinois Public Finance*. Urbana: University of Illinois Press.

Ginsberg, B. 1976. "Elections and Public Policy." *American Political Science Review* 70: 41–49.

Hansen, S. B. 1978. "The Politics of State Tax Innovation." Paper presented at the annual meeting of the Midwest Political Science Association, Chicago.

Hardin, R. 1976. "Hollow Victory: The Minimum Winning Coalition." *American Political Science Review* 70: 1202–1214.

Howe, F. C. 1896. *Taxation and Taxes in the United States under the Internal Revenue System 1791–1895*. New York: Crowell.

Hughes, J. R. T. 1977. *The Governmental Habit*. New York: Basic Books.

Lambert, W. F. 1970. "New Deal Revenue Acts: The Politics of Taxation." Ph.D. dissertation, University of Texas at Austin.

Lineberry, R., and E. P. Fowler. 1967. "Reformism and Public Policies in American Cities." *American Political Science Review* 61: 701–716.

Manley, J. 1970. *The Politics of Finance*. Boston: Little, Brown.

Mosher, F. C., and O. F. Poland. 1964. *The Costs of American Government*. New York: Dodd, Mead.

Musgrave, R. A. 1969. *Fiscal Systems*. New Haven: Yale University Press.

Neuman, W. L., and A. Hicks. 1977. "Public Policy, Party Platforms, and Critical Elections: A Reexamination." *American Political Science Review* 71: 277–280.

Niskanen, W. A., Jr. 1971. *Bureaucracy and Representative Government*. Chicago: Aldine-Atherton.

O'Connor, J. 1973. *The Fiscal Crisis of the State*. New York: St. Martin's.

Paul, R. E. 1954. *Taxation in the United States*. Boston: Little, Brown.

Peacock, A. T., and J. Wiseman. 1961. *The Growth of Public Expenditures in the United Kingdom*. Princeton: Princeton University Press (National Bureau of Economic Research).

Pierce, L. C. 1971. *The Politics of Fiscal Policy Formation*. Pacific Palisades, Calif.: Goodyear.

Pryor, F. L. 1968. *Public Expenditures in Communist and Capitalist Nations*. Homewood, Ill.: Richard D. Irwin.

Ratner, S. 1942. *A Political and Social History of Federal Taxation 1789-1913*. New York: W. W. Norton.

Ricker, W. 1962. *The Theory of Political Coalitions*. New Haven: Yale University Press.

Schattschneider, E. E. 1942. *Party Government*. New York: Holt, Rinehart & Winston.

Schlesinger, A. M., Jr. 1946. *The Age of Jackson*. Boston: Little, Brown.

Seligman, L. G., and M. R. King. 1980. "Political Realignments and Recruitment to the U.S. Congress 1870-1970," in Bruce A. Campbell and Richard J. Trilling, eds., *Realignment in American Politics: Toward a Theory*. Austin: University of Texas Press.

Sharkansky, I. 1969. *The Politics of Taxing and Spending*. Indianapolis: Bobbs-Merrill.

Shultz, G., and K. Dam. 1977. *Economic Policy beyond the Headlines*. Stanford: Stanford Alumni Association.

Stewart, C. A. 1976. "Tax Policy 1893-1913: A Case Study of Conflict and Consensus." Manuscript, University of North Carolina.

Sundquist, J. 1973. *Dynamics of the Party System: Alignment and Realignment of Political Parties in the United States*. Washington, D.C.: Brookings Institution.

Tarschys, D. 1975. "The Growth of Public Expenditures: Nine Modes of Explanation." *Scandinavian Political Studies* 10: 9-31.

Taussig, F. W. 1966. *The Tariff History of the United States*. New York: Capricorn Books. (Originally published by G. P. Putnam, 1892.)

Trescott, P. B. 1957. "Some Historical Aspects of Federal Fiscal Policy 1790-1956." In U.S. Congress, Joint Economic Committee, *Federal Expenditure Policy for Growth and Stability*, 85th Congress, 1st session, pp. 60-83. Washington, D.C.: G.P.O.

United States, Bureau of the Census. 1975. *Historical Statistics of the United States: Colonial Times to 1970*. Bicentennial edition, pts. 1 and 2. Washington, D.C.: G.P.O.

Walker, J. 1969. "The Diffusion of Innovation among the American States." *American Political Science Review* 63: 880-899.

Waltman, J. L. 1976. "Linkage Politics and Public Policy: An Analysis of the American Social Security and Income Tax Adoptions." Ph.D. dissertation, Indiana University.

Winters, R. T. 1976. "Party Control and Policy Change." *American Journal of Political Science* 20: 597-636.

3B.3. From Redistributive to Hegemonic Logic
The Transformation of American Tax Politics, 1894–1963

RONALD FREDERICK KING

Whereas the preceding essay stressed democratic control of taxes and argued that party control was the key mechanism of change, this essay, echoing James O'Connor's, stresses ideological (hegemonic) control by a capitalist elite and considers changes in party control less important than the common beliefs of those in both parties.

Ronald King is primarily interested in the redistributional effects of taxation. He argues that when the income tax was first imposed, its burden fell heavily on the rich, arousing expectations that it would become a major means of income redistribution. This, King claims, led capitalist elites to search for a means to prevent this effect. In order to do so, they had to persuade politicians that it was not in the interests of the majority to use the income tax as a major redistributive weapon against the wealthy minority.

The key event for King is the general acceptance by both Republican and Democratic policymakers of an argument made in the 1920s by Treasury Secretary Andrew Mellon, a forerunner of the supply-side economists of the 1980s. Mellon argued that it was important to consider the effects of taxation on economic growth, and that heavy taxation of capital, by reducing savings, would reduce investment and growth. This, in King's view, converted a zero-sum argument over the distribution of the economic pie, to a non–zero-sum argument about how the growth of the economic pie could be secured.

In assessing the significance of King's theory, it clearly matters a great deal whether Mellon's argument is true or false. If false, then acceptance of the view reduces redistribution without increasing growth. If true, then the majority faces a trade-off between current and future benefits.

Reprinted with permission from *Politics and Society* 12, no. 1 (1983): 1–52 (with deletions). Copyright 1983 by Geron-X, Inc.

"The present assault upon capital is but the beginning." Thus wrote Justice Stephen J. Field in a concurring opinion to the 1895 Supreme Court decision declaring unconstitutional a 2 percent income tax on corporate profits and individual earnings over $4,000. "It will be but the stepping-stone to others, larger and more sweeping, till our political contests will become a war of the poor against the rich; a war constantly growing in intensity and bitterness."[1] Now, over eighty-five years later, federal income taxes appropriate considerably more than 2 percent of receipts and raise hundreds of billions of dollars annually. Yet the politics of fiscal policy formation can hardly be said to correspond to the early prognostications. There has been no "communistic march" to "confiscate wealth," "spoliate private property," and "ultimately wreck the American republic."[2] Tax politics has become routinized. It displays little of the divisive fervor that characterized the redistributive struggles of an earlier era. Allocational equity, much less equality, now constitutes just one among several ends of taxation and, indeed, is often compromised in the pursuit of objectives promising social benefits for all. Effective burdens are far less progressive than one might infer from the nominal rate schedules, and the notion of ability to pay, although an accepted part of American political ideology, does not operate as an absolute standard, serving instead to put the onus of proof on those wishing to introduce special exemptions and dispensations into the revenue code.

This essay seeks to explain why Justice Field's dire prediction did not come to pass, why contemporary American tax politics has not, after all, taken the form of a bitter class conflict over the apportionment of short-run liabilities. I base my explanation on two alternative perspectives on fiscal controversies that have been derived, by loose analogy, from mathematical models of distributional games. The first perspective corresponds to a strict zero-sum opposition, in which the total payoff is fixed and fungible: any benefit received by one player reduces the amount available to others. The second corresponds to an asymmetric and non-zero-sum game model, in which a marginal shift of resources to one sort of player potentially but with risk offers enhanced net discounted payoffs to all players over time.

Although further game analogies are possible, these two perspectives hold special importance for understanding tax struggles in the U.S., especially when viewed from a temporal, and not merely analytical, standpoint. Federal income taxation did once seriously threaten to promote zero-sum redistribution. Such tax redistribution was considered by many the only way to protect the people against undemocratic accumulations of wealth and power and to compel the rich to contribute their just share to the support of the government. However, the introduction of an investment-dependent logic stressing market consequences, represented by the second of our game models, effectively ended any redistributive hopes. It gradually altered the purposes attached to taxation policy and thus modified the way groups calculated their interest when revenue matters reached the political agenda. Grounded in the structural asymmetries of modern capitalism, this revised fiscal outlook was neither necessary to nor inherent in the taxation arena per se. Instead, it became established only after much struggle and as the result of a series of strategic choices. By the end of the Second World War, fiscal policy had become almost synonymous with macroeconomic policy. Prosperity subordinated apportionment, and the federal government fully accepted its role as indirect stimulator, regularly awarding incentives to both demand and supply yet possessing scant control over the private economic institutions expected to respond. The story to follow, therefore, chronicles certain major transformations in the game of U.S. federal taxation politics and the effects these have had on the range of predictable distributional outcomes. . . .

The emergence of hegemonic* tax logic

The political struggles over the passage of the initial federal income tax in the United States reflected fundamental conflict regarding the distribution of immediate government fiscal burdens. To income tax proponents, existing consumption taxes, which bore primarily upon the mass of citizens, were seen as being the product of undemocratic elite domination of the political process and as relieving avaricious wealth of its just obligations. To income tax opponents, by contrast, the subjection of a single class of taxpayers to discriminatory penalties simply because of their higher earnings demonstrated the dangers that an aroused populace could pose when the precept of equal treatment before the law was contradicted by short-run advantage. The conflict over taxation was certainly symbolic of a wider struggle over the development of the American society. Yet taxes, in themselves, were featured merely as representative of the perceived bias of public policy and the abuses of class legislation. The issue was defined on both sides in terms of distributional equity versus myopic greed. The principles of proper allocation were determined solely by the arrangement of current liabilities, and all wider, economic implications of tax impositions were explicitly denied.

Some initial supporters of the tax did start to express reservations, even though the original income levy was quite modest, with only 10 percent of federal receipts in 1914 garnered from this new revenue source and barely 1 percent of reported net incomes and profits appropriated. Already they feared mass persecution of business. Theodore Roosevelt, for example, wrote to his cousin in 1915 that "my withers are unwrung" and that he concurred with the assault upon this income tax law.[3] Potential splits within the protax movement, however, did not prove historically significant. Under the pressure of military preparedness and war, the income tax was raised to levels entirely unforeseen by even its stongest advocates. In the postwar return to normalcy, the debate over fiscal obligations resumed, but it was recast in a structurally different, non-zero-sum form.

With the decline in tariff revenues caused by the outbreak of World War I in Europe and with the need for funds to finance rearmament at home, an emergency

---

Hegemony is a term derived from the work of Antonio Gramsci. It refers to the process through which the working class internalizes the values of the ruling class and comes to think that what is good for the rich is good for them.—Ed.

income tax increase was approved in 1914 and extended the following year. The agreement was that new legislation would be proposed shortly. In contrast to the Wilson administration's subsequent recommendation to lower the personal exemption, the 1916 act doubled the normal tax rate and raised the surtax to 13 percent, while leaving exemptions untouched. It further imposed a graduated inheritance tax and levied a special tax on the profits of munitions manufacturers.

Paradoxically, it was the insurgents opposed to foreign intervention who were the most emphatic proponents of the revenue measure designed to pay for war preparedness. In addition to the customary justifications based upon distributional equity, agrarian Democrats believed that northeastern manufacturers would take a less aggressive stand on foreign policy if the cost of such a stand were greater. As Warren Bailey (Democrat, Pennsylvania) declared, "if the forces of big business are to plunge this country into a saturnalia of extravagance for war purposes at a time of peace, it is my notion that the forces of big business should put up the money."[4] The principal Republican complaint was that the 1916 act represented a new and dangerous direction in fiscal policy. Employment of the income tax had not been reserved for dire national emergency, nor merely to compensate for downward revisions of the tariff. The tax could no longer be seen just as a secondary fiscal tool to be used when traditional sources of revenue proved inadequate. Critics claimed, with much prescience, that income taxation was attaining an autonomous development that increased the possibility of its use for redistributive ends.

America's entry into the war placed great strains upon the nation's economy and supplied the pretext for an enormous expansion of the income tax as virtually the only elastic source of federal funds. Two sizable war revenue bills were enacted, in October 1917 and in December 1918, both of which were approved by overwhelming majorities and endorsed by the leaderships of both parties. Treasury Secretary McAdoo, determined not to follow the example of Chase during the Civil War, organized the broad distribution of Liberty Bonds and resolved to finance at least one-third of government expenditures out of current receipts. An economically rational fiscal policy would have been far more regressive, since it would have reduced consumer spending to encourage a shift to war production and to help curb demand inflation. Such a policy, however, would not have been acceptable to the dominant political coalition in the Congress, which was concerned primarily with preventing war profiteering and with forcing the wealthy to bear a just share of expenses.

As a result of the war revenue acts, income and profits taxes in 1918 generated 63.1 percent of total federal receipts, customs duties only 4.9 percent, and miscellaneous excises 23.8 percent. The maximum personal income tax rate of 77 percent (12 percent plus a 65 percent surtax) was five times the prewar level and eleven times the 7 percent maximum rate originally imposed just six years before. As for corporations, 37.2 percent of net reported profits went to the government, as compared to merely 2.0 percent in 1916.[5] Part of this increased corporate burden came from an excess profits tax on surplus business income, termed by one newspaper "the first attempt in a country whose industries are organized under capitalist leadership to limit profits as part of its economic system."[6] Ways and Means Chairman Claude Kitchen had wanted to follow the Canadian model, which was based on profits as a percentage of invested capital, rather than the British model, which was based on prewar average returns. Kitchen hoped that the former approach would permit the tax to become a permanent feature of the campaign for revenue equity. The Wilson administration and Senate Democrats disagreed, claiming that the Canadian system demanded a complex and hazy definition of capital, encouraged overinvestment, and discriminated against growing and risky enterprises. The final provision embodied a compromise combining bits of both principles in an ad hoc fashion.

Among the problems confronted by the Congress was an unavoidable ignorance regarding the amount of taxation the nation would willingly bear. Never before had so much been taken, both directly and indirectly, from incomes and profits. Given the highly progressive rate structure, concern was for the first time expressed that a level might be reached where business would lose its incentive to invest. Academic moderates began to remind their radical colleagues demanding the conscription of wealth as well as soldiers that some profits were necessary if industry was to carry out the expansion required for war production. The Congressional opinion was that, with net profits more than double the prewar average, it was unreasonable to assert that business could not stand increased taxes. Yet a few conservatives in debate registered their dissent from the Republican strategy of cooperation. "Unnecessary taxation," said Warren Harding, "only halts and hampers the needed activity of capital."[7] An indication of the new attention to the possible economic consequences of heavy taxation can be seen in the Finance Committee minority report in 1918. Already knowing that they would control the next Congress, Republicans objected that it would be wrong to fix rates as far ahead as 1920, not merely because of the difficulty of estimating government needs, but especially because it was impossible to forecast postwar business conditions and because an inflexible policy might "disarrange our industrial system."[8]

Spokesmen for private industry were surprisingly restrained in their remonstrations that very high taxes were destructive of the capitalized energy necessary to keep the war machine functioning. Business was being extremely careful to avoid all action that might cast aspersions on corporate motives. There was still considerable feeling in the country that this was a rich man's war, entered into for imperialistic gain and windfall profits. The example of the Russian Revolution was a caution for those who wished that mass attitudes could be ignored and the cost of the war shifted downward. The business campaign against progressive taxation was thus reserved for after the close of hostilities, when it emerged with vehemence. For example, the National Industrial Conference Board and the National Tax Association arranged educational seminars on high taxes as they contributed to rising prices and fettered industrial expansion; a movement was launched on behalf of a national sales tax, sponsored by organizations such as the

Business Men's National Tax Committee and the Tax League of America; and a United States Chamber of Commerce referendum resulted in a 1718-to-44 vote against the retention of the excess profits tax.[9] The outgoing Wilson administration gave some support to the campaign for tax reduction, but no legislation was advanced. Tax relief for the wealthy had to wait until after the inauguration of Harding.

Thus the first public consideration of taxation's economic effects on the private market, and therefore the initial shift away from taxation as a narrow zero-sum struggle solely over the immediate allocation of government burdens, occurred at the end of World War I. Business agitation for reductions in tax rates entailed far more than a reactionary dream of returning to normalcy. Finding its best spokesman in the incoming Secretary of the Treasury, Andrew Mellon, a new conservatism arose that accepted the principle of graduated taxation but proclaimed that rates on profits and high incomes ought not be set so as to restrict economic expansion. There had always been complaints that the income tax penalized thrift and discouraged industriousness. But the thrust of these objections was that the tax violated normative values fundamental to American life. Now, however, the very existence of the income tax was not in question, and certain political actors began to evaluate the marginal effects of tax changes on such critical economic variables as growth, prices, and unemployment. The fiscal tools were rudimentary, economic understanding limited, and it was more assumed than proved that tax reduction for the wealthy would have the desired stimulative effects. Nevertheless, the application of a non-zero-sum logic to internal revenues gave conservatives a new, more sophisticated position from which to resist the possible redistributive uses of income taxation.

The most comprehensive statement of the new tax ideology is to be found in Mellon's book, *Taxation: The People's Business*, published in 1924. According to Mellon, "the principle that a man should pay tax in accordance with his 'ability to pay' is sound, but like other general statements, has its practical limitations and qualifications, and when, as a result of an excessive or unsound basis of taxation, it becomes evident that the source of taxation is drying up and wealth is being diverted into unproductive channels, yielding neither revenue to the Government nor profit to the people, then it is time to readjust our basis of taxation upon sound principles."[10] In contrast to the situation just a few years before, the income tax was no longer seen as confiscation and progressive rates were not indicative of encroaching communism. The problem with the tax system was merely that it contained inefficient provisions that required readjustment. The existing high levels of taxation, an inheritance from the war, were said to violate sound principles in three ways: they drove investment funds away from gainful employment and into such unproductive sources as tax-exempt securities; they hampered incentives and quashed the spirit of enterprise; and they reduced the total amount of private investment capital. In order to unleash economic growth, the secretary recommended, the maximum level of taxation must never diminish after-tax profits on investment to a lower point than can be obtained from speculation or from tax-free bonds. Thus he proposed a complete repeal of the excess profits tax, a reduction in the top-bracket personal surtax to 25 percent on incomes over $100,000, and a major slash in the estate tax. By encouraging private capital to contribute more fully to the nation's well being, government policy could generate long-run economic prosperity that would permit sufficient government receipts under low nominal rates, a gradual reduction in the public debt, ample profits, and full employment.

According to Mellon, what had been missing from earlier fiscal theories, which focused entirely upon zero-sum struggles over public contributions, was the recognition that the consequences of taxation extended beyond the individual called upon to pay, affecting the economic development of the nation as a whole. Even workers, he contended, would be better off supporting the kind of regressive tax cuts sought by the Harding administration. "The hardship of suffering resulting from business depressions and unemployment inevitably falls most seriously not upon those paying high income taxes, but upon the great body of the people of small incomes. Under our form of government there is, and very rightly so, little danger of any undue burden from the taxes imposed directly upon those of small means, but there is danger of serious hardship and suffering to them because of high prices, unemployment, and high living costs, resulting from unjust or unwise tax laws."[11] Mellon's conclusion is a full statement of the integrative, cooperative aspect of business-stimulative tax policy arising from the new conservative fiscal ideology. "The prosperity of each individual," he wrote, "is, after all, dependent upon the prosperity of the whole country; and anything that endangers or retards the country's normal development also jeopardizes to that extent the prosperity of each individual taxpayer."[12]

While explanations for this rapid shift in basic ideology must be tentative, four interrelated causes emerge from the account given above. First, the state of economic knowledge changed considerably over these thirty years, and politicians became more sensitive to academic teachings during the war. Nevertheless, there is certainly no automatic correlation between economic pedagogy and political practice, and one should always look for concrete inducements when politicians adopt the categories of professionals.

Second, the huge increases during the war in the size of the state and the amount of taxation meant both that a greater percentage of the income of the wealthy was publicly appropriated and that, for the first time, progressive taxation could have substantial effects on the social distribution of income. As one Washington attorney euphemistically stated, "In 1917 and 1918, when the rates very suddenly went way up, we realized with equal suddenness the importance of fundamental, sound, right principles both in the provisions and in the administration of the income tax."[13]

Third, the very concept of an excess profits tax presented a challenge to the assumed right of a firm to whatever it receives, demanding a clear ideological response from capital. As James Emery of the National Association of Manufacturers said, "I think the excess profits tax carries, first of all, a false social implication. It insidiously insinuates, in the phrase that qualifies the tax, that the amount which is exempted from the operation of the tax comprises a fair, normal return, all above which is in its nature an excessive and socially improper return. In this hour, in this day, we cannot be too careful about the social implications of the phraseology of our taxation, for that carries a dangerous and incorrect idea into the public mind.[14] In replying to the connotation that earnings above a certain base are illegitimate, it was logical to claim that profits, even very high profits, serve a necessary and useful social function. The direct attack upon unlimited returns brought forth an answer based upon economics rather than equity, that the accumulation of surplus corporate income was a precondition to the investment needed initially for war production and later for national economic growth and progress.

Fourth, the new emphasis upon the effect taxation can have on industry came not merely from an awareness of the greater percentage of the national income now taken and from a business reaction and protest. It also came from a recognition that government policies can have an impact upon social relations. If subordinate classes could be convinced that the private market gains secured by means of tax-stimulated increases in productivity were greater than those possible through tax redistribution, they would be more likely to accept and participate in the emerging system of corporate capitalism. Thus the changes in the pattern of tax politics beginning during the 1920s can be seen as part of the movement toward the integration rather than the repression of organizations representing workers' material interests. This also found expression in, for example, Herbert Hoover's corporatist vision of a voluntarily self-regulating society.

It had taken thirty years, from the origin of the redistributive threat posed by income taxation, for hegemonic, capital-dependent considerations to emerge as a defense used by dominant groups in society. Under capitalism, savings and investment out of profits are necessary preconditions for generating future income streams to all social classes. To the extent that the manipulation of taxation influences capital decisions, through adjustments in the level and allocation of burdens, it provides a useful technique for any state seeking ways to affect private economic performance. Yet given the explicit prewar denials of such a broad impact, it was not at all obvious that this functional tax logic would appear. Moreover, once admitted into the revenue discourse, its acceptance was not immediate and it became an object of controversy during the interwar era. Hegemonic taxation theory did quickly become a central tenet of mainstream Republicanism, but the positions adopted by others were inconsistent. For the coming period, the enactment of fiscal policies based upon hegemonic principle would depend upon the number of moderate and conservative Republicans in Congress and upon the responses of Democrats, insurgent Progressives, and the leaders of labor and agrarian interest organizations. . . .

Conclusion

The issues relevant to taxation politics have become much more complex since the time of Andrew Mellon. Yet the non-zero-sum logic basic to his program and the hegemonic concerns that he articulated remain essential to any analysis of the contemporary federal revenue system. They exercise significant influence over nondecisions, restricting demands for greater effective tax progressivity and limiting the sorts of distributive claims responsible groups can make. Correspondingly, hegemonic, class-cooperative yet capital-dependent arguments also provide the principal defense for a number of the most well-entrenched and expensive of current tax preferences. Special tax stimulants to business investment have been proposed and passed by every single American president since Eisenhower, a surprising record of bi-partisanship. Ability to pay has thus been substantially eroded, and the equitable apportionment of burdens has virtually ceased to be a politically potent doctrine. In other words, the federal income tax has gradually been tamed. It has lost its initial radical potential, has failed to reapportion incomes, and is now even being used to support capitalist accumulation.

Conventional zero-sum models of tax politics would explain this taming of the federal income tax by saying that a preponderance of legislative resources are held by business elites and that, while workers persistently oppose the awarding of fiscal advantages to the wealthy, they lack the political power to prevent it. Such a zero-sum game would certainly be very risky for dominant classes, for with any appreciable shift in class capacities, especially in a democracy where representatives responsible to the voting populace have an institutionalized say, they might lose all privileges. Historically, in fact, American income taxation did once portend real redistribution, and elites responded by taking the matter to the least democratic branch of government, the Supreme Court, to proscribe changes in the revenue base.

The important point, however, is that our story did not stop there. The 1895 tactic of legal prohibition was defeated by the passage of the Sixteenth Amendment, and a graduated tax was eventually levied. Yet income and wealth have not been expropriated. Instead, federal taxation politics has been slowly transformed. Strictly allocative concerns have been supplemented by, even subordinated to, a market philosophy that gives priority to capital investment and that emphasizes the cooperative national benefits to be derived from business stimulants for expanded productive potential. As a result, a relatively steep nominal tax progressivity is counterbalanced by numerous targeted erosions and inducements, many of which are intended to promote allegedly desirable social ends and have sometimes been approved with a degree of consensus inconsistent with traditional theory.

Actors do not appear sui generis in the political arena, and moreover, the institutional and ideological constitution of that arena affects the capacity of those actors to define and satisfy their interests. In this sense, the structured mode of insertion becomes an essential element in understanding political practice. Using terms of analogy to alternative types of rational games, this paper has argued that between 1921 and 1963 the ideological insertion of classes into tax politics was reformulated, which affected the pattern of conflict and the expected range of outcomes. After 1913, it was not the formal rules governing the aggregation of citizen preferences that constrained popular egalitarianism. Participation was left open through the normal channels of access and influence. However, a change gradually occurred in how classes viewed fiscal issues, affecting the objectives sought through taxation, the factors relevant to the calculation of net advantage, and the possible appeal of class conciliation.

From the strictly zero-sum perspective, distributional struggles appear merely as private matters. Particularistic factions seek their own benefit at the expense of others, and no inherent merit resides in any group. The only restriction is that outcomes remain within relatively wide boundaries so that none can foresee such striking and persistent losses that they withdraw support from the prevailing social system. For example, during the late nineteenth and early twentieth centuries, certain reformers believed we had drifted sufficiently close to one boundary as to advocate state redistribution for purposes of public safety. Heeding the protests of farmers and workers about the inequity of revenue burdens, an income tax was urged, in the words of Benton McMillin, to "diminish the antipathies that now exist between the classes," by removing the basis of that "iconoclastic complaint which finds expression in violence and threatens the very foundations upon which our whole institutions rest."[15]

The situation is substantially altered, however, once dynamic, non-zero-sum market ramifications are introduced. Under the rules of a taxation game played by actors seeking to maximize revenues stemming from interconnected public and private spheres, those who control the mechanism that determines the size of the economic pie are the privileged ones. To protect after-tax profits and to insure their use in productive investment, the distributive interests of the capitalist minority can become the interest of all. Thus the terrain inside the boundaries gets structured, and effective tax progressivity disappears not simply because of the extraordinary power of an economic elite, nor because of any abstract purpose given to the state apparatus, but because of the organization of competitive tax politics in a capitalist democracy.

Nevertheless, and this has been fundamental to my narrative, there is no *a priori* reason for federal taxation to have become dominated by the goal of insuring stable growth for the American corporate economy. The restructuring of tax politics away from zero-sum redistribution was not unilaterally imposed upon an unwilling mass populace. Rather, the institutionalization of a revised fiscal outlook occurred over four decades, was itself an object of struggle among social forces, and was the culmination of a series of reasonable strategic choices. Only in retrospect does it appear inevitable that taxation would become the primary location for aggregate state macroeconomic interventions, within which an asymmetric class coalition dependent upon capitalist investment would emerge fundamental in patterning policy outcomes. . . .

Notes

1. Pollock vs. Farmers' Loan and Trust Co., 157 U.S. 429 (1895), p. 607.

2. Phrases used by William Guthrie and William Choate, counsels for the appellants, in Pollock vs. Farmers' Loan and Trust Co., *The Records and Briefs of the Supreme Court of the United States, 1782–1896*, microfilm edition (Wilmington, Dela: Scholarly Resources, Inc.), vol. 939, roll 427.

3. Theodore Roosevelt, Letter to William Emlen Roosevelt, January 24, 1915, *The Letters of Theodore Roosevelt*, ed. Elting Morrison (Cambridge: Harvard University Press, 1952), 8:884.

4. Bailey quoted in Link, *Woodrow Wilson*, p. 194.

5. Calculated from the historical tables found in U.S. Treasury Department, *Statistical Appendix to the Report of the Secretary of the Treasury on the State of the Finances*, fiscal year 1979 (Washington, D.C.: U.S. Government Printing Office, 1980), p. 8; and in U.S. Treasury Department, Bureau of Internal Revenue, *Statistics of Income for 1932* (Washington, D.C.: U.S. Government Printing Office, 1934), pp. 38, 47.

6. *New York Globe*, in *Literary Digest*, 54, no. 4 (January 27, 1917): 176.

7. *Congressional Record*, August 31, 1917; 55: 6471.

8. U.S. Congress, Senate, Committee on Finance, *Senate Report* no. 617, December 6, 1918, 65th Cong., 3rd sess., pt. 3, p. 2.

9. Chamber of Commerce of the United States, *Annual Report of the Board of Directors*, 9th Annual Meeting, April 1921, Report on the Results of Referendum no. 34 (Washington, D.C.: Chamber of Commerce, 1921), pp. 26–7. For a review of the sales tax debate, see K. M. Williamson, "The Literature on the Sales Tax," *Quarterly Journal of Economics* 35, no. 4 (August 1921): 618–33.

10. Andrew Mellon, *Taxation: The People's Business* (New York; Macmillan, 1924), pp. 15–16.

11. Andrew Mellon, U.S. Treasury Department, *Annual Report of the Secretary of the Treasury on the State of the Finances*, fiscal year ending June 30, 1921, transmitted November 28, 1921 (Washington, D.C.: U.S. Government Printing Office, 1922), p. 13.

12. Andrew Mellon, *Taxation: The People's Business*, p. 138.

13. J. C. Peacock, "Revision of the Income Tax to Promote Equity and Develop Sources of Taxable Income," *Proceedings, Second National Industrial Conference*, New York City, October 22, 1920, Special Report no. 17 (New York: National Industrial Conference Board, 1920), p. 14.

14. James A. Emery, "Address," *Proceedings, National Industrial Tax Conference*, Chicago, April 16, 1920, Special Report no. 9 (Boston: National Industrial Conference Board, 1920), pp. 8–9.

15. *Congressional Record*, January 29, 1894; 26: appendix 415.

3B.4 Changes in the Distribution of Tax Burdens 1966–85

JOSEPH A. PECHMAN

The three preceding essays would lead us to expect that little change should have occurred in tax policy outcomes in the last few years. There has not been a major realignment and there is little reason for thinking that the view that taxation has important implications for growth has been undermined. Nonetheless, there appear to have been significant changes in the tax system during the Reagan years. Major personal and corporate income tax reductions in 1981 were followed by a moderate tax increase in 1982, minor tax increases in the next two years, and a major revision of the income tax code in 1986. At the state level a series of property tax reductions in the 1979–1981 period were followed by sales and income tax increases in the years that followed.

But some of this change has been more apparent than real. The balance between the different types of taxes has not shifted radically. Nor has the amount paid in taxes changed radically: the American people paid 25.3 percent of their income in taxes in 1980 and 24.5 percent in 1985. Nevertheless, as Buchanan would point out, this small decrease in taxes, combined with increasing expenditures, led to federal deficits unprecedented in peacetime. Nor have there been major changes in the degree to which taxes redistribute income. This article by Joseph A. Pechman shows the changes that did occur. The most important of these changes is an easing of the tax burden for the wealthiest members of the population. This change has been accompanied by an increase in the use of a modern version of Mellon's supply-side logic, and, some argue, by a very slow realignment toward the Republican party. It has also been accompanied by a great deal of rhetoric calling for a new and fairer system of taxes. It remains to be seen whether these trends, or the changes in tax redistribution, will be lasting.

The reader should know that, subsequent to the publication of this work, the author issued revised versions of some of the tables. The revisions are explained in an editor's note at the end of the essay.

Calculations of tax burdens . . . were made for the years 1966, 1970, 1975, and 1985. The 1966, 1970, and 1975 calculations were prepared on the basis of the MERGE files* for those years; the 1980 and 1985 calculations are based on projections of the 1975 file.[1] The 1985 tax calculations are estimates based on federal, state, and local tax legislation enacted as of January 1, 1984. Taken together, these figures provide a series of snapshots depicting tax burdens for the U.S. population over a period of almost two decades. Before analyzing the trends in the distribution of tax burdens, it will be useful to identify the more significant changes in tax policy affecting tax burdens during this period.[2]

Legislative history

It is useful to start with the Revenue Act of 1964, which set the structural features of the federal income taxes for the rest of the 1960s. The act reduced individual income tax rates by an average of 20 percent, with the botttom rate going from 20 percent to 14 percent and the top rate from 91 percent to 70 percent. An investment tax credit and liberalized depreciation allowances had been introduced in 1962 and the 1964 act reduced the general corporation tax rate from 52 to 48 percent. These changes were the first of many during the period covered by this study that greatly reduced the effective corporation tax rates.

In 1965, Congress passed a major excise tax reduction bill, effective in mid-1965. This bill scaled down the Korean war excise taxes to all but a few major taxes levied for sumptuary and regulatory reasons and user charges. Many of the excise taxes are levied on a specific basis (for example, cents per gallon or per 100 cigarettes) and remained at the level enacted in 1965 until 1982. Because of the large intervening inflation, receipts from federal excise taxes did not keep pace with the growth of nominal incomes throughout the period.

The only major change made in the excise tax structure since 1965 was the introduction of special taxes to finance the Airport and Airway Trust Fund in 1970. In 1982, taxes to finance the highways and airways were raised and the cigarette tax was increased from eight cents to sixteen cents for the period from January 1, 1983, to September 30, 1985.

The Tax Reform Act of 1969 was enacted in response to public pressure for tax revision generated by a statement from outgoing Secretary of the Treasury Joseph J. Barr that 155 taxpayers with incomes above $200,000 had not paid any tax in 1967. The act relieved a large number of low-income people from paying federal income taxes by increasing the personal exemption and standard deduction, introduced a minimum tax for high-income individuals and corporations, and reduced the maximum tax rate on earnings (wages and salaries and self-employment incomes) from 70 percent to 50 percent.

During the early 1970s, federal tax bills were passed frequently, some of relatively minor significance but cumulating to significant change. The Revenue

---

*The MERGE files Pechman uses are sets of data describing the effects of different taxes on the income of a random sample of U.S. citizens.—Ed.

Act of 1971 introduced the Accelerated Depreciation Range (ADR) system of depreciation, continuing the trend toward more liberal depreciation allowances begun a decade earlier. The Pension Reform Act of 1974 initiated the use of Individual Retirement Accounts (IRAs) to permit the accumulation of tax-free saving for retirement purposes by those who were not covered by employer retirement plans. The Tax Reduction Act of 1975 increased the personal exemptions through the use of a tax credit, introduced an earned income credit for low-income recipients, and raised the investment tax credit from 7 percent to 10 percent.

The Tax Reform Act of 1976 lengthened the holding period for the reduced rate on capital gains from six months to a year. The Tax Reduction and Simplification Act of 1977 increased the amount of nontaxable income that could be earned by introducing the zero bracket amount at a higher level than the previous low-income allowance. The Revenue Act of 1978 converted the credit enacted two years earlier to the equivalent exemption. It also reduced the tax rate on long-term capital gains from 50 percent to 40 percent of the tax rates on ordinary income. Energy tax credits were introduced in 1980, and a windfall profits tax on oil and gas was enacted in 1980.

The major piece of legislation affecting the 1980s was the Economic Recovery Tax Act of 1981 (ERTA). This act reduced individual income tax rates by 23 percent over a period of three years, cut the top rate on unearned income from 70 percent to 50 percent, and adjusted the individual income tax rate brackets, exemptions, and zero bracket amounts for inflation beginning in 1985. It also permitted individuals not covered by private pension plans to invest in tax-free IRAs, and introduced a deduction for net interest received beginning in 1985.[3]

Depreciation allowances for tax purposes were further liberalized in 1981 by the substitution of the Accelerated Cost Recovery System (ACRS) for ADR. The Tax Equity and Fiscal Responsibility Act of 1982 (TEFRA) reduced these allowances somewhat (but they remained much more liberal than the ADR allowances), required taxpayers to reduce the basis for depreciation purposes by half the investment credit, and introduced a new, somewhat higher minimum tax for both individuals and corporations.[4]

Aside from income tax legislation, the major influence on the distribution of tax burdens has been the increase in payroll taxes. From 1966 to 1985 the social security payroll tax rate for both employers and employees increased from 4.2 percent to 7.05 percent, and the maximum taxable earnings level rose from $6,600 in 1966 to an estimated $39,000 in 1985, about twice as fast as the change in the consumer price index. Payroll taxes for the unemployment compensation system also increased during the period. The rate for this tax increased from 3.1 percent on wages up to $3,000 in 1966 to a scheduled 6.2 percent on wages up to $7,000 in 1985.

State and local governments raised their income and sales tax rates during the period, while the effective rate of property taxation declined. On balance, state and local taxes rose from 9.4 percent of the gross national product in 1966 to 12.2 percent in 1977, and then declined to 11.3 percent in 1980.

The net effect of these changes on the roles of the various taxes is summarized in Table 1, using the aggregates based on the variant 1c* assumptions. Total federal, state, and local taxes varied only slightly during this period as a percentage of adjusted family income, rising from 25.2 percent in 1966 to 26.1 percent in 1970 and then declining to 24.5 percent in 1985. However, there were significant changes in the relative importance of the various tax sources. Federal, state, and local individual income taxes increased gradually from 8.5 percent of adjusted family income in 1966 to 10.9 percent in 1985. Payroll taxes rose sharply between these years, from 4.4 percent to 6.2 percent. On the other hand, the corporation income tax declined from 3.9 percent to 1.8 percent of adjusted family income, sales and excise taxes from 5.1 percent to 3.4 percent, and the property tax from 3.0 percent to 2.0 percent. Thus there was a decline in two major progressive sources (the corporation income tax and the property tax) and a rise in a major regressive source (the payroll tax), which was only partially offset by the decline in the regressive sales and excise taxes and the increase in the individual income taxes. Moreover, federal individual tax rates in the top brackets were reduced sharply in 1981. These broad trends suggest that the progressivity of the tax system declined between 1966 and 1985.

Changes in effective tax rates

The data in Table 2, which summarize the changes in the effective rates of tax by population decile for variants 1c and 3b, confirm the decline in the progressivity of the tax system from 1966 to 1985. In 1966, federal, state, and local taxes rose from 16.8 percent of adjusted family income in the lowest decile to 30.1 percent in the top decile under the most progressive assumptions (variant 1c). Between 1966 and 1985 the tax burdens increased in the two lowest deciles, remained about the same in the third and fourth deciles, rose slightly in the fifth to the ninth deciles, but declined in the highest decile. By 1985 the effective tax rate had risen

---

*Some taxes can be passed on to others by raising prices—for example, a landlord might raise rents after receiving a property tax increase. In such cases, the final burden of a tax is different from its initial incidence. The tables in this article show the impact of taxes based on two different sets of assumptions about who bears the final burden of the corporate income tax and the property tax. Variant 1c assumes that the property tax falls on property owners and that the corporate income tax falls on shareholders and other capital owners. Variant 3b assumes that half of the property tax is passed along to consumers, primarily in the form of increased rents, and that half of the corporate income tax is passed on to consumers in the form of higher prices for goods produced by the firms. Pechman sees variant 1c as the more accurate of the two.—Ed.

Table 1

Ratio of Federal and of State and Local Taxes to Adjusted Family Income under Variant 1c, Selected Years, 1966–85[a] (percent)

Year	Individual income taxes	Corpora- tion income tax	Property tax	Sales and excise taxes	Payroll taxes	Personal property and motor vehicle taxes	Total taxes
			Total taxes				
1966	8.5	3.9	3.0	5.1	4.4	0.3	25.2
1970	9.7	2.6	3.3	5.3	4.9	0.3	26.1
1975	9.3	2.5	2.8	4.5	5.7	0.3	25.0
1980	10.8	2.5	2.0	4.0	5.8	0.2	25.2
1985	10.9	1.8	2.0	3.4	6.2	0.2	24.5
			Federal taxes				
1966	7.7	3.7	—	1.8	4.4	—	17.6
1970	8.6	2.3	—	1.6	4.9	—	17.4
1975	8.0	2.1	—	1.0	5.7	—	16.7
1980	9.2	2.1	—	0.7	5.8	—	17.7
1985	9.0	1.4	—	0.6	6.2	—	17.2
			State and local taxes				
1966	0.8	0.3	3.0	3.3	—	0.3	7.6
1970	1.1	0.3	3.3	3.7	—	0.3	8.7
1975	1.4	0.3	2.8	3.5	—	0.3	8.3
1980	1.6	0.3	2.0	3.3	—	0.2	7.5
1985	1.9	0.4	2.0	2.9	—	0.2	7.3

Source: Brookings MERGE files. Figures are rounded.

a. Variant 1c is the most progressive set of incidence assumptions used in this study.

to 21.9 percent in the lowest decile and declined to 25.3 percent at the top. Thus the ratio of the tax burden in the highest to that in the lowest decile fell from 1.79 to 1.16.

The least progressive set of assumptions (variant 3b) tells a similar story. Between 1966 and 1985 the tax burdens remained about the same in the third to the ninth decile, but they changed at the top and bottom of the income distribution. In the lowest decile the effective tax rate rose from 27.5 percent in 1966 to 28.2 percent in 1985. In the highest decile the effective rate declined from 25.9 percent to 23.3 percent. The ratio of the tax burden in the highest to that in the lowest decile declined from 0.94 to 0.83.

Table 2

Effective Rates of Federal, State, and Local Taxes under Variants 1c and 3b, by Population Decile, Selected Years, 1966–85[a] (percent)

Population decile	1966	1970	1975	1980	1985
			Variant 1c		
First[b]	16.8	18.8	21.2	20.6	121.9
Second	18.9	19.5	19.9	20.4	21.3
Third	21.7	20.8	20.5	20.6	21.4
Fourth	22.6	23.2	22.0	21.9	22.5
Fifth	22.8	24.0	23.0	22.8	23.1
Sixth	22.7	24.1	23.3	23.3	23.5
Seventh	22.7	24.3	23.6	23.6	23.7
Eighth	23.1	24.6	24.4	25.0	24.6
Ninth	23.3	25.0	25.3	25.7	25.1
Tenth	30.1	30.7	27.1	27.3	25.3
All deciles[c]	25.2	26.1	25.0	25.2	24.5
			Variant 3b		
First[b]	27.5	25.8	29.6	28.9	28.2
Second	24.8	24.2	24.2	25.7	25.6
Third	26.0	24.2	23.4	24.6	24.6
Fourth	25.9	25.9	24.6	25.2	25.2
Fifth	25.8	26.4	25.3	25.8	25.3
Sixth	25.6	26.2	25.3	25.9	25.6
Seventh	25.5	26.2	25.5	26.0	25.4
Eighth	25.5	26.4	26.0	27.1	26.3
Ninth	25.1	26.1	26.3	27.2	26.1
Tenth	25.9	27.8	24.2	24.9	23.3
All deciles[c]	25.9	26.7	25.5	26.3	25.3

Source: Brookings MERGE files. Figures are rounded.

a. Variant 1c is the most progressive and 3b is the least progressive set of incidence assumptions used in this study.

b. Includes only units in the sixth to tenth percentiles.

c. Includes negative incomes not shown separately.

Changes in the burdens of various taxes

The major reason for the increase in the tax burden at the lower end of the income scale from 1966 to 1985 was the rise in payroll taxes. In the first decile, payroll taxes amounted to 2.6 percent of adjusted family income in 1966 under variant 1c and 9.4 percent in 1985. Individual income taxes also rose significantly—in the first decile from 1.1 percent to 4.2 percent of adjusted family income—partly as a result of the failure to adjust the personal exemptions and standard deduction for the inflation in the late 1970s and partly as a result of income growth during the entire period. These increases were partially offset by reductions in both the corporation and property taxes (from a combined total of 3.8 percent of adjusted family income in 1966 to 1.2 percent in 1985), but the increases outweighed the reductions.

In the top decile the effective rate of tax fell between 1966 and 1985 mainly because of reductions in the corporation and property taxes. Under variant 1c the corporation income tax declined from 8.1 percent of adjusted family income in 1966 to 3.6 percent in 1985, and the property tax declined from 5.1 percent to 3.3 percent. Individual income, sales, and payroll taxes rose in this decile, but not enough to offset the large reductions in the corporation and property taxes.

Effect of the 1981 federal tax cuts

The changes in effective rates of tax resulting from the federal tax reductions enacted in 1981 are reflected primarily in the tax burdens of the top decile. Between 1980 and 1985 effective federal individual income tax rates under variant 1c rose in the first seven deciles by an average of about 1 percentage point, remained about the same in the eighth and ninth deciles, and declined 1.2 points in the top decile (Table 3). The higher tax burdens at the lower end of the income scale is the result of increases in effective tax rates generated by inflation;[5] and these increases were enough to offset the effect of the 23 percent reduction in individual income tax rates that became effective during this period. At the top end, the federal individual income tax burden declined from 11.5 percent of adjusted family income to 10.3 percent because the rate reductions and other structural changes of the 1981 act (notably the reduction in the long-term capital gains rate and the increase in deductions for IRAs) more than offset the effect of income increases in this decile. The changes in effective federal individual income tax rates during this period are roughly the same under variant 3b because the incidence assumptions are the same under variants 1c and 3b.

Effective federal corporation income tax rates under variant 1c declined throughout the income distribution between 1980 and 1985 (Table 3), but the decline was significant only in the top decile, where it fell from 4.3 percent to 2.9 percent of income, or by almost a third. The decline was most pronounced at the top end of the distribution because under variant 1c the corporation income tax is assumed to be borne by property income, which is heavily concentrated in the highest income classes. The decline in effective federal corporation income tax rates is more pronounced in all deciles except the top two under variant 3b than under 1c because half the corporation tax is assumed to be shifted to consumers under this set of assumptions.

Table 3

Effective Rates of Federal Individual Income Tax and Corporation Income Tax under Variants 1c and 3b, by Population Decile, 1980 and 1985[a] (percent)

Population decile	Individual income tax		Corporation income tax	
	1980	1985	1980	1985
		Variant 1c		
First[b]	1.1	3.1	0.5	0.4
Second	3.0	4.5	0.5	0.4
Third	4.4	5.8	0.6	0.5
Fourth	5.7	6.9	0.7	0.5
Fifth	6.7	7.6	0.7	0.5
Sixth	7.4	8.1	0.8	0.6
Seventh	8.0	8.5	1.0	0.7
Eighth	9.3	9.4	1.0	0.7
Ninth	10.3	10.0	1.4	1.0
Tenth	11.5	10.3	4.3	2.9
All deciles[c]	9.2	9.0	2.1	1.4
		Variant 3b		
First[b]	1.1	2.9	3.6	2.2
Second	2.8	4.5	2.9	1.8
Third	4.3	5.7	2.6	1.6
Fourth	5.5	6.7	2.4	1.6
Fifth	6.6	7.4	2.3	1.5
Sixth	7.2	8.0	2.3	1.5
Seventh	7.8	8.3	2.3	1.5
Eighth	9.0	9.2	2.3	1.5
Ninth	10.1	9.8	2.4	1.5
Tenth	11.7	10.5	2.9	1.8
All deciles[c]	9.1	9.0	2.6	1.7

Source: Brookings MERGE files.

a. Variant 1c is the most progressive and 3b is the least progressive set of incidence assumptions used in this study.

b. Includes only units in the sixth to tenth percentiles.

c. Includes negative incomes not shown separately.

Changes in the federal and the state and local tax systems

The decline in the progressivity of the tax system between 1966 and 1985 is accounted for entirely by changes in the federal tax system. The state-local tax system remained slightly U-shaped or regressive, depending on the incidence assumptions, and the effective rates in each decile did not change much.

Under variant 1c, federal taxes in 1966 rose from 7.8 percent of adjusted family income in the first decile to 21.1 percent in the top decile. By 1985, largely as a result of the decline in the corporation income tax and the rise in payroll taxes, federal taxes increased to 13.9 percent of adjusted family income in the first decile, but declined to 17.1 percent in the top decile. State and local taxes declined slightly as a share of income during this period, but the decline was distributed throughout the income scale and thus did not alter the U-shaped character of the effective rate curve under this variant (Table 4).

Federal taxes are much less progressive under variant 3b than under 1c, while state and local taxes are distinctly regressive under 3b. Between 1966 and 1985, federal taxes became even less progressive under variant 3b, while state and local taxes became somewhat less regressive.

Taxes and sources and uses of income

The data in the MERGE files permit an allocation of the burden of taxation among the sources and uses of income, as shown in Table 5.[6] In 1966, the tax burden under variant 1c was almost twice as heavy on capital income than it was on labor income—33.0 percent versus 17.6 percent. The burden on capital income declined by almost 50 percent from 1966 to 1985, while the burden on labor income rose slightly. Thus labor income was taxed more heavily than capital income in 1985—20.6 percent versus 17.5 percent (Table 5).

The shift in tax burdens from capital to labor income between 1966 and 1985 is even more dramatic under variant 3b, which distributes a major share of the corporation income, property, and payroll taxes to consumption. Under this variant, the effective rate of tax was slightly larger on capital income than on labor income in 1966, but in 1985 it was almost twice as large on labor income.

As might be expected, the effective tax rate on consumption is much lower than it is on either capital or labor income under variant 1c. By contrast, under variant 3b, consumption is taxed about as heavily as labor income in all years, almost as heavily as capital income in 1966 and 1970, and much more heavily thereafter. Under both variants, the tax on consumption rose from 1966 to 1975 an then declined from 1975 to 1985, ending the period at a somewhat lower level than at the beginning.

Changes in the distribution of income

The effect of changes in relative tax burdens on the distribution of income since

Table 4

Effective Rates of Federal and of State and Local Taxes under Variants 1c and 3b, by Population Decile, 1966 and 1985[a] (percent)

Population decile	Federal		State and local	
	1966	1985	1966	1985
	Variant 1c			
First[b]	7.8	13.9	9.1	8.0
Second	10.2	14.5	8.6	6.8
Third	13.5	15.0	8.2	6.5
Fourth	15.1	16.0	7.5	6.5
Fifth	15.9	16.7	6.9	6.4
Sixth	16.1	16.9	6.6	6.6
Seventh	16.2	17.0	6.5	6.7
Eighth	16.6	17.8	6.5	6.9
Ninth	16.7	18.0	6.6	7.1
Tenth	21.1	17.1	9.0	8.1
All deciles[c]	17.6	17.2	7.6	7.3
	Variant 3b			
First[b]	13.8	16.9	13.7	11.3
Second	13.7	16.7	11.1	8.9
Third	15.8	16.7	10.2	7.9
Fourth	16.8	17.4	9.1	7.8
Fifth	17.4	17.7	8.4	7.6
Sixth	17.4	17.9	8.2	7.7
Seventh	17.5	17.8	8.0	7.7
Eighth	17.7	18.5	7.9	7.8
Ninth	17.6	18.4	7.5	7.7
Tenth	19.2	16.4	6.6	6.9
All deciles[c]	17.9	17.7	8.0	7.6

Source: Brookings MERGE files.

a. Variant 1c is the most progressive and 3b is the least progressive set of incidence assumptions used in this study.

b. Includes only units in the sixth to tenth percentiles.

c. Includes negative incomes not shown separately.

1966 is shown in Table 6. To highlight changes in broad segments of the distribution, the income shares shown in this table are by quintiles rather than by deciles of the population.

According to the data in Table 6, the distribution of income *before* taxes remained virtually unchanged from 1966 to 1985. There were small variations in the income shares received by the various quintiles, but these variations were

Table 5

Effective Rates of Federal, State, and Local Taxes on Sources and Uses of Income under Variants 1c and 3b, Selected Years, 1966–85[a] (percent)

	Variant 1c			Variant 3b		
Year	Income from labor[b]	Income from capital[c]	Consumption[d]	Income from labor[b]	Income from capital[c]	Consumption[d]
1966	17.6	33.0	8.3	16.0	21.0	17.6
1970	19.7	29.4	9.8	18.0	19.7	19.1
1975	22.6	22.2	10.6	20.6	13.9	21.9
1980	19.9	21.5	9.7	18.1	14.4	20.5
1985	20.6	17.5	7.7	18.6	10.8	17.0

Sources: Brookings MERGE files. For an explanation of the methods used to allocate taxes among sources and uses of income see text note 6.

a. Variant 1c is the most progressive and 3b is the least progressive set of incidence assumptions used in this study.

b. The sum of wages, salaries, wage supplements, and portion of nonfarm and farm business income regarded as labor income.

c. The sum of interest, corporation profits before tax, rents, royalties, capital gains, and portion of nonfarm and farm business income regarded as capital income.

d. The sum of total expenditures on consumption items generally subject to state sales and excise taxes.

unsystematic and tended to be reversed in later years. Thus, for example, the share of adjusted family income before taxes under variant 1c in the bottom quintile of the population rose from 3.9 percent in 1966 to 4.6 percent in 1975, and then declined to 4.2 percent in 1985. The before-tax share of the top quintile was 47.7 percent in 1966; it then declined to 46.5 percent in 1970, rose to 48.9 percent in 1980, and declined again to 47.7 percent in 1985.[7]

It should be noted that adjusted family income includes transfer payments, which increased sharply from 1966 to 1985. Consequently, the distribution of market incomes (that is, adjusted family incomes less transfers) must have become more unequal. Unfortunately, the change during this period cannot be provided because size distributions of market incomes were not tabulated from 1966 and 1970 MERGE files.

Since the distribution of adjusted family income before tax remained unchanged and the tax system became less progressive, the distribution of income *after* taxes became somewhat more concentrated during this period. Under variant 1c, the after-tax income shares in the first two quintiles were virtually the same in 1966 and 1985, but the shares of the next two quintiles declined while the share of the top quintile rose.

Similar conclusions may be drawn from the distributions calculated under the variant 3b assumptions. The income shares before tax of the bottom quintile were

Table 6

Distribution of Adjusted Family Income before and after Federal, State, and Local Taxes under Variants 1c and 3b, by Population Quintile, Selected Years, 1966–85[a] (percent)

Population quintile	1966	1970	1975	1980	1985
			Variant 1c		
Before tax					
First	3.9	4.1	4.6	4.1	4.2
Second	10.0	10.1	10.2	9.7	10.0
Third	16.3	16.2	15.6	15.4	15.8
Fourth	22.0	23.0	21.8	21.9	23.3
Fifth	47.7	46.5	47.9	48.9	47.7
After tax					
First	4.3	n.a.	4.8	4.3	4.4
Second	10.3	n.a.	10.5	10.1	10.2
Third	16.4	n.a.	15.8	15.6	15.8
Fourth	23.3	n.a.	22.0	22.0	22.4
Fifth	45.7	n.a.	46.8	48.0	47.3
			Variant 3b		
Before tax					
First	4.0	4.1	4.6	4.1	4.2
Second	10.2	10.2	10.3	9.8	10.0
Third	16.7	16.5	15.8	15.6	15.9
Fourth	22.6	23.5	22.1	22.1	22.5
Fifth	46.6	45.7	47.2	48.4	47.3
After tax					
First	4.1	n.a.	4.6	4.1	4.2
Second	10.1	n.a.	10.4	9.9	10.0
Third	16.3	n.a.	15.7	15.4	15.6
Fourth	23.2	n.a.	21.9	21.8	22.2
Fifth	46.3	n.a.	47.5	48.8	48.0

Source: Brookings MERGE files. Figures are rounded.

n.a. Not available.

a. Variant 1c is the most progessive and 3b is the least progressive set of incidence assumptions used in this study. The cumulative percentages are based on distributions of adjusted family income before tax and then reranked by adjusted family income after tax.

4.0 percent in 1966 and 4.2 percent in 1985; the shares of the top quintile in these years were 46.6 percent and 47.3 percent, respectively. While the after-tax shares of the bottom quintiles remaind virtually unchanged between 1966 and 1985 and the shares of the next two quintiles declined, that of the top quintile rose from 46.3 percent in 1966 to 48.0 percent in 1985.

Summary

The distribution of total tax burdens was less progressive in 1985 than in 1966 under the most progressive incidence assumptions and more regressive under the least progressive assumptions. This was the result mainly of the rise in payroll tax rates, which increased tax burdens at the lower end of the income scale, and the reduction in corporation income and property taxes, which reduced tax burdens at the top end. The individual and corporation income tax cuts enacted in 1981 also contributed to the decline in progressivity.

Federal taxes declined in progressivity between 1966 and 1985, while the burden of state and local taxes remained either U-shaped or regressive, depending on the incidence assumptions.

Taxes on capital income were heavier than those on labor income in 1966, but as a result of the reductions in the corporation income and property taxes, the tax burden on labor income was higher in 1985. Taxes on consumption were twice as high or higher under the least progressive incidence assumptions than under the most progressive.

The distribution of income *before* taxes was virtually the same in 1985 as it was in 1966. As a result of the decline in the progressivity of the tax system, the disbribution of income *after* taxes was more unequal in 1985.

Editor's Note

As this book was going to press, Dr. Pechman's office provided me with revised versions of tables 2 and 5. I have reprinted these below as tables 2a and 5a.

The revisions to Table 5 serve primarily to reinforce the major point made by Dr. Pechman in the text. In the article, he shows that income from capital has been taxed at a steadily lower rate over time, while income from labor has been taxed at a steadily higher rate. The result has been to shift the burden of taxation away from unearned income and toward earned income. The revisions show that this shift has been even greater than shown in Table 5.

The revisions made to Table 2 confirm some parts of Pechman's argument but change other parts. They confirm that the share of taxes paid by the wealthiest 10% of the population has declined over time, although the decline is a little less than shown in the original table. They do not confirm the increased burden on the lowest 30% of the population shown in the original table. Instead they show a slight increase in tax burden for the bottom 10% (the poor), combined with reductions in the tax

Table 2a

Effective Rates of Federal, State, and Local Taxes under Variants 1c and 3b, by Population Decile, Selected Years, 1966–85[a] (percent)*

Population decile	1966	1970	1975	1980	1985
			Variant 1c		
First[b]	16.8	18.8	19.7	17.1	17.0
Second	18.9	19.5	17.6	17.1	15.9
Third	21.7	20.8	18.9	18.9	18.1
Fourth	22.6	23.2	21.7	20.8	21.2
Fifth	22.8	24.0	23.5	22.7	23.4
Sixth	22.7	24.1	23.9	23.4	23.8
Seventh	22.7	24.3	24.2	24.4	24.7
Eighth	23.1	24.6	24.7	25.5	25.4
Ninth	23.3	25.0	25.4	26.5	26.2
Tenth	30.1	30.7	27.8	28.5	26.4
All deciles[c]	25.3	26.1	25.0	25.2	24.5
			Variant 3b		
First[b]	27.5	25.8	27.9	25.9	24.0
Second	24.8	24.2	21.7	22.2	20.1
Third	26.0	24.2	21.0	22.5	20.7
Fourth	25.9	25.9	24.0	25.5	23.2
Fifth	25.8	26.4	25.4	24.7	24.4
Sixth	25.6	26.2	25.5	25.1	25.0
Seventh	25.5	26.2	25.8	25.8	25.5
Eighth	25.5	26.4	26.1	26.7	26.2
Ninth	25.1	26.1	26.6	27.4	26.7
Tenth	25.9	27.8	25.9	26.8	25.0
All deciles[c]	25.9	26.7	25.5	26.3	25.3

Source: Brookings MERGE files [revised]. Figures are rounded.

a. Variant 1c is the most progressive and 3b is the least progressive set of incidence assumptions used in this study.

b. Includes only units in the sixth to tenth percentiles.

c. Includes negative incomes not shown separately.

*Corrected data have been inserted in the columns for 1975, 1980, and 1985. The effect of the corrected figures is to make the table less regressive in the lower deciles than in the original published version.—Ed.

Table 5a

Effective Rates of Federal, State, and Local Taxes on Sources and Uses of Income under Variants 1c and 3b, Selected Years, 1966–85[a] (percent)*

	Variant 1c			Variant 3b		
Year	Income from labor[b]	Income from capital[c]	Consump- tion[d]	Income from labor[b]	Income from capital[c]	Consump- tion[d]
1966	17.6	33.0	8.3	16.0	21.0	17.6
1970	19.7	29.4	9.8	18.0	19.7	19.1
1975	23.9	22.3	10.6	21.9	13.9	21.9
1980	25.3	21.8	9.7	23.6	15.4	20.5
1985	25.9	18.1	7.7	23.8	11.9	17.0

Sources: Brookings MERGE files [revised]. For an explanation of the methods used to allocate taxes among sources and uses of income, see text note 6, page 2 of Joseph A. Pechman, *Who Paid the Taxes, 1966–85?*

a. Variant 1c is the most progressive and 3b is the least progressive set of incidence assumptions used in this study.

b. The sum of wages, salaries, wage supplements, and portion of nonfarm and farm business income regarded as labor income.

c. The sum of interest, corporation profits before tax, rents, royalties, capital gains, and portion of nonfarm and farm business income regarded as capital income.

d. The sum of total expenditures on consumption items generally subject to state sales and excise taxes.

*Corrected data have been inserted in the rows for 1975, 1980, and 1985.—Ed.

burden of those in the 10th to 30th percentiles (the near-poor). The table also shows increases in tax burden for those in the 40th to 90th percentiles (the middle classes).

Over all, the best interpretation of Table 2a is that suggested by the data in Table 5a. Most of the middle-class families in the 40th to 90th percentiles are wage and salary earners. Many of the near-poor rely on Social Security or other transfer payments for their income, and pay only sales taxes. The wealthier individuals in the top 10% of the income distribution are more likely to receive income from rents and dividends. Because wage and salary income is bearing more of the tax burden, those groups in the population that include the most employed people have an increased tax burden. Groups that include more people who receive income from transfers or capital have a decreased tax burden.

For an understanding of the controversy that sparked these revisions in the tables, see Edgar K. Browning, "Pechman's Tax Incidence Study: A Note on the Data," *American Economic Review* 76 (December 1986): 1214–18, and Joseph A. Pechman, "Pechman's Tax Incidence Study: A Response," *American Economic Review* 76 (December 1986): 1219–20.

Notes

1. For the assumptions used in the projections, see chapter 2 of *Who Paid the Taxes, 1966–85?*

2. Clearly, a brief review of tax developments over two decades can hardly do justice to the subject. The interested reader is encouraged to consult more detailed references. See, for example, Joseph A. Pechman, *Federal Tax Policy* (Brookings, 1983).

3. The deduction, which was 15 percent of total interest reported less interest paid up to a maximum of $6,000 for married couples and $3,000 for single people, was repealed in 1984 (see note 4).

4. The Tax Reform Act of 1984 was enacted after the calculations for this study were completed. The major change in the act was repeal of the net interest deduction enacted in 1981, reduction of the holding period for capital gains from a year to six months, and an increase in the period over which depreciation for real estate is calculated. The effect of these changes on the 1985 distribution of tax burdens is small.

5. Between 1980 and 1985 the average adjusted family income under variant 1c rose 24 percent. This compares with an estimated increase in the gross national product deflator of more than 30 percent.

6. In these calculations taxes were allocated to labor income, income from capital, or consumption in proportion to the amounts assumed to be subject to tax. Farm income and nonfarm business income were assumed to represent partly a return to labor and partly a return to capital. All taxes were allocated in accordance with the particular assumptions applicable to each incidence variant. For details see Joseph A. Pechman and Benjamin A. Okner, *Who Bears the Tax Burden?* (Brookings, 1974), pp. 79–80.

7. The constancy of the before-tax distribution has been observed in data derived from field surveys, but these surveys understate the shares of top incomes in the income distribution. Since the highest incomes in the MERGE files were obtained from income tax returns that are a more accurate representation of the top tail of the distribution, the constancy of the income shares on the basis of these data is all the more remarkable.

3C. Monetary Policy

Economists long regarded monetary policy as, at best, a rather weak and ineffective economic policy tool, and relegated it to a supporting role under fiscal policy. The rise of the Chicago school and neoclassical economics has led to a complete reevaluation of the role of monetary policy. There is now a range of views, with monetarists generally holding that monetary policy is the major determinant of inflation and hence possible growth, and neo-Keynesians assigning it a more or less equal role with fiscal policy. There is, however, general agreement that controlling the quantity of money is of first importance and that, under a number of circumstances, monetary policy can severely limit what fiscal policy can achieve.

Monetary policies determine the amount of money and credit that is available in a society. When the amount of money and credit is reduced, the price borrowers have to pay for money (the interest rate) goes up. When the money supply is increased, the interest rate is driven down. People borrow more when the interest rate is lower; they use the borrowed money to purchase goods, such as cars and houses, and invest in machinery and factories. Thus, increasing the money supply stimulates the economy. Of course, beyond some point the economy can be overstimulated. With more money in their pockets, people bid up the prices of goods and the result is inflation. Reducing the amount of money available to borrowers tends to depress the economy and reduce inflation. Many analysts think it was the rapid money growth during the Administration of President Jimmy Carter that led to the high inflation of the 1979 to 1982 period, while it was the restrictive monetary policies pursued by Federal Reserve Board Chairman Paul Volcker that led to the lower inflation, and the major recession, of the first Reagan term.

The political aspects of monetary policy, long neglected by political scientists, have in recent years attracted considerable interest. Most of the new work has revolved around two topics: who controls monetary policy and why we get the

283

kind of monetary policy that we do. Interest in the first topic was sparked by the fact that the United States, like many other democracies, has chosen to take formal responsibility for this vital policy out of the hands of elected officials, lodging it instead in the Federal Reserve Board, a small body appointed by the President for thirteen-year terms. This naturally leads to the related questions of whether, and why, this important policy has been left in the control of an undemocratic body. Actually, as we shall see, there is general agreement that the President and the Congress are more powerful monetary policy actors than might at first appear to be the case, but considerable disagreement concerning the extent of their power (Weintraub 1978; Kane 1982; Beck 1982).

The literature on the determinants of monetary policy has also focused on two primary questions. The larger body of research looks at the short-term determinants of monetary policy, seeking to determine why the Federal Reserve Board chooses to switch from stimulative to restrictive policies and vice versa. This inquiry has been prompted by the observation that both stimulation and restriction have often taken place well after they were justified economically. There is also some research that asks why the policies pursued by the Federal Reserve Board are in general more restrictive and anti-inflationary than the fiscal policies undertaken by the President and the Congress.

The article below by Michael Reagan outlines the structure of power within the Federal Reserve and argues, on grounds of accountability, that power over monetary policy should reside in the White House. Nathaniel Beck, on the other hand, believes that the Federal Reserve Board has less power over monetary policy than is commonly assumed, and that the President, rather than the Federal Reserve Board, is responsible for many policy shifts. As proof Beck offers evidence that key policy changes have shortly followed the election of a new President. The selection by Edward Kane argues that real power over monetary policy lies with the President and the Congress. However, because it is often necessary to pursue deflationary policies, which are unpopular, elected officials have preferred to assign formal responsibility to the Federal Reserve Board, permitting them to evade the blame for recessions.

For further reading

The best introduction to this field is John T. Woolley's well-written book *Monetary Politics: The Federal Reserve and the Politics of Monetary Policy*. A brief introduction to the area can be found in Nathaniel Beck's article "Domestic Politics and Monetary Policy." Milton Friedman and Anna J. Schwartz's *A Monetary History of the United States, 1867–1960* is a classic history of monetary policy formation. A still useful book on monetary policy in the 1950–1970 period is George L. Bach's *Making Monetary and Fiscal Policy*. Robert Weintraub's article "Congressional Supervision of Monetary Policy" offers a good account of Congress's role in the recent period.

Bibliography

Bach, George L., *Making Monetary and Fiscal Policy* (Washington D.C.: The Brookings Institution, 1971).

Beck, Nathaniel, "Presidential Influence on the Federal Reserve in the 1970s," *American Journal of Political Science* 26 (August 1982):415–45.

Beck, Nathaniel, "Domestic Politics and Monetary Policy," in Thomas D. Willett, ed., *Political Business Cycles: The Economics and Politics of Stagflation* (San Francisco: Pacific Institute for Public Policy Research, 1987).

Friedman, Milton, and Anna J. Schwartz, *A Monetary History of the United States* (Princeton N.J.: Princeton University Press, 1963).

Kane, Edward, "External Pressures and the Operation of the Fed," in Raymond E. Lombra and Willard E. Witte, eds., *Political Economy of International and Domestic Monetary Relations* (Ames, Iowa: Iowa State University Press, 1982).

Weintraub, Robert, "Congressional Supervision of Monetary Policy," *Journal of Monetary Economics* 4 (April 1978):341–62.

Woolley, John T., *Monetary Politics* (New York: Cambridge University Press, 1984).

3C.1. The Political Structure of the Federal Reserve System

MICHAEL D. REAGAN

Monetary policy is unique among the major areas of public policy, in that formal authority over the policy lies with two bodies—the Federal Reserve Board and the Federal Open Market Committee—neither of which includes any members directly elected by the public at large. This means that there is no direct accountability to the public for monetary policy outcomes.

In this article Michael D. Reagan briefly outlines how this peculiar governmental arrangement came about, who exercises power within the Federal Reserve system, and the interests those people represent. He argues that the mixed public–private nature of the policy-making system arose in an era when the importance of monetary policy for the national economy was not understood. He then looks at the arguments for continuing this arrangement, paying particular attention to the notion that the independence of the system must be maintained if it is to be able to keep inflation in check. Reagan concludes that, despite the danger that elected officials would not make the hard choices that are required in monetary policy, there is a strong argument for bringing it more directly under the control of the President.

Public policy is not self-generating; it emerges from institutions. Foremost among the institutions charged with monetary and credit policy formation—an area, like fiscal policy, that has not received from political scientists the attention accorded to micro-economic regulation of particular firms or industries—is the Federal Reserve System. The purpose of this paper is to examine the "fit" of the system's formal structure to (1) the policy functions and the informal policy-forming mechanisms of the "Fed," and (2) the pattern of interests and values

Reprinted with permission from *The American Political Science Review* 55, *1* (September 1966), pp. 64–76 (with deletions). Copyright 1961 by the American Political Science Association.

affected by monetary policy. Its thesis is that a substantial gap has developed between these elements.

A brief sketch of the formal structure of authority and the historical development of system functions is needed to begin with; this is followed by analysis of the formal and the effective roles of each component of the System along with the internalized interest representation at each level. Then the linkage between the Federal Reserve System and general economic policy is explored. Finally, the conclusion summarizes the findings and suggests briefly how formal structure and policy functions might be brought into closer, more effective alignment.

I. Structural and functional development

The pyramid

The Federal Reserve System[1] can be described as a pyramid having a private base, a mixed middle level and a public apex. At the apex stands the Board of Governors (frequently referred to as the Federal Reserve Board or FRB). Its seven members are appointed by the President, with the consent of the Senate, for fourteen-year, overlapping terms, one term expiring at the end of January in each even-numbered year. Members are removable for cause, but the removal power has not been exercised. In making appointments, the President must give due regard to "fair representation of financial, agricultural, industrial, and commercial interests, and geographical divisions of the country," and not more than one member can be appointed from a single Federal Reserve District. The Chairman is selected by the President for a renewable four-year term. The board is independent of the appropriations process, for its operating funds come from semi-annual assessments upon the twelve Reserve Banks.

At a level of equivalent authority to the Board itself, but in the "middle" of the public-private pyramid, stands the statutory Federal Open Market Committee. It is composed of all FRB Members plus five of the twelve Reserve Bank Presidents, with the President of the New York Reserve Bank always one of the five and the others serving in rotation. The Chairman of the Board of Governors is, by custom, the Chairman of the Committee. . . .

The Reserve Bank Presidents are not government appointees; they are elected by the boards of directors of their respective Banks, subject to FRB veto; and their compensation—far above civil service levels—is fixed in the same way. Thus their selection is initially private, but with public supervision. The Board of Directors of each Reserve Bank consists of nine persons, six of whom are elected by the member commercial banks of that District (these banks, the "owners" of the Reserve Banks, constituting the private base of the pyramid), while three (including the Chairman and Deputy Chairman) are appointed by the FRB in Washington.

Off to the side stands the final element of statutory organization, the Federal Advisory Council (FAC). This group of twelve men is composed of one commercial-banker representative from each District, annually elected by the respective regional Boards. The FAC meets quarterly with the FRB to discuss general business conditions and may make recommendations to the Board on matters of policy. The twelve Reserve Bank Presidents constitute a non-statutory Conference of Presidents that meets three times a year; a Conference of Reserve Bank Chairmen meets annually with the FRB.

The location of policy powers

The three major tools of monetary policy are the rediscount rate charged by Reserve Banks to member bank borrowers on their loans from the System; the setting of reserve requirement levels for the member banks; and—most important today—open market operations in securities of the federal government. Decisions regarding each of these instruments is formally located in a different organ of the System, although (as will be developed below) channels for advice and influence cause a mingling of the decisional powers in fact. The levels of reserve requirements are set by the FRB; open market policy is a function of the Open Market Committee (OMC), thus providing the regional and quasi-private elements of the System with formal access to the heart of monetary policy formation; and the Reserve Bank Boards of Directors share with the FRB formal authority over the discount rate. The rate is "established" every fourteen days by each regional Bank, but "subject to the review and determination" of the Board of Governors. In addition the FRB shares with the Comptroller of the Currency, the FDIC and state authorities a very considerable list of regulatory and supervisory powers over member banks and their officers.

Functional change since 1913

When established, the Federal Reserve System was thought of as exercising only the technical function of quasi-automatic adjustment of an elastic currency supply to the fluctuating needs of commerce and industry. The System was pictured as a "cooperative enterprise" among bankers for the purpose of increasing the security of banks and providing them with a reservoir of emergency resources.[2] To this day the Federal Reserve Act mandate reflects this view: it instructs that the discount rate and open market policy shall be operated with "a view of accommodating commerce and business," and that reserve requirements shall be handled so as to prevent "excessive use of credit for the purchase or carrying of securities." Nothing in the Act relates the monetary authority to the function of national economic stabilization; yet this is its prime task today.

In 1913, it was not foreseen that the techniques of monetary policy would become instruments of economic stabilization with their consequences for employment, growth and price stability overtaking their specific banking objectives in importance. Yet this is what has happened, beginning in the Twenties but more strongly and with more explicit recognition in the policy process since the Great

Crash. With this shift, the operation of the Federal Reserve System necessarily moved into the political mainstream, for the goal of stabilization requires making choices among alternatives that have important and visible consequences for substantial interests and community values. Once macro-economic policy had become the primary *raison d'être* of the System, the breadth of interests involved became coterminous with the nation, not just with the bankers; and monetary policy, as well as depositors' safety, became a public concern rather than a private convenience.

A corollary of the rise of stabilization to stage center is that the scope of FRB action has become essentially national, belying the assumption of relative regional independence that underlay the original legislation. Divergent policies for each region become undesirable—even impossible—if national stabilization is to be achieved in an increasingly interdependent national economy.

II. Roles and interests of the components

We turn now to a comparison of formal roles and interest composition with the informal roles and interest-impact of each level of the System's structure.

The commercial bank base

The formal role of the member banks is that of an electoral constituency in the selection of six of the nine directors for each Reserve Bank. While the member banks have no direct policy voice, this electoral role originally gave them an indirect one, on the assumption that the regional boards would be policy-making bodies through their authority over the discount rate. That authority is negligible today. Furthermore, the "ownership" of the Reserve Banks by the commercial banks is symbolic; they do not exercise the proprietary control associated with the concept of ownership nor share beyond the statutory dividend, in Reserve Bank "profits." . . .

Bank ownership and election at the base are therefore devoid of substantive significance, despite the superficial appearance of private bank control that the formal arrangement creates.

Reserve Bank Boards of Directors

The Reserve Bank Boards' authority to set rediscount rates, subject to "review and determination" by the FRB, is considerably diminished by the ultimate formal authority of the latter, for "determination" includes final decision and even initiation of rate changes. It is further reduced by informal practice: to avoid the embarrassments of public disputes, discount rate policy is discussed at OMC meetings and the determinations settled upon therein are usually followed through uniformly at the next meetings of the respective regional Boards of Directors.[3] The special formalities are "of little significance: rediscount policy is made in much the same way and on essentially the same considerations as is reserve and open-market policy.''[4] The nationalization of function has thus removed the basis for the assumption of regional autonomy that underlay the original grant of authority to the Reserve Banks. The major tasks of the Directors now are to provide information on regional conditions for OMC and the FRB to take into account, and to serve as a communications and public relations link between the System and local communities—both the general community and the specific ''communities'' of commercial banking, industry, merchants and other financial institutions. They do not exercise important substantive authority.

This may be fortunate in view of the structure of interests that prevails at this level. For the range of interests, reflecting the banker-business orientation of 1913, is narrow by legal specification and narrower still in fact. By statute, each regional Board has three classes of membership: Class A consists of three commercial bankers; Class B of three men active in commerce, agriculture or ''some other industrial pursuit''; and Class C, without occupational restriction. Class C members are appointed by the FRB; the others are elected by the member banks of each region. . . .

The Reserve Bank Presidents

The Presidents, by virtue of the membership of five of their number on the OMC (and the participation of all twelve in OMC discussions) are more significantly related to the policy process than are their nominal superiors, the regional Boards.

Selection of the Presidents is by the respective Boards, but subject to FRB veto: initially private but finally public. Increasingly, they are men with substantial Reserve System experience. Two-thirds of the incumbents have had such experience; one-third have come to their posts from careers in commercial banking. Their daily contacts are with private bankers and one observer suggests that they have been ''inclined to favor more cautious, mild policies that would be less disturbing to the normal courses of banking and the money markets'' than has the FRB.[5] Yet another writer, granting a ''commercial banker mentality'' in the early days of the System, argues that a public, central banking view is coming to prevail as a majority come up through the System.[6] In one respect the Presidents have clearly differed from the FRB: in their support of a change urged by commercial bankers that would place authority for all monetary actions in the OMC—a change the FRB has opposed.

As a statutory minority on the OMC, the views of the Presidents cannot be controlling in themselves. In the apparently unlikely event of a split within the FRB segment of the Committee, however, a solid front by the five President-members would enable them to determine public policy. Since they are not appointed by the President, nor removable for policy differences with either the President or the FRB within their five-year terms, the present structure allows the possibility that policy with a highly-charged political potential may be made by men who lack even indirect accountability to the national public affected. Former FRB Chairman Marriner Eccles has pointed out the uniqueness of the arrangement in these words: "there is no other major governmental power entrusted to a Federal agency composed in part of representatives of the organizations which are the subject of regulation by that agency."[7]

The situation of the Reserve Presidents reverses that of the regional Boards: while the latter's structurally important place has been downgraded by loss of function, the former's structurally inferior position has been upgraded by increased authority.

The Board of Governors and the Board Chairman

The gap between formal and informal roles in the Federal Reserve is readily apparent at the FRB level. By statute, it controls by itself only one of the major monetary instruments, the setting of reserve requirements. In fact, it is in a position to, and does, exercise authority in varying degrees over all three instruments of policy—and is popularly recognized as *the* monetary policy authority. Further, the effective voice within the Board is that of the Chairman, despite the formal equality of all seven Members—and this too is popularly recognized. William McChesney Martin's name may not be a household word, but it is far better known than those of his colleagues. Over the years, the Board has seldom contained, besides the Chairman, more than one or two members at a time whose stature commanded independent respect.

The Board has final authority over discount rates through its power to "review and determine" the decisions of the Reserve Directors. The Members of the FRB constitute a seven-to-five majority in the OMC and thus—barring defections—control the most important of monetary tools. In fact, decisions on all three instruments of policy are taken on the basis of discussion within OMC. Since 1955 the Committee has been used as a "forum, a clearinghouse for all of the aspects of policy determination in the System."[8] Thus the formal distribution of authority is belied in practice by unified consideration. Unified control seems inevitable, since the types of decision are logically related and it would be unthinkable to have them operating in contradictory directions. Because of the political importance of monetary policy, however, and the desirability of fiscal-monetary coordination, it is questionable whether a twelve-man, quasi-private body provides an adequate or appropriate locus for policy determination; of this, more presently.

The size, length of term and interest composition of the FRB have been the subject of considerable Congressional attention and have undergone some change over the years. The Board began with five appointed Members with staggered ten-year terms and two *ex officio*—the secretary of the Treasury and the Comptroller of the Currency. Both the latter were removed in the 1935 revision of the Banking Act, at the insistence of Senator Carter Glass, then chairman of the Banking and Currency Committee. Now there are seven Presidential appointees, and the term is fourteen years. No Member, incidentally, has yet served a full fourteen-year term, but a few have served *more than* fourteen years through successive appointments to unexpired terms.

The Chairman is selected by the President for a four-year, renewable term. This definite term was adopted in 1935, apparently with the intent that an incoming President should have a free hand. Resignations and new appointments have not coincided with presidential inaugurations, however, with the result that the incumbent's appointment, for example, expires in 1963.

The Federal Reserve Act has from the beginning stipulated group-interest qualifications for FRB Members. Originally, two had to be experienced in banking or finance, and the total membership had to provide "fair representation" of industrial, commercial and financial interests—as well as a regional balance designed to avoid eastern "domination." In 1922 the requirement of financial experience was dropped and agriculture was added to the list of represented interests. The actual composition for the 1914–50 period was as follows: thirteen from banking, five each from business and agriculture, and four from law.[9] Those appointed since 1950 have included one from private banking, two from business, two from agriculture and one each from the deanship of a business school and from a government career. Two of the post–1950 group also had experience of several years each on a Reserve Bank Board and one appointee's major experience had been as a Reserve Bank officer. "Promotion from within" is the trend. Among the major organized interests, labor is conspicuous by its absence. Business has been represented, but by substantial independents (ranchers, lumbermen, realtors) rather than by executives of large industrial corporations.

The size, length of term, interest composition and geographic distribution are all of questionable value to the System's policy functions and administrative effectiveness. It has been argued that fourteen-year terms provide an opportunity for Members to develop a knowledge of monetary economics and that they insulate the Board from partisan considerations. But many posts of equal technical complexity in other agencies are adequately staffed on a much shorter basis and, more importantly, insulation from politics is as impossible as it is democratically undesirable for an agency functioning so near the center of national economic policy. I shall return to this point later.

Although replacement of the Board by a single executive has been suggested only rarely, many observers, including Chairman Martin, are on record as favoring a smaller group than seven, on the ground that more capable men might then be attracted to the Board.[10] Clearly a seven-man board cannot collectively negotiate effectively with the President, the Secretary of the Treasury, the Chairman of the Council of Economic Advisers, or the lending agencies whose programs impinge on economic stability; yet coherent policy requires negotiation, consultation and program coordination constantly. Nor would a five-man board be notably better in this respect.

As it is now, the Chairman *is* the Federal Reserve Board for purposes of negotiation. In recent years he has lunched with the Secretary of the Treasury weekly,[11] and has sat in with the President's informal inner council on economic policy.[12] Congressional committees rely upon the Chairman to speak for the Board and rarely bother to interrogate other Board members. These arrangements apparently work because none of the other members is strong enough, personally or politically, to challenge the Chairman; and also, it seems reasonable to suggest, because there is no alternative save chaos. It is supported too by the tradition of secrecy that attends the actions of central banks, and that is defended as necessary to prevent the exploitation of leaks to private advantage: the fewer the negotiators, the less the likelihood of leaks. The gap between formal structure and the necessities of action reflected in the informal but decisive accretion of power to the Chairman (not only to the incumbent, but to McCabe and Eccles before him) is too great to be bridged by a minor adjustment in the size of the group.

Because of the importance of the Chairmanship, and the necessity for cordial relations between the head of the FRB and the President, Martin and McCabe have both suggested that the four-year term of the Chairman should end on March 31 of the year in which a President begins his term of office. Simpler still is the suggestion that the Chairman's term should be at the President's pleasure, as with most other national regulatory commissions. Whichever way the matter is handled, the need is for a relationship of mutual trust between President and Chairman, both for the sake of consistent economic policy and for democratic accountability through the President as chief elected representative of the public.[13] The present system of a fixed four-year term that (accidentally) does not coincide with Presidential inaugurations is unfortunate on both counts. Moreover, since the staggered 14-year terms of members expire in January of even-numbered years, a new President—even if the Chairman stepped aside—would be confined to the membership he inherits, in choosing a new Chairman, unless some member resigned to create a vacancy.

The policy suitability of geographic and interest qualifications for membership on the Board is a question that would become moot if the Board were replaced by a single head. If not, the answer must be that such qualifications are unsuitable because they are irrelevant and, in their present form, inequitable as well. They are irrelevant because the function of the Board is no longer simply to accommodate business, but to stabilize the national economy. The Board is not engaged in mediating group conflicts where the direct representation of parties-in-interest may be an irresistible political demand, but in a task of economic analysis and political judgment affecting the interests and values of *all* groups and individuals. Given the agency's function, independence of mind and familiarity with government finance and money markets, and with macro-economic analysis, are far more desirable qualifications than group representation.[14] Sensitivity to basic political currents—a quite different kind of "expertise"—is also pertinent, but not sensitivity only to the needs of a few special segments of the economy. . . .

The inequity of existing group representation requirements lies in the exclusion of interests as much affected by monetary policy as those that are included by statute. The present range reflects the original, restricted concept of the system. Today if groups are to be represented as such labor has as strong a claim as the farmers or industrialists, because employment levels are dependent on monetary policy to a significant extent; fixed-income receivers, whether corporate bond-clippers or Social Security pensioners, are directly and adversely affected if the tools of the FRB are not used with sufficient vigor to combat inflationary tendencies. Chairman Martin has even defined the objectives of monetary policy as providing job opportunities for wage earners and protection of those who depend upon savings or fixed incomes.[15] . . .

Even if labor and pensioner representation were added, however, the list of affected interests would be far from exhausted. As Emmette Redford has written of interest representation in regulatory agencies generally, "It is difficult, if not impossible, to include representation of all the interests which might legitimately make a claim for some representation.[16] A non-interest or "general interest" criterion for appointments would be the simplest way to avoid the problem entirely if a multi-member Board is retained. A statement expressing the views of the House Committee on Banking and Currency in 1935 sums up the matter nicely:

> It is important to emphasize in the law that Board Action should reflect, not the opinion of a majority of special interests, but rather the well considered judgment of a body that takes into consideration all phases of the national economic life.[17]

The Open Market Committee and policy unification

In origin and development, the OMC represents the leading structural response of the Federal Reserve System to its change in function. But the response has not been entirely adequate and further modifications in the structure and scope of authority of the Committee have been advanced from a number of quarters.

When the System began operations, the discount rate and the levels of reserves were thought to be the major tools of policy. As the public debt grew, and as the macro-economic function of stabilization developed, open market operations by the Reserve Banks increased in importance. The initial structural response came in 1922 when an Open Market Committee was established informally, more under the leadership of President Benjamin Strong of the New York Reserve Bank than of the FRB. The Banking Act of 1933 gave the OMC statutory recognition as a twelve-man group, selected by the Reserve Banks, to carry on open market operations under rules laid down by the FRB, thus substantially increasing the power of the national, public component. The Banking Act of 1935, largely written by then-Chairman Eccles as an effort to enhance the centralized, public character of the monetary authority, reorganized the Committee into its present form: the seven FRB members and five Reserve Presidents.[18]

(The House version—not enacted—of the 1935 Act would have gone further with the centralizing process by transferring authority for open market operations to the Board alone, with a requirement of consultation with an advisory committee of the regional Banks.) In short, change in economic circumstance, i.e., the growth of a large federal debt as an inescapable component of the nation's financial structure, and the development of a new function led to an institutional addition to the System. Informally, the change has gone one step further: as mentioned earlier, the OMC is used as a forum for discussion of the entire range of monetary actions, not just for decisions regarding the tool that lies formally within its jurisdiction.

There is widespread agreement among participants and observers that unified handling of the three major techniques is essential for coherence; but there is sharp disagreement over the appropriate composition of the OMC and over the division of labor between OMC and FRB. The disagreements involve in a politically sensitive way the central-regional and public-private balances in the policy process. The range of specific proposals is as follows:

(1) Consolidate all instruments in a publicly appointed Board, either the present FRB or a smaller one, abolishing the OMC but requiring consultation with the Reserve Bank Presidents. Variants of this have been suggested by the Hoover Commission Task Force, Eccles, and Bach, who see this approach as the proper way to secure the advantages of both public responsibility and "grass roots" information.[19]

(2) Consolidate by merging the OMC and FRB into a single Board constituted of three Members appointed by the President and two Reserve Bank Presidents, each of the latter group serving full time for a year on a rotating basis. This was proposed by former Chairman McCabe in 1949 as the proper change if any were to be made at all[20]; it would have the effect of displacing the New York Bank President from his present permanent seat on the OMC.

(3) Consolidate in the OMC as presently constituted. This is the position once favored by the regional Presidents.[21]

(4) Consolidate reserve requirements and open market policy in a reconstituted OMC consisting of the present five Reserve Bank representatives and a smaller FRB of five Members—thus creating an even balance between central and regional, publicly and semiprivately appointed elements. This proposal was advanced by the New York Clearing House Association, which also urged that in case of a disagreement between a Reserve Bank and the FRB over the rediscount rate, either party should be allowed to refer the question to the OMC for final decision.[22] The Association apparently felt that commercial bank influence was greater with the Presidents than with the national Board.

Those preferring no change at all include Martin, who has defended the existing arrangement as consistent with the "basic concept of a regional" System and as a way of promoting close relations between the Presidents and the Board.[23] The Patman subcommittee saw no reason, as of 1952, to disturb the *status quo*, but Representative Patman has more recently proposed consolidation in an enlarged FRB of twelve Presidential appointees.[24]

The rationale underlying the all-powers-to-the-Board approach can be summarized in the principle that public functions should be lodged in public bodies, and the assertion that open market operations are in no sense regional in character. Eccles has pointed out that the Reserve Presidents are not appointed by or accountable to either the President or Congress, and for this reason argues that their participation in national, public policy formation is inappropriate.[25] Bach has emphasized the national character of open market policy,[26] and he is joined in this view by Jacob Viner, who has said that:

> The regional emphasis in central banking is an obsolete relic of the past. No country, not even Canada, which is much more a collection of distinct economic regions than is the United States, has thought it expedient to follow our initial example of introducing regionalism into central banking.[27]

The argument for OMC as the top body derives from the importance attributed to regionalism and (inferentially at least) from a belief in the financial community that the Committee is more sympathetic than the FRB to the felt needs of bankers. The regional case has been most strongly stated by President Delos C. Johns of the St. Louis Reserve Bank:

> Each Reserve bank president is in a position to judge possible alternatives of national monetary policy with due regard to the particular characteristics of his reigon. This makes for adoption of national monetary policy that squares realistically with actual conditions in the regions. . . .[28]

Macro-stabilization as the major function of the System clearly forecloses regional devolution in the making of policy, yet regional circumstances should be considered. The valid claims of regionalism, however, require only a consultative voice, not a decisional one. And public policy, I would agree with Eccles, should not be made by a body containing men who are not accountable to the national public whose welfare is affected by the decisions made.

In *operations*, as distinct from policy determination, regionalism may well possess continued utility; and centralization of policy is entirely compatible with a considerable degree of regional diversification in operations. The point of greatest overlap between national policy and Reserve Bank operations appears to be in the handling of the "discount window," that is, the ease or difficulty with which a member bank may avail itself of the rediscount privilege. A uniform national policy could, for example, suggest "easier" loan conditions in any District whose area rate of unemployment was "x" percentage points above the national average, and thus provide for regional differentiation while maintaining central policy control.

Federal Advisory Council

The Federal Advisory Council began as a compensation to the commercial bankers for their failure to obtain direct representation on the FRB.[29] Its function today has been described as providing "firsthand advice and counsel from people who are closely in touch with the banking activities of their particular districts,"[30] although available information does not explain how these bank representatives are able to contribute something that the Reserve Bank Presidents, with their extensive staff aids, could not supply as well or better. Assuming that their advice is not redundant, however, it is questionable whether the FRB should accord *statutory* advisory status to commercial bankers only, now that the System's policy may affect many other social groups just as significantly as the bankers; *e.g.*, non-bank financial institutions, home builders, state and local governments, Golden Age Clubs, wage-earners, and so on. The board has at times used formal consultants from outside the commercial banking sphere, as when consumer credit regulations were being formulated[31]; but this is apparently infrequent. Once again, we see that the System's structure has become outmoded by the change in scope of function.

III. The Federal Reserve and national economic policy

The analysis to this point has focused upon internal factors. We come now to the questions: What is the source of the Federal Reserve's policy goals? Does existing structure adequately relate the monetary authority to the President and to the monetary management operations of the Treasury, to lending agency decisions, and to the Council of Economic Advisers? Does an adequate mechanism exist for resolving disputes that threaten the coherence of an Administration's over-all economic policy? These can only be answered by going beyond the internal organization of the Fed to a consideration of its external relationships.

The first place to look for the mandate of an agency is in its organic statute; but the Federal Reserve Act deals sparsely with the matter of goals, and has in any case, as already noted, been outpaced by events. Since the law does not provide a mandate fitted to the modern concerns of the System, it is to the Employment Act of 1946 that one must look for goals written in macro-economic language: "it is the continuing policy and responsibility of the Federal Government to use all practicable means . . . to promote maximum employment, production, and purchasing power." This declaration applies to the Federal Reserve as to all other agencies of the national government, and is often mentioned in FRB descriptions of the system's role. But as a policy guide it is less than complete. For one thing, it does not mention price stability, although it has been widely interpreted as including this goal by logical extrapolation from those explicitly specified. For another, it leaves open such questions as, should employment be maximized today by measures that may bring on unemployment tomorrow by over-stimulating a "boom," or conversely, contribute to unemployment today lest inflation come tomorrow?

Thus the Employment Act mandate shares the imprecision of most such statements. While it could perhaps be sharpened, a need for interpretive subsidiary definition probably cannot be eliminated because any language tight enough to do this would inevitably place too inflexible a straight-jacket on agency operation. Elaboration of goals at later stages of the policy process may be expected to continue. The President, who enters office with a vague mandate that is partly personal, partly party doctrine, commonly sets at least the tone for the specific interpretation of statutory directives, by the nature of his appointees. But the President's authority over the Federal Reserve is restricted, unless vacancies occur, to one appointment of a member (for fourteen years) every other year starting a year after his own term begins; and to appointment of the Chairman for a fixed four-year term. The independence of the agency conflicts with the President's responsibilities for overall economic policy.

In support of the position that independence should prevail—*i.e.*, that the FRB should not take its mandate from the President—the argument is advanced that anti-inflationary measures are unpopular though necessary; that "hard" decisions are more acceptable "if they are decided by public officials who, like the members of the judiciary, are removed from immediate pressures"[32]; and that the accountability of the system to the electorate is adequately achieved through its responsibility to Congress.[33] On the other side, the President is required by the Employment Act to submit a program for achieving the Act's goals; such a program must include recommendations on monetary policy to be meaningful; and thus the President must be "the coordinating agent for the whole national economic program."[34] Men on both sides agree on one point: there should be a strong advocate within the government for the monetary stability viewpoint, and the central bank is the logical home for such advocacy. The major disagreements are whether a substantial degree of insulation from other agencies engaged in economic policy determination helps or hinders the expression of that viewpoint, and whether a clear locus of authority is required for settlement of disputes between the institutions variously responsible for monetary and fiscal policies.

The issue of FRB accountability to Congress is a false one and should be exposed as such. Contrary to a myth strongly held by System spokesmen—and many Congressmen—the FRB, even more than the other regulatory commissions, is *less* accountable to Congress than are the line departments in the Presidential hierarchy. The Federal Reserve does not depend on appropriations and thus is freed from the most frequently used tool of Congressional administrative supervision. And Congress has exercised an unusual degree of restraint in even suggesting its policy views to the Board. All executive agencies that have statutory bases may be said to be "creatures of Congress," and those with single heads are more easily held accountable than those with boards that diffuse responsibility.[35] For agencies with substantive powers, the price of accountability to Congress is accountability to the President.

On the need for a coordinating authority, Martin's position has been to grant the need for coordination but to argue that it can be achieved adequately through informal consultation.[36] The Advisory Board on Economic Growth and Stability established by President Eisenhower in 1953 would appear to be in line with his thinking: ABEGS (under leadership of the then CEA Chairman Arthur Burns) could bring about full exchange of information and full discussion, but could not *commit* the participating agencies to a unified course, even before it fell into desuetude after Burns' departure. The same was true of the Treasury Secretary-FRB Chairman luncheons and the President's informal economic policy discussions with agency heads during the Eisenhower Administration. Thus the problem of a possible stalemate or contradiction between Presidential and FRB policy is not resolved by these consultative arrangements.[37] . . . Only if the FRB Chairman served at the will of the President, and a centralized authority directed the use of all credit instruments, would a formal basis for cohesion and accountability be laid.

Would a proposal of this kind mean the subordination of monetary stability to a frequently assumed low-interest, easy money predilection in the Treasury Department and the White House? While an unambiguous "No" cannot be given in reply, the weight of argument is in the negative direction. Independence may mean isolation rather than strength, for independent agencies lack the power of Presidential protection and Presidential involvement. Paradoxically, the real ability of the Fed to influence national economic policy might very well be increased if its formal independence were diminished. Have not the informal steps taken in the past seven or eight years toward closer liaison between the FRB and Presidential policy makers already made the Board (*i.e.*, the Chairman) somewhat stronger than was the case during the Truman Administration?

In addition to Presidential elaboration of Congressional policy statements, further interpretation is invariably made at the agency level. When the FRB or OMC decides to change, or not to change, the degree of restraint or ease in credit policy it is deciding—*necessarily*—whether to place emphasis for the short-run on the price stability or the maximum-employment-and-growth side of its imprecise mandate. The question of internal interpretation, therefore, is whether the policy preferences of the monetary authority are likely to coincide with those of the politically accountable originators and interpreters of the mandate. The probability is that the central banking agency will be to some extent more conscious of the monetary than of the employment-and-growth aspects of stabilization, the major reasons being (1) the role of the institution, (2) the inevitably close relationships of the policy makers to their commercial banking "clientele" as the focal point of immediate policy impact, and (3) the social backgrounds of the policy makers. The Administration (of whichever party) and Congress, however, are likely to give greater weight to employment than are the central bankers, simply because the political consequences of unemployment are likely to be—and are even more likely to be perceived as—more unfortunate for elected office holders than those of price inflation. This difference may be pronounced or slight, depending on the personal emphasis and understandings of the men involved; but that they will continue to exist even when the general orientation of both sides is similar was shown by the occasional disputes between the President's economic advisers and the FRB during the Eisenhower Administrations.[38] . . .

In the absence of any but the traditional instruments the FRB is faced with a cruel choice: its own rationale calls for it to fight inflation, but doing so would create rising unemployment. If it refrains from acting, in order to preserve high employment, it may fail to stop inflation. Does it have a mandate to make such a choice? One could be extrapolated from the general stabilization directive, but not with any clear political sanction. As economist Gardiner C. Means has said, "there is a good deal of question whether such a momentous decision should rest with the Federal Reserve Board."[39]

IV. Conclusion

The basic finding of the analysis presented above is that the formal structure of the Federal Reserve System is inappropriate to its functions and out of line with informal arrangements that have the logic of necessity behind them. These gaps flow from changes in the monetary authority's function and in the structure of the economy. Devised as a service agency for banking and commerce—to achieve a semi-automatic adjustment of the money supply—the Federal Reserve has become as well a policy-making institution with major responsibility for national eocnomic stabilization. Ancillary arrangements for interest representation based on an assumption that monetary actions were of important concern only to bankers and businessmen now have the appearance of unjustified special access because the range of affected interests and values is seen to be as broad as the nation itself.

Informal developments—most notably the unified handling of major monetary techniques and the preeminence of the Chairman's position—and the formal changes of 1935 that in a degree public-ized and nationalized the Open Market Committee did something to improve the fit of form to function. But these alterations have not been sufficient to ensure adequate accountability for what is today an authority of first rank political importance; they have not brought the quasi-private "face" of the System into line with its public responsibilities; and they do not provide a sufficient organizational base for coherent integration of the fiscal and monetary components of national economic policy. A more complete face-lifting is in order.

The Chairmanship is the key both to accountability and to effective performance. The four-year fixed term, having produced a result contradictory to the one intended, should be repealed in favor of service at the pleasure of the President. The informal preeminence of the Chairman should be recognized formally by abolishing the Board and the OMC and centralizing authority over the discount rate, reserve requirements and open market operations in the hands of the Chairman, who might be re-titled the Governor of the Federal Reserve System. The need for information from below could be handled through regularized reporting from the Reserve Bank Presidents on regional conditions, and by strengthened staff analysis in the Office of the Governor. By these alterations, the public, i.e., political, quality of monetary policy would be accorded appropriate recognition; responsibility would be clearly located; a means of settling possible disputes between fiscal policy under the President and monetary under the Fed would be created; and the process of consultation and negotiation by the Fed with the Treasury, the CEA and the lending agencies would be made more effective. In short, a single head, enjoying the confidence of the President, would be able to speak with vigor for the central banking viewpoint in the formation of economic policy; yet once the deliberations had been completed an assurance would exist that the Fed would be at one with the rest of the government in executing the policy determined upon.

A second, lesser category of structural change would have the object of revising the Fed's appearance to fit the public nature of its responsibilities. Election of two-thirds of the Reserve Bank Directors by commercial banks, and "ownership" of the Reserve Banks by commercial banks, are admittedly matters of no great substantive importance today. But since they are functionless elements, and their appearance of special interest access is harmful to the legitimacy of monetary actions, the Reserve Boards should be eliminated (or, at least, all of their members should be publicly appointed) and the commercial banks' shares in the Reserve Banks should be bought out by the government—thus making the Reserve Banks in form what they largely are in fact: field offices of the national, public monetary authority.

Adoption of this series of proposals—or others, perhaps milder in form but having the same essential consequences—would significantly improve the economic policy machinery of the national government. These changes represent a logical extension of the premises of the Employment Act:

> In no major country of the world today, except in the United States, is there a central bank that can legally, if it wishes, tell the head of its own Government to go fly a kite. It seems to me that if we are to hold Government responsible for carrying out the new doctrine of economic stabilization, there must be a chain of responsibility reaching through the Presidency to all the instumentalities that do the stabilizing.[40]

Notes

1. For more detailed description of the formal organization, see Board of Governors, *The Federal Reserve System* (Washington, D.C., 1961) and G. L. Bach, *Federal Reserve Policy-Making* (New York, 1950).

2. E. A. Goldenweiser, *American Monetary Policy* (New York, 1951), p. 295.

3. Joint (Patman) Committee on the Economic Report, *Monetary Policy and the Management of the Public Debt, Replies to Questions*, Sen. Doc. 123, 82d Cong. 2d sess., 1952, pp. 278–79. Cited hereafter as Sen. Doc. 123.

4. Bach, pp. 81–82.

5. Bach, pp. 57–58.

6. Goldenweiser, p. 296.

7. Joint (Douglas) Committee on the Economic Report, *Hearings, Monetary, Credit and Fiscal Policies*, 81st Cong., 1st sess., 1949, p. 221.

8. Chairman Martin in Senate Committee on Finance, *Hearings, Investigation of the Financial Condition of the United States*, 85th Cong., 1st sess., 1957, p. 1260. Cited hereafter as Senate Finance Committee *Hearings*.

9. Bach, p. 119.

10. Sen. Doc. 123, p. 30.

11. Senate Finance Committee *Hearings*, 1959, p. 2180.

12. Conversation with staff members, Council of Economic Advisers.

13. Bach, pp. 227–28.

14. See Chairman Martin's remarks, Sen. Doc. 123, p. 300, and Bach, p. 121.

15. Senate Finance Committee *Hearings*, p. 1262.

16. *Administration of National Economic Control* (New York, 1952), p. 270; and see ch. 9 generally.

17. House Report No. 742, 74th Cong., 1st sess. (April 19, 1935), p. 6.

18. Marriner S. Eccles, *Beckoning Frontiers* (New York, 1951), pp. 167–71. These pages contain an excellent capsule summary of OMC development.

19. Commission on Organization of the Executive Branch of the Government, *Task Force Report on Regulatory Commissions*, Appendix N, January 1949, pp. 113–14; Eccles, pp. 224–26; Bach, pp. 234–35.

20. Joint Committee on the Economic Report, *Monetary, Credit, and Fiscal Policies, A Collection of Statements*, 81st Cong., 1st sess., 1949, pp. 68–69.

21. Ibid., p. 162. By 1952, the Presidents were less enthusiastic for change (see Sen. Doc. 123, p. 673). They perhaps feared that the unified control might go to the FRB rather than to the OMC if the subject were opened up at all.

22. New York Clearing House Association, *The Federal Reserve Reexamined* (New York, 1953), pp. 138–39.

23. Sen. Doc. 123, p. 294.

24. Subcommittee on General Credit Control and Debt Management, Joint Committee on the Economic Report, *Monetary Policy and the Management of the Public Debt*, Sen. Doc. 163, 82d Cong., 2d sess. (1952), p. 54; H. R. 2790, 86th Cong., 1st sess. (1959).

25. Joint Committee on the Economic Report, *Hearings, Monetary, Credit and Fiscal Policies*, 81st Cong., 1st sess. (1949), p. 221.

26. Bach, p. 234.

27. Subcommittee on General Credit Control and Debt Management, Joint Committee on the Economic Report, *Hearings, Monetary Policy and the Management of the Public Debt*, 82d Cong., 2d sess. (1952), p. 756, cited hereafter as General Credit Control Subcommittee *Hearings*, 1952. Regionalism in the Federal Reserve—or at least its modern defense—perhaps owes more to an unexamined bias in favor of "federalism" as a matter of political ideology than to an empirical examination of the national economic structure.

28. Sen. Doc. 123, pp. 677–79.

29. Robert E. Cushman, *The Independent Regulatory Commissions* (New York, 1941), p. 160.

30. Martin, in Senate Finance Committee *Hearings*, 1957, p. 1261.

31. Letter, Kenneth A. Kenyon, Assistant Secretary, Board of Governors, to the author, August 17, 1960.

32. Martin, in Sen. Doc. 123, p. 242.

33. See, for example, FRB Research Director Ralph A. Young's remarks, Antitrust Subcommittee, Senate Committee on the Judiciary, *Hearings, Administered Prices*, 86th Cong., 1st sess. (1959), Part 10, pp. 4887–91.

34. See H. Christian Sonne's comments, from which the quotation is taken, in General Credit Control Subcommittee *Hearings*, 1952, pp. 848–50.

35. For discussion of this and other pertinent administrative myths, see Harold Stein's remarks in General Credit Control Subcommittee *Hearings*, 1952, pp. 758–59.

36. Sen. Doc. 123, pp. 263–73.

37. See the remarks of Leon H. Keyserling and Roy Blough in Sen. Doc. 123, pp. 848–51.

38. *E.g.*, in the spring of 1956; see discussion in Senate Finance Committee *Hearings*, 1957, pp. 1361–63.

39. Antitrust Subcommittee, Senate Committee on the Judiciary, *Hearings, Administered Prices*, 86th Cong., 1st sess. (1959), Part 10, p. 4917.

40. Elliott V. Bell, "Who Should Manage Our Managed Money?" An address before the American Bankers Association Convention, Los Angeles, California, October 22, 1956.

3C.2. Presidential Influence on the Federal Reserve in the 1970s

NATHANIEL BECK

As we have seen, formal authority over monetary policy lies with the Federal Reserve Board. In recent years, however, many observers have argued that the President has considerably more power over monetary policy than his formal powers would suggest. They argue that the same lack of legitimacy that Michael Reagan complains about often leads Federal Reserve system officials to defer to the wishes of the President. This viewpoint is usually supported by interviews in which current or former Federal Reserve officials claim to have followed the President's priorities.

In this article Nathaniel Beck takes this approach a step further. He argues that if the President were in fact a major influence on Federal Reserve actions, we would expect to see sharp changes in monetary policy when a new President comes into office, especially if the new President is of a different party. Beck uses changes in the federal funds rate as an indicator of the direction of monetary policy. He tries to correct for nonpolitical influences on the federal funds rate, such as changes in unemployment and inflation. He then looks at the changes that remain and shows that there do appear to be the expected sharp breaks when a new President comes into office. This, he argues, provides evidence to support those who claim that the President has a major influence on monetary policy.

The middle part of this paper uses advanced quantitative analysis, which many readers will find difficult (the most difficult material appears in the appendix). The reader should note that Beck's evidence is not conclusive: other events could have caused some of the breaks, and Beck is looking at only a very restricted time period. Nor does he show that the President has an effect on policy at times other than when he comes into office. Nonetheless, Beck's careful study provides solid evidence for the view that the President influences monetary policy.

Reprinted, in edited version, from *American Journal of Political Science*. Vol. 26, No. 3, August 1982, by permission of the author and the University of Texas Press.

As public concern over the decline of America's economic performance grows, political scientists and economists are examining how American political institutions affect economic performance. These examinations have usually dealt either with the impact of the economy on political variables (e.g., Kramer, 1971; Kernell, 1978) or with how politicians manipulate economic outcomes to achieve some goal, which may be electoral (Tufte, 1978) or ideological (Hibbs, 1977). Implicit in this work is the assumption that politicians have the tools to manipulate economic outcomes. Most research connecting politics and economic policy has taken a rather simple view of the policy-making process, generally assuming that the president can get any economic outcome he desires. Because these works have not looked explicitly at the economic policy-making process and because they have not taken into account contraints on policymakers imposed by the private economy, their conclusions linking political behavior and economic policy are often open to question.

A few researchers have attempted to build models of economic policymaking that explicitly include both economic and political variables. Cowart (1978) modeled the monetary policy of several European countries as a function of economic and political variables. Golden and Poterba (1980) studied the behavior of American macroeconomic variables as functions of electoral and economic variables. However, these works have a fairly simplistic model of the policy-making process, with respect to which instruments policymakers attempt to control and how those instruments are controlled. Alt and Woolley (1980) set forth a much more sophisticated model of the politics of macroeconomic policy making; however, they have not applied their model to the study of American economic policy.

Presumably, economic policymakers are trying to accomplish something; the question becomes whether politics affects either the goals of policymakers or the means by which they try to reach those goals. To answer this question, we need a precise notion of what instruments policymakers manipulate and a model of how they manipulate those instruments. This paper explores the question in terms of recent American monetary policy, focusing in much more detail on policy-making institutions than has been typical. In particular, the paper examines the impact of elections, party, administration, and individual policymakers on monetary policy as it is actually made, rather than on its outcomes. By focusing on the behavior of decision makers (constrained by factors beyond their control), we can achieve a better understanding of the forces shaping economic policy.

This study is restricted to an examination of the impact of politics on monetary policy because it seems possible to specify a model of how such policy is made and what policy instruments are under the control of policymakers. At present, the same is not possible for fiscal policy. There are also other reasons for focusing on monetary policy. First, it is clearly important. Wherever one stands on the debate between the monetarists and the Keynesians, few deny that monetary policy has at least a short-run impact on the economy. Second, monetary policy has been largely ignored by political scientists. The few political studies of the

Federal Reserve System (Fed) have either been overly legalistic (e.g., Reagan, 1961) or have been based primarily on qualitative evidence (e.g., Woolley, 1977, 1980). Other studies of the politics of the Fed have either been insider accounts (e.g., Maisel, 1973) or journalistic (e.g., Rose, 1974). Third, it is expected that if politics has any impact on economic policy, it should appear in a study of monetary policy. Monetary policy, unlike fiscal policy, is made by a relatively small group of actors, who leave a fairly accurate record of the parts they play. The fiscal policy-making process is considerably more complex and involves bargaining among a much more diverse set of actors. Fourth, the few quantitative empirical studies that have carefully examined some of the political influences on monetary policy (e.g., Golden and Poterba, 1980) have looked at what, we shall see, is an outcome, rather than an indicator of policy, namely, money supply.

In the United States, monetary policy is officially made by the Fed. This body is nonpartisan and legally independent of the president (see Reagan, 1961, for details). The next section gives a brief introduction to both (internal) Fed policy making and its (external) role in the political system. The second section presents a brief discussion of data and methods used in the paper. The last section preceding the summary examines the impact of the White House on Fed policy making.

The Federal Reserve and monetary policy

In common parlance, we talk of the Fed "printing money," in particular, to finance the government deficit. Strictly speaking, of course, it does no such thing. To understand the Fed's role in determining money supply, we must look briefly at the American banking system (see Bach, 1971, for a more complete discussion). This system is what is called a "fractional reserve system." Banks are required only to keep a fraction of their total deposits on reserve (on the theory that all people will not want to withdraw their deposits at the same time). If someone deposits $1,000, the bank is free to lend most of that amount, keeping only a fraction of that $1,000 on reserve. Presumably, the borrower of the portion of $1,000 puts that amount on deposit in another bank, which is then free to lend a portion, and so on. Thus a deposit of $1,000 can create many thousands of dollars in additional deposit. The Fed makes the rules on what reserves banks are required to hold. Lowering the reserve ratio (that of reserves to total deposits) increases the total amount of funds on deposit, assuming that banks are able and willing to lend all that they legally can. Such, of course, is not always the case. In practice, the Fed seldom changes the reserve ratio, and it is not a tool of short-term policy making.[1]

Given a constant (or near constant) reserve requirement, the Fed can influence total deposits by influencing bank reserves. To meet their reserve requirements, banks are allowed to borrow reserves either from other banks or from the Fed. By raising the discount rate (the interest rate it charges banks) the Fed makes it more costly for banks to borrow reserves and hence should cause banks to desire to decrease reserves, which then leads banks to carry fewer deposits.

In practice, the discount rate is not a major tool of short-run policy because it is cumbersome to change. The discount rate *is* an important signal to the financial community of Fed intentions, and, indeed, the Fed has often signaled major turnarounds in policy by changes in the discount rate, although not always so dramatically as in October of 1979 when the Fed raised the discount rate by an unprecedented full percentage point. However, its symbolic use does not mean that it is a powerful tool of monetary policy—just the opposite is true. Moreover, banks are not encouraged to use the discount window to obtain funds for normal use. Almost all bank-borrowed reserves are borrowed in the so-called Federal Funds (Fed Funds) market. This market consists primarily of large (over $1 million) overnight loans between banks, with banks having excess reserves making loans to banks with insufficent reserves.[2] This means that we should not focus on the discount rate as the principal indicator of American monetary policy. Therefore, this paper will not replicate Cowart's study of European monetary policy for the United States, since he used only the discount rate as a policy indicator.

Rather than the reserve requirement or the discount rate, the Fed's major monetary policy tool is the so-called open market operation. Briefly, the Fed owns a portfolio of government securities. Open market operations consist of the buying and selling of securities from this portfolio to and from government bond dealers. When the Fed buys a bond from a dealer, it credits his bank account with a check drawn on the Federal Reserve Bank of New York; this increases the reserves held by the dealer's bank, and hence enables that bank to make more loans, which makes more deposits and so on. Similarly, if the Fed sells a bond from its portfolio, the bond dealer pays for it with a check drawn on his account. This payment reduces the reserves of that bank, and hence causes the bank to contract its loan portfolio, with an ensuing decrease in deposits. These open market operations constitute the major short-run tool of monetary policy.

Before discussing how the Fed makes decisions about open market policy, it is necessary to discuss what is meant by ''money.'' Although discussions of what money is can become painfully Byzantine, it can be thought of as anything that can be used to settle a commercial transaction. Thus in the United States, commercial transactions can be settled by either currency or a check drawn on a commercial bank. The sum of all deposits in checking accounts (demand deposits) and all currency in circulation is called M1 and is the most common measure of the money supply.[3] However, other types of financial instruments, such as money market mutual fund shares, can be easily turned into demand deposits or generally used to settle transactions. Thus the Fed has defined various other monetary aggregates (M2 through M5) to take account of this ''near'' money. In this study, I look at M1 since this is the aggregate that the Fed appears to look at and also the aggregate that the financial markets appear to consider most important.

What then is the relationship between open market operations and M1? We have seen that when the Fed sells a security, bank reserves decrease. Presumably, this leads to a decrease in deposits and hence a decrease in M1. But M1 is a function of decisions made by banks and corporations as well as those by the Fed. To see this, imagine that the economy is at the peak of a boom period. Suppose the Fed sells a security. The bank might well borrow in the Fed Funds market rather than contract its loan portfolio, if borrowers are willing to pay the bank more than the Fed Funds rate for the money. Therefore, selling a security might not decrease M1. Similarly, imagine the economy at the bottom of a trough. Suppose that the Fed attempts to increase M1 by buying a security. If no one wishes to make additional loans, then there will be a rather small increase in M1 (and perhaps none at all if the bank simply uses the payment for the bond to decrease its borrowings in the Fed Funds market). M1 is not under the direct control of the Fed; it is a function of actions of the Fed and decisions of private actors in the economy. M1 might increase rapidly in spite of Fed efforts to tighten the money supply or it might fall in spite of Fed efforts to ease the money supply. *Thus M1 is not a good measure of what policy the government is pursuing. M1 is not a policy instrument that is under the control of the government. The government can have an impact on M1, but so can nongovernmental agents.* Studies that use money supply as a maeasure of Fed policy (e.g., Golden and Poterba, 1980) are, therefore suspect.

Given that the Fed cannot use open market operations simply to achieve a desired money stock, how does the Fed make open market policy? If we can answer this question, we can then examine whether changes in political variables seem to affect the process. Formally, open market policy is made by the Federal Open Market Committee (FOMC), which consists of the seven governors of the board, the president of the Reserve Bank of New York, and four other regional bank presidents who serve on a rotating basis. The committee meets every three weeks and determines policy for the ensuing three weeks; in between meetings, the chairman of the board is authorized to take emergency measures. Theoretically decisions are made by majority vote, but practically decisions are consensual, and in general the chairman gets what he proposes (although he often must be clever enough to propose what he can get). Until the Accord of 1951, the FOMC basically served the needs of Treasury, accommodating Treasury's need to borrow.[4]

In 1951 the Fed's objection to this policy of accommodation led President Truman to arrange an agreement between Treasury and the Fed that would allow the Fed to act independently of Treasury as long as it consulted with Treasury. This is the famous Accord. At the same time, William McChesney Martin was appointed as chairman of the board of governors, a position he would hold for twenty years. Under Martin, the FOMC was very sensitive to something called the "tone" of the market, that is, whether money appeared to be "tight" or "easy." According to Maisel's (1973) and Borins' (1972) accounts, Martin disdained simple quantitative measures and felt that his feeling for the market would be a better guide to policy making than would any set of economic or financial indicators. Towards the end of Martin's tenure, the FOMC did start looking more at various financial indicators.

When Arthur Burns took over as chairman in 1970, the FOMC was already moving towards using quantitative economic tools. Under Burns, the FOMC used a "targets and instruments" approach (see Friedman, 1975) by which it attempted to manipulate an instrument under its control to come close to some goal (target). The FOMC was somewhat vague about its targets, although it was clearly interested in such long-run targets as low unemployment, low inflation, and a strong dollar. In addition to these long-run targets, the FOMC also pursued, if rather desultorily, intermediate targets such as growth rates for the monetary aggregates.[5]

The instrument used by the FOMC to try to hit these targets was the Fed Funds rate, the interest rate on large overnight borrowings between member banks. This rate can be effectively and continuously manipulated by the open market desk, making possible policy changes that do not introduce major shocks into the markets. Thus at each meeting, the FOMC would issue instructions to the open market account manager in New York telling him to keep the Fed Funds rate within a certain band (usually between one-half and one-percentage point wide). The open market desk had little trouble in keeping the Fed Funds rate within the desired range. Thus, in the decade of the 1970s, the Fed used an instrument, the Fed Funds rate, which was effectively under its control, to try to achieve what-ever goals it desired.[6] The Fed Funds rate can thus serve as an indicator of monetary policy, with money stock (M1) as an indicator of the intermediate target and unemployment, inflation, and the balance of payments as indicators of long-run targets.

Burns's departure from the Fed in 1978 brought few changes in these basic operating procedures. Under the chairmanship of William Miller, the FOMC continued to use the Fed Funds rate as the major tool of monetary policy.[7] Furthermore, since 1975 Congress has required the FOMC to set and defend quarterly targets before Senate and House committees. Thus we have a fairly good idea about both targets the Fed was trying to hit and how it manipulated instruments under its control. This understanding enables us to estimate a reaction function relating the instrument used by the FOMC to target deviations. We can then study whether that reaction function changed with changes in the political environment.

The FOMC manipulated the Fed Funds rate to accomplish whatever it was trying to accomplish. What was it trying to accomplish? During the 1970s, the FOMC generally tried for a growth rate of M1 somewhere near 6 percent. Why did it choose this particular target, and how did it make trade-offs among the final macroeconomic targets? Clearly, decisions about targets and trade-offs are political decisions. How does decison making at the Fed fit in with other political decisions made in the United States?

Observers of the Fed (e.g., Maisel, 1973; Weintraub, 1978) are unanimous in saying that the president is the major determinant of Fed policy. The president has great power simply because he is president. Monetary policy is not made in a policy vacuum. The president, by fiscal policy, can undo much of what the Fed does. A president who supports the Fed's monetary policy with a coordinate fiscal policy greatly simplifies the task of the Fed. (This assertion is considered later.)

In addition the president appoints the chairman of the Fed and the other governors. While governors of the Fed have been granted long tenure (fourteen years) in order to guarantee their independence, in practice most governors serve about six years; the term of the chairman is four years. Thus a president might have a strong influence on the board by appointments. One check on the president's power is that he does not have the authority to appoint a new chairman until one year after taking office. (Whether the appointment of a chairman by a new president affects FOMC decision making is also considered later.)

The Fed could potentially play a great role in aiding (or hurting) an incumbent president's chances for reelection. Given that the Fed needs the cooperation of the president, it might choose to help him. On the other hand, the Fed benefits greatly by an appearance of being nonpartisan. Much of the power of the Fed comes from its ability to speak for the "national interest." A partisan Fed would probably soon find itself stripped of much of its power. (See Woolley, 1980; Borins, 1972; or Kane, 1980, for further discussion of this point.) . . .

Data and methods[8]

This research estimated reaction functions for the FOMC and then investigated whether those functions shifted at politically relevant times (change of President, change of party, change of chairman, election time). The reaction function used here is similar to one developed by Diggins (1978). The reader interested in a more complete discussion of that particular function should see Diggins's dissertation. As discussed above, the FOMC under Martin did not consider quantitative economic evidence and instead relied on the "tone" of the markets. In that period, the FOMC's instructions to the open market account manager consisted of orders to "ease," "firm," or maintain market conditions. Thus it would seem to be a mistake to try to fit a reaction function for interest rates or money stocks for this period. In this research, reaction functions were only estimated for the post-Martin period (i.e., from March 1970). The final data point used is August 1979, the month Miller resigned. The Volcker period is not included in this study because of the major changes that took place in FOMC procedure in October 1979. There simply were not enough data points after this change to allow inclusion of the Volcker period in the estimations. Monthly data from this time period (March 1970–August 1979) were used, yielding 114 data points.

A reaction function tells how an instrument that is under the control of FOMC (and is manipulated by its members to achieve a target or goal) changes as a function of either changes in the environment of prior target misses. It was argued above that the appropriate instrument to look at is the Federal Funds rate, the interest rate on large overnight loans between banks. Following Diggins, I used the monthly change in the Fed Funds rate as the dependent variable in the reaction function. One can tell what factors the FOMC appeared to consider by looking at FOMC records and congressional hearings, as well as by talking to Fed personnel. Based on these considerations, the independent variables used in the reaction function (the goals) were unemployment rates, inflation rates, and, as a measure of the strength of the dollar, the value of the mark.[9] These variables were lagged one month, to take into account information lags in the system. . . .

I assumed that the Fed desired low unemployment and inflation and a strong dollar. In the absence of knowledge of the specific target values for these variables, I simply assumed that the long-run targets did not vary much during the period under study. Given constant targets and a linear specification, the actual values of the targets only affect the value of the constant term. Therefore, in this research, unemployment, inflation, and the mark were measured in absolute terms, rather than as deviations from a target. This simply means that the constant term cannot be easily interpreted.[10] The coefficient on unemployment should be negative; the coefficients on inflation and the mark, positive.

The Fed also had intermediate targets for the money supply. Over the period of study, this target was generally about 6 percent for M1 (the targets were given in ranges rather than as single numbers). However, unlike the long-run targets, monetary targets did vary over the latter part of the 1970s; therefore, I used target deviations for the independent monetary variables.[11] If prior values for M1 exceeded that target, the FOMC should presumably have tightened the money supply by increasing the Fed Funds rate, and acted conversely if M1 was too low.[12] Thus the reaction function included a variable (M1L) to measure the difference between the previous month's M1 and the target value for M1 as given in the policy directive and another variable (M6L) to measure that deviation averaged over the prior half year. Each of those variables should have a positive sign. The reaction function estimated is then

$$DFF = c + b_1 M1L + b_2 M6L + b_3 UNL + b_4 INFL + b_5 MARKL + e, \quad (1)$$

where DFF is the monthly change in the Fed Funds rate, b is the regression coefficient, c is a constant, UNL is the unemployment rate, $INFL$ is the inflation rate, $MARKL$ is the value of the mark (all with L to indicate one-month lag), and e is an error term.

Before estimating (1), several comments are in order. Equation (1) assumes that the *change* in the Funds rate is a function of the *level* of the state of the economy. I focus on change in the dependent variable because most decision makers follow an incrementalist scheme (i.e., they make month-to-month changes in a variable, rather than setting the level of the variable anew each month). The use of a level independent variable is harder to justify. One justification is that estimating reaction functions with change independent variables gives decidedly inferior fits. This choice is consistent with my other work (Beck, 1981b), which found that changes in the monetary base could be better explained by the level of unemployment than changes in that level.

This finding is surprising in that it means that the Fed continues to tighten up (from its perspective) in bad times, even if the state of the economy is improving. The result is somewhat less surprising for the inflation variable, which measures the rate of change in the Consumer Price Index, but no such easy explanation is available for either the unemployment level or the value of the mark. . . .

In Table 1, the results of estimating (1) using ordinary least squares are shown. The Durbin-Watson statistic indicates that the errors are serially correlated. Thus most of the results reported here use the Cochran-Orcutt estimation procedure that corrects for the inefficiency of ordinary least squares in the presence of autocorrelated error terms. The results of this reestimation of (1) are also reported in Table 1.

While the prime interest was in whether the coefficients of (1) were stable over time, the estimates themselves were of some interest. The estimates were quite consistent with Diggins's (1978) estimates even though his estimates were based on 1970–1976. My estimates were also roughly consistent with the estimates reported by Abrams et al. (1980). As they did, I found that the FOMC was sensitive to the growth rate of the money supply in that failure to hit target growth rates of M1 caused it to adjust the Fed Funds rate in the appropriate direction. It also appears that the Fed was sensitive to recent target misses and misses over the last half year. Neither of the estimates for the value of the mark or the unemployment rate was significant (although they did have the expected sign); however, higher rates of inflation did appear to cause the FOMC to increase the Fed Funds rate. The intermediate monetary target variables appeared to have a greater impact on the Fed Funds rate than did the long-run macroeconomic target variables. . . .

There are two approaches to studying whether the reaction function shifted: one can test for a specified shift point or the data can indicate when shifts appear to be occurring. Both approaches were used. The first approach rests on the common Chow test. This test compares the squared prediction error from running separate subperiod regressions with one overall regression and uses an F statistic to test the statistical significance of this difference.

The second approach is based on a set of procedures designed by Brown, Durbin, and Evans (1975). One of their procedures is to carry out Quandt's (1960) likelihood ratio test for the shift of a regression at each time point. The Quandt procedure is the maximum likelihood analogue of the Chow test described above. A graph of the Quandt statistic (against time) indicates fairly clearly where shifts occurred. Their second procedure is based on the idea of calculating regressions on moving (temporally continuous) subsets of the data. Graphs of the estimated subset coefficients against time indicates where those coefficients appear to shift.

The most complicated of their procedures is based on what Brown et al. call "recursive residuals," w_r. The factor w_r is the standardized prediction error at time r based on a regression estimated from time 1 to $r - 1$. The statistic S_r is

Table 1

Estimation of Reaction Function for DFF, March 1970–August 1979

Variable	OLS[a]		CORC[b]	
	b	SE	b	SE
Constant	0.049	0.24	0.155	0.42
M1L[d]	0.045**	0.008	0.038**	0.007
M6L[e]	0.096**	0.02	0.088**	0.028
UNL[f]	−0.046	0.036	−0.061	0.056
INFL[g]	0.006	0.012	0.020*	0.011
MARKL[h]	0.005	0.006	0.0026	0.008
R[2]	0.40		0.51	
Standard error	0.40		0.35	
SSR[i]	17.05		13.07	
DW[j]	1.09		2.00	
df[k]	108		107	
Rho			0.48	

a. OLS, ordinary least squares.
b. CORC, Cochrane-Orcutt pseudogeneralized least squares.
c. Short-run targets used for M1 (CORC) [omitted].
d. M1L, difference between previous month's M1 and target M1.
e. M6L, deviation of M1L averaged over prior six months.
f. UNL, unemployment rate lagged one month.
g. INFL, inflation rate lagged one month.
h. MARKL, value of mark lagged one month.
i. SSR, sum of squared residuals.
j. DW, Durbin-Watson test for serially correlated errors.
k. df, degrees freedom.
*Significant at .05.
**Significant at .01.

then calculated; it is the sum of the squared recursive residuals up to r. From S_r another statistic called the Cusum Square S_r, which is simply S_r/S_T (T being the final data point), is calculated. This statistic is plotted against r; if the regression does not shift, the graph should resemble a straight line. Confidence bands around the straight line to allow tests of the null hypothesis that a regression did not shift are also provided. Finally, the Brown-Durbin-Evans procedures assume the absence of autocorrelation; thus all data were transformed so as to eliminate autocorrelation before use in this set of procedures. . . .

The President and monetary policy

Observers of the Fed have noted the power that the president has over monetary policy. Robert Weintraub (1978, p. 349) of the House Banking Committee staff states, "The dominant guiding force behind monetary policy is the President." Former governor Maisel (1973, p. 111) states that the "most significant influence on the Federal Reserve comes from the President and other members of the Administration.'' Presumably this power stems from the president's appointment power, his control over nonmonetary financial policy, and his status as an elected official (as contrasted to the unelected and relatively unknown board of governors). In another context, Hibbs (1977) has argued that Democratic administrations generate less unemployment and more inflation than do Republican administrations. Since monetary policy is a strong determinant of inflation and unemployment (at least in the short run), if Hibbs' argument is correct, then the president must be able to get the Fed to do his bidding.

The powers of the president over the Fed are not limitless. The Fed enjoys great legitimacy among the financial community. Insofar as the president needs the support of that community, he is limited in the actions he can take in opposition to the Fed. It can be argued that Carter needed Volcker to give him some semblance of credibility on Wall Street. Even the president's appointment powers are limited. Martin was appointed by a Democrat, reappointed by a Republican, reappointed by a relatively conservative Democrat (Kennedy), and then reappointed by the liberal Johnson. A former Fed staffer suggested to me that even Arthur Burns was almost reappointed by Carter. The Martin reappointments and the Burns near reappointment came about at least partly because of (implicit) pressure put on the president by members of the financial community.

Furthermore, the president is more limited in making partisan appointments to the board of governors than he is in making such appointments to other economic policy-making positions. Just as it would be difficult to appoint a Supreme Court Justice without the approval of the legal community, so it is difficult for the president to appoint a member to the board without the approval of either the academic or the financial community. All recent appointees to the board (with the partial exception of vice-chairman Schultz) have come from relatively nonpartisan backgrounds. The most common route to membership on the board recently has been through the ranks of Fed staff positions. Five of the seven current governors served at one time or another as Fed staffers. Six of the seven hold advanced degrees in economics.

Given the decision to estimate reaction functions only for the 1970s, the quantitative evidence on the impact of the president on monetary policy can hardly be conclusive. We can only check whether the reaction function changed between the Nixon, Ford, and Carter administrations. Presumably, if party is the appropriate independent political variable, (i.e., if Fed policy changes with shifts in the party controlling the White House), there should be no shift in the reaction function when Ford took office, but there should be such a shift soon after Carter took office. This question was investigated both by Chow tests and by examining the graphs produced by the Brown-Durbin-Evans procedures. Turning first to the Chow tests, which test for the presence of a prespecified change point, we tested whether the reaction function shifted right after Ford or Carter took office. The results of those tests are shown in the appendix.

The null hypothesis that any shift in administration (Nixon-Ford or Ford-

Carter) makes no difference can be tested by examining the first F ratio in the appendix. Quite clearly, administration did make a difference. The changes in the magnitudes of the coefficients between administrations was not large, but the change was statistically significant. Looking at the cusum of squares graph (Figure 1a), it again appears that the reaction function was not stable over the whole period. The maximum deviation of the graph from a 45° angle is 0.22. Using Durbin's test as described by Brown et al., we can reject the null hypothesis of stability at the .01 level. The cusum squares graph, as well as the graph of the Quandt likelihood ratios (Figure 1b), also indicates where the shift seemed to occur. Interestingly, this shift occurred soon after the Ford administration took office. Neither of the figures indicates a shift in the reaction function during the Ford-Carter transition.

This finding is confirmed by the Chow tests reported in section II and section III of the appendix, reporting tests for single shifts in the reaction function after the ascensions of Ford and Carter. Section II indicates that the reaction function did shift soon after Ford took office, but section III is consistent with no shift in the reaction function when Carter took office. Moreover, estimating the reaction functions over two administrations rather than three (eg., Nixon-Ford and Ford-Carter) produced identical results. Also, the Brown-Durbin-Evans tests applied to the Ford-Carter period showed no shift in the reaction function over that period.[13] The reaction function for the Fed Funds rate in the 1970s appeared to shift between two consecutive presidents of the same party but did not similarly shift during the changeover in party control of the White House.

The methods of this research do not allow us to infer from the data that the change in monetary policy in 1974 was caused by the transition from Nixon to Ford. The period 1973–74 was, of course, a period of great economic turmoil, marked by a tripling of the Organization of Petroleum Exporting Countries' oil prices and the dismemberment of the Bretton Woods international monetary system. Certainly, these international events could explain the observed change in monetary policy. (See Beck, 1981b, for further discussion of this question). We cannot conclude, therefore, that had Ford entered the White House in less turbulent economic times, we would have observed a major shift in monetary policy. However, the findings were consistent with my earlier work that showed that administration was a better predictor of unemployment rates than was party (Beck, 1982). Perhaps the most interesting finding of this section is not the discontinuity between the Nixon and Ford Feds, but rather the lack of differentiation between the Ford and Carter Feds.

Perhaps some of this continuity can be explained by noting that Burns was chairman of the FOMC for over a third of the Carter period (under study here). Thus perhaps the Democrat Carter did not get to exert his influence over the Fed until his own chairman (Miller) came to the Fed in March of 1978. To test for this, we used the Brown-Durbin-Evans procedures and performed Chow tests for the period October 1974-August 1979. The Chow tests were for a break point one month after Miller became chairman (April 1980). The F tests for such a shift

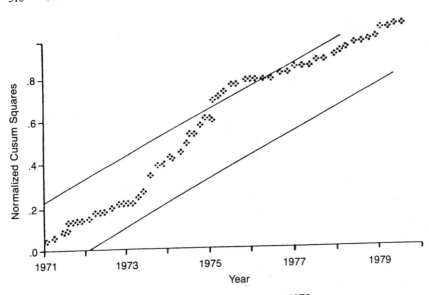

Figure 1a **Plot of Cusum Squares, March 1970–August 1979**

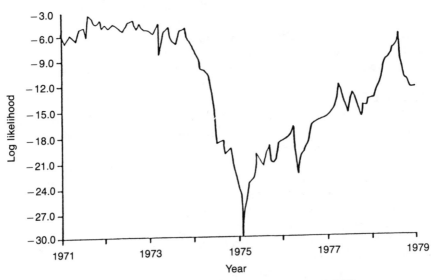

Figure 1b **Plot of Quandt's Log Likelihood, March 1970–August 1979**

were not significant (appendix, section IV). Moreover, the Brown-Durbin-Evans tests indicated a shift in the reaction function very early in the Ford administration and no shift around the Burns-Miller changeover. Again, a sample of two chairmen is rather small, but the lack of shift from Burns to Miller is interesting. (This finding is consistent with impressionistic evidence from the Martin era. Martin appeared to serve the needs of the liberal Johnson as well as the conservative Eisenhower. As Maisel [1973] shows in several anecdotes, Johnson made it quite clear who was boss. Also, several of my informants at the Fed indicated that Burns, had he kept a lower profile, could have been reappointed chairman by Carter.)

Over the decade of the 1970s, it appears that monetary policy differed by administration. It does not seem to have varied systematically by party. While unfortunately it is not possible to compare the reaction functions of earlier periods with those of the 1970s, it is possible to compare the growth rate of M1 during the various administrations. Following Golden and Poterba (1980), I compared both actual growth rates of M1 and those growth rates adjusted for inflation (on the grounds that a 6 percent growth rate in M1 means different things when the inflation rate is 2 percent and when it is 12 percent. The results are presented in Table 2. Carter and Nixon had the highest growth rates in nominal money with Johnson and Ford next and Kennedy and Eisenhower showing the least growth in M1. The administrations differed from highest to lowest growth by about five points. The interadministration differences were significant. Clearly, there was no pattern to the growth rates by party.

Looking at the more sensible real growth rates, we see the ordering of the administrations is Johnson, Kennedy, Nixon, Eisenhower, Carter, and Ford, with Johnson one point over Kennedy and Ford two and one-half points under Carter. The Democrats appear to show a higher growth rate in real money, but there were significant interadministration, intraparty differences in that rate; the difference between Kennedy and Johnson was one point and the difference between Nixon and Ford was three and one-half points; Kennedy was only half a point above Nixon. This set of findings was consistent with my prior work, showing party does appear to make a difference in the making of monetary policy, but administration makes more of a difference than does party.

Finally, it is of interest to look at the graphs of the moving regression (Figure 2). These graphs plot the coefficients of regressions based on 18-month periods (against the midpoint of the period) as that period is moved along the entire decade. Looking at Figure 2, we see that misses in the monetary target had maximal impact in early 1974. This variable had least impact before 1972 and from 1976 on. Since monetarist economists would stress that this variable should be an important determinant of policy, it would appear that the Fed acted most consistently monetarist during the late Nixon and Ford regimes.

The impact of unemployment on the Fed Funds rate remained roughly constant after the 1972 election. The impact of inflation was highest on the Nixon Fed, with a decline in impact during the Ford Fed. This is perhaps a surprising finding,

Table 2

Nominal and Real Growth Rates in M1 by Administration

Administration	Annual growth rate Nominal M1[a]	Annual growth rate Real M1[a] (Deflated by CPI)[b]
Eisenhower	1.73	0.37
Kennedy	2.31	1.20
Johnson	4.78	2.21
Nixon	6.17	0.63
Ford	4.76	−3.03
Carter[c]	6.61	−0.60

a. M1, sum of all deposits in checking accounts and all currency in circulation.
b. CPI, Consumer Price Index.
c. Through August 1979.

since inflation seemed to be perceived as an increasingly serious problem as the decade wore on. Finally, the Fed appeared to pay most attention to the value of the mark during 1972–75. This is perhaps not too surprising, since this was the period in which the United States was learning how to live with the new post-Bretton Woods era of international monetary agreements. Overall, the moving regression results did not indicate a clear picture of stable Fed policies followed by sharp breaks in those policies. Different variables seemed to have had different impacts on FOMC policy making at different times during the decade.

Summary and conclusions

The Fed views itself as a neutral, nonpolitical decision-making body. This statement can only be true if we take a very limited view of politics. This paper has shown that the Fed . . . did appear to respond to the desires of the incumbent president. Fed policy changed when Ford took office.

The results of this paper are consistent with the view that presidential administration, rather than party, is the prime determinant of Fed policy. Fed policy shifted between two consecutive Republican administrations but did not appear to shift during the Ford-Carter transition. Perhaps too much should not be made of this. A sample of three administrations is not large. Moreover, the shift in Fed policy in 1974 occurred soon after the OPEC oil price increases and barely a year after the breakup of the Bretton Woods international monetary system. The data do not allow ruling out the hypothesis that it was exogenous changes in the world political-economy, rather than a change of administration, that caused the Fed policy shift.

Moreover, we do not have a good explanation of why the president should have such power over Fed policy. Based on the data presented here, it does not appear that the president's power to appoint the chairman of the Fed caused large

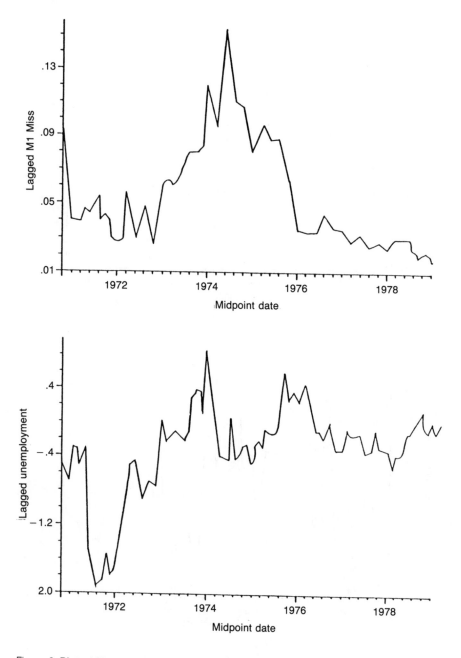

Figure 2 **Plot of Moving Regressions Coefficients (18-month regressions)**

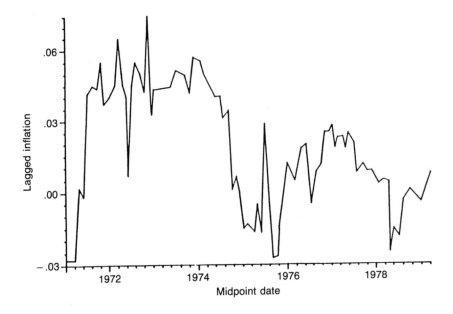

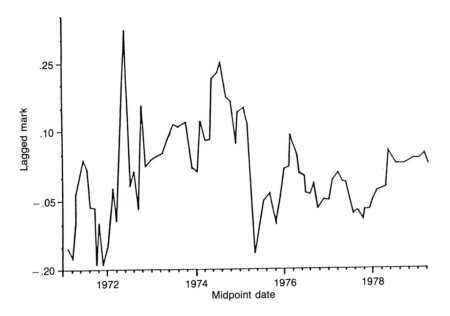

Figure 2

changes in Fed policy. Somehow, political demands, and particularly presidential political demands, are transmitted to the Fed. Exactly how they are transmitted, as well as why the Fed accedes to them, is a question that clearly needs further study, but that presidential preferences are an important determinant of Fed policy making seems clear.

Notes

1. This is not to say it is never used. For example, in March, 1980 the Fed imposed a reserve requirement on Eurodollar deposits in overseas branches of American banks and on some institutions that had come to resemble banks, money market mutual funds. However, such actions are rare.

2. In the last two decades, borrowings in the Fed Funds market have far surpassed borrowings at the discount window. To look at one unexceptional week, that ending July 14, 1976, 46 large money market (N.Y.) banks borrowed $135 million at the discount window and $17 billion in the Fed Funds market.

3. This paper talks about the monetary aggregates as defined during the period under study. In late 1980, the Fed redefined the monetary aggregates to take account of various changes in financial institutions such as NOW accounts (interest paying accounts at the "thrifts" that resemble checking accounts) and money market mutual funds. This paper focuses on M1, which is the same as the new M1a. The new aggregate M1b is designed to be theoretically similar to the former M1.

4. Treasury would decide how much it wanted to borrow and at what rate; the job of the FOMC was to buy enough securities to allow the new securities to be sold at the desired rate. This policy was an outgrowth of World War II, in which there was general agreement that the goal of government financial policy could be financing the war.

5. This is not meant to imply that the FOMC was good at hitting its targets; it was not. Nor is this meant to imply that the FOMC adopted a "monetarist" position; it did not. All that this statement means is that if inflation was too high, the FOMC attempted (in its own way) to tighten up. It may have done this in the wrong way, and it may not have been successful, but it did try. Similarly, when the FOMC did overshoot its monetary target, it did increase the Fed Funds rate. It also changed the target. But again, the important point is that the Fed Funds rate was moved in accord with prior target misses. See Hetzel (1981) for a further discussion of FOMC policy making.

6. Does the FOMC have any more control over the Funds rate than it does over M1? After all, the Funds rate is determined by the forces of supply and demand in the private market for funds, a market that the Fed can influence but not control. The Fed can, in practice, determine either the quantity of Fed Funds borrowed or the Fed Funds rate, but not both. As Pierce (1978) and Hetzel (1981) have shown, in the 1970s the FOMC attempted to peg the Funds rate, and, in general, the open market desk at the New York Fed was able to keep the Funds rate within the band set by the FOMC.

7. Since our quantitative study stops with Miller's move to Treasury in August 1979, we need not inquire at this point into the new FOMC operating procedures, which focus more on reserves and less on interest rates.

8. Further econometric details on the behavior of the reaction function may be found in Beck (1981a). In that paper, I report results showing that the linear forms used in this paper perform as well as various nonlinear forms.

9. All data were obtained from the National Bureau for Economic Research's TROLL data file. All data were seasonally adjusted. The unemployment rate is that reported by the Bureau of Labor Statistics; the inflation measure is the monthly percentage increase in the Comsumer Price Index (at an annualized rate) as reported by the Department of Commerce; the monthly average value of the mark (in cents) is from the New York

foreign exchange market. The value of the mark is used because it is an important currency and is reported monthly. Balance of payments accounts are only reported quarterly.

10. To see this, note that if U^* is target unemployment, which is constant over the period, then the correct equation:

$$DFF = c + b(UNL - U^*) + e_t$$

is equivalent to

$$DFF = c + b(UNL - U^*) + e_t$$

where DFF is the monthly change in the Fed Funds rate, b is the regression coefficient, UNL is the unemployment rate lagged one month, c is a constant, e is an error term, and $c^* = c - bU^*$.

11. By 1975, the FOMC was setting long-run targets explicitly (or at least giving ranges for those targets). I use a value of 6.25 as the target up until 1975. The midpoint of the target range was not reset until 1977, and it moved very slowly until 1979. Thus the 6.25 percent figure for the nonexplicit targets seems reasonable (and is also the target used by Pierce, 1978).

12. The term "tighten" must be used with great caution here. As a referee kindly pointed out, increasing interest rates could be associated with any "easy" monetary policy. In addition, if inflation is increasing faster than interest rates, an increase in nominal interest rates could be associated with a decrease in real interest rates. All that I actually need to say is that the FOMC focused (rightly or wrongly) on the Fed Funds rate, and that they adjusted that rate according to perceived economic conditions. They may have been operating incorrectly, but this is how the FOMC did behave. See Hetzel (1981) for more details.

13. The subperiod results are available from the author on request.

Appendix

Tests for Shifts in Reaction Function, March 1970-August 1979

I. Test of H_0: No shift in reaction function in entire period against
H_1: Reaction function shifts either in October 1974 (Ford) or February 1977 (Carter)
Under H_0: Sum of squared residuals = 13.06   Degrees of freedom = 107
Under H_1: Sum of squared residuals = 11.96   Degrees of freedom = 95
F (6,101) = 1.5 (not significant at .05). Do not reject H_0.

II. Test of H_0: No shift in reaction function, March 1970-August 1979, against H_1:
Reaction function shifts in October 1974
(beginning of Ford administration).
Under H_0: Sum of squared residuals = 13.06   Degrees of freedom = 107
Under H_1: Sum of squared residuals = 10.89   Degrees of freedom = 101
F (6,101) = 3.4 (significant at .01). Reject H_0.

III. Test of H_0: No shift in reaction function, March 1970-August 1979 against
H_1: Reaction function shifts in February 1977
(beginning of Carter administration)

Under H_0: Sum of squared residuals = 13.06   Degrees of freedom = 107
Under H_1: Sum of squared residuals = 11.96   Degrees of freedom = 101
F (6,101) = 1.5 (not significant at .05). Do not reject H_0.

IV. Test of H_0: No shift in reaction function, October 1974-August 1979 against
H_1: Reaction function shifts in April 1978
(beginning of Miller chairmanship)
Under H_0: Sum of squared residuals = 2.50   Degrees of freedom = 52
Under H_1: Sum of squared residuals = 2.05   Degrees of freedom = 46
F (6,46) = 1.7 (not significant at .05). Do not reject H_0.

All tests have a null hypothesis that the reaction function coeficients were stable over the entire period and alternative hypothesis that at least one coefficient shifted at the indicated time, in the sense that its values differ in the two subperiods.

References

Abrams, Richard, Richard Froyen, and Roger Waud. 1980. Monetary policy reaction functions, consistent expectations, and the Burns era. *Journal of Money, Credit and Banking*, 12 (February 1980): 30–42.

Alt, James, and John Woolley. 1980. Reaction functions and institutional differences: Sources of variation in the political economy of macroeconomic policy. Paper presented for delivery at the seventy-sixth Annual Meeting of the American Political Science Association, Washington, D.C., September 1–4, 1980.

Bach, G. L. 1971. *Making monetary and fiscal policy*. Washington, D.C.: Brookings Institution.

Beck, Nathaniel. 1980. Did Arthur Burns manipulate the money supply so as to aid Nixon's re-election? Discussion paper 80–81. Department of Political Science, University of California, San Diego.

—————. 1981a. Political influences on Federal Reserve policy in the 1970s. Paper prepared for delivery at the Annual Meeting of the Public Choice Society, New Orleans, La., March 13–16, 1981.

—————. 1981b. Linkages between political pressures and economic policy-making: Monetary and fiscal policy in the post-war United States. Paper prepared for delivery at the seventy-seventh Annual Meeting of the American Political Science Association, New York, September 3–6, 1981.

—————. 1982. Parties, administrations and macroeconomic outcomes. *American Political Science Review*, 76 (March 1982), in press.

Borins, Sanford. 1972. The political economy of the Fed. *Public Policy*, 20 (Spring 1972): 175–198.

Brimmer, Andrew. 1974. Letter. *Fortune*, 90 (August 1974): 113.

Brown, R., J. Durbin, and J. Evans. 1975. Techniques for testing the constancy of regression relationships over time. *Journal of the Royal Statistical Society (series B)*, 37 (1975): 149–163.

Cowart, Andrew. 1978. The economic policies of European governments, part I: Monetary policy. *British Journal of Political Science*, 8 (July 1978): 285–311.

Diggins, J. 1978. A short term model of Federal Reserve behavior in the 1970s. Ph.D. dissertation, Harvard University.

Freidman, Benjamin. 1975. Targets, instruments and indicators of monetary policy. *Journal of Monetary Economics*, 1 (October 1975): 443–473.

—————. 1977. Empirical issues in monetary policy: A review of monetary aggregates and monetary policy. *Journal of Monetary Economics*, 3 (January 1977): 87–101.

Garbade, Kenneth. 1977. Two methods for estimating the stability of regression coefficients. *Journal of the American Statistical Association*, 72 (March 1977): 54–63.

Golden, David, and James Poterba. 1980. The price of popularity: The political business cycle reexamined. *American Journal of Political Science*, 24 (November 1980): 696–714.

Hetzel, Robert. 1981. The Federal Reserve System and control of the money supply in the 1970s. *Journal of Money, Credit and Banking*, 13 (February 1981): 31–43.

Hibbs, Douglas. 1977. Political parties and macroeconomic policy. *American Political Science Review*, 71 (December 1977): 1467–1487.

Kane, Edward. 1980. Politics and Fed policy-making: The more things change the more they remain the same. *Journal of Monetary Economics*, 6 (April 1980): 199–212.

Kernell, Samuel. 1978. Explaining presidential popularity. *American Political Science Review*, 72 (June 1978): 506–522.

Kramer, Gerald. 1971. Short term fluctuations in U.S. voting behavior. *American Political Science Review*, 65 (March 1971): 131–143.

Lombra, Raymond. 1980. Reflections on Burns's reflections: A review article. *Journal of Money, Credit and Banking*, 12 (February 1980): 94–104.

Lombra, Raymond, and Michael Moran. 1980. Policy advice and policymaking at the Federal Reserve. *Journal of Monetary Economics: Conference Series on Public Policy*, 13 (Autumn 1980): 9–68.

Maisel, Sherman. 1973. *Managing the Dollar*. New York: Norton.

Pierce, James. 1978. The myth of congressional supervision of monetary policy. *Journal of Monetary Economics*, 4 (April 1978): 363–370.

—————. 1979. The political economy of Arthur Burns. *Journal of Finance*, 34 (May 1979): 485–496.

Poole, William. 1979. Burnsian monetary policy: Eight years of progress? *Journal of Finance*, 34 (May 1979): 473–484.

Quandt, Richard. 1960. Tests of the hypothesis that a linear regression obeys two separate regimes. *Journal of the American Statistical Association*, 55 (June 1960): 324–330.

Reagan, Michael. 1961. The political structure of the Federal Reserve System. *American Political Science Review*, 55 (March 1961): 64–76.

Robertson, J. R. 1974. Letter. *Fortune*, 90 (August 1974): 113.

Rose, Sanford. 1974. The agony of the Fed. *Fortune*, 90 (July 1974): 90–93, 180–190.

Tufte, Edward. 1978. *Political control of the economy*. Princeton, N.J.: Princeton University Press.

Weintraub, Robert. 1978. Congressional supervision of monetary policy. *Journal of Monetary Economics*, 4 (April 1978): 341–362.

Woolley, John. 1977. Monetary policy instruments and the relationship of central banks and governments. *Annals of the American Academy of Political and Social Science*, 434 (November 1977): 151–173.

—————. 1980. The Federal Reserve System and the political economy of monetary policy. Ph.D. dissertation, University of Wisconsin.

3C.3. External Pressure and the Operations of the Fed

EDWARD J. KANE

As both Michael Reagan and Nathaniel Beck note, there is something extraordinary about the fact that, in one of the world's oldest democracies, something as important as monetary policy should be formally under the control of a nonelected body. The mystery is in no way resolved by saying that the President has more power here than he appears to, as this merely raises the question of why such a cumbersome arrangement should be retained.

In this paper Edward Kane argues that the arrangement is retained in order to protect members of Congress and the President from having to bear the responsibility for taking unavoidable but unpopular decisions. It is often necessary, in order to cool inflation, to pursue a tight monetary policy—which will drive up interest rates, slow business expansion, and increase unemployment. Such outcomes are unpopular with the electorate; if they were thought to have been brought about by a particular politician, he might have trouble getting reelected. Thus, it is in the interest of elected officials to have a scapegoat that can be blamed for these unpopular consequences of necessary policies.

Scapegoats can of course have real power, but Kane does not think that the Federal Reserve has the predominant influence on monetary policy. Rather, he argues, the real power over policy is largely retained by the President and Congress, with the Federal Reserve having little independent power and serving largely to deflect blame from the real policy makers.

The reader should note that Kane attributes more power to Congress than do most other observers and that he has been criticized for underestimating the degree to which formal institutional arrangements can result in real power shifts (Meltzer 1982). Nonetheless, even Kane's critics find his thesis insightful and thought-provoking.

Adapted from *Political Economy of International and Domestic Monetary Relations*, edited by Raymond E. Lombra and Willard E. Witte, pp. 211–232 (with deletions). Copyright © 1982 by Iowa State University Press.

Introduction

Fed goals do not hatch full formed like Athena from the brow of Zeus. They are hammered and shaped on the anvil of national politics by artisans who never cease to reheat and touch up their work.

Nor is any particular macroeconomic goal absolutely good. Reputed macroeconomic public enemies such as unemployment, inflation, stagnation, and payments imbalance are neither entirely bad for the national economy nor bad at all for every sector. Unemployment probably retards inflation and strengthens the balance of payments; inflation reduces repayment burdens borne by debtors and encourages many types of investment; economic stagnation makes it easier to preserve the quality of the physical environment; and international payments imbalances lower the cost of living, reduce shortages, and generate profits for importers.

No logically coherent strategy exists for promoting every macroeconomic goal at the same time. Policies meant to promote one goal tend to interfere—either in the short or the long run—with efforts to achieve at least one other. Typically, the difference between macroeconomic good and macroeconomic level depends principally on how political power is distributed. Macroeconomic goal formation is inevitably a political process of trade-offs, in which the economic interests and political clout of different groups of citizens are, along with the timing of the next election, carefully weighed and balanced.

Elected and appointed politicians use constitutionally granted market power to resolve, to their personal and professional satisfaction, sectoral conflicts over the distribution of economic resources. Fiscally underrestrained sectoral demands on government resources combine with cyclically shifting electoral payoffs to incumbent politicians to induce accommodative monetary policies that squeeze private-sector real incomes and impose a politically induced overlay on the ordinary business cycle. In the United States, the trade-offs made in formulating monetary policy are seldom openly admitted either by elected politicians or by Federal Reserve officials. Surreptitious politics clouds the process of central-bank goal formation and encourages Fed officials to describe their decisions in a ludicrously sanctimonious kind of code. To understand the workings of the Federal Reserve System one must learn both to sort out political events affecting Fed policy decisions and to crack the several codes in which political communication takes place.

This paper develops the hypothesis that political events—not economic events—are the proximate determinants of Fed actions. It focuses on the elaborate system of contacts, threats, rewards, and punishments by which incumbent politicians in Congress and in the executive branch transmit monetary policy instructions to the Fed. Four main classes of relevant political events can be discerned: impacts of individual sectors on incumbent politicians; incumbents' impacts on Fed officials; Fed dealings with incumbent officials and individual sectors, includng those that comprise the operative constituency against inflation; and internal Fed dealings: transactions among Fed officials and with and among component staffs. The analysis offered here concentrates on events of the second and third type.

To maintain the unfavorable trends in inflation and in the foreign exchange value of the dollar that the United States has experienced during the last fifteen years, U.S. politicians had to revise institutional arrangements for selecting monetary policy priorities. Incumbent federal politicians and political appointees preferred to ratify excessive sectoral demands on government fiscal resources in the short run, relying on taxation levied covertly by inflation to rebalance sectoral demands over the longer run. Moreover, incumbents found that they could at least occasionally curry votes by pursuing slight preelection improvements in macroeconomic indices at the expense of substantial postelection deterioration (Gordon 1975; Nordhaus 1975; Tufte 1978). To carry out these policies, incumbents had to persuade Fed officials to monetize a succession of federal deficits. Political pressure on the Fed fostered monetary policies that allowed incumbents to take credit for distributing current sectoral benefits and for bringing about short-run decreases in unemployment without requiring them to accept consonant blame for the inflationary consequences that these policies generated over the longer haul.

Analysis of the political economy of Fed decision making suggests that the Fed's role in this process of blame displacement is carefully scripted. Underlying this hypothesis is the principle that adjustments in Fed procedures and structural arrangements must be politically optimal at the time they are made. By revealed preference, authorities with jurisdiction (i.e., incumbent politicians or top Fed officials) have rejected other feasible approaches as less desirable than those chosen. Over time, legislation amending the Federal Reserve Act and extending the Fed's stabilization responsibilities via the Employment Act (and amendments thereto) have produced a U.S. central bank very different from the one originally conceived. This legislation, while undermining the Fed's ability to carry out its primordial assignment of acting as a roadblock to short-sighted economic policies, has left the Fed just enough apparent autonomy to provide incumbent politicians with a plausible scapegoat for all untoward macroeconomic events. By accommodating, year after year, a cumulative fiscal deficit, the Fed has come to function like a chaperone at a fraternity party. It legitimizes the process without changing it very much. Time after time, Fed officials accept the contradictory policy assignment of singlehandedly bringing inflation and unemployment down to satisfactory levels, stoically accepting the blame when these impossible goals fail to materialize. That intelligent observers continue to be swayed by Fed promises is a phenomenon for which (in contrast to P. T. Barnum) modern theories of expectations formation have no good answer.

Fed appearances versus Fed reality

The place that the Federal Reserve System holds today in the macroeconomic policy formation process calls to mind Chesterton's conception of politics as the art of not telling the truth without actually lying. To decipher the Federal Reserve Act and most official Fed statements, one needs to recognize that key words have come to mean almost precisely the opposite of what they would mean in ordinary discourse. For example, Fed independence is now a code word for Fed political subservience and a Fed stock certificate no longer represents anything more than a nonmarketable, fixed-coupon bond of indefinite maturity.

In all too many cases, disguised politics transform the appearances of contemporary Fed practices, processes, and reasoning into the opposite of underlying realities. Fed fiction begins with its legal form of organization as a quasiprivate corporation. Formal ownership of Federal Reserve stock certificates by so-called ''member'' banks makes the Fed look suspiciously like a bank-owned corporation. In reality, the Fed operates as an agency of the federal government. Fed staff members see themselves as government employees, and members of the Fed's Board of Governors are appointed by the president of the United States subject to the consent of the Senate. Fed stockholders have no proxy decisions to make and no beneficial interest in Fed earnings. . . .

Federal Reserve "independence" is greatly exaggerated

Although the Federal Reserve is generically just another federal agency, it *is* a species unto itself. Bureaucratically, the Fed enjoys a set of formal privileges that in the short run insulate its budget from partisan incursion and its highest officials from the threat of dismissal.

Federal Reserve governors are granted a degree of autonomy surpassed only by the Supreme Court, in the form of long terms of appointment and an independent source of operating funds (Burns 1978). The seven members of the Federal Reserve Board enjoy 14-year terms in office, staggered to make it hard—at least in theory—for a president (in his maximum eight years in office) to dominate the board by threats of nonreappointment. Moreover, neither the president's Office of Management and Budget nor the Congress can influence Federal Reserve decisions through the conventional discipline of the budgetary process. The Federal Reserve is chartered as a quasiprivate corporation with first call on the interest that accrues on its portfolio of over $125 billion in U.S. Treasury and agency securities.

At best, this special bureaucratic shielding works *only* in the short run. Unlike Supreme Court justices who are appointed for life, Federal Reserve governors must concern themselves with postseparation career planning. Unless they are appointed at an advanced age, they must regularly review alternative job opportunities. This need to consider their future career profiles increases the separation rate and the number of partial-term appointments available over time. Governors appointed to unexpired partial terms are particularly susceptible to reappointment pressure.

Moreover, in the long run, successive presidents and Congresses must be persuaded to maintain the statutory armorplate. Fed officials possess a narrow political base. What political strength they have is drawn from the Fed's client banks, backed up by constituencies against inflation and for bank regulation. On the issue of inflation, popular allegiance has been weak and becomes even weaker when and as a recession develops. This is when the Fed—whose previous antiin-flationary policies inevitably take the blame for surging unemployment—is most vulnerable. In boom and recession, Fed officials must struggle in Congress to turn aside or to soften bills (such as H.R. 7001 in the 1980 Congressional session) that threaten to chip away at various pieces of the Fed's suit of armor. The necessity to campaign continually for the preservation of Fed autonomy makes Fed officials far more submissive to the short-run political interests of incumbent presidents and congressmen than they care to admit.

Debate about the desirability of an independent Federal Reserve system proceeds from a dangerously false premise. The Fed is approximately as independent as a college student whose room and board is financed by a parentally revocable trust fund. Some conflict will be tolerated, but the limits of the benefactors' patience must always be kept in mind.

Just as other federal agencies, the Fed is fully accountable to representatives elected by people (Board of Governors of Federal Reserve System 1974, p. 3). The difference lies in the intricate pattern of accountability and in the precise rewards and punishments elected officials are able to manipulate. Although dissatisfied politicians can't discipline recalcitrant Fed officials by forcing their dismissal or even by cutting next year's budget, they can and do restrain them by threatening to make unfriendly new appointments and to take back various elements of the Fed's vaunted independence.

Therefore, in addition to coping with the System's nominal responsibilities for economic policy and for facilitating the flow of domestic payments, Federal Reserve officials worry about avoiding public confrontations and preserving the System's structural autonomy. Each regime wants to bequeath to its successors an agency at least as strong in structure as the one they inherited. No regime wants to be recorded as gaining a string of Pyrrhic policy victories for which the System itself is made to pay dearly in the long run.

Political events and forces influencing Fed decisions

As scientists, economists are interested in observable phenomena. Unfortunately, external influences on the Fed and Fed reactions to these influences leave a deliberately muddled trail behind them. How to read this trail is the focus of this paper.

Political action for and against the Fed emanates from many sources and occurs along a broad spectrum of events. Presidential scoldings, special-interest attacks or pleas for help, and formal votes to approve or to reject legislative proposals are merely the most visible of these events. Private interests and elected officials work at the day to day task of influencing Fed officials by subtle means. These less dramatic tools include promises of jobs, public praise, use of rumors and trial balloons, informal meetings, hearings on legislative recommendations of various kinds, and redistribution of bureaucratic privileges.

Congress and the president impact on Fed officials formally and informally through the link of their shared responsibility for macroeconomic and financial events. Private interests act through governmental agencies sensitized to their needs, through the press, and through channels of social and economic contact.

A framework for assessing incumbent self-interest

In the tradition of Anthony Downs (1957), we may conceive of elected officials as managing a production process, whose inputs consist of their own time, wealth, and office budgets and whose output is the probability of reelection. For a congressional incumbent, at least four intermediate products enter the reelection-probability production functions:

1. A record of individual achievement in office, as perceived by constituents. This record may be decomposed into different elements of constituent service (broadly considered).

a. Service to the constituent business community in sponsoring important legislation or in shepherding it toward enactment

b. Positions and votes taken on important issues, as reflected in favorable ratings by special interest groups, including so-called public interest groups

c. Casework for individual constituents in dealing with the federal bureaucracy, e.g., in clearing claims for lost veterans' pensions or social security checks and following up constituent appeals against denials of benefits

d. Providing responsive answers to opinionated mail from irate constituents

e. Name recognition—keeping his or her name before constituents in as many ways as possible

2. The prestige which the office and particular mix of committee assignments currently enjoys

3. The size of the campaign budget

4. The short-term performance of the national economy, as represented (say) in Okun's "discomfort index," which sums the current rates of inflation and unemployment

Holding hearings on legislation threatening to impose new congressional controls on Fed procedures enhances incumbents' ability to influence Fed thinking about what adjustments in the monetary aggregates would prove desirable.[1] It also elevates the status of service on a banking committee and, if legislation is enacted, raises the chairman's and committee members' record of achievement (Woolley 1980). In addition, raising manifold possibilities for restructuring Fed regulatory powers triggers greater involvement by bank and savings and loan lobbies, increasing the flow and selectivity of campaign contributions from these institutions' political action committees (PACs).[2]

Statutory framework within which the Fed operates

Fed officials' legal authority to make macroeconomic policy decisions on their own is contained in two frequently amended pieces of legislation: the Federal Reserve Act (1913) and the Employment Act of 1946. Proposed readjustments in the scope of Fed autonomy and responsibilities under these acts can be manipulated as a system of rewards and punishments, to increase or to diminish the prestige and quality of life enjoyed by Fed bureaucrats.

The president

As the hub of the executive branch, the office of the presidency provides numerous points of contact with Fed officials. Presidents can steer Fed decision makers in the direction they desire by holding out carrots of accommodation or by beating them with administrative sticks.

Appeals for policy coordination serve as tasty carrots. The ideal of assisting in the design of unified macroeconomic policies plays directly upon the ego of Fed officials by promising to enlarge their scope of activity. Governors and staff representatives may be invited to participate in policy formation over a broad field of economic issues with top officials from the Treasury, State Department, Commerce Department, Council of Economic Advisers, and Office of Management and Budget. Given that governors are drawn from a pool of predominantly idealistic and public spirited persons who see their service as a personal sacrifice made for the greater good, such appeals and opportunities are hard to resist.

The president appoints members of the Federal Reserve Board (FRB) and designates one member to serve as chairman. Economists widely regard the FRB chairmanship as the single most powerful economic policy post in the federal government. However, because a chairman's power is predicated on the cooperation of a majority of other board members, a president can punish an FRB chairman by appointing "difficult" but loyal persons to the board when and as vacancies arise. Less formally, he can make life in Washington uncomfortable in many ways for any set of government officials who stubbornly refuse to bend toward his view of the common good. Since such pressure should increase board turnover, it can reinforce the president's appointment power precisely when it promises to be most useful.

Every chairman is anxious to influence new appointments to the board. In the 1970s, when accelerating inflation drove levels of compensation for competitive positions in the private economy far above board salaries, board turnover soared. President Carter's first three and a half years saw six resignations. This turnover magnified the president's leverage on his FRB chairman and, early in Volcker's chairmanship, may have been used to make appointments specifically intended to blunt a politically uncomfortable policy thrust.

During the 1950s and 1960s, Fed officials were publicly called on the carpet by two different sitting presidents (Truman and Johnson) for resisting broad macroeconomic policy recommendations. The first such incident (in early 1951) cost Chairman McCabe his job, although two months later (see Clifford 1965) it led to an accord with the Treasury that strengthened the Fed. On the other hand, the second incident marked the high-water mark of Fed power, after which Chairman Martin never publicly challenged a president's economic policies again. In 1972, Chairman Burns permitted an election-year spurt in the monetary aggregates that assisted President Nixon's reelection campaign (Kane 1974a). In July 1975, President Ford pointedly celebrated his birthday with the board. Under Carter, beginning with the presidential press conference of November 1, 1978, the Federal Reserve Board chairman began to appear at the president's side to pledge in advance Fed support for the latest changes in Presidential economic policy strategy.

This increased receptiveness to shows of presidential attention reflected in part the Fed's increasing need for presidential support both to stop the inflation-accelerated exodus of member banks from the System and to fend off the accelerating congressional criticisms of its policies. As Fed problems became embodied in the concrete form of individual bills that would either extend or limit the Fed's powers, it became important to have the ability to call on a presidential *veto* in the clutch.[3]

Congress

Congressional power over the Fed also resides in ability to grant or to withhold rewards (legislative changes that Fed officials want) and to impose punishments (legislative changes that they don't want). Besides simple praise, the class of congressional rewards consists principally of two items. First, Congress could allow the salaries of Fed governors (which are currently constrained by those of Cabinet officers) to move as freely as those of the Reserve Bank presidents (which are tied instead to salaries received by local commercial-bank presidents). More competitive salaries for members of the Board of Governors would strengthen the Fed politically. It would increase the board's prestige and reduce its turnover. It would permit top staff salaries to be more competitive as well. Second, Congress could increase the degree of Fed authority over nonmember banks and savings institutions. Through the 1970s, Fed officials were especially anxious to gain the power to set reserve requirements for nonmember depository institutions.

Congressional restraints on governor salaries strongly limit the population of individuals for whom FRB service poses an attractive career opportunity. For individuals of a given age, salary levels for FRB governors are more adequate for academics and career bureaucrats than for lawyers and bank executives. Similarly, low current salaries are less unattractive for youngish individuals, who can extract substantial implicit income by planning to parlay board service either into the name recognition required to campaign for elective office or into many years of higher-paying jobs in the private sector. Recently, Congress has taken action to reduce the present value of even this implicit or steppingstone income. The Ethics in Government Act of 1978 (as amended in May 1980) applies specifically to FRB members and serves to restrict their postseparation employment even more than the stringent "Boy Scout rules" the Fed adopted in 1973. Postemployment conflict-of-interest restrictions are especially severe for board members who fail to serve out the (possibly partial) term to which they were appointed. They are prohibited for two years from taking a wide class of jobs in the financial industry. Moreover, since the early 1960s, the board's own rules have prevented sitting governors from earning outside income from speaking fees. Taken together, congressional and in-house restrictions on FRB members' ability to earn explicit and implicit income make it hard to recruit competent governors with broad experience and make it uneconomic for all but a narrow class of FRB members to plan to serve more than a fraction of a full fourteen-year term.

Accelerating inflation tends to reduce the after-tax real value of governors' salaries and to increase the differential burden of reserve requirements on member banks. By letting the membership problem fester through the 1970s, Congress kept Fed officials under constant pressure. The Fed's fundamental membership problem was that declining membership (which for economic reasons was concentrated among small- to medium-sized banks) simultaneously reduced and narrowed its political base. This undermined Fed clout with Congress by impairing its ability to rally widespread bank lobbying activity in support of its policies. To close the Fed's longstanding political wound, in March 1980, Congress extended Fed-imposed reserve requirements to nonmember institutions, but permitted reserve balances to be held in the form of correspondent balances at member banks. This legislation denies the correspondent-balance option to all banks that were members on July 1, 1979. To establish incentives to restore the blood the system lost in the years prior to July 1, 1979, the Fed proposes to administer the statute by requiring a 100 percent passthrough of correspondent-held reserve balances to Fed accounts.

Although the class of congressional deprivations is virtually unbounded, recent threats have focused on the following issues:

1. Expanded Congressional oversight of decisions made by the Federal Open Market Committee, FOMC. Starting in 1975, the Fed was required to report quarterly (now semiannually) to the congressional banking committees on interim FOMC policy targets for the next twelve months and, since February 1979 (under the Humphrey-Hawkins amendment to the Employment Act), to square these targets verbally with administration plans. Related controversy has centered on the number and identity of the targets reported, on the desirability of simultaneously reporting interim targets, on whether the Fed should adopt a monetarist strategy, and on the contents and timely release of FOMC minutes, including the possibility of opening FOMC meetings under the Government in the Sunshine Act.

2. Reducing Fed budgetary autonomy. Congressman Wright Patman's overarching objective was to force the Fed to obtain its operating funds from annual appropriations from Congress. He urged retirement of Fed stock and regular

audits of Federal Reserve accounts and policies by the Government Accounting Office, GAO. In 1977, a GAO audit was finally established, but the scope of the audit was limited to the Fed's bank supervisory functions. H.R. 7001 sought to redeem Fed stock and to end Federal Reserve bank presidents' membership in the FOMC.

3. Full-cost pricing for Fed banking services. This is now required by 1980 legislation. Although intended nominally to help private banks compete more effectively with Federal Reserve banks in the market for correspondent services, it affects the Fed's ability to tailor offers of implicit interest to the advantage or disadvantage of individual banks.

4. The propriety of having Federal Reserve bank directors and Board Chairmen lobby members of Congress. Although lobbying expense is legal for the Fed, government agencies that are restricted to congressionally appropriated funds are disallowed from spending funds in this way. This issue is designed to restrain the political activity of Fed officials.

5. Realigning the four-year term of FRB chairman to coincide with that of incoming presidents. This would ensure each new president a chance to place his own person in this top policymaking post. Although it incorporated a one-year delay, such a bill passed the House in 1980.

6. Extending the need for Senate confirmation to cover Reserve Bank presidents (because they are potential members of the FOMC) and to require new confirmation for an FRB chairman who had been confirmed previously as a board member. The first part of this proposal (which has not been enacted) would reduce the FRB's power to select Reserve Bank presidents and would allow Congress to screen all members of the FOMC. The second part addressed a loophole that could have allowed the president and the FRB to make an end run around the process of congressional screening. Since 1977, it has been necessary for all FRB chairman and vice-chairman to be explicitly confirmed in their posts.

7. Broader representation of women, minorities, and regional nonfinancial interests on F.R. bank boards and on the Board of Governors itself. For example, in May, 1980, before granting approval of Lyle Gramley's appointment to the FRB, the Senate passed a resolution decrying "Eastern" domination of recent board appointments. Except that this issue impinges slightly on presidential and Fed official's freedom of appointment, it is essentially symbolic.

8. Transferring the Fed's supervisory authority over member banks and bank holding companies (BHCs) to a new agency, which would consolidate in a single office all federal bank regulatory functions, including those currently exercised by the U.S. Comptroller of the Currency and the Federal Deposit Insurance Corporation (FDIC). By segregating the locus of monetary control from that of bank and BHC regulation, this change would deprive the Fed of a major element of leverage over credit policy at individual banks (Kane 1973).

9. Pressures to allocate credit in favor of specific sectors. These range from proposed bailouts of troubled industries, cities, and firms to proposals meant to provide better access to credit for small businesses and would-be homeowners.

These pressures for sectoral relief constrain the Fed's ability to impose sharp or sustained increases in nominal interest rates on the macroeconomy.

One consequence of the assault in 1975 by post-Watergate freshman legislators on executive branch autonomy and on the congressional seniority system was an intensification of interest in reassessing Fed officials' rights and duties (Kane 1975; Weintraub 1978). Prior to Wright Patman's being stripped in 1975 of the House Banking Committee chairmanship, he had perennially pushed these same issues without effect. In the rush to build can-do records, his successor Henry Reuss, and his Senate counterpart William Proxmire (who succeeded John Sparkman in the same year), transformed what had been widely perceived as Patman's personal vendetta against the Fed into a careful reevaluation of congressional oversight responsibilities.

Since 1975, Fed officials have found themselves besieged simultaneously on many fronts. Month after month, House and Senate banking committees and subcommittees have held hearings to consider a series of bills that would either strengthen the Fed by relieving its membership problem or weaken it by chipping away at one or another of the Fed's special bureaucratic privileges. Few weeks pass in which a contemporary Fed chairman does not spend time preparing or delivering testimony for committee hearings. Legislation passed during this era has reduced the Fed's ability to keep internal procedures and debates from public scrutiny.

Beyond the statutory framework: the scapegoat hypothesis

As a matter of legislative formula, the Fed is "merely a creature of Congress" in the same sense that Mary Shelley's fictional green monster was a "creature of Frankenstein." In both cases, the issue is whether the "creator" can ever truly bring the creature back under control.

Although a few congressmen and senators work very hard for this result, one can legitimately question whether the Congress as a whole has any taste for the task (Kane 1975; Roberts 1978; Weintraub 1978; Woolley 1980). In practice, the ponderous multilayered structure of congressional decision making and the economic naivete of the great preponderance of elected officials provide effective limitations on congressional ability to dominate a reluctant Fed. Members who cannot to any great extent interpret current macroeconomic information fear the possibility that a Fed chairman's election-year counterattack might tar them with the label of "inflationists," while the slowness and unwieldiness of Congress itself virtually insure that its influence even on quarter-to-quarter decisions by the Fed will prove more apparent than real.

At election time, incumbent congressmen find it extremely convenient to be free to blame the economic ills of the country on the "misguided" policies of an "independent" Federal Reserve system. A skeptic would say that the knowledgeable congressional leaders consent to small adjustments in Fed powers and responsibilities just often enough to keep the activist reformers among them hard at their job of reminding Fed officials of their accountability to Congress.

As this suggests, congressional dealings with the Fed have levels of meaning quite different from their surface appearance. Many of the most important transactions occur away from the public eye. The most palpable transactions take place when Fed witnesses testify at open hearings of congressional committees. A closely related type of encounter takes the form of sparring in the press and on TV over the severity and causes of alleged macroeconomic problems and the workability of reputed "solutions." Such public transactions are theatrically disputatious. They involve a great deal of posing and game playing, some of which is carefully rehearsed. Harsh exchanges are sometimes initiated solely for symbolic effect, to assure some troubled Fed or party constituency that its plight (which in most cases will continue to be neglected) has not been forgotten.

Private meetings occur frequently at the staff level. When necessary, congressional and Fed staff members negotiate legislative compromises for their principals, but in most cases they meet merely to exchange analysis and information about matters of "mutual interest." These meetings are generally friendly ones, but reluctance, resistance, and hostility are not unknown. In top-level contacts, persuasion is applied and deals are sealed. Fed officials lobby key congressmen and senators much as other special interests do, except that they are severely limited in the kind of inducements they can offer. Still, with what they have to work with Fed officials try—just as private contractors and other federal agencies do—to build up a coterie of friendly congressmen and senators.

In open forums, congressional criticisms of Fed policy vary predictably over the business and electoral cycles. At the top of a boom when unemployment first begins to increase, legislators focus on the Fed's "inhumane" willingness to sacrifice unemployed workers to the cause of slowing inflation and on the tendency of monetary restraint to reduce the flow of credit to small businesses and participants in housing markets (builders, construction workers, and would-be homeowners). Although these sectors tend to lobby for low interest rates at all times, a guilty suspicion exists that the social costs of using tight money to fight inflation falls disproportionately on them, and on the automobile industry as well. Reinforcing this view is a perennial complaint that, no matter how tight money becomes, loans of "low social value" somehow get made. In times of recession when unemployment is high and inflation begins to relent, congressional critics tend to accuse Fed officials of aggravating and then aborting the previous boom instead of keeping the economy moving along on a smooth path of "sustainable growth." They demand that the Fed relent in its "pathological" concern with fighting inflation and assist troubled firms or cities and fight singlemindedly the now-pressing problem of unemployment. Especially in election years, congressmen tend to continue this pressure until long after the recovery has begun and strong inflationary pressure has built up once more. As the recovery solidifies and turns into an inflationary boom, the foreign exchange and gold value of the dollar weakens and monetary policy is discovered to have been too easy for too long. At this stage, Fed officials are ceremonially urged to tighten up monetary discipline. The intertwining cycles run on and on, but this brings the analysis full circle.[4]

Although at each point of the cycle Fed officials offer ritualistic defenses against each charge, they cannot fail to recognize that political benefits accrue to them from allowing incumbents to use the Fed as a scapegoat. Bearing such criticism patiently contributes to the stereotype of Fed decisions as a continuing series of policy errors, but Fed officials are compensated by the survival of the unique bureaucratic privileges the Fed enjoys.

Lesser sources of external pressure on the Fed officials

Almost everyone has an opinion about the state of the national economy and what could be done to improve it. Some opinions are better informed and less self-serving than others, but all of them are affected by the owner's perspective as an interested member of various political and economic groups. Perspectives on many macroeconomic issues differ markedly between creditors and debtors, between workers and employers, between jobholders and the unemployed, between landlords and tenants, between a product's producers and its consumers, between bureaucrats and the public that pays their salaries, between Fed staff economists and their counterparts in academe, and between incumbent politicians and those seeking to unseat them. The best-articulated opinions come from the business, financial, and foreign central-banking communities and from various elements of the economics profession.

Central bankers in other countries

As the events of October 6, 1979, and Fed documents (e.g., Board of Governors of Federal Reserve System, 1974) testify, Fed officials maintain important points of regular contact with the international central-banking community. The detailed features of these connections adapt to the flow of political and economic events, with structural changes becoming clear only after the passage of time (Coombs 1976; Solomon 1977). The Board of Governors and New York Reserve Bank are linked formally to counterparts in Europe, Canada, and Japan through a network of daily telephone calls and through face-to-face meetings held under the aegis of various international organizations. The principal organizations are the Bank for International Settlements (which except in August, conducts monthly meetings in Basel), the International Monetary Fund (which holds a high-level meeting once a year in one or another major world capital), and the Organization for Economic Cooperation and Development (headquartered in Paris).

Since the tribe of central bankers is genetically encoded to resist inflation, they operate as an explicit part of the constituency against inflation. Just as any domestic interest group, the central-banking community seeks to impact politically on incumbent U.S. politicians. They do this primarily through their powers of persuasion and their power to improve or to worsen the dollar's standing on foreign exchange markets.

As the world's major reserve and vehicle currency, the dollar is inherently vulnerable to speculative attack. Fed officials labor long and hard to maintain an assured capacity to coordinate central-bank intervention against any large scale flight from dollars. For this reason, as the dollar has weakened secularly, the foreign central-banking community has gained more amd more leverage over Fed officials and, through them (at least on occasions—such as October 6, 1979—when the dollar is highly vulnerable), over U.S. politicians as well.

Domestic business and financial community

Because monetary policy affects the income statements and balance sheets of every kind of business firm, managers and stockholders strive energetically to communicate their policy perspectives to Fed officials. Whereas most members of Congress openly confess their inability to make sense of macroeconomic developments, spokespersons for the domestic and international business and financial communities profess to understand economic events and policies per- haps too well. On the symbolic level, businessmen regard the Fed as a restraining force in federal policymaking and the chairman as a spokesperson for their view of the public interest. Many lobby simultaneously against inflation and big gov- ernment and for measures to strengthen the dollar and to grant relief to their own troubled industries. They firmly expect the Fed to value these same goals. In return, they support the Fed in its struggles with Congress to maintain its "inde- pendence" and urge the retention of "proven" Fed leaders when an unsympathe- tic president has a chance to make a change.

This mutuality develops partly because Fed officials and executives are of the same social class. Top and middle managers at the Fed are alumni of the same schools, live in the same types of neighborhoods, and float in the same executive labor pool as those in the private economy. Between this pool and the Federal Reserve, regular interchange occurs in both directions. In particular, stints of employment at the Fed add gloss to a career as a securities dealer or commercial banker. For this and the following list of other reasons, dealers and bankers influence Fed policies more than any other industry groups.

1. *They serve as sources of information about the distribution of policy burdens that may help guide open-market policy in the short run.* First, banks and dealers bear the initial impact of open-market policy. Their impressions of how that policy is working and their observable reaction to Federal Reserve actions are important pieces of distributional information. Monitoring these responses provides feedback that can be used to guide short-run policy adjustments and to evaluate long-run issues concerning the appropriate institutional framework of monetary control.

Officials that manage the Fed's open-market account in New York describe the ease or difficulty with which banks and dealers can adjust to policy actions as the "tone" or "feel" of the money market. For years, this subjective tone or feel occupied an untoward and politically sensitive central place in the FOMC's assessment of whether or not its policies were realizing its intentions.

2. *Banker and dealer interpretations of events can contribute to the system's understanding of its own policies.* One element of Fed stabilization policy is to discover more about how its policy instruments actually work. To produce better effects, Fed officials need better theories of how its instruments link up with intermediate targets and goals. Although one may debate how well Fed officials learn from experience, evolutionary changes in FOMC strategy have developed as pragmatic adaptions to lessons taught by past mistakes.

From a research perspective, each business-cycle turning point begins a fresh scientific experiment from which to learn something new about how monetary policy works. Bankers' and dealers' self-interest makes them keen (if biased) observers of these experiments. By publicizing their developing forecasts and critical insights, bank and securities-industry analysts (such as Henry Kaufman) can put a great deal of pressure on the FOMC.

3. *Regulator-regulatee symbiosis.* To some extent, regulators tend to think of regulatees as customers or clients whose approval needs to be cultivated. Prior to the 1980 extension of Fed reserve requirements to nonmember banks, this tendency exemplified itself in Fed discussions of its membership problem. Membership in the system is wholly voluntary for state-chartered banks. Even though national banks are required to join the system, their ability to convert to a state charter made even their continued membership a quasivoluntary decision. This "exit option" gave member banks leverage they could use to soften Fed supervisory and regulatory policies. Persistent failure to respond to widespread banker criticisms could embarrass Fed officials by reducing the very reach of the system. To keep at least a semblance of an exit option open, commercial banks lobbied successfully against instituting compulsory membership *per se*.

This clientele orientation explains a parallel tendency for regulatees and regulators to view themselves as victims of a common enemy: the unreasoned demands of well-intentioned but naive legislators. Far more often than not, U.S. banking firms and their federal regulators stand together for or against proposed reforms in banking regulation.

Such solidarity is useful to both parties. In backroom legislative showdowns, bankers have considerable political power. They pointedly contribute funds to the election campaigns of state, local, and national candidates, giving special attention to the needs of candidates who serve on banking committees. More subtly, some congressmen and senators have been induced to make investments in bank stock. Such holdings create an unavoidable conflict of interest, by linking industry profits with the legislators' personal financial welfare.

On the other hand, in dealing with issues that capture the public's imagination, bankers' grasping (if not villainous) image in American folklore puts them at a severe disadvantage. With the general public, the media, and most politicians easily confused about how financial markets and monetary policy work, it is hard for bankers to argue the economic merits of their own case. Their obvious self-interest makes observers skeptical of their motives and arguments.

A political fire storm develops whenever bankers make cumulative increases in their *prime rate*,[5] even when anticipated inflation is accelerating very quickly and prime rate increases merely defend banks' real incomes. In times of tight credit, borrowers whose loan requests are turned down tend to band together to blame refusals on bankers' greedy disregard for the national interest. The event of raising the rate on bank loans and reducing availability is taken as prima facie evidence of a banker conspiracy to exploit monopoly power. In the popular press, bankers' fiduciary responsibilities to stockholders and the risks and returns available on alternative assets are seen as pretexts for tightening credit terms rather than as causes.

Bankers' need for assistance in media politics and the Fed's inability to offer financial incentives impart a symbiotic character to their mutual relationships with Congress. When legislation is introduced to hold down bank interest rates or to channel bank loan funds toward or away from favored or disfavored classes of borrowers, sponsors inevitably seek to involve the Fed in administering the program.

When called to testify on the subject, Fed officials underscore the administrative difficulties and long-run economic problems that would almost certainly attend such control programs. Fed officials' willingness to help bankers resist gross regulatory incursions creates a political debt on which the Fed sometimes calls to resist attacks (often from the same regulatory activists) on its bureaucratic autonomy. On issues of Fed reform, bankers' solid lines of communicaiton and influence into Congress and the administration can be used more openly. Bankers' less direct interest makes it easier for them to lay out the Fed's case. To argue convincingly that "good intentions" will produce bad effects, it is nice to possess hands that appear relatively clean.

4. *Points of formal contact.* Although of minor practical significance, business and financial interest have three points of formal contact with Fed officials. These occur in the Reserve Bank Directorates, the Federal Advisory Council, and the Consumer Advisory Council.

Reserve Bank boards of directors consist of six persons (three bankers and three other persons actively engaged in commerce, agricultural, or industrial pursuits) elected by the member banks in that district (usually after considerable prior screening by Fed officials) and three "class C directors" appointed from the public at large by the Board of Governors in Washington. These regional boards meet regularly to "supervise and control" Reserve Bank operations. This gives a director many opportunities to exchange views on Fed policies with the Reserve Bank president, who represents the district in the FOMC.

Directors also elect each district's member of the Federal Advisory Council. This council meets at least four times a year with the Board of Governors in Washington, to confer about the economic outlook and any elements of Fed policies and operations its members wish to discuss. The council is specifically empowered to make oral and written representations on these matters and to collect information and issue policy recommendations as well. It (and a larger counterpart Consumer Advisory Council that focuses on consumer-related banking issues) are widely thought not to exercise important influence.

Economists

In policy debates, an economist's role depends both on the nature of the issues and on where he or she is employed. Labor and business economists function principally as advisors and advocates. After advising their clients of the advantages and disadvantages of current and prospective policies, they help their clients to state their side of an issue as clearly and as forcefully as they can. They may or may not have much role in deciding what stand their employer takes on a given issue. They may not even agree with the position they are called upon to represent.

On issues where political pressure or ideological bias predetermines their employer's stand, presidential, congressional, and Fed staff economists function in much the same way—the major difference being that they are expected to gather and process statistically a great many numbers to support their principals' case. Still, government economists feel a responsibility to their craft (nurtured by their academic colleagues) to represent their professional perceptions of the public interest to some degree as well.

On some issues and under some chairmen, Fed staff economists play a leading role in policy formation (Wallich [1982]). As a matter of tradition, even on controversial issues Fed staff economists play an active and politically nonpartisan role in system decision making (Maisel 1973; Pierce 1979; Lombra and Moran 1980). Fed economists are jealous of this role and of their reputation for preparing for internal consumption an objective analysis of even the most controversial problems facing the Fed. When a chairman resists what staff members firmly believe to be the public interest (as, for example, when a chairman thinks of himself as the "best economist in the system"), the more adventurous among them may supply helpful arguments and data to dissident governors or district bank presidents. When board and FOMC decisions run seriously counter to their conception of the public interest, at least a few individual staff members will regard it as their right (if not their duty) to explain matters to their colleagues in the academic or banking communities. On rare occasions (and usually only after another job has been lined up), some have gone so far as to "leak" their independent analysis of a given issue to the press.

In most bureaucracies, habitual violation of administrative secrecy is tantamount to mortal sin. During the Burns era, a siege mentality, featuring a narrow view of proper staff lines of communication, took root at the Fed. But, though impaired, a more open, public-interest tradition survives among the professional staff. Many staff members remain eager to debate Fed policies informally with outside observers.

By fostering this tradition and engaging in such debates, academic economists pose an indirect influence on Fed decision making. Formally, the governors and their senior staff meet several times a year with a panel of distinguished academic consultants to discuss Fed policies and the national economic outlook. Informally, staff members exchange views with academic economists in professional assemblies and during looser contacts of a diverse sort. A particularly interesting forum is the Shadow Open Market Committee (SOMC) formed in 1973 by academic economists Karl Brunner and Allan Meltzer. The SOMC is a group of prominent monetarist economists who gather twice a year to evaluate Fed open market policy in the light of contemporaneous monetary policy recommendations of their own. Their goal is to produce academic criticism in which elements of "Monday morning quarterbacking" play a minimal role.

The media and Main Street

Because of what may be described as the "gross economic illiteracy" of the American journalistic establishment, the Fed and its political, business, and academic critics set the tone and dimensions of jounalistic discussions of macroeconomic goal formation. For the most part, the press concentrates on what financial and governmental *celebrities* have to say. The space allocated to items of monetary policy news tends to be proportional to the public standing of the celebrity newsmaker and to bear little relation to the intellectual quality of the case developed. Journalists act as a channel for disseminating and explaining the positions of the contending parties rather than as agents for skeptically investigating and reconciling competing claims.

Contemporary economic journalism is almost completely an exercise initiated by—and focusing on—a media event or press release of some kind. This concentration on reportable events rather than on evidence and logical argument reinforces politicians' tendency to focus on the quick-to-develop effects of policies rather than on their long-run implications. To enhance their effect, distributors of official handouts often support their documents with individual background interviews. These are offered both to guard against embarrassing misundertandings and to reward individual journalists for friendly reports in the past.

The Fed's internal workings are adapted to its scapegoat role

The Federal Reserve System is a political institution designed by politicians to serve politicians. Framers of the Federal Reserve Act deliberately dispersed jurisdiction over Fed actions among 12 regional (district) banks and a coordinating Board of Governors in Washington, D.C. Precise control over the Fed's various policy instruments is statutorily fractionated among 127 individuals: the nine-member boards of directors at each Reserve Bank, the twelve-regional bank presidents, and the seven governors. Intricate legislative formulas differentiate among bodies that may initiate policy actions and bodies that must review these initiatives. By these formulas, the chairman of the Federal Reserve Board appears as a governor only to be "first among equals" and not obviously more powerful than the president of the Federal Reserve Bank of New York, who also has a permanent place on the FOMC and whose salary (usually a reliable index of organizational authority) runs about twice that of the chairman.

Such contrived structural confusion must serve a political purpose. Government institutions evolve by natural selection, albeit without a genetic overlay. In bureaucracies, although change is often painfully slow, structural innovations occur principally as creative ways of relieving external and internal pressure on top management. Form follows function in the sense that organizational changes that serve continuing agency purposes survive while those that do not are eventually eliminated.

Elements of the Fed's bureaucratic structure are best seen as rational adaptations to ongoing and sporadic political pressures on the Fed's management team. As their principal functions, these adaptations serve to establish a cautious posture vis-a-vis incumbent politicians, to blur internal responsibility for controversial decisions, and to diffuse external blame for policy mistakes widely among system personnel.

Although the office of Federal Reserve Board chairman has come to occupy—in practice and over time—the predominant position in the hierarchy of the Fed, formally all Fed policy decisions are made jointly. Reinforced by the ambiguous formal dispersal of jurisdiction over the Fed's major policy instruments, the jointness makes it easier for Fed chairmen to let congressmen and senators blame them unfairly after the fact for whatever financial or macroeconomic developments their constituents dislike. The Fed's internal structure rolls the blame displaced from elected politicians into a thin film that spreads smoothly across a host of internal committees, councils, and boards.

The duality and ambiguity enshrined in the language of the Federal Reserve Act erect a uniquely confusing bureaucratic structure that makes the Fed appear both independent of short-run political influence and decentralized in its internal organization. The Employment Act of 1946, as amended by the Humphrey-Hawkins Act of 1978, enlarges the Fed's statutory mission while providing no specific guidance as to how Fed officials should execute politically sensitive trade-offs among conflicting goals. In accepting a series of impossible economic policy tasks, Fed officials set themselves up as shields for elected politicians, institutionally absorbing and distributing the blame for repeatedly choosing shortsighted policies. When the Fed fails to achieve its contradictory goals, how sharply these politicians and their successors attack (and whether or not they try to impose punitive damages) depends on the quality of Fed efforts to get along.

Being programmed to fail repeatedly at their policy assignments, Fed officials find it useful to express their intentions in a code that makes it hard for hindsighted critics to score cleanly. Fed officials consistently refuse congressional requests to identify their implicit short-term targets for inflation and unemployment. They won't even commit themselves as to which combination of the many values reported in their ranges of tolerable monetary aggregate growth rates they would most prefer. This obfuscation masks the Fed's openness to political influence and facilitates the formulation of quasicontradictory explanations both of the mechanics of their policies and of the rationale behind them. To protect the system from criticism and bureaucratic punishment, Fed chairmen are systematically led to employ their bully pulpit to miseducate the U.S. public about the macroeconomic consequences of alternative economic policies.

Why does the Fed end up having a procyclical impact?

Despite the FOMC's progressive adoption since 1970 of countercyclical targets for monetary growth rates, U.S. monetary aggregates continue to move procyclically (Kaminow 1979a). In fact, in the presence of accelerating inflation, deposit-rate ceilings and the structure of bank reserve requirements and FDIC insurance premiums make observed movements in monetary aggregates understate the procyclical thrust of Fed monetary policy (Kane 1978). These regulations make the stock of money substitutes expand rapidly whenever interest rates rise.

In a now-classic piece, Brunner and Meltzer (1964) show that the Fed's procyclical impact can be traced to "money-market myopia," i.e., to the Fed's obsessive concern with damping the size of short-run increases in nominal interest rates. What I wish to add to their analysis is the hypothesis that Federal Reserve officials aren't fooled into thinking that focusing on short-term interest rates is sound policy. I maintain that the political response system, driven by sectors that are ill-served by rising interest rates (including firms and individuals that consciously or unconsciously speculate against interest rate increases), makes it necessary for the Fed to follow nominal interest rates closely and to increase them less rapidly in the face of accelerating inflation than farsighted, independent policymaking would require (Kane 1980a). It is merely convenient internally and externally for Fed officials to rationalize their interest rate focus as they have.

Experience teaches that when the inflation rate varies over time, the policy effects of changes in the level of nominal interest rates become hard to interpret. Nominal interest rates treat loan repayments of *future* dollars as the equivalent in value of *current* dollars. But with inflation, future dollars have increasingly less purchasing power. To account for this, it is better to focus on real interest rates. These are nominal interest rates minus the anticipated rate of price inflation. for example, with 10 percent of anticipated inflation, a 12 percent Treasury bond rate would pay only 2 percent real.

Although real and inflation-adjusted interest rates would measure the thrust of monetary policy more accurately, in the popular mind and in the popular press the Fed's chief task is to act as the arbiter of nominal interest rates. During times of monetary restraint, this adversary perception subjects the Fed to political pressures from sectors that are hurt by rising interest rates. These sectors' political action leads elected officials to resist increases in nominal interest rates.

Fed efforts to reassure its antiinflation constituency focus attention on observed changes in nominal interest rates and reinforce the mistaken popular notion that changes in the level of nominal interest rates are reliable indicators of the macroeconomic thrust of monetary policy. In times of gathering inflation, to placate the Fed's natural constituency in the business and financial communities, Fed officials tend to emphasize that they are fighting inflation with high and rising nominal rates of interest. However, unexpectedly accelerating inflation would push up nominal rates anyway. The issue is how hard the Congress and the administration are simultaneously pushing Fed officials to fight unemployment by expanding the money stock.

Money market myopia is rooted in an underlying political and societal myopia with respect to the long-run and short-run consequences of economic policy. To end money market myopia, the fundamental need is not just to change Fed operating procedures and to disentangle the Federal Reserve System from excessively short-term political influences, but also to help the American public to understand who is responsible for bad monetary policy performance. Accountability for our economic policies, and for monetary policy in particular, should flow through to elected officials. What I find offensive in the current U.S. situation is that the Federal Reserve tries to convince people that it is independent. Every senator and congressman knows that the Fed responds to political pressures, as indeed every agency should under our system of government. Why should the Fed take the blame institutionally for mistakes of policy that are forced on it? The problem is not so much that the Federal reserve fails to flatten out business cycles, but that it acts in ways that aggravate the cycle in economic activity. As a minimum, voters should insist that the Fed not be made to serve as a mechanism for injecting politically induced, procyclical influences that make business cycle swings wider.

Despite their efforts to do the best job humanly possible, given the political constraints they accept, Fed officials end up adopting policies that reinforce rather than offset cyclical influences. An important part of the difficulty is the emphasis Fed officials place on nourishing the false image of ''the independence of the monetary authority within the structure of government'' (Burns 1978, p. 381). In the 1970s, the desire to preserve this independence locked Fed officials into a ''Caesar's wife'' syndrome, in which they became more sensitive to political pressure than even a less ''independent'' central bank would need to be. They sought to avoid the controversy that would attend their making hard decisions about the sectoral distribution of income precisely in order to maintain a latent capacity to make such decisions at some unspecified future date. If Fed officials could accept openly either in their charter or in their hearts that they are fundamentally servants of the elected representatives of the people no different from any other bureaucrats, the electorate would have a fairer chance to punish inflationists and to reward farsighted economic statesmanship.

Because recurring sectoral and election-year pressures lead policymakers to adopt an inappropriately short-run horizon, somewhat longer terms of elected office might prove helpful. But frequent elections are not the major source of stop and go monetary policy. The ultimate sources are the exaggerated expectations that voters (as pressure groups) have as to what government can do for them economically and the lack of constraints on the ability of special interests to beg benefits from the federal government. In the final analysis, lawmakers register and balance the distribution and intensity of voter opinion. Inflation will not slow appreciably until the constituency against inflation becomes a political majority. For this to occur, interest groups must learn, as parts of a "constituency of the whole," that society's relying habitually and permanently on the government to improve on demand the lot of any individual sector produces in the long run not more wealth for some sectors but less for everybody. . . .

Summary statement

External pressure is to politics what arbitrage is to economics and finance. It is a force that explains how individuals and groups of individuals manage their affairs. As applied to the operations of the Fed, external pressure is a stress that helps the Fed officials to decide what priorities to assign to conflicting macroeconomic goals.

In resolving any of the dilemmas of monetary policymaking, the key pressure points are Congress and the president. Every other group is subsidiary. To have a genuine effect, arguments for changing the operative set of monetary policy priorities must first impact politically on elected or appointed politicians.

Conceiving of the Fed as a willing scapegoat, whose task is to absorb guilt efficiently, explains very well the complicated, arbitrary-looking structure of the Federal Reserve system. Most of the Fed's special bureaucratic features (its independence, its acceptance of contradictory policy assignments, and its murky lines of internal authority) and its incomplete policy strategies serve definite political ends. If one accepts the hypothesis that the Fed's main function is to serve as a policy scapegoat for elected officials, these apparent anomalies may be seen to be intelligible adaptations to recurring political pressures.

Fed officials desire good monetary policy performance even more than anyone else. With the best of intentions, they revise the structure of Fed decision making and modify procedures for conducting their operations and for monitoring their effects. However, as long as these changes have no perceptible impact on the relevant political forces, they can have precious little effect on the short-run compromises Fed leaders find it prudent to make among alternative policy goals.

On the other hand, the Depository Institution Deregulation and Monetary Control Act of 1980 does affect the balance of political forces. Because it removes an important source of external pressure on Fed officials, it is potentially far more important than the largely cosmetic past pledges of Fed allegiance to monetary aggregate targets. Extending Fed-administered reserve requirements to nonmember deposit institutions lessens the value of member banks' exit option and increases the Fed's ability to command their political support. This enhanced political muscle makes it politically feasible for the Fed to take more effective action against secular inflation in the 1980s than it has at any time during the last two decades.

Notes

This paper brings together in a single source analysis developed earlier in Kane (1973, 1974a, 1974b, 1975, 1978, 1979a, 1979b, 1980a, 1980b). The author wishes to thank Benjamin Friedman, Benson Hart, George Kaufman, Allan Meltzer, Thomas Mayer, Anna Schwartz, and the editors of this volume for valuable comments on an earlier draft and to acknowledge the impact on his thinking of repeated conversations with Richard C. Aspinwall, Robert Eisenbeis, Raymond Lombra, and Edward J. McCarthy. All opinions expressed are those of the author and not those of the National Bureau of Economic Research.

1. Consider this statement about election year monetary policy by House Banking Committee Chairman Henry Reuss: "I think a build-up in the money supply during the Presidential election is a good thing. It would have helped in 1970, actually; but when you continued it into 1973 and made it worse, and continued in 1974, I and others did protest" (Committee *Hearings*, February 19, 1975, p. 21).

2. The great spurt in the number of bills introduced in the last two Congresses (which approached 20,000 pieces of legislation in the 1979–80 Congress) suggests a larger strategy of shaking down PACs of all kinds.

3. In private correspondence, Stephen V. O. Clarke has emphasized that the importance to the Fed of maintaining friendly relations with the White House was appreciated even in the early 1920s. In a 1922 letter to Montagu Norman, Benjamin Strong wrote:

In the face of a powerfully organized antagonism in Congress, the Federal Reserve System must, to a considerable extent, rely for its protection against political attack and interference upon the present administration. . . . We cannot afford, practically or politically, to embark upon a course which ignores the policy of the administration, which would possibly antagonize the administration and place us in the position where we would be quite helpless to resist the repeated efforts which have been made in Congress to effect important and possibly vital modifications in the underlying principles of the Federal Reserve System (Clarke 1967, p. 30).

4. It is instructive to compare the cyclical shifts in banking committee members' evaluations of current monetary policies with contemporaneous *Policy Statements* put out semiannually by the nonpolitical Shadow Open Market Committee led by Karl Brunner and Allan Meltzer.

5. This is the lowest rate of interest that banks *admit* collecting on funds lent to their best business customers.

Bibliography

Board of Governors of Federal Reserve System. 1974. *The Federal Reserve System: Purposes and Functions*. 6th ed. Washington, D.C.: Board of Governors, Federal Reserve System.

Brunner, K., and A. H. Meltzer, 1963. "Predicting velocity: Implications for theory and policy." *Journal of Finance* (May):319–54.

—————. 1964. The Federal Reserve's attachment to the free reserve concept. U.S. House of Representatives, Committee on Banking and Currency, Subcommittee on Domestic Finance, May 7. Washington, D.C.: Government Printing Office.

Burns, Arthur R. 1978. *Reflections of an Economic Policy Maker: Speeches and Congressional Statements, 1969–1978*. Washington, D.C.: American Enterprise Institute.

Clarke, Stephen V. O. 1967. *Central Bank Cooperation: 1924–31*. New York: Federal Reserve Bank of New York.

Clifford, Jerome A. 1965. *The Independence of the Federal Reserve System*. Philadelphia: University of Pennsylvania Press.

Coombs, Charles A. 1976. *The Arena of International Finance*. New York: Wiley.

Downs, Anthony, 1957. *An Economic Theory of Democracy*. New York: Harper and Row.

Gordon, Robert J. 1975. "The demand and supply of inflation." *The Journal of Law and Economics* (December):807–36.

Kaminow, Ira P. 1979. "Fed policy under resolution 133 (1975–1978): Is what they said what they did?" Government Research Corporation, Working Paper.

Kane, Edward J. 1973. "The central bank as big brother." *Journal of Money, Credit and Banking* 5 (November):979–81.

———. 1974a. "The re-politicization of the Fed." *Journal of Financial and Quantitative Analysis* 9 (November):743–52.

———. 1974b. "All for the best: The Federal Reserve Board's 60th Annual Report." *American Economic Review* 64 (December):835–50.

———. 1975. "New congressional restraints and Federal Reserve independence." *Challenge* 18 (November-December):37–44.

———. 1978. "EFT and monetary pollicy." *Journal of Contemporary Business* 7 (Spring):29–50.

———. 1979a. Statement. In U.S. Senate, Committee on Banking, Housing and Urban Affairs, *Hearings, Federal Reserve's First Monetary Policy Report for 1979*, February 20 and 23, 1979, pp. 154–60.

———. 1979b. "The three faces of commercial-bank liability management." In M.P. Dooley, H.M. Kaufman, and R.E. Lombra, eds. *The Political Economy of Policy Making*. Beverly Hills: Sage, pp. 149–74.

———. 1980a. "Politics and Fed policymaking: The more things change, the more they remain the same." *Journal of Monetary Economics* 6 (April):199–211.

———. 1980b. Accelerating inflation and the distribution of savings incentives. Mimeographed. Columbus: Ohio State University.

Lombra, Raymond E., and Michael Moran. 1980. "Policy advice and policymaking at the Federal Reserve." In K. Brunner and A. Meltzer, eds. *Monetary Institutions and the Policy Process*. Carnegie-Rochester Conference Series on Public Policy, vol. 13, pp. 9–68.

Maisel, Sherman J. 1973. *Managing the Dollar*. New York: W. W. Norton.

Meltzer, Allen. 1982. "Politics and Economics at the Federal Reserve, in Raymond E. Lombra and Willard E. Witte, *Political Economy of International and Domestic Monetary Relations*. Ames, Iowa: Iowa State University Press.

Nordhaus, William D. 1975. "The political business cycle." *Review of Economic Studies* 42 (April):169–90.

Pierce, James. 1979. "The political economy of Arthur Burns." *Journal of Finance* 34 (June):485–96.

Roberts, Steven M. 1978. "Congessional oversight of monetary policy." *Journal of Monetary Economics* 4 (August):543–56.

Solomon, Robert. 1977. *The International Monetary System 1946–1976: An Insider's View*. New York: Harper and Row.

Tufte, Edward. 1978. *Political Control of the Economy*. Princeton: Princeton University Press.

Wallich, Henry C. 1982. "Policy research, policy advice and policy making." in Raymond E. Lombra and Willard E. Witte, *Political Economy of International and Domestic Monetary Relations*. Ames, Iowa: Iowa State University Press.

Weintraub, Robert E. 1978. Congressional supervision of monetary policy. *Journal of Monetary Economics* 4 (August):341–62.

Woolley, John T. 1980. "Congress and the conduct of monetary policy in the 1970s." Political Science Paper, no. 52, April. St. Louis: Washington University.

4. The Relationship between Government and the Economy

4A. The Political Business Cycle

In the last thirty years a considerable literature has developed which examines the general effects of government on the economy and vica versa. Much of this literature looks at the long-term causes of government growth, a topic we shall take up in part 4B. There is an even larger literature focused on the short- term interactions between politics and economics. Most of these studies examine one or another aspect of the theory of the political business cycle.

This theory has four parts. The first holds that the state of the economy is the major factor in the reelection of public officials, especially the President. The second is the assertion that voters place greatest weight on the state of the economy in the year immediately preceding the election when deciding their votes. Third, this gives politicians an incentive to use fiscal and monetary policy tools to stimulate the economy around election time, in order to improve their chances of getting reelected. Fourth, elected officials are able to implement this desire. Together, these should result in a political business cycle: the economy booms just before elections and goes into recession after elections.

While this sort of phenomenon has been observed since Greek and Roman times, and while there have been sporadic impressionistic attempts to test the theory of the political business cycle since the 1920s (Monroe 1979), it is only since Gerald Kramer's (1971) article using time-series analysis that a serious literature has emerged. It has become clear, as the literature has grown, that all four parts of the theory are controversial, but some more than others. The evidence seems strongest for the first part of the theory, especially the view that voting in presidential elections is affected by economic conditions. However, even here, the tendency has been in the direction of concluding that economic conditions are one of a number of important factors, not the single dominant factor as first asserted. There has been much less support for the notion that incumbents always attempt to stimulate the economy before elections, or indeed that they are always capable of doing so. The general trend in the literature is toward the position that some presidents sometimes act in the way the theory predicts and that they are sometimes successful.

In the last few years there have been two major developments on the voting side of the literature. One is a questioning of the assumption that economic voting occurs on the basis of pure self-interest (Kinder and Kiewit 1979; Kiewit 1983); the other is investigation of the idea that different groups in the population watch different economic indicators and hence reward different economic outcomes (Hibbs 1982; Peretz 1983). On the policy side of the literature two interesting developments have been attempts to extend the cycle to monetary policy (Beck 1987) and attempts to weigh the relative importance of political, economic, and international causes of business cycles (Alt 1985).

The selection included here by Edward Tufte is an excerpt from his book *Political Control of the Economy*, generally seen as the most committed defense of the political business cycle theory. Tufte argues that all parts of the theory are true and that the theory explains a lot about who gets elected and why economic policy changes. The piece by Alt and Crystal, a chapter from their book *Political Economics*, assesses the validity of the political business cycle theory by taking the arguments put forward by a number of its proponents, including Tufte, and examining the reasons and evidence that they advance.

For further reading

The best known book advocating a political business cycle is Edward Tufte's *Political Control of the Economy*. More skeptical accounts are contained in Alt and Crystal's *Political Economics* and my own *The Political Economy of Inflation in the United States*. A review of the early literature is Kristin Monroe's article "Econometric Analyses of Electoral Behavior: A Critical Review." A good review of the later literature can be found in the Richard Winters *et al.* article "Political Behavior and American Public Policy: The Case of the Political Business Cycle."

Bibliography

Alt, James, "Political Parties, World Demand and Unemployment: Domestic and International Sources of Economic Activity," *American Political Science Review* (December 1985):1016–40.

Alt, James and Alex Crystal, *Political Economics* (Berkeley, Ca.: University of California Press, 1983).

Beck, Nathaniel, "Elections and the Fed: Is there a Political Monetary Cycle," *American Journal of Political Science* 31 (February 1987):194–216.

Hibbs, Douglas "The Dynamics of Political Support for American Presidents Among Occupational and Partisan Groups," *American Journal of Political Science* 26 (May 1982):312–333.

Kiewit, D. Roderick, *Macroeconomics and Micropolitics* (Chicago: University of Chicago Press, 1983).

Kinder, Donald and Roderick Kiewit, "Economic Discontent and Political Behavior: The Role of Collective Economic Judgements in Congressional Voting," *American Journal of Political Science* 31 (August 1979):495–527.

Kramer, Gerald, "Short Run Fluctuations in U.S. Voting Behavior, 1896–1964," *American Political Science Review* 65 (March 1971): 131–43.

Monroe, Kristin, "Econometric Analyses of Electoral Behavior: A Critical Review," *Political Behavior* 1 (Summer 1979): 137–73.

Peretz, Paul, *The Political Economy of Inflation in the United States* (Chicago: University of Chicago Press, 1983).

Tufte, Edward, *Political Control of the Economy* (Princeton, N.J.: Princeton University Press, 1978).

Winters, Richard C. et al. "Political Behavior and American Public Policy: The Case of the Political Business Cycle." in Samuel Long, ed., *Handbook of Political Behavior*, Vol. V (New York: Plenum Publishing, 1981).

4A.1. The Electoral-Economic Cycle

EDWARD R. TUFTE

"A Government is not supported a hundredth part so much by the constant, uniform, quiet prosperity of the country as by those damned spurts which Pitt used to have just in the nick of time."
Brougham, 1814

"The year 1972 ended with considerable forward momentum in economic activity. According to preliminary fourth quarter data, GNP rose by $32 billion, or at a seasonally adjusted rate of 11½ percent. . . . Judging from monthly indicators such as industrial production, the course of output was strongly upward through the quarter."
Annual Report of the Council of Economic Advisers, 1973

"Some circumstantial evidence is very strong, as when you find a trout in the milk."
Henry David Thoreau

Edward Tufte was one of the earliest and strongest proponents of the view that there is a political business cycle. In this excerpt from his book Political Control of the Economy, *Tufte outlines his idea of the electoral-economic cycle and provides evidence to support it.*

He begins by showing, with judicious use of quotations, that some American political actors have claimed to act in ways that fit the theory. He then looks at some comparative evidence from 27 democracies which appears to support the idea that the cyclical economy predicted by the theory occurred more often than could be expected by chance. Then Tufte looks more closely at the United States, in an effort to show that people's real incomes increase more, and unemployment decreases more, in election years, and that the so-called "prosperity index," which adds the rate of inflation to the rate of unemployment, has been lower in election than nonelection years. He also tries to demonstrate that the effects of the political business cycle will be greatest in elections in which the President has the greatest stake.

The evidence contained in this excerpt has been attacked on a variety of grounds (many of them outlined in the next reading). Most of the criticisms concern Tufte's selective choice of data and his exclusion of data from years that do not fit the theory. However, while one can object to much of his evidence, the reader should note that Tufte has been careful to provide a range of evidence, precisely to allow for possible weaknesses in individual indicators.

The government of a modern democratic country exerts very substantial control over the pace of national economic life and the distribution of economic benefits. While it cannot always dilute the consequences of exogenous shocks, reduce unemployment or inflation below certain levels, or protect its citizens from the vicissitudes of world markets, the government's control over spending, taxes, transfers, money stock, and the like enables it to direct the short-run course of the economy to a significant degree. We need not, therefore, be as agnostic as the Council of Economic Advisers' 1973 *Report* with respect to the causes of "considerable forward momentum in economic activity"—in this case, an 11.5 percent growth rate—occurring in the fourth quarter of a presidential election year. It is hardly a novel hypothesis that an incumbent administration, while operating within political and economic constraints and limited by the usual uncertainties in successfully implementing economic policy, may manipulate the short-run course of the national economy in order to improve its party's standing in upcoming elections and to repay past political debts. In particular, incumbents may seek to determine the *location* and the *timing* of economic benefits in promoting the fortunes of their party and friends.

The hypothesis of an electoral-economic cycle is nearly integrated into the folklore of capitalist democracies; political motives are regularly attributed to economic policies in election years. Furthermore, the formal possibilities for such a cycle have been developed in some technical detail in economic analysis.[1] As is often the case with folklore and with economic theory, however, little empirical evidence bearing on the question is available. A few case studies of a single country over a short period of time have found some evidence for the acceleration of the national economy in an election year, but these studies leave one wondering if other times or places would testify differently. After all, no investigators have sought to find the *lack* of a link between economic policy and elections. The only analysis comparing a number of countries, after a casual review of unemployment data, yielded very mixed findings: "The overall results indicate that for the entire period a political cycle seems to be implausible as a description for Australia, Canada, Japan, and the UK. Some modest indications of a political cycle appear for France and Sweden. For three countries—Germany, New Zealand and the United States—the coincidence of business and political cycles is very marked."[2] In short, virtually no evidence confirming even the existence of an electoral-economic cycle is at hand, let alone considerations on its measurement, causes, and consequences. The absence of evidence, however, is not convincing evidence of absence.

Let us begin by seeking a motive, an initiating cause for an electoral-economic cycle. It is obvious enough: incumbent politicians desire re-election and they believe that a booming pre-election economy will help to achieve it.

The economic theory of elections held by politicians and their economic advisers

It has been a political commonplace since the massive political realignment growing out of the Great Depression that the performance of the economy affects the electoral fate of the dominant incumbent party. Ample evidence confirms that politicians and high-level economic advisers appreciate what they see as an economic fact of political life. At hand is the rueful testimony of politicians and the more self-important pronouncements of their economic advisers that short-run economic fluctuations are very important politically. Walter Heller, the chairman of the Council of Economic Advisers from 1961 to 1964, wrote:

> As a political leader, President Johnson has found in modern economic policy an instrument that serves him well in giving form and substance to the stuff of which his dreams for America are made, in molding and holding a democratic consensus, and in giving that consensus a capital "D" in national elections. That the chill of recession may have tipped the Presidential election in 1960, and that the bloom of prosperity boosted the margin of victory in 1964, is widely acknowledged, especially by the defeated candidates.[3]

Richard Nixon expressed a similar view in *Six Crises*:

> I knew from bitter experience how, in both 1954 and 1958, slumps which hit bottom early in October contributed to substantial Republican losses in the House and Senate. The power of the "pocket-book" issue was shown more clearly perhaps in 1958 than in any off-year election in history. On the international front, the Administration had had one of its best years. . . . Yet, the economic dip in October was obviously uppermost in the people's minds when they went to the polls. They completely rejected the President's appeal for the election of Republicans to the House and Senate.[4]

And, with regard to the 1960 presidential contest, Nixon wrote:

> Unfortunately, Arthur Burns turned out to be a good prophet. The bottom of the 1960 dip did come in October and the economy started to move up in November—after it was too late to affect the election returns. In October, usually a month of rising employment, the jobless rolls increased by 452,000. All the speeches, television broadcasts, and precinct work in the world could not counteract that one hard fact.[5]

The matter was put most bluntly in a memorandum that Paul Samuelson wrote to President Kennedy and the Council of Economic Advisers:

> When my grandchildren ask me: "Daddy, what did you do for the New Frontier?," I shall sadly reply: "I kept telling them down at the office, in December,

January, *and* April that, WHAT THIS COUNTRY NEEDS IS AN ACROSS THE BOARD RISE IN DISPOSABLE INCOME TO LOWER THE LEVEL OF UNEMPLOYMENT, SPEED UP THE RECOVERY AND THE RETURN TO HEALTHY GROWTH, PROMOTE CAPITAL FORMATION AND THE GENERAL WELFARE, INSURE DOMESTIC TRANQUILITY AND THE TRIUMPH OF THE DEMOCRATIC PARTY AT THE POLLS.''[6]

A month before the 1976 presidential election, L. William Seidman, a top economic adviser and confidant of President Ford, commented on the slight downturn in the leading economic indicators for September: ''. . . the economic issue could be important. It had been one of the strongest things we had going for us. When things turn sluggish, we lose some of the advantage.''[7] A week before the election, Seidman again expressed his concern about the fall pause in the economy: ''I think Mr. Ford's chances for re-election are very good. As for the economic lull, we considered the use of stimulus to make sure we didn't have a low third quarter, but the President didn't want anything to do with a short-term view.''[8]

News reports, memoirs, and internal political documents abound with similar analyses by politicians, their economic advisers, and journalists.[9] In fact, since the 1930s only one administration has seemingly taken exception to the hypothesis that economic growth and stimulative fiscal policy are the important things politically. President Eisenhower and most of his cabinet officers (other than Richard Nixon), perhaps projecting their own ideological views on the electorate, felt that what voters wanted was a balanced federal budget—or, even better, a budget in surplus—and protection against inflation. But the belief in the political value of big budget surpluses and muted economic growth never took hold among politicians and economic policy-makers, particularly since they attributed the Republican losses of 1954, 1958, and 1960 to economic declines during those election years.[10]

The main propositions, in summary, of the politicians' theory of the impact of economic conditions on election outcomes emphasize short-run economic shifts:

1. Economic movements in the months immediately preceding an election can tip the balance and decide the outcome of an election.

2. The electorate rewards incumbents for prosperity and punishes them for recession.

3. Short-run spurts in economic growth in the months immediately preceding an election benefit incumbents.

What are the consequences of the politicians' economic theory of elections? Do incumbent administrations act on the theory and attempt to engineer election-year economic accelerations? Do macroeconomic fluctuations ride the electoral cycle? If so, what instruments of economic policy are deployed in election years?

My first concern [here will be] to show that electoral-economic cycles actually do exist.

Electoral-economic cycles in 27 democracies

How is an electoral-economic cycle to be detected and measured? A whole range of economic indicators might be matched up with election dates in a shotgun search for correlations. Instead of cycle-searching through economic time-series, however, let us try to obtain some theoretical guidance to the electoral-economic cycle by considering the perspective of the incumbent administration on election-year economics. If the administration seeks a pre-election economic stimulation, it seems likely that the economic policy instruments involved must be easy to start up quickly and must yield clear and immediate economic benefits to a large number of voters—or at least to some specific large groups of voters if the benefits are targeted as well as timed. Increased transfer payments, tax cuts, and postponements in tax increases—all of which have a widespread impact and can be legislated and implemented quickly—are the policy instruments that come to mind. Election-year economics is probably not often a matter of sophisticated macroeconomic policy. The politicians' economic theory of election outcomes gives great weight to economic events in the months before the election; thus the politicians' strategy is to turn on the spigot surely and swiftly and fill the trough so that it counts with the electorate.

These considerations suggest that short-run fluctuations in real disposable income might be a good aggregate signal of the pre-election stimulation of the economy. Real disposable income, unlike other major aspects of aggregate economic performance (such as unemployment, inflation, or real growth), can be immediately and directly influenced by short-run government action through taxes and transfers with little uncertainty about the time lag between activation of the policy instruments and the resulting change in real disposable income. For example, a few days after increased social security or veterans checks are in the mail, real disposable personal income has increased. In fact, in normal economic times, taxes and transfers have more to do with determining real disposable income than whether the economy goes faster or slower. Changes in real disposable income, furthermore, have special political relevance: several studies have found that upswings in real disposable income per capita are highly correlated with greater electoral support for incumbents.[11]

It is appropriate to look at the rate of change in real disposable income in relation to elections in *all* the world's democratic countries. Earlier we saw evidence that U.S. politicians believed that pre-election prosperity would help them retain office when they sought re-election. No doubt similar beliefs—as well as the desire to be re-elected—animate members of the political elite in almost any democracy. Consequently, I assembled electoral and economic time-series (election dates, disposable income, price changes, and population) for all 29 countries classified as "democracies" circa 1969—those nations with both widespread participation in free elections and an effective political opposition.[12] For 27 of the 29 (missing were Lebanon and Trinidad-Tobago), data sufficient to compute changes in real disposable income per capita for each year from 1961 to 1972 were found. Then the yearly acceleration-deceleration in real disposable income per capita was compared with the timing of elections in each of the 27 democracies.

The findings are clear. Evidence for an electoral-economic cycle was found in 19 of the 27 countries; in those 19, short-run accelerations in real disposable income per capita were more likely to occur in election years than in years without elections. Table 1 shows the results. Combining all the experience of the 27 countries over the period 1961–1972 reveals that real disposable income growth accelerated in 64 percent of all elections years ($N = 90$) compared to 49 percent of all the years without elections ($N = 205$). Furthermore, for those 19 countries whose economies ran faster than usual in election years, the effect was substantial: real disposable income growth accelerated in 77 percent of election years compared with 46 percent of years without elections.

The data in Table 1 provide only aggregate testimony; to convince ourselves that in *each* of the 19 individual countries a political-economic cycle occurs would require considerably more evidence—a longer data series, more detail about the structure of the cycle, and a deeper understanding of the politics of economic policy in the various democracies. The fundamental point of the aggregate evidence is that 70 percent of the countries showed some signs of a political business cycle.[13]

A few countries have been studied more systematically. For Israel, Ben-Porath reports:

> In following the timing of discrete policy decisions, one can observe a fairly consistent pattern. Thus, for example, of the seven devaluations that took place in the period [1952–1973], the closest that one ever came to preceding an election was eighteen months. (The eighth devaluation took place in November 1974 approximately three years before the next scheduled elections.) When a public committee recommended reducing income tax rates and imposing a value added tax the government proceeded to implement the first in April 1973, expecting elections in November 1973, but waited with the second.[14]

For the six parliamentary elections from 1952 to 1973, per capita annual consumption accelerated during the year before the election five out of six times; the average pre-election increase in consumption was 7.4 percent compared to 2.0 percent in the post-election periods. Similarly, per capita GNP increased a pre-election average of 7.9 percent as against a post-election 3.7 percent.

In the Philippines, the economy moved with the electoral cycle in a "biennial lurch" from 1957 to 1966 according to Averch, Koehler, and Denton. They sketch out a fairly complete pattern of political economies:

> Although it is growing rapidly, the Philippine economy also appears to be rather unstable. At least until 1966, the reported rate of growth of real GNP alternately rose and fell in a two-year cycle. . . . The survey data . . . suggest that both

Table 1

Elections and Economic Acceleration, 27 Democracies, 1961–1972

	Percentage of years in which rate of growth of real disposable income increased				Did acceleration in real income growth occur more often in election years compared to years without an election?
	election years	N	years without elections	N	
Australia	75%	4	29%	7	yes
Austria	25%	4	86%	7	no
Belgium	67%	3	63%	8	yes
Canada	100%	5	57%	7	yes
Chile	50%	2	44%	9	yes
Costa Rica	100%	2	50%	8	yes
Denmark	25%	4	43%	7	no
Finland	67%	3	50%	8	yes
France	60%	5	33%	6	yes
Germany	33%	3	38%	8	no
Iceland	33%	3	75%	8	no
India	50%	2	43%	7	yes
Ireland	67%	3	63%	8	yes
Israel	67%	3	50%	8	yes
Italy	33%	3	50%	8	no
Jamaica	100%	2	44%	9	yes
Japan	100%	4	29%	7	yes
Luxembourg	100%	2	56%	9	yes
Netherlands	50%	4	57%	7	no
New Zealand	75%	4	43%	7	yes
Norway	100%	2	33%	9	yes
Philippines	60%	5	67%	6	no
Sweden	67%	3	50%	8	yes
Switzerland	67%	3	50%	8	yes
United Kingdom	67%	3	38%	8	yes
United States	83%	6	40%	5	yes
Uruguay	33%	3	50%	8	no

politicians and voters perceive election strategy in terms of allocating public works, jobs, and various other payoffs to maximize votes . . . the unevenness we observe is in part the consequence of fiscal and monetary policies that work together to destabilize the economy. The instability does not reflect the impact of uncontrollable events but is built into the Philippine political system. As Philippine policymakers pursue and *achieve* their goals, they generate the cycles we have observed.[15]

The policy instrument implicated was the government budget: deficits were run in six straight election years and surpluses in the five intervening years.

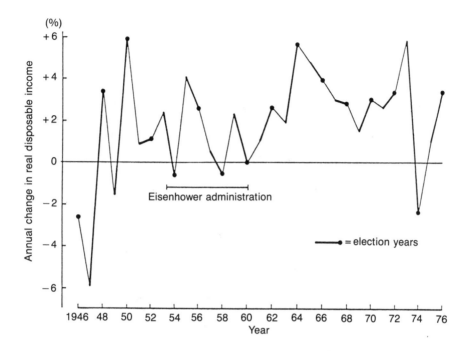

Figure 1 **Yearly Changes in Real Disposable Income per Capita, 1946–1976**

The studies of Israel and the Philippines help shore up the wishy-washy results for these two countries recorded in Table 1. All the available material combined—the case studies of Israel and the Philippines, Nordhaus's report on the coincidence of unemployment and electoral cycles in Germany, New Zealand, and the United States, and, most importantly, the reuslts of Table 1—yields evidence of electoral-economic cycles in 21 of the world's 27 democracies.[16]

The political history of real disposable income in the United States

Incumbent administrations in postwar America have generally enjoyed quite a perky electoral-economic cycle. Figure 1 displays the path of yearly changes in real disposable income per capita in the United States since 1947. During the Truman, Kennedy, Johnson, Nixon, and Ford administrations, the short-run growth in real disposable income per capita tended to swing up in election years and drop down in odd-numbered years. The tie between elections and a quickening economy is a strong one: in those five administrations, real income growth accelerated in eight of eleven election years (73 percent) compared to only two of ten years (20 percent) without elections.

Things were different during the Eisenhower administration. Real income growth declined in every election year (1954, 1956, 1958, and 1960), but rose in three of the four intervening years without elections. Things were different because the economic goals and the evaluations of what was politically sound economic policy were different. The dominant political-economic goals of the Eisenhower presidency, unlike those of other postwar administrations, were the reduction of inflation and a balanced (and small) federal budget. These economic beliefs were initially reinforced by the election returns: Eisenhower read his landslide victory in 1952 as the voters' express approval of these goals and as the rejection of the Democratic focus on governmental intervention to reduce unemployment. The Eisenhower administration memoirs, fiscal histories, and diaries—unlike those of any other postwar administration—bristle with determined statements on the need to avoid inflation and reduce the federal budget. Stimulative interventionist policies by the government were to be avoided because they ultimately stifled creative business initiative and because they served little purpose, since economic downturns and unemployment were seen as self-curing.[17] These doctrines held firm even in the face of the deep pre-election economic slump of 1958 and the Burns-Nixon proposal to the cabinet to stimulate the economy in the months before the 1960 election.[18] In fact, going into the elections of 1954, 1956, and 1960, the federal budget was less stimulative than in the previous odd-numbered years; for two of those election years, moreover, the federal budget was in surplus. Perhaps there was a political budget cycle.[19] That policy, if it was a policy, may have grown out of a conviction that voters cared as strongly about a balanced federal budget as those who shaped economic policy. Certainly the economic outcomes differed; the results for all 15 election years from 1948 to 1976 were:[20]

	Number of election years in which growth in real disposable income	
	accelerated	decelerated
Eisenhower administration	0	4
Other administrations	8	3

The Eisenhower years demonstrated that when the administration's views on political economy changed the political-economic cycle also changed. Once a new administration came into office in 1961 with a contrary doctrine about what was politically important as far as the economy was concerned, the match of the ups and downs of real income growth to election years was restored.[21]

A four-year cycle in unemployment

Let us examine another indicator of economic well-being, the unemployment rate, in relation to the U.S. electoral cycle. Nordhaus found that unemployment has tended to reach a low point around election time in Germany, New Zealand, the United States, and perhaps France and Sweden.[22] Evidence for the United States is shown in Figure 2, where the path of monthly unemployment is centered

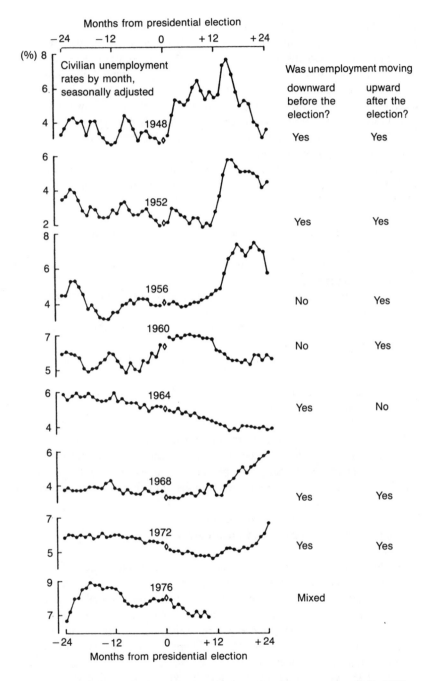

Figure 2 **Unemployment Rates and the Cycle of Presidential Elections, 1946–1976**

around the schedule of presidential elections from 1948 to 1976. In the main, unemployment has bottomed out every fourth November.[23] Unemployment levels twelve to eighteen months before presidential elections have exceeded unemployment levels at election time in six of the last eight presidential elections. (If the planned economic targets from 1977 to 1980 are achieved, the score will be up to seven out of nine by 1980.[24]) The elections during the Eisenhower administration, 1956 and 1960, are the only exceptions: while unemployment dipped slightly in 1956, everything was wrong, politically, with the pre- and post-election shifts in unemployment in 1960.

Omitting the two presidential elections taking place during the Eisenhower administration, the pre-election downturn in the unemployment rate in all the other postwar presidential elections is quite phenomenal:

—The unemployment rate in November 1948 was lower than in *all but five* of the preceding twenty-four months.
—The unemployment rate in November 1952 was lower than in *all but one* of the preceding twenty-four months.
—The unemployment rate in November 1964 was lower than in *all but two* of the preceding twenty-four months.
—The unemployment rate in November 1968 was lower than in *all* of the preceding twenty-four months.
—The unemployment rate in November 1972 was lower than in *all* of the preceding twenty-four months.
—The unemployment rate in November 1976 was lower than in *eleven* of the preceding twenty-four months.

Except in the Eisenhower years, the election-day unemployment rate has averaged about one percentage point below the rate twelve to eighteen months before the election and nearly two percentage points below the post-election unemployment rate twelve to eighteen months after the presidential election.

Presidential elections in relation to the trade-off between inflation and unemployment

Since 1946, the American economy has beaten the putative trade-off between inflation and unemployment—by having less of both—in only six years. Four of these six great economic successes were delivered in presidential election years.

The trade-off broke down in four other years when both inflation and unemployment increased. None of these failures took place in a presidential election year, although three of them—in 1946, 1970, and 1974—did occur at the time of off-year congressional elections.

Table 2 shows the joint inflation-unemployment movements in relation to presidential elections for all thirty-one years from 1946 to 1976. It is apparent

Table 2

Inflation, Unemployment, and Presidential Elections, 1946–1976

Yearly change in unemployment rate and inflation (real GNP deflator):	Presidential election years	All other years
less unemployment and less inflation	50%	9%
less unemployment, but more inflation	13	30
less inflation, but more unemployment	38	43
more inflation and more unemployment	0	17
	101%	99%
	(8)	(23)

that the way to defeat the trade-off between inflation and unemployment in the short-run is to hold a presidential election.

The electoral stakes and the electoral-economic cycle

Elections differ in how much is at stake. An election year in which an incumbent president seeks re-election is far more important, from the perspective of the incumbent administration, than a midterm congressional election. The incentives for producing a booming pre-election economy are greater in some election years than in others. Is it true, then, that the greater the electoral stakes, the greater the likelihood and the greater the magnitude of pre-election economic acceleration?

The short-run stimulation of the economy for electoral purposes involves several possible costs to an administration: inflationary pressures, destabilization, political attacks on deficit spending or the other policy instruments used to stimulate the economy, disruption of governmental programs due to shifts in the rate of government spending, political attacks on the fact of the stimulation itself, and having to forego stimulation at other times when it might be useful for long-run economic management. Such costs are more tolerable, of course, when the potential electoral benefits are greater.

From the vantage point of the incumbent administration—particularly the incumbent president—years can be ordered from maximum to minimum electoral importance:

1. On-years, incumbent president seeking re-election
2. Midterm congressional elections

3. On-years, incumbent president not seeking re-election

4. Odd-numbered years

There are surely special incentives to the administration in those on-years when the incumbent president seeks re-election; his direct personal interest in political survival coincides with what must be a particularly tempting opportunity to hit the economic accelerator. In those on-years when the incumbent president is not seeking re-election, his interest is not so clear. While his political party would inevitably consider more important all on-year over all off-year elections, a president might quite reasonably consider the congressional elections in the middle of his term as more important than an election at the conclusion of his political career. Success at midterm—or at least curbing the losses of his congressional allies, which is about the best the president can expect in an off-year—may allow him to maintain the force and continuity of his program, and may also serve as the beginnings of a drive for re-election. The downgrading of the electoral importance (from the president's point of view) of the on-year when he is retiring is reinforced by the apparent ambivalence that presidents seem to have felt toward their party's nomination of a successor (consider Truman-Stevenson in 1952, Eisenhower-Nixon in 1960, and Johnson-Humphrey in 1968—the only relevant cases in many years). Finally on our list, there is no doubt that odd-numbered years are the least important electorally.

Having ranked the electoral importance of each year of a president's term, we can test the prediction that the greater the political importance of the year, the greater the efforts that an administration will make to accelerate the economy. Table 3 shows the clear link between the extent of economic well-being and the electoral importance of the year: *the greater the electoral stakes, the greater the economic improvement.* Real disposable income increased an average of 3.4 percent in years when the incumbent president sought re-election, 2.6 percent in midterm election years, 2.0 percent in those on-years when the incumbent president did not seek re-election, and a dismal 1.5 percent in odd-numbered years.[25]

The most important finding here—the difference between presidential elections when an incumbent seeks re-election and other years—holds over the entire set of elections from 1946 to 1976, *including* the Eisenhower years. During those thirty-one years the median rate of growth in real disposable income per capita was *3.3 percent in years when the incumbent president sought re-election* compared to *1.7 percent in all other years.*

The rhetoric of policy initiatives matches the reality of the electoral-economic cycle. A content analysis of presidential State of the Union messages from 1946 to 1969 revealed that the most important topic after international relations was social welfare and allocative policy, and that its importance varied with the presidential election cycle and the term of the president:

> . . . the modal activity in this policy area is for the president to respond to the claim of a single segment of American society by asking Congress to pass legislation to confer some benefit on them.

Table 3

Annual Change in Real Disposable Income per Capita in Relation to the Political Complexion of the Years, all Postwar Administrations Except Eisenhower's

	No election	On-year incumbent president not seeking re-election	Midterm election	On-year incumbent president seeking re-election
1946			−2.6%	
1947	−5.9%			
1948				3.4%
1949	−1.5%			
1950			5.9%	
1951	0.9%			
1952		1.1%		
1961	1.0%			
1962			2.6%	
1963	1.9%			
1964				5.6%
1965	4.8%			
1966			3.9%	
1967	3.0%			
1968		2.8%		
1969	1.5%			
1970			3.0%	
1971	2.6%			
1972				3.3%
1973	5.9%			
1974			−2.3%	
1975	1.0%			
1976				3.3%
Median amount	1.5%	2.0%	2.8%	3.4%

The temporal pattern in this policy area is almost the opposite to that characteristic of international involvement. The distribution of social benefits is primarily a first term phenomenon. It rises gradually, but does not overshadow the more important international policy area until the president's fourth year in office. When faced with re-election needs, he is likely to be bountiful. But during a president's second term, the loadings on this factor fall sharply.

One might argue that a second term president does not have much influence with Congress and hence is less likely to urge them to undertake new activities. Whether or no, it does seem clear that there are political gains accruing from giving population groupings benefits they want: health, welfare assistance, housing, consumer protection, and so forth. Presidents attempt to distribute this largess when they have the greatest need to increase their political support.[26]

Conclusion

There is, then, an electoral rhythm to the national economic performance of many capitalist democracies. The electoral cycle causes substantial macroeconomic fluctuations.

In the United States, the electoral-economic cycle from 1948 to 1976 (other than the Eisenhower years) has consisted of:

—A two-year cycle in the growth of real disposable income per capita, with accelerations in even-numbered years and decelerations in odd-numbered years.

—A four-year presidential cycle in the unemployment rate, with downturns in unemployment in the months before the presidential election and upturns in the unemployment rate usually beginning from twelve to eighteen months after the election.

These patterns are consistent with the character of the economic tools available to control real disposable income and unemployment. Real disposable income— which is directly and immediately affected by taxes and transfer payments—can be manipulated in the short run. The unemployment rate, by contrast, is affected by fiscal and monetary policies that act more slowly and with more uncertain time lags on unemployment than do taxes and transfers on real disposable income.

Further, the greater the electoral stakes, the greater the economic stimulation. In particular, those years when incumbent presidents sought re-election enjoyed the most favorable short-run economic conditions. It comes as no surprise, however, to discover that upon re-election several of those incumbent presidents had to undertake, as their first economic priority, deflationary policies.

Like a detective in a murder mystery, I have tried so far to establish a motive and to find a pattern. The questions that remain are those of means and opportunity: How is the electoral-economic cycle produced? What specific instruments of economic policy are involved?

Notes

1. The three fundamental papers, each with a very different perspective on political economics, are M. Kalecki, "Political Aspects of Full Employment," *Political Quarterly*, 14 (October-December 1943), 322–331; William D. Nordhaus, "The Political Business Cycle," *Review of Economic Studies*, 42 (April 1975), 169–190; and Assar Lindbeck,

"Stabilization Policy in Open Economies with Endogenous Politicians," *American Economic Review*, 66 (May 1976), 1–19. Other major developments are found in C.A.E. Goodhart and R. J. Bhansali, "Political Economy," *Political Studies*, 18 (March 1970), 43–106; W. Miller and M. Mackie, "The Electoral Cycle and the Asymmetry of Government and Opposition Popularity," *Political Studies*, 21 (September 1973), 263–279; C. Duncan MacRae, "A Political Model of the Business Cycle," working paper, December 1971, The Urban Institute, Washington, D.C.; Raford Boddy and James Crotty, "Class Conflict and Macro-Policy: The Political Business Cycle," *Review of Radical Political Economics*, 7 (Spring 1975), 1–19; and the many papers of Frey and his co-workers, including Bruno S. Frey and Friedrich Schneider, "On the Modelling of Politico-Economic Interdependence," *European Journal of Political Research*, 3 (1975), 339–360. Suggestions for further research are developed in Ryan C. Amacher, William J. Boyes, Thomas Deaton, and Robert D. Tollison, "The Political Business Cycle: A Review of Theoretical and Empirical Evidence," manuscript, 1977.

2. Nordhaus, "Political Business Cycle," p. 186. Similar mixed results are reported in Martin Paldam, "Is There an Electional Cycle? A Comparative Study of National Accounts," Institute of Economics, University of Aarhus, Denmark, 1977, no. 8.

3. Walter W. Heller, *New Dimensions of Political Economy* (Cambridge, Mass.: Harvard University Press, 1966), p. 12.

4. Richard M. Nixon, *Six Crises* (Garden City, N.Y.: Doubleday, 1962), p. 309.

5. Ibid., pp. 310–311.

6. Paul Samuelson, "Memorandum for the President and the Council of Economic Advisers: That 'April Second Look' at the Economy," March 21, 1961 (John F. Kennedy Presidential Library).

7. Hobart Rowen, "Ford Aide Sees Lag in GNP Aiding Carter," *Washington Post*, October 6, 1976, p. A17.

8. Vartanig G. Vartan, "Seidman Expects Leveling in Leading Economic Index: Ford Adviser Says Pause Is Now Lull," *New York Times*, October 26, 1976, p. 51.

9. The best guides are Herbert Stein, *The Fiscal Revolution in America* (Chicago: University of Chicago Press, 1969) and James L. Sundquist, *Politics and Policy: The Eisenhower, Kennedy, and Johnson Years* (Washington, D.C.: The Brookings Institution, 1968). For Britain, David Butler and Donald Stokes report: ". . . how deeply rooted in British politics is the idea that the Government is accountable for good and bad times. Popular acceptance of this idea means that the state of the economy has loomed large in the minds of all modern Prime Ministers as they pondered on the timing of a dissolution. And in the post-Keynesian era more than one government has been tempted to seek a favorable context for an election by expanding the economy, although dissolutions are more easily timed to coincide with expansion than the other way round" (*Political Change in Britain*, 2nd ed. [New York: St. Martin's Press, 1974], p. 369).

10. Nixon pointed to economic downturns in the few months before the elections of 1954, 1958, and 1960 (*Six Crises*, pp. 309–312). Sundquist makes a similar point: "Three elections [1954, 1958, and 1960] had taught the politicians that they *must* respond to the issue of unemployment whenever it appears. In a more positive sense, experience since 1964 had also taught them that a full employment economy provides the greater revenues from which the politicians' dreams are realized" (*Politics and Policy*, p. 56). And James Tobin sharpens the observation: "Recessions of course are politically dangerous, as Republican defeats in 1932, 1954, 1958, 1960—we might add 1970—indicate. But a first-derivative mentality is strong in American politics. Provided economic indicators are moving up, their level is secondary. Incidentally, politico-econometric studies of the influence of economic variables on elections confirm this instinctive feeling of politicians: the current growth rate of GNP counts for votes, but not the level of unemployment" (*The New Economics One Decade Older* [Princeton: Princeton University Press, 1974], p. 20).

11. Gerald Kramer, "Short-Term Fluctuations in U.S. Voting Behavior, 1896–1964,"

American Political Science Review, 65 (March 1971), 131–143; and Edward R. Tufte, "Determinants of the Outcomes of Midterm Congressional Elections," *American Political Science Review*, 69 (September 1975), 812–826. Further evidence is discussed in Chapters 4 and 5 below.

12. The list is from Robert A. Dahl, *Polyarchy: Participation and Opposition* (New Haven: Yale University Press, 1971), pp. 231–248. The data sources for each table and figure are described in the Appendix, "Data Sources," p. 155.

13. Since election dates in these democracies are scattered over the years, the observed relationship between the occurrence of elections and short-run economic stimulation is not the artifactual product of common worldwide changes in economic conditions. At least such was the case in the 1960s. In Chapter 3, however, I shall present evidence for the increasing synchronization since 1970 of election timing in the major capitalist democracies.

14. Yoram Ben-Porath, "The Years of Plenty and the Years of Famine—A Political Business Cycle?" *Kyklos*, 28 (1975), 400.

15. Harvey A. Averch, John E. Koehler, and Frank H. Denton, *The Matrix of Policy in the Philippines* (Princeton: Princeton University Press, 1971), pp. 95–96. The capital-intensive character of Philippine elections, election-stimulated inflation, and post-election retrenchment appear to have combined to produce both an unstable economy and unstable ruling coalitions. On this, see the excellent analysis in Thomas C. Nowak, "The Philippines before Martial Law: A Study in Politics and Administration," *American Political Science Review*, 71 (June 1977), 522–539.

16. I investigated the possibility that electoral-economic cycles might be more likely to occur in countries having irregular election schedules, where the date of the election is set by the incumbent government. The cycle, however, appeared with nearly equal frequency in countries with flexible election dates and in countries with fixed dates. A more subtle possibility is that countries with non-periodic election dates have elections called at economic extremes, with the incumbent government seizing the opportunity for electoral gains in prosperous times and crumbling in times of economic crisis. The hypothesis is too subtle to test with the data of Table 1. For countries with non-periodic elections, the direction of the causal arrow must remain ambiguous: does a buoyant economy produce elections or does the prospect of elections produce stimulative economic policies? Such questions, which depend among other things on the time horizons of politicians and how politicians perceive the time horizons of voters, pose difficult problems of model specification and estimation.

17. Full details are in Stein, *Fiscal Revolution*, chapters 11–14, and Sundquist, *Politics and Policy*. See also Edward S. Flash, Jr., *Economic Advice and Presidential Leadership* (New York: Columbia University Press, 1965) and Eisenhower's memoirs *Mandate for Change* (Garden City, N.Y.: Doubleday, 1963) and *Waging Peace* (Garden City, N.Y.: Doubleday, 1965).

18. See Eisenhower, *Waging Peace*, pp. 307–310; and Nixon, *Six Crises*, pp. 309–311.

19. Evidence on this point is found in a letter from the Secretary of the Treasury, George M. Humphrey, to President Eisenhower on December 6, 1956 (Eisenhower Presidential Library):

> These are a few thoughts I hope you may have in mind as you think of the problem of the budget. The matter of timing is of very great importance as to both politics and economics.
>
> *As to politics*: I believe we can resist any major tax reductions this coming year provided there is a real prospect of an important reduction to be effective in 1958. . . .
>
> Barring a war, I think there will have to be a substantial general tax reduction sometime during the next four years and, politically, the best time to have it will be in

1958. If this occurs, we will be in approximately the same situation as in the past four years and the voters will actually have the benefit of a tax cut for a couple of years before the next Presidential election.

20. The exact probability (via the hypergeometric distribution) of observing an outcome as extreme as that shown in the two-by-two table in the text, under the null hypothesis that there is no difference between the Eisenhower and the other administrations, is only 1/ 39 or about 0.026 (under the assumptions of fixed marginals and independence of observations). Consequently we reject either the null hypothesis or the assumptions. The Eisenhower case is bothersome, naturally raising questions about the selective use of evidence. It appears that the Eisenhower administration did make electoral cycle calculations in formulating its economic policies, but that other priorities—preventing inflation, limiting government intervention in the economy, seeking a budget surplus—were far more important than the all-out stimulation of the economy in election years. Given Eisenhower's assured re-election in 1956 and his quite limited devotion to the 1960 Nixon campaign, it is not surprising that ideological priorities in economic policy substituted for heating up the pre-election economy. Finally, in this chapter as well as the next two we shall see a great deal of additional evidence (mostly not dependent on the Eisenhower exclusion) that details the structure and content of the electoral-economic cycle.

21. A sharp contrast between the two administrations is provided in Paul Samuelson, "Economic Policy for 1962," *Review of Economics and Statistics*, 44 (1962), 3–6; and in Seymour E. Harris, *The Economics of the Two Political Parties* (New York: Macmillan, 1962). See also Tobin, *The New Economics One Decade Older*.

22. Nordhaus, "Political Business Cycle," p. 186. I have borrowed the arrangement for my Figure 2 from an unpublished draft of Nordhaus's paper.

23. The unemployment rates reported here are seasonally adjusted, thereby removing (among other things) the normal downturn in unemployment (unadjusted) occurring in the fall of each year. Thus the actual, unadjusted unemployment rates would show a sharper pre-election improvement. This becomes an interesting issue in understanding how the electorate responds to pre-election economic changes: Do voters seasonally adjust? If not, then the normal autumn economic upswing benefits incumbents in those countries holding elections late in the year.

24. In his press conference on November 16, 1976, President-elect Carter said: "We believe that we can get the unemployment rate down over a fairly long period of time— two, three or perhaps four years—to the 4 to 4½ percent figure before excessive inflation will be felt. But I will reveal my plans as they are evolved. They are not final enough now to discuss further" (*New York Times*, November 16, 1976, p. 32). Later, the 1980 unemployment goal became 4.75 percent. See James T. Wooten, "Carter Delay on Endorsing Bill Linked to 4% Unemployment Provision," *New York Times*, October 20, 1977, p. A12.

25. Let E_i = real disposable income per capita in year i. The annual change (in percentage terms) in real disposable income per capita is simply

$$\Delta E = \frac{E_i - E_{i-1}}{E_{i-1}} \times 100.$$

In Chapter 5 [of *Political Control of the Economy*] ΔE [is] related to the national vote for members of the incumbent (White House) party.

26. John H. Kessel, "The Parameters of Presidential Politics," *Social Science Quarterly* (June 1974), 8–24, at pp. 11–14.

4A.2. Political Business Cycles

JAMES E. ALT and K. ALEC CRYSTAL

Over time a considerable literature has grown up on the topic of political business cycles. Some writers argue for the existence of such cycles, others that such cycles do not exist. In this excerpt from their book Political Economics, *Alt and Crystal assess the arguments for and against the theory.*

They divide the literature according to two criteria. One is whether the author assumes that the electorate's preferences are always the same or that they vary over time. The other is whether the government seeks to reward its supporters or acts so as to get the most votes at the next election. Tufte's work is categorized as an example of the second variant, holding that the preferences of the electorate may change and that the government will seek to maximize the votes it receives at the next election.

Alt and Crystal then look at the arguments and evidence advanced by some of the best-known authors on each variant and outline some of the possible objections to the arguments and the evidence. In general, they conclude that the evidence for the political business cycle theory taken as a whole is much weaker than is generally supposed, but that there are some data that support some parts of the theory.

Economic phenomena are commonly cyclical. Since economic fluctuations may cause hardship and uncertainty, much research has been devoted to their origins. Some academics have, naturally enough, wondered if economic cycles could be tied to political cycles. Early investigations relied on a mixture of observation and commentary and, unsurprisingly, reached no strong conclusions. More recent efforts have tried to derive a politically induced business cycle from theories that assume governments make economic policy with an eye on economic conditions at election time. This implies that certain economic indicators will fluctuate over time so that peaks (or troughs) in the series are synchronized with elections. They are consequently known as *political business cycle* models. They purport to show that at any given time the level of aggregate demand or general economic activity depends at least in part on how long there is until the next election. It is curious that the literature on political business cycles is widely invoked, even though there is little evidence for the existence of such cycles.

If political business cycles exist, economists need to know about them to understand the economy fully. Furthermore, political business cycle models usually imply that economic outcomes are *suboptimal*, that is, the public is worse off than if there were no manipulation of the economy by the government in pursuit of reelection. The most extreme version of the political business cycle model is the one where electoral manipulation of the economy creates an "inflationary bias" in democratic systems.

Political business cycle theories also have a number of political implications. First, economic conditions affect election outcomes. Otherwise, governments would not gain electorally from manipulating the economy. These models frequently assume that a high level of economic activity, whether measured by low unemployment or fast real growth, increases the popularity of governments. Second, many assume that the electorate is *myopic*, or short-sighted, in evaluating economic conditions. An extreme version is that the electorate is concerned only with economic conditions at the time of elections. A more common assumption is that the electorate has no expectations about the future. The electorate does not fully understand the economy. Finally, politicians are taken to be *self-seeking manipulators* who mortgage the future for current electoral advantage. They show no concern for the welfare of the citizenry or their own long-term reputations. Whether evidence supports these theories is, of course, another question entirely.

Common core of the models

All political business cycle models have a common core, though they can be subclassified. There are three common arguments:

1. Governments aim to win elections. In order to win elections, they attempt to maximize votes.

2. Among economic outcomes, electors have preferences that are reflected in their voting behavior.

3. Governments can manipulate the economy to improve their chances of reelection.

These statements are controversial. Take the first. It would be surprising if politicians had no concern for winning elections, but this need not be their only or dominant motivation. Moreover, elected politicians are not the only actors who affect policy outcomes. The power of bureaucracies and the influence of party systems and the media constrain politicians. The assumption that citizens vote their economic policy preferences is also controversial. Finally, the degree of control over the economy is questionable, given uncertainties of timing and effects of interventions. These need not deter politicians from attempting an election-oriented economic policy, though they may impede its successful execution.

Table 1 represents variations in political business cycle models as dichotomies. How governments form policy is one difference. On the one hand (II, IV), *responsive* governments adopt the policy preferences of their supporters. *Strategic* governments (I, III) calculate policy to provide the greatest number of potential votes. This calculation may disregard the preferences of their own supporters. Strategic governments may appear responsive by attempting to shape popular preferences to the government's own policy preferences.

The second distinction relates to popular preferences. Some models (I, II) assume that popular preferences for economic outcomes are *fixed* for each individual elector, possibly by socioeconomic class. That is, electors' preferences do not evolve, and so available majorities do not shift. Other models (III, IV) assume the electorate has *varying* preferences. They vary because people change their minds about policy, whether or not politicians' persuasion causes the change. The formal consequence of varying popular preferences is some uncertainty about the "demand" for economic outcomes. The underlying assumptions have major empirical consequences. We take the quadrants one at a time. In each case we review first the theory, then evaluate the evidence.

Models of the political business cycle

Quadrant I: Strategic governments, fixed preferences

Theory. Quadrant I contains models that assume strategic governments and fixed electoral preferences. The best known of these models is after Nordhaus (1975). It is built around a Phillips curve analysis and deals with unemployment and inflation but is in fact quite general. It applies to any intervention whose effects come only with a lag. Such policies can be exploited by a government, provided it understands the economy and the electorate does not. Strategic governments exploit an asymmetric distribution of information resulting from institutionally defined incentives. Decisions are taken for short-run gains, and long-run adverse consequences are ignored.

It is worth discussing Nordhaus's model in some detail. It has two central conclusions. One is:

> Under conditions where voting is an appropriate mechanism for social choice, democratic systems will choose a policy on the long-run trade-off (between unemployment and inflation) that has lower unemployment and higher inflation than is optimal. (p. 178)

The other is:

Table 1

Models of Political Business Cycles

Electorate preferences	Government capability	
	Strategic	Responsive
Fixed	I	II
Varying	III	IV

The unemployment rate must be falling over the entire electoral regime. . . . immediately after an election the victor will raise unemployment to some relatively high level in order to combat inflation. As elections approach, the unemployment rate will be lowered. . . . (p. 184)

Because obvious difficulties surround an "immediate" postelection rise in unemployment to some high level, the second implication is weakened in empirical tests to be that unemployment should rise in the first half of an incumbency and fall in the second half.

In the model, an expectations-augmented Phillips curve relates inflation and unemployment:

$$I_t = f(u_t) + cv_t. \tag{1}$$

I_t (the rate of inflation) is a function of the contemporaneous level of unemployment (u_t) and expected inflation (v_t). The expected rate of inflation is a function of the difference between inflation and previous expectations. Expectations rise whenever actual inflation exceeds that expected. There is a short-term Phillips curve labeled S in Figure 1, and a long-term Phillips curve, labeled L.[1] The slope of the long-term curve is *steeper* than that of the short-term curve, though not vertical in the Nordhaus analysis. In the long term, inflation is responsive to unemployment because of the cumulative impact of expectations. In the short term, the inflationary cost of reductions in unemployment is relatively small.

On the political side, a government that has been democratically elected and has wide economic policy powers can use these powers to choose a level of unemployment for the economy on the short-run curve but *not* to alter the short-run trade-off during its incumbency. Incumbent politicians choose policies to maximize their votes at the next election. They are assumed to know the preferences of voters. Voters evaluate policies at the end of each incumbency on the basis of levels of inflation and unemployment. The evaluations result in incumbents receiving some proportion of the vote at any combination of unemployment and inflation. The proportion decreases as unemployment or inflation increases. The line connecting all combinations of inflation and unemployment giving rise to *some* specific vote percentage can be called an "iso-vote" line (examples are

Inflation

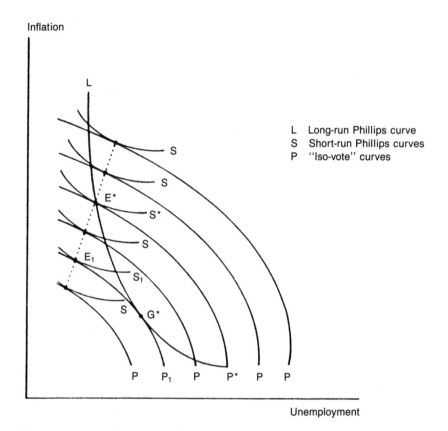

L   Long-run Phillips curve
S   Short-run Phillips curves
P   "Iso-vote" curves

Unemployment

Figure 1   **Expectations-Augmented Phillips Curve in the Nordhaus Model**

drawn in Figure 1). These "iso-vote" lines are assumed to be quasi-concave.

The government searches for combinations of inflation and unemployment that are *optimal* with respect to the popular vote function, subject to the economic constraint reflected in the Phillips curve. Nordhaus argues that the government chooses the point on the *short-run* Phillips curve tangent to the highest available "iso-vote" curve. In other words, unemployment is set to the value giving the highest possible number of votes. If S_1 is the relevant short-term Phillips curve, then E_1 is the point on the highest "iso-vote" curve. The government chooses E_1 as its policy, knowing it will receive P_1 percent of the votes and could do no better.

If E_1 lies to the left of the long-term Phillips curve, it represents a combination of unemployment and inflation that can be sustained only in the *short term* and will ultimately produce higher levels of inflation. The short-term Phillips curve must shift *up*, giving more inflation at any level of unemployment. Thus, E_1 will not be feasible at the next election. A new tangency point will be chosen. This will continue until the chosen policy E^* on the short-term Phillips curve S^* also lies on the long-term curve. If the first choice had been to the right of the long-term curve, subsequent choices would converge on E^* from above rather than from below.

There is a point G^* on the long-run curve which gives the maximum long-term level of support to the government. This is the most popular combination of inflation and unemployment *sustainable indefinitely*. E^* was reached by a series of decisions in which the future was entirely discounted and only the present considered. Thus, the government steers the economy to a higher level of inflation than if it chose the most popular point on the long-run trade-off.[2] This yields the first implication, that long-run inflation rates in democratic societies are higher than socially optimal. However, it follows not just from electoral considerations but also from economic management being treated as a series of short-run decisions, with the long term being discounted entirely.

The second implication is that unemployment must be continuously falling through the election period. This arises from discarding the static treatment outlined above in favor of a continuous model.[3] Now treated as a continuous optimization problem, attention is switched from decisions of government to the behavior over time of unemployment and inflation. Nordhaus does not show that the implication of higher long-term inflation follows from total future discounting in the continuous model, but it does. Nordhaus substitutes a specific welfare function (by an arbitrary but important assumption, it is quadratic in unemployment but linear in inflation) for the specification in Figure 1. He supplies an actual function for the $f(u)$ in equation (1) above (linear so that $I_t = a - bu_t + cv_t$). The problem is to maximize $-u^2 - dI$ (the welfare function, with two negatively valued economic states), subject to the constraint that $I_t = a - bu_t + cv_t$, where the welfare function is considered to be weighted more heavily close to the election but to carry no weight at all beyond the next election. It is then possible to deduce the optimal movement of unemployment over time. Its rate of change is shown to be everywhere negative *within* each election period. Since the rate of unemployment does not fall forever, it is raised immediately after each election and falls continuously until the next. Just how it is raised or how its continual fall is ensured is not clarified.

Unemployment falls throughout the incumbency because the future is totally discounted. Nordhaus himself points out that expectations of inflation in the economic evaluation underlying voting decisions alters the cycle and pulls the system toward the "golden rule" point or long-term vote-maximizing outcome. This myopic discounting of the future is very important since it guarantees that the government incurs no electoral penalty from inflation after the election.[4] *Myopia* describes a process in which expectations are derived entirely from observations of the past. Myopia has nothing to do with amnesia, the rate at which people forget the past. Any rate of memory decay is compatible with the myopic expectations Nordhaus uses in his model. Myopic expectations always underestimate accelerating inflation. This allows the government to escape any penalty at election time for the inflation which is about to occur. Any expectations which include extra information, whether about the tendency of inflation to accelerate at election time or about the role of unemployment in generating inflation, will undo the cycle if people vote their expectations as well as their observations of past inflation. Myopia in Nordhaus's model makes the question of expectations moot, for even if people did vote their expectations, these expectations contain only past observations. Of course, empirical support for the Nordhaus model would be evidence that people actually do vote myopically.

Evidence. Nordhaus does not present any estimates of his model. No suggestions are made about the origins of the welfare function, why it is quadratic in unemployment but linear in inflation, how its weights could be determined, or whether the actual values in the economic constraint matter. The only empirically contingent point is whether or not unemployment rates conform to the pattern implied by qualitative analysis of the continuous model, namely, that they should always fall. Thus, the model focuses entirely on the behavior of unemployment rates, not on the behavior of governments.

Nordhaus looked at interelection rates of unemployment in nine countries. He found the expected pattern of unemployment rates rising in the first half of incumbencies and falling in the second half in only three of the nine, Germany, the United States, and New Zealand. The substitute proposition that unemployment should simply be higher in the first half of incumbencies does no better. This formulation picks up support largely from the trend of declining unemployment in the United States in the 1960s. Other attempts also fail to find significant differences in unemployment rates between years of incumbencies (Golden and Poterba, 1980).

Moreover, of the nine countries, two of the three where the cycles appear to exist, Germany and the United States, have among the *lowest* long-term inflation. Germany is lowest of all in average inflation from 1951 to 1974, and the United States is second lowest. It is true that the assumption that the government treats economic policy decisions with a short-term horizon only entails that inflation would be higher than the "optimal" inflation produced under less extreme discounting of the future. It would be odd if those countries where inflation was higher than "optimal" were also those with the lowest inflation rates. Even if electorally induced cycles produced some extra inflation in these countries, they do not appear to have suffered from it. So the Nordhaus model fails in this additional sense. Its principal *suboptimality*, extra inflation, is also inconsistent with the evidence.

Do governments operate with a one-election time horizon? Alternatively, is the weight attached to economic conditions beyond the next election zero? G. D. MacRae's (1977) model empirically tests the assumption of myopia, contrasting it with the "strategic" hypothesis that governments maximize support over an indefinite time horizon. MacRae suggests that of four American administrations, in two cases policy was characterized by the assumption of electoral myopia and in two cases by strategic behavior. Alt's (1979) replication of the MacRae model for British administrations since 1951 produced no evidence at all of a political business cycle of either description in two of five administrations. In two of the other three cases, the indefinite time horizon hypothesis outperformed the myopic hypothesis, and in the final case both were equally plausible. British administrations may thus occasionally have practiced giving the electorate what the government thought the electorate wanted. There was no evidence that governments had ever attempted to steal reelection by taking advantage of the lag with which inflation follows reduced unemployment.

Quadrant II: Responsive governments, fixed preferences

Theory. Quadrant I assumed that a government was free to choose any combination of unemployment and inflation and derive support from it. Electors had fixed preferences for unemployment and inflation, but changes in economic outcomes would make them change party allegiance. If people are not so flexible, then political authorities cannot be unconstrained strategic agents. Their actions will be largely constrained by the preferences of their supporters. Authorities can still be optimizing and indeed vote-maximizing. The optimal decision will assume that the best they can do is to implement programmatically a set of policies on the basis of which they were elected.

Such "programmatic" behavior on the part of the political authorities in a competitive electoral system can be rational. It requires at least that each party's supporters have different but stable preferences over some policy alternatives. If a party's supporters can find alternative parties within the system to implement their preferences, responsiveness becomes likelier. Followers enforce it if they do not switch parties but abstain if their party did not implement their preferences, accepting short-term defeat in return for longer-term adherence of the party to its supporters' goals. The changes of economic priority which arise when there are partisan changes in incumbency will produce a "political business cycle." In this case, economic conditions will change after rather than before elections. The cycles will have a periodicity which is at least one interelection period long.[5]

Hibbs (1977, 1979, 1982a, 1982b) proposes a model of the political business cycle along these lines. Each country faces a Phillips curve trade-off between unemployment and inflation. The trade-offs faced by all countries are sufficiently similar to allow one to characterize long-run outcomes among countries as choices along such a trade-off curve. Left-wing parties' programs should place greater emphasis on providing high levels of employment. Countries with greater long-run socialist or left-party participation in government should have lower long-run unemployment and higher inflation than countries predominantly governed by right-of-center parties.

Hibbs presents evidence that this is so. For instance, in the 1960s Scandinavian countries, with predominantly socialist governments, had average annual inflation rates around 4 to 5 percent and unemployment rates of 1 to 2 percent whereas the United States and Canada, with little or no left-wing control of government, had inflation rates of 2 to 3 percent but unemployment rates around 5 percent. Such long-run characteristics could also result from economic-structural variations. Therefore, Hibbs provides a model of unemployment in both the United States and Britain which shows that partisan changes in incumbency in each country are accompanied by the predicted change in unemployment rate. The long-run or steady-state rate of unemployment under the Democrats is approximately 2.5 percentage points lower than under the Republicans. There is a similar kind of difference in unemployment rates between Labor and Conservatives of slightly less than 1 percent. Support for socialist parties is strongest among those in working-class occupational grades. Preferences for reduced unemployment and indeed the incidence of actual unemployment are greatest in these occupational classes. The working class is most hurt by unemployment and possibly less hurt by inflation. Their policy preferences for reduced unemployment at the cost of inflation correspond to their objective interests. They support left-wing parties which implement policies reflecting these preferences. Both short-run and long-run outcomes reflect these partisan differences.

Evidence. Hibbs's empirical conclusions have been widely, if not always fairly or usefully, criticized. The "cross-national Phillips curve" is a useful heuristic device, but it is not clear what economic theory underlies an international trade-off. Under the Bretton Woods system, no country could have lower long-run inflation that the United States unless either its currency appreciated against the dollar or its nontraded (service) industries' prices rose slower than those in the United States. Although there is clear contrast between the extreme cases Hibbs discusses, it is less clear how much information the curve gives about differences between countries in the middle of the curve. Moreover, it is a time-bound creature. As Figure 2 shows, the same countries displayed no systematic trade-off between unemployment and inflation over the next decade. This reflects varying domestic responses to major shocks and indeed changes in inflation under floating exchange rates. Perhaps the fixed exchange rate period of the late 1950s and 1960s was the only period in which countries actually can be seen as having had a choice along an inflation-unemployment frontier of the sort Hibbs describes.

Nevertheless, the underlying rank ordering of 1970s unemployment rates in Figure 2 is still much as it was in the 1960s, though Belgium and France have higher levels of unemployment. Hibbs is probably right to interpret these unemployment rates as reflecting structural characteristics and long-term labor market policies as well as the cumulative effects of short-term interventions.

N. Beck (1982) reestimates Hibbs's model of American unemployment rates and finds smaller differences between the parties, though the qualitative differences remain. Part of their dispute is technical.[6] However, differences in unemployment rates are greater between some incumbents of the same party than between many incumbents of opposite parties.

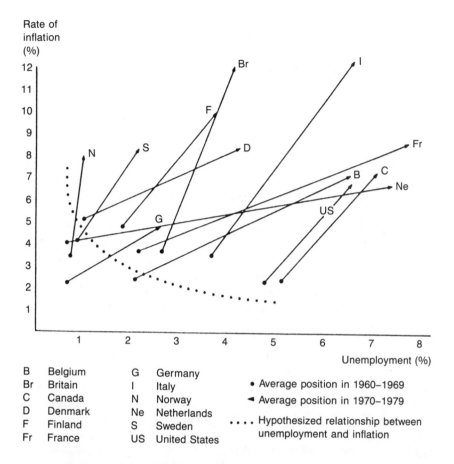

Figure 2 **Inflation and Unemployment in the 1960s and 1970s**

Source: OECD, Main Economic Indicators, 1960-1979.

In the postwar United States, only Truman and Johnson look like the Democrats described by Hibbs; similarly, only Ford really fits Hibbs's Republican pattern. Looking at the unemployment rates only, it would be quite hard to tell that Carter was a Democrat. . . . (N. Beck, 1982, p. 91)

It is surely no coincidence, given the changes in economic theory and institutions in the 1970s, that at the same time Carter was not acting like a traditional Democrat, the British Labor government in the late 1970s abandoned low unemployment as a target in favor of controlling inflation.

I do not think this [increase in unemployment] will be reduced for some time. . . . as long as we try to squeeze inflation out of the economy . . . this is one of

> the consequences we have to bear. . . . (Prime Minister Callaghan, quoted in the *London Times*, January 26, 1977)[7]

Party commitments to a core of policies are not invariant over long periods, certainly not in the face of major changes in economic theory and the international context.

Even the party differences in Britain are not well established by Hibbs's model. There are only three changes of incumbency in Britain in this period: 1951 (Conservatives take over), 1964 (Labor), 1970 (Conservatives). Estimates of party differences in his model depend largely on unemployment trends at these critical times. Britain is a small open economy. Its level of economic activity responds to world (or U.S.) trends. The U.S. economy was in an upswing after 1964 but was slowing down in 1952 and 1971. The first two postwar British Labor administrations were in office at the same time as the Truman and Johnson administrations, which Beck finds to be the two American administrations which most successfully produced low unemployment. If wars are removed from the American unemployment series, should not the effects of the U.S. economy be removed from the British series?

Hibbs argues that the rise of unemployment in Britain after 1966 should be ascribed to the reform of social benefits enacted in that year, which made earnings-related benefits available to the unemployed, reducing the personal economic cost of unemployment. Although this reform may have had some effect, 1966–1970 was also a period in which the Labor government had a consistently deflationary economic policy. This policy produced in 1969 and 1970 the last budget surpluses in recent British history and the highest levels of government revenue relative to national income and expenditure since 1955.[8] Ignoring the effects of this deflation—which the Wilson government acknowledged publicly but claimed was necessary to restore balance of payments equilibrium—weakens Hibbs's case. Reducing the supposed impact of social benefits on unemployment rates diminishes the estimated interparty differences.

Looking only at indicators like unemployment risks missing polical interventions whose effects were canceled out before working through to the ultimate targets. The Kennedy administration, as Beck notes, had little effect on unemployment but made an effort to reduce it. Their early strategy was built around the investment tax credit rather than orthodox Keynesian policy. Only after this policy failed to reduce unemployment were the Johnson tax cuts passed. Actual interventions require looking at the instruments rather than the targets of policy with models in which policymakers react systematically to the economy (see Golden and Poterba, 1980).

Parties' goals change even if the British parties maintain more ideological coherence than the "impermanent coalitions between the various sectors of society, with elections offering a choice between temporary alliances," which Beck describes in the American case. The next two quadrants discuss models of the political business cycle where popular preferences vary. First, however, a word in defense of Hibbs's model. Members of the British electorate differ along class and partisan lines over the importance of unemployment and inflation as issues, whether it is worth reducing unemployment if the cost is increased inflation, and what means should be used to fight inflation (Alt, 1979). In all cases Labor supporters display greater aversion to unemployment. We doubt whether any account of the steep rise of British unemployment from 6 to 12 percent between 1979 and 1981 will be written with no mention of the change to a Conservative incumbency. Thus, there is still some power in Hibbs's account even if his estimates do not clearly establish interparty differences in the earlier period of fixed exchange rates and consensus in economic management.

Quadrant III: Strategic governments, varying preferences

Theory. Electors may vary in their preferences according to circumstances, the presentation of circumstances in the media, or even in response to government persuasion. Tufte's model of the political business cycle contained in his book *Political Control of the Economy* (1978) exemplifies this case. We drop for the moment the idea that governments are constrained to respond to the preferences of a core of supporters. Suppose instead that governments have the latitude to carry out strategic macroeconomic manipulation. However, assume there are a variety of preferences which they could satisfy rather than known penalties being attached to particular outcomes.

Nothing as specific in its parameters and terms as the Nordhaus model is put forward. Indeed, Tufte has at different points in his book three distinct ideas about the political business cycle. In part of his work he uses Hibbs's fixed preference/responsiveness model. At another point he suggests a decision rule of "attack whatever problem the electorate considers most important" which is identical to Mosley's varying preference/responsiveness model (next section). His central assertion is that incumbent politicians seek to win elections by staging the most favorable possible conditions with respect to two key economic variables: real disposable incomes (that is, personal incomes net of taxes in constant prices) and the rate of unemployment. There are "accelerations" of real disposable incomes in election years. In the United States this gives a two-year cycle. Real disposable income always grows more quickly in the (even numbered) election year than in the year before. The rate of unemployment declines over the twelve to eighteen months before a presidential election. This is expected to produce a four-year cycle.

Electors are sufficiently discerning to respond to rates of change rather than levels. Popularity accrues to a *decline* in unemployment and *faster* real income growth in the election year regardless of previous levels. Policy choices do not require the optimizing calculations of the Nordhaus and MacRae models. Rather the model assumes that politicians have sufficient policy instruments to make any situation better in the year before an election. How do they do it? Tufte suggests two ways: taxation (particularly tax rates) and transfer payments. Exactly how these instruments are controlled is not elaborated, though in one place Tufte describes how a strong president can affect the timing of veterans' benefits and Social Security payments.

Since cycles in economic aggregates are observed rather than deduced from first principles of behavior, Tufte mobilizes a lot of quantitative evidence. He argues that: (1) accelerations of real disposable income occur more frequently in election years than nonelection years in nineteen of twenty-seven countries studied having elections between 1961–1972; (2) such accelerations were more common in the United States in election years from 1946–1976, at least provided the Eisenhower years are ignored;[9] (3) unemployment levels have been lower at election time than twelve to eighteen months before in six of eight recent presidential elections (again the Eisenhower incumbency—1956 and 1960—is deviant); (4) there are only a few years in which both unemployment and inflation have declined, but most of these are presidential election years; (5) increases in real disposable income in the United States are, on average, largest in election years when an incumbent president stands for reelection, slightly smaller in midterm election years, smaller still in presidential election years with no incumbent standing, and smallest of all in years with no election; (6) within-year increases in Social Security benefits tend to occur in election years whereas beginning-of-year increases occur in nonelection years; (7) unusually large increases in veterans' benefits occur in the fourth quarters of election years; (8) "windows" are created between Social Security increases in benefits (timed for before the election) and contributions (timed for after the election), with the 20 percent increase in benefits in October 1972 and consequent increase in contributions in January 1973 a prominent example; (9) transfer payments tend to "heap" such that in presidential election years with a strong president in the White House, there are peaks in payments for the last month (sometimes October, sometimes November) whose check would arrive before the election; and (10) the amount of currency in circulation has tended (again outside the Eisenhower years) to increase faster in the two years before a presidential election than in the two years after.

Evidence. Tufte's simultaneous concern for the outcomes and instruments of economic policy is a strong point. He deals not only with electorally timed movements in unemployment and incomes but also with how politicians bring these cycles about. The problem with Tufte's results is that more formal studies do not find the expected cyclical patterns. One weakness is his observational method. Many of Tufte's observed periodic contrasts require an "all other things being equal" assumption which cannot be sustained. Furthermore, many of his propositions rest on categorical judgments of what are quantitatively very small differences.

For instance, adding up cases in Tufte's Table [1] shows that (across all countries) income accelerations are a fifty-fifty bet in nonelection years but occur in fifty-eight of ninety or 64 percent of election years. But several of these countries do not have fixed election periods. If such governments choose to call elections at favorable opportunities, growth will coincide with elections. This does not entail political control of the economy. Only a dozen such cases make the overall difference between election and nonelection years disappear. Whether the unemployment series supports or rejects the hypothesis of declining rates before elections and rising rates after is frequently a marginal choice. For instance, Tufte claims post-1972 as a confirming case, although unemployment actually fell for a few months after the election, stayed below October-November 1972 levels for eighteen months, and only rose above them in September 1974. In the same way, he counts the *February* 1968 Social Security increase as "within-year" but the *January* 1965 increase counts as "beginning of the year." Long trends in unemployment cloud the picture further. Unemployment in the United States declined (because of fiscal policy and the Vietnam War) more or less continuously from 1961 to 1969, confirming several preelection cycle expectations on the way. His evidence on transfer payments is equally shaky. His "windows" certainly exist, but most of the largest ones occur far away from election times (Winters et al., 1981). While 1972 exemplifies "heaping," his figures for 1964 and 1970 do not conform to published Commerce Department data, and 1962, the only other supporting case, involves an extremely small difference in monthly levels of benefit (Brown and Stein, 1982). Finally, nearly all the expected relationships failed to materialize between 1976 and 1980. Real incomes fell before the election. Unemployment fell continuously after the 1976 election and through 1979 but rose before the 1980 election.

Not all of Tufte's evidence can or should be discredited. Sometimes there is observable evidence of a cycle and sometimes not. The Eisenhower and Carter years are disconfirming cases. The Nixon years (especially 1972) and less clearly but possibly the Truman years (especially 1948) in the United States and the Conservatives' 1955 budget in Britain appear to be supporting cases. The Kennedy-Johnson years offered sustained rather than cyclic economic expansion. Care must be taken to demonstrate the existence of electoral cycles independent of trends. The Ford years are overshadowed by response to the oil crisis of 1973, though 1976 like 1964 does not refute the hypothesis of an electoral business cycle. Preelection stimulation of the economy could be a strategy which may or may not be adopted, but no theory says why the strategy sometimes is and sometimes is not adopted.

Something which occasionally works is an unsatisfactory model of the politics of economic policy. Eclecticism is part of Tufte's problem. He has at least four behavioral rules for the authorities (support your core clients, do whatever the public finds most important, get unemployment down for the presidential election, and get real incomes up for any election) with no lexicographic ordering among them. Conflict between them is clearly possible. Whatever happens can probably be interpreted as supporting one of these rules.

Finally, Tufte's account is also institutionally inconsistent. He stresses presidential influence rather than Congress's. Four presidential elections come closest

to sustaining his case—1948, 1964, 1972, and 1976. In at least three of these—
1948, 1964 and 1976—tax changes rather than transfer payments created the
economic stimulation. The 1964 tax cut came in an election year because Congress resisted the tax cuts Kennedy sought earlier. In 1976, the tax cut which
passed Congress was larger than the one President Ford had sought. In 1948, a
Republican Congress passed the tax cut over Democratic President Truman's
veto! If Congress is sometimes so important, why not the rest of the time?

Quadrant IV: Responsive governments, varying preferences

Theory. Suppose we drop the assumption of strategic governments and assume that governments only respond to conditions and popular preferences but
that these preferences vary from time to time. Mosley's (1976) political model of
economic policymaking allows motivations of policymakers to transcend the
prescriptions of economic advice. His model involves "satisficing." *Satisficing*
models, in contrast to *optimizing* models, have at least one of three main characteristics: information is taken to be limited and costly, preferences over alternative outcomes are partial and not necessarily transitive, and the desire for goods is
satiable and may reflect subjective levels of aspiration. There are conditions
under which such behavior is nevertheless still optimal decision-making. Though
Mosley does not develop this point, we will return to it in the next chapter.

In Mosley's model the government and electorate are crisis-averters. The
government does not fine-tune or steer the economy toward long-term goals. The
actual workings of the economy are only relevant when some economic variable
goes into "crisis." Crises only reflect negatively valued states. The electorate is
aware of the economy (or so the government assumes) only when things are
sufficiently bad. Such concern adversely affects the government's reelection
prospects. Governments do not benefit by doing particularly well in economic
management. The only political purpose of economic policy is thus to steer the
economy out of crisis. Mosley claims his model describes accurately how governments actually involve themselves in economic policy. In his model governments
consider at most one target at a time, unlike the simultaneous optimization of the
Nordhaus model. Any relevant target is identified by popular concern, which
varies with the severity of bad economic conditions. Intermittent interventions
characterize policymaking, which is geared neither to core constituency preferences nor the electoral calendar.

British bank rate, tax rate, and public investment changes identify crises from
1946 to 1971. Changes of more than £100 million in tax revenues (at 1946 prices)
or deviations of more than 50 percent from trend (investment) or 20 percent from
trend (bank rate) are the thresholds. Years in which at least two of these three
instruments had above-threshold changes are defined as crises. Mosley selects
unemployment and the balance of payments as the targets which caused changes
in the instruments. The selection rests on regressing changes in taxes and public
investment on deviations of unemployment and the balance of payments from

trend. Mosley (1978) extends the model to the electorate by considering whether government popularity is particularly affected by economic crises. If government popularity is only affected by economic crisis, it is appropriate for the government to follow a satisficing strategy.

Evidence. Mosley's model contains an important insight into the sporadic nature of interventions and the variability of popular preferences. Cycles could arise from government (possibly rationally) pursuing a strategy of considering only one target at a time and for a substantial period. Such behavior is indeed optimal under reasonable assumptions about politicians' intervention costs and the uncertainty of popular demand for economic outcomes. Cycles could then follow directly from optimizing behavior but without Nordhaus's extra assumption that the government tries to exploit an information advantage or Hibbs's assumption that politicians rigidly serve the fixed interests of their core constituencies.

Mosley starts from observed interventions. His empirical problem is therefore to estimate the decision threshold. Deviations from trends do this badly. Consider the case of "threshold" levels of inflation. Mosley regresses inflation on a time trend and claims the fitted values give levels of inflation which were satisfactory at the time. But only the high levels of inflation of the mid-1970s make many of the earlier years appear not to be crisis periods. Trend values of British inflation calculated over a period including the 18 to 25 percent levels of 1974–1976 are going to be substantially higher across the 1960s than would be the case if the trend calculation stopped even in 1973. For instance, the inflation rate in the final quarter of 1964 is 4.4 percent. This is above the trend value of inflation for that quarter calculated from 1955 to 1964, which is 2.3 percent. Indeed, inflation at the end of 1964 exceeds its trend values until the calculation period includes 1974. But in Mosley's model inflation was only satisfactory in 1964 because of the higher inflation experienced ten full years later! Satisfaction cannot reflect events many years ahead and should be affected by what has happened recently. A moving average of recent inflation levels would be a better guide to satisfactory levels. Any such formulation produces a different set of crises from Mosley's. An a priori model of "acceptable standards," without which there are no testable predictions, is needed.

Summary

No one could read the political business cycle literature without being struck by the lack of supporting evidence. There must be cases where politicians have undertaken electorally motivated interventions. It is difficult to imagine politicians not exploiting some extra information or other resources. But while this clearly happens, and happens particularly clearly in some cases, such cycles may be trivial in comparison with other economic fluctuations. Incumbents may be able to give themselves significant advantages relative to challengers. But the ability to intervene economically is only one of many possible incumbency advantages. The existence of such advantages may not make anything worse overall or in the long run.

Available trade-offs as well as the goals of different administrations appear to vary considerably, contrary to fixed preference models. Models of movements of the ultimate targets of policy like unemployment have not been empirically confirmed. On the evidence we cannot say whether this is because the authorities did not attempt a political business cycle or tried but failed. This distinction requires looking systematically at how policymakers respond to their economic environment. The next chapter discusses models which explain economic policy as a systematic set of responses to economic conditions, built around the core of policy optimizing.

Notes

1. A natural rate of unemployment implies that there is no unique long-run trade-off between unemployment and inflation. This would be depicted in Figure 1 by a vertical line. The long-run trade-off in Nordhaus's analysis is not vertical, though the cumulative impact of expectations means that the inflationary cost of reducing unemployment is greater in the long run than in the short run.

2. Nordhaus refers to a social welfare optimum point in between E^* and G^*, implying that some rate of discounting the future *is* appropriate, but he does not clarify why or how much.

3. It is just as well that the first treatment of the problem is discarded. In no recognizable institutional framework do governments make one policy choice per incumbency. The static and continuous models are not logically inconsistent. The short-term/long-term Phillips curve is present in both. In the continuous model, the short-term curve has slope b whereas the long-term curve has slobe $b/1 - c$ (steeper if c is less than 1). There is also one major intervention per incumbency, driving up unemployment after the election rather than taking an optimal choice along the short-term Phillips curve. In the continuous model, it is less clear where the suboptimality arises. The "extra" inflation does not come from inconsistencies between short-term and long-term tradeoffs. The inflation that results from lowered unemployment comes only after some delay, allowing the creation of a "window" during which unemployment and inflation are temporarily low. Because this window occurs when the welfare function is most heavily weighted and because the increase in unemployment (and inflation from the previous low unemployment) come later in a more discounted future, the system produces more inflation than if the weights were evenly distributed throughout time into the indefinite future. Some of the cycle, as well as the extra inflation, arises from Nordhaus's wholly arbitrary choice of making inflation linear but unemployment quadratic in the welfare function.

4. The Nordhaus model does not say whether myopia is a desirable characteristic of government policy, simply the way governments make decisions, a feature of the electorate in evaluating economic policies, or a feature the government imputes to the electorate's evaluation, or what. It is simply present in the system.

5. We should note at this point that there is a model, owing largely to the work of Frey (1978) which subsumes both quadrants I and II and also provides a criterion by which to decide which sort of behavior the government will adopt. In particular, he argues that governments which feel secure about their reelection prospects will be responsive whereas governments which are not secure will become strategic.

6. Beck argues that Hibbs may have misspecified the underlying process of unemployment rate changes, thereby obtaining estimates of the adjustment speed of unemployment which were excessively slow. On the other hand, Beck omits the effects of wars, which are hardly economic policies, and his discussion appears to confuse instantaneous and cumulative impacts of partisan changes.

7. We believe there was a major policy shift in this period, even if one does not always wish to take politicians' pronouncements at face value. Some might argue that Callaghan's statement was a strategic announcement in the light of Labor's need to shore up the support of the financial community in order to secure a massive loan from the IMF in 1976–1977. It seems at least as likely, given that under a floating exchange rate regime the need for such a loan is questionable, that Labor's seeking a loan with tight economic policy conditions attached from the IMF was a strategic attempt to shift the blame for contractionary policies onto a third party.

8. This underscores the problems which accrue to Hibbs's decision to model the effects of party changes as occurring only at the beginning of incumbencies. The effects of any major policy changes (midterm U-turns) at other times are absorbed more by the parameters of the underlying economic series and less by the party impact parameters.

9. Without omitting the Eisenhower years, "accelerations" become a fifty-fifty proposition both in and out of election years.

References

Alt, J. E. *The Politics of Economic Decline*. Cambridge: Cambridge University Press, 1979.

Beck, N. "Parties, Administrations, and American Macroeconomic Outcomes." *American Political Science Review* 76 (1982):83–93.

Brown, T., and A. Stein. "The Political Economy of National Elections. *Comparative Politics* 14 (1982):479–97.

Frey, B. *Modern Political Economy*. London: Martin Robertson, 1978.

Golden, D., and J. Poterba. "The Price of Popularity: The Political Business Cycle Reexamined." *American Journal of Political Science* 24 (1980):696–714.

Hibbs, D. "Political Parties and Macroeconomic Policy." *American Political Science Review* 71 (1977):1467–87.

————. Letter. *American Political Science Review*. 73 (1979):185–90.

————. "The Dynamics of Political Support for American Presidents among Occupational and Partisan Groups." *American Journal of Political Science* 26 (1982):312–32.

————. "Economic Outcomes and Political Support for British Governments Among Occupational Classes: A Dynamic Analysis." *American Political Science Review* 76 (1982):259–79.

MacRae, G. D. "A Political Model of the Business Cycle." *Journal of Political Economy* 85 (1977):239–63.

Mosley, P. "Towards a Satisficing Theory of Economic Policy." *Economic Journal* 86 (1976):59–72.

————. "Images of the Floating Voter, or the 'Political Business Cycle,' Revisited." *Political Studies* 26 (1978):375–94.

Nordhaus, W. "The Political Business Cycle." *Review of Economic Studies* 42 (1975):169–90.

Tufte, E. *The Political Control of the Economy*. Princeton: Princeton University Press, 1978.

Winters, R., C. Johnson, P. Nowosadko, and J. Rendini. "Political Behavior and American Public Policy: The Case of the Political Business Cycle." In *Handbook of Political Behavior*, vol. 5, edited by S. Long. New York: Plenum Publishing, 1981.

4B. Government Growth

The role of government in the economy has increased drastically in all the developed countries in the last century. Many functions once performed by the family, nonprofit institutions, and industry are now considered the responsibility of government. Although government has grown less in the United States than in most other countries, government spending as a share of all economic activity has increased dramatically—from 7.3% in 1902, and 23.1% in 1950, to 34.4% in 1984; and, contrary to popular belief, this growth has continued under the Reagan Administration.

Ever since this trend became clear in the 1890s, academics have been producing theories to explain it. In 1889 Adolph Wagner advanced two theories that continue to dominate the field. One held that the increasing complexity of social life increased the number of what economists later came to call *externalities*, situations in which, in the absence of government action, individuals had incentives to act in ways that would harm the social whole. The other held that as income increased, people would satisfy their basic needs for those things (such as food and clothing) that are most easily provided by the free market and would demand more public goods (such as defense and education), which are the purview of government.

While Wagner's theories remain important, a vast number of other explanations have since been offered. These include the well-known contributions of Baumol and Oates (1967, 1975) (the price of government goods rises faster than private goods because of slower productivity improvements in the government sector); Peacock and Wiseman (1961) (citizens' willingness to bear taxes increases in wartime and stays up after wars, allowing greater postwar spending); and Wildavsky (1975) (there is a natural tendency to small steady increases in government spending).

In recent years three major trends are noticeable in the burgeoning literature. One is a breaking down of government spending into its component parts, with many arguing that different explanations are needed for different kinds of government spending (Fischer and Kamlet 1984). A second is the contention, put forward by Beck (1979) and Alt and Crystal (1983), for example, that nontransfer government spending is *not* growing after all, when one allows for the fact that the cost of government services is increasing faster than the cost of other goods. A third, exemplified by our final reading, is an attempt to reduce the number of explanations by testing them against one another to see which are truly important and which explain only insignificant amounts of change. Finally, there is some attempt being made to link particular theories to the particular revenue or spending category they should best explain, in order to test them more accurately (Ostrom and Marra 1986).

The reading by Peacock and Wiseman in this section outlines both Wagner's ideas and the authors' own fascinating theory that wars lead to sharp increases in government spending because they generate an increased willingness to pay taxes. The reading by David Cameron is an attempt to take many of the more recent explanations of government growth and test them against one another. Cameron argues that the domestic reasons usually cited for government growth are less important than international factors.

For further reading

The classic books in this area are Adolph Wagner's *Finanzwissenschaft* and Peacock and Wiseman's *The Growth of Public Expenditure in the United Kingdom*. A good early review of the literature is Daniel Tarchys's article "The Growth of Public Expenditures: Nine Modes of Explanation." A recent, somewhat crude test of the degree to which these theories explain government growth in the United States can be found in David Lowery and William Berry's article "The Growth of Government in the United States: An Empirical Assessment of Competing Explanations." The most comprehensive recent reviews of the literature are Patrick Larkey *et al.*, "Theorizing About the Growth of Government: A Research Assessment," and the last few chapters of James Alt and Alec Crystal's *Political Economics*.

Bibliography

Alt, James E. and K. Alec Crystal, *Political Economics* (Berkeley, Ca.: University of California Press, 1983).
Baumol, W.J. "Macro Economics of Unbalanced Growth," *American Economic Review* 57 (1967): 415–26.
Baumol, W.J. and W.E. Oates, *The Theory of Environmental Policy* (Englewood Cliffs, N.J.: Prentice Hall, 1975).
Beck, Morris. "Public Sector Growth: A Real Perspective," *Public Finance* 34 (1979): 313–56.
Fischer, Gregory W. and Mark S. Kamlet, "Explaining Presidential Priorities: The Competing Aspiration Levels Model of Macrobudgetary Decision Making," *American Political Science Review* 78 (June 1984): 356–71.

Larkey, Patrick D., Chandler Stolp and Mark Winer, "Theorizing About the Growth of Government: A Research Assessment," *Journal of Public Policy* 1 (May 1981): 157–220.

Lowery, David and William D. Berry, "The Growth of Government in the United States: An Empirical Assessment of Competing Explanations," *American Journal of Political Science* 27 (November 1983): 665–94.

Ostrom, Charles W. and Robin F. Marra, "U.S. Defense Spending and the Soviet Estimate," *American Political Science Review* 80 (September 1986): 819–42.

Peacock, Alan and Jack Wiseman, *The Growth of Public Expenditure in the United Kingdom* (Princeton, N.J.: Princeton University Press, 1961).

Tarschys, Daniel, "The Growth of Public Expenditures: Nine Modes of Explanation," *Scandinavian Political Studies* 10 (1975): 9–31.

Wagner, Adolph, *Finanzwissenschaft*, 1883. Portions of this work have been translated and reprinted as "Three Extracts on Public Finance," in R. A. Musgrave and Alan T. Peacock, eds., *Classics in the Theory of Public Finance* (London: MacMillan, 1962).

Wildavsky, Aaron, *Budgeting: A Comparative Theory of Budgetary Processes* (Boston: Little Brown, 1975).

4B.1. The Growth of Public Expenditures in the United Kingdom

ALAN T. PEACOCK and JACK WISEMAN

In this reading from their classic book, Peacock and Wiseman outline a fascinating two-part theory to explain the growth of government in Britain. In normal times, they argue, government spending rises roughly in line with the expansion of the economy. Taxes rise, but because incomes also rise, people pay roughly the same percent of their income in taxes. Taxpayers are generally unwilling to allow government to increase this percent, and this prevents government expenditures from rising faster than economic growth.

However, in periods of major dislocation, especially during wars, people are willing to pay higher taxes to help their country. If the emergency lasts several years, people become accustomed to higher tax rates. When the emergency is over, tax rates may fall somewhat, but they will remain above the levels obtaining when the emergency began.

This theory was formulated to explain the pattern of government growth in Britain, but it has since been applied to other countries, including the United States. While few analysts think it explains all of government growth, many consider that it explains a substantial part of it. The reader should note that if this theory is correct, we should expect tax levels after major wars to be considerably higher than before them. This appears to be true in the United States, although it could be for other reasons.

Approaches to interpretation of expenditure growth

At present, there are few fields of applied economic study which lack some useful general, albeit frequently incomplete, frame of reference; for example, there are plenty of business cycle theories to test against the facts. But it is difficult to find

Reprinted with permission of the National Bureau of Economic Research, Inc., from *The Growth of Public Expenditures in the United Kingdom* by Alan T. Peacock and Jack Wiseman (Princeton, N.J.: Princeton University Press, 1961), pp. xxii–xxxi, 44 and 49 (with deletions).

theories of public expenditure that explain rather than justify or condemn the facts of expenditure growth.

It is obvious why attempts to provide a satisfactory general theory of government economic behavior, or of collective behavior in the provision of public goods, should run into difficulties. To be general, such a theory must inevitably become highly abstract. Consider the attempt by Pigou to reduce the problem to manageable proportions by assuming that the government was a "unitary being," capable of determining the "correct level" of government expenditure by reference to the marginal principle.[1] In reality, governments are complex organisms whose functions and objectives may change greatly even over short periods of time. If any general theory is to be useful, it must somehow take these things into account.

In other contexts, where economic analysis requires that some recognition be given to the role of the public sector, government is usually treated as an exogenous factor outside the particular model's area of mutual interdependence, or is incorporated into it by postulating simple relationships between such magnitudes as government expenditure and the other variables in the model. In the latter case, the relationship assumed appears usually to be determined by analytical convenience rather than by the facts. From our present point of view, such a procedure has little or no value.

A somewhat different approach—at one time much discussed, but now referred to only in textbooks on public finance—is Adolph Wagner's attempt at the turn of the century to relate government expenditure growth to economic development. Briefly, Wagner's "law" asserts that government expenditures in any society will grow at a faster rate than community output. It was not expected necessarily to be valid for all time, but was certainly believed relevant both to the periods that Wagner studied and to the near future, which includes a large part of our own period. Wagner adduced a number of reasons for the existence of his "law," concerned not only with the nature of the state but also with such things as the essential complementarity of demand for and supply of private and public goods. In our view, Wagner's general approach seems more productive than those discussed above. Since, however, we do not accept it entirely, a brief summary of his argument may be a useful preliminary to the explanation of our own position.

Starting from observable facts in a number of countries, Wagner asks what general causes there might be for a rising trend in public expenditures. He divides expenditures into four broad groups and, considering each in turn, produces reasons why the rate of growth of expenditures in the group should be faster than the rate of growth of community output. The arguments are held to be valid irrespective of the political and social nature of the society concerned; the more rapid rate of growth of public spending is inherent in the nature of the public economy.

On the positive side, Wagner's approach starts from the facts and tries to explain them. This appeals to us more than other analyses which, while logically more satisfying, have no relevance to the facts. Further, Wagner draws attention to the importance of the permanent influences upon public spending and to the effect of the increasing complexity of economic life upon the necessary functions of government.

Against this, Wagner's argument suffers from two serious defects. First, he adopts an organic theory of the state which we do not believe to be superior to other explanations of the character of the state, or to be equally applicable to different societies. Second, Wagner's interest is in the secular trend of public expenditures. There are other aspects of the development of public expenditures, such as the time pattern of expenditure growth, which seem to us equally significant.

Our own approach acknowledges the influences to which Wagner directs attention, but does not regard them as inevitably causing expenditures to grow faster than GNP in all societies or at all times. Indeed, if there are generalizations to be made about the relation between public expenditures and GNP, they should be concerned with the characteristics of social and economic change that require examination, and not with the "inevitable" results of such change. Also, we do not confine our attention to secular change, as Wagner did, but also consider (and attempt to explain) the time pattern of expenditure growth to be observed in the British statistics. We believe that the hypothesis we offer about this time pattern may be of some value for the explanation of the behavior of public expenditures. Finally, we do not base our discussion upon any all-embracing theory of the state; our sole "political" propositions are that governments like to spend more money, that citizens do not like to pay more taxes, and that governments need to pay some attention to the wishes of their citizens.

Working hypotheses developed in this study

It is fundamental to our thesis that decisions about public expenditure are taken politically, and so can be influenced through the ballot box or by whatever media citizens use to bring pressure to bear upon the government. Political choices about the use of resources differ from choices made through the market system. In particular, citizens can have ideas about desirable public expenditure which are quite different from, and perhaps incompatible with, their ideas about reasonable burdens of taxation.

When societies are not being subjected to unusual pressures, people's ideas about tolerable burdens of taxation, translated into ideas of reasonable tax rates, tend also to be fairly stable. Fixed, if low, rates of taxation are obviously compatible with growing public expenditure if real output is growing, so that there may be some connection between the rate of growth of real output and the rate of growth of public expenditure. Much more rapid rates of expenditure growth are unlikely; in settled times, notions about taxation are likely to be more influential than ideas about desirable increases in expenditure in deciding the size and rate of growth of the public sector. There may thus be a persistent divergence between ideas about desirable public spending and ideas about the limits of taxation. This divergence may be narrowed by large-scale social disturbances, such as major wars. Such disturbances may create a displacement effect, shifting public revenues and expenditures to new levels. After the disturbance is over new ideas of tolerable tax levels emerge, and a new plateau of expenditure may be reached, with public expenditures again taking a broadly constant share of gross national product, though a different share from the former one.

This displacement effect has two aspects. People will accept, in times of crisis, methods of raising revenue formerly thought intolerable, and the acceptance of new tax levels remains when the disturbance has disappeared. It is harder to get the saddle on the horse than to keep it there. Expenditures which the government may have thought desirable before the disturbance, but which it did not then dare to implement, consequently become possible. At the same time, social upheavals impose new and continuing obligations on governments both as the aftermath of functions assumed in wartime (e.g., payments of war pensions, debt interest, reparation payments) and as the result of changes in social ideas. Wars often force the attention of governments and peoples to problems of which they were formerly less conscious—there is an "inspection effect," which should not be underestimated.

Alongside the displacement effect, there is another influence, called here the concentration process. It is concerned not so much with changes in the total volume of public expenditures as with changes in the responsibility for such expenditures. In many societies, the functions of government are shared between a central authority and other (state and local) authorities whose powers may be protected by statute (as in legal federations) or conferred by the central government. In such countries local autonomy usually has many defenders, and its preservation is frequently a matter of political importance. At the same time, economic development produces changes in the technically efficient level of government, and also produces demands for equality of treatment (e.g., in services such as education) over wider geographical areas. These opposing pressures are reflected in the relative evolution of the expenditures undertaken at different levels of government. Clearly, this evolution is distinct from the displacement effect, since the forces just described operate in normal as well as in disturbed times. Nevertheless, given the political importance of local autonomy and the barrier it may create to change, periods of displacement are also going to be periods of interest from the viewpoint of the concentration process.

There are subsidiary aspects of this analysis not considered in detail here. For example, we do not assert that social disturbances inevitably produce lasting upward changes in government expenditure, nor do we suggest that the more permanent influences on the behavior of government (such as population change) can be ignored. We do suggest that, given a period when increasing state activity has been the rule rather than the exception and in which social disturbances have occurred, the concept of a displacement effect helps to explain the time pattern by which the expenditure growth takes place, and that no explanation that ignores it can be very satisfactory.

We believe these concepts provide a means of profitable organization of study of the statistics of the evolution of public expenditures, by use of which we can obtain some understanding of the processes of change. As a corollary, we believe it to provide a useful approach to that neglected aspect of economic history concerned with the evolution of fiscal systems. An explanation follows of our use of these ideas in the examination of the British statistics, and of our results.

Use of conceptual framework for examination of British statistics

Our approach must incorporate examination of the time pattern of expenditure growth as well as consideration of the secular trend of public expenditures. At the same time, it must take into account both the displacement effect upon expenditures of periods of social disturbance (here the periods of the two world wars) and other more "permanent" influences (such as those suggested by Wagner) that may have affected the development of public expenditures.

We have tried to meet these requirements, first, by examining the other factors that might have affected public spending during the period, and then by eliminating these from the total expenditure series and considering how far the displacement idea is capable of explaining the data so adjusted. We then deal with the behavior of expenditures classified by responsible authority (the concentration effect) and with the expenditures of nationalized industries. [Our] final chapter considers methods of projecting future British government expenditure.

We have already pointed out that the curve of total government expenditures (in current money terms) shows a peak and rising plateau pattern, which suggests that the growth in expenditures has come about through upward displacements in the periods of war (See Figure 1). Our first task is to see whether this inference is destroyed when we take account of the more permanent influences. Two such influences, population and price changes, can be disposed of easily. The growth in population from the turn of the century until the present day has been about 22 per cent, which is certainly slower then the absolute rate of growth in government expenditure in money terms. Moreover, the irregular time pattern associated with the incidence of wars still remains in the statistics of government expenditure per head. Further, although there are many difficulties associated with the elimination of price changes, the peaks and plateaus still occur when the influence of price changes has also been removed. This elimination of population and price changes, however, reveals the real rate of growth of public expenditures per head of population to be much slower than the rate of growth of total money spending (See Figure 2).

Another possible influence might be the business cycle as manifested in changes in the level of employment. But we show that, while there may be short-term increases in the ratio of government expenditure to GNP when there is a considerable rise in the unemployment index (particularly in the 1930's), no

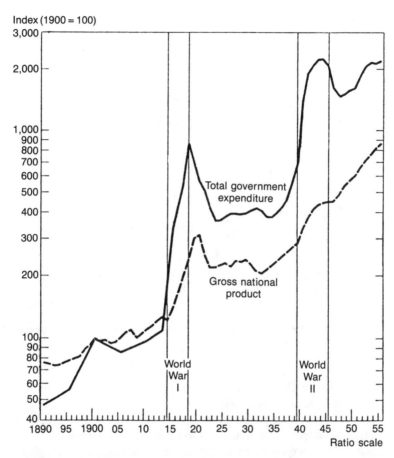

Figure 1 **Indexes of Total Government Expenditure and Gross National Product, at Current Prices, 1890–1955**

permanent upward shift in government expenditure can plausibly be attributed to the cycle. This is not to say that the Great Depression may not have had a profound influence upon attitudes toward public intervention, but rather that any such influence is not manifested in a permanent shift in public spending related to the periods of unemployment. It is possible to conclude, then, that the "permanent" factors influencing the level of government spending cannot satisfactorily explain the pattern of growth in public expenditures. We must look elsewhere.

Upward displacement of government expenditure has come during and after two major wars. The next possibility to consider, therefore, is how far the growth in expenditure can be explained simply as the direct and inevitable consequence of war for the continuing level of government spending in the postwar periods. Wars clearly affect public expenditures outside the immediate period of hostilities. We also need to consider the influence of peacetime spending on defense, which

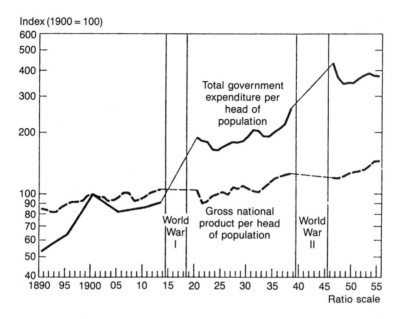

Figure 2 **Indexes of Government Expenditure and Gross National Product, per Head of Population, at 1900 Prices, 1890–1955**

shares some common characteristics with the last group, but is sufficiently differ-ent to require separate examination.

We cannot know what government expenditures would have been in some hypothetical situation in which no wars had occurred. Nevertheless, if we find that ''war-related'' expenditures cannot account entirely for the displacement effect, we shall know that war itself cannot provide a complete explanation of the growing size of public expenditures. In fact, we find that as the influence of different types of war-related expenditure is cumulatively removed (even includ-ing peacetime defense expenditures, not specifically war related), the residual expenditures of government continue to show the peak and plateau sequence.

We can now examine the displacement effect over the period of the two wars in more detail. We begin by breaking down the national statistics; a classification by functional and economic categories gives insight into the changes that occurred at these times, and directs our attention, among other things, to the growing impor-tance of social welfare spending. But the statistics cannot tell the whole story. Their value in the form just described is to guide us toward the facts of history that have been significant in encouraging the growth of public expenditures. The short survey which follows picks out some of those facts.

About the changed possibilities of government spending that have resulted from the two wars there can be little doubt. The exigencies of war produced significant improvements in tax administration, under the compulsion to increase government revenues. These changes, which would have been politically impossible earlier, were borne without protest. More to the point, the new burdens and methods became a lasting feature of British society.[2]

The government came out of the two wars, then, with the possibility of undertaking public expenditures on a much wider scale than before. But why should it wish to do so? There are two reasons, of the general kind earlier elaborated, and to which our statistical classifications direct attention.

In the first place, there is reason to believe that ideas about "desirable" expenditures and about "tolerable" taxation did begin to diverge over the period. From at least the time of the election of the Liberal Government of 1906, there was growing agreement about the desirability of increased public expenditure, particularly for purposes of social welfare. At the same time, the extension of the franchise began to increase the political power of those with most to gain from increased spending on social services. Also, there were important changes in the character of Treasury control of expenditure; we count it to the credit of our approach that it has forced this neglected aspect of British fiscal history before our attention.

As we should expect, however, these developments give a less than complete picture. They provide a part of the explanation of the secular growth in public spending, but tell us little about the time pattern of growth, and particularly about the effect of wars in changing social ideas. The second group of reasons for the growth of British Government expenditure, then, concerns those developments that relate to periods of war; all we can do here is to illustrate how the concept of displacement provides a useful guide to the relevant and important facts of history.

As major wars have come more and more to affect all sections of the community, both through demands of the military services and through such things as air raids on the homeland, the lasting social effects of war have become more profound. In the first place, wars generate an "inspection process"; the emergency brings the government and the citizens new knowledge about the nature of society. This phenomenon has roots in the past; it was the Napoleonic Wars which first laid bare the deficiencies in education of the "lower orders." More recent wars have been the means of directing attention to deficiencies not only in education but also in health services and housing conditions. At the same time, war produces a feeling of community, encouraging support for extensions of the public sector increasingly as its effects come to be more directly felt by the whole community. Indeed, as Titmuss has shown, provision of social services in World War II became an integral part of the British war effort and war aims.[3] The development of the National Health Service was thus the immediate outcome of wartime bombing which made the replacement of voluntary hospital services a necessity, and also the response to a community desire for continuing provision of state health services on a larger scale. . . .

Bearing on future research

It is appropriate to conclude with a consideration of the possible bearing of our study on future research. To reiterate our general position: We are not trying to formulate some general "law" which governs the growth of public expenditure in all circumstances. Nor do we believe that our concepts of displacement and concentration will be equally significant, in all countries and at all times, and relative to the "permanent" influences on expenditure growth, as guides to the evolution of public spending. Not all countries have been equally affected by social disturbances, and not all countries have the same political system. Nevertheless, we feel that the general approach, using these concepts alongside the facts about absolute expenditure growth and its historical time pattern, provides a useful technique for imposing order upon the study of government expenditure generally. Indeed, we feel sufficiently confident of the value of our approach to have embarked on a comparative analysis of a number of other countries, using the same general technique.[4] It is perhaps of particular interest to compare our conclusions with those reached in recent studies of government expenditure growth in the United States.

We can draw upon four recent studies.[5] Most of the authors rely upon the *Historical Statistics of the United States, 1789–1945, 1949*,[6] and the Department of Commerce national income series, which show only selected years for the period before 1929. The exception is Kendrick, who is concerned solely with the federal government, which played a much smaller role than the British central government did in the overall development of public expenditures in the same period. All these studies point to the importance of the two World Wars as influences upon the growth and structure of government expenditures. Kendrick notes the same plateau effect with reference to federal expenditures, and Musgrave and Culbertson show that war-related expenditures cannot account entirely for the trend increase in expenditure.

Most interesting from our point of view is the study of Colm and Helzner. These writers demonstrate the importance of war in the evolution of United States expenditure patterns. They note that if defense expenditure and social insurance are excluded from consideration, the relative proportions of the remaining federal and state expenditures have not altered over the period, but as a result of war—and this is interesting in view of British experience—the distribution of tax receipts has shifted in favor of the federal government. Moreover, their explanation of government expenditure changes, while placing much more emphasis on the changing structure of the economy accompanied by spectacular urban development, is similar. They state that "the traditional resistance to central government control has weakened only in time of war or serious depression. Thus, government functions do not always respond gradually to the needs of an industrial and urban (suburban) society. An increase in government activity or responsibility often depends on events happening which dramatize the need for such measures and help to overcome traditional resistance."[7] Our views receive support from their emphasis on the increase in tax rates and the broadening of the income tax base during World War II.

This is one striking difference between the United States and the United Kingdom. The Great Depression had surprisingly little effect on the trend of government expenditures in the United Kingdom; there was no displacement effect. On first examination, the depression in the United States would seem clearly to come within our category of social disturbance of a major character; the upward displacement particularly in federal expenditures was most marked.

It would also be interesting to investigate and compare further the influence of the growth and the distribution of population on government expenditure in both countries. Probably the proper parallel for the influence of urbanization on public expenditure would be mid-nineteenth-century Britain with mid-twentieth-century United States.

However, these are questions for future examination. All we wish to suggest is that the technique developed in this study of Britain, if applied to other countries, gives promise of illuminating results.

Notes

1. Dalton's famous attempt to apply the Pigovian approach in formulating his principle of maximum social advantage ends with the significant words: "Those who are oppressed by a sense of difficulty of this calculus should console themselves with the saying of the Ancient Greeks that 'it is not the easy things, but the difficult things, which are beautiful.'" See his *Principles of Public Finance*, 4th ed., London, 1954, p. 1.

2. Parliamentary discussion of the first Conservative Government budget after World War II, for example, was concerned, not so much about the continuance of a tax burden so much larger than that of 1937, but rather with the right distribution of the marginal gains and losses that would result from the budget changes. Such facts support the concept of a notion of taxable capacity that is "customary" in character, i.e., broadly unchanging in time of stability, but liable to violent adjustment in periods of upheaval. Further backing is provided by the contemporary observations of other economists (Bastable, Giffen, Clark) concerning the "limits" of taxable capacity.

3. See, R. M. Titmuss, "Problems of Social Policy," *History of the Second World War*, Civil Series, London, 1950, Chapter XV.

4. A comparative study of twenty to twenty-five countries is now under way, sponsored jointly by the University of Edinburgh and the London School of Economics and Political Science and financed out of a Ford Foundation grant. Findings so far confirm the value of the general approach, though of course the character and importance of displacement vary from country to country.

5. Solomon Fabricant, assisted by Robert E. Lipsey, *The Trend in Government Activity in the United States since 1900*, New York, National Bureau of Economic Research, 1952; R. A. Musgrave and J. M. Culberston, "The Growth of Public Expenditures in the United States, 1890–1948," *National Tax Journal*, June 1953; M. Slade Kendrick, *A Century and a Half of Federal Expenditures*, Occasional Paper 48, New York, NBER, 1955; G. Colm and M. Helzner, "The Structure of Government Revenue and Expenditure in Relation to the Economic Development of the United States," in *L'Importance et la Structure des Recettes et des Dépenses Publiques*, International Institute of Public Finance, Brussels, 1960.

6. Supplement to *Statistical Abstract of the United States*, Bureau of the Census, Department of Commerce.

7. Colm and Helzner, *op. cit.*, pp. 60–61. They illustrate their point with reference to the growth in education expenditures.

4B.2. The Expansion of the Public Economy
A Comparative Analysis

DAVID R. CAMERON

A host of competing explanations for government growth have grown up in the last thirty years. In this article David Cameron summarizes much of the previous literature and then attempts to test different types of explanation.

Cameron outlines five kinds of explanation. Economic explanations, such as Adolph Wagner's, hold that economic growth is an important determinant of government growth. Fiscal explanations hold that government growth depends on the degree to which the tax burden is visible to the voter. Political explanations hold that the degree of electoral competition, and/or the parties that hold power, are key determinants. Institutional explanations argue that bureaucratic empire-building or fiscal decentralization can increase spending. International explanations hold that the openness of the domestic economy to international competition is of central importance.

Having outlined the explanations, Cameron runs some simple statistical tests using cross-national data, in order to see which type of explanation is most useful. In general, he finds that the international explanation is best supported by his data, that there is some evidence for political factors having some effect, and that there is very little evidence to support the other possible explanations.

Cameron's critics have generally focused on whether he fully controls for other important variables and whether the particular period he examined is typical. The reader should also note that Cameron leaves many important theories untested. Nonetheless, this is a useful and provocative essay.

During the three decades following World War II, the role of government in most advanced capitalist economies increased dramatically. With the maturation of the ''welfare state,'' governments increased their provision of social services and income transfers for the unemployed, the sick, the elderly, and the poor.

Reprinted with permission from the *American Political Science Review*, 72, 4 (December 1978), pp. 1243–61. Copyright 1978 by the American Political Science Association.

Furthermore, governments have become important producers of goods, and in several European nations publicly owned corporations dominate the petroleum, automotive, and transportation industries. In addition, by using a variety of fiscal and monetary instruments such as public spending programs, taxes, and discount rates, governments have attempted to manipulate the levels of unemployment and inflation and dampen the effects of business cycles. They have also sought to guide the long-term development of the economy through the creation of planning institutions and, occasionally, through their control of the assets of financial institutions. And in order to finance their activities in each of these domains, governments have instituted new taxes and raised the levels of old taxes, Indeed, the growth of the extractive role of public authorities has been so great that Schumpeter's words, written half a century ago and pertaining to the historical development of Europe, seem even more appropriate today: "Tax bill in hand, the state penetrated the private economies and won increasing dominion over them" (1918, p. 19).

This article explores the causes of the expansion of the extractive role of government during the recent past in 18 relatively developed capitalist nations. The first section presents several alternative explanations of that expansion. Following the argument developed, rather imprecisely, by Wagner (1883) in the late nineteenth century, most economists have concentrated on the impact of economic growth in accounting for the inexorable increase in government activity. In addition to outlining the Wagnerian argument, I will discuss several alternative causes of the expansion of public revenues. In particular, the analysis examines the impact on taxation of two aspects of the policy-making environment whose effects have been frequently disputed or neglected in many comparative studies of public policy: (1) the electoral politics of a nation—for example, the existence of electoral competition and the partisan composition of government; and (2) the institutional structure of government—for example, the existence of unitary or federal government, and the extent of fiscal centralization. The analysis also considers the extent to which the scope of government activity within a nation is influenced by the position of the domestic economy vis-à-vis the world economy. In this regard, the analysis investigates whether the openness, or exposure, of a nation's economy to the international marketplace stimulates an expansion in the role of government.

The several explanations of the expansion of the public economy[1] will be evaluated by analyzing the experience of 18 nations since 1960. All 18 have capitalist economies; this criterion allows the inclusion of nations for which the expansion of the public economy might represent a source of tension and conflict with the traditional reliance on, and legitimation of, the market economy for the allocation of goods. The nations are: the United States, Canada, Britain, Ireland, Australia, Japan, the Federal Republic of Germany, France, Italy, Spain, the Netherlands, Austria, Belgium, Switzerland, Sweden, Norway, Denmark, and Finland.

Measuring the scope of the public economy

The scope of activity of public authorities can be described by enumerating the programs and types of expenditures carried out by government (King, 1973). However, in the contemporary era in the nations considered here, the increase in the level of expenditure and the multiple uses of funds has been accompanied by an expansion of the revenue-generating capacity of government. Although imbalances occasionally occur between the aggregate totals of all government revenues and expenditures, the two have usually moved in tandem. Thus, the scope of the public economy can be compared as well by considering the revenues of governments rather than their expenditures—that is, by considering the extractive aspect of government.[2] The public economy is defined in terms of the total of all revenues obtained by all levels of government in a nation. Included are all direct taxes, e.g., those on personal and corporate incomes and property; all indirect taxes, e.g., those on sales and value added; all social insurance contributions by employers and employees; and all other fees, taxes, rents, and withdrawals from enterprises which flow into governmental treasuries. To convey the relative importance of the funds which are appropriated (and subsequently distributed) by public authorities, and to control for the obvious differences among nations in the size of the economy, I have calculated the ratio of all governmental revenues to Gross Domestic Product (GDP). This ratio, calculated for all years between 1960 and 1975 (the latest for which data are available), is treated as a measure of the scope of the public economy.[3] In order to measure and compare across nations the degree of expansion in the scope of the public economy, I have calculated the first-order difference in this ratio for the earliest and latest years.[4]

There has been significant variation in both the level and rate of change in the scope of the public economy among these 18 nations. In 1960, for example, the scope of the public economy, which averaged 28.5 percent of GDP, varied from 18 percent in Spain to 35.4 in Germany. By 1975, the average scope of the public economy increased to 38.5 percent of GDP and the variation among the nations also increased, ranging from 23.5 percent in Japan to 53.5 percent in the Netherlands. Thus, while there was a general trend of expansion of the public economy at work in all the nations, there were also great differences among them in the rate of expansion. Why that rate of expansion varied as much as it did is the question to which we now turn.

Five explanations of the expansion of the public economy

Several distinct explanations of why the scope of the public economy changes over time can be identified. This section elaborates five types of explanation—one economic, the second fiscal, the third political, the fourth institutional, and the fifth international in character—and derives predictions to account for the considerable differences in the rate of expansion of the public economy in the 18 nations.

The economic explanation

The most frequently mentioned explanation of the increase in the scope of the public economy is that derived from Wagner's "law of expanding state activity" (1883, pp. 1–8). The "law" holds that, among European nations, the "pressure for social progress" leads inevitably to the growth of the public sector. Writing in the midst of a period of rapid urbanization and industrialization, and just as Bismarck was developing the first programs of the welfare state, Wagner recognized the growing role of the state as a provider of social overhead investments in such areas as transportation and education and the need, even in an authoritarian state, for the state to retain legitimacy by providing public funds to compensate for the human costs of economic development.

As elaborated by numerous scholars of public finance,[5] Wagner's "law" suggests that citizens' demands for services and willingness to pay taxes are income-elastic, and therefore bound to increase with the increase in economic affluence. If this "law" is correct, one would expect that, in comparing the experiences of a number of nations, the greater the increment in economic affluence of a nation during a given period, the greater the expansion of the public economy.

Several scholars have rejected the logic and evidence in support of Wagner's "law." Bird (1971, p. 19), Musgrave (1969, pp. 112–13), and Gupta (1968) find that any positive cross-national relationship between economic growth and government share in the economic product disappears when analysis is confined to the wealthier nations of the world. Apparently there exists an upper threshold to the scope of public economy; beyond certain levels of income, international demonstration effects and internally derived perceptions of marginal benefit are less likely to generate increases in spending. Peacock and Wiseman (1967) also reject the "historical determinism" implicit in Wagner's "law" and in their discussion of the "displacement effect" emphasize the importance of crises such as war and depression in inducing infrequent but large changes in the tolerable burden of taxation. This provides little assistance in explaining a secular upward trend during periods of prosperity and peace (both of which existed in most of the 18 nations during most of the period between 1960 and 1975). However, the Peacock and Wiseman argument, taken with the findings of Bird, Musgrave, and Gupta, might lead one to expect a negligible relationship between economic growth and state expansion.

Wildavsky (1975, pp. 232–35) provides a third perspective on the economic sources of public sector expansion. In what might be termed a "counter-Wagner" law, Wildavsky suggests that the degree of expansion in the scope of the public economy varies inversely, rather than directly, with economic growth. Where national affluence increases very rapidly, as in Japan, any increased demand for public funds can be met by the added revenues obtained by applying a constant public share to a larger economic product. But where economic growth is so modest that it generates insufficient revenues to meet demands for additional public goods, as in Britain, those demands must be met through an expansion of the public share of the economic product. In short, Wildavsky's argument would predict that the relationship between growth and public sector expansion would be negative, indicating the greatest expansion of the public economy in low-growth nations.[6]

The fiscal explanation

The second type of explanation of public sector growth is fiscal in nature. As elaborated by Downs (1960) and Buchanan and Wagner (1977), this perspective emphasizes the structure of the system of revenue generation as a determinant of how much revenue can be raised. Downs argues that because public goods are inherently nondivisible, costs and benefits are not directly linked. Benefits frequently are uncertain (as in preventive or long-term policies). In addition, public goods are, when taken as a whole, inevitably suboptimal, since each citizen will pay for some programs that provide no individual benefit. As a result, the costs, i.e., taxes, are perceived to exceed the benefits of public goods. Therefore, it is only when public officials can conceal the costs of policies in a "fiscal illusion" that they can spend large amounts without incurring the wrath of the electorate. As Buchanan and Wagner (1977) argue, "complex and indirect payment structures create a fiscal illusion that will systematically produce higher levels of public outlay than those that would be observed under simple payments structures" (p. 129).

The major form of tax concealment, according to Downs (1960, p. 558), Wildavsky (1975, pp. 235–39), and Wilensky (1975, p. 52), is indirect taxation. In addition to taxes on value added or sales, relatively invisible forms of revenue generation might include taxes which are paid before individuals receive income, e.g., social insurance contributions by employees, and taxes which can be passed on to third parties, e.g., the social insurance contributions of employers. Applying this "fiscal illusion" argument to the present analysis, one might expect that the nations with the largest increase in the scope of the public economy would be ones in which there is a large and increasing reliance on indirect taxes and social insurance contributions.[7]

The political explanation

A third type of explanation of the expansion of the public economy involves politics. The impact of politics on the scope of the public sector has seldom been recognized, in spite of Downs' assertion (1960, p. 541) that "in a democratic society, the division of resources between the public and private sector is roughly determined by the desires of the electorate." Recently, however, studies by Kramer (1971), Nordhaus (1975), Tufte (1975, 1978), and Hibbs (1978) have suggested that politics—especially electoral politics—exerts a significant influence on the public economy. Two aspects of politics may influence the magnitude of expansion of the public economy: (1) the effect of electoral competition in "bidding up" the scope of expenditure programs; and (2) the effect of variations in the partisan composition, and presumably the ideological preferences, of government.

In his revision of the classical doctrine of democracy, Schumpeter (1950, p. 269) defined democracy in terms of electoral competition: "the democratic method is that institutional arrangement for arriving at political decisions in which individuals acquire the power to decide by means of a competitive struggle for the people's vote." As elaborated by Downs (1957), this theory of democracy implies that the contenders for political office alter their programs in order to enhance their electoral appeal. An important weapon in this competitive struggle is the public economy: some political contenders will attempt to garner votes by promising cuts in taxes; others will promise increases in spending; and others will promise both (see Downs, 1960; Buchanan and Wagner, 1977).

Ever since Key (1949) noted the propensity of political opponents to appeal to the "have-not" voters by promising more spending, scholars have been virtually unanimous in attributing to electoral competition an expansionist impulse (see Brittan, 1975, pp. 139–40). Empirical studies of the American electorate by Kramer (1971) and Tufte (1975) have demonstrated that voters have tended to provide short-term electoral rewards to incumbents who can effect, through their tax, fiscal, and monetary policies, increases in real personal income. And as Tufte (1978, Ch. 2) demonstrates, because incumbents are aware of this relationship, most adopt policies in anticipation of elections which stimulate the economy and increase personal income by pumping funds into the economy. As a result, periodic electoral competition frequently produces a long-term cyclical effect on the economy. The most important consequence, for our concerns here, is that this "political business cycle" is marked by increased spending and other reflationary policies in the period immediately before and after an election (Nordhaus, 1975; Lindbeck, 1976).

The existence of a "political business cycle," the likelihood that incumbents will attempt to use spending policies to enhance their support in anticipation of elections, as well as the tendency of opposition parties to build electoral support by promising more spending on particular government policies, all tend to suggest that public spending increases at an unusually rapid rate immediately before elections (and immediately afterward, if the opposition takes control of government). One application of this argument to the cross-national perspective is to consider the impact of variations among nations in the frequency of national elections. Since the measure of the scope of the public economy relies on revenues (i.e., taxes) rather than expenditures, frequent electoral competition might be expected to dampen the growth of the public economy. However, because revenues and expenditures moved in tandem in most, if not all, of the nations during the period under consideration, the effects of electoral competition on public spending tended to be reflected in tax increases (often in the post-election period). Therefore, one might expect that nations with frequent elections during

1960-75 experienced larger increases in the public economy than nations with infrequent elections, since there were more opportunities for government and opposition elites to indulge in "competitive bidding."[8]

One of the most contested issues in political science is whether or not partisanship influences public policy, and if so, how. Many scholars conclude that parties do not differ significantly in their positions on major issues. Proponents of the "decline of ideology" thesis argue, for example, that parties—particularly those on the left—have forsaken traditional ideologies in order to assemble larger electorates.[9] Even if parties resist the temptation of assembling socially and ideologically heterogeneous electorates and retain some measure of ideological distinctiveness, they may be unable to implement their preferences when in office. The complexities of the internal processes of revenue and spending decisions (Klein, 1976), the vagueness of campaign proposals and the frequent lack of experience, and turnover, of ministers (Gordon, 1971), the importance of policy professionals in the civil service (Heclo, 1974, p. 301), the impulse of incrementalism and the tendency to follow established routines (Wildavsky, 1974), as well as the occasional movement by governments in directions not consistent with their traditional ideologies (King, 1969, p. 136) all do much to circumscribe the impact of party. Largely for these reasons, King concludes that the policy role of parties is "sharply restricted. . . . While organized party generally remains one of the forces . . . in the formation of public policy . . . it has never been the only one, and there is reason to suppose that in many countries in the late 1960's it is not even a major one" (pp. 136-37).

In spite of the support which can be mustered for the skeptical view of the importance of parties in the policy process, some evidence suggests that parties may be relevant in defining the scope of the public economy. For example, Hibbs (1978) contends that strike activity decreased in European nations where Social Democratic and Labor parties increased their representation in cabinets in the 1930s and 1940s. This decrease occurred, says Hibbs (p. 165), because of the propensity of leftist parties to provide funding for new and expanded welfare programs. This caused a much larger portion of the national income to flow through the public sector, thereby shifting the focus of the distributional struggle from the private sector, where labor and capital compete through industrial conflict, to the public sector, where these economic actors compete through electoral mobilization and political bargaining with each other and with government.[10]

The budgetary studies of Davis, Dempster, and Wildavsky (1966, 1974) provide additional evidence that the partisanship of government may influence public policy. In their first study, the authors found "shift points" in the incremental drift of spending which coincided with changes in the control of the White House. Wildavsky's analysis (1975, p. 371) of British budgets during 1964-74 found that the direction of the trend line of public spending shifted when the Conservatives replaced the Labour party in government in 1970.[11] Also, Davis, Dempster, and Wildavsky (1974) found that the magnitude of the increments granted to American federal agencies was influenced by such partisan variables as the strength of the liberal wing of the Democrats in Congress and Democratic control of the presidency.

The Hibbs and Wildavsky studies suggest that as the partisan composition of government varies over time, within a nation, and among nations, so too the priorities and substance of policy vary, including the definition by governments of the "proper" scope of the public economy. One might expect, therefore, that the considerable variation among nations in the rate of expansion of the public economy reflects differences in the frequency of control of national governments over a period of years by parties which, in general, favor that expansion. Following Downs (1957, p. 116), who viewed leftist parties as more favorable than others to the extension of governmental intervention in the economy, one might expect that the rate of expansion of the public economy was positively associated with the extent to which governments relied for their support on leftist parties during 1960-75.[12]

The institutional explanation

A fourth type of explanation of the expansion of the public economy involves the institutional structure of government. Two aspects of that structure are considered here: (1) the formal relationship among levels of government within a nation—in particular, the existence of multiple, independent centers of public authority; and (2) the degree of fiscal centralization.

Downs (1964), Niskanen (1971), Wildavsky (1974), and Tarschys (1975) argue that government bureaucracies develop internal pressures for self-aggrandizement and expansion. If that is true, then a multiplicity of autonomous governmental bureaucracies would enhance this tendency. Thus, in nations where no single authority controls the bulk of public spending—where, in other words, spending authority is fragmented—and where the institutional structure guarantees that some units and levels spend funds that were raised by other units or levels (Tarschys, 1975, p. 25), the rate of increase in spending should be unusually high. The institutional arrangement of government which most closely approximates this situation is federalism: that arrangement provides considerable autonomy for subnational and local governments, fragments the control of public spending, allows some levels or units the luxury of spending funds which have been raised by other levels or units, and multiplies the number of self-aggrandizing bureaucracies. Therefore, one might expect the nations with a federal structure of government experienced larger increases in the scope of the public economy than those with a unitary structure.

A second aspect of the institutional structure of government that may influence the expansion of the public economy is the degree of fiscal centralization. Centralization, defined here as the proportion of all governments' revenues generated by the central government, reflects, to some extent, the formal institutional structure of government; nations with unitary government tend to be more centralized than federal nations. Nevertheless, the degree of centralization varies widely among both the federal and the nonfederal nations considered here, and it is plausible to think that it exerts an impact on the scope of the public economy that is independent of the formal structure of government. [13]

Several studies conclude that government spending tends to increase most rapidly at subnational and local levels of government. Wagner (1883, p. 8) was perhaps the first to note that local authorities' requirements for funds were most likely to expand when administration was decentralized. Recent studies of the United States (Freeman, 1975, p. 208), Britain (Bacon and Eltis, 1976), and Sweden (Tarschys, 1975, p. 25) have found that increases in public spending were greater at the subnational and local, rather than at the national, levels of government. Heidenheimer (1975, p. 28) suggests a reason for these findings in his comparison of the difference in spending for health care in Britain and Sweden: "The monopolistic control of the national Treasury and the Health Ministry over financing sources enabled Britain, much better than Sweden [where health financing is decentralized and the responsibility of the counties], to hold down the proportion of national income allocated to the health sector." In other words, the ability of central government decision makers to oversee spending and, presumably, their awareness of the cost-benefit tradeoffs among policy sectors serve to limit aggregate spending. These studies support a contention that, for the same reasons mentioned in regard to the impact of federalism, relatively decentralized nations experienced larger increases in the scope of the public economy than did highly centralized nations.

The international explanation

The four alternative explanations of the expansion of the public economy presented thus far share a common element. The rate of economic growth, the degree of "invisibility " in the revenue-generating mechanism of the state, electoral politics, and the institutional structure of government all involve internal aspects of nations. However, nations are not wholly autonomous and entirely independent of the external world. In fact, certain nations are highly dependent on their external environments as markets for export goods or sources of capital. [14] To the extent that there is a high degree of substitution of foreign and domestic goods, with domestic prices of commodities, labor, and capital established by supply and demand in the international rather than the domestic market, these economies are "open" (see Lindbeck, 1976, p. 2). They are, in other words, exposed to pressures on markets and prices which are transmitted from other nations via international exchange.

The concept of the open economy is applicable, in varying degrees, to almost all of the advanced capitalist societies considered here, but it is especially relevant for the smaller nations. As Dahl and Tufte (1973) note, trade dependence— one aspect of openness—is strongly, and inversely, related to the size of a nation:

> By free trade, small political systems can achieve the same economies of scale as large systems. . . . [Thus] a partial solution to the problem for small systems [is] to engage in foreign trade. . . . In general, the smaller a political system the higher the proportion of foreign trade to total trade. . . . Few relationships with size hold up more uniformly than this one (p. 115).

In several of the smaller nations considered here, such as Belgium and the Netherlands, the value of imports and exports is almost as large as the Gross Domestic Product. In fact, the value of trade exceeded 50 percent of GDP in 12 of the 18 nations in 1975.[15] Even in the larger nations, such as the United States and Japan, however, the economies are not impervious to the international economy. Like the smaller nations, they depend on external producers for important commodities such as oil and other raw materials, and they depend on external consumers to provide the markets for export goods.

The most important political consequence of an ''open'' economy is the constraint it imposes on the effectiveness of a variety of macroeconomic policies (see Krasner, 1976, p. 319). To quote Dahl and Tufte again (1973, pp. 116, 130):

> economies of scale tend to erode the independence and autonomy of the smaller democracy, making it dependent—officially or not—on the actions of people outside the country. . . . In order to develop and maintain a relatively high standard of living, the small country must go beyond its own boundaries in search of markets, and often in search of raw materials, labor, and capital investment as well. As a consequence, the small country is highly dependent on the behavior of foreign actors not subject to its authority.

Lindbeck (1975, 1977) and Aukrust (1977) have noted the several ways in which the trade dependence of the Scandinavian economies has limited the ability of national officials to manage aggregate demand and control inflation. Aggregate demand in small, open economies is, in part, a function of the demand in the world market for domestically produced export goods; thus, unemployment, which is a function of demand relative to operating capacity in the economy, is somewhat uncontrollable. And since price levels in export industries are set in the world market, they may not move in accordance with changes in domestic costs, causing either low profitability (if external demand, and prices, do not increase with increases in domestic costs) or high profitability (if external demand, and prices, increase more than domestic costs). Whether export profits are small or large, they may destabilize the economy: a lack of profits in the export sector may cause a reduction in the funds available for capital investment and, ultimately, a reduction in the rate of growth; a high level of export profits may, on the other hand, contribute to inflation, since they may be used to justify higher wages in the export industries and these wage increases may, in turn, be generalized to the nonexport sector through centralized collective bargaining.[16]

Just as a high degree of dependence on the international economy for markets for export industries may limit a government's ability to manage aggregate demand and control levels of unemployment and capital formation, a high degree of penetration of the domestic market by external producers also limits the control by the national government over the economy. High levels of imports tend to remove decisions regarding the production, and pricing, of goods for domestic consumption to external actors. In addition, import penetration may transmit inflationary pressures from the rest of the world—particularly if the domestic demand for particular commodities is relatively inelastic with regard to price, as, for example, oil (see Aukrust, 1977; Lindbeck, 1975). Furthermore, high levels of imports may contribute to balance of payments deficits, the solution of which usually requires the funding of deficits with foreign borrowings, devaluation, and the institution of deflationary "austerity" programs—all of which may be unattractive to national policy makers.

Several scholars have suggested that the vulnerability of the open economy can be lessened by an assertion of the role of the state. Gilpin (1975, p. 45) concludes, for example, that a likely result of the national anxieties and insecurities produced by economic interdependence will be a resurgence of mercantilism—that is, of states intervening between the domestic and international economy on behalf of national economic objectives. Myrdal (1960) suggested a similar development nearly two decades ago when noting that in order to protect national objectives of internal stability, employment of workers, and undisturbed domestic production and consumption in a world of more chaotic economic relations, "all states have felt themselves compelled to undertake new, radical intervention, not only in the sphere of their foreign trade and exchange relations, but also in other sectors of the national economy" (pp. 70–72). More recently, Lehmbruch (1977) reached a similar conclusion, arguing that

> in a national economy subject to strong interpenetration with international markets, monetary policies often are of rather limited effectiveness. The same is more and more true of "Keynesian" techniques of macroeconomic budgetary and fiscal demand management. . . . Faced with "control deficits" of this sort, governments increasingly turn to more direct attempts at influencing the economic behavior of business and/or labor (p. 98).

Lindbeck (1975, p. 56) argues that governments can dampen the effects of the open economy on production, employment, and consumption by increasing the scope of the public economy. He notes that the growth of social insurance and tax systems represent "built-in stabilizers" which allow policy makers to "smooth out" the peaks and valleys of business cycles. And through extensive labor market policies which include not only unemployment compensation but also subsidies to firms to retain and retrain workers who might otherwise be laid off, as well as through large increases in public employment, governments can maintain near-full employment in spite of the uncertainties of demand inherent in an open economy. In addition, through the provision of capital funds to the private sector (Lindbeck, 1974, pp. 9, 214–27), governments may be able to dampen the effect on capital accumulation of volatile profits in export industries as well as stimulate the development of import substitution industries.[17]

It may not always be the case that an expansion of the role of the state provides a sufficient means by which governments can enhance their control over open economies. Indeed, Vernon (1974) suggests that the efforts by European states to formally "plan" their economies failed because of increasing openness produced by the creation of the EEC and EFTA and the maturation of multinational enterprises: "None of these efforts to shore up the idea of the independent comprehensive national plan had much chance of succeeding; the contradiction between independent national plans of that sort and open national boundaries was simply too strong" (p. 16). In spite of this caveat, it is reasonable to expect that the arguments of Myrdal, Lehmbruch, and Lindbeck may be reflected in the experience of the 18 nations during the last two decades. Applying their arguments about the response of governments to a condition of external economic dependence, one might expect that the expansion of the public economy was most pronounced in nations in which the economy is relatively "open," in the sense of being exposed to the vagaries of the international economy. Using the ratio of imports and exports as a proportion of GDP as a measure of "openness," this argument would predict a strong positive association between the level, and the rate of increase, of "openness" and the expansion of the public economy.

Findings: Why the public economy expanded in 1960–75

Table 1 presents the result of an analysis of the five plausible explanations of the expansion of the public economy. That analysis, based on data for the 18 nations, supports the following conclusions:

(a) Contrary to Wagner's "law," the rate of growth in the economic affluence of a nation does not contribute to the expansion of the public economy. Apparently citizens' demands for services and their willingness to accept higher levels of taxes, or both, are not income-elastic. Instead, the analysis supports Wildavsky's argument that the public economy grows, in relative terms, when economic growth is modest ($B = -.35$). In high-growth nations such as Japan and France, the demands of government for funds can be met with the "dividend" produced by applying a constant share to an expanding economic product. In low-growth nations, where governments do not enjoy that dividend, however, the almost inevitable increase in funding required for "uncontrollable" costs associated with mandated programs, as well as discretionary increments and new programs, absorbs a larger share of the economic product.

(b) Contrary to Downs and to Buchanan and Wagner, budgets do not expand most easily when taxes are concealed in a "fiscal illusion." A high and increasing reliance on "hidden" taxes exerted a significant dampening effect on the degree of expansion of the public economy, as indicated by the strong negative coefficients in Table 1. Instead, the public economy expanded most rapidly after 1960

Table 1

The Expansion of the Public Economy: Economic, Fiscal, Political, Institutional, and International Explanations

Variable	Level and rate of increase in economic output		Reliance on indirect and Social Security taxes		Partisanship of government and the frequency of elections		Inter-governmental structure and degree of centralization		Openness of the economy	
	Regression coefficient	Beta coefficient	Regression coefficient	Beta coefficient	Regression coefficient	Beta coefficient	Regression coefficient	Beta coefficient	Regression coefficient	Beta coefficient
Governments' revenues as percent of GDP, 1960	0.28 (0.91)[a]	.25	0.42 (1.49)	.36	0.09 (0.34)	.08	0.52 (1.78)	.46	0.09 (0.45)	.08
GDP per capita, 1960	−0.002 (0.77)	−.22								
Average annual increase, 1960–75, in real GDP	−1.34 (1.16)	−.35								
Percent of all governments' revenues from indirect taxes and Social Security contributions, 1960			−0.15 (1.10)	−.27						
Increase in percent of all governments' revenues from indirect taxes and Social Security contributions, 1960–75			−0.17 (0.75)	−.18						

Independent variable										
Percent of governments' electoral base composed of Social Democratic or Labor parties, 1960–75					0.10 (2.15)	.54				
Number of national legislative elections, 1960–75					0.21 (0.29)	.07				
Federal structure of government							−2.56 (0.82)	−.23		
Percent of all governments' revenues received by central government, 1960							0.13 (0.92)	.28		
Exports and imports as a percent of GDP, 1960									0.19 (4.86)	.79
Increase in percent of GDP represented by exports and imports, 1960–75									0.00 (0.00)	.00
Coefficient of determination (R²)	.19	(.02)b	.20	(.03)	.37	(.24)	.31	(.16)	.67	(.60)

a. Parentheses contain the regression coefficient divided by its standard error.
b. Parentheses contain the R^2 adjusted for degrees of freedom (R^2).

in nations which relied heavily, and to an increasing degree, on wealth-elastic taxes, such as those on personal and corporate incomes.

(c) Contrary to the skeptics' view, politics is important in influencing the scope of the public economy. The partisanship of government is associated with the rate of expansion, and whether a nation's government was generally controlled by Social Democrats (and their leftist allies), or by nonleftist parties, provides a strong clue to the relative degree of change in the scope of the public economy ($B = .54$). Thus, nations such as Sweden, Norway, and Denmark, in which leftist parties tended, on average, to possess a majority of the government's electoral base, experienced increases in public revenues which were much larger, as a proportion of GDP, than those in nations such as Japan, Italy, or France, where the Left either participated in government only as the minority partner of nonleftist parties or was excluded from government altogether.

The frequency of electoral competition dispalys a modest positive correlation with the increase in the public economy, indicating that competition may indeed exert an inflationary impact on budgets. However, after we control for the effects associated with the partisan composition of government, the impact of the frequency of electoral competition is negligible ($B = .07$).

(d) Contrary to our predictions, federalism tends to dampen the degree of expansion of the public economy and centralization tends to facilitate that expansion. Any inherent tendency for aggregate revenues to increase in federal systems because of the fragmentation of spending authority among several quasi-autonomous levels of government is apparently more than offset by other effects. Among these may be the larger number of access points which federalism provides for those who wish to intervene in public policy making in order to oppose the extension of government activity (Heidenheimer, 1975, pp. 20–29, 48–65). Also, the fragmentation of authority which characterizes federalism may contribute to an aggregate pattern of offsetting policy developments among the subnational units that lessens the magnitude of change in the nation taken as a whole. A high degree of centralization, on the other hand, seems to facilitate the expansion of the public economy ($B = .28$). Thus, it appears that that expansion was greatest in unitary, highly centralized nations. We might speculate that that institutional arrangement minimizes the effects of fragmentation and provides the means by which national elites can insure uniformity in existing policies and can most easily avoid the institutional obstacles to policy innovation.

(e) As the discussion of the concept of the open economy suggested, a high degree of trade dependence is conducive to a relatively large expansion of the public economy. Nations with open economies were far more likely to experience an increase in the scope of public funding than were nations with relatively closed economies ($B = .79$). Apparently, governments in nations with open economies have sought to counter the effects of external dependence by expanding their control over the domestic economy through the "nationalization" of a large portion of consumption (Lindbeck, 1974, p. 9).[18]

In order to ascertain the importance of each of the explanations presented in

Table 2

The Relative Importance of the Economic, Fiscal, Political, Institutional, and International Explanations of the Expansion of the Public Economy

	Increase, 1960–75 All Governments' Revenues as a Percent of GDP		
	Simple correlation	Regression coefficient	Beta coefficient[a]
Level of public economy, 1960, (governments' revenues as percent of GDP)	.35	0.11 (0.46)	0.10
Average annual percentage increase, 1960–75, in real GDP	−.31	0.06 (0.09)	0.02
Percent of governments' revenues obtained from indirect taxes and Social Security contributions, 1960	−.23	−0.06 (0.68)	−0.12
Percent of government's electoral base composed of Social Democratic or Labor parties, 1960–75	.60	0.07 (1.75)	0.34
Percent of all governments' revenues received by central governments, 1960	.21	0.08 (0.97)	0.17
Exports and imports of goods and services as percent of GDP, 1960	.78	0.13 (3.22)	0.58

Coefficient of determination ($R^2 = .75$. $\bar{R}^2 = .61$).
a. Beta coefficient is the standarized regression coefficient.

Table 1, I performed a regression analysis which included the six variables most closely associated with the expansion of the public economy. Table 2 presents the results of that analysis. The analysis suggests that about 75 percent of the variation among the nations in the degree of expansion can be accounted for by the six variables. The analysis also suggests that two variables are far more important to the explanation than the others; the two are the partisanship of government ($B = .34$) and the openness of the economy ($B = .58$).

Figure 1 arrays the measure of the expansion of the public economy with that for the partisanship of government. The array provides a clue as to why the strong bivariate relationship between the two ($r = .60$) is reduced in the regression analysis. It suggests that the dominance in government of leftist parties was a sufficient condition for a relatively large increase in the scope of public activity; there was no nation in which the Left had a large share of the government's electoral base which did not also experience a relatively large increase in the public economy. However, leftist domination was not a necessary condition, since several nations experienced large increases in spite of the absence of a strong leftist representation in government. Included in this latter group are the

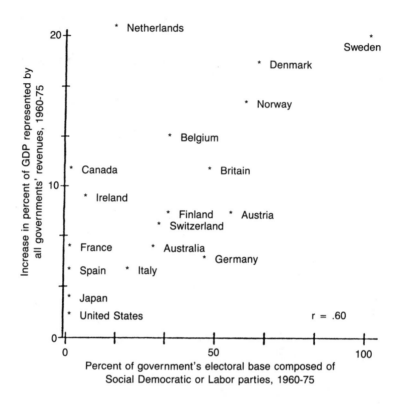

Figure 1 **The Partisan Composition of Government and the Expansion of the Public Economy**

Netherlands, Belgium, Ireland, and Canada. All share at least one common trait: their economies are relatively open. To some extent, then, the impact of partisanship on the scope of the "tax state" is more pronounced in larger nations with more closed economies than in the smaller nations with more open economies. In the latter, apparently, all governments—whether formed by leftist or nonleftist parties—have been impelled by the exigencies of the open economy to expand the role of the state. To illustrate this, Table 3 presents the year-by-year change in the measure of the public economy in four nations in which the partisan control of government alternated between leftist and nonleftist parties. In the two larger nations, Britain and Germany, a clear partisan effect is noted. In Britain, for example, the change was positive in every year in which the Labour party was in power (1964-70, 1974-75), and was negative in five of the seven years during which the Conservatives governed. Similarly, in Germany, the years of Christian Democratic government, particularly when Ludwig Erhard, the former minister of economics and proponent of the neoliberal "social market policy," was chancellor (1963-66), were marked by modest increases or decreases, while the period of Social Democratic control was marked by a cumulative increase in the

Table 3

The Partisan Composition of Government and Change in the Scope of the Public Economy in Four Nations[a]

Year	Britain[b]	Germany	Denmark	Norway
1961	0.5	0.8	−0.5	**1.1**
1962	1.7	0.6	**1.5**	**1.4**
1963	−0.5	−0.1	**1.5**	**−0.1**
1964	−0.2	−0.4	**0.1**	**−0.5**
1965	**1.7**	−0.8	**1.3**	**1.2**
1966	**1.0**	0.5	**2.2**	1.1
1967	**1.8**	*0.6*	**0.6**	1.6
1968	**1.6**	*−0.5*	2.9	0.4
1969	**2.1**	*1.8*	0.2	2.1
1970	**1.3**	**−0.8**	4.5	0.5
1971	−1.9	**0.9**	3.4	**3.1**
1972	−1.7	**0.3**	**0.2**	**2.1**
1973	−0.8	**2.4**	**0.1**	**1.2**
1974	**3.3**	**0.3**	**2.1**	−1.2
1975	**0.8**	−0.4	**−3.1**	**1.5**

a. Entries are the first-order changes between successive years in the percent of GDP received by all governments.

b. Boldface entries indicate that the Social Democratic or Labor parties controlled government for at least six months during the year. The British entry for 1970 is credited to Labour, in spite of its defeat in the June election. Italicized entries for Germany denote the period of the Grand Coalition between the SPD and CDU/CSU (1966-69).

scope of the public economy. In contrast, in Denmark and Norway, nonleftist governments were no less inclined than those dominated by the Social Democratic and the Labor parties to increase the public revenues at a rapid rate, relative to the rate of economic growth. Thus, while the size of the public economy grew considerably in Denmark during the Social Democratic minority government and subsequent "red coalition" of 1964-67, the largest increase occurred during the nonleftist coalition government of 1968-71. Likewise, in Norway, the bourgeois coalition which governed during 1966-71 and again during 1972-73 expanded the scope of state activity at a rate which in some years approached that achieved by Labor governments.

The regression analysis presented in Table 2 suggests that the openness of the economy is the best single predictor of the growth of public revenues relative to the economic product of a nation. In Figure 2, the measure of openness is displayed with that of the change in the scope of the public economy. A strong relationship is observed and no major exceptions appear to the pattern of covariation: larger nations with more closed economies experienced relatively modest increases in the scope of the public economy compared to the smaller nations with

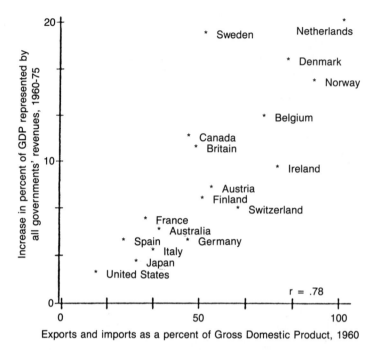

Figure 2 **The Openness of the Economy and the Expansion of the Public Economy**

open economies.[19] Within the latter group, one finds some distinction between the Scandinavian nations, where the Left frequently governed, and Belgium and Ireland, where centrists or conservatives usually dominated government. But the overall message is clear: the best explanation of why public authorities in some nations have expanded their control over the appropriation and allocation of resources while those in other nations have not is international in character. Among the nations considered here, the expansion of the public economy was most closely associated with a relatively high exposure to, and dependence upon, external producers and consumers.[20]

Discussion

The domestic consequences of the open economy

Why is the degree of trade dependence the best predictor of the extent of expansion of the public economy? Is it simply the force of the exigencies posed by exposure to the international economy that causes government to extract and allocate a large share of the economic product? Or does openness generate certain structural characteristics in advanced capitalist economies which are conducive to an expansion of the scope of the public economy? We shall attempt to provide an answer to these questions by identifying a sequence of economic, sociological,

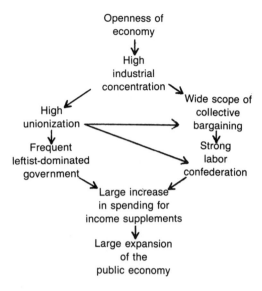

Figure 3 **The Domestic Consequences of an Open Economy**

and political characteristics that derive, ultimately, from the openness of the economy. This sequence, presented in Figure 3, includes the following: (a) the degree of industrial concentration; (b) the density of unionization; (c) the scope of collective bargaining; and (d) the strength of labor confederations.

One of the structural attributes that frequently characterizes small, open economies is a high degree of industrial concentration—that is, an unusually large share of production and employment in a few large firms. According to Ingham (1974, pp. 40–41), "those societies in which industrialization was based upon exports because of too small a domestic market have tended to develop highly concentrated industries. Sharp competition in the export field has, in these countries, tended to force out the smaller and less-efficient companies which were less able to contend with fluctuations in world markets."

High levels of industrial concentration appear, in turn, to facilitate the formation of employers' associations and labor confederations which include a relatively large portion of all firms and employees. Ingham notes, for example, that small, open, and highly concentrated economies tend to have "a small number of oligopolistic and non-competitive sectors . . . which facilitates collective organization" (p. 42). And the labor force in such economies tends to be somewhat less differentiated in terms of occupation and skill levels and, as a result, less fragmented (p. 43). The existence of such a labor force—relatively homogeneous and relatively concentrated in large firms in a small number of non-competitive sectors—is conducive to the growth of union organization. The existence of a relatively high level of unionization is, in turn, an important prerequisite for enduring leftist government, since unionized workers provide the core of the electoral base of most Social Democratic and Labor parties (see Stephens, 1978). Thus, in following the left-hand branch in Figure 3, we see that the openness of the economy contributes to an expansion of the public economy by facilitating the development of the social infrastructure upon which Social Democratic and Labor party electoral support rests.[21]

In addition to its effects on unionization and, ultimately, the structure of the party system, industrial concentration influences the scope of collective bargaining. The existence of "a small number of oligopolistic and non-competitive sectors," composed of a relatively small number of large firms, coupled with the proliferation of labor and employer organizations, widens the scope of collective bargaining. In some nations considered here, bargaining is decentralized and usually conducted at the level of the enterprise, either by enterprise unions as in Japan, or by national unions as in the United States. In most European nations, on the other hand, bargaining is conducted at the industry level with important additional negotiations at the enterprise level, as in Britain and Italy, or the regional level, as in Germany. But in the smaller open economies, industry bargaining often follows guidelines established in national negotiations (see Mouly, 1967; Schregle, 1974; Elvander, 1974; Lehmbruch, 1977; Hibbs, 1976). Thus, in Norway, Sweden, and Denmark, economy-wide "framework" agreements are formally negotiated between labor and employer confederations. And in Austria, Belgium, and the Netherlands, institutions exist in which representatives of the major confederations consult about, and occasionally negotiate, collective bargaining guidelines.[22]

One of the more important consequences of industrial and economy-wide collective bargaining is the power it bestows on labor confederations. Since they are the representatives of organized labor in economy-wide consultations and negotiations, they have tended to acquire formal powers over their affiliates in regard to collective bargaining. In Norway, Sweden, Finland, Austria, Belgium, and the Netherlands, for example, the major confederations can withhold strike funds from affiliates, thereby weakening the latter's ability to use the threat of strike action. In Austria, Norway, and the Netherlands, confederations can veto wage settlements obtained by their affiliates, and in these and most of the other open economies in Europe confederations have, *de jure* or *de facto*, the right to consult with affiliates prior to negotiations (Headey, 1970, pp. 421-25).[23]

The ability of labor confederations to intervene in collective bargaining makes them major actors in the political economy. This is especially true in nations where the domain of macroeconomic issues about which confederations consult with employers and/or government has been extended beyond collective bargaining in recent decades. This occurred in some nations through the creation of consultative institutions, such as the Austrian Parity Commission and the Dutch Foundation of Labor and the Social and Economic Council; in other nations, consultation is less institutionalized but equally important, as in Norway and Sweden where the confederation and the Labor party have traditionally represented the two arms of the labor movement (see Lehmbruch, 1977). This access to government can be used by labor confederations in many ways, but two are of special relevance here. Acting as representatives of the labor movement, confederations may advocate policies that will enhance the economic condition of their members by supporting programs that provide income supplements. On the other hand, confederations may act as allies of government—particularly when it is formed by Social Democratic or Labor parties—to moderate wage demands in the export sector in order to maintain international competitiveness. For example, they may voluntarily participate in programs of wage restraint negotiated between themselves, employer federations, and government (see Rall, 1975; Ulman and Flanagan, 1971; Galenson, 1973; Headey, 1970; and Lehmbruch, 1977). More frequently than not, labor confederations involved in such cooperative programs of wage restraint have felt compelled to use their access to government to obtain increments to the disposable income of their members, thereby compensating them for wage sacrifices. Whether they act as the representatives of organized labor or as allies of government, then, the existence of strong labor confederations tends to produce the same effect—an unusually large increase in publicly funded income supplements. And this, in turn, requires a comparable expansion in the scope of the public economy.[24]

The consequences of the expansion of the public economy

Does it matter that in some nations the public economy expanded to the range of 50 percent of GDP, while in others it increased only slightly in the years since 1960?[25] Thus far, this article has examined the reasons for the large cross-national variation in the degree of expansion of the public economy. It is appropriate to conclude, however, by shifting our attention from cause to consequence and examining the impact of changes in the scope of the public economy. A variety of effects might be considered, ranging from macroeconomic policy to electoral behavior; we have chosen two related effects which demonstrate the magnitude of the impact of different rates of cumulative change and the value dilemmas that accompany policy choices in this domain. The two involve economic equality and private capital accumulation.

In Figure 4, we illustrate the relationship among 12 of the 18 nations between the cumulative expansion of the public economy and measures of economic equality and private capital accumulation. A strong positive correlation (r = .83) exists beween the size of the increase in the public economy and a measure of economic equality involving the difference in the proportion of all national income received, after taxes, by the top and bottom 20 percent of households. A strong negative correlation (r = −.89) exists between the size of the cumulative increase in the public economy and the change in the proportion of GDP represented by private capital accumulation.[26]

The data in Figure 4 suggest the existence of a tradeoff between relatively high degrees of economic equality and increasing rates of private capital accumulation.[27] And they suggest that the collective choice of a nation in regard to this

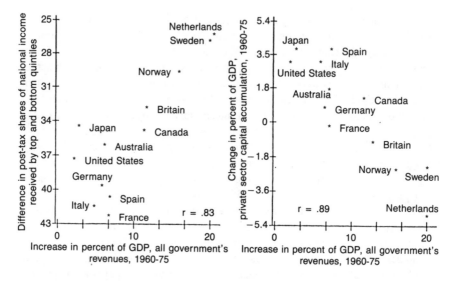

Figure 4 **The Tax Tradeoff: The Expansion of the Public Economy, Economic Equality, and Capital Accumulation**

tradeoff is strongly influenced by choices made in regard to taxation policy. Nations such as the United States, Japan, Spain, and Italy, where the extractive capacity of government did not significantly increase, relative to the economic product, have, in a sense, opted for a relatively inegalitarian distribution of income and an increasing rate of private capital accumulation.[28] Other nations, however, have, in the cumulative effect of their policies, made a different choice and have attained a relatively greater degree of economic equality at the cost of lower rates of private capital accumulation. Given the structural features that tend to accompany economic openness—a high degree of unionization, relatively frequent government by Social Democratic and Labor parties, strong labor confederations, and, ultimately, a large increase in taxation—it is perhaps not surprising that the nations which tended to favor distributional equity rather than private accumulation were those with open economies.

Conclusion

Most studies of public policy in advanced industrial society confine themselves to an analysis of internal, or domestic, causes and consequences. Only rarely, and only recently, have students of public policy examined the linkage between the international economy and domestic policy (Katzenstein, 1976, 1977). The predominant image implicit in most policy studies is that of political autarky—of autonomous states whose policy processes are wholly insulated from external influences. Yet in a world marked by "complex interdependence" (Keohane and Nye, 1977) such an image is increasingly anachronistic; because, as Cooper argues, "increased economic interdependence . . . erodes the effectiveness of national economic policies and hence threatens national autonomy in the determination and pursuit of economic objectives,'' governing elites are likely to feel compelled to use public policy to confront the challenges posed by the international economy (1972, p. 164).

Governments use a variety of policy instruments to shelter their economics from the competitive risks of the international economy. Some states adopt explicitly neo-mercantilist policies (Katzenstein, 1978, pp. 879–920); others favor certain enterprises, whether in the private or public sector, as "national champions" (Vernon, 1974, Ch. 1); still others adopt a variety of industry-specific protectionist measures. Each type of policy has occurred in one or more of the nations considered here during the past decade. However, neo-mercantilism, support of "national champions," and protectionism are often ineffective for nations with open economies, given their small size relative to some of their most important trading partners. For such nations, another type of response is more feasible—one which is more defensive in character and involves a relatively large public economy. Governments in small open economies have tended to provide a variety of income supplements in the form of social security schemes, health insurance, unemployment benefits, job training, employment subsidies to firms, and even investment capital. Prompted in part by the incentive to maintain price competitiveness of export goods in the world market and accentuated by the social structural features generated by economic openness, this expansion of the role of government in the distribution and comsumption of national income has dramatically enlarged the scope of the "tax state" in contemporary advanced capitalist society.

Notes

1. The term "public economy" refers here to that portion of a nation's economic product which is consumed or distributed by all public authorities.

2. In most nations, during most years, the total of all governments' revenues exceeds the total of all governments' expenditures. During the world recession of 1975, the aggregate of all governments' expenditures exceeded all revenues in six nations—the United States, Belgium, Germany, Ireland, Italy, and Britain. In the prior half-decade (1970–74), however, only two nations (the United States in 1971 and Italy in 1971–74) experienced an aggregate deficit. Thus, a measure of the public economy based on revenues is less likely to understate the fiscal scope of governmental activity than one based on expenditures. See Organisation for Economic Co-operation and Development (O.E.C.D.) (1977a).

3. The data were obtained from O.E.C.D. (1973, 1977a). The measure includes withdrawals from, but not operating revenues of, public enterprises, which in some nations (for example, Austria, Finland, Britain, and Italy) are among the largest industrial firms.

4. First-order differences, rather than percentage changes, are used in order to avoid artificially deflating the magnitude of change in nations with a relatively *high* value in the initial year. To control for the tendency of first-order differences to deflate the magnitude of change in nations with relatively *low* initial values, regression analyses will include both the value in the initial year and the measure of change.

5. See Bird (1970, p. 70; 1971), Musgrave (1969, p. 74), and Gupta (1968).

6. The data for the level of per capita Gross Domestic Product are reported in United Nations (1976, pp. 701–02). The data for the average annual increase in real GDP were obtained from O.E.C.D. (1977b, Technical Annex).

7. Data pertaining to the structure of governments' revenues, and the portion that was generated through indirect taxes and social security contributions, are reported in O.E.C.D. (1973, 1977a).

8. During 1960–75, the number of national legislative elections ranged from zero in Spain to seven in Australia and Denmark. During this period, of course, Spain was nondemocratic; thus our arguments concerning the impact of electoral competition on fiscal policy are irrelevant for that case. For purposes of comparability with the other nations, we treat only the four American presidential elections rather than all eight congressional elections. It is, of course, true that the argument regarding the effect of electoral competition on fiscal policy is relevant to the latter elections; see Kramer (1971) and Tufte (1975).

9. See Lipset (1960, pp. 439–56) and Bell (1960). For rejoinders, see LaPalombara (1966) and Putnam (1973).

10. The most dramatic instances of reduced industrial conflict after World War II are found in Scandinavia. For discussions of the institutionalization of industrial conflict in those nations, see Elvander (1974) and Ingham (1974).

11. The effect is less pronounced when one considers the trend in British expenditures, in part because the government of Edward Heath ran down the surplus of funds allocated to capital formation. The result was a marked increase in borrowings from abroad, beginning in 1972, and actual deficits beginning in 1975. See Klein (1976, p. 418) and Brittan (1975).

12. Leftist parties are defined as those which are Social Democratic, Labor, or Communist. Thus, the American Democratic party is not considered to be leftist; it is, of course, true that the party is to the left of the Republican party and that it does matter whether Republicans or Democrats control the executive and legislative branches. (In this regard, see Tufte [1978, pp. 71–83].) Nevertheless, it is also true that it differs considerably from most European Socialist and Social Democratic-Labor parties—for example, in its electoral support among middle-class voters and in its unusually large body of self-declared "middle-of-the-roaders" and "conservatives." See, on the former point, Hamilton (1972, pp. 190–93). In regard to the latter point, Flanigan and Zingale (1975, p. 114) find that 66 percent of 1972 Democratic identifiers called themselves "conservative" or "middle-of-the-road" rather than "liberal." The measure of the partisan composition of government was calculated as follows: in each year, I summed the votes received in the previous national legislative election by all parties participating in government (i.e., holding cabinet positions) and divided the total into the number of votes received by all Social Democratic, Socialist, Labor, Communist, and smaller leftist parties (such as the Dutch Radicals and the Danish Socialist Peoples' parties) that were participants in government. This proportion ranges from 0 (when no leftist parties were in government) to 100 (when the government was composed entirely of leftist parties). I then summed the values for the 16 years between 1960–75 and calculated the average. That average represents the average proportion of the government's electoral base that was accounted for by leftist parties. It is highly correlated (on the order of $r = .99$) with a measure of the proportion of Cabinet portfolios held by leftist parties. The electoral data were obtained from Mackie and Rose (1974, 1975, 1976).

13. The measure of the formal structure of government is binary: 0 for unitary nations; 1 for federal nations. The measure of centralization was obtained from O.E.C.D. (1973). The degree of centralization in 1960 for the federal nations varied between 38.2 percent (Germany) and 79.7 percent (Australia). Among the unitary nations, the measure of centralization varied from 59 percent (Italy) to 85.8 percent (Ireland). The correlation between the measure of federalism and that of centralization is $r = -.53$.

14. See Lindbeck (1975, 1976, 1977); Aukrust (1977); Cooper (1972); and Keohane and Nye (1977).

15. The figures refer to exports and imports of all goods and services, and are derived from data reported in O.E.C.D. (1973, 1977a).

16. Recent Swedish experience confirms the argument here. Capitalizing on the rise in prices in several of the nations to which it exports goods, Swedish exports enjoyed high profits in 1973–74. Subsequent wage negotiations in late 1974 provided unusually large increments. As a result, prices for Swedish goods rose in the world market and, even with slender profit margins, firms lost markets. The result has been large balance of trade deficits, three devaluations since 1976, and negative growth in 1977.

17. More recently, Lindbeck (1977, pp. 13, 42) notes that the increased internationalization of the economy has caused an upsurge in international coordination of economic policy. Two recent examples are the development of protectionist limitations on imports and domestic capacity restrictions in the European steel industry (the Davignon plan), and the institution of annual economic summit conferences of western heads of state (Rambouillet, 1975; Puerto Rico, 1976; London, 1977; Bonn, 1978).

18. Lindbeck notes here the distinction—relevant to Sweden and several other small open economies—between the nationalization of the consumption of income, which implies a large "tax state," and the nationalization of the production of income, which implies, instead, a large number of publicly owned enterprises.

19. As Dahl and Tufte (1973, p. 130) suggest, there is a strong inverse correlation between the population of a nation and the degree of economic openness ($r = -.65$).

20. Contrary to our expectation, the extent of increase in openness during 1960–75 is not related to the extent of increase in the public economy. While all 18 nations became increasingly open during this period (in terms of exports and imports as a percent of GDP), the wide variation among the 18 nations was unaltered and the ordering of the nations remained, in 1975, almost as it was in 1960 ($r = .95$ between the measures of openness in 1960 and 1975). The findings reported here imply that it is the extent of openness, rather than the rate of change, that stimulates an expansion of the public economy.

21. This argument is supported by the existence of a positive correlation between the measure of the openness of the economy and the proportion of the work force that belong to labor unions ($r = .41$), and the positive correlation ($r = .56$) between the extent of unionization and the extent of government by leftist parties. Unfortunately, no satisfactory data exist with which cross-nationally comparable measures of concentration might be constructed. Data on unionization were obtained from Europa Publications (1977). We might note that our argument here implies a more complex relationship between the openness of the economy and the partisanship of government than is suggested by the assumption of independence in the regression analysis reported in Table 2. In fact, there is a positive, albeit modest, correlation between the two measures ($r = .37$).

22. The argument in this paragraph is supported by the very strong correlation between the measure of openness and a measure of the scope of collective bargaining derived from Mouly (1967), Schregle (1974), Lehmbruch (1977), and Hibbs (1976). The correlation is $r = .74$.

23. The argument that labor confederations are stronger, in terms of their ability to intervene in collective bargaining, in nations in which the scope of collective bargaining is relatively broad is supported by the strong correlation of $r = .65$ between the measure of the scope of collective bargaining (which ranges from 1 for Japan where collective bargaining often involves enterprise unions, to 6 for Austria, Ireland, Denmark, Norway, and Sweden, where economy-wide "framework" agreements, or similar consultations, take place) and a measure of the formal right of labor confederations to intervene in collective bargaining through prior consultation, post-negotiation approval, and/or control of strike funds.

24. This argument is supported by the high correlation between the measure of the

right of labor confederations to intervene in collective bargaining and a measure of the increase in the proportion of GNP spent on social security schemes (as defined by the International Labour Organisation) between 1960 and 1971. The correlation is r = .74. That increase in spending effort for social security schemes is, in turn, highly correlated with the measure of the expansion of the public economy (r = .72). The data on the increase in Social Security spending are reported in I.L.O (1964, 1976).

25. By 1975, the public economy absorbed 53.5 percent of the Dutch GDP, 50.2 percent of the Norwegian GDP, 52.2 percent of the Swedish GDP, and 45.0 percent of the Danish GDP. To a very large extent the scope of the public economy in 1975 was determined by the magnitude of the increase between 1960 and 1975. Thus the correlation between the measure of expansion in 1960–75 and the scope of the public economy in 1975 was r = .89, compared to a correlation of r = .35 between the 1960 and 1975 measures.

26. The data on the size distribution of income are reported in O.E.C.D. (1976). The data used here represent the first-order difference between the proportion of all after-tax income received by the top 20 percent and the bottom 20 percent of households. To control for national differences in the size of households and enhance the cross-national comparability of the data, the O.E.C.D. reports standardized figures. These are the data used here. The measure of the change in the proportion of GDP that represents all private capital accumulation (i.e., savings and consumption of fixed capital) is the first-order difference of the proportions in 1960 and 1975. The data are reported in O.E.C.D. (1973, 1977a).

27. That a trade-off exists between equality and accumulation is further suggested by the high negative correlation between the two measures (r = −.74).

28. In spite of the increase in the rate of capital accumulation in the private sector, the low rate of governmental savings—and indeed aggregate government deficits in several years—caused the proportion of gross capital accumulation in GDP to drop in Italy and the United States between 1960 and 1975. See O.E.C.D. (1977a).

References

Aukrust, Odd (1977), "Inflation in the Open Economy." In Lawrence B. Krause and Walter S. Salant (eds.), *Worldwide Inflation: Theory and Recent Experience*. Washington, D.C.: Brookings, pp. 107–53.

Bacon, Robert and Walter Eltis (1976). *Britain's Economic Problem: Too Few Producers*. London: Macmillan.

Bell, Daniel (1960). *The End of Ideology*. Glencoe: Free Press.

Bird, Richard M. (1970). *The Growth of Government Spending in Canada*. Toronto: Canadian Tax Foundation.

————. (1971). "Wagner's 'Law' of Expanding State Activity." *Public Finances/Finances Publiques* 26:1–26.

Brittan, Samuel (1975). "The Economic Contradictions of Democracy." *British Journal of Political Science* 5:129–59.

Buchanan, James M. and Richard E. Wagner (1977). *Democracy in Deficit: The Political Legacy of Lord Keynes*. New York: Academic Press.

Collier, David and Richard E. Messick (1975). "Prerequisites vs. Diffusion: Testing Alternative Explanations of Social Security Adoption." *American Political Science Review* 69:1299–1315.

Cooper, Richard N. (1972). "Economic Interdependence and Foreign Policy in the Seventies." *World Politics* 24:159–81.

Dahl, Robert and Edward Tufte (1973). *Size and Democracy*. Stanford: Stanford University Press.

Davis, Otto A., M. A. H. Dempster, and Aaron Wildavsky (1966). "A Theory of the Budgetary Process." *American Political Science Review* 60:529–47.

—————. (1974). "Toward a Predictive Theory of the Federal Budgetary Process." *British Journal of Political Science* 4:419–52.

Downs, Anthony (1957). *An Economic Theory of Democracy*. New York: Harper and Row.

—————. (1960). "Why the Government Budget is Too Small in a Democracy." *World Politics* 12:541–63.

—————. (1964). *Inside Bureaucracy*. Boston: Little, Brown.

Elvander, Nils (1974). "The Role of the State in Settlement of Labor Disputes in the Nordic Countries: A Comparative Analysis." *European Journal of Political Research* 2:363–83.

Europa Publications (1977). *Europa Yearbook 1977*. London: Europa.

Flanigan, William H. and Nancy Zingale (1975). *Political Behavior of the American Electorate*, 3rd ed. Boston: Allyn and Bacon.

Freeman, Roger A. (1975). *The Growth of American Government*. Stanford: Hoover Institute.

Galenson, Walter, ed. (1973). *Incomes Policy: What Can We Learn from Europe?* Ithaca: Cornell University Press.

Gilpin, Robert (1975). "Three Models of the Future." In C. Fred Bergsten and Lawrence B. Krause (eds.), *World Politics and International Finance*. Washington, D.C.: Brookings, pp. 37–60.

Gordon, Michael (1971). "Civil Servants, Politicians, and Parties." *Comparative Politics* 4:29–58.

Gupta, Shibshankar P. (1968). "Public Expenditure and Economic Development." *Finanzarchiv* 28:26–41.

Hamilton, Richard (1972). *Class and Politics in the United States*. New York: Wiley.

Headey, Bruce W. (1970). "Trade Unions and National Wages Policies." *Journal of Politics* 32:407–39.

Heclo, Hugh (1974). *Modern Social Politics in Britain and Sweden*. New Haven: Yale University Press.

Heidenheimer, Arnold J. et al. (1975). *Comparative Public Policy*. New York: St. Martin's.

Hibbs, Douglas A., Jr. (1976). "Industrial Conflict in Advanced Industrial Societies." *American Political Science Review* 70:1033–58.

—————. (1977). "Political Parties and Macroeconomic Policy." *American Political Science Review* 71:467–87.

—————. (1978). "On the Political Economy of Long-Run Trends in Strike Activity." *British Journal of Political Science* 8:153–75.

Ingham, Geoffrey K. (1974). *Strikes and Industrial Conflict*. London: Macmillan.

International Labour Organisation (1964). *The Cost of Social Security 1958–60*. Geneva: I.L.O.

—————. (1976). *The Cost of Social Security 1966–71*. Geneva: I.L.O.

Katzenstein, Peter J. (1976). "International Relations and Domestic Structure: Foreign Economic Policies of Advanced Industrial States." *International Organization* 30:4–13.

—————, ed. (1977). "Between Power and Plenty: Foreign Economic Policies of Advanced Industrial States." *International Organization* 31:587–920.

Keohane, Robert O. and Joseph S. Nye (1977). *Power and Interdependence: World Politics in Transition*. Boston: Little, Brown.

Key, V. O. (1949). *Southern Politics*. New York: Knopf.

King, Anthony (1969). "Political Parties in Western Democracies: Some Skeptical Reflections." *Polity* 2:111–41.

—————. (1973). "Ideas, Institutions and the Policies of Governments: A Comparative Analysis: I, II." *British Journal of Political Science* 3:291–313.

Klein, Rudolf (1976). "The Politics of Public Expenditure: American Theory and British Practice." *British Journal of Poltical Science* 6:401–32.

Kramer, Gerald H. (1971). "Short-Term Fluctuations in U.S. Voting Behavior, 1896–1964." *American Poltical Science Review* 65:131–43.

Krasner, Stephen D. (1976). "State Power and the Structure of International Trade." *World Politics* 28:317–47.

LaPalombara, Joseph (1966). "Decline of Ideology: A Dissent and an Interpretation." *American Political Science Review* 60:5–16.

Lehmbruch, Gerhard (1977). "Liberal Corporatism and Party Government." *Comparative Political Studies* 10:91–126.

Lindbeck, Assar (1974). *Swedish Economic Policy*. Berkeley: University of California Press.

————. (1975). "Business Cycles, Politics and International Economic Dependence." *Skandinaviska Enskilden Bank Quarterly Review* 2:53–68.

————. (1976). "Stabilization Policy in Open Economies with Endogenous Politicians." *American Economic Review* 66:1–19.

————. (1977). "Economic Dependence and Interdependence in the Industrialized World." Stockholm: Institute for International Economic Studies, University of Stockholm.

Lipset, Seymour Martin (1960). *Political Man*. Garden City: Doubleday.

Mackie, Thomas, T. and Richard Rose (1974). *International Almanac of Election Statistics*. London: Macmillan.

————. (1975). "General Elections in Western Nations During 1974." *European Journal of Political Research* 3:319–28.

————. (1976). "Election Data: General Elections in Western Nations During 1975." *European Journal of Political Research* 4:329–32.

Mouly, Jean (1967). "Wage Determination: Institutional Aspects." *International Labour Review* 96:497–526.

Musgrave, Richard A. (1969). *Fiscal Systems*. New Haven: Yale University Press.

Myrdal, Gunnar (1960). *Beyond the Welfare State*. New Haven: Yale University Press.

Niskanen, William A. (1971). *Bureaucracy and Representative Government*. Chicago: Aldine.

Nordhaus, William D. (1975). "The Political Business Cycle." *Review of Economic Studies* 42:160–90.

Organisation for Economic Co-operation and Development (1973). *National Accounts of OECD Countries: 1960–71*. Paris: O.E.C.D.

————. (1976). *Occasional Studies: Income Distribution in OECD Countries*. Paris: O.E.C.D.

————. (1977a). *National Accounts of OECD Countries: 1975*, Vol. 2. Paris: O.E.C.D.

————. (1977b). *Economic Outlook*, Vol. 22. Paris: O.E.C.D.

Peacock, Alan R. and Jack Wiseman (1967). *The Growth of Public Expenditure in the United Kingdom*, 2nd ed. London: Allen and Unwin.

Putnam, Robert D. (1973). *The Beliefs of Politicians*. New Haven: Yale University Press.

Rall, Wilhelm (1975). *Zur Wirksamkeit der Einkommenspolitik*. Tübingen: Mohr.

Schregle, Johannes (1974). "Labour Relations in Western Europe: Some Topical Issues." *International Labour Review* 109:1–22.

Schumpeter, Joseph (1918). "The Crisis of the Tax State." *International Economic Papers* 4:5–38.

————. (1950). *Capitalism, Socialism and Democracy*. New York: Harper and Row.

Shonfield, Andrew (1969). *Modern Capitalism*. New York: Oxford University Press.

————. (1976). *International Economic Relations of the Western World, 1959–1971*, 2 Vols. London: Oxford University Press.

Stephens, John D. (1978). *The Transition from Capitalism to Socialism*. London: Macmillan.

Tarschys, Daniel (1975). "The Growth of Public Expenditures: Nine Modes of Explanation." *Scandinavian Political Studies* 10:9–31.

Tufte, Edward (1975). " Determinants of the Outcome of Midterm Congressional Elections." *American Political Science Review* 69:812–26.

——————. (1978). *Political Control of the Economy*. Princeton: Princeton University Press.

United Nations (1976). *Statistical Yearbook 1975*. New York: United Nations.

Vernon, Raymond, ed. (1974). *Big Business and the State*. Cambridge: Harvard University Press.

Wagner, Adolf (1883). "The Nature of the Fiscal Economy." In Richard A. Musgrave and Alan R. Peacock, eds., *Classics in the Theory of Public Finance*. London: Macmillan, 1958, pp. 1–8.

Wildavsky, Aaron (1974). *The Politics of the Budgetary Process*, 2nd ed. Boston: Little, Brown.

——————. (1975). *Budgeting: A Comparative Theory of Budgetary Processes*. Boston: Little, Brown.

Wilensky, Harold (1975). *The Welfare State and Equality*. Berkeley: University of California Press.

5. Recent Trends in Economic Policy

It is always interesting to follow changes in policy. Looking at events in the recent past brings an immediacy, and a sense of the relation to one's own affairs, that is often lacking in theoretical work based on past events. In addition, there are two especially strong reasons to look at the events of this decade. One is that the 1980s have brought major changes in the way economic policy is made, and it is important that we look at the reasons for these innovations and their effects on economic outcomes. A second is that, precisely because there has been considerable change, it may be possible to test theories about economic and political behavior that cannot readily be tested in an era when little fluctuates.

There have been significant policy changes in all the areas examined in this book. A hitherto untried economic theory, supply-side theory, had many converts in the Reagan Administration and was used as the rationale for many of the administration's fiscal policy changes. Monetarism also influenced monetary policy more than in any previous era. The administration placed a strong emphasis on free-market principles, and made a determined effort to roll back much of the social and environmental regulation imposed during the previous two decades. There was a prolonged, albeit unintended, experiment with running a tight monetary policy while pursuing an expansive fiscal policy. There were two major tax changes along with several minor ones. While the administration worked to cut and redirect federal expenditures, it ran up the largest peacetime deficits in history.

The essay that follows will examine the reasons for all these changes and attempt to assess their effects.

The events of the eighties also have implications for many of the theories presented in this collection, particularly some of the theories in the tax and expenditure area. Since many of these theories were designed to explain the *lack* of change in earlier eras, they receive a real test in the 1980s. To what extent do they remain valid? In recent years we have also seen more open conflict between the Federal Reserve Board and the Presidency. What does this tell us about the locus of power over monetary policy? The 1980 and 1984 presidential elections were the first to occur after the idea of a political business cycle became widely known. Did events bear out this theory? The Reagan Administration was more opposed to increasing government expenditures than almost any preceding it; and it was the first Republican presidency in decades to control the Senate. What effect did this have on government growth? While no one could tackle all these questions comprehensively in a single essay, the reading that follows makes a rough attempt to assess some of the available evidence.

For further reading

Much of the published work on economic policy making in the 1980s has arisen from projects at Princeton University and the Urban Institute devoted to examining the economic policies of the Reagan Administration, and from work at the Brookings Institution and the American Enterprise Institute. Among the most recent books on monetary and fiscal policy are Aaron *et al.*, *Economic Choices 1987*; Cagan, *Essays in Contemporary Economic Problems 1986*; Mills and Palmer, *Federal Budget Policy in the 1980s*; Stone and Sawhill, *Economic Policy in the Reagan Years*; and Hulten and Sawhill, *The Legacy of Reaganomics*. Daneke and Lemak, *Regulatory Reform Considered* and Eads and Fix, *The Reagan Regulatory Strategy* contain some good articles on recent regulatory policy; Derthick and Quirk, *The Politics of Deregulation* is also interesting. *Market Based Public Policy* by Hula examines privatization. Norton's article "Industrial Policy and American Renewal" and articles in *Revitalizing the U.S. Economy* (Redburn *et al.*) look at industrial policy. William Greider's *The Education of David Stockman* and Stockman's own *The Triumph of Politics* give an unusually frank picture of day-to-day policy making in the Reagan Administration.

Bibliography

Aaron, Hency *et al.*, *Economic Choices 1987* (Washington D.C.: The Brookings Institution, 1986).

Cagan, Phillip, ed., *Essays in Contemporary Economic Problems 1986: The Impact of the Reagan Program* (Washington D.C.: American Enterprise Institute, 1986).

Daneke, Gregory A. and David J. Lemack, eds., *Regulatory Reform Reconsidered* (Boulder, Co.: Westview, 1985).

Eads, George C. and Michael Fix, *The Reagan Regulatory Strategy: An Assessment* (Washington D.C.: The Urban Institute Press, 1985).

Greider, William, *The Education of David Stockman and Other Americans* (New York: E. P. Dutton, 1986).

Hula, Richard ed., *Market Based Public Policy* (New York: Macmillan, 1987).

Hulten, Charles R. and Isabel V. Sawhill, eds., *The Legacy of Reagonomics: Prospects for*

Long-term Growth (Washington D.C.: The Urban Institute Press, 1984).

Mills, Gregory B. and John L. Palmer, eds., *Federal Budget Policy in the 1980s* (Washington D.C.: The Urban Institute Press, 1984).

Norton, Patrick, "Industrial Policy and American Renewal," *Journal of Economic Literature* 26 (March 1986): 1–40.

Redburn, F. Stevens, Terry F. Buss, and Larry Ledbur, *Revitalizing the U.S. Economy* (New York: Praeger, 1986).

Stockman, David, *The Triumph of Politics: How the Reagan Revolution Failed* (New York: Harper and Row, 1986).

Stone, Charles F. and Isabel V. Sawhill, *Economic Policy in the Reagan Years* (Washington D.C.: The Urban Institute Press, 1984).

5.1 Economic Policy in the 1980s

PAUL PERETZ

At the beginning of the 1980s there appeared to be promise that the economic situation would improve. Many of the factors that had resulted in poor economic performance during the 1970s seemed poised for change. Oil prices, which had risen sharply in the 1970s, had begun a long downward slide. Rapid food price increases were over. And a new administration—one with an activist orientation toward economic policy—was about to take office.

The 1980s have seen an extraordinary number of changes in economic policy. There have been two major and several minor changes in the tax code, a concentrated attempt to shift spending priorities, a prolonged experiment with monetarist monetary policy, and spasmodic attempts to deregulate the private economy. It seems only appropriate to conclude this volume of readings on economic policy making with an assessment of the recent changes in economic policy, the reasons for and the results of the changes, and the implications of these events in terms of the theories that have been devised to explain the relation between government and the economy.

The policy environment

The economic policy changes of the 1980s did not take place in a vacuum. Many factors which normally constrain economic policy changed, and these changes had important effects on what was possible.

The most important of these changes occurred in the relation of the United States to the outside world. A long-term trend of relative decline in American economic power continued. This was a result not so much of what happened in this country, as of faster economic growth in other countries. Although growth in Europe and Japan in the 1980s slowed somewhat relative to that in the United States, the nations of the Pacific rim achieved extremely rapid growth in this period.

The growing economic maturity of the rest of the world, together with the

436

lowering of American tariff barriers over the previous two decades, fostered a significant export of manufacturing jobs to countries with lower labor costs, including Japan, Korea, and Taiwan. This process was accelerated by the phenomenon of "outsourcing" by U.S.-based corporations which, in the face of foreign competition, became increasingly multinational, shifting more and more of their manufacturing capacity overseas (Zysman and Cohen 1986). Overvaluation of the dollar until 1987 magnified the U.S. trade deficits for much of this period.

Internally, the effects of these phenomena were a weakening of the union movement, job loss, and slower growth in income for the blue-collar workforce (Krugman 1984). As the upper ranks of industrial workers and other groups lost ground, the American middle class appeared to be shrinking (Thurow 1984; Rosenthal 1985).

The slow collapse of the OPEC oil cartel was another important factor. Many attributed the high inflation and slow growth of the 1970s in part to a series of petroleum price increases imposed by oil-producing countries. In the 1980s the situation reversed: oil prices fell considerably, helping to reduce inflation in all the industrialized countries, and growth rates began to recover.

The domestic economy also constrained options. Here perhaps the most important single factor was the high rate of inflation prevailing at the end of the 1970s. This combined with the low growth rates to produce what was referred to as stagflation. As we shall see, much of economic policy, especially monetary policy, in the early 1980s was a reaction to this constraint.

New theories in economics also played some part in the economic changes of the 1980s. Monetarist theories were given an extensive test by the Federal Reserve Board in the 1979–1985 period. Supply-side theories were used to justify the early fiscal policy of the Reagan Administration.

The shift to Republican rule was also important. Ronald Reagan was one of very few Presidents to place changes in economic policy high on his personal agenda. Almost as important was the fact that the Senate, normally the more liberal branch of Congress, was controlled by the Republicans from 1980 to 1986. These two factors in combination favored a shift in the tax burden and a shift in spending priorities.

The private sector

A brief history

As might be expected during a conservative Republican administration, the 1980s saw a new emphasis on the encouragement of free market forces and reliance on the market to achieve public ends. This theme was acted out in both positive and negative ways.

On the negative side, repeated calls for an industrial policy of the sort described by Reich and Etzioni were stoutly resisted. In a similar vein, the Reagan

Administration persistently fought attempts by Democrats in Congress to secure protection for American industry.

On a more positive note, there were some interesting initiatives aimed at helping private industry. One example is the attempt to create "economic enterprise zones"—industrial parks, primarily in depressed areas, that try to attract business with lower taxes and reduced regulation (Fasenfest 1986). The use of industrial development bonds, which make relocation more attractive to industry, also increased in the early 1980s (Peretz 1986). However, these efforts were cut back considerably in the second half of the 1980s.

There were also attempts to apply market incentives to the production of public goods, an idea long advocated by economists (Niskanen 1971). Examples are the use of housing vouchers in place of public housing, and government contracts with private firms to provide medical care, correctional facilities, and sanitation services (Fitzgerald 1986, Palumbo 1986).

Most observers at the beginning of the Reagan era expected that the administration would give highest priority to a rollback of government regulation of private business (Weidenbaum 1980). What is striking, however, is that, although deregulation was a major theme in the President Reagan's 1980 campaign and his subsequent rhetoric (Congressional Quarterly 1980), in two terms he has achieved less in the way of deregulation than did President Carter in one—and for Carter, deregulation was a relatively minor priority (Lemak 1985).

The key to this apparent paradox is a recognition that there are two distinct types of regulation—what I have termed *producer regulation* and *consumer regulation*. In producer regulation, as in the cases of the trucking, airline, taxi cab, and undertaking industries, what we have primarily is government enforcement of high prices and entry barriers on an industry's behalf (Stigler 1971). By contrast, consumer regulation, including environmental, utility, product safety, and food and drug regulation, is primarily aimed at constraining actors in the market system from causing harm to the public.

The deregulatory efforts of the Carter Administration were mainly aimed at lifting producer regulation. Modest successes were achieved in deregulation of the rail, trucking, financial, and oil industries and a major success in deregulation of the airline industry. By contrast, the Reagan Administration focused its attention on consumer regulation, arguing that the costs imposed on the economy far outweighed the benefits. This campaign ran into considerable opposition from the public, from public-interest groups, and from a Democratic House of Representatives that did not favor this kind of deregulation.

This is not to say that the Reagan Administration did not have an important short-term impact on business regulation. Perhaps the most innovative single step was the establishment in the Office of Management and Budget of a review process for proposed regulations (DeMuth 1985). This led to some limited centralization of power in this area and increased the effort to weigh the benefits of proposed regulations against the costs (Tolchin and Tolchin 1985). But the real impact of the change has been questioned, on the grounds that the OMB approved

98 percent of all regulations submitted (Eads and Fix 1984; Weidenbaum 1984).

Two other Reagan initiatives were more immediate in their impact. One was the appointment of strong proponents of deregulation to positions of power in the regulatory agencies—for example, the appointments of Mark Fowler as chairman of the Federal Communications Commission and of Ann Gorsuch-Burford as director of the Environmental Protection Agency. Such appointees substantially reduced regulatory activity in the first few years of the administration. However, in the longer term, the actions of these opponents of regulation seemed to provoke a public backlash which made more permanent changes harder to achieve (Weidenbaum 1985). The other successful initiative was a 14 percent reduction in the budgets of regulatory agencies between 1980 and 1985, leading to a decline in staffing by around one-sixth (Weidenbaum 1985). This hampered the agencies' ability to enforce regulations.

There was also a spate of executive orders (Weidenbaum 1985) aimed at reducing the costs to industry of compliance with regulations—for example, by delaying enforcement of the gasoline mileage and air-bag regulations in the automobile industry. While some of these achieved their goal, many of the orders were later reversed by the courts.

This reliance on dubious executive orders was prompted by the failure of the Reagan Administration to get most of its reform legislation through Congress. While substantial progress was made in the area of financial deregulation, which had bipartisan support, and there was some further deregulation in the transportation area, the Reagan Administration got little cooperation from Congress in its attempts to roll back consumer regulation (Foreman 1984).

The failure was due primarily to three factors. One was that the House of Representatives remained under Democratic control throughout the period. The second was that industry failed to give strong backing to the deregulatory legislation, partly because it feared a consumer backlash and partly because many of the larger firms had already invested in compliance—for example, by installing pollution control equipment—and did not want competition from others who had not. The final factor was simply that the Reagan Administration did not make deregulatory legislation a top priority (Weidenbaum 1984).

Over all, one can best characterize the 1980s as a period of temporary reductions in business regulation, which may have increased productivity a miniscule 0.1 percent (Christiansen and Haveman 1984), but accomplished little in the way of long-term change. Considerable deregulation took place at the administrative level, but the inability of the Reagan Administration to convert its deregulatory program into legislation meant that the long-term effects of the program could not be extensive or lasting.

The theories

How do the three major regulatory theories we looked at earlier in this volume stand up in light of the events of the 1980s? Recent history seems to provide some support for all three, but strong support for none of them.

The "capture" theory developed by Huntington and Stigler is contradicted at least on its face by the extensive deregulation and reform that has taken place in the late 1970s and early 1980s, precisely in those agencies considered most prone to capture. Even more remarkable is the fact that much of this reform has been implemented by the high-level staffs of the agencies; this is particularly true in the case of the Interstate Commerce Commission (Derthick and Quirk 1985). On the other hand, one could argue that Huntington's more basic point, that agencies act to preserve themselves, receives some support. At a time when deregulation pressures were strong, the ICC bent with the wind in order to preserve itself. By initiating limited deregulation, the ICC remained intact, and suffered relatively low budget cuts compared with other agencies.

Downs's theory too seems to receive mixed support. While the downturn in environmental regulation that his theory appears to predict has indeed taken place, this seems to be due not to a heavier weighing of costs by the general public, but to pressure from industry and the actions of the Reagan Administration. In fact, most of the legislation passed in the 1960s and early 1970s remains in place, and public support for that legislation seems as high as ever.

The notion outlined in the Meier piece—i.e., that regulatory agencies are self-contained entities with an internalized sense of mission and can do much to control their own destiny—also seems only partially borne out. In support is the fact that after ten years of deregulatory effort, only one medium-sized agency, the Civil Aeronautics Board, had been abolished. On the other hand, it has become obvious that the people appointed to head agencies can change their direction significantly. This was as apparent in the case of Carter's appointees who had public-interest and environmental backgrounds as of Reagan's conservative, pro-industry appointees. For example, in a ten-year period the Federal Trade Commission went from being a sleepy inactive agency, to a champion of the consumer, to a pro-industry position (Meier 1985).

In sum, the events of the late 1970s and the 1980s support parts of each theory but cannot be said to validate any of them completely.

The public sector

The 1980s have been a period characterized by poor coordination of monetary, tax, and expenditure policies. Indeed, there has been less policy coordination in recent years than at any time since the end of the Second World War, and this despite the creation of new mechanisms designed to promote coordination. This situation is responsible for the two most obvious economic problems of the 1980s—a federal deficit larger than any other in peacetime, and the transformation of the United States from a net creditor to the world's leading debtor nation.

Because monetary policy and fiscal policy have been pushing in opposite directions for much of this period, the 1980s provide a test of policy dominance: which policy prevails when policies are in conflict? The evidence seems to support the notion that monetary policy is predominant. As James Tobin puts it, "Over the past 40 years, particularly over the last 15, monetary policy has overtaken fiscal policy as the principal regulator of macroeconomic performance" (Tobin 1986, 33).

Monetary policy

In October 1979 the Federal Reserve Board, under the chairmanship of Paul Volcker, began an experiment with monetarism. Instead of paying primary attention to interest rates, the board instead concentrated on the total amount of money in the economy. This experiment was sparked by the rapid rise in inflation in the late 1970s, reaching 13.4 percent in 1979. Monetarists felt that the root problem was a rapid increase in the supply of money, and that the only solution was to curb that increase by keeping the money supply constant. Although the Fed did not keep the money supply as constant as monetarists would have liked, it nonetheless paid far more attention to this goal than had been the case before 1979.

This change was reinforced by the fact that the Reagan administration in its early years advocated a monetarist monetary policy as an antidote to what it saw as the stop-and-go policies of the 1970s (Congressional Quarterly 1985, 61). The tight monetary policies instituted in 1980 reduced the real money supply by 2.7 percent in 1980 and 3.3 percent in 1981. Owing in part to unanticipated declines in the velocity of money, by 1981 this policy brought on the largest recession since the Great Depression. With coincident declines in oil prices and food prices, inflation fell from 12.4 percent in 1980 to 3.8 percent by 1982, and since then it has stayed around that level. At the same time, unemployment climbed from 5.8 percent in 1979 to 9.7 percent in 1982 and did not fall back to 6 percent until 1987 (C.E.A. 1987).

It has been estimated that the recession cost as much as $886 billion in lost output (Stone and Sawhill 1984). Somewhat chastened by this experience, both the Reagan Administration and, to a lesser degree, the Federal Reserve Board turned more expansionary after October 1982. Under pressure from the administration, and with a series of Reagan appointees with supply-side leanings joining the Board, the Fed began a slow retreat from monetarism. Monetary policy became gradually more stimulatory after 1982, accelerating somewhat in 1985 and 1986. Then, in the spring of 1987, there was some tightening, in an effort to curb the precipitous drop in the value of the dollar and to retain overseas financing for the federal deficit. Yet, even in this more liberal period, monetary policy was somewhat tighter than in previous decades. In the early 1980s this was primarily because of fears of inflation. In the middle 1980s the driving force was the need to maintain high real interest rates to assure financing of record federal deficits.

The events of the 1980s tend to confirm the view of most observers that Congress has little independent power over monetary policy, but do not provide a good test of the extent of the President's power in this area. For much of the period, the Fed and the Administration favored similar policies, making it hard to decide who was more influential. Yet it is clear that the Federal Reserve Board pursued tighter monetary policies than were favored by the administration for the latter part of the period. Reagan retained Paul Volcker as Fed chairman in 1983, despite the fact that Volcker presumably would not have been Reagan's first choice, and replaced him with another conservative, Alan Greenspan, in 1987. On the other hand, the Reagan appointment of supply-side sympathizers to the Federal Reserve Board was certainly partly responsible for the board's retreat from monetarism, so that the administration's urging of more expansionary policies had some effect. Furthermore, continued pressure *from* the Fed for action to reduce the deficit had virtually no effect. Overall, it seems fair to say that while the Federal Reserve Board was fairly independent in the 1980s, the President clearly had considerable power to affect monetary policy.

Fiscal policy

During his 1980 election campaign Ronald Reagan promised to cut taxes significantly, raise spending on defense, and reduce the federal deficit. His efforts to fulfill these promises resulted in major changes in fiscal policy during the decade. Because (as most economists pointed out at the time) it is virtually impossible to achieve these three ends simultaneously, the attempt to do so resulted in major economic distortions.

The natural result of raising spending while cutting taxes is a growing deficit. This could have been avoided only if domestic spending had been cut sufficiently to compensate for the increases in defense spending, or if the tax cuts had stimulated enough economic growth to make up the revenue shortfall, as some supply-side economists claimed—and the Reagan Administration appeared to believe—would happen. For those who did not consider either of these optimistic scenarios to be possible, the question was which promise would give way. It was the promise to lower the federal deficit.

Taxes

On the tax side, Ronald Reagan's campaign promises were faithfully carried out. In 1981 the President endorsed a version of the Kemp-Roth tax-cut proposal which cut the federal income tax by 25 percent over a three-year period and cut the effective rate of the corporation income tax. This was not such a major cut as it might at first appear. Inflation, which had reached a historic peacetime high, had driven up the effective rates of both taxes, and even the Carter Administration was proposing a cut of around 10 percent to compensate for this. Nonetheless, the Reagan tax cut was one of the largest in American history, and more than double the amount most mainstream economists recommended. The benefits of the cuts were disproportionately concentrated on those with the highest incomes.

For a tax cut of this magnitude not to lead to massive deficits, it was necessary that the kind of increased work effort discussed in the reading by Wanniski actually take place. By 1982 it was apparent that the anticipated large increase was not taking place and that the deficit was indeed growing. This prompted Congress and the administration to pass a series of small tax increases. Some of the business tax cuts of 1981 were repealed in 1982. Gasoline taxes were raised in 1982. Payroll taxes were raised in 1983. Some minor tax loopholes were closed in 1984. But these small increases failed to offset the effects of the original reductions, and the deficit continued to climb.

From 1984 onward, most observers expected Congress and the Administration to reach a compromise that would combine some further domestic spending cuts with considerable tax increases (Mills and Palmer 1984). Congress, usually reluctant even to consider tax increases, made a number of proposals along these lines, but was unwilling to take the unpopular step of passing a major tax increase until the President was willing to share the responsibility. This the President would not do, despite the urging of advisers such as OMB Director David Stockman and the Chairman of the Council of Economic Advisers, Martin Feldstein. Reagan undoubtedly regarded the deficit as a check on a Democratic Congress's propensity to spend, was unwilling to reverse the 1981 cuts which he regarded as a major achievement of his administration, and in any case did not need to court further unpopularity as his administration drew to a troubled close. The fact that his 1984 opponent, Walter Mondale, had been defeated after promising to raise taxes and predicting that Reagan would break his "no new taxes" promise after the election, was probably a contributory factor.

Instead President Reagan pushed for a major revision in the federal tax code, which lowered individual tax rates again, removed many loopholes, and increased the corporation income tax. While on balance this reform, too, favored the wealthy, it also benefited those with low incomes. The program was enacted in 1986.

It was anticipated that the reform would be revenue-neutral overall. The effect of the changes was greatly to simplify the tax code and to remove many of the loopholes that had been distorting incentives in the economy. Most of the changes had been proposed by economists for the previous twenty years. What was new was the willingness of a conservative administration to make a priority of ending tax breaks, and the ability of the leaders of the Finance and Ways and Means committees to push the changes through Congress in the face of determined opposition from some of the most active interest groups in the country. The basic compromise which ensured passage of the legislation was a trade incorporating the lower personal tax rates desired by conservatives, along with the removal of loopholes and the increase in business taxes desired by liberals and moderates.

Unlike the first Reagan tax change, which most economists regarded as a mistake both at the time and afterward, this one was generally applauded by mainstream economists and received support from both liberals and conservatives. However, because it did nothing to solve the deficit problem, many regarded it as the right program at the wrong time. The ultimate impact of the tax reform remains to be determined. At the time it was passed, many liberals expected that the lowering of income tax rates would eventually be reversed in an attempt to reduce the deficit, so that the removal of loopholes would be the only lasting effect. At the same time, many interest groups hoped gradually to reintroduce many of the special exemptions they had lost, leaving only the rate cuts in place. Only time will tell who was correct.

It is clear that the dramatic changes of the 1980s raise problems for all the theories we looked at in the section on taxes. The consensus over tax policy discussed by Buchanan does not seem to be evident. Slow change, as described by by Downs and Winters (see Susan Hansen's essay) does not seem to characterize the eighties at all.

Hansen's theory fares somewhat better. On the down side, important changes were made in the tax code in the absence of a major party realignment. Nevertheless, it does appear that it was changes in the party composition of the Presidency and the Senate that facilitated the change.

King's theory also receives mixed support. In its favor is the fact that most of the changes benefited the well-off and were justified as promoting economic growth. If one believes Stockman's famous remark about supply-side rationales being a "Trojan Horse" to justify tax cuts for those in the highest brackets, then this was intended. However, against the theory is the fact that change of the party in power made such a difference in permitting tax reform. The sort of control that King discusses should change little from administration to administration.

Expenditures

The changes in expenditure policy during the first half of the 1980s were almost as dramatic as the changes in tax policy. Two major changes dominated the period. There was a large expansion of the defense buildup commenced by President Carter at the end of the 1970s and there was a considerable reduction in many federal domestic expenditures. Defense spending increased from 25.8 percent of the total budget in 1980 to 30.2 percent in 1987, whereas domestic programs excluding Social Security and Medicare fell from 34.8 percent in 1980 to 32.4 percent in 1987 (O.M.B. 1987).

The increase in defense spending had begun under Carter, partly in response to an extensive arms buildup by the Soviet Union. Nonetheless, the need for increased defense spending was a major theme of the 1980 Reagan campaign. After the election of Reagan and of a Republican Senate, the buildup was accelerated. Between 1982 and 1986 national security spending increased at an average rate of 7.1 percent per year. After 1985, procurement scandals, the increasing unpopularity of the defense buildup, and Democratic congressional gains slowed the growth of the defense budget (Wehr 1987). The rate of increase of real defense spending dropped from 8.9 percent in 1985 to 6 percent in 1986 and 2.3 percent in 1987 (O.M.B. 1987).

The second major component of the federal budget, Social Security spending, underwent little change during the 1980s. The fairly rapid increase of previous decades was slowed. Nonetheless, Social Security spending as a percent of GNP continued to rise, driven by the growth in the numbers of elderly and the political popularity of the program. The Reagan Administration tried at a number of points to cut back various aspects of the Social Security program, but succeeded only at the margins due to the strong public support for Social Security and strong opposition to the cuts in Congress.

One of the key achievements of the Reagan Administration was the reduction of spending on domestic programs other than Social Security. As was the case with defense spending and taxation, the major changes occurred during the so-called honeymoon period, the first two years of the Reagan Administration. In 1981 major reductions were enacted for almost all domestic programs, with the cuts generally in the 8 to 15 percent range. Smaller but still substantial cuts were made in 1982. After the 1982 elections, when Democrats made gains in the House and five Republican Senators won by less than 2 percent of the vote, little further erosion took place, and there was some modest restoration of previous cuts. However, it was notable that no major new domestic programs were introduced in the period up to 1987 and that the cuts made in 1981 and 1982 were generally not reversed.

The domestic spending reductions were achieved for four major reasons. The first was that Reagan Administration made the cuts a priority. Second was that most of the cuts came during the honeymoon period after the 1980 election, in which the new President had carried 44 of the 50 states against an incumbent President and the Senate had become Republican. Members of the Democrat-controlled House, who are elected every two years, feared to oppose what seemed to be the will of the people. The third factor was the prior reform of the budgetary process in Congress, especially the creation of the budget committees. This centralization permitted David Stockman, the President's exceptionally able OMB director, and his allies in Congress, to cut all domestic programs simultaneously, rather than having to undertake the more difficult task of working on cuts with an array of committees one at a time. The fourth factor was the fear of a huge federal deficit. Given the huge tax cuts and the buildup in defense, failure to cut domestic spending would have made an already bad deficit problem even worse.

In many ways the failure of Congress to restore the program budgets after the President's power began to wane was just as remarkable as the initial cuts. Here the key factor was the ever-increasing federal deficit. While it is hard to believe that the Reagan Administration wanted a huge deficit, its presence made it difficult for congressional Democrats to increase spending without running into claims of fiscal irresponsibility.

The deficit also gave rise to one of the more bizarre policy changes of the 1980s, the adoption of the Gramm-Rudman-Hollings deficit reduction plan in December 1985. The idea behind the bill was that automatic spending cuts would take place if Congress and the President failed to meet the prescribed deficit reduction targets. Viewed charitably, this could be seen as an attempt by Congress to curb its own tendencies. But, as almost everyone understood when it was passed, the mechanism enforcing the automatic cuts was unconstitutional. Although the bill had passed with massive support in 1985, its passage was due largely to a desire on the part of the members of Congress to be seen as doing something to solve the deficit problem. By 1987 most of the bill's provisions were being circumvented by the same President and Congress that had adopted it.

On balance, the changes in expenditure policy in the 1980s do not seem kind to the theory of incrementalism, although parts of the theory fare better than others. The sharp reductions in domestic spending at the beginning of the eighties do not fit well with the idea of a base level of spending that remains unexamined, or with the notion of inevitable slow increases in spending. Just as problematic is the fact that the cuts that were made varied widely from program to program, apparently contradicting the notion that budget makers lacked the information to make differentiated cuts.

Another problem with the theory is that in this period the three major components of federal spending moved in very different directions. Budget makers reduced domestic spending while increasing defense spending, and left Social Security to increase at a slow but steady pace. This does not fit well with incrementalism's view that all components of the budget tend to move at similar rates.

However, not all of incrementalist theory has been disconfirmed by recent events. As Davis, Dempster, and Wildavsky predict, the major nonincremental changes occurred soon after a change of administration. Further, after 1982, expenditures grew in essentially incrementalist fashion. It seems wise to view incrementalist theory as a reasonable description of the process that occurs when an administration is not trying to reorder spending priorities, but the theory is flawed as a general explanation of expenditure growth.

Economic outcomes

While the economic policies pursued during the 1980s are interesting in their own right, what is most important is their connection to economic outcomes. What were the major economic trends of the 1980s and to what degree can what happened be attributed to changes in policy?

Economic growth

The great success story of the 1980s with respect to economic goals was the reduction of inflation from 13.3 percent in 1979 to an average of 3.3 percent in the four years from 1982 to 1986. Around half of this reduction was due to fortuitous decreases in energy and food prices (Stone and Sawhill 1984). The other half was largely due to the sharp recession of 1981–1982. The primary credit for this must be given to the tight monetary policies of the Federal Reserve Board (and to their failure to foresee the drop in the velocity of money), which served to counteract the Reagan Administration's somewhat expansionary fiscal policies. However, some credit is also due to the Reagan Administration, which gave priority to reducing inflation and encouraged the Fed's tight money policies in the first few years.

Economists generally believe that the most reliable way to reduce inflation is to throttle back on growth, allowing unemployment to rise. The events of the eighties tended to confirm this grim belief. Despite favorable developments in energy prices, real per capita GNP growth in the period 1980–1986 was actually lower than in the 1970s, averaging 1.5 percent, versus 1.8 percent in the 1970s and 2.5 percent in the 1960s. This is a case where the average figure is somewhat misleading, however. The years 1980 to 1982 had virtually no growth at all. After 1982 there was erratic but unspectacular expansion at a rate that averaged 2.8 percent per year (C.E.A. 1987). On the other hand, the growth figures overstate the benefits to the average family. Real family income averaged $29,029 in 1979 (in 1985 dollars). It dropped to a low of $26,116 in 1982, before rising slightly to 27,735 in 1985 (U.S. Department of Commerce 1986a).

If growth was a little below the average for the postwar period, unemployment was markedly higher. The average unemployment rate in the 1980–1986 period was 7.8 percent, around 9 million workers. In the peak year of 1983, 10.7 million people were out of work. This contrasts with rates of 6.1 percent in the 1970s, 4.7 percent in the 1960s and 4.4 percent in the 1950s. Not all of this was due to policy. Demographic changes had made the work force somewhat more vulnerable to unemployment. But a lot of the rise in unemployment can reasonably be laid at the feet of the Federal Reserve Board and its fears that rapid expansion would reignite inflation.

Other than unemployment, the three major negative developments of the 1980s were the increase in the federal deficit, the rise in real interest rates, and the rapid increase in the amount owed abroad. In the 1970s the federal debt averaged 2.1 percent of GNP, a figure sufficiently high that the deficit was made a major theme of the Reagan 1980 campaign. However, the deficit grew to an average of 4.5 percent of GNP in the period 1980 to 1986, when it stood at 5.3 percent of GNP (C.E.A. 1987). This led to upward pressure on interest rates, raised the value of the dollar, and undermined U.S. industrial competitiveness, while slowing capital formation and growth (Gramlich 1984; Aaron et al. 1986).

Real interest rates were abnormally high during the 1980s. In the early part of the decade, expectations that inflation would take off again played an important part in keeping rates high. In the latter half of the eighties, as fears of inflation diminished, the ever-increasing federal deficit kept rates high. Whereas the real prime rate of interest in the 1970s was 1.0 percent, in the 1980–1986 period it averaged 7.3 percent (C.E.A. 1987).

Net foreign investment also became negative during the 1980s for the first time since the Second World War. In 1980 Americans owned $106 billion more in foreign investments than foreigners owned in the United States. By 1986 foreigners owned $264 billion more in the United States than Americans owned in their countries.

Despite the fact that the Reagan Administration's supply-side goal was to foster increases in investment and productivity, neither did very well during the period (Marshall 1986). Nonresidential fixed investment, which rose from 10.1 percent of GNP in 1976 to 11.8 percent of GNP in 1980, fell back to 10.9 percent of GNP in 1986. Output per hour dropped from a low 1.3 percent annual increase in the 1970s to an even lower 1.1 percent in the 1980–1985 period.

Allocation: Public/Private

One of the continuing themes of the 1980s was the need to reduce the size of government. We have already seen that substantial real cuts were made in federal domestic programs. It might therefore be expected that the size of government was reduced during the period. Such was not the case.

If one considers all levels of government, including state and local, government expenditures constituted 32.6 percent of GNP in 1980. This figure had risen to 35.3 percent by 1986. This increase was *not* due to state and local governments taking up the slack as the federal government trimmed down. State and local spending as a percent of GNP was constant at 13.3 percent of GNP between 1980 and 1986. Federal spending, on the other hand, rose from 21.6 percent of GNP in 1980 to 24.4 percent in 1986 (C.E.A. 1987).

Although the cuts made in federal domestic expenditures were quite substantial, they affected only about a third of the budget. Expenditures rose in the Social Security and Medicare component, in the national security component, and in the interest payments component of the budget. Together the increased expenditures in these areas outbalanced the cuts in domestic spending.

Granted that the role of government in the economy increased during the Reagan years, can one at least assume that it did so at a slower rate? The answer is no. Between 1970 and 1976, under the Republican administrations of Nixon and Ford, government expenditures as a percent of GNP rose from 31.3 percent in 1970 to 33 percent in 1976. In what are generally regarded as the spendthrift Carter years, government expenditures as a percent of GNP actually fell from 33 percent in 1976 to 32.6 percent in 1980. Under Reagan, a dedicated foe of government growth, government expenditures as a percent of GNP rose from 32.6 percent in 1980 to 35.3 percent in 1985 (C.E.A. 1987).

Allocation: Public/Public

As has already been noted, there was extensive change in the type of government programs at the federal level during the 1980s. National security spending increased from 25.8 percent of the federal budget in 1980 to 30.2 percent in 1987. Interest payments increased from 8.9 percent to 13.5 percent of the budget in the same period. Social Security and Medicare spending also increased in this period, rising from 25.5 percent of the budget to 27.2 percent. Domestic programs, however, dropped from 34.8 percent of the budget in 1980 to 32.4 percent in 1987 (O.M.B. 1987).

Looking more closely at this last category, one can divide it into health and income security, general government and law enforcement, and other domestic programs such as transportation, agriculture, education, natural resources, and community development programs. Health and income security payments rose from 16.8 percent of the budget in 1980 to 18.8 percent in 1987, but the rate of increase slowed from the level of the 1970s (Weicher 1986). General government and law enforcement spending levels also rose slowly, from 1.3 percent of the budget in 1980 to 1.5 percent in 1987. But other domestic programs fell from 16.8 percent to 12.1 percent between 1980 and 1987 (O.M.B. 1987). Thus, most of the drop in spending was concentrated in substantive domestic programs, with manpower programs being hit especially hard.

Redistribution

Many observers, including David Stockman (Greider 1986), have identified redistribution from the poor and the middle class to the better-off segments of society as one of the hidden aims of the Reagan Administration. If so, it was one of the few aims that was successfully accomplished.

In an article in this reader, Joseph Pechman shows that the tax burden on the wealthy declined markedly in the 1980–1985 period. And, although spending on transfer payments to the poor rose in the 1980s, the number of poor rose even more. This did not, as many welfare advocates have claimed, lead to a reduction of benefits for those on public assistance. It is true that monthly cash payments to welfare mothers (measured in 1986 dollars) declined from $383 in 1980 for a family of four, to $348 in 1985; but increases in food stamp, housing, and Medicaid payments made up the gap. Rather, what happened was a reduction in the percentage of the poor who receive welfare benefits. While the number of persons below the poverty level rose from 29.3 million in 1980 to 33.1 million in 1985, the number receiving benefits from Aid to Families with Dependent Children, the major cash program, fell from 10.923 million in 1980 to 10.74 million in 1985 and the number receiving food stamps fell from 22.028 million in 1980 to 19.193 million in 1985 (U.S. Department of Commerce 1986b).

The impact of these changes, however, is probably far outweighed by the effects of the macroeconomic policies pursued by the administration. The most important factor here was the high rate of unemployment, which falls disproportionately upon those who earn the least. For example, when unemployment among managers is 3 percent unemployment among laborers is normally 15 percent (Peretz 1983). Slow growth and the loss of high-paying blue-collar jobs to overseas workers all hurt lower-income groups more than the rich, while the huge increase in real interest rates was a major boost to those with large assets.

Taken together, the specific program changes and macroeconomic policy changes of the Reagan Administration appear to have had important effects on the distribution of income in the United States. Between 1980 and 1985 the percent of all income received by the bottom 20 percent of families (those earning less than $13,192 in 1985) declined from 5.3 percent to 4.6 percent. The percent of all income received by the lowest 40 percent of families (those earning less than $22,725 in 1985) declined from 16.7 percent to 15.5 percent.

At the other end of the income scale, the percent of all income received by the top 20 percent of families (those with incomes over $48,000 in 1985) rose from 41.6 percent of all income in 1980 to 43.5 percent in 1985. The percent received by the top 5 percent (those earning over $77,706 in 1985) rose from 15.3 percent in 1980 to 16.7 percent in 1985 (U.S. Department of Commerce 1986a).[1]

While these do not at first appear to be massive shifts, they are the largest shifts since 1947. They left the share of income received by the top 20 percent at a postwar high, and reduced the share of the bottom 20 percent to a level not seen since 1950.

Not all of this shift should be attributed to policy changes. Certainly overseas competition played an important part. Still, there does appear to be a significant policy effect. The economic policy changes of the 1980s have resulted in considerable changes in the welfare of Americans.

Political business cycles

To what degree do recent events validate the theories about the interaction between government and the economy propounded in the last section of this book?

Looking first at the theory of political business cycles, the events of the 1980s, taken at face value, appear to lend reasonable support to the theory. It will be recalled that political business cycle theory has three parts. It argues that voting is based on the state of the economy, that politicians try to expand the economy before elections and depress it afterwards, and that public officials have sufficient control of the economy that they can manipulate it successfully.

The first part of the theory receives the most support. President Carter's term can be characterized as three years of economic expansion followed by one year of economic downturn in 1980. As the theory would lead us to expect, Carter lost the 1980 election. President Reagan's tenure included a major downturn in 1981–1982 followed by a rapid growth spurt in 1984 and slow growth thereafter. Republicans suffered losses in the 1982 congressional elections, but Reagan won a landslide reelection in 1984.

Yet things may not be as simple as they appear. Carter might perhaps have won reelection but for adverse developments in the hostage crisis in Iran. The Republican losses in 1982 were less than the theory would lead one to expect in the greatest recession since the Great Depression. The Republicans suffered losses again in 1986, despite four years of continued growth. Overall, the evidence in support of the theory seems better for presidential than for congressional elections, and debatable even there.

What of the second and third parts of the theory? Here the evidence appears even weaker. One should note that President Carter seems to have performed in the reverse of the way the theory predicts. He expanded the economy in nonelection years and contracted it in his reelection year. This shows either that he was prepared to risk a recession in 1980, or that he was not able to control the economy.

On the other hand, the first Reagan term initially appears to fit this part of the theory very well. There was a major recession in the early part of his term, reducing inflation, followed by mild expansion in 1983 and rapid expansion in 1984. However, examination of the intentions of the administration casts some doubt on this fit. It is clear that the great recession of 1981–1982 was not intended either by the administration or by the Federal Reserve Board (Greider 1986). Indeed, the administration seems to have believed that the combination of tight money and supply-side tax cuts would usher in a period of continued expansion like that of the 1960s, rather than a recession. Likewise, the expansion after 1982 can reasonably be seen as due to adjustments by the Federal Reserve Board to compensate for its earlier miscalculation about the velocity of money, which was largely responsible for the recession.

In a similar vein, the administration did not contract the economy in the early part of its second term. Rather, it actively tried to convince the Federal Reserve Board to increase the money supply more rapidly in order to speed up growth.

The most reasonable interpretation of the Reagan Administration, as of most others, is that it wanted continuous rapid expansion throughout its term, but did not pursue the policies necessary to realize this end.

In sum, the events of the eighties do not appear to support the political business cycle theory very strongly, although one can make a reasonable case that the economic condition of the country does have some effect on voting in presidential elections.

The growth of government

As we have seen, the size of the government sector in the United States grew both absolutely and relative to GNP in the 1980s. But, as is true of previous decades, the events of the eighties do little to settle the debate about the causes of that growth.

For example, Wagner's theories can reasonably be seen to hold. The economy did grow more complex in this period. National defense needs did increase. The economy's growth did allow more to be spent on transfer payments. However, none of these things were any more true in the 1980s than they were in the 1976–1980 period when government did not grow relative to GNP.

The growth in this decade does not seem compatible with Peacock and Wiseman's view that in peacetime government would grow at roughly the same rate as GNP. On the other hand, the peaceful eighties afford no test of their more central theory about the effects of wars and other crises on people's willingness to bear tax burdens.

Cameron's notion that government growth is linked to the need to control the economy receives little support. In the 1976–1980 period, when government declined a bit in size, exports and imports grew sharply as a share of GNP grew (from 13.4 percent to 17.4 percent of GNP). By contrast, in the 1980–1986 period, during which the government share of GNP *rose*, exports and imports as a share of GNP fell from 17.4 percent in 1980 to 13.9 percent in 1986 (C.E.A. 1987). Further, the sort of neo-Keynesian manipulation that Cameron talks about was not characteristic of policymaking in the eighties.

Nor does Cameron's other major assertion, the idea that the ideology of the party in power is a key determinant, receive strong support. It is true that the more conservative Reagan Administration made much more determined efforts than its Democratic predecessor to cut both taxes and government spending, and was successful in doing so. However, it is still true that government expenditures as a percent of GNP grew more in the Reagan than in the Carter era.

In short, we appear to be as much in the dark about the causes of government growth as we were when the decade began. The issue awaits better, more sophisticated testing.

Conclusions

Economic policymaking in the 1980s has had three major themes. One is the return to free-market principles. This was especially evident in the avoidance of planning and the attempts at deregulation, but can also be seen in the heavy tax cuts and the experiments with such devices as housing vouchers and enterprise zones. The second theme is the reordering in spending priorities, with cuts in exhaustive domestic programs such as transportation and energy, and large increases in defense spending. And not only were there changes in spending priorities, there were also marked changes in the way budgets were made. The third theme was redistribution in favor of the well-off, which was achieved by the huge tax cuts for the wealthy, the weakening of labor unions, and the shift in spending priorities.

However, it is unlikely that any of these changes will be permanent. The next Democratic administration can be expected to experiment with industrial planning and to expand the budgets of regulatory agencies. Public opinion has already swung against defense spending increases and in favor of social spending. Finally, if the decision is made to raise taxes in order to reduce the deficit, it seems likely that the well-off will be made to bear more of the burden. Only time will tell the true legacy of the eighties.

Notes

1. These figures slightly overstate the increase at the top levels. A change in the way income was measured affected the results (U.S. Department of Commerce 1986a, p. 5) To get a true comparison one should probably add around .3 to the top 20 percent figure and .4 to the top 5 percent figure in 1980.

Bibliography

Aaron, Henry *et al.*, *Economic Choices 1987* (Washington D.C.: The Brookings Institution, 1986)

Christiansen, Gregory B. and Robert H. Haveman, "The Reagan Administration's Regulatory Relief Effort: A Mid-term Assessment," in George C. Eads and Michael Fix, eds., *The Reagan Regulatory Strategy* (Washington D.C.: The Urban Institute Press, 1984).

Congressional Quarterly Weekly Report, July 19, 1980, pp. 2038- 46.

Congressional Quarterly, *Reagan: The Next Four Years* (Washington D.C.: Congressional Quarterly Press, 1985).

Council of Economic Advisers (C.E.A.), *Economic Report of the President*, January 1987 (Washington, D.C.: U.S. Government Printing Office, 1987).

DeMuth, Christopher, "Regulation, Productivity, and the Reagan Administration's Regulatory Reform Program," in Gregory A. Daneke and David J. Lermak, *Regulatory Reform Reconsidered* (Boulder, Co., Westview Press, 1985).

Derthick, Martha and Paul J. Quirk, *The Politics of Deregulation* (Washington D.C.: The Brookings Institution, 1985).

Eads, George C. and Michael Fix, "Introduction," in George C. Eads and Michael Fix , eds., *The Reagan Regulatory Strategy* (Washington D.C.: The Urban Institute Press, 1984).

Fasenfest, David, "Using Producer Incentives to Achieve Social Objectives: An Assessment of the Marketplace and Public Policies," *Policy Studies Review* 5 (February 1986): 598–605.

Fitzgerald, Michael R.,"The Promise and Performance of Privatization: The Knoxville Experience," *Policy Studies Review* 5 (February 1986): 606–13.

Foreman, Christopher H., "Congress and Social Regulation in the Reagan Era," in George C. Eads and Michael Fix, eds., *The Reagan Regulatory Strategy* (Washington D.C.: The Urban Institute Press, 1984).

Gramlich, Edward M., "How Bad are the Large Federal Deficits?," in Gregory B. Mills and John L. Palmer, eds., *Federal Budget Policy in the 1980s* (Washington D.C.: The Urban Institute Press, 1984).

Greider, William, *The Education of David Stockman and Other Americans* (New York, E.P. Dutton, 1986).

Krugman, Paul "The Effects of International Competition on Economic Growth," in Charles R. Hulten and Isabel V. Sawhill, eds., *The Legacy of Reaganomics: Prospects for Long-Term Growth* (Washington D.C.: The Urban Institute Press, 1984).

Lemak, David J., "Social Regulation: A Swing of the Pendulum," in Gregory A. Daneke and David J. Lermak, *Regulatory Reform Reconsidered* (Boulder, Co., Westview Press, 1985).

Marshall. Ray, "Working Smarter," in David R. Obey and Paul Sarbanes, eds., *The Changing American Economy* (New York: Basil Blackwell, 1986).

Meier, Kenneth, *Regulation: Politics, Bureaucracy and Economics* (New York, St. Martins Press, 1985).

Mills, Gregory and John L. Palmer, "The Federal Budget in Flux," in Gregory B. Mills and John L. Palmer, eds., *Federal Budget Policy in the 1980s* (Washington D.C.: The Urban Institute Press, 1984).

Niskanen, William, *Bureaucracy and Representative Government* (New York: Aldine Atherton, 1971).

Office of Management and Budget (O.M.B.), *Budget of the United States Government*. Fiscal Year 1988—Supplement (Washington, D.C.: U.S. Government Printing Office, 1987).

Palumbo, Dennis J., "Privatization and Corrections Policy," *Policy Studies Review* 5 (February 1986): 598–605.

Peretz, Paul, *The Political Economy of Inflation in the United States* (Chicago: University of Chicago Press, 1983).

Peretz, Paul, "The Market for Industry: Where Angels Fear to Tread," *Policy Studies Review* 5 (February 1986): 624–633.

Rosenthal, Neal, "The shrinking middle class; myth or reality," *Monthly Labor Review* (1985).

Stigler, George, "The Theory of Economic Regulation," *Bell Journal of Economics and Management Service* 2 (Spring 1971): 3- 21.

Stone, Charles F. and Isabel V. Sawhill, *Economic Policy in the Reagan Years* (Washington D.C.: The Urban Institute Press, 1984).

Thurow, Lester, "The disappearance of the middle class: it's not just demographics," *New York Times*, February 5, 1984, p. F3.

Tobin, James, "The Economic Experience," in David R. Obey and Paul Sarbanes, eds., *The Changing American Economy* (New York: Basil Blackwell, 1986).

Tolchin, Susan J. and Martin Tolchin, "Presidential Power Over the Regulatory Process," in Gregory A. Daneke and David J. Lermak, *Regulatory Reform Reconsidered* (Boulder, Co.: Westview, 1985).

U.S. Department of Commerce, *Money Income and Poverty Status of Families and Persons in the United States 1985* (Washington D.C.: U.S. Government Printing Office, 1986a).

U.S. Department of Commerce, *Statistical Abstract of the United States 1987* (Washington, D.C.: U.S. Government Printing Office, 1986b).

Wehr, Elizabeth, "Signals of Fiscal Restraint from Democrats May Presage New Strength for the Budget," *Congressional Quarterly Weekly* 45:20 (May 16, 1987): 986–87.

Weicher, John C., "The Reagan Domestic Budget Cuts: Proposals, Outcomes and Effects," in Phillip Cagan ed., *Essays in Contemporary Economic Problems: The Impact of the Reagan Program* (Washington D.C.: American Enterprise Institute, 1986).

Weidenbaum, Murray L., "Regulatory Reform Under the Reagan Administration," in George C. Eads and Michael Fix, eds., *The Reagan Regulatory Strategy* (Washington D.C.: The Urban Institute Press, 1984).

Weidenbaum, Murray L., *The Future of Business Regulation* (New York: Amacom, 1980).

Zysman, John and Stephen Cohen, "The International Experience," in David R. Obey and Paul Sarbanes, eds., *The Changing American Economy* (New York: Basil Blackwell, 1986).

About the Editor

Paul Peretz completed his B.A. in economics and political science at the Victoria University of Wellington and a Ph.D. in political science at the University of Chicago. He is assistant professor of political science at the University of Washington. His previous publications include *The Political Economy of Inflation in the United States* (1983) and a number of articles.